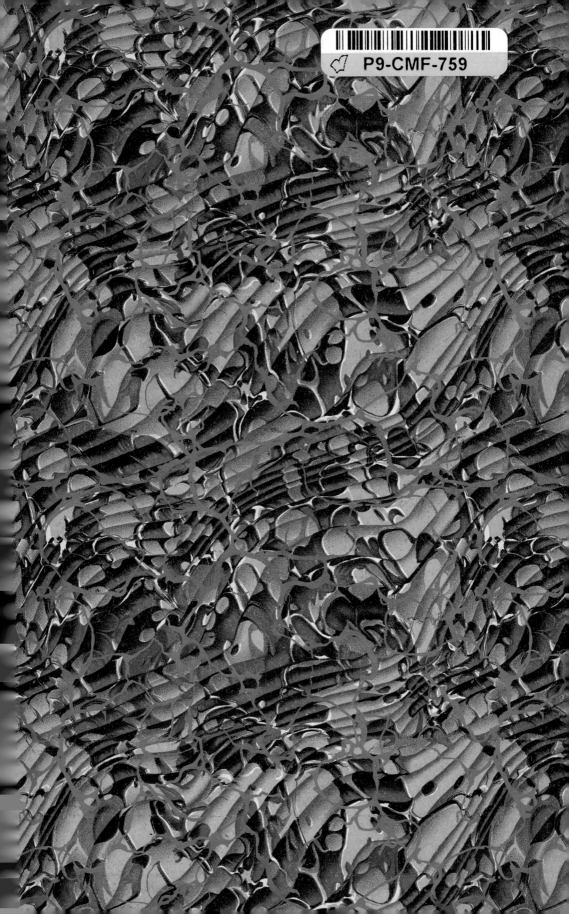

Smithsonian Institution.

THE SMITHSONIAN INSTITUTION is the result of the philanthropy of an Englishman, James Smithson, a younger son of the Duke of Northumberland, who in 1829 bequeathed a fortune of over $500,000 to the United States "to found an institution at Washington for the increase of knowledge." The fund now amounts to over a million. The building was designed by Renwick, architect of St. Patrick's Cathedral in New York.

A COMPILATION

OF THE

MESSAGES AND PAPERS

OF THE

PRESIDENTS

1789–1897

BY

JAMES D. RICHARDSON

A REPRESENTATIVE FROM THE STATE OF TENNESSEE

VOLUME X

PUBLISHED BY
AUTHORITY OF CONGRESS
1900

Prefatory Note

This volume closes the task, entered upon by me in April, 1895, of compiling all the official papers of the Presidents. Instead of finding it the labor of a year, as I supposed it would be when I undertook it, the work has occupied me closely for more than four years. A great portion of this time has been consumed in the preparation of the Index. The Index is mainly the work of my son, James D. Richardson, jr., who prepared it with such assistance as I could give him. He has given his entire time to it for three years. Every reference in it has been examined and compared with the text by myself. We have endeavored to make it full, accurate, and comprehensive, with numerous cross references. There will be found in this Index a large number of encyclopedic articles, which are intended, in part at least, to furnish the reader definitions of politico-historical words and phrases occurring in the papers of the Chief Magistrates, or to develop more fully questions or subjects to which only indirect reference is made or which are but briefly discussed by them. There will also be found short accounts of several hundred battles in which the armies of the United States have been engaged; also descriptions of all the States of the Union and of many foreign countries. We have striven earnestly to make these encyclopedic articles historically correct, and to this end have carefully compared them with the most eminent authorities. This feature was not within the scope of the work as contemplated when the resolution authorizing the compilation was passed, nor when the act was passed requiring the preparation of the index; but with the approval of the Joint Committee on Printing I have inserted the articles, believing that they would be of interest. They contain facts and valuable information not always easily accessible, and it is hoped that they will serve to familiarize the young men of the country who read them with its history and its trials and make of them better citizens and more devoted lovers of our free institutions. There has been no effort or inclination on my part to give partisan bias or political coloring of any nature to these articles. On the other hand, I have sought only to furnish reliable historical data and well-authenticated definitions and to avoid even the appearance of an expression of my own opinion. It is proper to add that these articles have all been read and approved by Mr. A. R. Spofford, Chief Assistant Librarian of Congress, to whom I now make acknowledgment of my indebtedness.

In pursuance of the plan originally adopted certain papers were omitted from the earlier volumes of this work. Referring to these papers, the following statement occurs in the Prefatory Note to Volume I: ''In executing the commission with which I have been charged I have sought to bring together in the several volumes of the series all Presidential proclamations, addresses, messages, and communications to Congress excepting those nominating persons to office and those which simply transmit treaties, and reports of heads of Departments which contain no recommendation from the Executive.'' In the Prefatory Note to Volume IX the statement was made that this course was a mistake, and ''that the work to be exhaustive should comprise every message of the Presidents transmitting reports of heads of Departments and other communications, no matter how brief or unintelligible the papers were in themselves, and that to make them intelligible I should insert editorial footnotes explaining them. Having acted upon the other idea in making up Volume I and a portion of Volume II, quite a number of such brief papers were intentionally omitted. Being convinced that all the papers of the Executives should be inserted, the plan was modified accordingly, and the endeavor was thereafter made to publish all of them. In order, however, that the compilation may be 'accurate and exhaustive,' I have gone back and collected all the papers—those which should have appeared in Volumes I and II as well as such as were unintentionally omitted from the succeeding volumes—excepting those simply making nominations, and shall publish them in an appendix in the last volume.'' These omitted papers, with editorial footnotes, have been inserted in the Appendix, and appear in the Index in alphabetical order, so that no serious inconvenience will result to the reader.

The compilation properly closed with President Cleveland's second Administration, March 4, 1897, but as the Spanish-American War excited great interest I determined, after conferring with the Joint Committee on Printing, to publish the official papers of President McKinley which relate exclusively to that war. These will be found in the Appendix.

I have been greatly assisted in the work of compilation by Mr. A. P. Marston, of the Proof Room of the Government Printing Office. Without his valuable assistance in searching for and obtaining the various papers and his painstaking care in the verification of data the work would not have been so complete. Mr. Charles T. Hendler, of the State Branch of the Government Printing Office, rendered timely aid in procuring proclamations from the archives of the State Department. To these gentlemen I make proper acknowledgments.

The work has met with public favor far beyond all expectations, and words of praise for it have come from all classes and callings. Those who possess it may be assured that they have in their libraries all the official utterances of the Presidents of the United States from 1789 to 1897 that could possibly be found after the most diligent search, and that these utterances are not to be found complete in any other publication.

I close by quoting from the Prefatory Note to Volume I: "If my work shall prove satisfactory to Congress and the country, I will feel compensated for my time and effort."

JAMES D. RICHARDSON.

JULY 4 1899.

APPENDIX

Messages, Proclamations, Executive Orders, etc., Omitted from Volumes I to IX

Messages, Proclamations, Executive Orders, etc., Omitted from Volumes I to IX

SPECIAL MESSAGES, ETC.

SATURDAY, *August 22, 1789.**

The President of the United States came into the Senate Chamber, attended by General Knox, and laid before the Senate the following state of facts, with the questions thereto annexed, for their advice and consent:

"To conciliate the powerful tribes of Indians in the southern district, amounting probably to 14,000 fighting men, and to attach them firmly to the United States, may be regarded as highly worthy of the serious attention of Government.

"The measure includes not only peace and security to the whole southern frontier, but is calculated to form a barrier against the colonies of a European power which in the mutations of policy may one day become the enemy of the United States. The fate of the Southern States, therefore, or the neighboring colonies may principally depend on the present measures of the Union toward the southern Indians.

"By the papers which have been laid before the Senate it will appear that in the latter end of the year 1785 and the beginning of 1786 treaties were formed by the United States with the Cherokees, the Chickesaws, and Choctaws. The report of the commissioners will show the reasons why a treaty was not formed at the same time with the Creeks.

"It will also appear by the papers that the States of North Carolina and Georgia protested against said treaties as infringing their legislative rights and being contrary to the Confederation. It will further appear by the said papers that the treaty with the Cherokees has been entirely violated by the disorderly white people on the frontiers of North Carolina.

"The opinion of the late Congress respecting the said violation will sufficiently appear by the proclamation which they caused to be issued on the 1st of September, 1788.

"By the public newspapers it appears that on the 16th of June last a truce was concluded with the Cherokees by Mr. John Steele on behalf of the State of North Carolina, in which it was stipulated that a treaty should be held as soon as possible and that in the meantime all hostilities should cease on either side.

*See message of August 21, 1789, Vol. I, p. 61.

5

"As the Cherokees reside principally within the territory claimed by North Carolina, and as that State is not a member of the present Union, it may be doubted whether any efficient measures in favor of the Cherokees could be immediately adopted by the General Government.

"The commissioners for negotiating with the southern Indians may be instructed to transmit a message to the Cherokees, stating to them as far as may be proper the difficulties arising from the local claims of North Carolina, and to assure them that the United States are not unmindful of the treaty at Hopewell, and as soon as the difficulties which are at present opposed to the measure shall be removed the Government will do full justice to the Cherokees.

"The distance of the Choctaws and Chickasaws from the frontier settlements seems to have prevented those tribes from being involved in similar difficulties with the Cherokees.

"The commissioners may be instructed to transmit messages to the said tribes containing assurances of the continuance of the friendship of the United States and that measures will soon be taken for extending a trade to them agreeably to the treaties of Hopewell. The commissioners may also be directed to report a plan for the execution of the said treaties respecting trade.

"But the case of the Creek Nation is of the highest importance and requires an immediate decision. The cause of the hostilities between Georgia and the Creeks is stated to be a difference in judgment concerning three treaties made between the said parties, to wit, at Augusta in 1783, at Galphinton in 1785, and at Shoulderbone in 1786. The State of Georgia asserts and the Creeks deny the validity of the said treaties.

"Hence arises the indispensable necessity of having all the circumstances respecting the said treaties critically investigated by commissioners of the United States, so that the further measures of Government may be formed on a full knowledge of the case.

"In order that the investigation may be conducted with the highest impartiality, it will be proper, in addition to the evidence of the documents in the public possession, that Georgia should be represented at this part of the proposed treaty with the Creek Nation.

"It is, however, to be observed, in any issue of the inquiry, that it would be highly embarrassing to Georgia to relinquish that part of the lands stated to have been ceded by the Creeks lying between the Ogeeche and Oconee rivers, that State having surveyed and divided the same among certain descriptions of its citizens, who settled and planted thereon until dispossessed by the Indians.

"In case, therefore, the issue of the investigation should be unfavorable to the claims of Georgia, the commissioners should be instructed to use their best endeavors to negotiate with the Creeks a solemn conveyance of the said lands to Georgia.

"By the report of the commissioners who were appointed under certain acts of the late Congress by South Carolina and Georgia it appears that they have agreed to meet the Creeks on the 15th of September ensuing. As it is with great difficulty the Indians are collected together at certain seasons of the year, it is important that the above occasion should be embraced if possible on the part of the present Government to form a treaty with the Creeks. As the proposed treaty is of great importance to the future tranquillity of the State of Georgia as well as of the United States, it has been thought proper that it should be conducted on the part of the General Government by commissioners whose local situations may free them from the imputation of prejudice on this subject.

"As it is necessary that certain principles should be fixed previously to forming instructions for the commissioners, the following questions arising out of the foregoing communications are stated by the President of the United States and the advice of the Senate requested thereon:

"First. In the present state of affairs between North Carolina and the United States will it be proper to take any other measures for redressing the injuries of the Cherokees than the one herein suggested?

"Second. Shall the commissioners be instructed to pursue any other measures respecting the Chickesaws and Choctaws than those herein suggested?

"Third. If the commissioners shall adjudge that the Creek Nation was fully represented at the three treaties with Georgia, and that the cessions of land were obtained with the full understanding and free consent of the acknowledged proprietors, and that the said treaties ought to be considered as just and equitable, in this case shall the commissioners be instructed to insist on a formal renewal and confirmation thereof, and in case of a refusal shall they be instructed to inform the Creeks that the arms of the Union shall be employed to compel them to acknowledge the justice of the said cessions?

"Fourth. But if the commissioners shall adjudge that the said treaties were formed with an inadequate or unauthorized representation of the Creek Nation, or that the treaties were held under circumstances of constraint or unfairness of any sort, so that the United States could not with justice and dignity request or urge a confirmation thereof, in this case shall the commissioners, considering the importance of the Oconee lands to Georgia, be instructed to use their highest exertions to obtain a cession of said lands? If so, shall the commissioners be instructed, if they can not obtain the said cessions on better terms, to offer for the same and for the further great object of attaching the Creeks to the Government of the United States the following conditions:

"First. A compensation, in money or goods, to the amount of $———, the said amount to be stipulated to be paid by Georgia at the period which shall be fixed, or in failure thereof by the United States.

"Second. A secure port on the Altamaha or St. Marys rivers, or at any other place between the same as may be mutually agreed to by the commissioners and the Creeks.

"Third. Certain pecuniary considerations to some and honorary military distinctions to other influential chiefs on their taking oaths of allegiance to the United States.

"Fourth. A solemn guaranty by the United States to the Creeks of their remaining territory, and to maintain the same, if necessary, by a line of military posts.

"Fifth. But if all offers should fail to induce the Creeks to make the desired cessions to Georgia, shall the commissioners make it an ultimatum?

"Sixth. If the said cessions shall not be made an ultimatum, shall the commissioners proceed and make a treaty and include the disputed lands within the limits which shall be assigned to the Creeks? If not, shall a temporary boundary be marked making the Oconee the line, and the other parts of the treaty be concluded? In this case shall a secure port be stipulated and the pecuniary and honorary considerations granted? In other general objects shall the treaties formed at Hopewell with the Cherokees, Chickesaws, and Choctaws be the basis of a treaty with the Creeks?

"Seventh. Shall the sum of $20,000 appropriated to Indian expenses and treaties be wholly applied, if necessary, to a treaty with the Creeks? If not, what proportion?"

Whereupon the Senate proceeded to give their advice and consent.

The first question, viz, "In the present state of affairs between North Carolina and the United States will it be proper to take any other measures for redressing the injuries of the Cherokees than the one herein suggested?" was, at the request of the President of the United States, postponed.

The second question, viz, "Shall the commissioners be instructed to pursue any other measures respecting the Chickesaws and Choctaws than those herein suggested?" being put, was answered in the negative.

The consideration of the remaining questions was postponed till Monday next.

MONDAY, *August 24.*

The President of the United States being present in the Senate Chamber, attended by General Knox—

The Senate resumed the consideration of the state of facts, and questions thereto annexed, laid before them by the President of the United States on Saturday last; and the first question, viz, "In the present state of affairs between North Carolina and the United States will it be proper to take any other measures for redressing the injuries of the Cherokees than the one herein suggested?" being put, was answered in the negative.

The third question, viz, "If the commissioners shall adjudge that the Creek Nation was fully represented at the three treaties with Georgia, and that the cessions of land were obtained with the full understanding and free consent of the acknowledged proprietors, and that the said treaties ought to be considered as just and equitable, in this case shall the commissioners be instructed to insist on a formal renewal and confirmation thereof, and in case of a refusal shall they be instructed to inform the Creeks that the arms of the Union shall be employed to compel them to acknowledge the justice of the said cessions?" was wholly answered in the affirmative.

The fourth question and its four subdivisions, "But if the commissioners shall adjudge that the said treaties were formed with an inadequate or unauthorized representation of the Creek Nation, or that the treaties were held under circumstances of constraint or unfairness of any sort, so that the United States could not with justice and dignity request or urge a confirmation thereof, in this case shall the commissioners, considering the importance of the Oconee lands to Georgia, be instructed to use their highest exertions to obtain a cession of said lands? If so, shall the commissioners be instructed, if they can not obtain the said cessions on better terms, to offer for the same and for the further great object of attaching the Creeks to the Government of the United States the following conditions: First. A compensation, in money or goods, to the amount of $———, the said amount to be stipulated to be paid by Georgia at the period which shall be fixed, or in failure thereof by the United States. Second. A secure port on the Altamaha or on St. Marys River, or at any other place between the same as may be mutually agreed to by the commissioners and the Creeks. Third. Certain pecuniary considerations to some and honorary military distinctions to other influential chiefs on their taking oaths of allegiance to the United States. Fourth. A solemn guaranty by the United States to the Creeks of their remaining territory, and to maintain the same, if necessary, by a line of military posts," was wholly answered in the affirmative. The blank to be filled at the discretion of the President of the United States.

The fifth question, viz, "But if all offers should fail to induce the Creeks to make the desired cessions to Georgia, shall the commissioners make it an ultimatum?" was answered in the negative.

The sixth question being divided, the first part, containing as follows, viz, "If the said cessions shall not be made an ultimatum, shall the commissioners proceed and make a treaty and include the disputed lands within the limits which shall be assigned to the Creeks?" was answered in the negative.

The remainder, viz: "If not, shall a temporary boundary be marked making the Oconee the line, and the other parts of the treaty be concluded?"

"In this case shall a secure port be stipulated and the pecuniary and honorary considerations granted?"

"In other general objects shall the treaties formed at Hopewell with the Cherokees, Chickesaws, and Choctaws be the basis of a treaty with the Creeks?'' were all answered in the affirmative.

On the seventh question, viz, ''Shall the sum of $20,000 appropriated to Indian expenses and treaties be wholly applied, if necessary, to a treaty with the Creeks? If not, what proportion?'' it was agreed to advise and consent to appropriate the whole sum, if necessary, at the discretion of the President of the United States.

The President of the United States withdrew from the Senate Chamber, and the Vice-President put the question of adjournment, to which the Senate agreed.

UNITED STATES, *September 26, 1789.*

Gentlemen of the Senate and of the House of Representatives:

Having yesterday received a letter written in this month by the governor of Rhode Island at the request and in behalf of the general assembly of that State, addressed to the President, the Senate, and the House of Representatives of the eleven United States of America in Congress assembled, I take the earliest opportunity of laying a copy of it before you.

G⁹ WASHINGTON.

STATE OF RHODE ISLAND AND PROVIDENCE PLANTATIONS,
In General Assembly, September Session, 1789.

To the President, the Senate, and the House of Representatives of the Eleven United States of America in Congress assembled:

The critical situation in which the people of this State are placed engage us to make these assurances on their behalf of their attachment and friendship to their sister States and of their disposition to cultivate mutual harmony and friendly intercourse. They know themselves to be a handful, comparatively viewed; and although they now stand, as it were, alone, they have not separated themselves or departed from the principles of that Confederation which was formed by the sister States in their struggle for freedom and in the hour of danger. They seek by this memorial to call to your remembrance the hazards which we have run, the hardships we have endured, the treasure we have spent, and the blood we have lost together in one common cause, and especially the object we had in view—the preservation of our liberty; wherein, ability considered, they may truly say they were equal in exertions with the foremost, the effects whereof, in great embarrassments and other distresses consequent thereon, we have since experienced with severity; which common sufferings and common danger we hope and trust yet form a bond of union and friendship not easily to be broken.

Our not having acceded to or adopted the new system of government formed and adopted by most of our sister States we doubt not have given uneasiness to them. That we have not seen our way clear to do it consistent with our idea of the principles upon which we all embarked together has also given pain to us. We have not doubted but we might thereby avoid present difficulties, but we have apprehended future mischief. The people of this State from its first settlement have been accustomed and strongly attached to a democratical form of government. They have viewed in the Constitution an approach, though perhaps but small, toward that form of government from which we have lately dissolved our connection at so much hazard and expense of life and treasure; they have seen with pleasure the administration thereof from the most important trust downward committed to men who have highly merited and in whom the people of the United States place unbounded confidence. Yet even in this circumstance, in itself so fortunate, they have apprehended danger by way of precedent. Can it be thought strange, then, that with these impressions they should wait to see the proposed system organized and in operation, to see what further checks and securities would be agreed to and established, by way of amendments, before they could adopt it as a constitution of government for themselves and their posterity? These amendments, we believe, have already afforded some relief and satisfaction to the minds of the people of this State, and we earnestly look for the time when they may with clearness and safety be again united with their sister States under a constitution and form of government so well poised as neither to need alteration or be liable thereto by a majority only of nine States out of thirteen—a circumstance which may possibly take place against the sense of a majority of the people of the United States. We are sensible of the extremes to which democratical government is sometimes liable, something of which we have lately experienced; but we esteem them temporary and partial evils compared with the loss of liberty and the rights of a free people. Neither do we apprehend they will be marked with severity by our sister States when it is considered that during the late trouble the whole United States, notwithstanding their joint wisdom and efforts, fell into the like misfortune; that from our extraordinary exertions this State was left in a situation nearly as embarrassing as that during the war; that in the measures which were adopted government unfortunately had not that aid and support from the moneyed interest which our sister States of New York and the Carolinas experienced under similar circumstances; and especially when it is considered that upon some abatement of that fermentation in the minds of the people which is so common in the collision of sentiments and of parties a disposition appears to provide a remedy for the difficulties we have labored under on that account. We are induced to hope that we shall not be altogether considered as foreigners having no particular affinity or connection with the United States, but that trade and commerce, upon which the prosperity of this State much depends, will be preserved as free and open between this and the United States as our different situations at present can possibly admit; earnestly desiring and proposing to adopt such commercial regulations on our part as shall not tend to defeat the collection of the revenue of the United States, but rather to act in conformity to or cooperate therewith, and desiring also to give the strongest assurances that we shall during our present situation use our utmost endeavors to be in preparation from time to time to answer our proportion of such part of the interest or principal of the foreign and domestic debt as the United States shall judge expedient to pay and discharge.

We feel ourselves attached by the strongest ties of friendship, kindred, and of interest with our sister States, and we can not without the greatest reluctance look to any other quarter for those advantages of commercial intercourse which we conceive to be more natural and reciprocal between them and us.

I am, at the request and in behalf of the general assembly, your most obedient, humble servant,   JOHN COLLINS, *Governor.*

His Excellency the PRESIDENT OF THE UNITED STATES.

Gentlemen of the Senate: UNITED STATES, *February 9, 1790.*

Among the persons appointed during the last session to offices under the National Government there were some who declined serving. Their names and offices are specified in the first column of the foregoing list.*

* Omitted.

I supplied these vacancies, agreeably to the Constitution, by temporary appointments, which you will find mentioned in the second column of the list. These appointments will expire with your present session, and, indeed, ought not to endure longer than until others can be regularly made. For that purpose I now nominate to you the persons named in the third column of the list as being, in my opinion, qualified to fill the offices opposite to their names in the first.

G? WASHINGTON.

UNITED STATES, *December 14, 1790.*

Gentlemen of the Senate and House of Representatives:

Having informed Congress of the expedition which had been directed against certain Indians northwest of the Ohio, I embrace the earliest opportunity of laying before you the official communications which have been received upon that subject.

G? WASHINGTON.

[The following was transmitted with the message of January 26, 1791 (see Vol. I, p. 95).]

[From Annals of Congress, Vol. II, 2116–2118.]

PARIS, *June 20, 1790.*

Mr. PRESIDENT:

The National Assembly has worn during three days mourning for Benjamin Franklin, your fellow-citizen, your friend, and one of the most useful of your cooperators in the establishment of American liberty. They charge me to communicate their resolution to the Congress of the United States. In consequence I have the honor to address to you, Mr. President, the extract from the proceedings of their session of the 11th which contains the deliberations.

The National Assembly have not been stopped in their decree by the consideration that Franklin was a stranger. Great men are the fathers of universal humanity; their loss ought to be felt as a common misfortune by all the tribes of the great human family; and it belongs without doubt to a nation still affected by all the sentiments which accompany the achievement of their liberty, and which owes its enfranchisement essentially to the progress of the public reason, to be the first to give the example of the filial gratitude of the people toward their true benefactors. Besides that, these ideas and this example are so proper to disseminate a happy emulation of patriotism, and thus to extend more and more the empire of reason and virtue, which could not fail promptly to determine a body devoted to the most important legislative combinations. Charged with assuring to the French the rights of men and citizens, it has believed without doubt that fruitful and great truths were likewise numbered among the rights of man.

The name of Benjamin Franklin will be immortal in the records of freedom and philosophy, but it is more particularly dear to a country where, conducted by the most sublime mission, this venerable man grew very soon to acquire an infinite number of friends and admirers as well by the simplicity and sweetness of his manners as by the purity of his principles, the extent of his knowledge, and the charms of his mind.

It will be remembered that every success which he obtained in his important negotiation was applauded and celebrated (so to express it) all over France as so many crowns conferred on genius and virtue.

Even then the sentiment of our rights existed in the bottom of our souls. It was easily perceived that it feelingly mingled in the interest which we took in America and in the public vows which we preferred for your liberty.

At last the hour of the French has arrived. We love to think that the citizens of the United States have not regarded with indifference our steps toward liberty. Twenty-six millions of men breaking their chains and seriously occupied in giving themselves a durable constitution are not unworthy the esteem of a generous people who have preceded them in that noble career.

We hope they will learn with interest the funeral homage which we have rendered the Nestor of America. May this solemn act of fraternal friendship serve more and more to bind the tie which ought to unite two free nations. May the common enjoyment of liberty shed itself over the whole globe and become an indissoluble chain of connection among all the people of the earth. For ought they not to perceive that they will march more steadfastly and more certainly to their true happiness in understanding and loving each other than in being jealous and fighting?

May the Congress of the United States and the National Assembly of France be the first to furnish this fine spectacle to the world! And may the individuals of the two nations connect themselves by a mutual affection worthy of the friendship which unites the two men at this day most illustrious by their exertions for liberty—Washington and Lafayette!

Permit me, Mr. President, to offer on this occasion my particular homage of esteem and admiration.

I have the honor to be, with respectful consideration, Mr. President, your most humble and most obedient servant, SIEYÈS, *President.*

DECREE OF THE NATIONAL ASSEMBLY OF THE IITH OF JUNE, 1790.

The National Assembly decree that their members shall wear during three days mourning for Benjamin Franklin, to commence on Monday next; that the discourse pronounced on this occasion be printed, and that the president write to the American Congress in the name of the National Assembly.

Compared with the original by us, president and secretaries of the National Assembly, at Paris, June 10, 1790.

> SIEYÈS, *President.*
> GOUDAU,
> FÉLIX DE PARDIEU,
> DUMOUCHET,
> > *Secretaries.*

UNITED STATES, *February 18, 1791.*

Gentlemen of the Senate and House.of Representatives:

I have received from the Secretary of State a report on the proceedings of the governor of the Northwestern Territory at Kaskaskia, Kahokia, and Prairie under the resolution of Congress of August 29, 1788, which, containing matter proper for your consideration, I lay the same before you.*

> G? WASHINGTON.

UNITED STATES, *February 22, 1791.*

Gentlemen of the Senate:

I lay before you a report of the Secretary of War, relative to the appointment of two brigadier-generals of militia in the territory of the United States south of the Ohio, and I nominate John Sevier to be

---

*Relating to land claimants in the Northwest Territory.

brigadier-general of the militia of Washington district and James Robertson to be brigadier-general of the militia of Miro district, both within the said territory.

G<u>O</u> WASHINGTON.

UNITED STATES, *December 28, 1791.*
Gentlemen of the Senate and of the House of Representatives:

I lay before you, for your consideration, the copy of a letter * which I have received from the Attorney-General of the United States.

G<u>O</u> WASHINGTON.

UNITED STATES, *January 2, 1792.*
Gentlemen of the Senate and of the House of Representatives:

I lay before you an official statement of the expenditures to the end of the year 1791 from the sum of $10,000 granted to defray the contingent expenses of Government by an act passed on the 26th of March, 1790.

G<u>O</u> WASHINGTON.

UNITED STATES, *November 7, 1792.*
Gentlemen of the Senate and of the House of Representatives:

I lay before you copies of certain papers relative to the Spanish interference in the execution of the treaty entered into in the year 1790 between the United States and the Creek Nation of Indians, together with a letter from the Secretary of State to the President of the United States on the same subject.

G<u>O</u> WASHINGTON.

UNITED STATES, *December 30, 1793.*
Gentlemen of the House of Representatives:

I now transmit you a report by the Secretary of State of such laws, decrees, and ordinances,† or their substance, respecting commerce in the countries with which the United States have commercial intercourse as he has received and had not stated in his report of the 16th instant.

G<u>O</u> WASHINGTON.

UNITED STATES, *December 30, 1793.*
Gentlemen of the Senate and of the House of Representatives:

I communicate to you the translation of a letter‡ received from the representatives of Spain here in reply to that of the Secretary of State to them of the 21st instant, which had before been communicated to you.

G<u>O</u> WASHINGTON.

---

* Respecting the relation between district attorneys and the Attorney-General.

† Decree of the National Assembly of France of March 26, 1793, "exempting from all duties the subsistence and other objects of supply in the colonies relatively to the United States," and extract of an ordinance of Spain of June 9, 1793, "for regulating provisionally the commerce of Louisiana and the Floridas."

‡ Relating to affairs with Indians on the southern frontier.

UNITED STATES, *December 31, 1793.*

Gentlemen of the Senate and of the House of Representatives:

I now lay before you a letter from the Secretary of State, with his account of the expenditure of the moneys appropriated for our intercourse with foreign nations from the 1st of July, 1792, to the 1st of July, 1793, and other papers relating thereto.

G? WASHINGTON.

UNITED STATES, *January 6, 1794.*

Gentlemen of the Senate:

I herewith transmit the copy of a letter from the Secretary of War, stating the circumstances which have hitherto prevented any explanation of the fourth article of the treaty with the Wabash Indians.

G? WASHINGTON.

UNITED STATES, *January 7, 1794.*

Gentlemen of the Senate and of the House of Representatives:

I lay before you an official statement of the expenditure to the end of the year 1793 from the sum of $10,000 granted to defray the contingent expenses of Government by an act passed on the 26th of March, 1790.

G? WASHINGTON.

UNITED STATES, *January 15, 1794.*

Gentlemen of the Senate and of the House of Representatives:

I lay before you, as being connected with the correspondence already in your possession between the Secretary of State and the minister plenipotentiary of the French Republic, the copy of a letter from that minister of the 25th of December, 1793, and a copy of the proceedings of the legislature of the State of South Carolina.*

G? WASHINGTON.

UNITED STATES, *January 16, 1794.*

Gentlemen of the Senate and of the House of Representatives:

I transmit for your information certain intelligence † lately received from Europe, as it relates to the subject of my past communications.

G? WASHINGTON.

UNITED STATES, *January 22, 1794.*

Gentlemen of the Senate and of the House of Representatives:

I forward to you extracts from the last advices from our minister in London,‡ as being connected with communications already made.

G? WASHINGTON.

* Relating to enlistments in South Carolina for the service of the French Republic.
† Respecting relations between the United States and France.
‡ Relating to commercial restrictions.

UNITED STATES, *January 30, 1794.*

Gentlemen of the House of Representatives:

I lay before you the copy of a letter from the governor of the State of North Carolina, together with two petitions,* to which it refers, and which I am requested by the legislature of that State and himself to transmit to Congress.

G⁰ WASHINGTON.

UNITED STATES, *March 12, 1794.*

Gentlemen of the Senate and of the House of Representatives:

I transmit to you the translation of two letters from the commissioners of His Catholic Majesty to the Secretary of State, and of their inclosures.†

G⁰ WASHINGTON.

UNITED STATES, *March 25, 1794.*

Gentlemen of the Senate and of the House of Representatives:

The two letters ‡ which I now forward to Congress were written by a consul of the United States, and contain information which will probably be thought to require some pecuniary provision.

G⁰ WASHINGTON.

UNITED STATES, *May 23, 1794.*

Gentlemen of the Senate and of the House of Representatives:

I lay before you the copy of a letter from the minister plenipotentiary of His Britannic Majesty, in answer to a letter from the Secretary of State communicated to Congress yesterday, and also the copy of a letter from the Secretary which is referred to in the above-mentioned letter of the minister.§

G⁰ WASHINGTON.

UNITED STATES, *June 4, 1794.*

Gentlemen of the Senate and of the House of Representatives:

I lay before Congress the copy of a letter, with its inclosures, from the Secretary of State to the minister plenipotentiary of His Britannic Majesty, it being an answer to a letter from the minister to him bearing date the 22d ultimo and already communicated.‖

G⁰ WASHINGTON.

---

*Relating to lands ceded to the United States by North Carolina.

† Relating to the declaration of war of March 23, 1793, against France by Spain and to expeditions of United States citizens against East Florida.

‡ Relating to the capture of American vessels by British ships of war.

§ Relating to a speech of Lord Dorchester, Governor-General of Canada, tending to an incitement of the Indians to hostilities against the United States, to complaints against alleged acts of violence by citizens of Vermont, etc.

‖ Relating to a speech of Lord Dorchester, Governor-General of Canada, tending to an incitement of the Indians to hostilities against the United States; justifying the measures pursued by the United States to enforce their neutrality, and rebutting the accusation of partiality to France.

UNITED STATES, *December 3, 1794.*

Gentlemen of the Senate and of the House of Representatives:

I transmit to you an official statement of the expenditure to the 30th of September last from the sums heretofore granted to defray the contingent expenses of Government by acts passed the 26th day of March, 1790, and the 9th of June, 1794.

GO WASHINGTON.

UNITED STATES, *December 11, 1794.*

Gentlemen of the Senate and of the House of Representatives:

I transmit to you, for consideration, a representation made to me by the Secretary of the Treasury on the subject of constituting an officer to be specially charged with the business of procuring certain public supplies.*

GO WASHINGTON.

UNITED STATES, *December 16, 1794.*

Gentlemen of the Senate and of the House of Representatives:

I transmit to Congress the copy of a letter from the Secretary of State, with his account, as adjusted with the Treasury Department, of the expenditure of moneys appropriated for our intercourse with foreign nations up to the 1st of July, 1794.

GO WASHINGTON.

UNITED STATES, *December 30, 1794.*

Gentlemen of the Senate:

I lay before you, for your consideration, certain additional articles of the treaty with the Cherokees, stipulated the 28th of June last, together with the conferences which occasioned the formation of the said articles.

GO WASHINGTON.

UNITED STATES, *January 12, 1795.*

Gentlemen of the Senate and of the House of Representatives:

I lay before Congress, for their consideration, the copy of a letter from the Secretary of War, accompanied by an extract from a memorandum of James Seagrove, agent of Indian affairs.†

GO WASHINGTON.

* For the Army and Navy.
† Relating to the justice of compensating owners of negroes taken by the Creek Indians from the conclusion of the Revolutionary War to 1790.

) [The following was transmitted with the message of January 4, 1796 (see Vol. I, pp. 189-190).]

[From American State Papers, Foreign Relations, Vol. I, pp. 527-528.]

PARIS, *30th Vendémiaire, Third Year of the French Republic, One and Indivisible* (*October 21, 1794*).

The Representatives of the French People composing the Committee of Public Safety of the National Convention, charged by the law of the 7th Fructidor with the direction of foreign relations, to the Representatives of the United States of America in Congress assembled.

CITIZENS REPRESENTATIVES: The connections which nature, reciprocal wants, and a happy concurrence of circumstances have formed between two free nations can not but be indissoluble. You have strengthened those sacred ties by the declarations which the minister plenipotentiary of the United States has made in your name to the National Convention and to the French people. They have been received with rapture by a nation who know how to appreciate every testimony which the United States have given to them of their affection. The colors of both nations, united in the center of the National Convention, will be an everlasting evidence of the part which the United States have taken in the success of the French Republic.

You were the first defenders of the rights of man in another hemisphere. Strengthened by your example and endowed with an invincible energy, the French people have vanquished that tyranny which during so many centuries of ignorance, superstition, and baseness had enchained a generous nation.

Soon did the people of the United States perceive that every victory of ours strengthened their independence and happiness. They were deeply affected at our momentary misfortunes, occasioned by treasons purchased by English gold. They have celebrated with rapture the successes of our brave armies.

None of these sympathetic emotions have escaped the sensibility of the French nation. They have all served to cement the most intimate and solid union that has ever existed between two nations.

The citizen Adet, who will reside near your Government in quality of minister plenipotentiary of the French Republic, is especially instructed to tighten these bands of fraternity and mutual benevolence. We hope that he may fulfill this principal object of his mission by a conduct worthy of the confidence of both nations and of the reputation which his patriotism and virtues have acquired him.

An analogy of political principles; the natural relations of commerce and industry; the efforts and immense sacrifices of both nations in the defense of liberty and equality; the blood which they have spilled together; their avowed hatred for despots; the moderation of their political views; the disinterestedness of their counsels, and especially the success of the vows which they have made, in presence of the Supreme Being, to be free or die, all combine to render indestructible the connections which they have formed.

Doubt it not, citizens, we shall finally destroy the combination of tyrants—you by the picture of prosperity which in your vast country has succeeded to a bloody struggle of eight years; we by that enthusiasm which glows in the breast of every Frenchman. Astonished nations, too long the dupes of perfidious kings, nobles, and priests, will eventually recover their rights, and the human race will owe to the American and French nations their regeneration and a lasting peace.

The members of the Committee of Public Safety,

J. S. B. DELMAS,
MERLIN (OF DOUAI), ETC., ETC.

The minister plenipotentiary of the French Republic to the President of the United States.

MR. PRESIDENT: I come to acquit myself of a duty very dear to my heart. I come to deposit in your hands and in the midst of a people justly renowned for their courage and their love of liberty the symbol of the triumphs and of the enfranchisement of my nation.

When she broke her chains; when she proclaimed the imprescriptible rights of man; when in a terrible war she sealed with her blood the covenant she had made with liberty, her own happiness was not alone the object of her glorious efforts; her views extended also to all free people. She saw their interest blended with her own, and doubly rejoiced in her victories, which in assuring to her the enjoyment of her rights became to them new guaranties of their independence.

These sentiments, which animated the French nation from the dawn of their revolution, have acquired new strength since the foundation of the Republic. France at that time, by the form of its Government, assimilated to, or rather identified with, free people, saw in them only friends and brothers. Long accustomed to regard the American people as her most faithful allies, she has sought to draw closer the ties already formed in the fields of America, under the auspices of victory, over the ruins of tyranny.

The National Convention, the organ of the will of the French nation, have more than once expressed their sentiments to the American people, but above all these burst forth on that august day when the minister of the United States presented to the National Representation the colors of his country. Desiring never to lose recollections as dear to Frenchmen as they must be to Americans, the Convention ordered that these colors should be placed in the hall of their sittings. They had experienced sensations too agreeable not to cause them to be partaken of by their allies, and decreed that to them the national colors should be presented.

Mr. President, I do not doubt their expectation will be fulfilled, and I am convinced that every citizen will receive with a pleasing emotion this flag, elsewhere the terror of the enemies of liberty, here the certain pledge of faithful friendship, especially when they recollect that it guides to combat men who have shared their toils and who were prepared for liberty by aiding them to acquire their own.

P. A. ADET.

Answer of the President of the United States.

UNITED STATES, *January 1, 1796.*

Born, sir, in a land of liberty; having early learned its value; having engaged in a perilous conflict to defend it; having, in a word, devoted the best years of my life to secure its permanent establishment in my own country, my anxious recollections, my sympathetic feelings, and my best wishes are irresistibly excited whensoever in any country I see an oppressed nation unfurl the banners of freedom. But above all, the events of the French Revolution have produced the deepest solicitude as well as the highest admiration. To call your nation brave were to pronounce but common praise. Wonderful people! Ages to come will read with astonishment the history of your brilliant exploits! I rejoice that the period of your toils and of your immense sacrifices is approaching. I rejoice that the interesting revolutionary movements of so many years have issued in the formation of a constitution designed to give permanency to the great object for which you have contended. I rejoice that liberty, which you have so long embraced with enthusiasm—liberty, of which you have been the invincible defenders—now finds an asylum in the bosom of a regularly organized Government, a Government which, being formed to secure the happiness of the French people, corresponds with the ardent wishes of my heart, while it gratifies the pride of every citizen of the United States by its resemblance to their own. On these glorious events accept, sir, my sincere congratulations.

In delivering to you these sentiments I express not my own feelings only, but those of my fellow-citizens, in relation to the commencement, the progress, and the issue of the French Revolution, and they will cordially join with me in purest wishes to the Supreme Being that the citizens of our sister Republic, our magnanimous allies, may soon enjoy in peace that liberty which they have purchased at so great a price, and all the happiness which liberty can bestow.

I receive, sir, with lively sensibility the symbol of the triumphs and of the enfranchisement of your nation, the colors of France, which you have now presented to the United States. The transaction will be announced to Congress, and the colors will be deposited with those archives of the United States which are at once the evidences and the memorials of their freedom and independence. May these be perpetual, and may the friendship of the two Republics be commensurate with their existence.

G̱ọ WASHINGTON.

UNITED STATES, *January 13, 1796.*

Gentlemen of the Senate and House of Representatives:

I lay before you an official statement of the expenditure to the end of the year 1795 from the sums heretofore granted to defray the contingent expenses of the Government.

G̱ọ WASHINGTON.

UNITED STATES, *February 29, 1796.*

Gentlemen of the Senate:

I send herewith the papers relating to the negotiation of the treaty with Spain, to which I referred in my message of the 26th instant.*

G̱ọ WASHINGTON.

Gentlemen of the Senate:

I send herewith a copy of the treaty of friendship, limits, and navigation between the United States and His Catholic Majesty, which has been ratified by me with your advice and consent. A copy of the treaty will be immediately communicated to the House of Representatives, it being necessary to make provision in the present session for carrying into execution the third and twenty-first articles, particularly the former, seeing that execution must commence before the next meeting of Congress.

Estimates of the moneys necessary to be provided for the purposes of this and several other treaties with foreign nations and the Indian tribes will be laid before you by the proper Department.

MARCH 29, 1796.

G̱ọ WASHINGTON.

UNITED STATES, *February 15, 1797.*

Gentlemen of the Senate and House of Representatives:

I lay before you an official statement of the expenditure to the end of the year 1796 from the sums heretofore granted to defray the contingent charges of the Government.

G̱ọ WASHINGTON.

*See Vol. I, p. 192.

UNITED STATES, *June 22, 1797.*

Gentlemen of the Senate:

Having sent the report and documents which accompany this message to the House of Representatives,* in compliance with their desire expressed in their resolution of the 10th of this month, I think it proper to send duplicates to the Senate for their information.

JOHN ADAMS.

UNITED STATES, *May 4, 1798.*

Gentlemen of the Senate and Gentlemen of the House of Representatives:

I now transmit to Congress copies of all the communications† from our envoys extraordinary received since their arrival in Paris, excepting those before presented by me to both Houses.

JOHN ADAMS.

UNITED STATES, *May 29, 1798.*

Gentlemen of the Senate:

An article explanatory of the treaty of amity, commerce, and navigation between the United States and His Britannic Majesty has been signed by the plenipotentiaries of the two powers, which I now submit to the Senate for their consideration.

JOHN ADAMS.

UNITED STATES, *June 5, 1798.*

Gentlemen of the Senate and Gentlemen of the House of Representatives:

I now transmit to both Houses the communications† from our envoys at Paris received since the last which have been presented by me to Congress.

JOHN ADAMS.

UNITED STATES, *June 18, 1798.*

Gentlemen of the Senate and Gentlemen of the House of Representatives:

I now transmit to Congress the dispatch No. 8 from our envoys extraordinary to the French Republic,‡ which was received at the Secretary of State's office on Thursday, the 14th day of this month.

JOHN ADAMS.

DECEMBER 31, 1798.

Gentlemen of the Senate and Gentlemen of the House of Representatives:

A report of the Secretary of War made to me on the 24th of this month, relative to the military establishment,§ I think it my duty to transmit to Congress and recommend to their consideration.

JOHN ADAMS.

---

*See message of June 22, 1797, Vol. I, p. 247.

†Relating to affairs between the United States and France.

‡Inclosing correspondence with the French minister of foreign relations relative to affairs between the United States and France.

§Reorganization of the Army.

JANUARY 8, 1799.

Gentlemen of the Senate and Gentlemen of the House of Representatives:

In obedience to the law, I now lay before you my annual account of the application of the grant made by Congress for the contingent charges of Government from the 1st of January to the 31st of December, 1798.

JOHN ADAMS.

JANUARY 21, 1799.

Gentlemen of the Senate and Gentlemen of the House of Representatives:

According to an intimation in my message of Friday last,* I now lay before Congress a report of the Secretary of State, containing his observations on some of the documents which attended it.

JOHN ADAMS.

Gentlemen of the Senate: JANUARY 30, 1799.

I send you, for your consideration, a treaty with the Oneida Nation of Indians, made on the 1st day of June, 1798, at their village.

JOHN ADAMS.

JANUARY 31, 1799.

Gentlemen of the Senate and Gentlemen of the House of Representatives:

I have received a report from the Director of the Mint on the state of the business committed to his superintendence, and a statement of the coinage of the Mint of the United States for the year 1798, which it is proper to lay before Congress.

JOHN ADAMS.

UNITED STATES, *December 13, 1799.*

Gentlemen of the Senate:

In conformity with your recommendation expressed in your resolution of March 6, 1798, I have entered into a friendly negotiation with the Bey and Government of Tunis on the subject † of the fourteenth article of the treaty of peace and friendship between the United States and that power. The result of that negotiation I now lay before the Senate for their consideration.

JOHN ADAMS.

UNITED STATES, *January 8, 1800.*

Gentlemen of the Senate and Gentlemen of the House of Representatives:

A report made to me on the 1st day of this month by the Director of the Mint, through the office of the Secretary of State, with the documents attending it, I transmit to both Houses of Congress for their consideration.

JOHN ADAMS.

*See message of January 18, 1799, Vol. I, p. 281.   † Commerce.

UNITED STATES, *January 20, 1800.*

Gentlemen of the Senate and Gentlemen of the House of Representatives:

In obedience to law, I transmit to Congress my annual account of the contingent fund.   JOHN ADAMS.

UNITED STATES, *February 7, 1800.*

Gentlemen of the House of Representatives:

In consequence of your request to me conveyed in your resolution of the 4th of this month, I directed the Secretary of State to lay before me copies of the papers intended.* These copies, together with his report, I now transmit to the House of Representatives, for the consideration of the members.   JOHN ADAMS.

UNITED STATES, *February 17, 1800.*

Gentlemen of the Senate:

I now lay before you the instructions given to our minister at the Court of Berlin, with the correspondence, respecting the negotiation of the treaty with Prussia, according to your request of the 12th of this month.   JOHN ADAMS.

UNITED STATES, *April 17, 1800.*

Gentlemen of the Senate:

In conformity with your request, I transmit you a return from the War Office of those officers who have been appointed under the act entitled "An act to augment the Army of the United States, and for other purposes," designating such officers who have accepted their appointments and those who have declined accepting, resigned their commissions, died, etc.

A report from the Secretary of War, which accompanied this return, as it contains observations which may throw some light upon the subject, I transmit with it.   JOHN ADAMS.

UNITED STATES, *December 22, 1800.*

Gentlemen of the Senate:

In conformity with your request in your resolution of the 19th of this month, I transmit you the instructions given to our late envoys extraordinary and ministers plenipotentiary to the French Republic.

It is my request to the Senate that these instructions may be considered in strict confidence and returned to me as soon as the Senate shall have made all the use of them they may judge necessary.   JOHN ADAMS.

---

* Relating to the surrender by the United States to Great Britain of Thomas Nash, charged with murder and piracy on the British frigate *Hermione.*

UNITED STATES, *January 16, 1801.*

Gentlemen of the Senate and Gentlemen of the House of Representatives:

I now transmit to both Houses of Congress, in conformity to law, my annual account of the application of grants for the contingent charges of Government for the year 1800.

JOHN ADAMS.

UNITED STATES, *February 20, 1801.*

Gentlemen of the Senate and Gentlemen of the House of Representatives:

The inclosed report* to me, made by the Acting Secretary of War on the 14th of this month, appears to be so well founded in all respects that I recommend it to the consideration of Congress.

JOHN ADAMS.

UNITED STATES, *February 20, 1801.*

Gentlemen of the Senate:

I request of the Senate that the letter and journal of our late envoys to France and the copy of their instructions and other documents relative to that negotiation may be returned to me or to the Office of State.

JOHN ADAMS.

UNITED STATES, *February 27, 1801.*

Gentlemen of the House of Representatives:

I transmit you a report of the Secretary of State, with sundry documents, relative to the subject of your resolution of the 24th instant.†

JOHN ADAMS.

UNITED STATES, *February 27, 1801.*

Gentlemen of the House of Representatives:

I transmit to you, in conformity with your request of the 17th instant, two reports, one from the Acting Secretary of War, the other from the Secretary of the Treasury, of the 26th,‡ with details of the·expenditure of the moneys appropriated by the acts of the 20th [4th] of May and 6th of July, 1798, and of the 10th of May, 1800.

JOHN ADAMS.

JANUARY 12, 1802.

Gentlemen of the House of Representatives:

According to the request in your resolution of the 8th instant, I now lay before you a letter from the Secretary of State, containing an estimate

*Relating to the inconveniences arising from the want of a competent general staff of the Army.

†Relating to depredations on American commerce by British ships of war; lists of captured American vessels, etc.

‡Estimates of the necessary expenditures for the purchase and fabrication of arms and cannon and establishment of foundries and armories, 1798–1801, and statement of appropriations for above purposes and of warrants drawn on same to December 31, 1800.

of the expenses necessary for carrying into effect the convention between the United States of America and the French Republic.

TH: JEFFERSON.

FEBRUARY 8, 1802.

Gentlemen of the House of Representatives:

In compliance with your resolution of the 2d instant, I have to inform you that early in the preceding summer I took measures for carrying into effect the act passed on the 19th of February, 1799, and that of the 13th of May, 1800, mentioned in your resolution. The objects of these acts were understood to be to purchase from the Indians south of the Ohio some portions of land peculiarly interesting to the Union or to particular States and the establishment of certain roads to facilitate communication with our distant settlements. Commissioners were accordingly appointed to treat with the Cherokees, Chickasaws, Choctaws, and Creeks. As these nations are known to be very jealous on the subject of their lands, the commissioners were instructed, as will be seen by the inclosed extract, to enlarge, restrain, or even to suppress propositions as appearances should indicate to be expedient. Their first meeting was with the Cherokees. The extract from the speech of our commissioners and the answers of the Cherokee chiefs will show the caution of the former and the temper of the latter, and that though our overtures to them were moderate and respectful of their rights, their determination was to yield no accommodation.

The commissioners proceeded then to the Chickasaws, who discovered at first considerable alarm and anxiety lest land should be asked of them. A just regard for this very friendly nation, whose attachment to us has been invariable, forbade the pressure of anything disagreeable on them, and they yielded with alacrity the road through their country which was asked and was essential to our communication with the Mississippi Territory.

The conferences with the Choctaws are probably ended, but as yet we are not informed of their result. Those with the Creeks are not expected to be held till the ensuing spring.

TH: JEFFERSON.

FEBRUARY 17, 1802.

Gentlemen of the Senate and of the House of Representatives:

I lay before both Houses of Congress, for their information, the report from the Director of the Mint, now inclosed.

TH: JEFFERSON.

MARCH 25, 1802.

Gentlemen of the Senate:

The act fixing the military peace establishment of the United States rendering it necessary that the officers retained in service should in most cases be transferred into regiments different from those to which their commissions attach them, new commissions are deemed necessary for them, as well as for those entitled to promotion and for the ensigns newly nominated. The inclosed report from the Secretary of War exhibits the transfers, promotions, and new appointments proposed in conformity with the law, and I accordingly nominate the several persons named in the report for commissions according to its tenor.

TH: JEFFERSON.

Gentlemen of the Senate: APRIL 3, 1802.

According to the request expressed in your resolution of yesterday, I now transmit to the Senate the proceedings of the court-martial lately held for the trial of Captain Cornelius Lyman, asking the favor of their return at the convenience of the Senate, as they are the originals.

TH: JEFFERSON.

Gentlemen of the Senate: APRIL 17, 1802.

I now transmit you a report of the Secretary of State, with the document accompanying it, on the subject of your resolution of the 12th instant, concerning the seventh article* of the treaty between the United States and Great Britain.

TH: JEFFERSON.

APRIL 20, 1802.

Gentlemen of the Senate and of the House of Representatives:

The object of the inclosed letter from the Director of the Mint at Philadelphia being within legislative competence only, I transmit it to both Houses of Congress.

TH: JEFFERSON.

JANUARY 11, 1803.

Gentlemen of the Senate and of the House of Representatives:

I transmit you a report received from the Director of the Mint on the subject of that institution.

TH: JEFFERSON.

Gentlemen of the House of Representatives: MARCH 1, 1803.

According to the request stated in your resolution of December 20, I communicated to you such returns of the militia of the different States as had then been received.† Since that date returns have been received from

---

*Relating to claims of American citizens against Great Britain and of British subjects against the United States for illegal captures of vessels, etc.

† See message of January 5, 1803, Vol. I, p. 350.

New Hampshire, Massachusetts, Connecticut, New York, North Carolina, Georgia, and Kentucky, which are now transmitted to you.

TH: JEFFERSON.

DECEMBER 7, 1803.

To the Senate and House of Representatives of the United States:

Since the last communication made to Congress of the laws of the Indiana Territory I have received those of which a copy is now inclosed for the information of both Houses.

TH: JEFFERSON.

JANUARY 13, 1804.

To the Senate and House of Representatives of the United States:

The Director of the Mint having made to me his report of the transactions of the Mint for the year 1803, I now lay the same before you for your information.

TH: JEFFERSON.

MARCH 7, 1804.

To the Senate and House of Representatives of the United States:

I communicate to Congress an extract of a letter from Governor Claiborne to the Secretary of State, with one which it covered, for their information as to the present state of the subject to which they relate.*

TH: JEFFERSON.

MARCH 15, 1804.

To the House of Representatives of the United States:

Agreeably to the request of the Senate and House of Representatives, delivered me by their Joint Committee of Enrolled Bills, I now return the enrolled bill entitled "An act for the relief of the captors of the Moorish armed ships *Meshouda* and *Mirboha*" to the House of Representatives, in which it originated.

TH: JEFFERSON.

[The same message was sent to the Senate.]

DECEMBER 6, 1804.

To the Senate and House of Representatives of the United States:

I communicate, for the information of Congress, a report of the Surveyor of the Public Buildings at Washington on the subject of those buildings and the application of the moneys appropriated for them.

TH: JEFFERSON.

* Importation of slaves into Louisiana.

JANUARY 25, 1805.

To the Senate and House of Representatives of the United States:

I communicate, for the information of Congress, the report of the Director of the Mint of the operations of that institution during the last year.

TH: JEFFERSON.

To the Senate of the United States: JANUARY 31, 1805.

According to the desire expressed in your resolution of the 28th instant, I now communicate a report of the Secretary of State, with documents, relative to complaints* against arming the merchant ships and vessels of the United States and the conduct of the captains and crews of such as have been armed.

TH: JEFFERSON.

FEBRUARY 23, 1805.

To the House of Representatives of the United States:

In further compliance with the desire of the House of Representatives, expressed in their resolution of December 31, I now transmit the report and map of Isaac Briggs referred to in my message of the 1st instant,† and received by the last post from New Orleans.

TH: JEFFERSON.

The PRESIDENT OF THE SENATE.   DECEMBER 6, 1805.

SIR: In order to give to Congress the details necessary for their full information of the state of things between Spain and the United States, I send them the communication and documents now inclosed. Although stated to be confidential, that term is not meant to be extended to all the documents, the greater part of which are proper for the public eye. It is applied only to the message itself and to the letters from our own and foreign ministers, which if disclosed might throw additional difficulties in the way of accommodation. These alone, therefore, are delivered to the Legislature in confidence that they will be kept secret.

TH: JEFFERSON.

[The same message was addressed to the Speaker of the House of Representatives.]

DECEMBER 10, 1805.

To the Senate and House of Representatives of the United States:

The inclosed documents,‡ relating to my message of the 6th instant, not being ready at that date, I thought it better not to detain the mes-

---

*By Great Britain and France.
† See Vol. I, pp. 376–377.
‡ Relating to depredations on American commerce by Spanish privateers, etc.

sage, but to communicate these papers afterwards, as supplementary to those then sent. They are not of a nature to be deemed confidential.

TH: JEFFERSON.

DECEMBER 27, 1805.

To the Senate and House of Representatives of the United States:

I lay before Congress a report of the Surveyor of the Public Buildings, stating the progress made on them during the last season and what may be expected to be accomplished in the ensuing one.

TH: JEFFERSON.

JANUARY 15, 1806.

To the Senate and House of Representatives of the United States:

I communicate, for the information of Congress, the report of the Director of the Mint of the operations of that institution during the last year.

TH: JEFFERSON.

JANUARY 24, 1806.

To the Senate of the United States:

According to the request of your resolution of yesterday, I again communicate the letter of the minister plenipotentiary of the United States at London to the secretary of that Government for foreign affairs dated October 18, 1805, with a postscript of October 25, but still in confidence that the matter of it shall not be made public.

TH: JEFFERSON.

FEBRUARY 4, 1806.

To the Senate of the United States:

I now transmit the letters desired by the resolution of the Senate of January 20 so far as they exist in the offices, to wit:

Extract of a letter from the Department of State to Mr. Eaton, May 20, 1801.

The letter from Mr. Cathcart to Mr. Eaton dated Leghorn, June 15, 1801, is not in the offices, but the substance of it is supposed to be recited in those of Mr. Cathcart to the Secretary of State of August 15, 1802, and July 2, 1801, extracts of both of which are transmitted.

The letter of Mr. Eaton of September 5, 1801, supposed to be that intended by the Senate, as it answers their description. There is no letter of his of September 15.

Extract of a letter from William Eaton to the Secretary of State, December 13, 1801.

Extract from Captain Murray's letter of August 18, 1802.

Extract of a letter from Mr. Cathcart to the Secretary of State, August 25, 1802.

Extract of a letter from Mr. Morris to the Secretary of the Navy, March 30, 1803.

The letter from the Swedish admiral to Hamet Bashaw designated in the resolution of the Senate is not in possession of the Executive.

The extracts above mentioned give the whole matter contained in the respective letters relating to Hamet B. Caramalli. The parts omitted are on subjects entirely foreign to what concerns him.

TH: JEFFERSON.

FEBRUARY 4, 1806.

To the House of Representatives of the L   States:

Sundry letters relative to Hamet Caramalli, in addition to the documents which accompanied my message of January 13,* having been sent to the Senate on their particular request, the same are now transmitted to the House of Representatives also, as the same subject is before them.

TH: JEFFERSON.

FEBRUARY 7, 1806.

To the Senate of the United States:

I transmit, for the consideration of the Senate, a treaty entered into on behalf of the United States with the Piankeshaw Indians, whereby our possessions on the north bank of the Ohio are entirely consolidated; and I ask the advice and consent of the Senate as to its ratification.

TH: JEFFERSON.

FEBRUARY 18, 1806.

To the House of Representatives of the United States:

I now communicate to the House of Representatives the information desired by their resolutions of January 24, relative to the fortifications erected at the several ports and harbors of the United States and their Territories and to the Navy and navy-yards of the United States.

TH: JEFFERSON.

FEBRUARY 18, 1806.

To the House of Representatives of the United States:

On the 13th instant I approved and signed the act entitled "An act making provision for defraying any extraordinary expenses attending the intercourse between the United States and foreign nations," which

* See Vol. I, pp. 392–394.

originated in the House of Representatives, and I shall in due season deposit it among the rolls in the office of the Secretary of State.

TH: JEFFERSON.

To the Senate and House of Representatives of the United States:

I communicate to Congress a letter recently received from the minister plenipotentiary of the United States at London, stating some circumstances which bear relation to the subject of my messages of January 17.* This paper being original and to be communicated to both Houses, the return of it is requested.

TH: JEFFERSON.

MARCH 24, 1806.

DECEMBER 15, 1806.

To the Senate of the United States:

I lay before Congress a report of the Surveyor of the Public Buildings, stating the progress made on them during the last season and what is proposed for the ensuing one.

TH: JEFFERSON.

DECEMBER 23, 1806.

To the House of Representatives of the United States:

I now lay before you accounts of the sums which have been expended by the United States on the Capitol, the President's house, the public offices, the navy-yard, and the marine barracks, respectively, and the amount expended on other objects of public expense within the city of Washington, as requested by your resolution of the 15th instant.

TH: JEFFERSON.

JANUARY 5, 1807.

To the House of Representatives of the United States:

In compliance with the request of the House of Representatives communicated in their resolution of the 26th of December, I now lay before them a report of the Secretary of the Navy on the state of the frigates, supplementary to his former report of January 28 of the last year, communicated to the House of Representatives.

TH: JEFFERSON.

JANUARY 27, 1807.

To the Senate and House of Representatives of the United States:

I communicate, for the information of Congress, the report of the Director of the Mint of the operations of that establishment during the last year.

TH: JEFFERSON.

*See Vol. I, pp. 395-396.

FEBRUARY 11, 1807.

To the Senate and House of Representatives of the United States:

I transmit to both Houses of Congress the laws adopted by the government and judges of the Territory of Michigan from the 1st day of July, 1806, to the 1st day of the present year.

TH: JEFFERSON.

JANUARY 8, 1808.

To the Senate and House of Representatives of the United States:

I communicate, for the information of Congress, the report of the Director of the Mint of the operation of that establishment during the last year.

TH: JEFFERSON.

To the Senate of the United States: JANUARY 30, 1808.

The Senate having advised and consented to the ratification of the treaty with the Ottaways, Chippeways, Wyandots, and Pottawattamies concluded at Detroit on the 17th day of November last, and also to the treaty concluded with the Choctaws at Pooshapukanuck on the 16th of November, 1805, I now lay them before both Houses of Congress for the exercise of their constitutional powers as to the means of fulfilling them.

TH: JEFFERSON.

To the Senate of the United States: MARCH 30, 1808.

I now transmit to the Senate the information requested in their resolutions of the 28th instant,* from the Secretaries of the Treasury and War.

TH: JEFFERSON.

To the Senate of the United States: MARCH 31, 1808.

The confidential papers† desired by the resolution of yesterday are now again sent to the Senate.

TH: JEFFERSON.

APRIL 1, 1808.

To the House of Representatives of the United States:

In answer to the inquiries of the resolution of the House of Representatives of the 30th of March, relative to certain dates,‡ I transmit a report of the Secretary of State to me on that subject.

TH: JEFFERSON.

---

* Relating to paying United States troops in the Territory of Michigan in bills issued by the Bank of Detroit after Congress had rejected the law of that Territory for establishing said bank, etc.

† Concerning the relations of the United States with England and France.

‡ Of certain letters from the French ministry to the United States minister at Paris, and the date of the receipt of said letters by said minister.

NOVEMBER 30, 1808.

To the House of Representatives of the United States:

According to the request of the House of Representatives expressed in their resolution of the 25th instant, I now lay before them a copy of my proclamation of the 19th of April last.*

TH: JEFFERSON.

DECEMBER 1, 1808.

To the Senate and House of Representatives of the United States:

I transmit to Congress a report from the Surveyor of the Public Buildings of the progress made on them during the last season, of their present state, and the expenditures incurred and of those that may be requisite for their further prosecution.

TH: JEFFERSON.

DECEMBER 23, 1808.

To the House of Representatives of the United States:

According to the request of the House of Representatives in their resolution of November 11 that copies should be laid before them of all acts, decrees, orders, and proclamations affecting the commercial rights of neutral nations issued or enacted by Great Britain and France or any other belligerent power since the year 1791, and also of an act placing the commerce of America in English ports upon the footing of the most favored nation, I now transmit them a report of the Secretary of State of such of them as have been attainable in the Department of State and are supposed to have entered into the views of the House of Representatives.

TH: JEFFERSON.

JANUARY 5, 1809.

To the Senate and House of Representatives of the United States:

I communicate, for the information of Congress, the report of the Director of the Mint of the operations of that establishment during the last year.

TH: JEFFERSON.

DECEMBER 4, 1809.

To the Senate and House of Representatives of the United States:

I now transmit a report of the Secretary of the Navy, containing statements† from that Department referred to in my message of the 29th ultimo.

JAMES MADISON.

* See Vol. I, pp. 450-451.
† Showing the condition of the Navy and the application of appropriations made for the Navy and Marine Corps.

DECEMBER 16, 1809.

To the Senate and House of Representatives of the United States:

I transmit to both Houses of Congress a report from the Surveyor of the Public Buildings of the progress made on them during the last season and of other explanations relative thereto.

JAMES MADISON.

JANUARY 5, 1810.

To the Senate and House of Representatives of the United States:

The Director of the Mint having made to me his report of the operations of the Mint for the year 1809, I lay the same before you for your information.

JAMES MADISON.

JANUARY 12, 1810.

To the House of Representatives of the United States:

I communicate to the House of Representatives the report* of the Secretary of State on the subject of their resolution of the 3d instant.

JAMES MADISON.

JANUARY 12, 1810.

To the House of Representatives of the United States:

I communicate to the House of Representatives the report† of the Secretary of State on the subject of their resolution of the 6th of December last.

JAMES MADISON.

JANUARY 22, 1810.

To the Senate and House of Representatives of the United States:

I now transmit to Congress an account of the contingent expenses of the Government for the year 1809.

JAMES MADISON.

FEBRUARY 1, 1810.

To the House of Representatives of the United States:

I lay before the House a report ‡ of the Secretary of the Treasury, conformably to their resolution of 18th January, 1810.

JAMES MADISON.

*Transmitting translations of a ukase of Russia relating to neutral commerce and regulations of Denmark for vessels commissioned as privateers.

†Relating to seizures, captures, and condemnations of ships and merchandise of citizens of the United States under authority of Denmark, Great Britain, and France.

‡Transmitting copies of instructions issued relative to foreign armed ships within the waters of the United States.

FEBRUARY 1, 1810.

To the House of Representatives of the United States:

I lay before the House a report * of the Secretary of War, conformably to their resolution of January 22. JAMES MADISON.

FEBRUARY 9, 1810.

To the House of Representatives of the United States:

I transmit to the House a report † of the Secretary of State, complying with their resolution of the 22d of January. JAMES MADISON.

FEBRUARY 17, 1810.

To the House of Representatives of the United States:

I transmit reports ‡ of the Secretaries of State and of the Treasury, complying with their resolution of the 5th instant.

JAMES MADISON.

To the Senate of the United States: FEBRUARY 17, 1810.

I transmit a report § of the Secretary of the Treasury, complying with their resolution of the 12th instant. JAMES MADISON.

To the Senate of the United States: FEBRUARY 22, 1810.

I transmit to the Senate a report ‖ of the Secretary of the Treasury, complying with their resolution of the 16th instant.

JAMES MADISON.

To the Senate of the United States: MARCH 14, 1810.

I transmit a report ** of the Secretary of War, complying with their resolution of the 22d January last. JAMES MADISON.

---

* Relating to the military force and its disposition in 1810.

† Relating to the free navigation of the Mobile River to its confluence with the ocean.

‡ Transmitting communications relative to certain orders and decrees of France and Great Britain violating the lawful commerce and neutral rights of the United States, etc.

§ Transmitting statement showing value and amount of duties which accrued in consequence of the duty of 2½ per cent laid on all goods, wares, and merchandise imported into the United States paying a duty *ad valorem* from July 1, 1804, to December 31, 1808, and statement showing amount of duties which accrued on merchandise imported into the United States from Mediterranean ports for years ending September 30, 1805, 1806, 1807, and 1808.

‖ Transmitting copy of instructions to collectors under the act to interdict commercial intercourse with Great Britain and France.

** Relating to the treaty with the Great and Little Osage Indians.

MARCH 20, 1810.

To the Senate and House of Representatives of the United States:

I lay before Congress a return of the militia of the United States as received by the Department of War from the several States and Territories.

JAMES MADISON.

MARCH 30, 1810.

To the Senate of the United States:

I transmit to the Senate a report* of the Secretary of State, complying with their resolution of the 22d instant.

JAMES MADISON.

APRIL 4, 1810.

To the House of Representatives of the United States:

I transmit to the House a report† of the Secretary of State, complying with their resolution of the 26th of March.

JAMES MADISON.

APRIL 27, 1810.

To the House of Representatives of the United States:

I transmit to the House a report ‡ of the Secretary of State, complying with their resolution of the 23d instant.

JAMES MADISON.

MAY 1, 1810.

To the House of Representatives of the United States:

I transmit to the House a report § of the Secretary of State, complying with their resolution of the 30th of April.

JAMES MADISON.

DECEMBER 28, 1810.

To the House of Representatives of the United States:

I lay before the House a report ‖ from the Secretary of State, complying with their resolution of the 21st instant.

JAMES MADISON.

DECEMBER 31, 1810.

To the House of Representatives of the United States:

I lay before the House of Representatives a supplemental report § of the Secretary of State, containing information received since the date of my late message on the subject of their resolution of the 21st instant.

JAMES MADISON.

---

* Relating to the capture of Danish vessels by United States war ships.
† Relating to the impressment of American seamen by British ships of war.
‡ Transmitting list of United States consuls and commercial agents, etc.
§ Relating to affairs between the United States and France.
‖ Transmitting a decree of the Emperor of France of July 15, 1810, and correspondence relative to affairs between the United States and France.

JANUARY 7, 1811.

To the Senate and House of Representatives of the United States:

I communicate, for the information of Congress, the report of the Director of the Mint of the operation of that establishment during the last year. JAMES MADISON.

JANUARY 12, 1811.

To the Senate and House of Representatives of the United States.

I transmit to Congress copies of a letter from the minister plenipotentiary of the United States at London to the Secretary of State, and of another from the same to the British secretary for foreign affairs.*

JAMES MADISON.

JANUARY 14, 1811.

To the House of Representatives of the United States:

I transmit to the House of Representatives reports of the superintendent of the city † and of the Surveyor of the Public Buildings on the subject of their resolution of the 28th of December last.

JAMES MADISON.

JANUARY 14, 1811.

To the House of Representatives of the United States:

I transmit to the House of Representatives copies of the documents ‡ referred to in their resolution of the 4th instant.

JAMES MADISON.

JANUARY 14, 1811.

To the Senate and House of Representatives of the United States:

I transmit to Congress an account of the contingent expenses of the Government for the year 1810. JAMES MADISON.

JANUARY 14, 1811.

To the Senate and House of Representatives of the United States:

I transmit to Congress a report from the Surveyor of the Public Buildings relative to the progress and present state of them.

JAMES MADISON.

---

*Relating to affairs between the United States and Great Britain.

† Washington.

‡ Proclamation of November 2, 1810 (see Vol. I, pp. 481-482), and circular letter from the Secretary of the Treasury to the collectors of the customs in pursuance of said proclamation.

To the Senate of the United States: JANUARY 25, 1811.

I transmit to the Senate a report* from the Secretary of the Treasury on the subject of their resolution of the 21st instant.

                                        JAMES MADISON.

                                        JANUARY 25, 1811.
To the House of Representatives of the United States:

I transmit to the House of Representatives a report of the superintendent of the city,† stating the expenditures under the act of April 28, 1810, for the better accommodation of the General Post-Office and Patent Office, and for other purposes.

                                        JAMES MADISON.

                                        JANUARY 31, 1811.
To the House of Representatives of the United States:

I transmit to the House of Representatives a report‡ of the Secretary of War, complying with their resolution of the 21st instant.

                                        JAMES MADISON.

To the Senate of the United States: FEBRUARY 4, 1811.

I transmit to the Senate a report§ of the Secretary of the Treasury, complying with their resolution of December 20, 1810.

                                        JAMES MADISON.

To the Senate of the United States: FEBRUARY 5, 1811.

I transmit to the Senate a report‖ of the Secretary of State, complying with their resolution of the 1st instant.

                                        JAMES MADISON.

To the Senate of the United States: FEBRUARY 7, 1811.

I transmit to the Senate a report** of the Secretary of the Treasury, complying with their resolution of the 21st January last.

                                        JAMES MADISON.

---

*Stating that there are no documents in his Department showing the amount of property of citizens or subjects of Great Britain or France confiscated under the acts of March 1, 1809, and May 1, 1810; that inquiry of the several district attorneys for such information has been made, and that the result will be communicated as soon as received; that an account of the goods, wares, and merchandise imported into the United States during the last three quarters of 1809 will be immediately prepared, but that such account for the year 1810 can not be prepared during the present session.

† Washington.

‡ Transmitting a general return of the Army.

§ Transmitting correspondence relative to the execution of the act to provide for surveying the coasts of the United States.

‖ Transmitting copies of the latest census of the Territory of Orleans and of the latest militia returns of said Territory.

** Transmitting a statement of importations in American and foreign vessels from April 1 to December 31, 1809.

FEBRUARY 11, 1811.

To the Senate of the United States:

I transmit to the Senate a report* of the Secretary of the Treasury, complying with their resolution of the 7th instant.

JAMES MADISON.

FEBRUARY 19, 1811.

To the Senate and House of Representatives of the United States:

I lay before Congress a return of the militia of the United States as received by the Department of War from the several States and Territories.

JAMES MADISON.

FEBRUARY 19, 1811.

To the House of Representatives of the United States:

I transmit to the House of Representatives a report† of the Secretary of State, complying with their resolution of the 18th instant.

JAMES MADISON.

FEBRUARY 25, 1811.

To the House of Representatives of the United States:

I transmit to the House of Representatives reports from the superintendent of the city ‡ and the Surveyor of the Public Buildings, complying with their resolution of the 14th of January.

JAMES MADISON.

FEBRUARY 28, 1811.

To the Senate and House of Representatives of the United States:

I transmit and recommend to the attention of Congress a report of the Secretary of State relative to deficiencies in the returns of the census.

JAMES MADISON.

NOVEMBER 7, 1811.

To the Senate and House of Representatives of the United States:

I now lay before Congress two letters§ to the Department of State—one from the present plenipotentiary of France, the other from his predecessor—which were not included among the documents accompanying my message of the 5th instant,|| the translation of them being not then completed.

JAMES MADISON.

* Transmitting account of George W. Erving relative to awards under the seventh article of the treaty with Great Britain of November 19, 1794.
† Relating to affairs between the United States and Great Britain.
‡ Washington.
§ Relating to affairs between the United States and France.
|| See Third Annual Message, Vol. I, pp. 491–493.

NOVEMBER 13, 1811.

To the Senate and House of Representatives of the United States:

I lay before Congress the result of the census lately taken of the inhabitants of the United States, with a letter from the Secretary of State relative thereto.

JAMES MADISON.

JANUARY 7, 1812.

To the Senate and House of Representatives of the United States:

I lay before Congress, for their information, a report of the Director of the Mint.

JAMES MADISON.

WASHINGTON, *January 15, 1812.*

To the House of Representatives of the United States:

I transmit to the House of Representatives a report* of the Secretary of State, complying with their resolution of the 29th of November.

JAMES MADISON.

JANUARY 16, 1812.

To the Senate of the United States:

I transmit to the Senate a report† of the Secretary of State, complying with their resolution of the 18th of November.

JAMES MADISON.

WASHINGTON, *January 17, 1812.*

To the Senate and House of Representatives of the United States:

I lay before Congress a letter from the envoy extraordinary and minister plenipotentiary of Great Britain to the Secretary of State, with the answer of the latter.‡

JAMES MADISON.

WASHINGTON, *January 22, 1812.*

To the Senate and House of Representatives of the United States:

At the request of the legislature of New Jersey, I communicate to Congress copies of its resolutions§ transmitted by the governor of that State.

JAMES MADISON.

---

* Relating to the impressment of American seamen by foreign powers.

† Relating to the commercial regulations of France applying to the trade of the United States.

‡ Relating to the agency of the British Government in the hostile measures of the Indian tribes toward the United States.

§ Expressing confidence in the wisdom and integrity of the President and Congress and pledging the support of New Jersey should the United States determine to resist by force the lawless aggressions by Great Britain.

FEBRUARY 1, 1812.

To the Senate and House of Representatives of the United States:

I lay before Congress a report of the Secretary of the Treasury, containing a statement of proceedings under the "act to regulate the laying out and making a road from Cumberland, in the State of Maryland, to the State of Ohio."

JAMES MADISON.

FEBRUARY 19, 1812.

To the House of Representatives of the United States:

I lay before the House of Representatives a report * of the Secretary of War, in pursuance of their resolution of the 17th of December, 1811.

JAMES MADISON.

MARCH 12, 1812.

To the Senate of the United States:

I transmit to the Senate a report † of the Secretary of State, complying with their resolution of the 10th instant.

JAMES MADISON.

MARCH 13, 1812.

To the Senate and House of Representatives of the United States:

I lay before Congress a letter ‡ from the envoy extraordinary and minister plenipotentiary of Great Britain to the Secretary of State.

JAMES MADISON.

APRIL 6, 1812.

To the House of Representatives of the United States:

I transmit to the House of Representatives a report of the superintendent of the city,§ in compliance with their resolution of the 24th of March, to which I add a letter from B. H. Latrobe, connected with that subject.

JAMES MADISON.

* Transmitting rules and regulations for training and disciplining the regular troops and militia of the United States.

† Stating that his Department is not in possession of any names of persons in the United States who entered into or countenanced the project for the fomentation of sectional divisions in the United States and the dissolution of the Union for the execution of which John Henry was in the year 1809 employed by Sir James Craig, then Governor-General of the British Provinces in North America.

‡ Disclaiming any knowledge of the employment of a secret agent by Great Britain to foment disaffection to the constituted authorities of the United States, etc. (See message of March 9, 1812, Vol. I, p. 498.)

§ Washington.

To the Senate of the United States: APRIL 23, 1812.

I transmit to the Senate a report* of the Secretary of State, complying with their resolution of the 4th of March last.

                                                    JAMES MADISON.

                                                    JUNE 4, 1812.

To the Senate and House of Representatives of the United States:

I transmit, for the information of Congress, copies of a correspondence of the minister plenipotentiary of Great Britain with the Secretary of State.†

                                                    JAMES MADISON.

                                                    JUNE 8, 1812.

To the Senate and House of Representatives of the United States:

I lay before Congress copies of letters ‡ which have passed between the Secretary of State and the envoy extraordinary and minister plenipotentiary of Great Britain.

                                                    JAMES MADISON.

                                                    JUNE 11, 1812.

To the Senate and House of Representatives of the United States:

I transmit, for the information of Congress, copies of letters§ which have passed between the Secretary of State and the envoy extraordinary and minister plenipotentiary of Great Britain.

                                                    JAMES MADISON.

                                                    JUNE 15, 1812.

To the Senate and House of Representatives of the United States:

I transmit, for the information of Congress, copies of letters† which have passed between the Secretary of State and the envoy extraordinary and minister plenipotentiary of Great Britain.

                                                    JAMES MADISON.

---

*Relating to captures by belligerent European Governments of American vessels bound to or from the Baltic or within that sea.

†Relating to the revocation of the Berlin and Milan decrees by France, to the British orders in council, etc.

‡Relating to impressment of American seamen in British ships of war, detention of British seamen in American ships of war, British orders in council, aid given by American citizens to deserters from British ships, etc.

§Relating to the alleged agency of British authorities in Canada in atrocities committed on the frontiers of the United States by Indians.

JUNE 16, 1812.

To the Senate and House of Representatives of the United States:

I transmit, for the information of Congress, copies of a letter to the Secretary of State from the chargé d'affaires of the United States at London, accompanied by a letter from the latter to the British minister of foreign affairs.*

JAMES MADISON.

JUNE 22, 1812.

To the Senate and House of Representatives of the United States:

I communicate to Congress copies of a letter to the Secretary of State from the chargé d'affaires of the United States at London and of a note† to him from the British secretary for foreign affairs.

JAMES MADISON.

JUNE 23, 1812.

To the Senate of the United States:

I transmit to the Senate a report ‡ of the Secretary of War, complying with their resolution of the 19th instant.

JAMES MADISON.

JULY 6, 1812.

To the House of Representatives of the United States:

I transmit to the House of Representatives a report § of the Secretary of State of this date, complying with their resolution of the 30th of January last.

JAMES MADISON.

NOVEMBER 6, 1812.

To the Senate and House of Representatives of the United States:

I transmit to Congress copies of the correspondence between the Department of War and the governors of Massachusetts and Connecticut referred to in my message of the 4th instant.||

JAMES MADISON.

* Relating to the British declaration and order in council of April 21, 1812, to the hostile attitude of Great Britain toward American commerce, etc.

† Inclosing copy of a declaration accompanying the British order in council of April 21, 1812.

‡ Transmitting extracts from letters of governors of Territories and other agents respecting the hostile and friendly movements and intentions of the Indians toward the United States.

§ Transmitting lists of captures, seizures, and condemnations of the ships and merchandise of citizens of the United States under authority of Governments of Europe.

|| Relating to the refusal of the governors of Massachusetts and Connecticut to furnish their quotas of militia.

NOVEMBER 18, 1812.

To the Senate and House of Representatives of the United States:

I transmit to Congress copies of a communication from Mr. Russell to the Secretary of State. It is connected with the correspondence accompanying my message of the 12th instant,* but had not at that date been received.

JAMES MADISON.

DECEMBER 21, 1812.

To the House of Representatives of the United States:

I transmit to the House of Representatives a report † of the Secretary of State, complying with their resolution of the 9th instant.

JAMES MADISON.

DECEMBER 22, 1812.

To the House of Representatives of the United States:

I transmit to the House of Representatives a report ‡ of the Secretary of the Navy, complying with their resolution of the 16th instant.

JAMES MADISON.

JANUARY 4, 1813.

To the Senate and House of Representatives of the United States:

I lay before Congress, for their information, a report of the Director of the Mint.

JAMES MADISON.

JANUARY 11, 1813.

To the Senate and House of Representatives of the United States:

I transmit to Congress an account of the contingent expenses of the Government for the year 1812.

JAMES MADISON

JANUARY 11, 1813.

To the Senate of the United States:

I transmit to the Senate a report § of the Secretary of War, complying with their resolution of the 24th December last.

JAMES MADISON.

---

* See Vol. I, p. 521.

† Relating to the conduct of British officers toward persons taken in American armed ships.

‡ Relating to the presentation to Commodore Edward Preble of a gold medal emblematical of the attacks on the town, batteries, and naval force of Tripoli by the squadron under his command, pursuant to a resolution of Congress of March 3, 1805.

§ Transmitting correspondence relative to murders committed by Indians in Tennessee and vicinity.

JANUARY 13, 1813.

To the Senate and House of Representatives of the United States:

At the request of the general assembly of Maryland, communicated by the governor of that State, I lay before Congress copies of their act passed on the 2d instant.* JAMES MADISON.

JANUARY 13, 1813.

To the Senate of the United States:

I transmit to the Senate copies of the correspondence† called for by their resolution of the 7th instant. JAMES MADISON.

JANUARY 14, 1813.

To the Senate of the United States:

I transmit to the Senate a report‡ of the Secretary of State, complying with their resolution of the 22d December. JAMES MADISON.

JANUARY 23, 1813.

To the Senate of the United States:

I transmit to the Senate a report§ of the Secretary of the Treasury, complying with their resolution of the 20th instant.

JAMES MADISON.

JANUARY 26, 1813.

To the Senate of the United States:

I transmit to the Senate a report‖ of the Secretary of State, complying with their resolution of the 18th instant. JAMES MADISON.

JANUARY 27, 1813.

To the Senate of the United States:

I transmit to the Senate a report** of the Secretary of War, complying with their resolution of the 7th instant. JAMES MADISON.

JANUARY 30, 1813.

To the Senate and House of Representatives of the United States:

At the request of the legislature of Pennsylvania, conveyed through the governor of that State, I transmit to Congress copies of its resolutions of the 16th December, 1812.†† JAMES MADISON.

*Relating to the Chesapeake and Delaware Canal Company.
†Relating to capture of the British brigs *Detroit* and *Caledonia* on Lake Erie October 8, 1812.
‡Relating to East Florida.
§Transmitting statements of purchases of Treasury notes by banks.
‖Transmitting correspondence, etc., relative to the revocation by France of the Berlin and Milan decrees in so far as they affected American vessels.
**Relating to enlistments under the "act authorizing the President of the United States to accept and organize certain volunteer military corps," etc.
††Approving of the declaration of war against Great Britain, etc.

FEBRUARY 13, 1813.

To the Senate and House of Representatives of the United States:

I lay before Congress a statement of the militia of the United States according to the latest returns received by the Department of War.

JAMES MADISON.

To the Senate of the United States: FEBRUARY 18, 1813.

I transmit to the Senate a report * of the Secretary of State, complying with their resolution of the 18th of January, 1813.

JAMES MADISON.

MARCH 1, 1813.

To the Senate and House of Representatives of the United States:

I lay before Congress a report of the Secretary of the Treasury, containing a statement of proceedings under the "act to regulate the laying out and making a road from Cumberland, in the State of Maryland, to the State of Ohio."

JAMES MADISON.

MARCH 3, 1813.

To the House of Representatives of the United States:

I transmit to the House of Representatives a report † of the Secretary of State, complying with their resolution of the 1st instant.

JAMES MADISON.

WASHINGTON, *May 29, 1813.*

To the Senate of the United States:

Commissions having been granted during the recess of the Senate to the following persons, I now nominate them to the same offices respectively annexed to their names: Albert Gallatin, John Quincy Adams, and James A. Bayard to be jointly and severally envoys extraordinary and ministers plenipotentiary to negotiate and sign a treaty of peace with Great Britain under the mediation of the Emperor of Russia, to negotiate and sign a treaty of commerce with Great Britain; and the said John Quincy Adams, Albert Gallatin, and James A. Bayard to be jointly and severally envoys extraordinary and ministers plenipotentiary to negotiate and sign a treaty of commerce with Russia.

   *   *   *   *   *   *   *

JAMES MADISON.

* Transmitting correspondence relative to affairs between the United States and Spain, etc.

† Transmitting correspondence relative to and text of decree of repeal of the Berlin and Milan decrees.

WASHINGTON, *June 3, 1813.*

To the Senate of the United States:

In compliance with their resolution of the 3d instant, the Senate are informed that the office of the Secretary of the Treasury is not vacated, and that in the absence of Albert Gallatin, commissioned as one of the envoys to treat with Great Britain and Russia, the duties of that office are discharged by William Jones, Secretary of the Navy, authorized therefor according to the provisions of the act of Congress entitled "An act making alterations in the Treasury and War Departments," passed May 8, 1792.   JAMES MADISON.

WASHINGTON, *June 5, 1813.*

To the Senate and House of Representatives of the United States:

I lay before Congress copies of certain legislative acts of Pennsylvania,* transmitted for that purpose by the governor of that State.

JAMES MADISON.

JUNE 7, 1813.

To the Senate of the United States:

I transmit to the Senate a report † of the Secretary of State, complying with their resolution of the 3d instant.

JAMES MADISON.

WASHINGTON, *July 12, 1813.*

To the House of Representatives of the United States:

I transmit to the House of Representatives a report ‡ of the Secretary of State, containing the information requested by their resolution of the 21st of June last.   JAMES MADISON.

WASHINGTON, *July 12, 1813.*

To the House of Representatives of the United States:

I transmit to the House of Representatives a report § of the Secretary of State, containing the information requested by their resolutions of the 21st of June last.   JAMES MADISON.

*"A supplement to an act to incorporate a company for the purpose of cutting and making a canal between the river Delaware and the Chesapeake Bay" and extracts from the act mentioned.

† Transmitting correspondence relative to an interchange of ministers with the Swedish Government.

‡ Relating to the British declaration and order in council of April 21, 1812.

§ Relating to the French decree of April 28, 1811, purporting to be a definitive repeal of the Berlin and Milan decrees, etc.

WASHINGTON, *July 28, 1813.*

To the Senate of the United States:

I transmit to the Senate a report* of the Acting Secretary of the Treasury, containing the information requested by their resolution of the 27th instant.

JAMES MADISON.

DECEMBER 20, 1813.

To the Senate of the United States:

I transmit to the Senate a report † of the Acting Secretary of the Treasury, complying with the resolution of the 13th instant.

JAMES MADISON.

JANUARY 6, 1814.

To the Senate and House of Representatives of the United States:

I communicate, for the information of Congress, the report of the Director of the Mint of the operation of that establishment during the last year.

JAMES MADISON.

JANUARY 10, 1814.

To the Senate of the United States:

I transmit to the Senate a report ‡ of the Acting Secretary of the Treasury, complying with their resolution of the 31st December, 1813.

JAMES MADISON.

JANUARY 14, 1814.

To the Senate and House of Representatives of the United States:

I transmit to Congress an account of the contingent expenses of the Government for the year 1813.

JAMES MADISON.

JANUARY 15, 1814.

To the Senate of the United States:

I transmit to the Senate a report § of the Acting Secretary of the Treasury, complying with their resolution of the 11th instant.

JAMES MADISON.

---

* Relating to the loan of $16,000,000 authorized by act of February 8, 1813.

† Transmitting statement of amount of duties accruing on goods, wares, and merchandise imported into the United States from July 1 to December 31, 1812, etc.

‡ Transmitting a statement of the quantity and estimated value of spirits distilled from materials other than grain imported into the United States from the West Indies and American colonies from October 1, 1804, to September 30, 1812.

§ Transmitting a digest of the number, nature, extent, situation, and value of the arts and manufactures of the United States.

JANUARY 18, 1814.

To the Senate and House of Representatives of the United States:

I lay before Congress a report of the Acting Secretary of the Treasury, containing a statement of proceedings under the "act to regulate the laying out and making a road from Cumberland, in the State of Maryland, to the State of Ohio."

JAMES MADISON.

JANUARY 18, 1814.

To the House of Representatives of the United States:

I transmit to the House of Representatives a report* of the Secretary of State, complying with their resolution of the 13th instant.

JAMES MADISON.

JANUARY 18, 1814.

To the House of Representatives of the United States:

I transmit to the House of Representatives a report† of the Secretary of State, complying with their resolution of the 11th instant.

JAMES MADISON.

JANUARY 19, 1814.

To the House of Representatives of the United States:

I transmit to the House of Representatives a report‡ of the Secretary of State, complying with their resolution of the 12th instant.

JAMES MADISON.

JANUARY 31, 1814.

To the House of Representatives of the United States:

I transmit to the House of Representatives a report§ of the Secretary of War, complying with their resolution of the 31st of December last.

JAMES MADISON.

FEBRUARY 3, 1814.

To the Senate of the United States:

I transmit to the Senate of the United States reports‖ of the Secretary of War and Secretary of the Navy, complying with their resolution of the 3d ultimo.

JAMES MADISON.

---

*Relating to the mediation of Russia in the war between the United States and Great Britain.

† Relating to the reception by the French Government of the United States minister to that court.

‡ Stating that no communication from the French minister prescribing the conditions on which his sovereign would treat of amity and commerce with the United States is on file in the Department of State.

§ Relating to the cause of the failure of the army on the northern frontier.

‖ Transmitting statements of foreign and domestic articles consumed in clothing the Army and Navy of the United States in 1813, and estimates for 1814.

FEBRUARY 10, 1814.

To the House of Representatives of the United States:

I transmit to the House of Representatives a report* of the Acting Secretary of the Treasury, complying with their resolution of the 30th July, 1813.

JAMES MADISON.

FEBRUARY 14, 1814.

To the Senate and House of Representatives of the United States:

At the request of the legislature of Pennsylvania, conveyed through the governor of that State, I transmit to Congress copies of its resolutions of the 18th ultimo.†

JAMES MADISON.

MARCH 22, 1814.

To the Senate and House of Representatives of the United States:

At the request of the legislature of Pennsylvania, conveyed through the governor of that State, I transmit to Congress copies of its resolutions of the 10th instant.‡

JAMES MADISON.

MARCH 28, 1814.

To the Senate of the United States:

I transmit to the Senate a report § of the Secretary of State, complying with their resolution of the 26th instant.

JAMES MADISON.

APRIL 9, 1814.

To the Senate of the United States:

I transmit to the Senate a report || of the Secretary of State, complying with their resolution of the 2d instant.

JAMES MADISON.

---

* Transmitting accounts of United States ministers, consuls, etc., from commencement of present Government; expenses incurred in and payments made under treaty with Algiers, and accounts of all other expenditures in relation to the Barbary Powers, including those occasioned by war with Tripoli and making of peace with that Regency.

† Commending the "decisive spirit and firmness which the national authorities have manifested in securing hostages for the safety of those defenders of the Republic who are threatened with the penalties of treason against Great Britain," and pledging under all circumstances to support the Government in every measure of just retaliation.

‡ Expressing disapprobation of the action of the governor of a sister State in issuing a proclamation ordering a detachment of militia of that State then in the United States service to desert and return to their respective homes, and also expressing disapprobation of the threatened resistance of another State to any action of Congress directing an inquiry by the President into the constitutionality of the act of said governor, and pledging to support the General Government in all lawful and constitutional measures to bring to justice all infractors of the Constitution and laws of the United States and all abettors and aiders of the enemies thereof.

§ Transmitting copies of certain commissions granted by Presidents Washington and Madison during the recess of the Senate.

|| Transmitting lists of ministers, their secretaries, and consuls appointed by the several Presidents during the recess of the Senate.

To the Senate of the United States: APRIL 16, 1814.

I transmit to the Senate a report* of the Secretary of State, complying with their resolutions of the 2d of February and 9th of March.

JAMES MADISON.

APRIL 16, 1814.

To the House of Representatives of the United States:

I transmit to the House of Representatives a report † of the Secretary of State, complying with their resolution of the 13th instant.

JAMES MADISON.

To the Senate of the United States: OCTOBER 3, 1814.

I transmit to the Senate a report ‡ from the Department of State, complying with their resolution of the 26th ultimo.

JAMES MADISON.

WASHINGTON, *October 13, 1814.*

To the Senate and House of Representatives of the United States:

I now transmit to Congress copies of the instructions to the plenipotentiaries of the United States charged with negotiating a peace with Great Britain, as referred to in my message of the 10th instant.§

JAMES MADISON.

OCTOBER 28, 1814.

To the House of Representatives of the United States:

I transmit to the House of Representatives a report ‖ from the Department of State, complying with their resolution of the 15th instant.

JAMES MADISON.

To the Senate of the United States: NOVEMBER 18, 1814.

I lay before the Senate, for their consideration whether they will advise and consent to the ratification thereof, a treaty concluded on the 22d day

---

* Transmitting list of American prisoners sent to England for trial by the British commander in Canada; statement of the grounds on which the British Government refused to deliver up American seamen impressed into the British service, and statement of the conduct of the British Government toward American seamen on board British ships of war.

† Transmitting extract of a letter from the United States minister at Paris touching relations with France.

‡ Stating that the relations of the United States with the continental powers of Europe continue to be those of peace and amity; that measures have been taken to continue diplomatic relations with France under the existing Government and to renew those with Spain and the United Provinces of the Low Countries.

§ See Vol. I, p. 551.

‖ Relating to retaliation upon prisoners of war.

of July last with the tribes of Indians called the Wyandots, Delawares, Shawanese, Senecas, and Miamies.

I lay before the Senate also, for the like purpose, an instrument entitled "Articles of agreement and capitulation made and concluded on the 9th day of August last between Major-General Jackson and the chiefs, deputies, and warriors of the Creek Nation of Indians."

These communications are accompanied by documents having relation to them.   JAMES MADISON.

JANUARY 2, 1815.

To the Senate and House of Representatives of the United States:

I lay before Congress a report of the Secretary of the Treasury, containing a statement of proceedings under the "act to regulate the laying out and making a road from Cumberland, in the State of Maryland, to the State of Ohio."   JAMES MADISON.

JANUARY 10, 1815.

To the Senate and House of Representatives of the United States:

I communicate, for the information of Congress, the report of the Director of the Mint of the operation of that establishment during the last year.   JAMES MADISON.

JANUARY 10, 1815.

To the Senate and House of Representatives of the United States:

I transmit to Congress an account of the contingent expenses of the Government for the year 1814.   JAMES MADISON.

JANUARY 14, 1815.

To the Senate of the United States:

I transmit to the Senate a report of the Secretary of War, complying with their resolution of the 19th December.*
JAMES MADISON.

FEBRUARY 16, 1815.

To the Senate of the United States:

I transmit to the Senate a report † of the Acting Secretary of State, complying with their resolution of yesterday.
JAMES MADISON.

---

*Relating to measures authorized by the President in pursuance of the "act to enable the President of the United States, under certain contingencies, to take possession of the country lying east of the river Perdido and south of the State of Georgia and the Mississippi Territory, and for other purposes," for the purpose of possessing and occupying any part of the country mentioned in said act.

†Transmitting correspondence and protocols of conferences between United States envoys at Ghent and ministers of Great Britain.

FEBRUARY 23, 1815.

To the House of Representatives of the United States:

I transmit to the House of Representatives a report * from the Acting Secretary of State, complying with their resolution of the 15th instant.

JAMES MADISON.

WASHINGTON, *February 28, 1815.*

To the Senate of the United States:

I transmit to the Senate a report † from the Postmaster-General, complying with their resolution of the 15th of December last.

JAMES MADISON.

WASHINGTON, *February 28, 1815.*

To the Senate of the United States:

I transmit to the Senate a report ‡ from the Acting Secretary of State, complying with their resolution of the 24th of October last.

JAMES MADISON.

JANUARY 8, 1816.

To the Senate and House of Representatives of the United States:

I communicate, for the information of Congress, the report of the Director of the Mint of the operation of that establishment during the last year.

JAMES MADISON.

JANUARY 26, 1816.

To the House of Representatives of the United States:

In compliance with the resolution of the 24th instant, I transmit two letters from the envoy extraordinary and minister plenipotentiary of Spain to the Secretary of State, with his answer.§

JAMES MADISON.

WASHINGTON, *January 31, 1816.*

To the House of Representatives of the United States:

I transmit a report ‖ of the Secretary of State, complying with the resolution of the 4th instant.

JAMES MADISON.

---

* Relating to affairs between the United States and the Barbary Powers.

† Transmitting statement of number of post-offices and miles of post-roads in each State, net amount of postages for six months ending June 30, 1814, etc.

‡ Relating to the sale of negroes taken from the United States by British forces.

§ Relating to demand of Spain for possession of West Florida; to unlawful expeditions against Spanish possessions; to the exclusion from ports of the United States of the flags of revolting provinces of Spain; to the attitude of the United States toward the Mexican revolution; to vessels of the United States condemned in ports of Spain; to the free navigation of the Mississippi; to the boundaries of Louisiana, etc.

‖ Relating to the massacre of American prisoners at Dartmoor prison, England.

To the Senate of the United States:　　　　February 13, 1816.

I transmit to the Senate a report from the Secretary of War, complying with their resolution of the 5th instant.*

JAMES MADISON.

March 11, 1816.

To the House of Representatives of the United States:

I transmit to the House of Representatives a report † of the Secretary of the Treasury, complying with their resolution of the 17th of February.

JAMES MADISON.

March 12, 1816.

To the Senate and House of Representatives of the United States:

I lay before Congress a report of the Secretary of the Treasury, containing a statement of proceedings under the act to regulate the laying out and making a road from Cumberland, in the State of Maryland, to the State of Ohio, with a statement of past appropriations and an estimate of required appropriations.

JAMES MADISON.

March 22, 1816.

To the House of Representatives of the United States:

I transmit to the House of Representatives a report ‡ from the Secretary of the Treasury, complying with their resolution of the 29th of February last.

JAMES MADISON.

March 26, 1816.

To the Senate of the United States:

I lay before the Senate, for their advice as to a ratification, articles of a treaty and of a convention which have been concluded with the Cherokee Nation, with documents relating to the losses by the Indians, for which indemnity is stipulated.

JAMES MADISON.

April 4, 1816.

To the Senate of the United States:

I transmit to the Senate a report § from the Secretary of the Treasury, complying with their resolutions of the 26th March last.

JAMES MADISON.

* Relating to the reduction of the late Army to a peace establishment.
† Transmitting statements of receipts and expenditures of the city of Washington from 1791 to 1815, inclusive, and of moneys advanced by the United States to said city.
‡ Relating to the employment of counsel to assist the Attorney-General in prosecuting cases in the Supreme Court, names of persons so employed, fees paid, etc.
§ Relating to the survey of the coasts of the United States.

APRIL 18, 1816.

To the House of Representatives of the United States:

I transmit to the House of Representatives a report* from the Secretary of State, complying with their resolution of the 17th February last.

JAMES MADISON.

APRIL 29, 1816.

To the House of Representatives of the United States:

I transmit to the House of Representatives a report † of the Secretary of State on the subject of their resolution of February 28, 1816.

JAMES MADISON.

JANUARY 6, 1817.

To the Senate and House of Representatives of the United States:

I communicate, for the information of Congress, the report of the Director of the Mint of the operation of that establishment during the last year.

JAMES MADISON

JANUARY 17, 1817.

To the Senate and House of Representatives of the United States:

I transmit to Congress an account of the contingent expenses of the Government for the year 1816.

JAMES MADISON.

JANUARY 23, 1817.

To the Senate of the United States:

I transmit to the Senate a report ‡ of the Acting Secretary of War, in compliance with their resolution of the 8th instant.

JAMES MADISON.

FEBRUARY 7, 1817.

To the Senate of the United States:

I transmit to the Senate a report § of the Secretary of State, complying with their resolution of the 28th of last month.

JAMES MADISON.

*Relating to obstructions to American commerce in the provincial and colonial possessions of Great Britain.

† Transmitting lists of impressed American seamen transferred from British ships of war to Dartmoor and other prisons in England and the West Indies and Nova Scotia, and those discharged in England since the treaty of peace.

‡ Transmitting statement of claims of New Hampshire, Rhode Island, Pennsylvania, Virginia, and North Carolina for militia services during the late war.

§ Relating to the deportation of slaves by Great Britain in contravention of the treaty of Ghent, etc.

To the Senate of the United States: FEBRUARY 22, 1817.

I transmit to the Senate a report* of the Secretary of State, complying with their resolution of the 20th instant.

JAMES MADISON.

WASHINGTON, *February 4, 1818.*

To the House of Representatives:

Pursuant to a resolution of the House of Representatives of the 31st of December last, requesting information of the number of States which had ratified the thirteenth article of the amendments to the Constitution of the United States,† I transmit to the House a detailed report from the Secretary of State, which contains all the information that has been received upon that subject.

No time will be lost in communicating to the House the answers of the governors of the States of South Carolina and Virginia to the inquiries stated by the Secretary of State to have been recently addressed to them when they are received at that Department.

JAMES MONROE.

WASHINGTON, *February 6, 1818.*

To the Senate of the United States:

In compliance with a resolution of the Senate of the 13th of February, 1817, I now transmit copies of the reports in relation to the surveys and examinations made by naval officers in cooperation with officers of the Corps of Engineers.

JAMES MONROE.

WASHINGTON, *February 12, 1818.*

To the House of Representatives of the United States:

Conformably with a resolution of the House of Representatives of the 6th of this month, I now lay before that House a report received from the Secretary of State, with the copy of the correspondence‡ referred to and requested by that resolution.

JAMES MONROE.

---

*Transmitting correspondence between the Governments of the United States and Spain relative to settlement of boundaries, to cession of East Florida by Spain, to indemnification for injuries to American commerce by Spanish vessels, etc.

†"If any citizen of the United States shall accept, claim, receive, or retain any title of nobility or honor, or shall, without the consent of Congress, accept and retain any present, pension, office, or emolument of any kind whatever from any emperor, king, prince, or foreign power, such person shall cease to be a citizen of the United States, and shall be incapable of holding any office of profit or trust under them, or either of them." This proposed amendment did not become a part of the Constitution, failing of ratification by three-fourths of the States.

‡Relating to a blockade of the Spanish coast in South America by Spanish forces.

WASHINGTON, *February 13, 1818.*

To the Senate of the United States:

In compliance with a resolution of the 28th of January last, I now transmit to the Senate a statement of the expenditures upon the public buildings and an account of their progress for the year 1818.

JAMES MONROE.

WASHINGTON, *February 18, 1818.*

To the House of Representatives of the United States:

Conformably with a resolution of the House of Representatives of the 12th instant, I lay before that House a report which I have received from the Department of State, with a copy of the letter communicated with it.*

JAMES MONROE.

MARCH 5, 1818.

To the Senate of the United States:

I lay before the Senate, for their consideration and the exercise of their constitutional power of advice and consent respecting the ratification thereof, a treaty concluded on the 22d of January last with the Creek Nation of Indians. This treaty is accompanied by certain documents having relation to it.

JAMES MONROE.

WASHINGTON, *March 24, 1818.*

To the House of Representatives of the United States:

In pursuance of a resolution of the House of Representatives of the 7th instant, I now transmit the report of the Secretary of State, with a statement of the expenses incurred under the fourth, fifth, sixth, and seventh articles of the treaty of Ghent, specifying the items of expenditure in relation to each.

JAMES MONROE.

NOVEMBER 26, 1818.

To the Senate of the United States:

I lay before the Senate a report from the Commissioner of the Public Buildings, made in compliance with a resolution of the 28th of January last, requiring a statement of the expenditures upon the public buildings and an account of their progress to be annually exhibited to Congress.

JAMES MONROE.

[The same message was sent to the House of Representatives.]

*Relative to the claims of the heirs of Caron de Beaumarchais.

NOVEMBER 30, 1818.

To the Senate of the United States:

In compliance with the resolution of the 17th of April, I transmit to the Senate a report * from the Acting Secretary of the Navy, which, with the documents accompanying it, will be found to contain all the information required.

JAMES MONROE.

DECEMBER 15, 1818.

To the House of Representatives of the United States:

I lay before the House of Representatives copies of the remainder of the documents † referred to in the message of the 17th of last month.

JAMES MONROE.

[The same message was sent to the Senate.]

DECEMBER 18, 1818.

To the Senate of the United States:

In compliance with the resolution of the Senate of the 10th instant, I transmit copies of the instructions to the commissioners who negotiated the Indian treaties now before it.

JAMES MONROE.

DECEMBER 28, 1818.

To the Senate of the United States:

In compliance with a resolution of the Senate of the 17th instant, I transmit to that House a report from the Secretary of State, with the papers and documents accompanying it. ‡

JAMES MONROE.

DECEMBER 28, 1818.

To the House of Representatives of the United States:

In compliance with a resolution of the 15th instant, I lay before the House of Representatives a report from the Secretary of State, with the papers and documents accompanying it. §

JAMES MONROE.

JANUARY 4, 1819.

To the Senate of the United States:

I lay before the Senate a report from the Secretary of State, accompanied with a copy of a letter from Governor Rabun, ‖ which was not communicated on a former occasion from that Department.

JAMES MONROE.

---

* Relating to the navy pension fund.

† Reports of Theodorick Bland and J. R. Poinsett, commissioners, on the condition of South America, correspondence between the Secretary of State and the Spanish minister relative to affairs between the United States and Spain, etc.

‡ Relating to affairs between the United States and Spain, the prosecution of Captain Obed Wright for the murder of friendly Indians, etc.

§ Relating to affairs between the United States and Spain.

‖ Relating to the case of Captain Obed Wright, charged with the murder of friendly Indians.

DECEMBER 24, 1819.

To the Senate and House of Representatives of the United States:

I transmit to Congress a report from the Commissioner of the Public Buildings, which, with the accompanying documents, will exhibit the present state of those buildings and the expenditures thereon during the year ending the 30th of September last.

JAMES MONROE.

JANUARY 18, 1820.

To the Senate of the United States:

In compliance with the resolution of the Senate of the 5th instant, the inclosed papers are transmitted to them *in confidence*, and contain all the information in possession of the Executive respecting the progress of the negotiation with the British Government in relation to the intercourse between the United States and the British colonies.

JAMES MONROE.

WASHINGTON, *March 8, 1820.*

The SPEAKER OF THE HOUSE OF REPRESENTATIVES:

I transmit to the House of Representatives, in pursuance of their resolution of the 22d of last month, a report from the Secretary of State, with the papers containing the information requested by that resolution.*

JAMES MONROE.

MARCH 10, 1820.

To the Senate of the United States:

I transmit to Congress a report from the Director of the Mint of the operations of that institution during the last year.

JAMES MONROE.

MARCH 17, 1820.

To the Senate of the United States:

I transmit to Congress a report from the Secretary of the Treasury, accompanied with statements of the annual expenditures made in the construction of the road leading from Cumberland, in the State of Maryland, to the State of Ohio from the year 1806 to the year 1820.

JAMES MONROE.

WASHINGTON, *March 23, 1820.*

To the Senate of the United States:

I transmit to the Senate, in pursuance of their resolution of the 1st of February, a report† from the Secretary of State, with the information required by that resolution.

JAMES MONROE.

* Relating to the Florida treaty.
†Relating to the construction of the first article of the treaty of Ghent, relative to slaves.

WASHINGTON, *March 28, 1820.*

To the House of Representatives:

I transmit to the House of Representatives, in pursuance of their resolution of the 31st of January last, a report* from the Secretary of the Treasury, with the documents which accompanied it.

JAMES MONROE.

To the Senate of the United States: MARCH 30, 1820.

I transmit to Congress a general abstract of the militia of the United States, in pursuance of the act of March 2, 1803.

JAMES MONROE.

WASHINGTON, *April 18, 1820.*

To the Senate of the United States:

I lay before the Senate, in pursuance of their resolution of the 21st of last month, the accompanying report and documents † from the Department of State.

JAMES MONROE.

WASHINGTON, *May 12, 1820.*

To the Senate and House of Representatives of the United States:

I communicate to Congress translations of letters from the minister of Spain to the Secretary of State, received since my message of the 9th instant.‡

JAMES MONROE.

The PRESIDENT OF THE SENATE: NOVEMBER 23, 1820.

In conformity with a resolution of the Senate passed the 28th of January, 1818, I communicate herewith to the Senate the report of the Commissioner of Public Buildings required by that resolution.

JAMES MONROE.

[The same message was addressed to the Speaker of the House of Representatives.]

To the Senate of the United States: JANUARY 26, 1821.

I lay before the Senate, for their consideration and advice as to a ratification, a treaty concluded between the United States and the Creek Nation of Indians.

JAMES MONROE.

---

* Relating to the marine-hospital fund.

† Relating to the seizure, sequestration, or confiscation of the ships or other property of citizens of the United States by authority of Sweden.

‡ See Vol. II, pp. 70–72.

WASHINGTON, *February 13, 1821.*

To the Senate of the United States:

I transmit herewith to the Senate a copy of a memorial received from Richard W. Meade,* together with a report of the Secretary of State concerning it. JAMES MONROE.

WASHINGTON, *February 14, 1821.*

To the Senate of the United States:

I transmit to Congress a report from the Director of the Mint, inclosing a statement of the Treasurer, submitting the operations of the Mint for the last year. JAMES MONROE.

DECEMBER 24, 1821.

To the Senate of the United States:

I transmit to the Senate a treaty recently concluded with the Indian tribes at Chicago, with the papers relating thereto, which is submitted for consideration as to its ratification. JAMES MONROE.

WASHINGTON, *January 7, 1822.*

To the Senate and House of Representatives of the United States:

I transmit to Congress a report from the Director of the Mint, with a statement of the operations for the last year. JAMES MONROE.

WASHINGTON, *January 15, 1822.*

To the Senate of the United States:

In compliance with a resolution of the Senate requesting the President "to cause a statement of expenditures upon the public buildings and an account of their progress to be annually laid before Congress at the commencement of each session," I herewith transmit the annual report of the Commissioner of the Public Buildings. JAMES MONROE.

[The same message was sent to the House of Representatives.]

WASHINGTON, *January 28, 1822.*

To the Senate of the United States:

I transmit to the Senate a report from the Secretary of State, containing the information required by the resolution of the Senate of the 3d instant, with the documents † which accompanied that report. JAMES MONROE.

* Relating to his claim against Spain for imprisonment.
† Relating to relief of sick, disabled, and destitute American seamen in foreign ports in 1818, 1819, and 1820.

WASHINGTON, *January 28, 1822.*

To the House of Representatives:

I transmit a report from the Secretary of War, together with the documents which accompany it, containing the information requested by a resolution of the House of Representatives of the 22d instant.*

JAMES MONROE.

WASHINGTON, *February 6, 1822.*

To the House of Representatives of the United States:

I transmit to the House of Representatives a report from the Secretary of State on the subject required by the resolution of that House of the 22d ultimo,† with the documents which accompanied that report.

JAMES MONROE.

WASHINGTON, *February 7, 1822.*

To the House of Representatives of the United States:

In compliance with a resolution of the 17th ultimo, I transmit a report from the Secretary of War, which, with the accompanying documents,‡ contains the information requested

JAMES MONROE.

To the Senate of the United States: FEBRUARY 8, 1822.

I transmit to the Senate a report from the Secretary of State, containing the information required by the resolution of the Senate of the 1st instant, with the documents which accompanied that report.§

JAMES MONROE.

WASHINGTON, *February 12, 1822.*

To the Senate of the United States:

I transmit to the Senate a report from the Secretary of State, containing the information ‖ required by the resolution of the Senate of the 4th instant.

JAMES MONROE.

* Relating to Indian affairs.

† Relating to that part of the boundary line between the United States and the British Provinces which extends "from the source of the river St. Croix to the northwesternmost head of Connecticut River."

‡ Statements of ordnance and ordnance stores in fortifications, arsenals, etc., and estimates of amounts required, contracted for, etc.

§ Relating to the appointment of William B. Irish as marshal of the western district of Pennsylvania.

‖ Relating to the lease of a building on Capitol Hill for the temporary use and accommodation of Congress.

WASHINGTON, *February 15, 1822.*

To the House of Representatives:

In compliance with a resolution of the House of Representatives "requesting the President of the United States to cause to be laid before this House any information which he may have of the condition of the several Indian tribes within the United States and the progress of the measures hitherto devised and pursued for their civilization," I now transmit a report from the Secretary of War. JAMES MONROE.

FEBRUARY 21, 1822.

To the Senate of the United States:

In compliance with a resolution of the Senate of the 7th instant, requesting the President of the United States to cause to be communicated to the Senate the instructions to the commissioners who negotiated the treaty concluded at Chicago with the Ottowa, Chippeway, and Potawatamie nations of Indians, I herewith transmit a report from the Secretary of War. JAMES MONROE.

WASHINGTON, *February 21, 1822.*

To the House of Representatives of the United States:

I transmit to the House of Representatives a report from the Secretary of State, with the documents* accompanying it, in pursuance of a resolution of the House of the 17th January last.

JAMES MONROE.

WASHINGTON, *March 4, 1822.*

To the House of Representatives of the United States:

I transmit a report from the Secretary of the Navy, communicating information in relation to the Navy of the United States† requested by a resolution of the House of Representatives of the 14th ultimo.

JAMES MONROE.

WASHINGTON, *March 15, 1822.*

To the Senate of the United States:

In compliance with a resolution of the Senate of the 29th of January, I herewith transmit reports‡ from the Treasury and War Departments, containing all the information in the possession of the Executive embraced by that resolution. JAMES MONROE.

*Correspondence leading up to and protocol of treaty of Ghent, etc.
†List of the navy yards and stations, number and grade of officers attached to each, etc.
‡Relating to lands granted to officers and soldiers of Virginia who served in the Revolutionary War.

WASHINGTON, *April 1, 1822.*

To the Senate of the United States:

In compliance with two resolutions of the 11th ultimo, requesting that the President of the United States cause to be furnished to that House certain detailed information from the Navy Department, I herewith transmit a report from the Secretary of the Navy, with other documents.*

JAMES MONROE.

APRIL 19, 1822.

To the Senate of the United States:

I transmit a letter from the Attorney-General on the subject of the resolution of the Senate of the 12th instant, which I have received this day, and which in consequence of his absence was not communicated with the message of the 15th instant.†

JAMES MONROE.

DECEMBER 10, 1822.

To the Congress of the United States:

I now transmit to both Houses of Congress the report of the Commissioner of Public Buildings made in obedience to a resolution of the Senate passed the 28th day of January, 1818.

JAMES MONROE.

WASHINGTON, *January 20, 1823.*

To the House of Representatives:

In compliance with the resolution of the 20th of December, requesting information "what appropriations will be required to fortify Thompsons Island, usually called Key West, and whether a naval depot established at that island, protected by fortifications, will not afford facilities in defending the commerce of the United States and in clearing the Gulf of Mexico and the adjacent seas from pirates," I transmit a report from the Secretary of the Navy, which communicates all the information which I am at this time able to give.

JAMES MONROE.

FEBRUARY 6, 1823.

To the Senate of the United States:

In compliance with a resolution of the Senate of the 28th of January, requesting the President to communicate the instructions to the commissioners nominated to treat with the Indians for the extinguishment of Indian titles in the State of Georgia, I transmit to the Senate a report from the Secretary of War, with the documents referred to in it.

JAMES MONROE.

---

*Statements showing names and number of officers belonging to the Navy attached to each navy-yard in the United States, and their compensation for two years ending January 1, 1822.
† See Vol. II, p. 136.

To the Senate of the United States:

In compliance with a resolution of the Senate of 28th January, 1818, I herewith transmit to Congress the report of the Commissioner of Public Buildings, showing the expenditures on public buildings and other objects committed to his care during the present year.

JAMES MONROE.

DECEMBER 19, 1823.

To the House of Representatives of the United States:

I transmit herewith to the House of Representatives a report from the Secretary of State, together with a digest of recent commercial regulations of foreign countries, prepared in compliance with a resolution of the House of the 30th of January, 1823.

JAMES MONROE.

FEBRUARY 2, 1824.

WASHINGTON, *February 2, 1824.*

The SPEAKER OF THE HOUSE OF REPRESENTATIVES OF THE UNITED STATES:

I transmit to the House of Representatives a report from the Secretary of State, agreeably to a resolution of that House of the 11th of December last, with the papers* which accompanied that report.

JAMES MONROE.

FEBRUARY 24, 1824.

To the Senate of the United States:

I herewith transmit a report from the Secretary of War, which communicates all the information in possession of the Department which was called for by a resolution of the Senate of the 21st of January, 1824.†

JAMES MONROE.

WASHINGTON, *March 19, 1824.*

To the House of Representatives of the United States:

I transmit to the House of Representatives a report from the Secretary of State, with the papers ‡ therein referred to, in compliance with a resolution of the House of the 27th of January last.

JAMES MONROE.

WASHINGTON, *May 7, 1824.*

To the Senate of the United States:

I communicate to the Senate copies of additional documents relating to the convention for the suppression of the African slave trade, which have this day been received at the Department of State.

JAMES MONROE.

*Relating to French spoliations.
†Relating to sites for fortifications at St. Marys and Patuxent rivers, plans for same, and estimates of cost of each fortification.
‡Relating to the suppression of the African slave trade.

MAY 24, 1824.

To the House of Representatives of the United States:

I transmit to the House of Representatives a report from the Secretary of State, with an appendix to a report * from him already communicated to the House.

JAMES MONROE.

WASHINGTON, *May 25, 1824.*

To the Senate of the United States:

I transmit to the Senate a report † from the Secretary of State, concerning two resolutions of the Senate of the 8th of January and 1st of March last, which had been referred to him.

JAMES MONROE.

MAY 25, 1824.

To the House of Representatives of the United States:

I transmit to the House of Representatives a report ‡ from the Secretary of State, concerning a resolution of that House of the 20th of April last, which was referred to him.

JAMES MONROE.

WASHINGTON, *December 13, 1824.*

To the Senate of the United States:

I transmit to the Senate, for its advice and consent as to the ratification, the treaties concluded and signed on the 4th day of August last between the United States and the Ioway, the Sock, and Fox tribes of Indians.

JAMES MONROE.

WASHINGTON, *December 13, 1824.*

To the Senate of the United States:

Agreeably to a resolution of the Senate of 28th January, 1818, requesting the President "to cause a statement of expenditures upon the public buildings and an account of their progress to be annually laid before Congress at the commencement of each session," I herewith transmit a report from the Commissioner of Public Buildings, which contains the information required.

JAMES MONROE.

[The same message was sent to the House of Representatives.]

---

* Addition to digest of foreign commercial law.

† Relating to foreign spoliations on American commerce.

‡ Stating that the correspondence relative to French spoliations and to the claims of France upon the United States for noncompliance with the treaties of alliance and commerce of February 6, 1778, would be communicated at the next session of Congress.

WASHINGTON, *January 5, 1825.*

To the Senate of the United States:

In compliance with the resolution of the Senate of the 17th May last, I transmit a report* from the Secretary of the Navy, which contains the information requested.

JAMES MONROE.

WASHINGTON, *January 17, 1825.*

To the House of Representatives of the United States:

I herewith transmit to the House a report from the Secretary of State, containing the information required by the resolution of the House of the 16th ultimo, relating to the western boundary of the United States.

JAMES MONROE.

WASHINGTON, *January 17, 1825.*

To the House of Representatives of the United States:

In compliance with a resolution of the House of Representatives of the 28th ultimo, requesting the President to inform that House what terms were offered by applicants for the stock created by the act of the 24th of May last and by whom such terms were offered, I herewith transmit a report from the Secretary of the Treasury, with accompanying papers, which contains the information called for.

JAMES MONROE.

WASHINGTON, *January 18, 1825.*

To the House of Representatives of the United States:

I herewith transmit to the House of Representatives a report of the Secretary of War, with a report made to that Department by the commissioners who were appointed under the act of the 3d of March, 1823, entitled "An act to establish an armory on the western waters."

· JAMES MONROE.

WASHINGTON, *January 18, 1825.*

To the House of Representatives of the United States:

I herewith transmit to the House of Representatives a report of the Secretary of War, with a report made to that Department by the commissioners who were appointed under the act of 3d March, 1823, entitled "An act to establish a national armory on the western waters."

JAMES MONROE.

* Relating to the use of canvas, cables, and cordage made of hemp grown in the United States in the equipment   vessels of the American Navy.

JANUARY 19, 1825.

To the Senate of the United States:

I transmit herewith to the Senate a report from the Secretary of State, with the documents desired by their resolution of the 13th instant.* In requesting that the originals may eventually be returned it may be unnecessary to add that the negotiations being by common consent to be hereafter resumed, it is important that this communication should be regarded by the Senate as strictly confidential.

JAMES MONROE.

WASHINGTON, *February 2, 1825.*

To the Senate and House of Representatives of the United States:

I herewith transmit a report from the Director of the Mint of the United States, showing the operations of that institution for the last year.

JAMES MONROE.

WASHINGTON, *March 1, 1826.*

To the Senate and House of Representatives of the United States:

I transmit herewith a report from the Director of the Mint of the United States, showing the operations of that institution for the year 1825.

JOHN QUINCY ADAMS.

WASHINGTON, *March 15, 1826.*

To the Senate and House of Representatives of the United States:

I now submit to the consideration of Congress the propriety of making the appropriation necessary for carrying into effect the appointment of a mission to the congress at Panama.

JOHN QUINCY ADAMS.

WASHINGTON, *December 8, 1826.*

To the Senate and House of Representatives of the United States:

In compliance with a resolution of the Senate of the 20th of January, 1818, I transmit a report of the Commissioner of the Public Buildings, containing the annual statement of expenditures on those buildings and the account of their progress, required by the said resolution.

JOHN QUINCY ADAMS.

WASHINGTON, *December 11, 1826.*

To the Senate and House of Representatives of the United States:

I transmit to Congress sundry additional papers appertaining to the report from the War Department relating to Indian affairs, communicated at the commencement of the session.

JOHN QUINCY ADAMS.

*Relating to commercial intercourse with the British colonies of the West Indies and Canada; to the boundary under the fifth article of the treaty of Ghent, and the navigation of the St. Lawrence River; to admission of United States consuls into British colonial ports; to the Newfoundland fishery; to maritime questions; to the northwest coast of America.

WASHINGTON, *December 28, 1826.*

To the House of Representatives of the United States:

I transmit to the House of Representatives a report from the Secretary of State, containing the information requested by two resolutions of the House relating to certain negotiations* with the Government of the United Mexican States.

JOHN QUINCY ADAMS.

WASHINGTON, *January 18, 1827.*

To the House of Representatives of the United States:

In compliance with a resolution of the House of Representatives of the 6th instant, I transmit herewith a report from the Secretary of State, together with copies of the correspondence with the Government of the Netherlands relating to discriminating duties.

JOHN QUINCY ADAMS.

WASHINGTON, *February 24, 1827.*

To the Senate and House of Representatives of the United States:

I transmit herewith to Congress a report from the Director of the Mint, with a statement of its operations during the year 1826.

JOHN QUINCY ADAMS.

WASHINGTON, *December 24, 1827.*

To the Senate of the United States:

I transmit to the Senate, for their consideration and advice, a convention of friendship, navigation, and commerce between the United States and the Free Hanseatic Republics of Lubeck, Bremen, and Hamburg, signed by the respective plenipotentiaries of the parties on the 20th instant at this city. A copy of the convention is likewise inclosed.

JOHN QUINCY ADAMS.

WASHINGTON, *January 3, 1828.*

To the Senate and House of Representatives of the United States:

I transmit to Congress the annual report of the Commissioner of the Public Buildings, made in conformity with a resolution of the Senate of the 28th January, 1818.

JOHN QUINCY ADAMS.

WASHINGTON, *January 11, 1828.*

To the Senate of the United States:

In answer to the inquiry contained in a resolution of the Senate of the 9th instant, I readily express the opinion that the publication of the

---

*Concerning the boundary line between the United States and Mexico and the return of slaves escaping from the former country into the latter.

message* and documents to which it alludes may be made without detriment to the public service.

JOHN QUINCY ADAMS.

WASHINGTON, *January 21, 1828.*

To the Senate and House of Representatives of the United States:

A report from the Director of the Mint, together with a statement of the operations of that institution during the year 1827, are herewith transmitted to Congress.

JOHN QUINCY ADAMS.

WASHINGTON, *December 8, 1828.*

To the Senate of the United States:

In compliance with a resolution of the Senate of the 26th of May last, I transmit a report of the Secretary of the Treasury, with statements relative to the estimates and appropriations for the expenses of the year 1828 at the last session of Congress.

JOHN QUINCY ADAMS.

WASHINGTON, *January 14, 1829.*

To the Senate and House of Representatives of the United States:

I transmit to Congress a report from the Director of the Mint, with the annual statement exhibiting the operations of that institution during the year 1828.

JOHN QUINCY ADAMS.

WASHINGTON, *February 25, 1829.*

To the Senate of the United States:

I transmit herewith a statement of the expenses of the General Land Office for the year 1827, as desired by a resolution of the Senate of the 23d instant.

JOHN QUINCY ADAMS.

WASHINGTON, *February 8, 1830.*

To the Congress of the United States:

I transmit to Congress a report from the Director of the Mint, exhibiting the operations of that institution during the year 1829.

ANDREW JACKSON.

JANUARY 12, 1831.

To the Senate and House of Representatives of the United States:

I transmit to Congress a report from the Director of the Mint, exhibiting the operations of that institution during the year 1830.

ANDREW JACKSON.

---

* Of December 24, 1827 (see Vol. II, p. 393), relative to the negotiation of the convention of November 13, 1826, with Great Britain.

JANUARY 25, 1831.

To the House of Representatives:

I beg leave to call the attention of Congress to the annual report of the inspectors of the penitentiary in the District of Columbia, herewith transmitted.

ANDREW JACKSON.

WASHINGTON, *January 16, 1832.*

To the Congress of the United States:

I transmit to Congress a report from the Director of the Mint, exhibiting the operations of that institution during the year 1831.

ANDREW JACKSON.

WASHINGTON, *January 31, 1832.*

To the Congress of the United States:

I herewith transmit, for the information of Congress, the third annual report of the inspectors of the penitentiary in the District of Columbia.

ANDREW JACKSON.

WASHINGTON, *January 19, 1833.*

To the Senate and House of Representatives:

I transmit herewith the fourth annual report of the board of inspectors of the penitentiary in the District of Columbia, which is required by the act of the 3d of March, 1829, to be laid before Congress.

ANDREW JACKSON.

WASHINGTON, *January 19, 1833.*

The Honorable the PRESIDENT OF THE SENATE UNITED STATES:

I transmit to Congress a report from the Director of the Mint, exhibiting the operations of that institution during the year 1832.

ANDREW JACKSON.

[The same message was sent to the House of Representatives.]

WASHINGTON, D. C., *January 15, 1834.*

The Honorable the PRESIDENT OF THE SENATE.

SIR: I transmit to Congress a report from the Director of the Mint, exhibiting the operations of that institution during the year 1833.

ANDREW JACKSON.

[The same message was addressed to the Speaker of the House of Representatives.]

WASHINGTON, *January 28, 1834.*
To the House of Representatives:

I herewith transmit the annual report of the inspectors of the penitentiary in the District of Columbia, which, agreeably to the act for the government and discipline of the same, is to be laid before Congress.

ANDREW JACKSON.

WASHINGTON, *January 10, 1835.*
The Honorable the PRESIDENT OF THE SENATE UNITED STATES.

SIR: I herewith transmit to the Senate a report from the Director of the Mint, showing the operations of that institution during the year 1834.

ANDREW JACKSON.

[The same message was addressed to the Speaker of the House of Representatives.]

WASHINGTON, *January 12, 1835.*
To the Congress of the United States:

I transmit, for the information of Congress, the sixth annual report of the inspectors of the penitentiary for the District of Columbia, made in compliance with the act of the 3d of March, 1829.

ANDREW JACKSON.

WASHINGTON, *December 10, 1835.*
To the Senate of the United States:

I transmit to the Senate of the United States a report* of the Secretary of State, to whom was referred the resolutions of that body passed on the 2d and 13th days of February last, together with such portion of the correspondence and instructions requested by the said resolutions as has not been heretofore transmitted and as can be communicated without prejudice to the public interest.   ANDREW JACKSON.

Hon. JAMES K. POLK,   WASHINGTON, *January 28, 1836.*
    Speaker of the House of Representatives.

SIR: I transmit herewith the seventh annual report of the board of inspectors of the penitentiary in the District of Columbia, which, in pursuance of the act of the 3d of March, 1829, is submitted to Congress.

ANDREW JACKSON.

---

*Transmitting correspondence which passed between the Governments of the United States and Spain in the negotiation of the treaty of February 17, 1834, instructions given to the minister of the United States during the course of the negotiation, etc.

JANUARY 16, 1838.

To the House of Representatives:

I herewith transmit a report from the Director of the Mint, showing the operations of that institution during the year 1837 and also the progress made toward the completion of the branch mints in North Carolina, Georgia, and Louisiana.   M. VAN BUREN.

WASHINGTON, *January 29, 1838.*

To the Senate and House of Representatives of the United States:

In compliance with the act of Congress of the 3d March, 1829, I herewith transmit to Congress the ninth annual report of the board of inspectors of the penitentiary of Washington.   M. VAN BUREN.

WASHINGTON, *January 18, 1839.*

To the Senate of the United States:

I transmit to the Senate a report of the Director of the Mint, exhibiting the operations of that institution during the year 1838.

M. VAN BUREN.

[The same message was sent to the House of Representatives.]

WASHINGTON, *February 6, 1839.*

To the Senate and House of Representatives of the United States:

In compliance with the act of Congress of the 3d March, 1829, I herewith transmit to Congress the tenth annual report of the board of inspectors of the penitentiary of Washington.   M. VAN BUREN.

WASHINGTON, D. C., *February 1, 1840.*

To the Senate of the United States:

I transmit to the Senate a report from the Director of the Mint, showing the operations of that institution for the year 1839.

M. VAN BUREN.

[The same message was sent to the House of Representatives.]

WASHINGTON, *February 5, 1840.*

To the Senate and House of Representatives of the United States:

In compliance with the act of Congress of the 3d of March, 1829, I herewith transmit to Congress the eleventh annual report of the board of inspectors of the penitentiary of the District of Columbia.

M. VAN BUREN.

To the Senate of the United States: FEBRUARY 10, 1840.

I transmit to the Senate a supplementary report received from the Director of the Mint, containing a complete statement of the operations of the branch mint at New Orleans for the year 1839.

                                                    M. VAN BUREN.

[The same message was sent to the House of Representatives.]

                                        WASHINGTON, *January 27, 1841.*

To the Senate and House of Representatives of the United States:

In compliance with an act of Congress of the 3d of March, 1829, I herewith transmit to Congress the twelfth annual report of the board of inspectors of the penitentiary of the District of Columbia.

                                                    M. VAN BUREN.

                                        WASHINGTON, *January 31, 1842.*

To the Senate of the United States:

I transmit herewith to the Senate a report of the Director of the Mint, showing the operations of the institution for the year 1841.

                                                    JOHN TYLER.

[The same message was sent to the House of Representatives.]

                                        WASHINGTON, *January 17, 1843.*

To the House of Representatives:

I transmit herewith the report of the inspectors of the penitentiary for the District of Columbia, made in pursuance of the act of Congress of the 3d March, 1829, with the accompanying documents.

                                                    JOHN TYLER

                                        WASHINGTON, *March 1, 1843.*

To the Senate of the United States:

I transmit herewith to the Senate a copy of a report received from the Director of the Mint, showing the operations of that institution for the year 1842.

                                                    JOHN TYLER.

[The same message was sent to the House of Representatives.]

                                        WASHINGTON, D. C., *January 19, 1844.*

To the House of Representatives:

I transmit herewith the report of the inspectors of the penitentiary of the District of Columbia for the past year, with the accompanying documents.

                                                    JOHN TYLER.

WASHINGTON, D. C., *January 20, 1844.*

To the House of Representatives:

I transmit herewith the annual report of the Director of the Mint at Philadelphia, exhibiting the operations of the Mint and branch mints for the past year.

JOHN TYLER.

WASHINGTON, *February 3, 1845.*

To the Senate of the United States:

I transmit herewith to the Senate a report from the Director of the Mint, showing the operations of the institution for the year 1844.

JOHN TYLER.

[The same message was sent to the House of Representatives.]

WASHINGTON, *February 11, 1845.*

To the House of Representatives:

I herewith transmit the annual report of the inspectors of the penitentiary for this District, together with accompanying documents.

JOHN TYLER.

WASHINGTON, *January 28, 1846.*

To the House of Representatives of the United States:

I herewith transmit the annual report of the inspectors of the penitentiary for the District of Columbia, made in compliance with the act of the 3d March, 1829.

JAMES K. POLK.

WASHINGTON, D. C., *February 10, 1846.*

To the Senate and House of Representatives of the United States:

I transmit herewith the report of the Director of the Mint at Philadelphia, showing the operation of the Mint and branch mints for the year 1845.

JAMES K. POLK.

WASHINGTON, *January 16, 1847.*

To the House of Representatives of the United States:

In compliance with the resolutions of the 3d of March, 1829, I transmit herewith the annual report of the inspectors of the penitentiary for the District of Columbia.

JAMES K. POLK.

WASHINGTON, *February 4, 1847.*

To the House of Representatives of the United States:

I transmit to the House of Representatives a report from the Director of the Mint, showing the operations of that institution for the year 1846.

JAMES K. POLK.

WASHINGTON, *January 18, 1848.*

To the House of Representatives of the United States:

I herewith transmit the annual report of the inspectors of the penitentiary for the District of Columbia, made in compliance with the act of the 3d March, 1829.

JAMES K. POLK.

WASHINGTON, *January 31, 1848.*

To the Senate and House of Representatives of the United States:

I transmit herewith the annual report of the Director of the Mint at Philadelphia, showing the operation of the Mint and branch mints for the year 1847.

JAMES K. POLK.

WASHINGTON, *January 11, 1849.*

To the House of Representatives:

I herewith transmit the annual report of the inspectors of the penitentiary for the District of Columbia, made in compliance with the act of the 3d March, 1829.

JAMES K. POLK.

WASHINGTON, *January 22, 1849.*

To the House of Representatives of the United States:

I transmit herewith the annual report of the Director of the Mint at Philadelphia, showing the operations of the Mint and branch mints for the year 1848.

JAMES K. POLK.

WASHINGTON, *January 28, 1850.*

To the Senate and House of Representatives of the United States:

I transmit herewith the annual report of the Director of the Mint at Philadelphia, showing the operations of the Mint and its branches for the year 1849.

Z. TAYLOR.

EXECUTIVE OFFICE, *February 5, 1850.*

To the House of Representatives of the United States:

I herewith transmit the annual report of the inspectors of the penitentiary for the District of Columbia, made in compliance with the act of the 3d March, 1829.

Z. TAYLOR.

WASHINGTON, *January 30, 1851.*

To the Senate and House of Representatives of the United States:

I transmit herewith the annual report of the Director of the Mint at Philadelphia, showing the operation of the Mint and branch mints for the year 1850.

MILLARD FILLMORE.

WASHINGTON, *February 15, 1851.*

The SPEAKER OF THE HOUSE OF REPRESENTATIVES:

I have the honor herewith to transmit to the House of Representatives the report of the inspectors of the penitentiary of the United States in this District for the year ending December 31, 1850.

MILLARD FILLMORE.

WASHINGTON, D. C., *February 10, 1852.*

To the Senate and House of Representatives of the United States:

I transmit herewith the annual report of the Director of the Mint at Philadelphia, showing the operations of the Mint and its branches for the year 1851.

MILLARD FILLMORE.

WASHINGTON, *April 2, 1852.*

To the House of Representatives:

I transmit herewith the report of the inspector of the penitentiary of the United States in the District of Columbia for the year ending the 31st of December last.

MILLARD FILLMORE.

WASHINGTON, *February 8, 1853.*

To the Senate and House of Representatives:

I herewith communicate, for the information of Congress, a copy of the report of the Director of the Mint for the past year.

MILLARD FILLMORE.

WASHINGTON CITY, *February 10, 1853.*

The SPEAKER OF THE HOUSE OF REPRESENTATIVES:

I transmit to the House of Representatives herewith a communication from the Secretary of the Interior, accompanied by the annual report of the board of inspectors of the penitentiary of the District of Columbia for the year ending 31st December, 1852, as required by law.

MILLARD FILLMORE.

WASHINGTON, *February 1, 1854.*

The SPEAKER OF THE HOUSE OF REPRESENTATIVES:

I transmit herewith the annual report of the Director of the Mint at Philadelphia, showing the operation of the Mint and branch mints for the year 1853.

FRANKLIN PIERCE.

WASHINGTON, *March 3, 1854.*
To the Senate and House of Representatives of the United States:

I transmit herewith the annual report of the board of inspectors of the penitentiary for the District of Columbia for the year ending December 31, 1853.

FRANKLIN PIERCE.

WASHINGTON, *February 8, 1855.*
To the House of Representatives:

I transmit herewith the report of the Director of the Mint, showing the operations of the Mint and its branches for the past year.

FRANKLIN PIERCE.

WASHINGTON, *March 27, 1856.*
To the Senate and House of Representatives of the United States:

I transmit herewith a report of the operations of the Mint of the United States and its branches, including the assay office, for the year 1855.

FRANKLIN PIERCE.

WASHINGTON, *February 3, 1857.*
To the Senate and House of Representatives of the United States:

I transmit herewith the report of the Director of the Mint, showing the operations of the Mint and its branches for the last year.

FRANKLIN PIERCE.

PROCLAMATIONS.

[From Laws of the United States of America (John Bioren and W. John Duane, Philadelphia, and R. C. Weightman, Washington City, 1815), Vol. V, p. 511.]

BY GEORGE WASHINGTON, PRESIDENT OF THE UNITED STATES.

A PROCLAMATION.

Whereas by an act supplementary to the act entitled "An act establishing a mint and regulating the coins of the United States," passed on the 3d day of March, 1795, "the President of the United States is authorized, whenever he shall think it for the benefit of the United States, to reduce the weight of the copper coin of the United States, provided such reduction shall not in the whole exceed 2 pennyweights in each cent and in like proportion in a half cent; of which he shall give notice by proclamation;" and

Whereas, on account of the increased price of copper and expense of coinage, I have thought it would be for the benefit of the United States to reduce the weight of the copper coin of the United States 1 pennyweight and 16 grains in each cent and in like proportion in each half cent, and the same has since the 27th day of December last been reduced accordingly:

I hereby give notice thereof and that all cents and half cents coined and to be coined at the Mint of the United States from and after the said 27th day of December are to weigh, the cents each 7 pennyweights and the half cents each 3 pennyweights and 12 grains.

In testimony whereof I, the said George Washington, President of the United States, have caused the seal of the United States to be hereto affixed and signed the same with my hand.

[SEAL.]   Done at the city of Philadelphia on the 26th day of January, A. D. 1796, and of the Independence of the United States the twentieth.   GO WASHINGTON.

By the President:
TIMOTHY PICKERING, *Secretary of State.*

[From Claypoole's American Daily Advertiser, Philadelphia, December 28, 1799.]

BY THE PRESIDENT OF THE UNITED STATES OF AMERICA.

A PROCLAMATION.

Whereas the Congress of the United States, "in honor of the memory of General George Washington," have this day "*Resolved*, That it be recommended to the people of the United States to wear crape on the left arm as mourning for thirty days," and "that the President of the United States be requested to issue a proclamation notifying to the people throughout the United States the said recommendation:"

Now, therefore, I, John Adams, President of the United States, do hereby proclaim the same accordingly.

Given under my hand and the seal of the United States, at Philadelphia, the 24th day of December, A. D. 1799, and of the Independence of the United States the twenty-fourth.

[SEAL.]

JOHN ADAMS.

By the President:
TIMOTHY PICKERING, *Secretary of State.*

[From the Daily National Intelligencer, December 15, 1860.]

TO THE PEOPLE OF THE UNITED STATES.

A RECOMMENDATION.

WASHINGTON, *December 14, 1860.*

Numerous appeals have been made to me by pious and patriotic associations and citizens, in view of the present distracted and dangerous condition of our country, to recommend that a day be set apart for humiliation, fasting, and prayer throughout the Union.

In compliance with their request and my own sense of duty, I designate

Friday, the 4th day of January, 1861, for this purpose, and recommend that the people assemble on that day, according to their several forms of worship, to keep it as a solemn fast.

The Union of the States is at the present moment threatened with alarming and immediate danger; panic and distress of a fearful character prevail throughout the land; our laboring population are without employment, and consequently deprived of the means of earning their bread. Indeed, hope seems to have deserted the minds of men. All classes are in a state of confusion and dismay, and the wisest counsels of our best and purest men are wholly disregarded.

In this the hour of our calamity and peril to whom shall we resort for relief but to the God of our fathers? His omnipotent arm only can save us from the awful effects of our own crimes and follies—our own ingratitude and guilt toward our Heavenly Father.

Let us, then, with deep contrition and penitent sorrow unite in humbling ourselves before the Most High, in confessing our individual and national sins, and in acknowledging the justice of our punishment. Let us implore Him to remove from our hearts that false pride of opinion which would impel us to persevere in wrong for the sake of consistency rather than yield a just submission to the unforeseen exigencies by which we are now surrounded. Let us with deep reverence beseech Him to restore the friendship and good will which prevailed in former days among the people of the several States, and, above all, to save us from the horrors of civil war and "blood guiltiness." Let our fervent prayers ascend to His throne that He would not desert us in this hour of extreme peril, but remember us as He did our fathers in the darkest days of the Revolution, and preserve our Constitution and our Union, the work of their hands, for ages yet to come.

An omnipotent Providence may overrule existing evils for permanent good. He can make the wrath of man to praise Him, and the remainder of wrath He can restrain. Let me invoke every individual, in whatever sphere of life he may be placed, to feel a personal responsibility to God and his country for keeping this day holy and for contributing all in his power to remove our actual and impending calamities.

JAMES BUCHANAN.

EXECUTIVE ORDERS.

[From Sparks's Washington, Vol. X, pp. 11–12.]

NEW YORK, *June 8, 1789.*

SIR:* Although in the present unsettled state of the Executive Departments under the Government of the Union I do not conceive it expedient to call upon you for information officially, yet I have supposed that some informal communications from the Office of Foreign Affairs might

*Addressed to the Secretary of Foreign Affairs, the Secretary of War, the Board of the Treasury, and the Postmaster-General.

neither be improper nor unprofitable. Finding myself at this moment less occupied with the duties of my office than I shall probably be at almost any time hereafter, I am desirous of employing myself in obtaining an acquaintance with the real situation of the several great Departments at the period of my acceding to the administration of the General Government. For this purpose I wish to receive in writing such a clear account of the Department at the head of which you have been for some years past as may be sufficient (without overburthening or confusing the mind, which has very many objects to claim its attention at the same instant) to impress me with a full, precise, and distinct general idea of the affairs of the United States so far as they are comprehended in or connected with that Department.

As I am now at leisure to inspect such papers and documents as may be necessary to be acted upon hereafter or as may be calculated to give me an insight into the business and duties of that Department, I have thought fit to address this notification to you accordingly.

I am, etc.,

GO WASHINGTON.

[From American State Papers, Indian Affairs, Vol. I, pp. 96–97.]

INSTRUCTIONS FROM THE PRESIDENT OF THE UNITED STATES TO THE GOVERNOR OF THE WESTERN TERRITORY—6TH OCTOBER, 1789.

ARTHUR ST. CLAIR, Esq.,
  Governor of the Territory of the United States Northwest of the
  Ohio and Superintendent of Indian Affairs for the Northern District.

SIR: Congress having by their act of the 29th of September last empowered me to call forth the militia of the States, respectively, for the protection of the frontiers from the incursions of the hostile Indians, I have thought proper to make this communication to you, together with the instructions herein contained.

It is highly necessary that I should as soon as possible possess full information whether the Wabash and Illinois Indians are most inclined for war or peace. If for the former, it is proper that I should be informed of the means which will most probably induce them to peace. If a peace can be established with the said Indians on reasonable terms, the interests of the United States dictate that it should be effected as soon as possible.

You will therefore inform the said Indians of the dispositions of the General Government on this subject and of their reasonable desire that there should be a cessation of hostilities as a prelude to a treaty. If, however, notwithstanding your intimations to them, they should continue their hostilities or meditate any incursions against the frontiers of Virginia and Pennsylvania or against any of the troops or posts of the United States, and it should appear to you that the time of execution would be so near as to forbid your transmitting the information to me and receiving my further orders thereon, then you are hereby authorized and empowered in my name to call on the lieutenants of the nearest counties of Virginia and Pennsylvania for such detachments of militia as you may judge proper, not exceeding, however, 1,000 from Virginia and 500 from Pennsylvania.

I have directed letters to be written to the executives of Virginia and Pennsylvania informing them of the before-recited act of Congress and that I have given you these conditional directions, so that there may not be any obstructions to such measures as shall be necessary to be taken by you for calling forth the militia agreeably to the instructions herein contained.

The said militia to act in conjunction with the Federal troops in such operations, offensive or defensive, as you and the commanding officer of the troops conjointly shall judge necessary for the public service and the protection of the inhabitants and the posts.

The said militia while in actual service to be on the continental establishment of pay and rations. They are to arm and equip themselves, but to be furnished with public ammunition if necessary; and no charge for the pay of said militia will be valid unless supported by regular musters, made by a field or other officer of the Federal troops, to be appointed by the commanding officer of the troops.

I would have it observed forcibly that a war with the Wabash Indians ought to be avoided by all means consistently with the security of the frontier inhabitants, the security of the troops, and the national dignity. In the exercise of the present indiscriminate hostilities it is extremely difficult, if not impossible, to say that a war without further measures would be just on the part of the United States.

But if, after manifesting clearly to the Indians the dispositions of the General Government for the preservation of peace and the extension of a just protection to the said Indians, they should continue their incursions, the United States will be constrained to punish them with severity.

You will also proceed, as soon as you can with safety, to execute the orders of the late Congress respecting the inhabitants at St. Vincennes and at the Kaskaskias and the other villages on the Mississippi. It is a circumstance of some importance that the said inhabitants should as soon as possible possess the lands to which they are entitled by some known and fixed principles.

I have directed a number of copies of the treaty made by you at Fort Harmar with the Wyandots, etc., on the 9th of January last to be printed and forwarded to you, together with the ratification and my proclamation enjoining the observance thereof.

As it may be of high importance to obtain a precise and accurate knowledge of the several waters which empty into the Ohio on the northwest and of those which discharge themselves in the Lakes Erie and Michigan, the length of the portages between, and nature of the ground, an early and pointed attention thereto is earnestly recommended.

Given under my hand, in the city of New York, this 6th day of October, A. D. 1789, and in the thirteenth year of the Sovereignty and Independence of the United States.

GᵠWASHINGTON.

[From The Freeman's Journal; or, The North American Intelligencer, Philadelphia, October 21, 1789.]

CONGRESS OF THE UNITED STATES.

AN ACT providing for the payment of the invalid pensioners of the United States.

Be it enacted by the Senate and House of Representatives of the United States of America in Congress assembled, That the military pensions which have been granted and paid by the States, respectively, in pursuance of the acts of the United States in Congress assembled, to the invalids who were wounded and disabled during the late war shall be continued and paid by the United States from the 4th day of March last for the space of one year under such regulations as the President of the United States may direct.

FREDERICK AUGUSTUS MUHLENBERG,
Speaker of the House of Representatives.
JOHN ADAMS,
Vice-President of the United States and President of the Senate.
Approved, September 29, 1789.

GᵠWASHINGTON,
President of the United States.

WAR OFFICE, *October 13, 1789.*

In pursuance of the above-recited law, information is hereby given to all the invalid pensioners of the United States that the amount of one year's pension from the 4th day of March last will be paid to them or their attorneys, respectively, in two equal payments, the first of which will be made on the 5th day of March, 1790, and the second on the 5th day of June following, at such places in each State and by such persons as shall hereafter in due season be publicly made known.

The payments will be made according to the following regulations, to wit:

The returns which have been or shall be made to the Secretary for the Department of War by the several States of the pensions which have been granted and paid by them, respectively, will, together with the vouchers herein required, be considered as the evidence whereon the payments are to be made.

Every application for payment must be accompanied by the following vouchers:

First. The certificate given by the State, specifying that the person possessing it is in fact an invalid and ascertaining the sum to which as such he is annually entitled.

Secondly. An affidavit agreeably to the following form, to wit:

A. B. came before me, one of the justices for the county of ———, in the State of ———, and made oath that he is the same A. B. to whom the original certificate in his possession was given, of which the following is a copy: [The certificate given by the State to be recited.]

That he served in ——— [regiment or vessel] at the time he was disabled, and that he now resides in the ——— and county of ———, and has resided there for the last ——— years, previous to which he resided in ———.

In case an invalid should apply for payment by an attorney the said attorney must, besides the certificate and oath before recited, produce a special letter of attorney agreeably to the following form:

I, A. B., of ———, county of ———, State of ———, do hereby constitute and appoint C. D., of ———, my lawful attorney to receive in my behalf ——— [the first or second moiety] of my annual pension as an invalid of the United States from the 4th day of March, 1789.

In testimony whereof I have hereunto set my hand and seal this ———.

Signed and sealed in the presence of ——— ———.

Acknowledged before me ——— ———.

Applications of executors or administrators must be accompanied with legal evidence of their respective offices and also the time the invalid died whose pension they may claim.

By command of the President of the United States of America:

H. KNOX,
Secretary for the Department of War.

[From Annals of Congress, Second Congress, 1247–1248.]

George Washington, President of the United States of America, to the Secretary of the Treasury for the time being:

By virtue of the several acts, the one entitled "An act making provision for the debt of the United States" and the other entitled "An act making provision for the reduction of the public debt," I do hereby authorize and empower you, by yourself or any other person or persons, to borrow on behalf of the United States, within the said States or elsewhere, a sum or sums not exceeding in the whole $14,000,000, and to make or cause to be made for that purpose such contract or contracts as shall be necessary and for the interest of the said States, subject to the restrictions and limitations in the said several acts contained; and for so doing this shall be your sufficient warrant.

In testimony whereof I have caused the seal of the United States to be hereunto affixed.

[SEAL.]   Given under my hand, at the city of New York, this 28th day of August, A. D. 1790.   GO WASHINGTON.

By the President:
TH: JEFFERSON.

[From Annals of Congress, Second Congress, 1249–1250.]

George Washington, President of the United States of America, to the Secretary of the Treasury for the time being:

Having thought fit to commit to you the charge of borrowing on behalf of the United States a sum or sums not exceeding in the whole $14,000,000, pursuant to the several acts, the one entitled "An act making provision for the debt of the United States," the other entitled "An act making provision for the reduction of the public debt"—

I do hereby make known to you that in the execution of the said trust you are to observe and follow the orders and directions following, viz: Except where otherwise especially directed by me you shall employ in the negotiation of any loan or loans which may be made in any foreign country William Short, esq. You shall borrow or cause to be borrowed, on the best terms which shall be found practicable (and within the limitations prescribed by law as to time of repayment and rate of interest), such sum or sums as shall be sufficient to discharge as well all installments or parts of the principal of the foreign debt which now are due or shall become payable to the end of the year 1791 as all interest and arrears of interest which now are or shall become due in respect to the said debt to the same end of the year 1791; and you shall apply or cause to be applied the moneys which shall be so borrowed with all convenient dispatch to the payment of the said installments and parts of the principal and interest and arrears of the interest of the said debt. You shall not extend the amount of the loan which you shall make or cause to be made beyond the sum which shall be necessary for completing such payment unless it can be done upon terms more advantageous to the United States than those upon which the residue of the said debt shall stand or be; but if the said residue or any part of the same can be paid off by new loans upon terms of advantage to the United States you shall cause such further loans as may be requisite to that end to be made and the proceeds thereof to be applied accordingly. And for carrying into effect the objects and purposes aforesaid I do hereby further empower you to make or cause to be made with whomsoever it may concern such contract or contracts, being of a nature relative thereto, as shall be found needful and conducive to the interest of the United States.

If any negotiation with any prince or state to whom any part of the said debt may be due should be requisite, the same shall be carried on through the person who in capacity of minister, chargé d'affaires, or otherwise now is or hereafter shall be charged with transacting the affairs of the United States with such prince or state, for which purpose I shall direct the Secretary of State, with whom you are in this behalf to consult and concert, to cooperate with you.

Given under my hand, at the city of New York, this 28th day of August, A. D. 1790.

Gⵔ WASHINGTON.

[From Annals of Congress, Second Congress, 1046.]

UNITED STATES, *January 16, 1792.*

The SECRETARY FOR THE DEPARTMENT OF WAR.

SIR: As the circumstances which have engaged the United States in the present Indian war* may some of them be out of the public recollection

* With certain tribes of Indians northwest of the Ohio.

and others perhaps be unknown, it may appear advisable that you prepare and publish from authentic documents a statement of those circumstances, as well as of the measures which have been taken from time to time for the reestablishment of peace and friendship.

When the community are called upon for considerable exertions to relieve a part which is suffering under the hand of an enemy, it is desirable to manifest that due pains have been taken by those intrusted with the administration of their affairs to avoid the evil.

G<u>O</u> WASHINGTON.

[From Annals of Congress, Sixth Congress, 1335.]

SEPTEMBER 29, 1792.

The President of the United States doth hereby order and direct that any lot or lots in the city of Washington may, after the public sale to commence on the 8th day of October, be sold and agreed for by the commissioners, or any two of them, at private sale for such price and on such terms as they may think proper.

G<u>O</u> WASHINGTON.

[From Sparks's Washington, Vol. X, pp. 546-548.]

RULES ADOPTED BY THE CABINET AS TO THE EQUIPMENT OF VESSELS IN THE PORTS OF THE UNITED STATES BY BELLIGERENT POWERS, AND PROCEEDINGS ON THE CONDUCT OF THE FRENCH MINISTER.

AUGUST 3, 1793.

1. The original arming and equipping of vessels in the ports of the United States by any of the belligerent parties for military service, offensive or defensive, is deemed unlawful.

2. Equipments of merchant vessels by either of the belligerent parties in the ports of the United States purely for the accommodation of them as such is deemed lawful.

3. Equipments in the ports of the United States of vessels of war in the immediate service of the Government of any of the belligerent parties which if done to other vessels would be of a doubtful nature, as being applicable either to commerce or war, are deemed lawful, except those which shall have made prize of the subjects, people, or property of France coming with their prizes into the ports of the United States pursuant to the seventeenth article of our treaty of amity and commerce with France.

4. Equipments in the ports of the United States by any of the parties at war with France of vessels fitted for merchandise and war, whether with or without commissions, which are doubtful in their nature, as being applicable either to commerce or war, are deemed lawful, except those which shall be made prize, etc.

5. Equipments of any of the vessels of France in the ports of the United States which are doubtful in their nature, as being applicable to commerce or war, are deemed lawful.

6. Equipments of every kind in the ports of the United States of privateers of the powers at war with France are deemed lawful.

7. Equipments of vessels in the ports of the United States which are of a nature solely adapted to war are deemed unlawful, except those stranded or wrecked, as

mentioned in the eighteenth article of our treaty with France, the sixteenth of our treaty with the United Netherlands, the ninth of our treaty with Prussia, and except those mentioned in the nineteenth article of our treaty with France, the seventeenth of our treaty with the United Netherlands, the eighteenth of our treaty with Prussia.

8. Vessels of either of the parties not armed, or armed previous to their coming into the ports of the United States, which shall not have infringed any of the foregoing rules, may lawfully engage or enlist their own subjects or citizens, not being inhabitants of the United States, except privateers of the powers at war with France and except those vessels which shall have made prize, etc.

The foregoing rules having been considered by us at several meetings and being now unanimously approved, they are submitted to the President of the United States.

> THOMAS JEFFERSON.
> ALEXANDER HAMILTON.
> HENRY KNOX.
> EDMUND RANDOLPH.

RESTITUTION OF PRIZES

AUGUST 5, 1793.

That the minister of the French Republic be informed that the President considers the United States as bound, pursuant to positive assurances given in conformity to the laws of neutrality, to effectuate the restoration of or to make compensation for prizes which shall have been made of any of the parties at war with France subsequent to the 5th day of June last by privateers fitted out of their ports.

That it is consequently expected that he will cause restitution to be made of all prizes taken and brought into our ports subsequent to the above-mentioned day by such privateers, in defect of which the President considers it as incumbent upon the United States to indemnify the owners of those prizes, the indemnification to be reimbursed by the French nation.

That besides taking efficacious measures to prevent the future fitting out of privateers in the ports of the United States they will not give asylum therein to any which shall have been at any time so fitted out, and will cause restitution of all such prizes as shall be hereafter brought within their ports by any of the said privateers.

That instructions be sent to the respective governors in conformity to the above communication.

The foregoing having been duly considered, and being now unanimously approved, they are submitted to the President of the United States.

> THOMAS JEFFERSON.
> ALEXANDER HAMILTON.
> HENRY KNOX.
> EDMUND RANDOLPH.

CONCERNING THE CONDUCT OF THE FRENCH MINISTER.

At a meeting of the heads of Departments and the Attorney-General at the President's on the 1st and 2d of August, 1793, on a review of the whole of M. Genet's correspondence and conduct, it was unanimously agreed that a letter should be written to the minister of the United States at Paris stating the same to him, resuming the points of difference which had arisen between the Government of the United States and M. Genet, assigning the reasons for the opinions of the former and desiring the recall of the latter; and that this letter, with those which have passed between M. Genet and the Secretary of State, and other necessary documents, shall be laid by Mr. Morris before the Executive of the French Government.

At a meeting of the same at the President's August 15 the rough draft of the said letter, having been prepared by the Secretary of State, was read for consideration, and it was agreed that the Secretary of the Treasury should take measures for obtaining a vessel, either by hire or purchase, to be sent to France express with the dispatches when ready.

At a meeting of the same at the President's August 20 the said letter was read and corrected by paragraphs, and finally agreed to.

At a meeting of the same at the President's August 23 it was agreed that the preceding letter should bear the date of the last document which is to accompany it, to wit, August 16; and the draft of a second letter to our minister at Paris was read and unanimously approved, and to bear date this day.

Sealed and signed, this 23d day of August, 1793.

> THOMAS JEFFERSON.
> ALEXANDER HAMILTON.
> HENRY KNOX.
> EDMUND RANDOLPH.

[From the original, Department of State.]

PHILADELPHIA, *August 4, 1793.*

The SECRETARY OF STATE.

SIR: If the heads of Departments and the Attorney-General, who have prepared the eight rules which you handed to me yesterday, are well satisfied that they are not repugnant to treaties or to the laws of nations, and, moreover, are the best we can adopt to maintain neutrality, I not only give them my approbation, but desire they may be made known without delay for the information of all concerned.

The same expression will do for the other paper, which has been subscribed as above and submitted to my consideration, for restoring or making restitution of prizes under the circumstances therein mentioned.

It is proper you should be informed that the minister of France intends to leave this city for New York to-morrow, and not amiss, perhaps, to know that in mentioning the seasonable aid of hands which the *Ambuscade* received from the French Indiaman the day preceding her meeting the *Boston* he added that seamen would no longer be wanting, as he had *now* 1,500 at his command. This being the case (although the allusion was to the subject he was then speaking upon), some of these men may be employed in the equipment of privateers other than those *now* in existence, as the right of fitting out such *in our ports* is asserted in unequivocal terms.

Was the propriety of convening the Legislature at an earlier day than that on which it is to assemble by law considered yesterday?

The late decree of the National Convention of France, dated the 9th of May, authorizing their ships of war and armed vessels to stop any neutral vessel loaded in whole or part with provisions and send them into their ports, adds another motive for the adoption of this measure.

G? WASHINGTON.

[From Annals of Congress, Seventh Congress, second session, 746–747.]

JOHN ADAMS, PRESIDENT OF THE UNITED STATES OF AMERICA.

INSTRUCTIONS TO THE COMMANDERS OF ARMED VESSELS BELONGING TO THE UNITED STATES, GIVEN AT PHILADELPHIA THIS 28TH DAY OF MAY, A. D. 1798, AND IN THE TWENTY-SECOND YEAR OF THE INDE-PENDENCE OF THE SAID STATES.

Whereas it is declared by an act of Congress passed the 28th day of May, 1798, that armed vessels sailing under authority or pretense of authority from the French Republic have committed depredations on the commerce of the United States and have recently captured the vessels and property of citizens thereof on and near the coasts, in violation of the law of nations and treaties between the United States and the French nation:

Therefore, and in pursuance of the said act, you are instructed and directed to seize, take, and bring into any port of the United States, to be proceeded against according to the laws of nations, any armed vessel sailing under authority or pretense of authority from the French Republic which shall have committed, or which shall be found hovering on the coasts of the United States for the purpose of committing, depredations on the vessels belonging to citizens thereof, and also to retake any ship or vessel of any citizen or citizens of the United States which may have been captured by any such armed vessel.

By command:

JAMES M'HENRY, *Secretary of War.*

[From American State Papers, Foreign Relations, Vol. II, pp. 365–367.]

INSTRUCTIONS FOR THE PRIVATE ARMED VESSELS OF THE UNITED STATES.

First. In exercising the powers granted by the act of Congress entitled "An act further to protect the commerce of the United States," passed the 9th day of July, 1798, and which is hereto annexed, the regulations therein prescribed are to be strictly attended to and observed.

Second. The powers of capturing and recapturing granted by the said act being pointed solely and exclusively against French armed vessels and those vessels, goods, and effects of citizens of the United States or of persons resident therein which shall have been captured by the French, the rights of all other nations are to be duly respected, and they are not to be molested in their persons or property; consequently American vessels and property captured by the commissioned vessels of such of those other nations as are at war are not to be recaptured by the armed vessels of the United States. Nevertheless, any vessels found on the high seas may be examined in such manner as shall be necessary to ascertain whether they are or are not armed French vessels, or "vessels the property of or employed by any citizen of the United States or person resident therein, or having on board any goods or effects belonging to any such citizen or resident," that have been captured by the French. But if they are of neither of these descriptions they are to be dismissed with as little delay as possible. And in making such examination care is to be taken that no injury be done to the vessel or to the persons or property on board her. It peculiarly becomes a nation like the American, contending for her just rights and defending herself against insults and injuries, to respect the rights of others and studiously to avoid not only the outrage and the inhumanity but even the incivility of which itself complains. It is hoped that Americans will be as distinguished for their justice and humanity as for their bravery and love of true liberty. If, on the contrary, any of the officers or crews of American armed vessels shall practice any cruelty or inhumanity contrary to the usage of civilized nations, the offenders will be severely punished.

Third. For the purposes of the act aforesaid you will consider the "high seas" to extend to low-water mark on all the coasts of France and her dominions and of all places subject to her power in any part of the world, and exercise accordingly the powers of capturing and recapturing granted by the act aforesaid. By the same rule, seeing a war exists between Great Britain and France, you may capture and recapture as aforesaid on all the coasts of the British dominions and of all places subject to the British power. But you are to refrain from exercising the aforesaid powers of capturing and recapturing in waters which are under the protection of any other nations, that their peace and sovereignty may remain unviolated. If, however, any armed French vessel, regardless of the rights of these other nations, shall within their jurisdictional limits attack or capture any vessel, goods, or effects the property of citizens of or residents in the United States, and you are able to attack and take such armed French vessel or to retake her prize within the jurisdictional limits of such nations, you are to do it, provided their governments, respectively, or the commanders or governors in chief in such places give their permission.

Fourth. The master or pilot and one or more of the principal persons of the company of every armed French vessel captured as aforesaid are to be sent as soon after the capture as may be to the judge or judges of the proper court in the United States to be examined upon oath touching the interest or property of the captured vessel and her lading, and at the same time are to be delivered to the judge or judges all passes, charter parties, bills of lading, invoices, letters, and other documents and writings found on board; the said papers to be proved by the affidavit of the commander of the capturing vessel or some other person present at the capture, to be produced as they were received, without fraud, addition, subduction, or embezzlement.

Fifth. The commanders of American private armed ships are by all convenient opportunities to send to the Secretary of the Navy written accounts of the captures they shall make, with the number and names of the captives and intelligence of what may occur or be discovered concerning the designs of the French and the destinations, motions, and operations of their fleets, cruisers, and armies.

Sixth. Where it can be done without injury or great inconvenience, the armed French vessels captured as aforesaid are to be sent to some port in the United States to be tried according to law. But such captures may happen in places remote from the United States or under circumstances which would render the sending of the captured vessels thither extremely inconvenient, while, from the vicinity of the ports of the British dominions or those of any other power in friendship with the United States, but at war with France, or from other circumstances, it would be easy to send such captured vessels into those friendly ports. In such cases it will be lawful to send such prizes into those friendly ports where they will find an asylum; and if the laws of those countries admit of it and it can be done to the satisfaction of the captors, there will be no objection on the part of the American Government to the libeling and trying such captured armed French vessels by the proper courts of those countries, where also may be delivered to the proper officers all French persons and others who shall be found acting on board of any French armed vessel which shall be captured or on board of any vessel of the United States which shall be recaptured as aforesaid.

Seventh. With respect to American vessels, goods, and effects recaptured, it seems not necessary to bring them immediately into a port of the United States. If brought in, they are to be restored to the owners on the payment of salvage. But such recaptured vessels, goods, and effects may at the time of recapture be so remote from the United States and so near a market, or the goods and effects may be of a nature so perishable, that to send such vessels, goods, and effects back to the United States may prove extremely injurious to the owners and recaptors, whereas, if permitted to proceed to their destined ports, or other places, to a market, greater advantages may result to all concerned therein; and as either the master, mate, or supercargo of any such recaptured vessel is usually left on board, and with the aid of the prizemaster and hands of the recaptors, which would be necessary to bring her home, might proceed and complete their original or other beneficial voyage, the commanders of the private armed vessels will in such case consider maturely the course most proper to be pursued, as well for the benefit of their fellow-citizens whose property they shall thus recapture as of themselves in respect to the salvage to which they and their crews and owners will be entitled. Nothing on this subject is enjoined; the commanders of the private armed vessels are to use their sound discretion.

Eighth. If any vessel of the United States, public or private, shall be found in distress by being attacked or taken by the French, the commanders, officers, and company of the private armed vessels aforesaid are to use their utmost endeavors to aid, succor, relieve, and free every such vessel in distress.

AN ACT further to protect the commerce of the United States.

SECTION 1. *Be it enacted by the Senate and House of Representatives of the United States of America in Congress assembled,* That the President of the United States shall be, and he is hereby, authorized to instruct the commanders of the public armed vessels which are or which shall be employed in the service of the United States to subdue, seize, and take any armed French vessel which shall be found within the jurisdictional limits of the United States or elsewhere on the high seas; and such captured vessel, with her apparel, guns, and appurtenances and the goods or effects which shall be found on board the same, being French property, shall be brought within some port of the United States and shall be duly proceeded against and condemned as forfeited, and shall accrue and be distributed as by law is or shall be provided respecting the captures which shall be made by the public armed vessels of the United States.

SEC. 2. *And be it further enacted,* That the President of the United States shall be, and he is hereby, authorized to grant to the owners of private armed ships and vessels of the United States who shall make application therefor special commissions in the form which he shall direct and under the seal of the United States; and such private armed vessels, when duly commissioned as aforesaid, shall have the same license and authority for the subduing, seizing, and capturing any armed French vessel and for the recapture of the vessels, goods, and effects of the people of the United States as the public armed vessels of the United States may by law have, and shall be in like manner subject to such instructions as shall be ordered by the President of the United States for the regulation of their conduct; and the commissions which shall be granted as aforesaid shall be revocable at the pleasure of the President of the United States.

SEC. 3. *Provided, and be it further enacted,* That every person intending to set forth and employ an armed vessel and applying for a commission as aforesaid shall produce in writing the name and a suitable description of the tonnage and force of the vessel and the name and place of residence of each owner concerned therein, the number of the crew, and the name of the commander and the two officers next in rank appointed for such vessel, which writing shall be signed by the person or persons making such application and filed with the Secretary of State, or shall be delivered to any other officer or person who shall be employed to deliver out such commissions, to be by him transmitted to the Secretary of State.

SEC. 4. *And provided, and be it further enacted,* That before any commission as aforesaid shall be issued the owner or owners of the ship or vessel for which the same shall be requested and the commander thereof for the time being shall give bond to the United States, with at least two responsible sureties not interested in such vessel, in the penal sum of $7,000, or, if such vessel be provided with more than 150 men, then in the penal sum of $14,000, with condition that the owners and officers and crews who shall be employed on board of such commissioned vessel shall and will observe the treaties and laws of the United States and the instructions which shall be given them for the regulation of their conduct, and will satisfy all damages and injuries which shall be done or committed contrary to the tenor thereof by such vessel during her commission, and to deliver up the same when revoked by the President of the United States.

SEC. 5. *And be it further enacted,* That all armed French vessels, together with their apparel, guns, and appurtenances and any goods or effects which shall be found on board the same, being French property, and which shall be captured by any private armed vessel or vessels of the United States duly commissioned as aforesaid, shall be forfeited and shall accrue to the owners thereof and the officers and crews by whom such captures shall be made, and on due condemnation had shall be distributed according to any agreement which shall be between them, or, in failure of such agreement, then by the discretion of the court before whom such condemnation shall be.

SEC. 6. *And be it further enacted,* That all vessels, goods, and effects the property of any citizen of the United States or person resident therein which shall be recaptured as aforesaid shall be restored to the lawful owners upon payment by them, respectively, of a just and reasonable salvage, to be determined by the mutual agreement of the parties concerned or by the decree of any court of the United States having maritime jurisdiction, according to the nature of each case: *Provided,* That such allowance shall not be less than one-eighth or exceeding one-half of the full value of such recapture, without any deduction. And such salvage shall be distributed to and among the owners, officers, and crews of the private armed vessel or vessels entitled thereto according to any agreement which shall be between them, or, in case of no agreement, then by the decree of the court who shall determine upon such salvage.

SEC. 7. *And be it further enacted,* That before breaking bulk of any vessel which shall be captured as aforesaid, or other disposal or conversion thereof, or of any articles which shall be found on board the same, such capture shall be brought into some port of the United States and shall be libeled and proceeded against before the district court of the same district; and if, after a due course of proceeding, such capture shall be decreed as forfeited in the district court, or in the circuit court of the same district in the case of any appeal duly allowed, the same shall be delivered to the owners and captors concerned therein, or shall be publicly sold by the marshal of the same court, as shall be finally decreed and ordered by the court; and the same court, who shall have final jurisdiction of any libel or complaint of any capture as aforesaid, shall and may decree restitution, in whole or in part, when the capture and restraint shall have been made without just cause as aforesaid, and if made without probable cause or otherwise unreasonably may order and decree damages and costs to the party injured, and for which the owners, officers, and crews of the private armed vessel or vessels by which such unjust capture shall have been made, and also such vessel or vessels, shall be answerable and liable.

SEC. 8. *And be it further enacted,* That all French persons and others who shall be found acting on board any French armed vessel which shall be captured, or on board of any vessel of the United States which shall be recaptured as aforesaid, shall be reported to the collector of the port in which they shall first arrive, and shall be delivered to the custody of the marshal or of some civil or military officer of the United States or of any State in or near such port, who shall take charge for their safe-keeping and support, at the expense of the United States.

Enacted into a law July 9, 1798.

By command of the President of the United States of America:

——— ———,
Secretary of State.

[From Annals of Congress, Seventh Congress, second session, 747.]

JOHN ADAMS, PRESIDENT OF THE UNITED STATES.

INSTRUCTIONS TO COMMANDERS OF ARMED VESSELS BELONGING TO THE UNITED STATES, GIVEN AT PHILADELPHIA THE 10TH DAY OF JULY, A. D. 1798, AND IN THE TWENTY-THIRD YEAR OF OUR INDEPENDENCE.

In pursuance of the acts of Congress passed the 27th day of May, the 20th day of June, and the 9th day of July—

You are hereby authorized, instructed, and directed to subdue, seize, and take any armed French vessel or vessels sailing under authority or pretense of authority from the French Republic which shall be found within the jurisdictional limits of the United States or elsewhere on the high seas, and such captured vessel, with her apparel, guns, and appurtenances and the goods and effects which shall be found on board of the same, to bring within some port of the United States; and also retake any vessel, goods, and effects of the United States or persons resident therein which may have been captured by any French vessel, in order that proceedings may be had concerning such capture or recapture in due form of law and as to right shall appertain.

By command of the President of the United States of America:

BEN. STODDERT.

[From C. F. Adams's Works of John Adams, Vol. IX, p. 160.]

CIRCULAR TO THE COMMANDERS OF ARMED VESSELS IN THE SERVICE OF THE UNITED STATES, GIVEN AT THE NAVY DEPARTMENT DECEMBER 29, 1798.

SIR: It is the positive command of the President that on no pretense whatever you permit the public vessel of war under your command to be detained or searched nor any of the officers or men belonging to her to be taken from her by the ships or vessels of any foreign nation so long as you are in a capacity to repel such outrage on the honor of the American flag. If force should be exerted to compel your submission, you are to resist that force to the utmost of your power, and when overpowered by superior force you are to strike your flag and thus yield your vessel as well as your men, but never your men without your vessel.

You will remember, however, that your demeanor be respectful and friendly to the vessels and people of all nations in amity with the United States, and that you avoid as carefully the commission of as the submission to insult or injury.

I have the honor to be, etc.,

BEN. STODDERT.

[From Annals of Congress, Seventh Congress, second session, 747-748.]

CIRCULAR INSTRUCTIONS TO THE CAPTAINS AND COMMANDERS OF VESSELS IN THE SERVICE OF THE UNITED STATES.

NAVY DEPARTMENT, *March 12, 1799.*

SIR: Herewith you will receive an act of Congress "further to suspend the commercial intercourse between the United States and France and the dependencies thereof," the whole of which requires your attention; but it is the command of the President that you consider particularly the fifth section as part of your instructions and govern yourself accordingly.

A proper discharge of the important duties arising out of this act will require the exercise of a sound and an impartial judgment. You are not only to do all that in you lies to prevent all intercourse, whether direct or circuitous, between the ports of the United States and those of France or her dependencies in cases where the vessels or cargoes are apparently, as well as really, American and protected by American papers only, but you are to be vigilant that vessels or cargoes really American, but covered by Danish or other foreign papers and bound to or from French ports, do not escape you. Whenever, on just suspicion, you send a vessel into port to be dealt with according to the aforementioned law, besides sending with her all her papers send all the evidence you can obtain to support your suspicions and effect her condemnation. At the same time that you are thus attentive to fulfill the objects of the law you are to be extremely careful not to harass or injure the trade of foreign nations with whom we are at peace nor the fair trade of our own citizens.

A misconstruction of his authority by Captain Nicholson in relation to vessels of friendly nations captured by the French renders it necessary that I should make some explanatory observations on that subject. Our laws direct the capture of all armed vessels sailing under authority or pretense of authority from the French Republic. A vessel captured by the citizens of France must be considered as sailing under the authority of France, and it is scarcely to be supposed that in times like the present, when few vessels sail without arms, a captured vessel in possession of the captors will be so circumstanced as not to come under the description of an armed vessel within the meaning of our laws. To justify a recapture nothing is necessary but that the vessel be provided with such means of annoyance as will render her dangerous to an unarmed American vessel in pursuit of lawful commerce. If, however, the vessel can not be considered an armed vessel within the meaning of our laws, you are not to recapture her unless you should have probable cause to suspect that the citizens of the United States or persons resident therein have some interest in the vessel or cargo.

It is always your duty to recapture American property and property of persons resident within the United States whenever found in possession of the French on the high seas.

I have the honor to be, sir, your most obedient servant,

BEN. STODDERT.

[From Claypoole's American Daily Advertiser, Philadelphia, December 20, 1799.]

The President with deep regret announces to the Army the death of its beloved chief, General George Washington. Sharing in the grief which every heart must feel for so heavy and afflicting a public loss, and desirous to express his high sense of the vast debt of gratitude which is due to the virtues, talents, and ever-memorable services of the illustrious deceased, he directs that funeral honors be paid to him at all the military stations, and that the officers of the Army and of the several corps of vol unteers wear crape on the left arm by way of mourning for six months. Major-General Hamilton will give the necessary orders for carrying into effect the foregoing directions.

Given at the War Office of the United States, in Philadelphia, this 19th day of December, A. D. 1799, and in the twenty-fourth year of the Independence of the said States.

By command of the President:

JAMES M'HENRY,
Secretary of War.

[From Claypoole's American Daily Advertiser, Philadelphia, December 21, 1799.]

NAVY DEPARTMENT, *December 20, 1799.*

The President with deep affliction announces to the Navy and to the marines the death of our beloved fellow-citizen, George Washington, commander of our armies and late President of the United States, but rendered more illustrious by his eminent virtues and a long series of the most important services than by the honors which his grateful country delighted to confer upon him.

Desirous that the Navy and marines should express, in common with every other description of American citizens, the high sense which all feel of the loss our country has sustained in the death of this good and great man, the President directs that the vessels of the Navy in our own and foreign ports be put in mourning for one week by wearing their colors half-mast high, and that the officers of the Navy and of the marines wear crape on the left arm below the elbow for six months.

BEN. STODDERT.

[From Claypoole's American Daily Advertiser, Philadelphia, December 24, 1799.]

Impressed with unspeakable grief and under the influence of an affectionate sympathy which must pervade the hearts of his beloved fellow citizen soldiers, the Blues, Brigadier-General MacPherson announces the following communication:

PHILADELPHIA, *December 21, 1799.*

Major-General Hamilton has received through the Secretary of War the following order from the President of the United States:

[For order see preceding page.]

The impressive terms in which this great national calamity is announced by the President could receive no new force from anything that might be added. The voice of praise would in vain endeavor to exalt a character unrivaled on the lists of true glory. Words would in vain attempt to give utterance to that profound and reverential grief which will penetrate every American bosom and engage the sympathy of an admiring world. If the sad privilege of preeminence in sorrow may justly be claimed by the companions in arms of our lamented Chief, their affections will spontaneously perform the dear though painful duty. 'Tis only for me to mingle my tears with those of my fellow-soldiers, cherishing with them the precious recollection that while others are paying a merited tribute to "The Man of the Age" we in particular, allied as we were to him by a closer tie, are called to mourn the irreparable loss of a kind and venerated patron and father!

In obedience to the directions of the President, the following funeral honors will be paid at the several stations of the Army:

At daybreak sixteen guns will be fired in quick succession and one gun at a distance of each half hour till sunset.

During the procession of the troops to the place representing that of the interment and until the conclusion of the ceremonial minute guns will be fired.

The bier will be received by the troops formed in line presenting their arms and the officers, drums, and colors saluting. After this the procession will begin, the troops marching by platoons in inverted order and with arms reversed to the place of interment, the drums muffled and the music playing a dead march.

The bier, carried by four sergeants and attended by six pallbearers, where there is cavalry will be preceded by the cavalry and will be followed by the troops on foot. Where there is no cavalry, a detachment of infantry will precede the bier, which itself will in every case be preceded by such of the clergy as may be present. The officers of the general staff will immediately succeed the bier.

Where a numerous body of citizens shall be united with the military in the procession, the whole of the troops will precede the bier, which will then be followed by the citizens.

When arrived near the place of interment, the procession will halt, the troops in front of the bier will form in line, and, opening their ranks, will face inwards, to admit the passage of the bier, which will then pass through the ranks, the troops leaning on their arms, reversed, while the bier passes. When the bier shall have passed, the troops will resume their position in line, and, reversing their arms, will remain leaning upon them until the ceremonial shall be closed.

The music will now perform a solemn air, after which the introductory part of this order shall be read.

At the end of this a detachment of infantry, appointed for the purpose, will advance and fire three volleys over the bier.

The troops will then return, the music playing the President's march, the drums previously unmuffled.

The uniform companies of militia are invited to join in arms the volunteer corps.

The commanders at particular stations, conforming generally to this plan, will make such exceptions as will accommodate it to situation. At places where processions of unarmed citizens shall take place it is the wish of the Major-General that the military ceremonial should be united, and the particular commanders at those places are authorized to vary the plan so as to adapt it to the circumstances.

Brigadier-General MacPherson is charged to superintend the ceremonial in the city of Philadelphia; Major Tousard will attend to Fort Mifflin and will cooperate with him.

The day of performing the ceremonial at each station is left to the particular commander.

Major-General Pinckney will make such further arrangements within his district as he shall deem expedient.

PHILIP CHURCH,
Aid-de-Camp.

In conformity to the above the volunteers of the city and county of Philadelphia in the service of the United States will parade, completely equipped, at the manege, in Chesnut street, on Thursday next, the 26th instant, at 10 o'clock a. m. The officers, together with the uniform companies of militia who may think proper to join on this mournful occasion, will please to signify their intention to Brigadier-General MacPherson at his quarters on or before Tuesday next at 1 o'clock p. m., in order that the necessary arrangement may be made to pay the last sad tribute of veneration to the manes of the late Commander in Chief of the Armies of the United States.

By order of Brigadier-General MacPherson:

JONATHAN WILLIAMS,
Aid-de-Camp.

[The following interesting paper is extracted from a speech of Senator W. C. Rives, of Virginia, delivered in the United States Senate February 12, 1839, on a bill to prevent the interference of certain Federal officers in elections. (See Congressional Globe, Twenty-fifth Congress, third session, Vol. VII, Appendix, p. 409.) This order President Jefferson caused to be issued by the heads of the several Departments shortly after his inauguration, March 4, 1801. References are made to it in several publications, but the originals could not be found.]

The President of the United States has seen with dissatisfaction officers of the General Government taking on various occasions active parts in elections of the public functionaries, whether of the General or of the State Governments. Freedom of elections being essential to the mutual independence of governments and of the different branches of the same government, so vitally cherished by most of our constitutions, it is deemed improper for officers depending on the Executive of the Union to attempt to control or influence the free exercise of the elective right. This I am instructed, therefore, to notify to all officers within my Department holding their appointments under the authority of the President directly, and to desire them to notify to all subordinate to them. The right of any officer to give his vote at elections as a qualified citizen is not meant to be restrained, nor, however given, shall it have any effect to his prejudice; but it is expected that he will not attempt to influence the votes of others nor take any part in the business of electioneering, that being deemed inconsistent with the spirit of the Constitution and his duties to it.

[From the Writings of Thomas Jefferson, Paul Leicester Ford, Vol. VIII, pp. 99-101.]

CIRCULAR TO THE HEADS OF THE DEPARTMENTS.

WASHINGTON, *November 6, 1801.*

DEAR SIR: Coming all of us into executive office new and unfamiliar with the course of business previously practiced, it was not to be expected we should in the first outset adopt in every part a line of proceeding so perfect as to admit no amendment. The mode and degrees of communication, particularly between the Presidents and heads of Departments, have not been practiced exactly on the same scale in all of them. Yet it would certainly be more safe and satisfactory for ourselves as well as the public that not only the best but also an uniform course of proceeding as to manner and degree should be observed. Having been a member of the first Administration under General Washington, I can state with exactness what our course then was. Letters of business came addressed sometimes to the President, but most frequently to the heads of Departments. If addressed to himself, he referred them to the proper Department to be acted on. If to one of the Secretaries, the letter, if it required no answer, was communicated to the President simply for his information. If an answer was requisite, the Secretary of the Department communicated the letter and his proposed answer to the President. Generally they were simply sent back after perusal, which signified his approbation. Sometimes he returned them with an informal note, suggesting an alteration or a query. If a doubt of any importance arose, he reserved it for conference. By this means he was always in accurate possession of all facts and proceedings in every part of the Union, and to whatsoever Department they related; he formed a central point for the different branches; preserved an unity of object and action among them; exercised that participation in the suggestion of affairs which his office made incumbent on him, and met himself the due responsibility for whatever was done. During Mr. Adams's Administration his long and habitual absences from the seat of Government rendered this kind of communication impracticable, removed him from any share in the transaction of affairs, and parceled out the Government, in fact, among four independent heads, drawing sometimes in opposite directions. That the former is preferable to the latter course can not be doubted. It gave, indeed, to the heads of Departments the trouble of making up once a day a packet of all their communications for the perusal of the President; it commonly also retarded one day their dispatches by mail; but in pressing cases this injury was prevented by presenting that case singly for immediate attention, and it produced us in return the benefit of his sanction for every act we did. Whether any change of circumstances may render a change in this procedure necessary a little experience will show us. But I can not withhold recommending to heads of Departments that we should adopt this course for the present, leaving any necessary modifications of it to time and trial. I am sure my conduct must have proved better than a thousand declarations would that my confidence in those whom I am so happy as to have associated with me is unlimited, unqualified, and unabated. I am well satisfied that everything goes on with a wisdom and rectitude which I could not improve. If I had the universe to choose from, I could not change one of my associates to my better satisfaction. My sole motives are those before expressed, as governing the first Administration in chalking out the rules of their proceeding, adding to them only a sense of obligation imposed on me by the public will to meet personally the duties to which they have appointed me. If this mode of proceeding shall meet the approbation of the heads of Departments, it may go into execution without giving them the trouble of an answer. If any other can be suggested which would answer our views and add less to their labors, that will be a sufficient reason for my preferring it to my own proposition, to the substance of which only, and not the form, I attach any importance.

TH: JEFFERSON.

[From Annals of Congress, Tenth Congress, second session, 332-333.]

By virtue of the act entitled ''An act making provision for defraying any extraordinary expenses attending the intercourse between the United States and foreign nations,'' passed on the 13th day of February, 1806, and of which the annexed is an official exemplification, I, Thomas Jefferson, President of the United States of America, do hereby authorize and empower Albert Gallatin, Secretary of the Treasury of the United States, to take all proper and necessary measures for placing the $2,000,000 appropriated by the act above recited at the joint disposal of John Armstrong and James Bowdoin, commissioners plenipotentiary and extraordinary for settling all matters of difference between the United States and the Government of Spain, and, in case of the death of one of them, at the disposal of the survivor, to be jointly applied by the said John Armstrong and James Bowdoin, or, in case of the death of one of them, by the survivor, to such purposes as I may think proper to direct in my instructions to them; and for so doing this shall be his sufficient warrant.

In testimony whereof I have caused the seal of the United States to be hereunto affixed.

[SEAL.] Given under my hand, at the city of Washington, this 18th day of March, 1806.

TH: JEFFERSON.

By the President:

JAMES MADISON, *Secretary of State.*

[From the Writings of Thomas Jefferson, Paul Leicester Ford, Vol. IX, pp. 34–35.]

CIRCULAR LETTER TO THE GOVERNORS OF KENTUCKY, TENNESSEE, OHIO, AND MISSISSIPPI.

WASHINGTON, *March 21, 1807.*

SIR: Although the present state of things on the western side of the Mississippi does not threaten any immediate collision with our neighbors in that quarter and it is our wish they should remain undisturbed until an amicable adjustment may take place, yet as this does not depend on ourselves alone it has been thought prudent to be prepared to meet any movements which may occur. The law of a former session of Congress for keeping a body of 100,000 militia in readiness for service at a moment's warning is still in force, but by an act of the last session, a copy of which I now inclose, the Executive is authorized to accept the services of such volunteers as shall offer themselves on the conditions of the act, which may render a resort to the former act unnecessary. It is for the execution of this act that I am now to solicit your zealous endeavors. The persons who shall engage will not be called from their homes until some aggression, committed or intended, shall render it necessary. When called into action it will not be for a lounging but for an active and perhaps distant service. I know the effect of this consideration in kindling that ardor which prevails for this service, and I count on it for filling up the numbers requisite without delay. To yourself I am sure it must be as desirable as it is to me to transfer this service from the great mass of our militia to that portion of them to whose habits and enterprise active and distant service is most congenial. In using, therefore, your best exertions toward accomplishing the object of this act you will render to your constituents as well as to the nation a most acceptable service.

With respect to the organizing and officering those who shall be engaged within your State the act itself will be your guide, and as it is desirable that we should be kept informed of the progress in this business I must pray you to report the same from time to time to the Secretary of War, who will correspond with you on all the details arising out of it.

I salute you with great consideration and respect.

TH: JEFFERSON.

[From American State Papers, Finance, Vol. II, p. 449.]

James Madison, President of the United States of America, to Albert Gallatin, Secretary of the Treasury:

By virtue of the act entitled "An act authorizing a loan of money for a sum not exceeding the amount of the principal of the public debt reimbursable during the year 1810," passed on the 1st day of May, 1810, I do hereby authorize and empower you, by yourself or any other person or persons, to borrow on behalf of the United States, of the Bank of the

United States, any sum not exceeding in the whole $3,750,000, and to make or cause to be made for that purpose such contract as shall be necessary and for the interest of the said States, pursuant to the act aforesaid; and for so doing this shall be your warrant.

Given under my hand, at Washington, this 28th day of May, A. D. 1810.

JAMES MADISON.

[From Annals of Congress, Thirteenth Congress, Vol. II, 2544–2545.]

NAVY DEPARTMENT, *July 29, 1813.*
Commanding Officers of Stations or Vessels of United States Navy:

The palpable and criminal intercourse held with the enemy's forces blockading and invading the waters and shores of the United States is, in a military view, an offense of so deep a dye as to call for the vigilant interposition of all the naval officers of the United States.

This intercourse is not only carried on by foreigners, under the specious garb of friendly flags, who convey provisions, water, and succors of all kinds (ostensibly destined for friendly ports, in the face, too, of a declared and rigorous blockade) direct to the fleets and stations of the enemy, with constant intelligence of our naval and military force and preparation and the means of continuing and conducting the invasion, to the greatest possible annoyance of the country, but the same traffic, intercourse, and intelligence is carried on with great subtility and treachery by profligate citizens, who, in vessels ostensibly navigating our own waters from port to port, under cover of night or other circumstances favoring their turpitude, find means to convey succors or intelligence to the enemy and elude the penalty of the law. This lawless traffic and intercourse is also carried on to a great extent in craft whose capacity exempts them from the regulations of the revenue laws and from the vigilance which vessels of greater capacity attract.

I am therefore commanded by the President of the United States to enjoin and direct all naval commanding officers to exercise the strictest vigilance and to stop and detain all vessels or craft whatsoever proceeding or apparently intending to proceed toward the enemy's vessels within the waters or hovering about the harbors of the United States, or toward any station occupied by the enemy within the jurisdiction of the United States, from which vessels or craft the enemy might derive succors or intelligence.

W. JONES.

[From Congressional Globe, Vol. V, p. 323.]

TREASURY DEPARTMENT, *February 22, 1836.*
To Receivers of Public Moneys, Collectors, Disbursing Officers, and the Deposit Banks of the United States:

The established policy of the Treasury Department, so far as may be practicable under its present powers over the collection, keeping, and disbursement of the public money, is to diminish the circulation of small bank notes and to substitute specie, and especially gold, for such notes, with the view of rendering the currency of the country, through which its fiscal operations are performed, more safe, sound, and uniform. In pursuance of that policy, a circular was issued last April which prohibited after the 30th September, 1835, the receipt on account of the Government of any bank notes of a less denomination than $5, and which intimated that other steps to promote the desirable objects before named would in due time be taken.

Consequently, in further pursuance of the same policy, you are hereby required after the 1st of May next not to pay the demands of any public officer or creditor in any bank notes of a less denomination than $5, and, except when it may be otherwise prescribed by law, after the 4th of July next not to receive or pay on account of the Government any bank notes of a less denomination than $10.

All the deposit banks are requested to supply themselves with such a quantity of American gold coin as to be able to pay, and when a public officer or creditor prefers it, and his demand does not exceed $500, to pay at least one-fifth of such demand in that coin. It is also requested that the deposit banks will not after the 4th of July next issue any notes of a less denomination than $5, and that after the 3d of March, 1837, they will not, unless the subject be otherwise regulated by Congress, issue any notes of a less denomination than $10. It is believed that the amount of gold which by that time shall be coined at the Mint will be sufficient to admit of the convenient substitution of it for small notes in a much greater extent than at present; and it is deemed reasonable that while the deposit banks have the use, without interest, of unusually large sums of the public money they should make some further temporary sacrifices to obtain and circulate gold and in other respects to enlarge the specie basis of our circulating medium.

From these considerations and from the liberal spirit evinced by most of the public depositories in a late correspondence with them on this subject, it is confidently expected that in this state of things they will cheerfully comply with the above requests and with all others which have been made by the Department with a view of improving the currency; nor will it, I trust, be considered unjust or impolitic, while the deposit banks shall continue to enjoy great privileges from the Treasury, to regard a neglect or refusal by any of them to comply with those requests as sufficient cause for discontinuing the employment of such banks as fiscal agents.

At a proper time it will be decided under what circumstances and at what periods these restrictions on the agents and officers of the Treasury shall be extended to notes of any denomination under $20.

This communication is made with the sanction of the President of the United States, and it is hoped that till otherwise prescribed by Congress or by this Department these requirements and requests will be faithfully complied with by all the fiscal agents of this Department and all the collecting and disbursing officers of the Government.

LEVI WOODBURY,

Secretary of the Treasury.

[From Senate Doc. No. 15, Twenty-fourth Congress, second session.]

CIRCULAR FROM THE SECRETARY OF THE TREASURY TO RECEIVERS OF PUBLIC MONEY AND TO THE DEPOSIT BANKS.

TREASURY DEPARTMENT, *July 11, 1836.*

In consequence of complaints which have been made of frauds, speculations, and monopolies in the purchase of the public lands, and the aid which is said to be given to effect these objects by excessive bank credits and dangerous, if not partial, facilities through bank drafts and bank deposits, and the general evil influence likely to result to the public interests, and especially the safety of the great amount of money in the Treasury, and the sound condition of the currency of the country from the further exchange of the national domain in this manner, and chiefly for bank credits and paper money, the President of the United States has given directions, and you are hereby instructed, after the 15th day of August next, to receive in payment of the public lands nothing except what is directed by the existing laws, viz, gold and silver, and in the proper cases Virginia land scrip: *Provided,* That till the 15th of December next the same indulgences heretofore extended as to the kind of money received may be continued for any quantity of land not exceeding 320 acres to each purchaser who is an actual settler or *bona fide* resident in the State where the sales are made.

In order to insure the faithful execution of these instructions, all receivers are strictly prohibited from accepting for land sold any draft, certificate, or other evidence of money or deposit, though for specie, unless signed by the Treasurer of the United States in conformity to the act of April 24, 1820; and each of those officers is required to annex to his monthly returns to this Department the amount of gold and of silver, respectively, as well as the bills, received under the foregoing exception; and each deposit bank is required to annex to every certificate given upon a deposit of money the proportions of it actually paid in gold, in silver, and in bank notes. All former instructions on these subjects, except as now modified, will be considered as remaining in full force.

The principal objects of the President in adopting this measure being to repress alleged frauds and to withhold any countenance or facilities in the power of the Government from the monopoly of the public lands in the hands of speculators and capitalists, to the injury of the actual settlers in the new States and of emigrants in search of new homes, as well as to discourage the ruinous extension of bank issues and bank credits by which those results are generally supposed to be promoted, your utmost vigilance is required and relied on to carry this order into complete execution.

LEVI WOODBURY,
Secretary of the Treasury.

[From American State Papers, Military Affairs, Vol. VII, p. 554.]

HERMITAGE, *September 7, 1836.*

General J. E. WOOL,
    East Tennessee.

SIR: Your letter of the 30th ultimo has just been handed to me by Mr. Rogers, the express. Being in a state of preparation for setting out for Washington and surrounded by much company, I have but a moment to reply to it.

In relation to your observations respecting the apportionment of the 10,000 volunteers, I need not say more here than that the requisition on the governor of the State was a sufficient guide for the organization of the part allotted to Tennessee. This requisition was for 2,500 men, to be raised in two brigades, one in the East and the other in West Tennessee, and there could be no authority to muster more into the service. The remainder of the 10,000 had been required from other States and Territories.

I have turned to the letter of the Adjutant-General to which you have called my attention. You will find, I think, that it relates to the volunteers called for agreeably to the requisition on the governor of Tennessee for 2,500. I can not suppose that it was expected of you to receive a greater number than this into the service.

As you have the treaty before you and the instructions of the Acting Secretary of War, I do not see that I can add anything more on this subject at present. The treaty is to be religiously fulfilled. You may assure all concerned that no modification or alteration in it will be made by me. Of this Mr. John Ross is fully advised. His friend, Mr. Standefer, who waited upon me at Washington and made the inquiry whether I would agree to a supplemental article admitting the Rosses and their delegation in as chiefs, was informed that I would not. You will therefore make known to the Cherokee people that no alteration in the treaty will be made, but that all its terms and conditions will be faithfully and fully executed. Should you find any evil-disposed white man in the nation exciting the Indians not to comply with the treaty, you will forthwith order him or them out of the nation, and if they refuse to go, the facts being thoroughly established, you will take the steps necessary to put them out. Such characters must be considered in the light of intruders, prohibited by the treaty from living within the limits of the nation.

You will caution John Ross from calling any council of the Cherokee people with the view of opposing or altering the treaty. He knows that there will be no further negotiation on the subject; that the Cherokees are to emigrate in two years from the ratification of the treaty, and will be obliged to go within that period; that the collisions between them and the whites have been too long continued for the gratification of himself at the expense of the poor in the nation.

I have had a letter from Governor Carroll. He will leave Pontotoc at as early a moment as he can, and expects to meet Governor Lumpkin early in October next.

With these hasty remarks, I remain, your obedient servant,

ANDREW JACKSON.

[From Congressional Globe, Vol. VII, Appendix, p. 245.]

DEPARTMENT OF STATE,
Washington, December 7, 1837.

SIR:* In the course of the contest which has commenced in a portion of the territory of Great Britain between portions of the population and the Government some of our citizens may, from their connection with the settlers and from their love of enterprise and desire of change, be induced to forget their duty to their own Government and its obligations to foreign powers. It is the fixed determination of the President faithfully to discharge, so far as his power extends, all the obligations of this Government, and that obligation especially which requires that we shall abstain under every temptation from intermeddling with the domestic disputes of other nations. You are therefore earnestly enjoined to be attentive to all movements of a hostile character contemplated or attempted within your district, and to prosecute without discrimination all violators of those laws of the United States which have been enacted to preserve peace with foreign powers and to fulfill all the obligations of our treaties with them.

I am, sir, your obedient servant,

JOHN FORSYTH.

[From Congressional Globe, Vol. VII, Appendix, p. 245.]

DEPARTMENT OF STATE,
Washington, December 7, 1837.

His Excellency WILLIAM L. MARCY,
Governor of the State of New York.

SIR: A contest having commenced in a territory of Great Britain adjoining the United States between portions of the population and government, during which attempts may be made to violate the laws of the United States passed to preserve the relations of amity with foreign

*Sent to the United States attorney at Rockingham, Vt., and to the district attorneys for the northern district of New York and the Michigan district.

powers and to fulfill the obligations of our treaties with them, by the directions of the President I have the honor to request the attention of your excellency to any movements of that character that may be contemplated in the State of New York and your prompt interference to arrest the parties concerned if any preparations are made of a hostile nature against any foreign power in amity with the United States.

I have the honor to be, sir, your obedient servant,

JOHN FORSYTH.

[Sent also to the governors of Vermont and Michigan.]

[From House Ex. Doc. No. 163, Fiftieth Congress, first session, p. 6.]

EXECUTIVE ORDERS TOUCHING DISPOSAL OF FLAGS CAPTURED IN WAR WITH MEXICO.

DECEMBER 26, 1848.

Pursuant to the second section of act approved April 18; 1814, directing that all flags, standards, and colors taken by the Army and Navy of the United States from their enemies be preserved and displayed under the direction of the President of the United States in such public place as he shall deem proper, the Secretary of War is directed to take measures to cause the flags, standards, and colors taken by the Army of the United States from their enemies in the recent war with Mexico to be deposited for the purpose specified in the act in the Military Academy at West Point.

JAMES K. POLK.

[From official records, War Department.]

WASHINGTON, *September 11, 1861.*

Major-General JOHN C. FRÉMONT.

SIR: Yours of the 8th, in answer to mine of the 2d instant, is just received. Assuming that you, upon the ground, could better judge of the necessities of your position than I could at this distance, on seeing your proclamation of August 30 I perceived no general objection to it. The particular clause, however, in relation to the confiscation of property and the liberation of slaves appeared to me to be objectionable in its nonconformity to the act of Congress passed the 6th of last August upon the same subjects, and hence I wrote you expressing my wish that that clause should be modified accordingly. Your answer, just received, expresses the preference on your part that I should make an open order for the modification, which I very cheerfully do. It is therefore ordered that the said clause of said proclamation be so modified, held, and construed as to conform to and not to transcend the provisions on the same subject contained in the act of Congress entitled "An act to confiscate property used for insurrectionary purposes," approved August 6, 1861, and that said act be published at length with this order.

Your obedient servant,

A. LINCOLN.

[From McPherson's History of the Rebellion, p. 248.]

DEPARTMENT OF STATE,
Washington, December 4, 1861.

Major-General GEORGE B. McCLELLAN,
Washington.

GENERAL: I am directed by the President to call your attention to the following subject:

Persons claimed to be held to service or labor under the laws of the State of Virginia and actually employed in hostile service against the Government of the United States frequently escape from the lines of the enemy's forces and are received within the lines of the Army of the Potomac.

This Department understands that such persons afterwards coming into the city of Washington are liable to be arrested by the city police upon the presumption, arising from color, that they are fugitives from service or labor.

By the fourth section of the act of Congress approved August 6, 1861, entitled "An act to confiscate property used for insurrectionary purposes," such hostile employment is made a full and sufficient answer to any further claim to service or labor. Persons thus employed and escaping are received into the military protection of the United States, and their arrest as fugitives from service or labor should be immediately followed by the military arrest of the parties making the seizure.

Copies of this communication will be sent to the mayor of the city of Washington and to the marshal of the District of Columbia, that any collision between the civil and military authorities may be avoided.

I am, General, your very obedient servant,

WILLIAM H. SEWARD.

[From McPherson's History of the Rebellion, p. 252.]

WAR DEPARTMENT,
Washington City, July 3, 1862.

Major-General B. F. BUTLER,
Commanding, etc., New Orleans, La.

GENERAL: I wrote you last under date of the 29th ultimo, and have now to say that your dispatch of the 18th ultimo, with the accompanying report of General Phelps concerning certain fugitive negroes that have come to his pickets, has been considered by the President.

He is of opinion that under the law of Congress they can not be sent back to their master; that in common humanity they must not be permitted to suffer for want of food, shelter, or other necessaries of life; that to this end they should be provided for by the Quartermaster's and Commissary's departments, and that those who are capable of labor should be set to work and paid reasonable wages.

In directing this to be done the President does not mean at present to settle any general rule in respect to slaves or slavery, but simply to provide for the particular case under the circumstances in which it is now presented.

I am, General, very respectfully, your obedient servant,

EDWIN M. STANTON,
Secretary of War.

[From official records, War Department.]

WASHINGTON, *May 1, 1863.*

Major-General WOOL,
Commanding at New York:

By virtue of the act of Congress authorizing the President to take possession of railroad and telegraph lines, etc., passed February 4, 1862, the President directs that you take immediate military possession of the telegraph lines lately established between Philadelphia and Boston, called the Independent Telegraph Company, and *forbid* the transmission of any intelligence relating to the movements of the Army of the Potomac or any military forces of the United States. In case this order is violated arrest and imprison the perpetrators in Fort Delaware, reporting to the Department. If the management of the line will stipulate to transmit no military intelligence without the sanction of the War Department, they need not be interfered with so long as the engagement is fulfilled. This order will be executed so as not to interfere with the ordinary business of the telegraph company.

By order of the President:

E. M. STANTON,
Secretary of War.

[From McPherson's History of the Rebellion, p. 436.]

Hon. ANDREW JOHNSON,
Military Governor of Tennessee:

You are hereby authorized to exercise such powers as may be necessary and proper to enable the loyal people of Tennessee to present such a republican form of State government as will entitle the State to the guaranty of the United States therefor and to be protected under such State government by the United States against invasion and domestic violence, all according to the fourth section of the fourth article of the Constitution of the United States.

ABRAHAM LINCOLN.

SEPTEMBER 19, 1863.

[From official records, War Department.]

GENERAL ORDERS, NO. 329.

WAR DEPARTMENT,
ADJUTANT-GENERAL'S OFFICE,
Washington, October 3, 1863.

Whereas the exigencies of the war require that colored troops should be recruited in the States of Maryland, Missouri, and Tennessee, it is—

Ordered by the President, That the chief of the bureau for organizing colored troops shall establish recruiting stations at convenient places within said States and give public notice thereof, and be governed by the following regulations:

First. None but able-bodied persons shall be enlisted.

Second. The State and county in which the enlistments are made shall be credited with the recruits enlisted.

Third. All persons enlisted into the military service shall forever thereafter be free.

Fourth. Free persons, and slaves with the written consent of their owners, and slaves belonging to those who have been engaged in or given aid and comfort to the rebellion may be now enlisted, the owners who have not been engaged in or given aid to the rebellion being entitled to receive compensation as hereafter provided.

Fifth. If within thirty days from the date of opening enlistments, notice thereof and of the recruiting stations being published, a sufficient number of the description of persons aforesaid to meet the exigencies of the service shall not be enlisted, then enlistments may be made of slaves without requiring consent of their owners; but they may receive compensation as herein provided for owners offering their slaves for enlistment.

Sixth. Any citizen of said States who shall offer his or her slave for enlistment into the military service shall if such slave be accepted receive from the recruiting officer a certificate thereof and become entitled to compensation for the service or labor of said slave, not exceeding the sum of $300, upon filing a valid deed of manumission and of release and making satisfactory proof of title; and the recruiting officer shall furnish to any claimant a descriptive list of any person enlisted and claimed under oath to be his or her slave, and allow anyone claiming under oath that his or her slave has been enlisted without his or her consent the privilege of inspecting the enlisted men for the purpose of identification.

Seventh. A board of three persons shall be appointed by the President, to whom the rolls and recruiting lists shall be furnished for public information, and on demand exhibited to any person claiming that his or her slave has been enlisted against his or her will.

Eighth. If any person shall within ten days after the filing of said rolls make a claim for the service of any person so enlisted, the board shall proceed to examine the proofs of title, and if valid shall award just compensation, not exceeding $300, for each slave enlisted belonging to the claimant, and upon the claimant's filing a valid deed of manumission and release of service the board shall give the claimant a certificate of the sum awarded, which on presentation shall be paid by the chief of the bureau.

Ninth. All enlistments of colored troops in the State of Maryland otherwise than in accordance with these regulations are forbidden.

Tenth. No person who is or has been engaged in rebellion against the Government of the United States, or who in any way has given or shall give aid or comfort to the enemies of the Government, shall be permitted to present any claim or receive any compensation for the labor or service of any slave, and all claimants shall file with their claim an oath of allegiance to the United States.

By order of the President:

E. D. TOWNSEND,
Assistant Adjutant-General.

[From McPherson's History of Reconstruction, p. 122.]

WASHINGTON, *March 3, 1865—12 p. m.*

Lieutenant-General GRANT:

The President directs me to say to you that he wishes you to have no conference with General Lee unless it be for the capitulation of General Lee's army or on some minor and purely military matter. He instructs me to say that you are not to decide, discuss, or confer upon any political question. Such questions the President holds in his own hands and will submit them to no military conferences or conventions. Meantime you are to press to the utmost your military advantages.

EDWIN M. STANTON,
Secretary of War.

[From McPherson's History of Reconstruction, p. 13.]

EXECUTIVE OFFICE, *August 16, 1865.*

O. O. HOWARD,
Major-General, Commissioner Freedmen's Affairs:

Respectfully returned to the Commissioner of Bureau Refugees, Freedmen, etc. The records of this office show that B. B. Leake was specially pardoned by the President on the 27th ultimo, and was thereby restored to all his rights of property except as to slaves. Notwithstanding this, it is understood that the possession of his property is withheld from him. I have therefore to direct that General Fisk, assistant commissioner at Nashville, Tenn., be instructed by the Chief Commissioner of Bureau of Freedmen, etc., to relinquish possession of the property of Mr. Leake held by him as assistant commissioner, etc., and that the same be immediately restored to the said Leake. The same action will be had in all similar cases.

ANDREW JOHNSON,
President United States.

[From McPherson's History of Reconstruction, p. 12.]

CIRCULAR NO. 15.

WAR DEPARTMENT,
BUREAU REFUGEES, FREEDMEN, AND ABANDONED LANDS,
Washington, D. C., September 12, 1865.

I. Circular No. 13, of July 28, 1865, from this Bureau, and all portions of circulars from this Bureau conflicting with the provisions of this circular are hereby rescinded.

II. This Bureau has charge of such "tracts of land within the insurrectionary States as shall have been abandoned or to which the United States shall have acquired title by confiscation or sale or otherwise," and no such lands now in its possession shall be surrendered to any claimant except as hereinafter provided.

III. Abandoned lands are defined in section 2 of the act of Congress approved July 2, 1864, as lands "the lawful owner whereof shall be voluntarily absent therefrom and engaged, either in arms or otherwise, in aiding or encouraging the rebellion."

IV. Land will not be regarded as confiscated until it has been condemned and sold by decree of the United States court for the district in which the property may be found, and the title thereto thus vested in the United States.

V. Upon its appearing satisfactorily to any assistant commissioner that any property under his control is not abandoned as above defined and that the United States has acquired no title to it by confiscation, sale, or otherwise, he will formally surrender it to the authorized claimant or claimants, promptly reporting his action to the Commissioner.

VI. Assistant commissioners will prepare accurate descriptions of all confiscated and abandoned lands under their control, keeping a record thereof themselves and forwarding monthly to the Commissioner copies of these descriptions in the manner prescribed in Circular No. 10, of July 11, 1865, from this Bureau.

They will set apart so much of said lands as is necessary for the immediate use of loyal refugees and freedmen, being careful to select for this purpose those lands which most clearly fall under the control of this Bureau, which selection must be submitted to the Commissioner for his approval.

The specific division of lands so set apart into lots and the rental or sale thereof, according to section 4 of the law establishing the Bureau, will be completed as soon as practicable and reported to the Commissioner.

VII. Abandoned lands held by this Bureau may be restored to owners pardoned by the President by the assistant commissioners, to whom applications for such restoration should be forwarded, so far as practicable, through the superintendents of the districts in which the lands are situated.

Each application must be accompanied by—

First. Evidence of special pardon by the President or a copy of the oath of amnesty prescribed in the President's proclamation of May 29, 1865,* when the applicant is not included in any of the classes therein excepted from the benefits of said oath.

Second. Proof of title.

Officers of the Bureau through whom the application passes will indorse thereon such facts as may assist the assistant commissioner in his decision, stating especially the use made by the Bureau of the land.

VIII. No land under cultivation by loyal refugees or freedmen will be restored under this circular until the crops now growing shall be secured for the benefit of the cultivators unless full and just compensation be made for their labor and its products and for their expenditures.

O. O. HOWARD,
Major-General, Commissioner.

Approved:

ANDREW JOHNSON,
President of the United States.

[From McPherson's History of Reconstruction, p. 8.]

War Department,
Adjutant-General's Office,
Washington, April 17, 1866.

Major-General N. A. Miles,
 Commanding, etc., Fortress Monroe, Va.:

Ordered, That Clement C. Clay, jr., is hereby released from confinement and permitted to return to and remain in the State of Alabama and to visit such other places in the United States as his personal business may render absolutely necessary, upon the following conditions, viz, that he takes the oath of allegiance to the United States and gives his parole of honor to conduct himself as a loyal citizen of the same and to report himself in person at any time and place to answer any charges that may hereafter be prepared against him by the United States.

Please report receipt and execution of this order.

By order of the President of the United States:

E. D. TOWNSEND,
Assistant Adjutant-General.

*See Vol. VI, pp. 310–312.

[From McPherson's History of Reconstruction, p. 198.]

GENERAL ORDERS, NO. 46.

WAR DEPARTMENT,
ADJUTANT-GENERAL'S OFFICE,
Washington, July 13, 1866.

Ordered, That all persons who are undergoing sentence by military courts and have been imprisoned six months, except those who are under sentence for the crimes of murder, arson, or rape, and excepting those who are under sentence at the Tortugas, be discharged from imprisonment and the residue of their sentence remitted. Those who belong to the military service and their term unexpired will be returned to their command if it is still in service, and their release is conditional upon their serving their full term and being of good behavior.

By order of the President of the United States:

E. D. TOWNSEND,
Assistant Adjutant-General.

[From Senate Ex. Doc. No. 82, Forty-ninth Congress, second session, pp. 3-5.]

Whereas, pursuant to the convention between the United States and Spain for the adjustment of the question of reclamation arising from the capture of the *Virginius*, entered into upon the 27th February, 1875, and duly ratified upon the 11th day of March, 1875, the Spanish Government engaged to deliver to the United States the sum of $80,000, or 400,000 pesetas, for the purpose of the relief of the families of those of the ship's company and of such of the passengers as were citizens of the United States who were executed, and to afford compensation to such of the ship's company and to such passengers as in like manner were citizens of the United States who were detained and suffered loss, excluding from any participation therein all individuals indemnified as British subjects; and

Whereas it was therein further provided that when such amount should have been received the President of the United States would proceed to distribute the same among the parties entitled thereto, in the form and manner which he may judge most equitable; and

Whereas such amount has been duly paid at Madrid and the proceeds thereof are now in possession of the Government of the United States:

Now, therefore, pursuant to the provisions of article 3 of said convention, I, Ulysses S. Grant, President of the United States, do hereby direct that such amount so received shall be distributed among the parties entitled thereto in the following amounts and proportions and pursuant to the following rules:

I. The amounts allowed are determined with a general reference to the rates of wages of officers and crew. All of the ship's company (constituting the crew) are to be regarded and considered as American seamen; but inasmuch as the British Government has demanded and received from

Spain certain indemnity and promises of further conditional indemnity for and on account of certain of the crew as being British subjects, those of the crew or passengers who were British subjects, or who have been claimed as such by the British Government, and for whom the British Government demanded or received indemnity from Spain, are to be excluded from the distribution to be made of the indemnity above referred to.

II. Distribution will be made on account of those who were executed as follows:

For each one (being thirteen in number) of the ship's company rated or serving as fireman, mariner, cook, cabin boy, or otherwise than as one of the officers or petty officers hereafter mentioned, who was executed, and excluding those referred to above, and also to each passenger who was executed, being at the time an American citizen, the sum of $2,500.

For each assistant engineer, second, third, fourth engineer or third mate, 40 per cent in addition to the above sum; that is to say, $3,500 each.

For the first mate and first engineer, 80 per cent in addition to the said above-mentioned sum; that is to say, $4,500 each.

For the captain, 150 per cent in addition to the said above-mentioned sum; that is to say, $6,250.

III. The several amounts allowed as above are to be paid to the widow, children, parents, or brothers and sisters of the deceased, as follows:

(1) To the widow of the deceased.

(2) If no widow, to the children of the deceased in equal shares.

Where such children shall be minors, the same shall be paid to a legally appointed guardian.

(3) If no children, then to the father; if no father, to the mother.

(4) If no father or mother, then to the brothers and sisters in equal shares.

(5) If the deceased shall have left no widow, child, parent, brother, or sister, no amount is to be paid on his account.

There shall be allowed to each of the ship's company and to such of the passengers as were citizens of the United States who were detained and suffered loss, to be paid on the conditions hereinafter provided, as follows:

To each of the ship's crew who was under the age of 21 years at the time of the capture, or who was reported at the time as under that age, and to each passenger who was an American citizen, the sum of $250.

To each of the ship's crew who was over the age of 21 years, and who was rated as being a fireman, mariner, cook, cabin boy, or otherwise than as one of the officers or petty officers hereafter mentioned, 40 per cent in addition to the above-allowed sum; that is to say, $350 each.

To any engineer, second or other assistant engineer, mate, purser, assistant purser, or surgeon, 86 per cent in addition to the above-allowed sum; that is to say, $450 to each.

In case any of such persons so entitled to payment shall have died, such amount shall be paid to the family of the deceased as provided in Article III.

IV. The proofs as to all the necessary facts in each case, including identity, relationship, and citizenship, shall be made to the satisfaction of the Department of State as a condition of payment, and a naturalized citizen, where proof of citizenship is necessary, shall produce his certificate of naturalization and furnish satisfactory proof, if required, as to residence and his right to such certificate.

V. Payments will be made to the parties entitled thereto through the Department of State, or in checks to their order, and will not be made to attorneys.

VI. Prior to any payment being made the party entitled thereto shall sign and duly acknowledge before some competent officer a receipt and release, stating that the sum so paid is received in full satisfaction of any claim or reclamations of any sort which may exist or which might be advanced against the Spanish Government by reason of the capture of the *Virginius* or the acts of the Spanish authorities connected therewith.

VII. Should any further order or direction be required, the same will hereafter be made as an addition hereto.

In witness whereof I have hereunto set my hand, at the city of Washington, this 21st day of July, A. D. 1875, and of the Independence of the United States of America the one hundredth.

U. S. GRANT.

[From Letters and Messages of Rutherford B. Hayes, pp. 19–22.]

WASHINGTON, *April 2, 1877.*

The Honorables CHARLES B. LAWRENCE, JOSEPH R. HAWLEY, JOHN M. HARLAN, JOHN C. BROWN, AND WAYNE MACVEAGH, *Commissioners.*

GENTLEMEN: I am instructed by the President to lay before you some observations upon the occasion and objects which have led him to invite you as members of the commission about to visit the State of Louisiana to undertake this public service.

Upon assuming his office the President finds the situation of affairs in Louisiana such as to justly demand his prompt and solicitous attention, for this situation presents as one of its features the apparent intervention of the military power of the United States in the domestic controversies which unhappily divide the opinions and disturb the harmony of the people of that State. This intervention, arising during the term and by the authority of his predecessor, throws no present duty upon the President except to examine and determine the real extent and form and effect to which such intervention actually exists, and to decide as to the time, manner, and conditions which should be observed in putting an end to it. It is in aid of his intelligent and prompt discharge of this duty that the President has sought the service of this commission to supply by means of its examination, conducted in the State of Louisiana, some information that may be pertinent to the circumspection and security of any measure he may resolve upon.

It will be readily understood that the service desired of and intrusted to this commission does not include any examination into or report upon the facts of the recent State election or of the canvass of the votes cast at such election. So far as attention to these subjects may be necessary the President can not but feel that the reports of the committees of the two Houses of Congress and other public information at hand will dispense with and should preclude any original exploration by the commission of that field of inquiry.

But it is most pertinent and important in coming to a decision upon the precise question of Executive duty before him that the President should know what are the real impediments to regular, legal, and peaceful procedures under the laws and constitution of the State of Louisiana by which the anomalies in government there presented may be put in course of settlement without involving the element of military power as either an agent or a makeweight in such solution. The successful ascertainment of these impediments the President would confidently expect would indicate to the people of that State the wisdom and the mode of their removal. The unusual circumstances which attended and followed the State election and canvass, from its relation to the excited feelings and interests of the Presidential election, may have retarded within the State of Louisiana the persuasive influences by which the great social and material interests common to the whole people of a State, and the pride of the American character as a law-abiding nation, ameliorate the disappointments and dissolve the resentments of close and zealous political contests. But the President both hopes and believes that the great body of the people of Louisiana are now prepared to treat the unsettled results of their State election with a calm and conciliatory spirit. If it be too much to expect a complete concurrence in a single government for that State, at least the President may anticipate a submission to the peaceful resources of the laws and the constitution of the State of all their discussions, at once relieving themselves from the reproach and their fellow-citizens of the United States from the anxieties which must ever attend a prolonged dispute as to the title and the administration of the government of one of the States of the Union.

The President therefore desires that you should devote your first and principal attention to a removal of the obstacles to an acknowledgment of one government for the purpose of an exercise of authority within the State and a representation of the State in its relations to the General Government under section 4 of Article IV of the Constitution of the United States, leaving, if necessary, to judicial or other constitutional arbitrament within the State the question of ultimate right. If these obstacles should prove insuperable, from whatever reason, and the hope of a single government in all its departments be disappointed, it should be your next endeavor to accomplish the recognition of a single legislature as the depositary of the representative will of the people of Louisiana. This great department of government rescued from dispute, the rest of the problem could gradually be worked out by the prevalent authority which the legislative power, when undisputed, is quite competent to exert in composing conflict in the coordinate branches of the government.

An attentive consideration of the conditions under which the Federal Constitution and the acts of Congress provide or permit military intervention by the President in protection of a State against domestic violence has satisfied the President that the use of this authority in determining or influencing disputed elections in a State is most carefully to be avoided. Undoubtedly, as was held by the Supreme Court in the case of Luther *vs.* Borden, the appeal from a State may involve such an inquiry as to the lawfulness of the authority which invokes the interference of the President in supposed pursuance of the Constitution; but it is equally true that neither the constitutional provision nor the acts of Congress were framed with any such design. Both obviously treated the case of domestic violence within a State as of outbreak against law and the authority of established government which the State was unable to suppress by its own strength. A case wherein every department of the State government has a disputed representation, and a State therefore furnishes to the Federal Government no internal political recognition of authority upon which the Federal Executive can rely, will present a case of so much difficulty that it is of pressing importance to all interests in Louisiana that it should be avoided. A single legislature would greatly relieve this difficulty, for that department of the State government is named by the Constitution as the necessary applicant, when it can be convened, for military intervention by the United States.

If, therefore, the disputing interests can concur in or be reduced to a single legislature for the State of Louisiana, it would be a great step in composing this unhappy strife.

The President leaves entirely to the commission the conciliatory influences which, in their judgment formed on the spot, may seem to conduce to the proposed end. His own determination that only public considerations should inspire and attend this effort to give the ascendency in Louisiana to the things that belong to peace is evinced by his selection of commissioners who offer to the country in their own character every guaranty of the public motives and methods of the transactions which they have undertaken. Your report of the result of this endeavor will satisfy the President, he does not doubt, of the wisdom of his selection of and of his plenary trust in the commission.

A second and less important subject of attention during your visit to New Orleans will be the collection of accurate and trustworthy information from the public officers and prominent citizens of all political connections as to the state of public feeling and opinion in the community at large upon the general questions which affect the peaceful and safe exercise within the State of Louisiana of all legal and political rights and the protection of all legal and political privileges conferred by the Constitution of the United States upon all citizens. The maintenance and protection of these rights and privileges by all constitutional means and by every just, moral, and social influence are the settled purpose of the President in his administration of the Government. He will hope to learn from your investigations that this purpose will be aided and not resisted by the substantial and effective public opinion of the great body of the people of Louisiana.

The President does not wish to impose any limit upon your stay in Louisiana that would tend to defeat the full objects of your visit. He is, however, extremely desirous to find it in his power at the earliest day compatible with a safe exercise of that authority to put an end to even the appearance of military intervention in the domestic affairs of Louisiana, and he awaits your return with a confident hope that your report will enable him promptly to execute a purpose he has so much at heart.

The President desires me to add that the publication of the results of your visit he shall hope to make immediately after their communication to him.

I have the honor to be, with great respect, your obedient servant,

WM. M. EVARTS.

[From Letters and Messages of Rutherford B. Hayes, p. 25.]

EXECUTIVE MANSION,
Washington, April 20, 1877.

Hon. GEO. W. McCRARY,
Secretary of War.

SIR: Prior to my entering upon the duties of the Presidency there had been stationed, by order of my predecessor, in the immediate vicinity of the building used as a statehouse in New Orleans, La., and known as Mechanics' Institute, a detachment of United States infantry. Finding them in that place, I have thought proper to delay a decision of the question of their removal until I could determine whether the condition of affairs is now such as to either require or justify continued military intervention of the National Government in the affairs of the State.

In my opinion there does not now exist in Louisiana such domestic violence as is contemplated by the Constitution as the ground upon which the military power of the National Government may be invoked for the defense of the State. The disputes which exist as to the right of certain claimants to the chief executive office of that State are to be settled and determined, not by the Executive of the United States, but by such orderly and peaceable methods as may be provided by the constitution and the laws of the State.

Having the assurance that no resort to violence is contemplated, but, on the contrary, the disputes in question are to be settled by peaceful methods under and in accordance with law, I deem it proper to take action in accordance with the principles announced when I entered upon the duties of the Presidency.

You are therefore directed to see that the proper orders are issued for the removal of said troops at an early date from their present position to such regular barracks in the vicinity as may be selected for their occupation.

R. B. HAYES.

EXPLANATORY NOTES TO SPECIAL MESSAGES, VOLUMES I AND II.

Message of February 8, 1792, Vol. I, p. 116: Transmitting an account of John B. Cutting for expenditures incurred in liberating seamen of the United States in British ports during the impressments by the British Government in 1790.

Message of February 7, 1794, Vol. I, p. 151: Extraordinary commission of Guadaloupe apply to Congress for aid in men, provisions, and ammunition.

Message of March 18, 1794, Vol. I, p. 152: Transmitting an application by the minister of France for an advance of $1,000,000 on account of the debt due by the United States, correspondence between the Secretary of State and the minister of France relative thereto, etc.

Message of February 4, 1795, Vol. I, p. 175: Transmitting letters from the Secretaries of State and the Treasury concerning the negotiation of a loan in Holland.

Message of January 5, 1798, Vol. I, p. 260: Transmitting a report of the Secretary of War stating that the five clerks in his office were insufficient to transact the business and asking a larger appropriation to enable him to increase the number.

Message of March 5, 1798, Vol. I, pp. 263–264: Transmitting a message of the Executive Directory of France to the Council of Five Hundred and decree of that council of January 11, 1798, declaring neutral vessels laden with English merchandise lawful prize.

Message of January 28, 1799, Vol. I, pp. 281–282: Edict declaring that "every individual, native of friendly countries allied to the French Republic, or neutral, bearing a commission granted by the enemies of France or making part of the crews of ships of war, and others, enemies, shall be by this single fact declared a pirate and treated as such without being permitted in any case to allege that he had been forced into such service by violence, threats, or otherwise."

Message of January 13, 1800, Vol. I, p. 301: Relating to the Military Academy and the reorganization of the Army.

Message of January 14, 1800, Vol. I, pp. 301–302: Letter from John Randolph, jr., demanding that certain officers of the Army or Navy be punished for grossly and publicly insulting him for advocating in the House of Representatives a reduction of the military establishment.

Message of April 20, 1802, Vol. I, p. 341: Relating to spoliations committed on the commerce of the United States under Spanish authority and to the imprisonment of the American consul at St. Jago de Cuba.

Message of December 22, 1802, Vol. I, p. 346: Transmitting letters from the governors of the Mississippi Territory and of Kentucky, etc., relative to the prohibition by authorities of Spain to land American cargoes at New Orleans, in violation of treaty rights.

Message of December 31, 1804, Vol. I, p. 375: Relating to the bombardment of Tripoli, vessels engaged, number of men, etc.

Message of December 30, 1808, Vol. I, p. 458: Resolutions of the legislature of Pennsylvania expressing confidence in the General Government in its attitude toward foreign powers, indorsing the embargo as a wise measure, etc.

Message of June 4, 1809, Vol. I, p. 471: Transmitting resolutions of the Pennsylvania assembly protesting against the decision of the Supreme Court in the case of Gideon Olmstead.

Message of December 16, 1809, Vol. I, p. 478: Transmitting documents connected with the arrangement between D. M. Erskine, minister plenipotentiary of Great Britain, and the Secretary of State of the United States, making reparation for the attack on the *Chesapeake* and providing for the suspension of the embargo and nonintercourse laws and the withdrawal of the orders in council, etc.

Message of January 31, 1811, Vol. I, p. 489: Transmitting documents relative to negotiations with France for the repeal of decrees violating the neutral commerce of the United States, etc.

Message of December 27, 1811, Vol. I, p. 497: Transmitting resolutions of the legislature of Pennsylvania expressing confidence in the wisdom, patriotism, and firmness of the President and Congress relative to affairs with Great Britain and pledging support in case of an appeal to arms.

Message of September 26, 1814, Vol. I, p. 551: Transmitting correspondence relative to an order of the British admiral, Alex. Cochrane, "to destroy and lay waste such towns and districts upon the coast as may be found assailable," in retaliation for acts of the United States Army in Upper Canada.

Message of February 5, 1821, Vol. II, p. 83: Transmitting correspondence with Great Britain relative to the commercial relations between the United States and the British colonies in the West Indies and in North America, etc.

Message of February 3, 1823, Vol. II, p. 200: Transmitting a memorial of the legislative council of Florida relative to the expediency and necessity for further legislative provision for the government and improvement of Florida.

Message of February 17, 1825, Vol. II, p. 284: Transmitting correspondence with France relative to the interpretation of the eighth article of the treaty for the cession of Louisiana.

William McKinley

Messages, Proclamations, and Executive Orders Relating to the Spanish-American War

WILLIAM McKINLEY

Engraved by special permission, from the original by Benziger

William McKinley

WILLIAM MCKINLEY, the twenty-fifth President of the United States, was born in Niles, Trumbull County, Ohio, January 29, 1843. His ancestors on the paternal side, who were Scotch-Irish, came from Scotland and located in Pennsylvania. His great-grandfather, David McKinley, after serving in the Revolution, resided in Pennsylvania until 1814, when he went to Ohio, where he died in 1840, at the age of 85. The grandmother of the President, Mary Rose, came from a Puritan family that fled from England to Holland and emigrated to Pennsylvania with William Penn. The father of the President, William McKinley, sr., was born in Pine Township, Mercer County, Pa., in 1807, and married Nancy Campbell Allison, of Columbiana County, Ohio, in 1829. Both the grandfather and father of the President were iron manufacturers. His father was a devout Methodist, a stanch Whig and Republican, and an ardent advocate of a protective tariff. He died during his son's first term as governor of Ohio, in November, 1892, at the age of 85. The mother of the President passed away at Canton, Ohio, in December, 1897, at the advanced age of 89. William McKinley was educated in the public schools of Niles, Union Seminary, at Poland, Ohio, and Allegheny College, at Meadville, Pa. Before attaining his majority taught in the public schools. At the age of 16 became a member of the Methodist Episcopal Church. At the beginning of hostilities in the War between the States Mr. McKinley, who was a clerk in the Poland post-office, volunteered his services, and on June 11, 1861, was enlisted as a private in the Twenty-third Ohio Volunteer Infantry. Participated in all the early engagements in West Virginia, and in the winter's camp at Fayetteville received his first promotion, commissary-sergeant, on April 15, 1862. In recognition of his services at Antietam, Sergeant McKinley was made second lieutenant, his commission dating from September 24, 1862, and on February 7, 1863, while at Camp Piatt, he was again promoted, receiving the rank of first lieutenant. In the retreat near Lynchburg, Va., his regiment marched 180 miles, fighting nearly all the time, with scarcely any rest or food. Lieutenant McKinley conducted himself with gallantry, and at Winchester won additional honors. The Thirteenth West Virginia Regiment failed to retire when the rest of Hayes's brigade fell back, and, being in great danger of capture, the young lieutenant was directed to go and bring it away, which he did in safety, after riding through a heavy fire. On July 25, 1864, at the age of 21, McKinley was promoted to the rank of captain. The brigade continued its fighting up and down the Shenandoah Valley. At Berryville, Va., September 3, 1864, Captain McKinley's horse was shot from under him. Served successively on the staffs of Generals R. B. Hayes, George Crook, and Winfield S. Hancock, and on March 14, 1865, was brevetted major of United States Volunteers by President Lincoln for gallantry in the battles of Opequan, Cedar Creek, and Fishers Hill. Was detailed as acting assistant adjutant-general of the First Division, First Army Corps, on the staff of General Samuel S. Carroll. At the close of the war was urged to remain in the Army, but, deferring to the judgment of his father, was mustered out of the service July 26, 1865, and returned to Poland. At once began the study of law under Glidden & Wilson, of Youngstown, Ohio, and later attended the law school in Albany, N. Y. Was admitted to the bar in March, 1867, at Warren, Ohio, and the same year removed to Canton, Ohio, which has since been his home. In 1867 his first political speeches were made in favor of negro suffrage. In 1869 was elected prosecuting attorney of Stark County, and served one term, being defeated two years later for the same office. Mr. McKinley took an active interest in State politics, and made speeches in many of the campaigns. On January 25, 1871, married Miss Ida Saxton. Two daughters were born to them, both of whom died in early childhood. In 1876 was elected a member of the National House of Representatives, and for fourteen years represented the Congressional district of which his county was a part, except for a portion of his fourth term, when he was unseated late in the first session. While in Congress served on the Committees on the Judiciary, Revision of the Laws, Expenditures in the Post-Office Department, Rules, and Ways and Means. As chairman of the last-named committee in the Fifty-first Congress, reported the tariff law of 1890. At the beginning of this Congress was defeated in the caucus of his party for the Speakership of the House. In the meantime, his district having been materially changed, he was defeated for reelection to Congress in November, 1890, though he largely reduced the usual majority against his party in the counties of which the new district was constituted. In 1891 was elected governor of Ohio by a plurality of 21,500, and in 1893 was reelected by a plurality of 80,995. In 1884 was a delegate at large to the Republican national convention, and supported James G. Blaine for President; was a member of the committee on resolutions, and presented the platform to the convention. Also attended the convention of his party in 1888 as a delegate at large from Ohio, supporting John Sherman for President, and as chairman of the committee on resolutions again reported the platform. In 1892 was again a delegate at large from Ohio, and supported the renomination of Benjamin Harrison, and served as chairman of the convention. At that convention 182 votes were cast for him for President, although he had persistently refused to have his name considered. On June 18, 1896, was nominated for President by the national convention of his party at St. Louis, receiving on the first ballot 661½ out of a total of 922 votes. Was chosen President at the ensuing November election by a plurality in the popular vote of over 600,000, and received 271 electoral votes, against 176 for William J. Bryan, of Nebraska.

SPECIAL MESSAGE.

EXECUTIVE MANSION, *May 17, 1897.*

To the Senate and House of Representatives of the United States:

Official information from our consuls in Cuba establishes the fact that a large number of American citizens in the island are in a state of destitution, suffering for want of food and medicines. This applies particularly to the rural districts of the central and eastern parts.

The agricultural classes have been forced from their farms into the nearest towns, where they are without work or money. The local authorities of the several towns, however kindly disposed, are unable to relieve the needs of their own people and are altogether powerless to help our citizens.

The latest report of Consul-General Lee estimates six to eight hundred Americans are without means of support. I have assured him that provision would be made at once to relieve them. To that end I recommend that Congress make an appropriation of not less than $50,000, to be immediately available, for use under the direction of the Secretary of State.

It is desirable that a part of the sum which may be appropriated by Congress should, in the discretion of the Secretary of State, also be used for the transportation of American citizens who, desiring to return to the United States, are without means to do so.

WILLIAM McKINLEY.

FIRST ANNUAL MESSAGE.

EXECUTIVE MANSION, *December 6, 1897.*

*   *   *   *   *   *   *

The most important problem with which this Government is now called upon to deal pertaining to its foreign relations concerns its duty toward Spain and the Cuban insurrection. Problems and conditions more or less in common with those now existing have confronted this Government at various times in the past. The story of Cuba for many years has been one of unrest, growing discontent, an effort toward a larger enjoyment of liberty and self-control, of organized resistance to the mother country, of depression after distress and warfare, and of ineffectual settlement to be followed by renewed revolt. For no enduring period since the enfranchisement of the continental possessions of Spain in the Western Continent has the condition of Cuba or the policy of Spain toward Cuba not caused concern to the United States.

The prospect from time to time that the weakness of Spain's hold upon the island and the political vicissitudes and embarrassments of the home Government might lead to the transfer of Cuba to a continental power called forth between 1823 and 1860 various emphatic declarations of the policy of the United States to permit no disturbance of Cuba's connection with Spain unless in the direction of independence or acquisition by us through purchase, nor has there been any change of this declared policy since upon the part of the Government.

The revolution which began in 1868 lasted for ten years despite the strenuous efforts of the successive peninsular governments to suppress it. Then as now the Government of the United States testified its grave concern and offered its aid to put an end to bloodshed in Cuba. The overtures made by General Grant were refused and the war dragged on, entailing great loss of life and treasure and increased injury to American interests, besides throwing enhanced burdens of neutrality upon this Government. In 1878 peace was brought about by the truce of Zanjon, obtained by negotiations between the Spanish commander, Martinez de Campos, and the insurgent leaders.

The present insurrection broke out in February, 1895. It is not my purpose at this time to recall its remarkable increase or to characterize its tenacious resistance against the enormous forces massed against it by Spain. The revolt and the efforts to subdue it carried destruction to every quarter of the island, developing wide proportions and defying the efforts of Spain for its suppression. The civilized code of war has been disregarded, no less so by the Spaniards than by the Cubans.

The existing conditions can not but fill this Government and the American people with the gravest apprehension. There is no desire on the part of our people to profit by the misfortunes of Spain. We have only the desire to see the Cubans prosperous and contented, enjoying that measure of self-control which is the inalienable right of man, protected in their right to reap the benefit of the exhaustless treasures of their country.

The offer made by my predecessor in April, 1896, tendering the friendly offices of this Government, failed. Any mediation on our part was not accepted. In brief, the answer read: ''There is no effectual way to pacify Cuba unless it begins with the actual submission of the rebels to the mother country.'' Then only could Spain act in the promised direction, of her own motion and after her own plans.

The cruel policy of concentration was initiated February 16, 1896. The productive districts controlled by the Spanish armies were depopulated. The agricultural inhabitants were herded in and about the garrison towns, their lands laid waste and their dwellings destroyed. This policy the late cabinet of Spain justified as a necessary measure of war and as a means of cutting off supplies from the insurgents. It has utterly failed as a war measure. It was not civilized warfare. It was extermination.

Against this abuse of the rights of war I have felt constrained on repeated occasions to enter the firm and earnest protest of this Government. There was much of public condemnation of the treatment of American citizens by alleged illegal arrests and long imprisonment awaiting trial or pending protracted judicial proceedings. I felt it my first duty to make instant demand for the release or speedy trial of all American citizens under arrest. Before the change of the Spanish cabinet in October last twenty-two prisoners, citizens of the United States, had been given their freedom.

For the relief of our own citizens suffering because of the conflict the aid of Congress was sought in a special message,* and under the appropriation of May 24, 1897,† effective aid has been given to American citizens in Cuba, many of them at their own request having been returned to the United States.

The instructions given to our new minister to Spain before his departure for his post directed him to impress upon that Government the sincere wish of the United States to lend its aid toward the ending of the war in Cuba by reaching a peaceful and lasting result, just and honorable alike to Spain and to the Cuban people. These instructions recited the character and duration of the contest, the widespread losses it entails, the burdens and restraints it imposes upon us, with constant disturbance of national interests, and the injury resulting from an indefinite continuance of this state of things. It was stated that at this juncture our Government was constrained to seriously inquire if the time was not ripe when Spain of her own volition, moved by her own interests and every sentiment of humanity, should put a stop to this destructive war and make proposals of settlement honorable to herself and just to her Cuban colony. It was urged that as a neighboring nation, with large interests in Cuba, we could be required to wait only a reasonable time for the mother country to establish its authority and restore peace and order within the borders of the island; that we could not contemplate an indefinite period for the accomplishment of this result.

No solution was proposed to which the slightest idea of humiliation to Spain could attach, and, indeed, precise proposals were withheld to avoid embarrassment to that Government. All that was asked or expected was that some safe way might be speedily provided and permanent peace

* See p. 127.   † See p. 126.

restored. It so chanced that the consideration of this offer, addressed to the same Spanish administration which had declined the tenders of my predecessor, and which for more than two years had poured men and treasure into Cuba in the fruitless effort to suppress the revolt, fell to others. Between the departure of General Woodford, the new envoy, and his arrival in Spain the statesman who had shaped the policy of his country fell by the hand of an assassin, and although the cabinet of the late premier still held office and received from our envoy the proposals he bore, that cabinet gave place within a few days thereafter to a new administration, under the leadership of Sagasta.

The reply to our note was received on the 23d day of October. It is in the direction of a better understanding. It appreciates the friendly purposes of this Government. It admits that our country is deeply affected by the war in Cuba and that its desires for peace are just. It declares that the present Spanish government is bound by every consideration to a change of policy that should satisfy the United States and pacify Cuba within a reasonable time. To this end Spain has decided to put into effect the political reforms heretofore advocated by the present premier, without halting for any consideration in the path which in its judgment leads to peace. The military operations, it is said, will continue, but will be humane and conducted with all regard for private rights, being accompanied by political action leading to the autonomy of Cuba while guarding Spanish sovereignty. This, it is claimed, will result in investing Cuba with a distinct personality, the island to be governed by an executive and by a local council or chamber, reserving to Spain the control of the foreign relations, the army and navy, and the judicial administration. To accomplish this the present government proposes to modify existing legislation by decree, leaving the Spanish Cortes, with the aid of Cuban senators and deputies, to solve the economic problem and properly distribute the existing debt.

In the absence of a declaration of the measures that this Government proposes to take in carrying out its proffer of good offices, it suggests that Spain be left free to conduct military operations and grant political reforms, while the United States for its part shall enforce its neutral obligations and cut off the assistance which it is asserted the insurgents receive from this country. The supposition of an indefinite prolongation of the war is denied. It is asserted that the western provinces are already well-nigh reclaimed, that the planting of cane and tobacco therein has been resumed, and that by force of arms and new and ample reforms very early and complete pacification is hoped for.

The immediate amelioration of existing conditions under the new administration of Cuban affairs is predicted, and therewithal the disturbance and all occasion for any change of attitude on the part of the United States. Discussion of the question of the international duties and responsibilities of the United States as Spain understands them is presented, with an apparent disposition to charge us with failure in this regard. This charge is without any basis in fact. It could not have been made if Spain had been cognizant of the constant efforts this Government has made, at the cost of millions and by the employment of the administrative machinery of the nation at command, to perform its full duty according to the law of nations. That it has successfully prevented the departure of a single military expedition or armed vessel from our shores in violation of our laws would seem to be a sufficient answer. But of this aspect of the Spanish note it is not necessary to speak further now. Firm in the conviction of a wholly performed obligation, due response to this charge has been made in diplomatic course.

Throughout all these horrors and dangers to our own peace this Government has never in any way abrogated its sovereign prerogative of reserving to itself the determination of its policy and course according to its own high sense of right and in consonance with the dearest interests and convictions of our own people should the prolongation of the strife so demand.

Of the untried measures there remain only: Recognition of the insurgents as belligerents; recognition of the independence of Cuba; neutral intervention to end the war by imposing a rational compromise between the contestants, and intervention in favor of one or the other party. I speak not of forcible annexation, for that can not be thought of. That, by our code of morality, would be criminal aggression.

Recognition of the belligerency of the Cuban insurgents has often been canvassed as a possible, if not inevitable, step both in regard to the previous ten years' struggle and during the present war. I am not unmindful that the two Houses of Congress in the spring of 1896 expressed the opinion by concurrent resolution that a condition of public war existed requiring or justifying the recognition of a state of belligerency in Cuba, and during the extra session the Senate voted a joint resolution of like import, which, however, was not brought to a vote in the House of Representatives. In the presence of these significant expressions of the sentiment of the legislative branch it behooves the Executive to soberly consider the conditions under which so important a measure must needs rest for justification. It is to be seriously considered whether the Cuban insurrection possesses beyond dispute the attributes of statehood, which alone can demand the recognition of belligerency in its favor. Possession, in short, of the essential qualifications of sovereignty by the insurgents and the conduct of the war by them according to the received code of war are no less important factors toward the determination of the problem of belligerency than are the influences and consequences of the struggle upon the internal polity of the recognizing state.

The wise utterances of President Grant in his memorable message of December 7, 1875, are signally relevant to the present situation in Cuba, and it may be wholesome now to recall them. At that time a ruinous conflict had for seven years wasted the neighboring island. During all those years an utter disregard of the laws of civilized warfare and of the just demands of humanity, which called forth expressions of condemnation from the nations of Christendom, continued unabated. Desolation and ruin pervaded that productive region, enormously affecting the commerce of all commercial nations, but that of the United States more than any other by reason of proximity and larger trade and intercourse. At that juncture General Grant uttered these words, which now, as then, sum up the elements of the problem:

A recognition of the independence of Cuba being, in my opinion, impracticable and indefensible, the question which next presents itself is that of the recognition of belligerent rights in the parties to the contest.

In a former message to Congress* I had occasion to consider this question, and reached the conclusion that the conflict in Cuba, dreadful and devastating as were its incidents, did not rise to the fearful dignity of war. * * * It is possible that the acts of foreign powers, and even acts of Spain herself, of this very nature, might be pointed to in defense of such recognition. But now, as in its past history, the United States should carefully avoid the false lights which might lead it into the mazes of doubtful law and of questionable propriety, and adhere rigidly and sternly to the rule, which has been its guide, of doing only that which is right and honest and of good report. The question of according or of withholding rights of belligerency must be judged in every case in view of the particular attending facts. Unless justified by necessity, it is always, and justly, regarded as an unfriendly act and a gratuitous demonstration of moral support to the rebellion. It is necessary, and it is required, when the interests and rights of another government or of its people are so far affected by a pending civil conflict as to require a definition of its relations to the parties thereto. But this conflict must be one which will be recognized in the sense of international law as war. Belligerence, too, is a fact. The mere existence of contending armed bodies and their occasional conflicts do not constitute war in the sense referred to. Applying to the existing condition of affairs in Cuba the tests recognized by publicists and writers on international law, and which have been observed by nations of dignity, honesty, and power when free from sensitive or selfish and unworthy motives, I fail to find in the insurrection the existence of such a substantial political organization, real, palpable, and manifest to the world, having the forms and capable of the ordinary functions of government toward its own people and to other states, with courts for the administration of justice, with a local habitation, possessing such organization of force, such material, such occupation of territory, as to take the contest out of the category of a mere rebellious insurrection or occasional skirmishes and place it on the terrible footing of war, to which a recognition of belligerency would aim to elevate it. The contest, moreover, is solely on land; the insurrection has not possessed itself of a single seaport whence it may send forth its flag, nor has it any means of communication with foreign powers except through the military lines of its adversaries. No apprehension of any of those sudden and difficult complications which a war upon the ocean is apt to precipitate upon the vessels, both commercial and national, and upon the consular officers of other powers calls for the definition of their relations to the parties to the contest. Considered as a question of expediency, I regard the accordance of belligerent rights still to be as unwise and premature as I regard it to be, at present, indefensible as a measure of right. Such recognition entails upon the country according the rights which flow from it difficult and complicated duties, and requires

*See Vol. VII, pp. 64-69.

the exaction from the contending parties of the strict observance of their rights and obligations. It confers the right of search upon the high seas by vessels of both parties; it would subject the carrying of arms and munitions of war, which now may be transported freely and without interruption in the vessels of the United States, to detention and to possible seizure; it would give rise to countless vexatious questions, would release the parent Government from responsibility for acts done by the insurgents, and would invest Spain with the right to exercise the supervision recognized by our treaty of 1795 over our commerce on the high seas, a very large part of which, in its traffic between the Atlantic and the Gulf States and between all of them and the States on the Pacific, passes through the waters which wash the shores of Cuba. The exercise of this supervision could scarce fail to lead, if not to abuses, certainly to collisions perilous to the peaceful relations of the two States. There can be little doubt to what result such supervision would before long draw this nation. It would be unworthy of the United States to inaugurate the possibilities of such result by measures of questionable right or expediency or by any indirection.

Turning to the practical aspects of a recognition of belligerency and reviewing its inconveniences and positive dangers, still further pertinent considerations appear. In the code of nations there is no such thing as a naked recognition of belligerency, unaccompanied by the assumption of international neutrality. Such recognition, without more, will not confer upon either party to a domestic conflict a status not theretofore actually possessed or affect the relation of either party to other states. The act of recognition usually takes the form of a solemn proclamation of neutrality, which recites the *de facto* condition of belligerency as its motive. It announces a domestic law of neutrality in the declaring state. It assumes the international obligations of a neutral in the presence of a public state of war. It warns all citizens and others within the jurisdiction of the proclaimant that they violate those rigorous obligations at their own peril and can not expect to be shielded from the consequences. The right of visit and search on the seas and seizure of vessels and cargoes and contraband of war and good prize under admiralty law must under international law be admitted as a legitimate consequence of a proclamation of belligerency. While according the equal belligerent rights defined by public law to each party in our ports disfavors would be imposed on both, which, while nominally equal, would weigh heavily in behalf of Spain herself. Possessing a navy and controlling the ports of Cuba, her maritime rights could be asserted not only for the military investment of the island, but up to the margin of our own territorial waters, and a condition of things would exist for which the Cubans within their own domain could not hope to create a parallel, while its creation through aid or sympathy from within our domain would be even more impossible than now, with the additional obligations of international neutrality we would perforce assume.

The enforcement of this enlarged and onerous code of neutrality would only be influential within our own jurisdiction by land and sea and applicable by our own instrumentalities. It could impart to the United States no jurisdiction between Spain and the insurgents. It would give the

United States no right of intervention to enforce the conduct of the strife within the paramount authority of Spain according to the international code of war.

For these reasons I regard the recognition of the belligerency of the Cuban insurgents as now unwise, and therefore inadmissible. Should that step hereafter be deemed wise as a measure of right and duty, the Executive will take it.

Intervention upon humanitarian grounds has been frequently suggested and has not failed to receive my most anxious and earnest consideration. But should such a step be now taken, when it is apparent that a hopeful change has supervened in the policy of Spain toward Cuba? A new government has taken office in the mother country. It is pledged in advance to the declaration that all the effort in the world can not suffice to maintain peace in Cuba by the bayonet; that vague promises of reform after subjugation afford no solution of the insular problem; that with a substitution of commanders must come a change of the past system of warfare for one in harmony with a new policy, which shall no longer aim to drive the Cubans to the "horrible alternative of taking to the thicket or succumbing in misery;" that reforms must be instituted in accordance with the needs and circumstances of the time, and that these reforms, while designed to give full autonomy to the colony and to create a virtual entity and self-controlled administration, shall yet conserve and affirm the sovereignty of Spain by a just distribution of powers and burdens upon a basis of mutual interest untainted by methods of selfish expediency.

The first acts of the new government lie in these honorable paths. The policy of cruel rapine and extermination that so long shocked the universal sentiment of humanity has been reversed. Under the new military commander a broad clemency is proffered. Measures have already been set on foot to relieve the horrors of starvation. The power of the Spanish armies, it is asserted, is to be used not to spread ruin and desolation, but to protect the resumption of peaceful agricultural pursuits and productive industries. That past methods are futile to force a peace by subjugation is freely admitted, and that ruin without conciliation must inevitably fail to win for Spain the fidelity of a contented dependency.

Decrees in application of the foreshadowed reforms have already been promulgated. The full text of these decrees has not been received, but as furnished in a telegraphic summary from our minister are: All civil and electoral rights of peninsular Spaniards are, in virtue of existing constitutional authority, forthwith extended to colonial Spaniards. A scheme of autonomy has been proclaimed by decree, to become effective upon ratification by the Cortes. It creates a Cuban parliament, which, with the insular executive, can consider and vote upon all subjects affecting local order and interests, possessing unlimited powers save as to matters of state, war, and the navy, as to which the Governor-General acts by his own authority as the delegate of the central Government. This parliament receives the oath of the Governor-General to preserve faithfully the liberties and privileges of the colony, and to it the colonial secretaries are responsible. It has the right to propose to the central Government, through the Governor-General, modifications of the national charter and to invite new projects of law or executive measures in the interest of the colony.

Besides its local powers, it is competent, first, to regulate electoral registration and procedure and prescribe the qualifications of electors and the manner of exercising suffrage; second, to organize courts of justice with native judges from members of the local bar; third, to frame the insular budget, both as to expenditures and revenues, without limitation of any kind, and to set apart the revenues to meet the Cuban share of the national budget, which latter will be voted by the national Cortes with the assistance of Cuban senators and deputies; fourth, to initiate or take part in the negotiations of the national Government for commercial treaties which may affect Cuban interests; fifth, to accept or reject commercial treaties which the national Government may have concluded without the participation of the Cuban government; sixth, to frame the colonial tariff, acting in accord with the peninsular Government in scheduling articles of mutual commerce between the mother country and the colonies. Before introducing or voting upon a bill the Cuban government or the chambers will lay the project before the central Government and hear its opinion thereon, all the correspondence in such regard being made public. Finally, all conflicts of jurisdiction arising between the different municipal, provincial, and insular assemblies, or between the latter and the insular executive power, and which from their nature may not be referable to the central Government for decision, shall be submitted to the courts.

That the government of Sagasta has entered upon a course from which recession with honor is impossible can hardly be questioned; that in the few weeks it has existed it has made earnest of the sincerity of its professions is undeniable. I shall not impugn its sincerity, nor should impatience be suffered to embarrass it in the task it has undertaken. It is honestly due to Spain and to our friendly relations with Spain that she should be given a reasonable chance to realize her expectations and to prove the asserted efficacy of the new order of things to which she stands irrevocably committed. She has recalled the commander whose brutal orders inflamed the American mind and shocked the civilized world. She has modified the horrible order of concentration and has undertaken to care for the helpless and permit those who desire to resume the cultivation of their fields to do so, and assures them of the protection of the Spanish Government in their lawful occupations. She has just released the *Competitor* prisoners, heretofore sentenced to death, and who have been the subject of repeated diplomatic correspondence during both this and the preceding Administration.

Not a single American citizen is now in arrest or confinement in Cuba of whom this Government has any knowledge. The near future will demonstrate whether the indispensable condition of a righteous peace, just alike to the Cubans and to Spain, as well as equitable to all our interests so intimately involved in the welfare of Cuba, is likely to be attained. If not, the exigency of further and other action by the United States will remain to be taken. When that time comes, that action will be determined in the line of indisputable right and duty. It will be faced, without misgiving or hesitancy, in the light of the obligation this Government owes to itself, to the people who have confided to it the protection of their interests and honor, and to humanity.

Sure of the right, keeping free from all offense ourselves, actuated only by upright and patriotic considerations, moved neither by passion nor selfishness, the Government will continue its watchful care over the rights and property of American citizens and will abate none of its efforts to bring about by peaceful agencies a peace which shall be honorable and enduring. If it shall hereafter appear to be a duty imposed by our obligations to ourselves, to civilization, and humanity to intervene with force, it shall be without fault on our part and only because the necessity for such action will be so clear as to command the support and approval of the civilized world.

*   *   *   *   *   *   *

WILLIAM McKINLEY.

JOINT RESOLUTION appropriating $50,000 for the relief of destitute citizens of the United States in the island of Cuba.

Resolved by the Senate and House of Representatives of the United States of America in Congress assembled, That the sum of $50,000 be, and the same is hereby, appropriated, out of any money in the Treasury not otherwise appropriated, for the relief of destitute citizens of the United States in the island of Cuba, said money to be expended at the discretion and under the direction of the President of the United States in the purchase and furnishing of food, clothing, and medicines to such citizens, and for transporting to the United States such of them as so desire and who are without means to transport themselves.

Approved, May 24, 1897.

SPECIAL MESSAGES.

EXECUTIVE MANSION, *March 28, 1898.*

To the Congress of the United States:

For some time prior to the visit of the *Maine* to Havana Harbor our consular representatives pointed out the advantages to flow from the visit of national ships to the Cuban waters, in accustoming the people to the presence of our flag as the symbol of good will and of our ships in the fulfillment of the mission of protection to American interests, even though no immediate need therefor might exist.

Accordingly, on the 24th of January last, after conference with the Spanish minister, in which the renewal of visits of our war vessels to Spanish waters was discussed and accepted, the peninsular authorities at Madrid and Havana were advised of the purpose of this Government to resume friendly naval visits at Cuban ports, and that in that view the *Maine* would forthwith call at the port of Havana.

This announcement was received by the Spanish Government with appreciation of the friendly character of the visit of the *Maine* and with notification of intention to return the courtesy by sending Spanish ships to the principal ports of the United States. Meanwhile the *Maine* entered the port of Havana on the 25th of January, her arrival being marked with no special incident besides the exchange of customary salutes and ceremonial visits.

The *Maine* continued in the harbor of Havana during the three weeks following her arrival. No appreciable excitement attended her stay. On the contrary, a feeling of relief and confidence followed the resumption of the long-interrupted friendly intercourse. So noticeable was this immediate effect of her visit that the consul-general strongly urged that the presence of our ships in Cuban waters should be kept up by retaining the *Maine* at Havana, or, in the event of her recall, by sending another vessel there to take her place.

At forty minutes past 9 in the evening of the 15th of February the *Maine* was destroyed by an explosion, by which the entire forward part of the ship was utterly wrecked. In this catastrophe 2 officers and 264 of her crew perished, those who were not killed outright by her explosion being penned between decks by the tangle of wreckage and drowned by the immediate sinking of the hull.

Prompt assistance was rendered by the neighboring vessels anchored in the harbor, aid being especially given by the boats of the Spanish cruiser *Alfonso XII* and the Ward Line steamer *City of Washington*, which lay not far distant. The wounded were generously cared for by the authorities of Havana, the hospitals being freely opened to them, while the earliest recovered bodies of the dead were interred by the municipality in a public cemetery in the city. Tributes of grief and sympathy were offered from all official quarters of the island.

The appalling calamity fell upon the people of our country with crushing force, and for a brief time an intense excitement prevailed, which in a community less just and self-controlled than ours might have led to hasty acts of blind resentment. This spirit, however, soon gave way to the calmer processes of reason and to the resolve to investigate the facts and await material proof before forming a judgment as to the cause, the responsibility, and, if the facts warranted, the remedy due. This course necessarily recommended itself from the outset to the Executive, for only in the light of a dispassionately ascertained certainty could it determine the nature and measure of its full duty in the matter.

The usual procedure was followed, as in all cases of casualty or disaster to national vessels of any maritime state. A naval court of inquiry was at once organized, composed of officers well qualified by rank and practical experience to discharge the onerous duty imposed upon them. Aided by a strong force of wreckers and divers, the court proceeded to make a thorough investigation on the spot, employing every available means for the impartial and exact determination of the causes of the explosion. Its operations have been conducted with the utmost deliberation and judgment, and, while independently pursued, no attainable source of information was neglected, and the fullest opportunity was allowed for a simultaneous investigation by the Spanish authorities.

The finding of the court of inquiry was reached, after twenty-three days of continuous labor, on the 21st of March instant, and, having been approved on the 22d by the commander in chief of the United States naval force on the North Atlantic station, was transmitted to the Executive.

It is herewith laid before the Congress, together with the voluminous testimony taken before the court.

Its purport is, in brief, as follows:

When the *Maine* arrived at Havana, she was conducted by the regular Government pilot to buoy No. 4, to which she was moored in from 5½ to 6 fathoms of water.

The state of discipline on board and the condition of her magazines, boilers, coal bunkers, and storage compartments are passed in review, with the conclusion that excellent order prevailed and that no indication of any cause for an internal explosion existed in any quarter.

At 8 o'clock in the evening of February 15 everything had been reported secure, and all was quiet.

At forty minutes past 9 o'clock the vessel was suddenly destroyed.

There were two distinct explosions, with a brief interval between them. The first lifted the forward part of the ship very perceptibly; the second, which was more open, prolonged, and of greater volume, is attributed by the court to the partial explosion of two or more of the forward magazines.

The evidence of the divers establishes that the after part of the ship was practically intact and sank in that condition a very few moments after the explosion. The forward part was completely demolished.

Upon the evidence of a concurrent external cause the finding of the court is as follows:

At frame 17 the outer shell of the ship, from a point 11½ feet from the middle line of the ship and 6 feet above the keel when in its normal position, has been forced up so as to be now about 4 feet above the surface of the water, therefore about 34 feet above where it would be had the ship sunk uninjured.

The outside bottom plating is bent into a reversed V shape (∧), the after wing of which, about 15 feet broad and 32 feet in length (from frame 17 to frame 25), is doubled back upon itself against the continuation of the same plating, extending forward.

At frame 18 the vertical keel is broken in two and the flat keel bent into an angle similar to the angle formed by the outside bottom plates. This break is now about 6 feet below the surface of the water and about 30 feet above its normal position.

In the opinion of the court this effect could have been produced only by the explosion of a mine situated under the bottom of the ship at about frame 18 and somewhat on the port side of the ship.

The conclusions of the court are:

That the loss of the *Maine* was not in any respect due to fault or negligence on the part of any of the officers or members of her crew;

That the ship was destroyed by the explosion of a submarine mine, which caused the partial explosion of two or more of her forward magazines; and

That no evidence has been obtainable fixing the responsibility for the destruction of the *Maine* upon any person or persons.

I have directed that the finding of the court of inquiry and the views of this Government thereon be communicated to the Government of Her Majesty the Queen Regent, and I do not permit myself to doubt that the sense of justice of the Spanish nation will dictate a course of action suggested by honor and the friendly relations of the two Governments.

It will be the duty of the Executive to advise the Congress of the result, and in the meantime deliberate consideration is invoked.

WILLIAM McKINLEY.

EXECUTIVE MANSION, *April 11, 1898.*

To the Congress of the United States:

Obedient to that precept of the Constitution which commands the President to give from time to time to the Congress information of the state of the Union and to recommend to their consideration such measures as he shall judge necessary and expedient, it becomes my duty to now address your body with regard to the grave crisis that has arisen in the relations of the United States to Spain by reason of the warfare that for more than three years has raged in the neighboring island of Cuba.

I do so because of the intimate connection of the Cuban question with the state of our own Union and the grave relation the course which it is now incumbent upon the nation to adopt must needs bear to the traditional policy of our Government if it is to accord with the precepts laid down by the founders of the Republic and religiously observed by succeeding Administrations to the present day.

The present revolution is but the successor of other similar insurrections which have occurred in Cuba against the dominion of Spain, extending over a period of nearly half a century, each of which during its progress has subjected the United States to great effort and expense in enforcing its neutrality laws, caused enormous losses to American trade and commerce, caused irritation, annoyance, and disturbance among our citizens, and, by the exercise of cruel, barbarous, and uncivilized practices of warfare, shocked the sensibilities and offended the humane sympathies of our people.

Since the present revolution began, in February, 1895, this country has seen the fertile domain at our threshold ravaged by fire and sword in the course of a struggle unequaled in the history of the island and rarely paralleled as to the numbers of the combatants and the bitterness of the contest by any revolution of modern times where a dependent people striving to be free have been opposed by the power of the sovereign state.

Our people have beheld a once prosperous community reduced to comparative want, its lucrative commerce virtually paralyzed, its exceptional productiveness diminished, its fields laid waste, its mills in ruins, and its people perishing by tens of thousands from hunger and destitution. We have found ourselves constrained, in the observance of that strict neutrality which our laws enjoin and which the law of nations commands, to police our own waters and watch our own seaports in prevention of any unlawful act in aid of the Cubans.

Our trade has suffered, the capital invested by our citizens in Cuba has been largely lost; and the temper and forbearance of our people have been so sorely tried as to beget a perilous unrest among our own citizens, which has inevitably found its expression from time to time in the National Legislature, so that issues wholly external to our own body politic engross attention and stand in the way of that close devotion to domestic advancement that becomes a self-contained commonwealth whose primal maxim has been the avoidance of all foreign entanglements. All this must needs awaken, and has, indeed, aroused, the utmost concern on the part of this Government, as well during my predecessor's term as in my own.

In April, 1896, the evils from which our country suffered through the Cuban war became so onerous that my predecessor made an effort to bring about a peace through the mediation of this Government in any way that might tend to an honorable adjustment of the contest between Spain and her revolted colony, on the basis of some effective scheme of self-government for Cuba under the flag and sovereignty of Spain. It failed through the refusal of the Spanish government then in power to consider any form of mediation or, indeed, any plan of settlement which did not begin with the actual submission of the insurgents to the mother country, and then only on such terms as Spain herself might see fit to grant. The war continued unabated. The resistance of the insurgents was in no wise diminished.

The efforts of Spain were increased, both by the dispatch of fresh levies to Cuba and by the addition to the horrors of the strife of a new and inhuman phase happily unprecedented in the modern history of civilized Christian peoples. The policy of devastation and concentration, inaugurated by the Captain-General's *bando* of October 21, 1896, in the Province of Pinar del Rio was thence extended to embrace all of the island to which the power of the Spanish arms was able to reach by occupation or by military operations. The peasantry, including all dwelling in the open agricultural interior, were driven into the garrison towns or isolated places held by the troops.

The raising and movement of provisions of all kinds were interdicted. The fields were laid waste, dwellings unroofed and fired, mills destroyed, and, in short, everything that could desolate the land and render it unfit for human habitation or support was commanded by one or the other of the contending parties and executed by all the powers at their disposal.

By the time the present Administration took office, a year ago, reconcentration (so called) had been made effective over the better part of the four central and western provinces—Santa Clara, Matanzas, Havana, and Pinar del Rio.

The agricultural population to the estimated number of 300,000 or more was herded within the towns and their immediate vicinage, deprived of the means of support, rendered destitute of shelter, left poorly clad, and exposed to the most unsanitary conditions. As the scarcity of food increased with the devastation of the depopulated areas of production, destitution and want became misery and starvation. Month by month the death rate increased in an alarming ratio. By March, 1897, according to conservative estimates from official Spanish sources, the mortality among the reconcentrados from starvation and the diseases thereto incident exceeded 50 per cent of their total number.

No practical relief was accorded to the destitute. The overburdened towns, already suffering from the general dearth, could give no aid. So-called "zones of cultivation" established within the immediate areas of effective military control about the cities and fortified camps proved illusory as a remedy for the suffering. The unfortunates, being for the most part women and children, with aged and helpless men, enfeebled by disease and hunger, could not have tilled the soil without tools, seed, or shelter for their own support or for the supply of the cities. Reconcentration, adopted avowedly as a war measure in order to cut off the resources of the insurgents, worked its predestined result. As I said in my message of last December, it was not civilized warfare; it was extermination. The only peace it could beget was that of the wilderness and the grave.

Meanwhile the military situation in the island had undergone a noticeable change. The extraordinary activity that characterized the second year of the war, when the insurgents invaded even the thitherto unharmed fields of Pinar del Rio and carried havoc and destruction up to the walls of the city of Havana itself, had relapsed into a dogged struggle in the central and eastern provinces. The Spanish arms regained a measure of control in Pinar del Rio and parts of Havana, but, under the existing conditions of the rural country, without immediate improvement of their productive situation. Even thus partially restricted, the revolutionists held their own, and their conquest and submission, put forward by Spain as the essential and sole basis of peace, seemed as far distant as at the outset.

In this state of affairs my Administration found itself confronted with the grave problem of its duty. My message of last December * reviewed the situation and narrated the steps taken with a view to relieving its acuteness and opening the way to some form of honorable settlement. The assassination of the prime minister, Canovas, led to a change of government in Spain. The former administration, pledged to subjugation without concession, gave place to that of a more liberal party, committed long in advance to a policy of reform involving the wider principle of home rule for Cuba and Puerto Rico.

The overtures of this Government made through its new envoy, General Woodford, and looking to an immediate and effective amelioration of the condition of the island, although not accepted to the extent of admitted mediation in any shape, were met by assurances that home rule in an advanced phase would be forthwith offered to Cuba, without waiting for the war to end, and that more humane methods should thenceforth prevail in the conduct of hostilities. Coincidentally with these declarations the new government of Spain continued and completed the policy, already begun by its predecessor, of testifying friendly regard for this nation by releasing American citizens held under one charge or another connected with the insurrection, so that by the end of November not a single person entitled in any way to our national protection remained in a Spanish prison.

While these negotiations were in progress the increasing destitution of the unfortunate reconcentrados and the alarming mortality among them claimed earnest attention. The success which had attended the limited measure of relief extended to the suffering American citizens among them by the judicious expenditure through the consular agencies of the money appropriated expressly for their succor by the joint resolution approved May 24, 1897,† prompted the humane extension of a similar scheme of aid to the great body of sufferers. A suggestion to this end was acquiesced in by the Spanish authorities.

On the 24th of December last I caused to be issued an appeal to the American people inviting contributions in money or in kind for the succor of the starving sufferers in Cuba, following this on the 8th of January by a similar public announcement of the formation of a central Cuban relief committee, with headquarters in New York City, composed of three

* See pp. 127-136.   † See p. 136.

members representing the American National Red Cross and the religious and business elements of the community.

The efforts of that committee have been untiring and have accomplished much. Arrangements for free transportation to Cuba have greatly aided the charitable work. The president of the American Red Cross and representatives of other contributory organizations have generously visited Cuba and cooperated with the consul-general and the local authorities to make effective distribution of the relief collected through the efforts of the central committee. Nearly $200,000 in money and supplies has already reached the sufferers, and more is forthcoming. The supplies are admitted duty free, and transportation to the interior has been arranged, so that the relief, at first necessarily confined to Havana and the larger cities, is now extended through most, if not all, of the towns where suffering exists.

Thousands of lives have already been saved. The necessity for a change in the condition of the reconcentrados is recognized by the Spanish Government. Within a few days past the orders of General Weyler have been revoked. The reconcentrados, it is said, are to be permitted to return to their homes and aided to resume the self-supporting pursuits of peace. Public works have been ordered to give them employment and a sum of $600,000 has been appropriated for their relief.

The war in Cuba is of such a nature that, short of subjugation or extermination, a final military victory for either side seems impracticable. The alternative lies in the physical exhaustion of the one or the other party, or perhaps of both—a condition which in effect ended the ten years' war by the truce of Zanjon. The prospect of such a protraction and conclusion of the present strife is a contingency hardly to be contemplated with equanimity by the civilized world, and least of all by the United States, affected and injured as we are, deeply and intimately, by its very existence.

Realizing this, it appeared to be my duty, in a spirit of true friendliness, no less to Spain than to the Cubans, who have so much to lose by the prolongation of the struggle, to seek to bring about an immediate termination of the war. To this end I submitted on the 27th ultimo, as a result of much representation and correspondence, through the United States minister at Madrid, propositions to the Spanish Government looking to an armistice until October 1 for the negotiation of peace with the good offices of the President.

In addition I asked the immediate revocation of the order of reconcentration, so as to permit the people to return to their farms and the needy to be relieved with provisions and supplies from the United States, cooperating with the Spanish authorities, so as to afford full relief.

The reply of the Spanish cabinet was received on the night of the 31st ultimo. It offered, as the means to bring about peace in Cuba, to confide the preparation thereof to the insular parliament, inasmuch as the concurrence of that body would be necessary to reach a final result, it being, however, understood that the powers reserved by the constitution to the central Government are not lessened or diminished. As the Cuban parliament does not meet until the 4th of May next, the Spanish Government would not object for its part to accept at once a suspension of hostilities if asked for by the insurgents from the general in chief, to whom it would pertain in such case to determine the duration and conditions of the armistice.

The propositions submitted by General Woodford and the reply of the Spanish Government were both in the form of brief memoranda, the texts of which are before me and are substantially in the language above given. The function of the Cuban parliament in the matter of "preparing" peace and the manner of its doing so are not expressed in the Spanish memorandum, but from General Woodford's explanatory reports of preliminary discussions preceding the final conference it is understood that the Spanish Government stands ready to give the insular congress full powers to settle the terms of peace with the insurgents, whether by direct negotiation or indirectly by means of legislation does not appear.

With this last overture in the direction of immediate peace, and its disappointing reception by Spain, the Executive is brought to the end of his effort.

In my annual message of December last I said:

Of the untried measures there remain only: Recognition of the insurgents as belligerents; recognition of the independence of Cuba; neutral intervention to end the war by imposing a rational compromise between the contestants, and intervention in favor of one or the other party. I speak not of forcible annexation, for that can not be thought of. That, by our code of morality, would be criminal aggression.

Thereupon I reviewed these alternatives in the light of President Grant's measured words, uttered in 1875, when, after seven years of sanguinary, destructive, and cruel hostilities in Cuba, he reached the conclusion that the recognition of the independence of Cuba was impracticable and indefensible and that the recognition of belligerence was not warranted by the facts according to the tests of public law. I commented especially upon the latter aspect of the question, pointing out the inconveniences and positive dangers of a recognition of belligerence, which, while adding to the already onerous burdens of neutrality within our own jurisdiction, could not in any way extend our influence or effective offices in the territory of hostilities.

Nothing has since occurred to change my view in this regard, and I recognize as fully now as then that the issuance of a proclamation of neutrality, by which process the so-called recognition of belligerents is published, could of itself and unattended by other action accomplish nothing toward the one end for which we labor—the instant pacification of Cuba and the cessation of the misery that afflicts the island.

Turning to the question of recognizing at this time the independence of the present insurgent government in Cuba, we find safe precedents in our history from an early day. They are well summed up in President Jackson's message to Congress, December 21, 1836, on the subject of the recognition of the independence of Texas. He said:

In all the contests that have arisen out of the revolutions of France, out of the disputes relating to the crowns of Portugal and Spain, out of the revolutionary movements of those Kingdoms, out of the separation of the American possessions of both from the European Governments, and out of the numerous and constantly occurring struggles for dominion in Spanish America, so wisely consistent with our just principles has been the action of our Government that we have under the most critical circumstances avoided all censure and encountered no other evil than that produced by a transient estrangement of good will in those against whom we have been by force of evidence compelled to decide.

It has thus been made known to the world that the uniform policy and practice of the United States is to avoid all interference in disputes which merely relate to the internal government of other nations, and eventually to recognize the authority of the prevailing party, without reference to our particular interests and views or to the merits of the original controversy.

* * * * * * *

* * * But on this as on every trying occasion safety is to be found in a rigid adherence to principle.

In the contest between Spain and her revolted colonies we stood aloof and waited, not only until the ability of the new States to protect themselves was fully established, but until the danger of their being again subjugated had entirely passed away. Then, and not till then, were they recognized. Such was our course in regard to Mexico herself. * * * It is true that, with regard to Texas, the civil authority of Mexico has been expelled, its invading army defeated, the chief of the Republic himself captured, and all present power to control the newly organized Government of Texas annihilated within its confines. But, on the other hand, there is, in appearance at least, an immense disparity of physical force on the side of Mexico. The Mexican Republic under another Executive is rallying its forces under a new leader and menacing a fresh invasion to recover its lost dominion.

Upon the issue of this threatened invasion the independence of Texas may be considered as suspended, and were there nothing peculiar in the relative situation of the United States and Texas our acknowledgment of its independence at such a crisis could scarcely be regarded as consistent with that prudent reserve with which we have heretofore held ourselves bound to treat all similar questions.

Thereupon Andrew Jackson proceeded to consider the risk that there might be imputed to the United States motives of selfish interest in view of the former claim on our part to the territory of Texas and of the avowed purpose of the Texans in seeking recognition of independence as an incident to the incorporation of Texas in the Union, concluding thus:

Prudence, therefore, seems to dictate that we should still stand aloof and maintain our present attitude, if not until Mexico itself or one of the great foreign powers shall recognize the independence of the new Government, at least until the lapse of time or the course of events shall have proved beyond cavil or dispute the ability of the people of that country to maintain their separate sovereignty and to uphold the Government constituted by them. Neither of the contending parties can justly complain of this course. By pursuing it we are but carrying out the long-established policy of our Government—a policy which has secured to us respect and influence abroad and inspired confidence at home.

These are the words of the resolute and patriotic Jackson. They are evidence that the United States, in addition to the test imposed by public law as the condition of the recognition of independence by a neutral state (to wit, that the revolted state shall "constitute in fact a body politic, having a government in substance as well as in name, possessed of the elements of stability," and forming *de facto*, "if left to itself, a state among the nations, reasonably capable of discharging the duties of a state"), has imposed for its own governance in dealing with cases like these the further condition that recognition of independent statehood is not due to a revolted dependency until the danger of its being again subjugated by the parent state has entirely passed away.

This extreme test was, in fact, applied in the case of Texas. The Congress to whom President Jackson referred the question as one "probably leading to war," and therefore a proper subject for "a previous understanding with that body by whom war can alone be declared and by whom all the provisions for sustaining its perils must be furnished," left the matter of the recognition of Texas to the discretion of the Executive, providing merely for the sending of a diplomatic agent when the President should be satisfied that the Republic of Texas had become "an independent state." It was so recognized by President Van Buren, who commissioned a chargé d'affaires March 7, 1837, after Mexico had abandoned an attempt to reconquer the Texan territory, and when there was at the time no *bona fide* contest going on between the insurgent province and its former sovereign.

I said in my message of December last:

It is to be seriously considered whether the Cuban insurrection possesses beyond dispute the attributes of statehood, which alone can demand the recognition of belligerency in its favor.

The same requirement must certainly be no less seriously considered when the graver issue of recognizing independence is in question, for no less positive test can be applied to the greater act than to the lesser, while, on the other hand, the influences and consequences of the struggle upon the internal policy of the recognizing state, which form important factors when the recognition of belligerency is concerned, are secondary, if not rightly eliminable, factors when the real question is whether the community claiming recognition is or is not independent beyond peradventure.

Nor from the standpoint of expediency do I think it would be wise or prudent for this Government to recognize at the present time the independence of the so-called Cuban Republic. Such recognition is not necessary in order to enable the United States to intervene and pacify the island. To commit this country now to the recognition of any particular government in Cuba might subject us to embarrassing conditions of international obligation toward the organization so recognized. In case of intervention our conduct would be subject to the approval or disapproval of such government. We would be required to submit to its direction and to assume to it the mere relation of a friendly ally.

When it shall appear hereafter that there is within the island a government capable of performing the duties and discharging the functions of a separate nation, and having as a matter of fact the proper forms and attributes of nationality, such government can be promptly and readily recognized and the relations and interests of the United States with such nation adjusted.

There remain the alternative forms of intervention to end the war, either as an impartial neutral, by imposing a rational compromise between the contestants, or as the active ally of the one party or the other.

As to the first, it is not to be forgotten that during the last few months the relation of the United States has virtually been one of friendly intervention in many ways, each not of itself conclusive, but all tending to the exertion of a potential influence toward an ultimate pacific result, just and honorable to all interests concerned. The spirit of all our acts hitherto has been an earnest, unselfish desire for peace and prosperity in Cuba, untarnished by differences between us and Spain and unstained by the blood of American citizens.

The forcible intervention of the United States as a neutral to stop the war, according to the large dictates of humanity and following many historical precedents where neighboring states have interfered to check the hopeless sacrifices of life by internecine conflicts beyond their borders, is justifiable on rational grounds. It involves, however, hostile constraint upon both the parties to the contest, as well to enforce a truce as to guide the eventual settlement.

The grounds for such intervention may be briefly summarized as follows:

First. In the cause of humanity and to put an end to the barbarities, bloodshed, starvation, and horrible miseries now existing there, and which the parties to the conflict are either unable or unwilling to stop or mitigate. It is no answer to say this is all in another country, belonging to another nation, and is therefore none of our business. It is specially our duty, for it is right at our door.

Second. We owe it to our citizens in Cuba to afford them that protection and indemnity for life and property which no government there can or will afford, and to that end to terminate the conditions that deprive them of legal protection.

Third. The right to intervene may be justified by the very serious injury to the commerce, trade, and business of our people and by the wanton destruction of property and devastation of the island.

Fourth, and which is of the utmost importance. The present condition of affairs in Cuba is a constant menace to our peace and entails upon this Government an enormous expense. With such a conflict waged for years in an island so near us and with which our people have such trade and business relations; when the lives and liberty of our citizens are in constant danger and their property destroyed and themselves ruined; where our trading vessels are liable to seizure and are seized at our very door by war ships of a foreign nation; the expeditions of filibustering that we are powerless to prevent altogether, and the irritating questions and entanglements thus arising—all these and others that I need not mention, with the resulting strained relations, are a constant menace to our peace and compel us to keep on a semi war footing with a nation with which we are at peace.

These elements of danger and disorder already pointed out have been strikingly illustrated by a tragic event which has deeply and justly moved the American people. I have already transmitted to Congress the report of the naval court of inquiry on the destruction of the battle ship *Maine* in the harbor of Havana during the night of the 15th of February.* The destruction of that noble vessel has filled the national heart with inexpressible horror. Two hundred and fifty-eight brave sailors and marines and two officers of our Navy, reposing in the fancied security of a friendly harbor, have been hurled to death, grief and want brought to their homes and sorrow to the nation.

The naval court of inquiry, which, it is needless to say, commands the unqualified confidence of the Government, was unanimous in its conclusion that the destruction of the *Maine* was caused by an exterior explosion—that of a submarine mine. It did not assume to place the responsibility. That remains to be fixed.

In any event, the destruction of the *Maine*, by whatever exterior cause, is a patent and impressive proof of a state of things in Cuba that is intolerable. That condition is thus shown to be such that the Spanish Government can not assure safety and security to a vessel of the American Navy in the harbor of Havana on a mission of peace, and rightfully there.

Further referring in this connection to recent diplomatic correspondence, a dispatch from our minister to Spain of the 26th ultimo contained the statement that the Spanish minister for foreign affairs assured him positively that Spain will do all that the highest honor and justice require in the matter of the *Maine*. The reply above referred to, of the 31st ultimo, also contained an expression of the readiness of Spain to submit to an arbitration all the differences which can arise in this matter, which is subsequently explained by the note of the Spanish minister at Washington of the 10th instant, as follows:

As to the question of fact which springs from the diversity of views between the reports of the American and Spanish boards, Spain proposes that the facts be ascertained by an impartial investigation by experts, whose decision Spain accepts in advance.

To this I have made no reply.

* See pp. 136–139.

President Grant, in 1875, after discussing the phases of the contest as it then appeared and its hopeless and apparent indefinite prolongation, said:

In such event I am of opinion that other nations will be compelled to assume the responsibility which devolves upon them, and to seriously consider the only remaining measures possible—mediation and intervention. Owing, perhaps, to the large expanse of water separating the island from the peninsula, * * * the contending parties appear to have within themselves no depository of common confidence to suggest wisdom when passion and excitement have their sway and to assume the part of peacemaker. In this view in the earlier days of the contest the good offices of the United States as a mediator were tendered in good faith, without any selfish purpose, in the interest of humanity and in sincere friendship for both parties, but were at the time declined by Spain, with the declaration, nevertheless, that at a future time they would be indispensable. No intimation has been received that in the opinion of Spain that time has been reached. And yet the strife continues, with all its dread horrors and all its injuries to the interests of the United States and of other nations. Each party seems quite capable of working great injury and damage to the other, as well as to all the relations and interests dependent on the existence of peace in the island; but they seem incapable of reaching any adjustment, and both have thus far failed of achieving any success whereby one party shall possess and control the island to the exclusion of the other. Under these circumstances the agency of others, either by mediation or by intervention, seems to be the only alternative which must, sooner or later, be invoked for the termination of the strife.

In the last annual message of my immediate predecessor, during the pending struggle, it was said:

When the inability of Spain to deal successfully with the insurrection has become manifest and it is demonstrated that her sovereignty is extinct in Cuba for all purposes of its rightful existence, and when a hopeless struggle for its reestablishment has degenerated into a strife which means nothing more than the useless sacrifice of human life and the utter destruction of the very subject-matter of the conflict, a situation will be presented in which our obligations to the sovereignty of Spain will be superseded by higher obligations, which we can hardly hesitate to recognize and discharge.

In my annual message to Congress December last, speaking to this question, I said:

The near future will demonstrate whether the indispensable condition of a righteous peace, just alike to the Cubans and to Spain, as well as equitable to all our interests so intimately involved in the welfare of Cuba, is likely to be attained. If not, the exigency of further and other action by the United States will remain to be taken. When that time comes, that action will be determined in the line of indisputable right and duty. It will be faced, without misgiving or hesitancy, in the light of the obligation this Government owes to itself, to the people who have confided to it the protection of their interests and honor, and to humanity.

Sure of the right, keeping free from all offense ourselves, actuated only by upright and patriotic considerations, moved neither by passion nor selfishness, the Government will continue its watchful care over the rights and property of American citizens and will abate none of its efforts to bring about by peaceful agencies a peace which shall be honorable and enduring. If it shall hereafter appear to be a duty imposed by our obligations to ourselves, to civilization, and humanity to intervene with force, it shall be without fault on our part and only because the necessity for such action will be so clear as to command the support and approval of the civilized world.

The long trial has proved that the object for which Spain has waged the war can not be attained. The fire of insurrection may flame or may smolder with varying seasons, but it has not been and it is plain that it can not be extinguished by present methods. The only hope of relief and repose from a condition which can no longer be endured is the enforced pacification of Cuba. In the name of humanity, in the name of civilization, in behalf of endangered American interests which give us the right and the duty to speak and to act, the war in Cuba must stop.

In view of these facts and of these considerations I ask the Congress to authorize and empower the President to take measures to secure a full and final termination of hostilities between the Government of Spain and the people of Cuba, and to secure in the island the establishment of a stable government, capable of maintaining order and observing its international obligations, insuring peace and tranquillity and the security of its citizens as well as our own, and to use the military and naval forces of the United States as may be necessary for these purposes.

And in the interest of humanity and to aid in preserving the lives of the starving people of the island I recommend that the distribution of food and supplies be continued and that an appropriation be made out of the public Treasury to supplement the charity of our citizens.

The issue is now with the Congress. It is a solemn responsibility. I have exhausted every effort to relieve the intolerable condition of affairs which is at our doors. Prepared to execute every obligation imposed upon me by the Constitution and the law, I await your action.

Yesterday, and since the preparation of the foregoing message, official information was received by me that the latest decree of the Queen Regent of Spain directs General Blanco, in order to prepare and facilitate peace, to proclaim a suspension of hostilities, the duration and details of which have not yet been communicated to me.

This fact, with every other pertinent consideration, will, I am sure, have your just and careful attention in the solemn deliberations upon which you are about to enter. If this measure attains a successful result, then our aspirations as a Christian, peace-loving people will be realized. If it fails, it will be only another justification for our contemplated action.

WILLIAM McKINLEY.

EXECUTIVE MANSION,
Washington, April 11, 1898.

To the Senate of the United States:

I transmit herewith, in response to a resolution of the Senate of the 14th of February last, calling for information and correspondence in regard to the condition of the island of Cuba and to negotiations for commercial relations between the United States and that island, a report of the Secretary of State, with its accompanying correspondence, covering the first inquiry of the resolution, together with a report of the special commissioner plenipotentiary charged with commercial negotiations under the provisions of the tariff act approved July 24, 1897, in response to the second inquiry.

WILLIAM McKINLEY.

DEPARTMENT OF STATE,
Washington, April 11, 1898.

The PRESIDENT:

The Secretary of State has had the honor to receive, by reference from the President, a resolution adopted in the Senate of the United States on the 14th of February last, reading as follows:

"*Resolved,* That the President is requested, if in his opinion it is not incompatible with the public service, to send to the Senate copies of the reports of the consul-general and of the consuls of the United States in Cuba written or received since March 4, 1897, which relate to the state of war in that island and the condition of the people there, or that he will send such parts of said reports as will inform the Senate as to these facts.

"Second. That the President inform the Senate whether any agent of a government in Cuba has been accredited to this Government or the President of the United States with authority to negotiate a treaty of reciprocity with the United States, or any other diplomatic or commercial agreement with the United States, and whether such person has been recognized and received as the representative of such government in Cuba."

This resolution contemplates answer being made to two separable inquiries: First, in relation to the present condition of affairs in Cuba, and, secondly, with regard to the action had in view of the overtures of the Government of Spain for a reciprocal commercial agreement covering particularly the trade between the United States and the island of Cuba.

The conduct of commercial negotiations under the authority and in accordance with the conditions found in sections 3, 4, and 5 of the existing tariff act, approved July 24, 1897, having been intrusted to a special commissioner plenipotentiary duly empowered by the President to that end, it has been deemed convenient to leave to the commissioner the preparation of a report in answer to the second part of the Senate resolution, the undersigned reserving to himself the response to the first part thereof, which concerns the political and consular functions of the Department of State. The separate report of the Hon. John A. Kasson, special commissioner plenipotentiary, is therefore herewith independently submitted to the President with a view to its transmission to the Senate, should such a course be, in the President's judgment, not incompatible with the public service.

The Senate resolution, while in terms calling for the submission to that honorable body of all or of a practical selection of the reports of the consul-general and consuls of the United States in Cuba written or received since March 4, 1897, which relate to the state of war in that island and the condition of the people there, appears to leave it to the discretion of the President to direct the scope of the information to be so reported and the manner of its communication. The undersigned, having taken the President's direction on both these points, has the honor to lay before him a selection of the correspondence received by the Department of State from the various consular representatives in Cuba, aiming thereby to show the present situation in the island rather than to give a historical account of all the reported incidents since the date assigned by the resolution.

Respectfully submitted.

JOHN SHERMAN.

DEPARTMENT OF STATE, WASHINGTON,
Office of Special Commissioner Plenipotentiary.

The PRESIDENT:

In response to the following resolution of the Senate, passed under date of February 14, 1898, and which was referred to the undersigned for report, viz—

"Second. That the President inform the Senate whether any agent of a government in Cuba has been accredited to this Government or the President of the United States with authority to negotiate a treaty of reciprocity with the United States, or any other diplomatic or commercial agreement with the United States, and whether such person has been recognized and received as the representative of such government in Cuba"—

I have the honor to submit the following report:

In October, 1897, the minister of Spain at this capital verbally advised the undersigned that so soon as the new government in Spain had leisure to take up the question he would probably be authorized to enter into negotiations with the undersigned for reciprocal trade arrangements with Spain, and that a representative of Cuba would probably be associated for the interests of that island.

Under date of December 9, 1897, the minister of the United States at Madrid was instructed to ascertain the disposition of the Spanish Government in respect to these negotiations.

Under date of January 24, 1898, a dispatch from Mr. Woodford (referred to this office) advised the Secretary of State that arrangements were made for the negotiation of a commercial treaty between Spain and the United States; that separate provisions would be made for Cuba, and that the Cuban insular government would appoint a delegate to represent that island in the negotiations. This was accompanied by a memorandum from the Spanish minister of colonies, stating that the same rules as for Cuba might be applied to Puerto Rico, and suggesting a basis for the negotiations. This communication was referred to this office on the 4th of February.

On the 6th of February the Spanish minister, Mr. Dupuy de Lôme, called on the undersigned and announced that he was authorized to represent Spain in the pending negotiations and that a special representative would arrive from Cuba, under appointment of the insular government, to act as far as the interests of that island were involved. He mentioned the name of Señor Angulo as the gentleman who had been suggested in Cuba for that appointment; but the delegate was not officially notified to this office.

On March 17 a note from the Spanish minister, Señor Polo y Bernabé, addressed, under date of the 16th instant, to the Secretary of State, was referred to this office. In that note his excellency advised this Government of his appointment by Her Majesty the Queen Regent of Spain to conduct these negotiations, assisted by Señor Manuel Rafael Angulo as special delegate of the insular government of Cuba, who would be aided by two technical assistants, also appointed by the Cuban government; and, further, that an officer from the treasury department would be added in the same character.

His excellency announced his readiness to commence the labors of the commission so soon as the Government of the United States should formulate the general plan for carrying on the work.

Respectfully submitted, March 17, 1898.

JOHN A. KASSON,
Special Commissioner Plenipotenitary.

EXECUTIVE MANSION, *April 12, 1898.*

To the Senate of the United States:

In response to a resolution of the Senate of the 4th instant, I inclose herewith a letter from the Secretary of the Navy, inclosing a copy of a report from the Chief of the Bureau of Navigation.

WILLIAM McKINLEY.

NAVY DEPARTMENT,
Washington, April 9, 1898.

The PRESIDENT OF THE UNITED STATES SENATE.

SIR: I have the honor to acknowledge the receipt of Senate resolution of April 4, directing that the Senate be informed "of the total number of human lives that were lost by the sinking of the United States battle ship *Maine* in Havana Harbor, Cuba, on the 15th day of February, 1898, the total number of dead bodies rescued from said ship, the total number remaining unrescued, and what effort, if any, is being made to rescue them," and in reply thereto inclose a copy of a report from the Chief of the Bureau of Navigation covering the above inquiry.

I have the honor to be, sir, very respectfully,

JOHN D. LONG, *Secretary.*

MEMORANDUM FOR THE SECRETARY.

BUREAU OF NAVIGATION,
Washington, D. C., April 8, 1898.

Number on board the U. S. S. *Maine* at the time of the disaster:
Officers	26	
Sailors	290	
Marines	39	
		355

Number saved:
Officers	24	
Sailors	60	
Marines	11	
		95

Number lost:
Officers	2	
Sailors	230	
Marines	28	
		260
		355

Bodies recovered:
Officers	1	
Sailors and marines	177	

Died from injuries:
Sailors and marines	8	
		186

Of the number recovered there were buried—
In the cemetery at Havana	166	
At Key West	19	
At Pittsburg, Pa. (officer)	1	
		186

Number of bodies not recovered:
Officers	1	
Enlisted men and marines	73	
		74

The work of recovery was continued until April 6, when the wrecking tugs were withdrawn, and nothing is now being done in that direction so far as is known; and the last bodies reported as recovered were sent to Key West on the 30th ultimo. No estimate has been made of the portions of bodies which were recovered and buried. The large percentage of bodies not recovered is due, no doubt, to the fact that the men were swinging in their hammocks immediately over that portion of the vessel which was totally destroyed.

A. S. CROWNINSHIELD,
Chief of Bureau.

EXECUTIVE MANSION,
Washington, April 25, 1898.

To the Senate and House of Representatives of the United States of America:

I transmit to the Congress, for its consideration and appropriate action, copies of correspondence recently had with the representative of Spain in the United States, with the United States minister at Madrid, and through the latter with the Government of Spain, showing the action taken under the joint resolution approved April 20, 1898, "for the recognition of the independence of the people of Cuba, demanding that the Government of Spain relinquish its authority and government in the island of Cuba and to withdraw its land and naval forces from Cuba and Cuban waters, and directing the President of the United States to use the land and naval forces of the United States to carry these resolutions into effect."*

Upon communicating to the Spanish minister in Washington the demand which it became the duty of the Executive to address to the Government of Spain in obedience to said resolution, the minister asked for his passports and withdrew. The United States minister at Madrid was in turn notified by the Spanish minister for foreign affairs that the withdrawal of the Spanish representative from the United States had terminated diplomatic relations between the two countries, and that all official communications between their respective representatives ceased therewith.

I commend to your especial attention the note addressed to the United States minister at Madrid by the Spanish minister for foreign affairs on the 21st instant, whereby the foregoing notification was conveyed. It will be perceived therefrom that the Government of Spain, having cognizance of the joint resolution of the United States Congress, and in view of the things which the President is thereby required and authorized to do, responds by treating the reasonable demands of this Government as measures of hostility, following with that instant and complete severance of relations by its action which by the usage of nations accompanies an existent state of war between sovereign powers.

The position of Spain being thus made known and the demands of the United States being denied, with a complete rupture of intercourse, by the act of Spain, I have been constrained, in exercise of the power and authority conferred upon me by the joint resolution aforesaid, to proclaim, under date of April 22, 1898,† a blockade of certain ports of the north coast of Cuba lying between Cardenas and Bahia Honda, and of the port of Cienfuegos, on the south coast of Cuba, and further in exercise of my constitutional powers and using the authority conferred upon me by the act of Congress approved April 22, 1898, to issue my proclamation dated April 23, 1898,‡ calling forth volunteers in order to carry into effect the said resolution of April 20, 1898. Copies of these proclamations are hereto appended.

In view of the measures so taken, and with a view to the adoption of such other measures as may be necessary to enable me to carry out the expressed will of the Congress of the United States in the premises, I now recommend to your honorable body the adoption of a joint resolution declaring that a state of war exists between the United States of

*See p. 155.   † See pp. 202–203.   ‡ See pp. 203–204.

America and the Kingdom of Spain, and I urge speedy action thereon, to the end that the definition of the international status of the United States as a belligerent power may be made known and the assertion of all its rights and the maintenance of all its duties in the conduct of a public war may be assured.*   WILLIAM McKINLEY.

JOINT RESOLUTION for the recognition of the independence of the people of Cuba, demanding that the Government of Spain relinquish its authority and government in the island of Cuba and to withdraw its land and naval forces from Cuba and Cuban waters, and directing the President of the United States to use the land and naval forces of the United States to carry these resolutions into effect.

Whereas the abhorrent conditions which have existed for more than three years in the island of Cuba, so near our own borders, have shocked the moral sense of the people of the United States, have been a disgrace to Christian civilization, culminating, as they have, in the destruction of a United States battle ship, with 266 of its officers and crew, while on a friendly visit in the harbor of Havana, and can not longer be endured, as has been set forth by the President of the United States in his message to Congress of April 11, 1898,† upon which the action of Congress was invited: Therefore,

Resolved by the Senate and House of Representatives of the United States of America in Congress assembled, First. That the people of the island of Cuba are and of right ought to be free and independent.

Second. That it is the duty of the United States to demand, and the Government of the United States does hereby demand, that the Government of Spain at once relinquish its authority and government in the island of Cuba and withdraw its land and naval forces from Cuba and Cuban waters.

Third. That the President of the United States be, and he hereby is, directed and empowered to use the entire land and naval forces of the United States and to call into the actual service of the United States the militia of the several States to such extent as may be necessary to carry these resolutions into effect.

Fourth. That the United States hereby disclaims any disposition or intention to exercise sovereignty, jurisdiction, or control over said island except for the pacification thereof, and asserts its determination, when that is accomplished, to leave the government and control of the island to its people.

Approved, April 20, 1898.

EXECUTIVE MANSION, *May 9, 1898.*

To the Congress of the United States:

On the 24th of April I directed the Secretary of the Navy to telegraph orders to Commodore George Dewey, of the United States Navy, commanding the Asiatic Squadron, then lying in the port of Hongkong, to proceed forthwith to the Philippine Islands, there to commence operations and engage the assembled Spanish fleet.

Promptly obeying that order, the United States squadron, consisting of the flagship *Olympia*, *Baltimore*, *Raleigh*, *Boston*, *Concord*, and *Petrel*, with the revenue cutter *McCulloch* as an auxiliary dispatch boat, entered the harbor of Manila at daybreak on the 1st of May and immediately engaged the entire Spanish fleet of eleven ships, which were under the protection of the fire of the land forts. After a stubborn fight, in which the enemy

* See p. 201.   † See pp. 139-150.

suffered great loss, these vessels were destroyed or completely disabled and the water battery at Cavite silenced. Of our brave officers and men not one was lost and only eight injured, and those slightly. All of our ships escaped any serious damage.

By the 4th of May Commodore Dewey had taken possession of the naval station at Cavite, destroying the fortifications there and at the entrance of the bay and paroling their garrisons. The waters of the bay are under his complete control. He has established hospitals within the American lines, where 250 of the Spanish sick and wounded are assisted and protected.

The magnitude of this victory can hardly be measured by the ordinary standard of naval warfare. Outweighing any material advantage is the moral effect of this initial success. At this unsurpassed achievement the great heart of our nation throbs, not with boasting or with greed of conquest, but with deep gratitude that this triumph has come in a just cause and that by the grace of God an effective step has thus been taken toward the attainment of the wished-for peace. To those whose skill, courage, and devotion have won the fight, to the gallant commander and the brave officers and men who aided him, our country owes an incalculable debt.

Feeling as our people feel, and speaking in their name, I at once sent a message to Commodore Dewey thanking him and his officers and men for their splendid achievement and overwhelming victory and informing him that I had appointed him an acting rear-admiral.

I now recommend that, following our national precedents and expressing the fervent gratitude of every patriotic heart, the thanks of Congress be given Acting Rear-Admiral George Dewey, of the United States Navy, for highly distinguished conduct in conflict with the enemy, and to the officers and men under his command for their gallantry in the destruction of the enemy's fleet and the capture of the enemy's fortifications in the bay of Manila.

WILLIAM McKINLEY.

EXECUTIVE MANSION, *June 1, 1898*.

To the Congress of the United States:

The resolution of Congress passed May 9, 1898, tendering to Commodore George Dewey, United States Navy, commander in chief of the United States naval force on the Asiatic station, the thanks of Congress and of the American people for highly distinguished conduct in conflict with the enemy, as displayed by him in the destruction of the Spanish fleet and batteries in the harbor of Manila, Philippine Islands, May 1, 1898, and through him extending the thanks of Congress and of the American people to the officers and men under his command for gallantry and skill exhibited by them on that occasion, required the President to communicate the same to Commodore Dewey, and through him to the officers and men under his command. This having been done, through the Secretary of the Navy, on the 15th of May, 1898, the following response has been received and is hereby transmitted to the Congress:

I desire to express to the Department, and to request that it will be transmitted to the President and to Congress, my most sincere thanks for the great compliment paid to me.

WILLIAM McKINLEY.

JOINT RESOLUTION tendering the thanks of Congress to Commodore George Dewey, United States Navy, and to the officers and men of the squadron under his command.

Resolved by the Senate and House of Representatives of the United States of America in Congress assembled, That, in pursuance of the recommendation of the President, made in accordance with the provisions of section 1508 of the Revised Statutes, the thanks of Congress and of the American people are hereby tendered to Commodore George Dewey, United States Navy, commander in chief of the United States naval force on the Asiatic station, for highly distinguished conduct in conflict with the enemy, as displayed by him in the destruction of the Spanish fleet and batteries in the harbor of Manila, Philippine Islands, May 1, 1898.

SEC. 2. That the thanks of Congress and the American people are hereby extended through Commodore Dewey to the officers and men under his command for the gallantry and skill exhibited by them on that occasion.

SEC. 3. *Be it further resolved*, That the President of the United States be requested to cause this resolution to be communicated to Commodore Dewey, and through him to the officers and men under his command.

Approved, May 10, 1898.

JOINT RESOLUTION authorizing the Secretary of the Navy to present a sword of honor to Commodore George Dewey, and to cause to be struck bronze medals commemorating the battle of Manila Bay, and to distribute such medals to the officers and men of the ships of the Asiatic Squadron of the United States.

Resolved by the Senate and House of Representatives of the United States of America in Congress assembled, That the Secretary of the Navy be, and he hereby is, authorized to present a sword of honor to Commodore George Dewey, and to cause to be struck bronze medals commemorating the battle of Manila Bay, and to distribute such medals to the officers and men of the ships of the Asiatic Squadron of the United States under command of Commodore George Dewey on May 1, 1898; and that to enable the Secretary to carry out this resolution the sum of $10,000, or so much thereof as may be necessary, is hereby appropriated out of any money in the Treasury not otherwise appropriated.

Approved, June 3, 1898.

EXECUTIVE MANSION, *June 27, 1898.*

To the Congress of the United States:

On the 11th of May, 1898, there occurred a conflict in the bay of Cardenas, Cuba, in which the naval torpedo boat *Winslow* was disabled, her commander wounded, and one of her officers and a part of her crew killed by the enemy's fire.

In the face of a most galling fire from the enemy's guns the revenue cutter *Hudson*, commanded by First Lieutenant Frank H. Newcomb, United States Revenue-Cutter Service, rescued the disabled *Winslow*, her wounded commander and remaining crew.   The commander of the *Hudson* kept his vessel in the very hottest fire of the action, although in constant danger of going ashore on account of the shallow water, until he finally got a line made fast to the *Winslow* and towed that vessel out of range of the enemy's guns—a deed of special gallantry.

I recommend that in recognition of the signal act of heroism of First Lieutenant Frank H. Newcomb, United States Revenue-Cutter Service, above set forth, the thanks of Congress be extended to him and to his officers and men of the *Hudson*, and that a gold medal of honor be presented to Lieutenant Newcomb, a silver medal of honor to each of his officers, and a bronze medal of honor to each member of his crew who served with him at Cardenas.

It will be remembered that Congress by appropriate action recognized the several commanders of ships of war for their services in the battle of Manila, May 1, 1898.

The commander of the revenue cutter *Hugh McCulloch*, present and in active cooperation with the fleet under Commodore Dewey on that occasion (by Executive order under the provisions of section 2757, Revised Statutes), is the only commander of a national ship to whom promotion or advancement was not and could not be given, because he already held the highest rank known to the Revenue-Cutter Service.

I now recommend that in recognition of the efficent and meritorious services of Captain Daniel B. Hodgsdon, United States Revenue-Cutter Service, who commanded the *Hugh McCulloch* at the battle of Manila (that officer being now in the sixty-third year of his age and having served continuously on active duty for thirty-seven years), he be placed upon the permanent waiting-orders or retired list of the Revenue-Cutter Service on the full-duty pay of his grade.

WILLIAM McKINLEY.

EXECUTIVE MANSION, *June 27, 1898.*

To the Congress of the United States:

On the morning of the 3d of June, 1898, Assistant Naval Constructor Richmond P. Hobson, United States Navy, with a volunteer crew of seven men, in charge of the partially dismantled collier *Merrimac*, entered the fortified harbor of Santiago, Cuba, for the purpose of sinking the collier in the narrowest portion of the channel, and thus interposing a serious obstacle to the egress of the Spanish fleet which had recently entered that harbor.   This enterprise, demanding coolness, judgment, and bravery amounting to heroism, was carried into successful execution in the face of a persistent fire from the hostile fleet as well as from the fortifications on shore.

Rear-Admiral Sampson, commander in chief of our naval force in Cuban waters, in an official report dated "Off Santiago de Cuba, June 3, 1898," and addressed to the Secretary of the Navy, referring to Mr. Hobson's gallant exploit, says:

As stated in a recent telegram, before coming here I decided to make the harbor entrance secure against the possibility of egress of the Spanish ships by obstructing the narrow part of the entrance by sinking a collier at that point. Upon calling upon Mr. Hobson for his professional opinion as to a sure method of sinking the ship, he manifested a most lively interest in the problem. After several days' consideration he presented a solution which he considered would insure the immediate sinking of the ship when she had reached the desired point in the channel. * * * The plan contemplated a crew of only seven men and Mr. Hobson, who begged that it might be intrusted to him.

As soon as I reached Santiago and had the collier to work upon, the details were commenced and diligently prosecuted, hoping to complete them in one day, as the moon and tide served best the first night after our arrival. Notwithstanding every effort, the hour of 4 o'clock in the morning arrived and the preparations were scarcely completed. After a careful inspection of the final preparations I was forced to relinquish the plan for that morning, as dawn was breaking. Mr. Hobson begged to try it at all hazards.

This morning proved more propitious, as a prompt start could be made. Nothing could have been more gallantly executed. * * * A careful inspection of the harbor from this ship showed that the *Merrimac* had been sunk in the channel.

I can not myself too earnestly express my appreciation of the conduct of Mr. Hobson and his gallant crew. I venture to say that a more brave and daring thing has not been done since Cushing blew up the *Albemarle*.

The members of the crew who were with Mr. Hobson on this memorable occasion have already been rewarded for their services by advancement, which, under the provisions of law and regulations, the Secretary of the Navy was authorized to make; and the nomination to the Senate of Naval Cadet Powell, who in a steam launch followed the *Merrimac* on her perilous trip for the purpose of rescuing her force after the sinking of that vessel, to be advanced in rank to the grade of ensign has been prepared and will be submitted.

Cushing, with whose gallant act in blowing up the ram *Albemarle* during the Civil War Admiral Sampson compares Mr. Hobson's sinking of the *Merrimac*, received the thanks of Congress, upon recommendation of the President, by name, and was in consequence, under the provisions of section 1508 of the Revised Statutes, advanced one grade, such advancement embracing 56 numbers. The section cited applies, however, to line officers only, and Mr. Hobson, being a member of the staff of the Navy, could not under its provisions be so advanced.

In considering the question of suitably rewarding Assistant Naval Constructor Hobson for his valiant conduct on the occasion referred to, I have deemed it proper to address this message to you with the recommendation that he receive the thanks of Congress and, further, that he be transferred to the line of the Navy and promoted to such position therein as the President, by and with the advice and consent of the Senate, may determine. Mr. Hobson's transfer from the construction corps to the line is fully warranted, he having received the necessary technical training as a graduate of the Naval Academy, where he stood No. 1 in his class; and such action is recommended partly in deference to what is understood to be his own desire, although, he being now a prisoner in the hands of the enemy, no direct communication on the subject has been received from him, and partly for the reason that the abilities displayed by him at Santiago are of such a character as to indicate especial fitness for the duties of the line.   WILLIAM McKINLEY.

SECOND ANNUAL MESSAGE.

EXECUTIVE MANSION, *December 5, 1898.*

To the Senate and House of Representatives:

Notwithstanding the added burdens rendered necessary by the war, our people rejoice in a very satisfactory and steadily increasing degree of prosperity, evidenced by the largest volume of business ever recorded. Manufacture has been productive, agricultural pursuits have yielded abundant returns, labor in all fields of industry is better rewarded, revenue legislation passed by the present Congress has increased the Treasury's receipts to the amount estimated by its authors, the finances of the Government have been successfully administered and its credit advanced to the first rank, while its currency has been maintained at the world's highest standard.   Military service under a common flag and for a righteous cause has strengthened the national spirit and served to cement more closely than ever the fraternal bonds between every section of the country.

A review of the relation of the United States to other powers, always appropriate, is this year of primary importance in view of the momentous issues which have arisen, demanding in one instance the ultimate determination by arms and involving far-reaching consequences which will require the earnest attention of the Congress.

In my last annual message* very full consideration was given to the question of the duty of the Government of the United States toward Spain and the Cuban insurrection as being by far the most important problem with which we were then called upon to deal.   The considerations then advanced and the exposition of the views therein expressed disclosed my sense of the extreme gravity of the situation.   Setting aside as logically unfounded or practically inadmissible the recognition of the Cuban insurgents as belligerents, the recognition of the independence of Cuba, neutral intervention to end the war by imposing a rational compromise between the contestants, intervention in favor of one or the other

*See pp. 127-136.

party, and forcible annexation of the island, I concluded it was honestly due to our friendly relations with Spain that she should be given a reasonable chance to realize her expectations of reform to which she had become irrevocably committed. Within a few weeks previously she had announced comprehensive plans which it was confidently asserted would be efficacious to remedy the evils so deeply affecting our own country, so injurious to the true interests of the mother country as well as to those of Cuba, and so repugnant to the universal sentiment of humanity.

The ensuing month brought little sign of real progress toward the pacification of Cuba. The autonomous administrations set up in the capital and some of the principal cities appeared not to gain the favor of the inhabitants nor to be able to extend their influence to the large extent of territory held by the insurgents, while the military arm, obviously unable to cope with the still active rebellion, continued many of the most objectionable and offensive policies of the government that had preceded it. No tangible relief was afforded the vast numbers of unhappy reconcentrados, despite the reiterated professions made in that regard and the amount appropriated by Spain to that end. The proffered expedient of zones of cultivation proved illusory. Indeed no less practical nor more delusive promises of succor could well have been tendered to the exhausted and destitute people, stripped of all that made life and home dear and herded in a strange region among unsympathetic strangers hardly less necessitous than themselves.

By the end of December the mortality among them had frightfully increased. Conservative estimates from Spanish sources placed the deaths among these distressed people at over 40 per cent from the time General Weyler's decree of reconcentration was enforced. With the acquiescence of the Spanish authorities, a scheme was adopted for relief by charitable contributions raised in this country and distributed, under the direction of the consul-general and the several consuls, by noble and earnest individual effort through the organized agencies of the American Red Cross. Thousands of lives were thus saved, but many thousands more were inaccessible to such forms of aid.

The war continued on the old footing, without comprehensive plan, developing only the same spasmodic encounters, barren of strategic result, that had marked the course of the earlier ten years' rebellion as well as the present insurrection from its start. No alternative save physical exhaustion of either combatant, and therewithal the practical ruin of the island, lay in sight, but how far distant no one could venture to conjecture.

At this juncture, on the 15th of February last, occurred the destruction of the battle ship *Maine* while rightfully lying in the harbor of Havana on a mission of international courtesy and good will—a catastrophe the suspicious nature and horror of which stirred the nation's heart profoundly. It is a striking evidence of the poise and sturdy good sense distinguishing our national character that this shocking blow, falling upon a generous people already deeply touched by preceding events in Cuba, did not move them to an instant desperate resolve to tolerate no longer the existence of a condition of danger and disorder at our doors that made possible such a deed, by whomsoever wrought. Yet the instinct of justice prevailed, and the nation anxiously awaited the result of the searching investigation at once set on foot. The finding of the naval board of inquiry established that the origin of the explosion was external, by a submarine mine, and only halted through lack of positive testimony to fix the responsibility of its authorship.

All these things carried conviction to the most thoughtful, even before the finding of the naval court, that a crisis in our relations with Spain and toward Cuba was at hand. So strong was this belief that it needed but a brief Executive suggestion to the Congress to receive immediate answer to the duty of making instant provision for the possible and perhaps speedily probable emergency of war, and the remarkable, almost unique, spectacle was presented of a unanimous vote of both Houses, on the 9th of March, appropriating $50,000,000 "for the national defense and for each and every purpose connected therewith, to be expended at the discretion of the President." That this act of prevision came none too soon was disclosed when the application of the fund was undertaken. Our coasts were practically undefended. Our Navy needed large provision for increased ammunition and supplies, and even numbers to cope with any sudden attack from the navy of Spain, which comprised modern vessels of the highest type of continental perfection. Our Army also required enlargement of men and munitions. The details of the hurried preparation for the dreaded contingency are told in the reports of the Secretaries of War and of the Navy, and need not be repeated here. It is sufficient to say that the outbreak of war when it did come found our nation not unprepared to meet the conflict.

Nor was the apprehension of coming strife confined to our own country. It was felt by the continental powers, which on April 6, through their ambassadors and envoys, addressed to the Executive an expression of hope that humanity and moderation might mark the course of this Government and people, and that further negotiations would lead to an agreement which, while securing the maintenance of peace, would afford all necessary guaranties for the reestablishment of order in Cuba. In responding to that representation I said I shared the hope the envoys had expressed that peace might be preserved in a manner to terminate the chronic condition of disturbance in Cuba, so injurious and menacing to our interests and tranquillity, as well as shocking to our sentiments of humanity; and while appreciating the humanitarian and disinterested character of the communication they had made on behalf of the powers, I stated the confidence of this Government, for its part, that equal appreciation would be shown for its own earnest and unselfish endeavors to fulfill a duty to humanity by ending a situation the indefinite prolongation of which had become insufferable.

Still animated by the hope of a peaceful solution and obeying the dictates of duty, no effort was relaxed to bring about a speedy ending of the Cuban struggle. Negotiations to this object continued actively with the Government of Spain, looking to the immediate conclusion of a six months' armistice in Cuba, with a view to effect the recognition of her people's right to independence. Besides this, the instant revocation of the order of reconcentration was asked, so that the sufferers, returning to their homes and aided by united American and Spanish effort, might be put in a way to support themselves and, by orderly resumption of the well-nigh destroyed productive energies of the island, contribute to the restoration of its tranquillity and well-being. Negotiations continued for some little time at Madrid, resulting in offers by the Spanish Government which could not but be regarded as inadequate. It was proposed to confide the preparation of peace to the insular parliament, yet to be convened under the autonomous decrees of November, 1897, but without impairment in any wise of the constitutional powers of the Madrid Government, which to that end would grant an armistice, if solicited by the insurgents, for such time as the general in chief might see fit to fix. How and with what scope of discretionary powers the insular parliament was expected to set about the "preparation" of peace did not appear. If it were to be by negotiation with the insurgents, the issue seemed to rest on the one side with a body chosen by a fraction of the electors in the districts under Spanish control, and on the other with the insurgent population holding the interior country, unrepresented in the so-called parliament and defiant at the suggestion of suing for peace.

Grieved and disappointed at this barren outcome of my sincere endeavors to reach a practicable solution, I felt it my duty to remit the whole question to the Congress. In the message of April 11, 1898,* I announced that with this last overture in the direction of immediate peace in Cuba and its disappointing reception by Spain the effort of the Executive was brought to an end. I again reviewed the alternative courses of action which had been proposed, concluding that the only one consonant with international policy and compatible with our firm-set historical traditions was intervention as a neutral to stop the war and check the hopeless sacrifice of life, even though that resort involved "hostile constraint upon both the parties to the contest, as well to enforce a truce as to guide the eventual settlement." The grounds justifying that step were the interests of humanity, the duty to protect the life and property of our citizens in Cuba, the right to check injury to our commerce and people through the devastation of the island, and, most important, the need of removing at once and forever the constant menace and the

*See pp. 139-150.

burdens entailed upon our Government by the uncertainties and perils of the situation caused by the unendurable disturbance in Cuba.   I said:

The long trial has proved that the object for which Spain has waged the war can not be attained.   The fire of insurrection may flame or may smolder with varying seasons, but it has not been and it is plain that it can not be extinguished by present methods.   The only hope of relief and repose from a condition which can no longer be endured is the enforced pacification of Cuba.   In the name of humanity, in the name of civilization, in behalf of endangered American interests which give us the right and the duty to speak and to act, the war in Cuba must stop.

In view of all this the Congress was asked to authorize and empower the President to take measures to secure a full and final termination of hostilities between Spain and the people of Cuba and to secure in the island the establishment of a stable government, capable of maintaining order and observing its international obligations, insuring peace and tranquillity and the security of its citizens as well as our own, and for the accomplishment of those ends to use the military and naval forces of the United States as might be necessary, with added authority to continue generous relief to the starving people of Cuba.

The response of the Congress, after nine days of earnest deliberation, during which the almost unanimous sentiment of your body was developed on every point save as to the expediency of coupling the proposed action with a formal recognition of the Republic of Cuba as the true and lawful government of that island—a proposition which failed of adoption—the Congress, after conference, on the 19th of April, by a vote of 42 to 35 in the Senate and 311 to 6 in the House of Representatives, passed the memorable joint resolution declaring—

First. That the people of the island of Cuba are, and of right ought to be, free and independent.

Second. That it is the duty of the United States to demand, and the Government of the United States does hereby demand, that the Government of Spain at once relinquish its authority and government in the island of Cuba and withdraw its land and naval forces from Cuba and Cuban waters.

Third. That the President of the United States be, and he hereby is, directed and empowered to use the entire land and naval forces of the United States and to call into the actual service of the United States the militia of the several States to such extent as may be necessary to carry these resolutions into effect.

Fourth. That the United States hereby disclaims any disposition or intention to exercise sovereignty, jurisdiction, or control over said island except for the pacification thereof, and asserts its determination when that is accomplished to leave the government and control of the island to its people.

This resolution was approved by the Executive on the next day, April 20.   A copy was at once communicated to the Spanish minister at this capital, who forthwith announced that his continuance in Washington had thereby become impossible, and asked for his passports, which were given him.   He thereupon withdrew from Washington, leaving the protection of Spanish interests in the United States to the French ambassador and the Austro-Hungarian minister.   Simultaneously with its communication to the Spanish minister here, General Woodford, the American minister at Madrid, was telegraphed confirmation of the text of the joint resolution and directed to communicate it to the Government of Spain with the formal demand that it at once relinquish its authority and government in the island of Cuba and withdraw its forces therefrom, coupling this demand with announcement of the intentions of this Government as to the future of the island, in conformity with the fourth clause of the resolution, and giving Spain until noon of April 23 to reply.

That demand, although, as above shown, officially made known to the Spanish envoy here, was not delivered at Madrid. After the instruction reached General Woodford on the morning of April 21, but before he could present it, the Spanish minister of state notified him that upon the President's approval of the joint resolution the Madrid Government, regarding the act as "equivalent to an evident declaration of war," had ordered its minister in Washington to withdraw, thereby breaking off diplomatic relations between the two countries and ceasing all official communication between their respective representatives. General Woodford thereupon demanded his passports and quitted Madrid the same day.

Spain having thus denied the demand of the United States and initiated that complete form of rupture of relations which attends a state of war, the executive powers authorized by the resolution were at once used by me to meet the enlarged contingency of actual war between sovereign states. On April 22 I proclaimed a blockade of the north coast of Cuba, including ports on said coast between Cardenas and Bahia Honda, and the port of Cienfuegos, on the south coast of Cuba,* and on the 23d I called for volunteers to execute the purpose of the resolution.† By my message of April 25 the Congress was informed of the situation, and I recommended formal declaration of the existence of a state of war between the United States and Spain.‡ The Congress accordingly voted on the same day the act approved April 25, 1898, declaring the existence of such war from and including the 21st day of April,§ and reenacted the provision of the resolution of April 20 directing the President to use all the armed forces of the nation to carry that act into effect.‖ Due notification of the existence of war as aforesaid was given April 25 by telegraph to all the governments with which the United States maintain relations, in order that their neutrality might be assured during the war. The various governments responded with proclamations of neutrality, each after its own methods. It is not among the least gratifying incidents of the struggle that the obligations of neutrality were impartially discharged by all, often under delicate and difficult circumstances.

In further fulfillment of international duty I issued, April 26, 1898, a proclamation announcing the treatment proposed to be accorded to vessels and their cargoes as to blockade, contraband, the exercise of the right of search, and the immunity of neutral flags and neutral goods

*See pp. 202–203.   †See pp. 203–204.   ‡See pp. 153–155.   §See p. 201.   ‖See p. 155.

under enemy's flag.* A similar proclamation was made by the Spanish Government. In the conduct of hostilities the rules of the Declaration of Paris, including abstention from resort to privateering, have accordingly been observed by both belligerents, although neither was a party to that declaration.

Our country thus, after an interval of half a century of peace with all nations, found itself engaged in deadly conflict with a foreign enemy. Every nerve was strained to meet the emergency. The response to the initial call for 125,000 volunteers† was instant and complete, as was also the result of the second call, of May 25, for 75,000 additional volunteers.‡ The ranks of the Regular Army were increased to the limits provided by the act of April 26, 1898.

The enlisted force of the Navy on the 15th day of August, when it reached its maximum, numbered 24,123 men and apprentices. One hundred and three vessels were added to the Navy by purchase, 1 was presented to the Government, 1 leased, and the 4 vessels of the International Navigation Company—the *St. Paul*, *St. Louis*, *New York*, and *Paris*—were chartered. In addition to these the revenue cutters and lighthouse tenders were turned over to the Navy Department and became temporarily a part of the auxiliary Navy.

The maximum effective fighting force of the Navy during the war, separated into classes, was as follows:

Four battle ships of the first class, 1 battle ship of the second class, 2 armored cruisers, 6 coast-defense monitors, 1 armored ram, 12 protected cruisers, 3 unprotected cruisers, 18 gunboats, 1 dynamite cruiser, 11 torpedo boats; vessels of the old Navy, including monitors, 14. Auxiliary Navy: 11 auxiliary cruisers, 28 converted yachts, 27 converted tugs, 19 converted colliers, 15 revenue cutters, 4 light-house tenders, and 19 miscellaneous vessels.

Much alarm was felt along our entire Atlantic seaboard lest some attack might be made by the enemy. Every precaution was taken to prevent possible injury to our great cities lying along the coast. Temporary garrisons were provided, drawn from the State militia; infantry and light batteries were drawn from the volunteer force. About 12,000 troops were thus employed. The coast signal service was established for observing the approach of an enemy's ships to the coast of the United States, and the Life-Saving and Light-House services cooperated, which enabled the Navy Department to have all portions of the Atlantic coast, from Maine to Texas, under observation.

The auxiliary Navy was created under the authority of Congress and was officered and manned by the Naval Militia of the several States. This organization patrolled the coast and performed the duty of a second line of defense.

Under the direction of the Chief of Engineers submarine mines were

* See pp. 204–205.   † See pp. 203–204.   ‡ See pp. 205–206.

placed at the most exposed points. Before the outbreak of the war permanent mining casemates and cable galleries had been constructed at nearly all important harbors. Most of the torpedo material was not to be found in the market, and had to be specially manufactured. Under date of April 19 district officers were directed to take all preliminary measures short of the actual attaching of the loaded mines to the cables, and on April 22 telegraphic orders were issued to place the loaded mines in position.

The aggregate number of mines placed was 1,535, at the principal harbors from Maine to California. Preparations were also made for the planting of mines at certain other harbors, but owing to the early destruction of the Spanish fleet these mines were not placed.

The Signal Corps was promptly organized, and performed service of the most difficult and important character. Its operations during the war covered the electrical connection of all coast fortifications, the establishment of telephonic and telegraphic facilities for the camps at Manila, Santiago, and in Puerto Rico. There were constructed 300 miles of line at ten great camps, thus facilitating military movements from those points in a manner heretofore unknown in military administration. Field telegraph lines were established and maintained under the enemy's fire at Manila, and later the Manila-Hongkong cable was reopened.

In Puerto Rico cable communications were opened over a discontinued route, and on land the headquarters of the commanding officer was kept in telegraphic or telephonic communication with the division commanders on four different lines of operations.

There was placed in Cuban waters a completely outfitted cable ship, with war cables and cable gear, suitable both for the destruction of communications belonging to the enemy and the establishment of our own. Two ocean cables were destroyed under the enemy's batteries at Santiago. The day previous to the landing of General Shafter's corps, at Caimanera, within 20 miles of the landing place, cable communications were established and a cable station opened giving direct communication with the Government at Washington. This service was invaluable to the Executive in directing the operations of the Army and Navy. With a total force of over 1,300, the loss was by disease in camp and field, officers and men included, only 5.

The national-defense fund of $50,000,000 was expended in large part by the Army and Navy, and the objects for which it was used are fully shown in the reports of the several Secretaries. It was a most timely appropriation, enabling the Government to strengthen its defenses and make preparations greatly needed in case of war.

This fund being inadequate to the requirements of equipment and for the conduct of the war, the patriotism of the Congress provided the means in the war-revenue act of June 13 by authorizing a 3 per cent popular loan not to exceed $400,000,000 and by levying additional imposts and taxes. Of the authorized loan $200,000,000 were offered and promptly taken, the subscriptions so far exceeding the call as to cover it many times over, while, preference being given to the smaller bids, no single allotment exceeded $5,000. This was a most encouraging and significant result, showing the vast resources of the nation and the determination of the people to uphold their country's honor.

It is not within the province of this message to narrate the history of the extraordinary war that followed the Spanish declaration of April 21, but a brief recital of its more salient features is appropriate.

The first encounter of the war in point of date took place April 27, when a detachment of the blockading squadron made a reconnoissance in force at Matanzas, shelled the harbor forts, and demolished several new works in construction.

The next engagement was destined to mark a memorable epoch in maritime warfare. The Pacific fleet, under Commodore George Dewey, had lain for some weeks at Hongkong. Upon the colonial proclamation of neutrality being issued and the customary twenty-four hours' notice being given, it repaired to Mirs Bay, near Hongkong, whence it proceeded to the Philippine Islands under telegraphed orders to capture or destroy the formidable Spanish fleet then assembled at Manila. At daybreak on the 1st of May the American force entered Manila Bay, and after a few hours' engagement effected the total destruction of the Spanish fleet, consisting of ten war ships and a transport, besides capturing the naval station and forts at Cavite, thus annihilating the Spanish naval power in the Pacific Ocean and completely controlling the bay of Manila, with the ability to take the city at will. Not a life was lost on our ships, the wounded only numbering seven, while not a vessel was materially injured. For this gallant achievement the Congress, upon my recommendation, fitly bestowed upon the actors preferment and substantial reward.

The effect of this remarkable victory upon the spirit of our people and upon the fortunes of the war was instant. A prestige of invincibility thereby attached to our arms which continued throughout the struggle. Reenforcements were hurried to Manila under the command of Major-General Merritt and firmly established within sight of the capital, which lay helpless before our guns.

On the 7th day of May the Government was advised officially of the victory at Manila, and at once inquired of the commander of our fleet what troops would be required. The information was received on the 15th day of May, and the first army expedition sailed May 25 and arrived off Manila June 30. Other expeditions soon followed, the total force consisting of 641 officers and 15,058 enlisted men.

Only reluctance to cause needless loss of life and property prevented the early storming and capture of the city, and therewith the absolute military occupancy of the whole group. The insurgents meanwhile had resumed the active hostilities suspended by the uncompleted truce of December, 1897. Their forces invested Manila from the northern and eastern sides, but were constrained by Admiral Dewey and General Merritt from attempting an assault. It was fitting that whatever was to be done in the way of decisive operations in that quarter should be accomplished by the strong arm of the United States alone. Obeying the stern precept of war which enjoins the overcoming of the adversary and the extinction of his power wherever assailable as the speedy and sure means to win a peace, divided victory was not permissible, for no partition of the rights and responsibilities attending the enforcement of a just and advantageous peace could be thought of.

Following the comprehensive scheme of general attack, powerful forces were assembled at various points on our coast to invade Cuba and Puerto Rico. Meanwhile naval demonstrations were made at several exposed points. On May 11 the cruiser *Wilmington* and torpedo boat *Winslow* were unsuccessful in an attempt to silence the batteries at Cardenas, a gallant ensign, Worth Bagley, and four seamen falling. These grievous fatalities were, strangely enough, among the very few which occurred during our naval operations in this extraordinary conflict.

Meanwhile the Spanish naval preparations had been pushed with great vigor. A powerful squadron under Admiral Cervera, which had assembled at the Cape Verde Islands before the outbreak of hostilities, had crossed the ocean, and by its erratic movements in the Caribbean Sea delayed our military plans while baffling the pursuit of our fleets. For a time fears were felt lest the *Oregon* and *Marietta*, then nearing home after their long voyage from San Francisco of over 15,000 miles, might be surprised by Admiral Cervera's fleet, but their fortunate arrival dispelled these apprehensions and lent much-needed reenforcement. Not until Admiral Cervera took refuge in the harbor of Santiago de Cuba, about May 19, was it practicable to plan a systematic naval and military attack upon the Antillean possessions of Spain.

Several demonstrations occurred on the coasts of Cuba and Puerto Rico in preparation for the larger event. On May 13 the North Atlantic Squadron shelled San Juan de Puerto Rico. On May 30 Commodore Schley's squadron bombarded the forts guarding the mouth of Santiago Harbor. Neither attack had any material result. It was evident that well-ordered land operations were indispensable to achieve a decisive advantage.

The next act in the war thrilled not alone the hearts of our countrymen but the world by its exceptional heroism. On the night of June 3 Lieutenant Hobson, aided by seven devoted volunteers, blocked the narrow outlet from Santiago Harbor by sinking the collier *Merrimac* in the channel, under a fierce fire from the shore batteries, escaping with their lives as by a miracle, but falling into the hands of the Spaniards. It is a most gratifying incident of the war that the bravery of this little band of heroes was cordially appreciated by the Spanish admiral, who sent a flag of truce to notify Admiral Sampson of their safety and to compliment them on their daring act. They were subsequently exchanged July 7.

By June 7 the cutting of the last Cuban cable isolated the island. Thereafter the invasion was vigorously prosecuted. On June 10, under a heavy protecting fire, a landing of 600 marines from the *Oregon, Marblehead*, and *Yankee* was effected in Guantanamo Bay, where it had been determined to establish a naval station.

This important and essential port was taken from the enemy, after severe fighting, by the marines, who were the first organized force of the United States to land in Cuba.

The position so won was held despite desperate attempts to dislodge our forces. By June 16 additional forces were landed and strongly intrenched. On June 22 the advance of the invading army under Major-General Shafter landed at Daiquiri, about 15 miles east of Santiago. This was accomplished under great difficulties, but with marvelous dispatch. On June 23 the movement against Santiago was begun. On the 24th the first serious engagement took place, in which the First and Tenth Cavalry and the First United States Volunteer Cavalry, General Young's brigade of General Wheeler's division, participated, losing heavily. By nightfall, however, ground within 5 miles of Santiago was won. The advantage was steadily increased. On July 1 a severe battle took place, our forces gaining the outworks of Santiago; on the 2d El Caney and San Juan were taken after a desperate charge, and the investment of the city was completed. The Navy cooperated by shelling the town and the coast forts.

On the day following this brilliant achievement of our land forces, the 3d of July, occurred the decisive naval combat of the war. The Spanish fleet, attempting to leave the harbor, was met by the American squadron under command of Commodore Sampson. In less than three hours all the Spanish ships were destroyed, the two torpedo boats being sunk and the *María Teresa, Almirante Oquendo, Vizcaya*, and *Cristóbal Colón* driven ashore. The Spanish admiral and over 1,300 men were taken prisoners. While the enemy's loss of life was deplorably large, some 600 perishing, on our side but one man was killed, on the *Brooklyn*, and one man seriously wounded. Although our ships were repeatedly struck, not one was seriously injured. Where all so conspicuously distinguished themselves, from the commanders to the gunners and the unnamed heroes in the boiler rooms, each and all contributing toward the achievement of this astounding victory, for which neither ancient nor modern history affords a parallel in the completeness of the event and the marvelous disproportion of casualties, it would be invidious to single out any for especial honor. Deserved promotion has rewarded the more conspicuous actors. The nation's profoundest gratitude is due to all of these brave men who by their skill and devotion in a few short hours crushed the sea power of Spain and wrought a triumph whose decisiveness and far-reaching consequences can scarcely be measured. Nor can we be unmindful of the achievements of our builders, mechanics, and artisans for their skill in the construction of our war ships.

With the catastrophe of Santiago Spain's effort upon the ocean virtually ceased. A spasmodic effort toward the end of June to send her Mediterranean fleet, under Admiral Camara, to relieve Manila was abandoned, the expedition being recalled after it had passed through the Suez Canal.

The capitulation of Santiago followed. The city was closely besieged by land, while the entrance of our ships into the harbor cut off all relief on that side. After a truce to allow of the removal of noncombatants protracted negotiations continued from July 3 until July 15, when, under menace of immediate assault, the preliminaries of surrender were agreed upon. On the 17th General Shafter occupied the city. The capitulation embraced the entire eastern end of Cuba. The number of Spanish soldiers surrendering was 22,000, all of whom were subsequently conveyed to Spain at the charge of the United States. The story of this successful campaign is told in the report of the Secretary of War, which will be laid before you. The individual valor of officers and soldiers was never more strikingly shown than in the several engagements leading to the surrender of Santiago, while the prompt movements and successive victories won instant and universal applause. To those who gained this complete triumph, which established the ascendency of the United States upon land as the fight off Santiago had fixed our supremacy on the seas, the earnest and lasting gratitude of the nation is unsparingly due. Nor should we alone remember the gallantry of the living; the dead claim our tears, and our losses by battle and disease must cloud any exultation at the result and teach us to weigh the awful cost of war, however rightful the cause or signal the victory.

With the fall of Santiago the occupation of Puerto Rico became the next strategic necessity. General Miles had previously been assigned to organize an expedition for that purpose. Fortunately he was already at Santiago, where he had arrived on the 11th of July with reenforcements for General Shafter's army.

With these troops, consisting of 3,415 infantry and artillery, two companies of engineers, and one company of the Signal Corps, General Miles left Guantanamo on July 21, having nine transports convoyed by the fleet under Captain Higginson with the *Massachusetts* (flagship), *Dixie*, *Gloucester*, *Columbia*, and *Yale*, the two latter carrying troops. The expedition landed at Guanica July 25, which port was entered with little opposition. Here the fleet was joined by the *Annapolis* and the *Wasp*, while the *Puritan* and *Amphitrite* went to San Juan and joined the *New Orleans*, which was engaged in blockading that port. The Major-General Commanding was subsequently reenforced by General Schwan's brigade of the Third Army Corps, by General Wilson with a part of his division, and also by General Brooke with a part of his corps, numbering in all 16,973 officers and men.

On July 27 he entered Ponce, one of the most important ports in the island, from which he thereafter directed operations for the capture of the island.

With the exception of encounters with the enemy at Guayama, Hormigueros, Coamo, and Yauco and an attack on a force landed at Cape San Juan, there was no serious resistance. The campaign was prosecuted with great vigor, and by the 12th of August much of the island was in our possession and the acquisition of the remainder was only a matter of a short time. At most of the points in the island our troops were enthusiastically welcomed. Protestations of loyalty to the flag and gratitude for delivery from Spanish rule met our commanders at every stage. As a potent influence toward peace the outcome of the Puerto Rican expedition was of great consequence, and generous commendation is due to those who participated in it.

The last scene of the war was enacted at Manila, its starting place. On August 15, after a brief assault upon the works by the land forces, in which the squadron assisted, the capital surrendered unconditionally. The casualties were comparatively few. By this the conquest of the Philippine Islands, virtually accomplished when the Spanish capacity for resistance was destroyed by Admiral Dewey's victory of the 1st of May, was formally sealed. To General Merritt, his officers and men, for their uncomplaining and devoted service and for their gallantry in action, the nation is sincerely grateful. Their long voyage was made with singular success, and the soldierly conduct of the men, most of whom were without previous experience in the military service, deserves unmeasured praise.

The total casualties in killed and wounded in the Army during the war with Spain were: Officers killed, 23; enlisted men killed, 257; total, 280; officers wounded, 113; enlisted men wounded, 1,464; total, 1,577. Of the Navy: Killed, 17; wounded, 67; died as result of wounds, 1; invalided from service, 6; total, 91.

It will be observed that while our Navy was engaged in two great battles and in numerous perilous undertakings in blockade and bombardment, and more than 50,000 of our troops were transported to distant lands and were engaged in assault and siege and battle and many skirmishes in unfamiliar territory, we lost in both arms of the service a total of 1,668 killed and wounded; and in the entire campaign by land and sea we did not lose a gun or a flag or a transport or a ship, and, with the exception of the crew of the *Merrimac*, not a soldier or sailor was taken prisoner.

On August 7, forty-six days from the date of the landing of General Shafter's army in Cuba and twenty-one days from the surrender of

Santiago, the United States troops commenced embarkation for home, and our entire force was returned to the United States as early as August 24. They were absent from the United States only two months.

It is fitting that I should bear testimony to the patriotism and devotion of that large portion of our Army which, although eager to be ordered to the post of greatest exposure, fortunately was not required outside of the United States. They did their whole duty, and, like their comrades at the front, have earned the gratitude of the nation. In like manner, the officers and men of the Army and of the Navy who remained in their departments and stations faithfully performing most important duties connected with the war, and whose requests for assignment in the field and at sea I was compelled to refuse because their services were indispensable here, are entitled to the highest commendation. It is my regret that there seems to be no provision for their suitable recognition.

In this connection it is a pleasure for me to mention in terms of cordial appreciation the timely and useful work of the American National Red Cross, both in relief measures preparatory to the campaigns, in sanitary assistance at several of the camps of assemblage, and later, under the able and experienced leadership of the president of the society, Miss Clara Barton, on the fields of battle and in the hospitals at the front in Cuba. Working in conjunction with the governmental authorities and under their sanction and approval, and with the enthusiastic cooperation of many patriotic women and societies in the various States, the Red Cross has fully maintained its already high reputation for intense earnestness and ability to exercise the noble purposes of its international organization, thus justifying the confidence and support which it has received at the hands of the American people. To the members and officers of this society and all who aided them in their philanthropic work the sincere and lasting gratitude of the soldiers and the public is due and is freely accorded.

In tracing these events we are constantly reminded of our obligations to the Divine Master for His watchful care over us and His safe guidance, for which the nation makes reverent acknowledgment and offers humble prayer for the continuance of His favor.

The annihilation of Admiral Cervera's fleet, followed by the capitulation of Santiago, having brought to the Spanish Government a realizing sense of the hopelessness of continuing a struggle now become wholly unequal, it made overtures of peace through the French ambassador, who, with the assent of his Government, had acted as the friendly representative of Spanish interests during the war. On the 26th of July M. Cambon presented a communication signed by the Duke of Almodóvar, the Spanish minister of state, inviting the United States to state the terms upon which it would be willing to make peace. On the 30th of July, by a communication addressed to the Duke of Almodóvar and handed to M. Cambon, the terms of this Government were announced substantially as in the protocol afterwards signed. On the 10th of August the Spanish reply, dated August 7, was handed by M. Cambon to the Secretary of State. It accepted unconditionally the terms imposed as to Cuba, Puerto Rico, and an island of the Ladrones group, but appeared to seek to introduce inadmissible reservations in regard to our demand as to the Philippine Islands. Conceiving that discussion on this point could neithei be practical nor profitable, I directed that in order to avoid misunderstanding the matter should be forthwith closed by proposing the embodiment in a formal protocol of the terms upon which the negotiations for peace were to be undertaken. The vague and inexplicit suggestions of the Spanish note could not be accepted, the only reply being to present as a virtual ultimatum a draft of protocol embodying the precise terms tendered to Spain in our note of July 30, with added stipulations of detail as to the appointment of commissioners to arrange for the evacuation of the Spanish Antilles. On August 12 M. Cambon announced his receipt of full powers to sign the protocol so submitted. Accordingly, on the afternoon of August 12, M. Cambon, as the plenipotentiary of Spain, and the Secretary of State, as the plenipotentiary of the United States, signed a protocol providing—

ARTICLE I. Spain will relinquish all claim of sovereignty over and title to Cuba.

ART. II. Spain will cede to the United States the island of Puerto Rico and other islands now under Spanish sovereignty in the West Indies, and also an island in the Ladrones to be selected by the United States.

ART. III. The United States will occupy and hold the city, bay, and harbor of Manila pending the conclusion of a treaty of peace which shall determine the control, disposition, and government of the Philippines.

The fourth article provided for the appointment of joint commissions on the part of the United States and Spain, to meet in Havana and San Juan, respectively, for the purpose of arranging and carrying out the details of the stipulated evacuation of Cuba, Puerto Rico, and other Spanish islands in the West Indies.

The fifth article provided for the appointment of not more than five commissioners on each side, to meet at Paris not later than October 1 and to proceed to the negotiation and conclusion of a treaty of peace, subject to ratification according to the respective constitutional forms of the two countries.

The sixth and last article provided that upon the signature of the protocol hostilities between the two countries should be suspended and that notice to that effect should be given as soon as possible by each Government to the commanders of its military and naval forces.

Immediately upon the conclusion of the protocol I issued a proclamation, of August 12,* suspending hostilities on the part of the United States. The necessary orders to that end were at once given by telegraph. The blockade of the ports of Cuba and San Juan de Puerto Rico was in like

* See pp. 206-207.

manner raised. On the 18th of August the muster out of 100,000 volunteers, or as near that number as was found to be practicable, was ordered.

On the 1st of December 101,165 officers and men had been mustered out and discharged from the service, and 9,002 more will be mustered out by the 10th of this month; also a corresponding number of general and general staff officers have been honorably discharged the service.

The military commissions to superintend the evacuation of Cuba, Puerto Rico, and the adjacent islands were forthwith appointed—for Cuba, Major-General James F. Wade, Rear-Admiral William T. Sampson, Major-General Matthew C. Butler; for Puerto Rico, Major-General John R. Brooke, Rear-Admiral Winfield S. Schley, Brigadier-General William W. Gordon—who soon afterwards met the Spanish commissioners at Havana and San Juan, respectively. The Puerto Rican Joint Commission speedily accomplished its task, and by the 18th of October the evacuation of the island was completed. The United States flag was raised over the island at noon on that day. The administration of its affairs has been provisionally intrusted to a military governor until the Congress shall otherwise provide. The Cuban Joint Commission has not yet terminated its labors. Owing to the difficulties in the way of removing the large numbers of Spanish troops still in Cuba, the evacuation can not be completed before the 1st of January next.

Pursuant to the fifth article of the protocol, I appointed William R. Day, lately Secretary of State; Cushman K. Davis, William P. Frye, and George Gray, Senators of the United States, and Whitelaw Reid to be the peace commissioners on the part of the United States. Proceeding in due season to Paris, they there met on the 1st of October five commissioners similarly appointed on the part of Spain. Their negotiations have made hopeful progress, so that I trust soon to be able to lay a definitive treaty of peace before the Senate, with a review of the steps leading to its signature.

I do not discuss at this time the government or the future of the new possessions which will come to us as the result of the war with Spain. Such discussion will be appropriate after the treaty of peace shall be ratified. In the meantime and until the Congress has legislated otherwise it will be my duty to continue the military governments which have existed since our occupation and give to the people security in life and property and encouragement under a just and beneficent rule.

As soon as we are in possession of Cuba and have pacified the island it will be necessary to give aid and direction to its people to form a government for themselves. This should be undertaken at the earliest moment consistent with safety and assured success. It is important that our relations with this people shall be of the most friendly character and our commercial relations close and reciprocal. It should be our duty to assist in every proper way to build up the waste places of the island, encourage the industry of the people, and assist them to form a government which shall be free and independent, thus realizing the best aspirations of the Cuban people.

Spanish rule must be replaced by a just, benevolent, and humane government, created by the people of Cuba, capable of performing all international obligations, and which shall encourage thrift, industry, and prosperity and promote peace and good will among all of the inhabitants, whatever may have been their relations in the past. Neither revenge nor passion should have a place in the new government. Until there is complete tranquillity in the island and a stable government inaugurated military occupation will be continued.

With the one exception of the rupture with Spain, the intercourse of the United States with the great family of nations has been marked with cordiality, and the close of the eventful year finds most of the issues that necessarily arise in the complex relations of sovereign states adjusted or presenting no serious obstacle to a just and honorable solution by amicable agreement.

A long unsettled dispute as to the extended boundary between the Argentine Republic and Chile, stretching along the Andean crests from the southern border of the Atacama Desert to Magellan Straits, nearly a third of the length of the South American continent, assumed an acute stage in the early part of the year, and afforded to this Government occasion to express the hope that the resort to arbitration, already contemplated by existing conventions between the parties, might prevail despite the grave difficulties arising in its application. I am happy to say that arrangements to this end have been perfected, the questions of fact upon which the respective commissioners were unable to agree being in course of reference to Her Britannic Majesty for determination. A residual difference touching the northern boundary line across the Atacama Desert, for which existing treaties provided no adequate adjustment, bids fair to be settled in like manner by a joint commission, upon which the United States minister at Buenos Ayres has been invited to serve as umpire in the last resort.

I have found occasion to approach the Argentine Government with a view to removing differences of rate charges imposed upon the cables of an American corporation in the transmission between Buenos Ayres and the cities of Uruguay and Brazil of through messages passing from and to the United States. Although the matter is complicated by exclusive concessions by Uruguay and Brazil to foreign companies, there is strong hope that a good understanding will be reached and that the important channels of commercial communication between the United States and the Atlantic cities of South America may be freed from an almost prohibitory discrimination.

In this relation I may be permitted to express my sense of the fitness of an international agreement whereby the interchange of messages over connecting cables may be regulated on a fair basis of uniformity. The world has seen the postal system developed from a congeries of independent and exclusive services into a well-ordered union, of which all countries enjoy the manifold benefits. It would be strange were the nations not in time brought to realize that modern civilization, which owes so much of its progress to the annihilation of space by the electric force, demands that this all-important means of communication be a heritage of all peoples, to be administered and regulated in their common behoof. A step in this direction was taken when the international convention of 1884 for the protection of submarine cables was signed, and the day is, I trust, not far distant when this medium for the transmission of thought from land to land may be brought within the domain of international concert as completely as is the material carriage of commerce and correspondence upon the face of the waters that divide them.

The claim of Thomas Jefferson Page against Argentina, which has been pending many years, has been adjusted. The sum awarded by the Congress of Argentina was $4,242.35.

The sympathy of the American people has justly been offered to the ruler and the people of Austria-Hungary by reason of the affliction that has lately befallen them in the assassination of the Empress-Queen of that historic realm.

On the 10th of September, 1897, a conflict took place at Lattimer, Pa., between a body of striking miners and the sheriff of Luzerne County and his deputies, in which 22 miners were killed and 44 wounded, of whom 10 of the killed and 12 of the wounded were Austrian and Hungarian subjects. This deplorable event naturally aroused the solicitude of the Austro-Hungarian Government, which, on the assumption that the killing and wounding involved the unjustifiable misuse of authority, claimed reparation for the sufferers. Apart from the searching investigation and peremptory action of the authorities of Pennsylvania, the Federal Executive took appropriate steps to learn the merits of the case, in order to be in a position to meet the urgent complaint of a friendly power. The sheriff and his deputies, having been indicted for murder, were tried, and acquitted, after protracted proceedings and the hearing of hundreds of witnesses, on the ground that the killing was in the line of their official duty to uphold law and preserve public order in the State. A representative of the Department of Justice attended the trial and reported its course fully. With all the facts in its possession, this Government expects to reach a harmonious understanding on the subject with that of Austria-Hungary, notwithstanding the renewed claim of the latter, after learning the result of the trial, for indemnity for its injured subjects.

Despite the brief time allotted for preparation, the exhibits of this country at the Universal Exposition at Brussels in 1897 enjoyed the singular distinction of a larger proportion of awards, having regard to the number and classes of articles entered than those of other countries.

The worth of such a result in making known our national capacity to supply the world's markets is obvious.

Exhibitions of this international character are becoming more frequent as the exchanges of commercial countries grow more intimate and varied. Hardly a year passes that this Government is not invited to national participation at some important foreign center, but often on too short notice to permit of recourse to Congress for the power and means to do so. My predecessors have suggested the advisability of providing by a general enactment and a standing appropriation for accepting such invitations and for representation of this country by a commission. This plan has my cordial approval.

I trust that the Belgian restrictions on the importation of cattle from the United States, originally adopted as a sanitary precaution, will at an early day be relaxed as to their present features of hardship and discrimination, so as to admit live cattle under due regulation of their slaughter after landing. I am hopeful, too, of favorable change in the Belgian treatment of our preserved and salted meats. The growth of direct trade between the two countries, not alone for Belgian consumption and Belgian products, but by way of transit from and to other continental states, has been both encouraging and beneficial. No effort will be spared to enlarge its advantages by seeking the removal of needless impediments and by arrangements for increased commercial exchanges.

The year's events in Central America deserve more than passing mention.

A menacing rupture between Costa Rica and Nicaragua was happily composed by the signature of a convention between the parties, with the concurrence of the Guatemalan representative as a mediator, the act being negotiated and signed on board the United States steamer *Alert*, then lying in Central American waters. It is believed that the good offices of our envoy and of the commander of that vessel contributed toward this gratifying outcome.

In my last annual message the situation was presented with respect to the diplomatic representation of this Government in Central America created by the association of Nicaragua, Honduras, and Salvador under the title of the Greater Republic of Central America, and the delegation of their international functions to the Diet thereof. While the representative character of the Diet was recognized by my predecessor and has been confirmed during my Administration by receiving its accredited envoy and granting exequaturs to consuls commissioned under its authority, that recognition was qualified by the distinct understanding that the responsibility of each of the component sovereign Republics toward the United States remained wholly unaffected.

This proviso was needful inasmuch as the compact of the three Republics was at the outset an association whereby certain representative functions were delegated to a tripartite commission rather than a federation possessing centralized powers of government and administration. In this view of their relation and of the relation of the United States to the several Republics, a change in the representation of this country in Central America was neither recommended by the Executive nor initiated by Congress, thus leaving one of our envoys accredited, as heretofore, separately to two States of the Greater Republic, Nicaragua and Salvador, and to a third State, Costa Rica, which was not a party to the compact, while our other envoy was similarly accredited to a union State, Honduras, and a nonunion State, Guatemala. The result has been that the one has presented credentials only to the President of Costa Rica, the other having been received only by the Government of Guatemala.

Subsequently the three associated Republics entered into negotiations for taking the steps forecast in the original compact. A convention of their delegates framed for them a federal constitution under the name of the United States of Central America, and provided for a central federal government and legislature. Upon ratification by the constituent States, the 1st of November last was fixed for the new system to go into operation. Within a few weeks thereafter the plan was severely tested by revolutionary movements arising, with a consequent demand for unity of action on the part of the military power of the federal States to suppress them. Under this strain the new union seems to have been weakened through the withdrawal of its more important members. This Government was not officially advised of the installation of the federation and has maintained an attitude of friendly expectancy, while in no wise relinquishing the position held from the outset that the responsibilities of the several States toward us remained unaltered by their tentative relations among themselves.

The Nicaragua Canal Commission, under the chairmanship of Rear-Admiral John G. Walker, appointed July 24, 1897, under the authority of a provision in the sundry civil act of June 4 of that year, has nearly completed its labors, and the results of its exhaustive inquiry into the proper route, the feasibility, and the cost of construction of an interoceanic canal by a Nicaraguan route will be laid before you. In the performance of its task the commission received all possible courtesy and assistance from the Governments of Nicaragua and Costa Rica, which thus testified their appreciation of the importance of giving a speedy and practical outcome to the great project that has for so many years engrossed the attention of the respective countries.

As the scope of the recent inquiry embraced the whole subject, with the aim of making plans and surveys for a canal by the most convenient route, it necessarily included a review of the results of previous surveys and plans, and in particular those adopted by the Maritime Canal Company under its existing concessions from Nicaragua and Costa Rica, so that to this extent those grants necessarily hold as essential a part in the deliberations and conclusions of the Canal Commission as they have held and must needs hold in the discussion of the matter by the Congress. Under these circumstances and in view of overtures made to the Governments of Nicaragua and Costa Rica by other parties for a new canal concession predicated on the assumed approaching lapse of the contracts of the Maritime Canal Company with those States, I have not hesitated to express my conviction that considerations of expediency and international policy as between the several governments interested in the construction and control of an interoceanic canal by this route require the maintenance of the *status quo* until the Canal Commission shall have reported and the United States Congress shall have had the opportunity to pass finally upon the whole matter during the present session, without prejudice by reason of any change in the existing conditions.

Nevertheless, it appears that the Government of Nicaragua, as one of its last sovereign acts before merging its powers in those of the newly formed United States of Central America, has granted an optional concession to another association, to become effective on the expiration of the present grant. It does not appear what surveys have been made or what route is proposed under this contingent grant, so that an examination of the feasibility of its plans is necessarily not embraced in the report of the Canal Commission. All these circumstances suggest the urgency of some definite action by the Congress at this session if the labors of the past are to be utilized and the linking of the Atlantic and Pacific oceans by a practical waterway is to be realized. That the construction of such a maritime highway is now more than ever indispensable to that intimate and ready intercommunication between our eastern and western seaboards demanded by the annexation of the Hawaiian Islands and the prospective expansion of our influence and commerce in the Pacific, and that our national policy now more imperatively than ever calls for its control by this Government, are propositions which I doubt not the Congress will duly appreciate and wisely act upon.

A convention providing for the revival of the late United States and Chilean Claims Commission and the consideration of claims which were duly presented to the late commission, but not considered because of the expiration of the time limited for the duration of the commission, was signed May 24, 1897, and has remained unacted upon by the Senate. The term therein fixed for effecting the exchange of ratifications having elapsed, the convention falls unless the time be extended by amendment, which I am endeavoring to bring about, with the friendly concurrence of the Chilean Government.

The United States has not been an indifferent spectator of the extraordinary events transpiring in the Chinese Empire, whereby portions of its maritime provinces are passing under the control of various European powers; but the prospect that the vast commerce which the energy of our citizens and the necessity of our staple productions for Chinese uses has built up in those regions may not be prejudiced through any exclusive treatment by the new occupants has obviated the need of our country becoming an actor in the scene. Our position among nations, having a large Pacific coast and a constantly expanding direct trade with the farther Orient, gives us the equitable claim to consideration and friendly treatment in this regard, and it will be my aim to subserve our large interests in that quarter by all means appropriate to the constant policy of our Government. The territories of Kiao-chow, of Wei-hai-wei, and of Port Arthur and Talienwan, leased to Germany, Great Britain, and Russia, respectively, for terms of years, will, it is announced, be open to international commerce during such alien occupation; and if no discriminating treatment of American citizens and their trade be found to exist or be hereafter developed, the desire of this Government would appear to be realized.

In this relation, as showing the volume and value of our exchanges with China and the peculiarly favorable conditions which exist for their expansion in the normal course of trade, I refer to the communication addressed to the Speaker of the House of Representatives by the Secretary of the Treasury on the 14th of last June, with its accompanying letter of the Secretary of State, recommending an appropriation for a commission to study the commercial and industrial conditions in the Chinese Empire and report as to the opportunities for and obstacles to the enlargement of markets in China for the raw products and manufactures of the United States. Action was not taken thereon during the late session. I cordially urge that the recommendation receive at your hands the consideration which its importance and timeliness merit.

Meanwhile there may be just ground for disquietude in view of the unrest and revival of the old sentiment of opposition and prejudice to alien people which pervades certain of the Chinese provinces. As in the case of the attacks upon our citizens in Szechuen and at Kutien in 1895, the United States minister has been instructed to secure the fullest measure of protection, both local and imperial, for any menaced American interests, and to demand, in case of lawless injury to person or property, instant reparation appropriate to the case. War ships have been stationed at Tientsin for more ready observation of the disorders which have invaded even the Chinese capital, so as to be in a position to act should need arise, while a guard of marines has been sent to Peking to afford the minister the same measure of authoritative protection as the representatives of other nations have been constrained to employ.

Following close upon the rendition of the award of my predecessor as arbitrator of the claim of the Italian subject Cerruti against the Republic of Colombia, differences arose between the parties to the arbitration in regard to the scope and extension of the award, of which certain articles were contested by Colombia, while Italy claimed their literal fulfillment. The award having been made by the President of the United States, as an act of friendly consideration and with the sole view to an impartial composition of the matter in dispute, I could not but feel deep concern at such a miscarriage, and while unable to accept the Colombian theory that I, in my official capacity, possessed continuing functions as arbitrator, with power to interpret or revise the terms of the award, my best efforts were lent to bring the parties to a harmonious agreement as to the execution of its provisions.

A naval demonstration by Italy resulted in an engagement to pay the liabilities claimed upon their ascertainment; but this apparent disposition of the controversy was followed by a rupture of diplomatic intercourse between Colombia and Italy, which still continues, although, fortunately, without acute symptoms having supervened. Notwithstanding this, efforts are reported to be continuing for the ascertainment of Colombia's contingent liability on account of Cerruti's debts under the fifth article of the award.

A claim of an American citizen against the Dominican Republic for a public bridge over the Ozama River, which has been in diplomatic controversy for several years, has been settled by expert arbitration and an award in favor of the claimant amounting to about $90,000. It, however, remains unpaid, despite urgent demands for its settlement according to the terms of the compact.

There is now every prospect that the participation of the United States in the Universal Exposition to be held in Paris in 1900 will be on a scale commensurate with the advanced position held by our products and industries in the world's chief marts.

The preliminary report of Mr. Moses P. Handy, who, under the act approved July 19, 1897, was appointed special commissioner with a view to securing all attainable information necessary to a full and complete understanding by Congress in regard to the participation of this Government in the Paris Exposition, was laid before you by my message of December 6, 1897, and showed the large opportunities opened to make known our national progress in arts, science, and manufactures, as well as the urgent need of immediate and adequate provision to enable due advantage thereof to be taken. Mr. Handy's death soon afterwards rendered it necessary for another to take up and complete his unfinished work, and on January 11 last Mr. Thomas W. Cridler, Third Assistant Secretary of State, was designated to fulfill that task. His report was laid before you by my message of June 14, 1898, with the gratifying result of awakening renewed interest in the projected display. By a provision in the sundry civil appropriation act of July 1, 1898, a sum not to exceed $650,000 was allotted for the organization of a commission to care for the proper preparation and installation of American exhibits and for the display of suitable exhibits by the several Executive Departments, particularly by the Department of Agriculture, the Fish Commission, and the Smithsonian Institution, in representation of the Government of the United States.

Pursuant to that enac ment I appointed Mr. Ferdinand W. Peck, of Chicago, commissioner-general, with an assistant commissioner-general and a secretary. Mr. Peck at once proceeded to Paris, where his success in enlarging the scope and variety of the United States exhibit has been most gratifying. Notwithstanding the comparatively limited area of the exposition site—less than one-half that of the World's Fair at Chicago— the space assigned to the United States has been increased from the absolute allotment of 157,403 square feet reported by Mr. Handy to some 202,000 square feet, with corresponding augmentation of the field for a truly characteristic representation of the various important branches of our country's development. Mr. Peck's report will be laid before you. In my judgment its recommendations will call for your early consideration, especially as regards an increase of the appropriation to at least one million dollars in all, so that not only may the assigned space be fully taken up by the best possible exhibits in every class, but the preparation and installation be on so perfect a scale as to rank among the first in that unparalleled competition of artistic and inventive production, and thus counterbalance the disadvantage with which we start as compared with other countries whose appropriations are on a more generous scale and whose preparations are in a state of much greater forwardness than our own.

Where our artisans have the admitted capacity to excel, where our inventive genius has initiated many of the grandest discoveries of these later days of the century, and where the native resources of our land are as limitless as they are valuable to supply the world's needs, it is our province, as it should be our earnest care, to lead in the march of human progress, and not rest content with any secondary place. Moreover, if this be due to ourselves, it is no less due to the great French nation whose guests we become, and which has in so many ways testified its wish and hope that our participation shall befit the place the two peoples have won in the field of universal development.

The commercial arrangement made with France on the 28th of May, 1898, under the provisions of section 3 of the tariff act of 1897, went into effect on the 1st day of June following. It has relieved a portion of our export trade from serious embarrassment. Further negotiations are now pending under section 4 of the same act with a view to the increase of trade between the two countries to their mutual advantage. Negotiations with other governments, in part interrupted by the war with Spain, are in progress under both sections of the tariff act. I hope to be able to announce some of the results of these negotiations during the present session of Congress.

Negotiations to the same end with Germany have been set on foot. Meanwhile no effort has been relaxed to convince the Imperial Government of the thoroughness of our inspection of pork products for exportation, and it is trusted that the efficient administration of this measure by the Department of Agriculture will be recognized as a guaranty of the healthfulness of the food staples we send abroad to countries where their use is large and necessary.

I transmitted to the Senate on the 10th of February last information touching the prohibition against the importation of fresh fruits from this country, which had then recently been decreed by Germany on the ground of danger of disseminating the San José scale insect. This precautionary measure was justified by Germany on the score of the drastic steps taken in several States of the Union against the spread of the pest, the elaborate reports of the Department of Agriculture being put in evidence to show the danger to German fruit-growing interests should the scale obtain a lodgment in that country. Temporary relief was afforded in the case of large consignments of fruit then on the way by inspection and admission when found noninfected. Later the prohibition was extended to dried fruits of every kind, but was relaxed so as to apply only to unpeeled fruit and fruit waste. As was to be expected, the alarm reached to other countries, and Switzerland has adopted a similar inhibition. Efforts are in progress to induce the German and Swiss Governments to relax the prohibition in favor of dried fruits shown to have been cured under circumstances rendering the existence of animal life impossible.

Our relations with Great Britain have continued on the most friendly footing. Assenting to our request, the protection of Americans and their interests in Spanish jurisdiction was assumed by the diplomatic and consular representatives of Great Britain, who fulfilled their delicate and arduous trust with tact and zeal, eliciting high commendation. I may be allowed to make fitting allusion to the instance of Mr. Ramsden, Her Majesty's consul at Santiago de Cuba, whose untimely death after distinguished service and untiring effort during the siege of that city was sincerely lamented.

In the early part of April last, pursuant to a request made at the instance of the Secretary of State by the British ambassador at this capital, the Canadian government granted facilities for the passage of four United States revenue cutters from the Great Lakes to the Atlantic coast by way of the Canadian canals and the St. Lawrence River. The vessels had reached Lake Ontario and were there awaiting the opening of navigation when war was declared between the United States and Spain. Her Majesty's Government thereupon, by a communication of the latter part of April, stated that the permission granted before the outbreak of hostilities would not be withdrawn provided the United States Government gave assurance that the vessels in question would proceed direct to a United States port without engaging in any hostile operation. This Government promptly agreed to the stipulated condition, it being understood that the vessels would not be prohibited from resisting any hostile attack.

It will give me especial satisfaction if I shall be authorized to communicate to you a favorable conclusion of the pending negotiations with Great Britain in respect to the Dominion of Canada. It is the earnest wish of this Government to remove all sources of discord and irritation in our relations with the neighboring Dominion. The trade between the two countries is constantly increasing, and it is important to both countries that all reasonable facilities should be granted for its development.

The Government of Greece strongly urges the onerousness of the duty here imposed upon the currants of that country, amounting to 100 per cent or more of their market value. This fruit is stated to be exclusively a Greek product, not coming into competition with any domestic product. The question of reciprocal commercial relations with Greece, including the restoration of currants to the free list, is under consideration.

The long-standing claim of Bernard Campbell for damages for injuries sustained from a violent assault committed against him by military authorities in the island of Haiti has been settled by the agreement of that Republic to pay him $10,000 in American gold. Of this sum $5,000 has already been paid. It is hoped that other pending claims of American citizens against that Republic may be amicably adjusted.

Pending the consideration by the Senate of the treaty signed June 16, 1897, by the plenipotentiaries of the United States and of the Republic of Hawaii, providing for the annexation of the islands, a joint resolution to accomplish the same purpose by accepting the offered cession and incorporating the ceded territory into the Union was adopted by the Congress and approved July 7, 1898. I thereupon directed the United States steamship *Philadelphia* to convey Rear-Admiral Miller to Honolulu, and intrusted to his hands this important legislative act, to be delivered to the President of the Republic of Hawaii, with whom the Admiral and the United States minister were authorized to make appropriate arrangements for transferring the sovereignty of the islands to the United States. This was simply but impressively accomplished on the 12th of August last by the delivery of a certified copy of the resolution to President Dole, who thereupon yielded up to the representative of the Government of the United States the sovereignty and public property of the Hawaiian Islands.

Pursuant to the terms of the joint resolution and in exercise of the authority thereby conferred upon me, I directed that the civil, judicial, and military powers theretofore exercised by the officers of the Government of the Republic of Hawaii should continue to be exercised by those officers until Congress shall provide a government for the incorporated territory, subject to my power to remove such officers and to fill vacancies. The President, officers, and troops of the Republic thereupon took the oath of allegiance to the United States, thus providing for the uninterrupted continuance of all the administrative and municipal functions of the annexed territory until Congress shall otherwise enact.

Following the further provision of the joint resolution, I appointed the Hons. Shelby M. Cullom, of Illinois, John T. Morgan, of Alabama, Robert R. Hitt, of Illinois, Sanford B. Dole, of Hawaii, and Walter F. Frear, of Hawaii, as commissioners to confer and recommend to Congress such legislation concerning the Hawaiian Islands as they should deem necessary or proper. The commissioners having fulfilled the mission confided to them, their report will be laid before you at an early day. It is believed that their recommendations will have the earnest consideration due to the magnitude of the responsibility resting upon you to give such shape to the relationship of those mid-Pacific lands to our home Union as will benefit both in the highest degree, realizing the aspirations of the community that has cast its lot with us and elected to share our political heritage, while at the same time justifying the foresight of those who for three-quarters of a century have looked to the assimilation of Hawaii as a natural and inevitable consummation, in harmony with our needs and in fulfillment of our cherished traditions.

The questions heretofore pending between Hawaii and Japan growing out of the alleged mistreatment of Japanese treaty immigrants were, I am pleased to say, adjusted before the act of transfer by the payment of a reasonable indemnity to the Government of Japan.

Under the provisions of the joint resolution, the existing customs relations of the Hawaiian Islands with the United States and with other countries remain unchanged until legislation shall otherwise provide. The consuls of Hawaii here and in foreign countries continue to fulfill their commercial agencies, while the United States consulate at Honolulu is maintained for all appropriate services pertaining to trade and the revenue. It would be desirable that all foreign consuls in the Hawaiian Islands should receive new exequaturs from this Government.

The attention of Congress is called to the fact that, our consular offices having ceased to exist in Hawaii and being about to cease in other countries coming under the sovereignty of the United States, the provisions for the relief and transportation of destitute American seamen in these countries under our consular regulations will in consequence terminate. It is proper, therefore, that new legislation should be enacted upon this subject in order to meet the changed conditions.

The interpretation of certain provisions of the extradition convention of December 11, 1861, has been at various times the occasion of controversy with the Government of Mexico. An acute difference arose in the case of the Mexican demand for the delivery of Jesús Guerra, who, having led a marauding expedition near the border with the proclaimed purpose of initiating an insurrection against President Diaz, escaped into Texas. Extradition was refused on the ground that the alleged offense was political in its character, and therefore came within the treaty proviso of nonsurrender. The Mexican contention was that the exception only related to purely political offenses, and that as Guerra's acts were admixed with the common crime of murder, arson, kidnaping, and robbery, the option of nondelivery became void, a position which this Government was unable to admit in view of the received international doctrine and practice in the matter. The Mexican Government, in view of this, gave notice January 24, 1898, of the termination of the convention, to take effect twelve months from that date, at the same time inviting the conclusion of a new convention, toward which negotiations are on foot.

In this relation I may refer to the necessity of some amendment of our existing extradition statute. It is a common stipulation of such treaties that neither party shall be bound to give up its own citizens, with the added proviso in one of our treaties, that with Japan, that it may surrender if it see fit. It is held in this country by an almost uniform course of decisions that where a treaty negatives the obligation to surrender the President is not invested with legal authority to act. The conferment of such authority would be in the line of that sound morality which shrinks from affording secure asylum to the author of a heinous crime. Again, statutory provision might well be made for what is styled extradition by way of transit, whereby a fugitive surrendered by one foreign government to another may be conveyed across the territory of the United States to the jurisdiction of the demanding state. A recommendation in this behalf made in the President's message of 1886* was not acted upon. The matter is presented for your consideration.

The problem of the Mexican free zone has been often discussed with regard to its inconvenience as a provocative of smuggling into the United States along an extensive and thinly guarded land border. The effort made by the joint resolution of March 1, 1895, to remedy the abuse charged by suspending the privilege of free transportation in bond across the territory of the United States to Mexico failed of good result, as is stated in Report No. 702 of the House of Representatives, submitted in the last session, March 11, 1898. As the question is one to be conveniently met by wise concurrent legislation of the two countries looking to the protection of the revenues by harmonious measures operating equally on either side of the boundary, rather than by conventional arrangements, I suggest that Congress consider the advisability of authorizing and inviting a conference of representatives of the Treasury Departments of the United States and Mexico to consider the subject in all its complex bearings, and make report with pertinent recommendations to the respective Governments for the information and consideration of their Congresses.

The Mexican Water Boundary Commission has adjusted all matters submitted to it to the satisfaction of both Governments save in three important cases—that of the "Chamizal" at El Paso, Tex., where the two commissioners failed to agree, and wherein, for this case only, this Government has proposed to Mexico the addition of a third member;

*See Vol. VIII, pp. 501–503.

the proposed elimination of what are known as "Bancos," small isolated islands formed by the cutting off of bends in the Rio Grande, from the operation of the treaties of 1884 and 1889, recommended by the commissioners and approved by this Government, but still under consideration by Mexico; and the subject of the "Equitable distribution of the waters of the Rio Grande," for which the commissioners recommended an international dam and reservoir, approved by Mexico, but still under consideration by this Government. Pending these questions it is necessary to extend the life of the commission, which expires December 23 next.

The coronation of the young Queen of the Netherlands was made the occasion of fitting congratulations.

The claim of Victor H. McCord against Peru, which for a number of years has been pressed by this Government and has on several occasions attracted the attention of the Congress, has been satisfactorily adjusted. A protocol was signed May 17, 1898, whereby, the fact of liability being admitted, the question of the amount to be awarded was submitted to the chief justice of Canada as sole arbitrator. His award sets the indemnity due the claimant at $40,000.

The Government of Peru has given the prescribed notification of its intention to abrogate the treaty of friendship, commerce, and navigation concluded with this country August 31, 1887. As that treaty contains many important provisions necessary to the maintenance of commerce and good relations, which could with difficulty be replaced by the negotiation of renewed provisions within the brief twelve months intervening before the treaty terminates, I have invited suggestions by Peru as to the particular provisions it is desired to annul, in the hope of reaching an arrangement whereby the remaining articles may be provisionally saved.

His Majesty the Czar having announced his purpose to raise the Imperial Russian mission at this capital to the rank of an embassy, I responded, under the authority conferred by the act of March 3, 1893, by commissioning and accrediting the actual representative at St. Petersburg in the capacity of ambassador extraordinary and plenipotentiary. The Russian ambassador to this country has since presented his credentials.

The proposal of the Czar for a general reduction of the vast military establishments that weigh so heavily upon many peoples in time of peace was communicated to this Government with an earnest invitation to be represented in the conference which it is contemplated to assemble with a view to discussing the means of accomplishing so desirable a result. His Majesty was at once informed of the cordial sympathy of this Government with the principle involved in his exalted proposal and of the readiness of the United States to take part in the conference. The active military force of the United States, as measured by our population, territorial area, and taxable wealth, is, and under any conceivable prospective conditions must continue to be, in time of peace so conspicuously less than that of the armed powers to whom the Czar's appeal is especially addressed that the question can have for us no practical importance save as marking an auspicious step toward the betterment of the condition of the modern peoples and the cultivation of peace and good will among them; but in this view it behooves us as a nation to lend countenance and aid to the beneficent project.

The claims of owners of American sealing vessels for seizure by Russian cruisers in Bering Sea are being pressed to a settlement. The equities of the cases justify the expectation that a measure of reparation will eventually be accorded in harmony with precedent and in the light of the proven facts.

The recommendation made in my special message of April 27 last is renewed, that appropriation be made to reimburse the master and owners of the Russian bark *Hans* for wrongful arrest of the master and detention of the vessel in February, 1896, by officers of the United States district court for the southern district of Mississippi. The papers accompanying my said message make out a most meritorious claim and justify the urgency with which it has been presented by the Government of Russia.

Malietoa Laupepa, King of Samoa, died on August 22 last. According to Article I of the general act of Berlin, "his successor shall be duly elected according to the laws and customs of Samoa."

Arrangements having been agreed upon between the signatories of the general act for the return of Mataafa and the other exiled Samoan chiefs, they were brought from Jaluit by a German war vessel and landed at Apia on September 18 last.

Whether the death of Malietoa and the return of his old-time rival Mataafa will add to the undesirable complications which the execution of the tripartite general act has heretofore developed remains to be seen. The efforts of this Government will, as heretofore, be addressed toward a harmonious and exact fulfillment of the terms of the international engagement to which the United States became a party in 1889.

The Cheek claim against Siam, after some five years of controversy, has been adjusted by arbitration under an agreement signed July 6, 1897, an award of 706,721 ticals (about $187,987.78), with release of the Cheek estate from mortgage claims, having been rendered March 21, 1898, in favor of the claimant by the arbitrator, Sir Nicholas John Hannen, British chief justice for China and Japan.

An envoy from Siam has been accredited to this Government and has presented his credentials.

Immediately upon the outbreak of the war with Spain the Swiss Government, fulfilling the high mission it has deservedly assumed as the patron of the International Red Cross, proposed to the United States and Spain that they should severally recognize and carry into execution, as a *modus vivendi*, during the continuance of hostilities, the additional articles proposed by the international conference of Geneva, October 20, 1868, extending the effects of the existing Red Cross convention of 1864 to the conduct of naval war. Following the example set by France and Germany in 1870 in adopting such a *modus vivendi*, and in view of the accession of the United States to those additional articles in 1882, although the exchange of ratifications thereof still remained uneffected, the Swiss proposal was promptly and cordially accepted by us, and simultaneously by Spain.

This Government feels a keen satisfaction in having thus been enabled to testify its adherence to the broadest principles of humanity even amidst the clash of war, and it is to be hoped that the extension of the Red Cross compact to hostilities by sea as well as on land may soon become an accomplished fact through the general promulgation of the additional naval Red Cross articles by the maritime powers now parties to the convention of 1864.

The important question of the claim of Switzerland to the perpetual cantonal allegiance of American citizens of Swiss origin has not made hopeful progress toward a solution, and controversies in this regard still continue.

The newly accredited envoy of the United States to the Ottoman Porte carries instructions looking to the disposal of matters in controversy with Turkey for a number of years. He is especially charged to press for a just settlement of our claims for indemnity by reason of the destruction of the property of American missionaries resident in that country during the Armenian troubles of 1895, as well as for the recognition of older claims of equal justness.

He is also instructed to seek an adjustment of the dispute growing out of the refusal of Turkey to recognize the acquired citizenship of Ottoman-born persons naturalized in the United States since 1869 without prior imperial consent, and in the same general relation he is directed to endeavor to bring about a solution of the question which has more or less acutely existed since 1869 concerning the jurisdictional rights of the United States in matters of criminal procedure and punishment under Article IV of the treaty of 1830. This latter difficulty grows out of a verbal difference, claimed by Turkey to be essential, between the original Turkish text and the promulgated translation.

After more than two years from the appointment of a consul of this country to Erzerum, he has received his exequatur.

The arbitral tribunal appointed under the treaty of February 2, 1897, between Great Britain and Venezuela, to determine the boundary line between the latter and the colony of British Guiana, is to convene at Paris during the present month. It is a source of much gratification to this Government to see the friendly resort of arbitration applied to the settlement of this controversy, not alone because of the earnest part we have had in bringing about the result, but also because the two members named on behalf of Venezuela, Mr. Chief Justice Fuller and Mr. Justice Brewer, chosen from our highest court, appropriately testify the continuing interest we feel in the definitive adjustment of the question according to the strictest rules of justice. The British members, Lord Herschell and Sir Richard Collins, are jurists of no less exalted repute, while the fifth member and president of the tribunal, M. F. De Martens, has earned a world-wide reputation as an authority upon international law.

The claim of Felipe Scandella against Venezuela for arbitrary expulsion and injury to his business has been adjusted by the revocation of the order of expulsion and by the payment of the sum of $16,000.

I have the satisfaction of being able to state that the Bureau of the American Republics, created in 1890 as the organ for promoting commercial intercourse and fraternal relations among the countries of the Western Hemisphere, has become a more efficient instrument of the wise purposes of its founders, and is receiving the cordial support of the contributing members of the international union which are actually represented in its board of management. A commercial directory, in two volumes, containing a mass of statistical matter descriptive of the industrial and commercial interests of the various countries, has been printed in English, Spanish, Portuguese, and French, and a monthly bulletin published in these four languages and distributed in the Latin-American countries as well as in the United States has proved to be a valuable medium for disseminating information and furthering the varied interests of the international union.

During the past year the important work of collecting information of practical benefit to American industries and trade through the agency of the diplomatic and consular officers has been steadily advanced, and in order to lay such data before the public with the least delay the practice was begun in January, 1898, of issuing the commercial reports from day to day as they are received by the Department of State. It is believed that for promptitude as well as fullness of information the service thus supplied to our merchants and manufacturers will be found to show sensible improvement and to merit the liberal support of Congress.

The experiences of the last year bring forcibly home to us a sense of the burdens and the waste of war. We desire, in common with most civilized nations, to reduce to the lowest possible point the damage sustained in time of war by peaceable trade and commerce. It is true we may suffer in such cases less than other communities, but all nations are damaged more or less by the state of uneasiness and apprehension into which an outbreak of hostilities throws the entire commercial world. It should be our object, therefore, to minimize, so far as practicable, this inevitable loss and disturbance. This purpose can probably best be accomplished by an international agreement to regard all private property at sea as exempt from capture or destruction by the forces of belligerent powers. The United States Government has for many years advocated this humane and beneficent principle, and is now in position to recommend it to other powers without the imputation of selfish motives. I therefore suggest for your consideration that the Executive be authorized to correspond with the governments of the principal maritime powers with a view of incorporating into the permanent law of civilized nations the principle of the exemption of all private property at sea, not contraband of war, from capture or destruction by belligerent powers.

The Secretary of the Treasury reports that the receipts of the Government from all sources during the fiscal year ended June 30, 1898, including $64,751,223 received from sale of Pacific railroads, amounted to $405,321,335, and its expenditures to $443,368,582. There was collected from customs $149,575,062 and from internal revenue $170,900,641. Our dutiable imports amounted to $324,635,479, a decrease of $58,156,690 over the preceding year, and importations free of duty amounted to $291,414,175, a decrease from the preceding year of $90,524,068. Internal-revenue receipts exceeded those of the preceding year by $24,212,067.

The total tax collected on distilled spirits was $92,546,999; on manufactured tobacco, $36,230,522, and on fermented liquors, $39,515,421. We exported merchandise during the year amounting to $1,231,482,330, an increase of $180,488,774 from the preceding year.

It is estimated upon the basis of present revenue laws that the receipts of the Government for the year ending June 30, 1899, will be $577,874,647, and its expenditures $689,874,647, resulting in a deficiency of $112,000,000.

On the 1st of December, 1898, there was held in the Treasury gold coin amounting to $138,441,547, gold bullion amounting to $138,502,545, silver bullion amounting to $93,359,250, and other forms of money amounting to $451,963,981.

On the same date the amount of money of all kinds in circulation, or not included in Treasury holdings, was $1,886,879,504, an increase for the year of $165,794,966. Estimating our population at 75,194,000 at the time mentioned, the per capita circulation was $25.09. On the same date there was in the Treasury gold bullion amounting to $138,502,545.

The provisions made for strengthening the resources of the Treasury in connection with the war have given increased confidence in the purpose and power of the Government to maintain the present standard, and have established more firmly than ever the national credit at home and abroad. A marked evidence of this is found in the inflow of gold to the Treasury. Its net gold holdings on November 1, 1898, were $239,885,162 as compared with $153,573,147 on November 1, 1897, and an increase of net cash of $207,756,100, November 1, 1897, to $300,238,275, November 1, 1898. The present ratio of net Treasury gold to outstanding Government liabilities, including United States notes, Treasury notes of 1890, silver certificates, currency certificates, standard silver dollars, and fractional silver coin, November 1, 1898, was 25.35 per cent, as compared with 16.96 per cent, November 1, 1897.

I renew so much of my recommendation of December, 1897, as follows:

That when any of the United States notes are presented for redemption in gold and are redeemed in gold, such notes shall be kept and set apart and only paid out in exchange for gold. This is an obvious duty. If the holder of the United States note prefers the gold and gets it from the Government, he should not receive back from the Government a United States note without paying gold in exchange for it. The reason for this is made all the more apparent when the Government issues an interest-bearing debt to provide gold for the redemption of United States notes— a non-interest-bearing debt. Surely it should not pay them out again except on demand and for gold. If they are put out in any other way, they may return again, to be followed by another bond issue to redeem them—another interest-bearing debt to redeem a non-interest-bearing debt.

This recommendation was made in the belief that such provisions of law would insure to a greater degree the safety of the present standard, and better protect our currency from the dangers to which it is subjected from a disturbance in the general business conditions of the country.

In my judgment the present condition of the Treasury amply justifies the immediate enactment of the legislation recommended one year ago, under which a portion of the gold holdings should be placed in a trust fund from which greenbacks should be redeemed upon presentation, but when once redeemed should not thereafter be paid out except for gold.

It is not to be inferred that other legislation relating to our currency is not required; on the contrary, there is an obvious demand for it.

The importance of adequate provision which will insure to our future a money standard related as our money standard now is to that of our commercial rivals is generally recognized.

The companion proposition that our domestic paper currency shall be kept safe and yet be so related to the needs of our industries and internal commerce as to be adequate and responsive to such needs is a proposition scarcely less important. The subject, in all its parts, is commended to the wise consideration of the Congress.

. The annexation of Hawaii and the changed relations of the United States to Cuba, Puerto Rico, and the Philippines resulting from the war, compel the prompt adoption of a maritime policy by the United States. There should be established regular and frequent steamship communication, encouraged by the United States, under the American flag, with the newly acquired islands. Spain furnished to its colonies, at an annual cost of about $2,000,000, steamship lines communicating with a portion of the world's markets, as well as with trade centers of the home Government. The United States will not undertake to do less. It is our duty to furnish the people of Hawaii with facilities, under national control, for their export and import trade. It will be conceded that the present situation calls for legislation which shall be prompt, durable, and liberal.

The part which American merchant vessels and their seamen performed in the war with Spain demonstrates that this service, furnishing both pickets and the second line of defense, is a national necessity, and should be encouraged in every constitutional way. Details and methods for the accomplishment of this purpose are discussed in the report of the Secretary of the Treasury, to which the attention of Congress is respectfully invited.

In my last annual message I recommended that Congress authorize the appointment of a commission for the purpose of making systematic investigations with reference to the cause and prevention of yellow fever. This matter has acquired an increased importance as a result of the military occupation of the island of Cuba and the commercial intercourse between this island and the United States which we have every reason to expect. The sanitary problems connected with our new relations with the island of Cuba and the acquisition of Puerto Rico are no less important than those relating to finance, commerce, and administration. It is my earnest desire that these problems may be considered by competent experts and that everything may be done which the most recent advances in sanitary science can offer for the protection of the health of our soldiers in those islands and of our citizens who are exposed to the dangers of infection from the importation of yellow fever. I therefore renew my recommendation that the authority of Congress may be given and a suitable appropriation made to provide for a commission of experts to be appointed for the purpose indicated.

Under the act of Congress approved April 26, 1898, authorizing the President in his discretion, "upon a declaration of war by Congress, or a declaration by Congress that war exists," I directed the increase of the Regular Army to the maximum of 62,000, authorized in said act.

There are now in the Regular Army 57,862 officers and men. In said act it was provided—

That at the end of any war in which the United States may become involved the Army shall be reduced to a peace basis by the transfer in the same arm of the service or absorption by promotion or honorable discharge, under such regulations as the Secretary of War may establish, of supernumerary commissioned officers and the honorable discharge or transfer of supernumerary enlisted men; and nothing contained in this act shall be construed as authorizing the permanent increase of the commissioned or enlisted force of the Regular Army beyond that now provided by the law in force prior to the passage of this act, except as to the increase of twenty-five majors provided for in section 1 hereof.

The importance of legislation for the permanent increase of the Army is therefore manifest, and the recommendation of the Secretary of War for that purpose has my unqualified approval. There can be no question that at this time, and probably for some time in the future, 100,000 men will be none too many to meet the necessities of the situation. At all events, whether that number shall be required permanently or not, the power should be given to the President to enlist that force if in his discretion it should be necessary; and the further discretion should be given him to recruit for the Army within the above limit from the inhabitants of the islands with the government of which we are charged. It is my purpose to muster out the entire Volunteer Army as soon as the Congress shall provide for the increase of the regular establishment. This will be only an act of justice and will be much appreciated by the brave men who left their homes and employments to help the country in its emergency.

In my last annual message I stated:

The Union Pacific Railway, main line, was sold under the decree of the United States court for the district of Nebraska on the 1st and 2d of November of this year. The amount due the Government consisted of the principal of the subsidy bonds, $27,236,-512, and the accrued interest thereon, $31,211,711.75, making the total indebtedness $58,448,223.75. The bid at the sale covered the first-mortgage lien and the entire mortgage claim of the Government, principal and interest.

This left the Kansas Pacific case unconcluded. By a decree of the court in that case an upset price for the property was fixed at a sum which would yield to the Government only $2,500,000 upon its lien. The sale, at the instance of the Government, was postponed first to December 15, 1897, and later, upon the application of the United States, was postponed to the 16th day of February, 1898.

Having satisfied myself that the interests of the Government required that an effort should be made to obtain a larger sum, I directed the Secretary of the Treasury, under the act passed March 3, 1887, to pay out of the Treasury to the persons entitled to receive the same the amounts due upon all prior mortgages upon the Eastern and Middle divisions of said railroad out of any money in the Treasury not otherwise appropriated, whereupon the Attorney-General prepared a petition to be presented to the court, offering to redeem said prior liens in such manner as the court might direct, and praying that thereupon the United States might be held to be subrogated to all the rights of said prior lien holders and that a receiver might be appointed to take possession of the mortgaged premises and maintain and operate the same until the court or Congress otherwise directed. Thereupon the reorganization committee agreed that if said petition was withdrawn and the sale allowed to proceed on the 16th of February, 1898, they would bid a sum at the sale which would realize to the Government the entire principal of its debt, $6,303,000.

Believing that no better price could be obtained and appreciating the difficulties under which the Government would labor if it should become the purchaser of the road at the sale, in the absence of any authority by Congress to take charge of and operate the road I directed that upon the guaranty of a minimum bid which should give the Government the principal of its debt the sale should proceed. By this transaction the

Government secured an advance of $3,803,000 over and above the sum which the court had fixed as the upset price, and which the reorganization committee had declared was the maximum which they would pay for the property.

It is a gratifying fact that the result of these proceedings against the Union Pacific system and the Kansas Pacific line is that the Government has received on account of its subsidy claim the sum of $64,751,223.75, an increase of $18,997,163.76 over the sum which the reorganization committee originally agreed to bid for the joint property, the Government receiving its whole claim, principal and interest, on the Union Pacific, and the principal of its debt on the Kansas Pacific Railroad.

Steps had been taken to foreclose the Government's lien upon the Central Pacific Railroad Company, but before action was commenced Congress passed an act, approved July 7, 1898, creating a commission consisting of the Secretary of the Treasury, the Attorney-General, and the Secretary of the Interior, and their successors in office, with full power to settle the indebtedness to the Government growing out of the issue of bonds in aid of the construction of the Central Pacific and Western Pacific bond-aided railroads, subject to the approval of the President.

No report has yet been made to me by the commission thus created. Whatever action is had looking to a settlement of the indebtedness in accordance with the act referred to will be duly submitted to the Congress.

I deem it my duty to call to the attention of Congress the condition of the present building occupied by the Department of Justice. The business of that Department has increased very greatly since it was established in its present quarters. The building now occupied by it is neither large enough nor of suitable arrangement for the proper accommodation of the business of the Department. The Supervising Architect has pronounced it unsafe and unsuited for the use to which it is put. The Attorney-General in his report states that the library of the Department is upon the fourth floor, and that all the space allotted to it is so crowded with books as to dangerously overload the structure. The first floor is occupied by the Court of Claims. The building is of an old and dilapidated appearance, unsuited to the dignity which should attach to this important Department.

A proper regard for the safety, comfort, and convenience of the officers and employees would justify the expenditure of a liberal sum of money in the erection of a new building of commodious proportions and handsome appearance upon the very advantageous site already secured for that purpose, including the ground occupied by the present structure and adjoining vacant lot, comprising in all a frontage of 201 feet on Pennsylvania avenue and a depth of 136 feet.

In this connection I may likewise refer to the inadequate accommodations provided for the Supreme Court in the Capitol, and suggest the wisdom of making provision for the erection of a separate building for the court and its officers and library upon available ground near the Capitol.

The postal service of the country advances with extraordinary growth. Within twenty years both the revenues and the expenditures of the Post-Office Department have multiplied threefold. In the last ten years they have nearly doubled. Our postal business grows much more rapidly than our population. It now involves an expenditure of $100,000,000 a year, numbers 73,000 post-offices, and enrolls 200,000 employees. This remarkable extension of a service which is an accurate index of the public conditions presents gratifying evidence of the advancement of education, of the increase of communication and business activity, and of the improvement of mail facilities leading to their constantly augmenting use.

The war with Spain laid new and exceptional labors on the Post-Office Department. The mustering of the military and naval forces of the United States required special mail arrangements for every camp and every campaign. The communication between home and camp was naturally eager and expectant. In some of the larger places of rendezvous as many as 50,000 letters a day required handling. This necessity was met by the prompt detail and dispatch of experienced men from the established force and by directing all the instrumentalities of the railway mail and post-office service, so far as necessary, to this new need. Congress passed an act empowering the Postmaster-General to establish offices or branches at every military camp or station, and under this authority the postal machinery was speedily put into effective operation.

Under the same authority, when our forces moved upon Cuba, Puerto Rico, and the Philippines they were attended and followed by the postal service. Though the act of Congress authorized the appointment of postmasters where necessary, it was early determined that the public interests would best be subserved, not by new designations, but by the detail of experienced men familiar with every branch of the service, and this policy was steadily followed. When the territory which was the theater of conflict came into our possession, it became necessary to reestablish mail facilities for the resident population as well as to provide them for our forces of occupation, and the former requirement was met through the extension and application of the latter obligation. I gave the requisite authority, and the same general principle was applied to this as to other branches of civil administration under military occupation. The details are more particularly given in the report of the Postmaster-General, and, while the work is only just begun, it is pleasing to be able to say that the service in the territory which has come under our control is already materially improved.

The following recommendations of the Secretary of the Navy relative to the increase of the Navy have my earnest approval:

1. Three seagoing sheathed and coppered battle ships of about 13,500 tons trial displacement, carrying the heaviest armor and most powerful

ordnance for vessels of their class, and to have the highest practicable speed and great radius of action. Estimated cost, exclusive of armor and armament, $3,600,000 each.

2. Three sheathed and coppered armored cruisers of about 12,000 tons trial displacement, carrying the heaviest armor and most powerful ordnance for vessels of their class, and to have the highest practicable speed and great radius of action. Estimated cost, exclusive of armor and armament, $4,000,000 each.

3. Three sheathed and coppered protected cruisers of about 6,000 tons trial displacement, to have the highest practicable speed and great radius of action, and to carry the most powerful ordnance suitable for vessels of their class. Estimated cost, exclusive of armor and armament, $2,150,000 each.

4. Six sheathed and coppered cruisers of about 2,500 tons trial displacement, to have the highest speed compatible with good cruising qualities, great radius of action, and to carry the most powerful ordnance suited to vessels of their class. Estimated cost, exclusive of armament, $1,141,800 each.

I join with the Secretary of the Navy in recommending that the grades of admiral and vice-admiral be temporarily revived, to be filled by officers who have specially distinguished themselves in the war with Spain.

I earnestly urge upon Congress the importance of early legislation providing for the taking of the Twelfth Census. This is necessary in view of the large amount of work which must be performed in the preparation of the schedules preparatory to the enumeration of the population.

There were on the pension rolls on June 30, 1898, 993,714 names, an increase of nearly 18,000 over the number on the rolls on the same day of the preceding year. The amount appropriated by the act of December 22, 1896, for the payment of pensions for the fiscal year of 1898 was $140,000,000. Eight million seventy thousand eight hundred and seventy-two dollars and forty-six cents was appropriated by the act of March 31, 1898, to cover deficiencies in army pensions, and repayments in the sum of $12,020.33, making a total of $148,082,892.79 available for the payment of pensions during the fiscal year 1898. The amount disbursed from that sum was $144,651,879.80, leaving a balance of $3,431,012.99 unexpended on the 30th of June, 1898, which was covered into the Treasury. There were 389 names added to the rolls during the year by special acts passed at the second session of the Fifty-fifth Congress, making a total of 6,486 pensioners by Congressional enactments since 1861.

The total receipts of the Patent Office during the past year were $1,253,948.44. The expenditures were $1,081,633.79, leaving a surplus of $172,314.65.

The public lands disposed of by the Government during the year reached 8,453,896.92 acres, an increase of 614,780.26 acres over the previous year. The total receipts from public lands during the fiscal year amounted to $2,277,995.18, an increase of $190,063.90 over the preceding year. The lands embraced in the eleven forest reservations which were suspended by the act of June 4, 1897, again became subject to the operations of the proclamations of February 22, 1897, creating them, which added an estimated amount of 19,951,360 acres to the area embraced in the reserves previously created. In addition thereto two new reserves were created during the year—the Pine Mountain and Zaca Lake Reserve, in California, embracing 1,644,594 acres, and the Prescott Reserve, in Arizona, embracing 10,240 acres—while the Pecos River Reserve, in New Mexico, has been changed and enlarged to include 120,000 additional acres.

At the close of the year thirty forest reservations, not including those of the Afognak Forest and the Fish-Culture Reserve, in Alaska, had been created by Executive proclamations under section 24 of the act of March 3, 1891, embracing an estimated area of 40,719,474 acres.

The Department of the Interior has inaugurated a forest system, made possible by the act of July, 1898, for a graded force of officers in control of the reserves. This system has only been in full operation since August, but good results have already been secured in many sections. The reports received indicate that the system of patrol has not only prevented destructive fires from gaining headway, but has diminished the number of fires.

The special attention of the Congress is called to that part of the report of the Secretary of the Interior in relation to the Five Civilized Tribes. It is noteworthy that the general condition of the Indians shows marked progress. But one outbreak of a serious character occurred during the year, and that among the Chippewa Indians of Minnesota, which happily has been suppressed.

While it has not yet been practicable to enforce all the provisions of the act of June 28, 1898, "for the protection of the people of the Indian Territory, and for other purposes," it is having a salutary effect upon the nations composing the five tribes. The Dawes Commission reports that the most gratifying results and greater advance toward the attainment of the objects of the Government have been secured in the past year than in any previous year. I can not too strongly indorse the recommendation of the commission and of the Secretary of the Interior for the necessity of providing for the education of the 30,000 white children resident in the Indian Territory.

The Department of Agriculture has been active in the past year. Explorers have been sent to many of the countries of the Eastern and Western hemispheres for seeds and plants that may be useful to the United States, and with the further view of opening up markets for our surplus products. The Forestry Division of the Department is giving special attention to the treeless regions of our country and is introducing species specially adapted to semiarid regions. Forest fires, which seriously interfere with production, especially in irrigated regions, are being studied, that losses from this cause may be avoided. The Department is inquiring into the use and abuse of water in many States of the West, and collating information regarding the laws of the States, the decisions of the courts, and the customs of the people in this regard, so that uniformity may be secured. Experiment stations are becoming more effective every year. The annual appropriation of $720,000 by Congress is supplemented by $400,000 from the States. Nation-wide experiments have been conducted to ascertain the suitableness as to soil and climate and States for growing sugar beets. The number of sugar factories has been doubled in the past two years, and the ability of the United States to produce its own sugar from this source has been clearly demonstrated.

The Weather Bureau forecast and observation stations have been extended around the Caribbean Sea, to give early warning of the approach of hurricanes from the south seas to our fleets and merchant marine.

In the year 1900 will occur the centennial anniversary of the founding of the city of Washington for the permanent capital of the Government of the United States by authority of an act of Congress approved July 16, 1790. In May, 1800, the archives and general offices of the Federal Government were removed to this place. On the 17th of November, 1800, the National Congress met here for the first time and assumed exclusive control of the Federal district and city. This interesting event assumes all the more significance when we recall the circumstances attending the choosing of the site, the naming of the capital in honor of the Father of his Country, and the interest taken by him in the adoption of plans for its future development on a magnificent scale.

These original plans have been wrought out with a constant progress and a signal success even beyond anything their framers could have foreseen. The people of the country are justly proud of the distinctive beauty and government of the capital and of the rare instruments of science and education which here find their natural home.

A movement lately inaugurated by the citizens to have the anniversary celebrated with fitting ceremonies, including, perhaps, the establishment of a handsome permanent memorial to mark so historical an occasion and to give it more than local recognition, has met with general favor on the part of the public.

I recommend to the Congress the granting of an appropriation for this purpose and the appointment of a committee from its respective bodies. It might also be advisable to authorize the President to appoint a committee from the country at large, which, acting with the Congressional and District of Columbia committees, can complete the plans for an appropriate national celebration.

The alien contract law is shown by experience to need some amendment; a measure providing better protection for seamen is proposed; the rightful application of the eight-hour law for the benefit of labor and of the principle of arbitration are suggested for consideration; and I commend these subjects to the careful attention of the Congress.

The several departmental reports will be laid before you. They give in great detail the conduct of the affairs of the Government during the past year and discuss many questions upon which the Congress may feel called upon to act. WILLIAM McKINLEY.

AN ACT declaring that war exists between the United States of America and the Kingdom of Spain.

Be it enacted by the Senate and House of Representatives of the United States of America in Congress assembled, First. That war be, and the same is hereby, declared to exist, and that war has existed since the 21st day of April, A. D. 1898, including said day, between the United States of America and the Kingdom of Spain.

Second. That the President of the United States be, and he hereby is, directed and empowered to use the entire land and naval forces of the United States and to call into the actual service of the United States the militia of the several States to such extent as may be necessary to carry this act into effect.

Approved, April 25, 1898.

EXECUTIVE MANSION,
Washington, February 10, 1899.

To the Senate and House of Representatives:

As a consequence of the ratification of the treaty of peace between the United States and Spain and its expected ratification by the Spanish Government, the United States will come into possession of the Philippine Islands, on the farther shores of the Pacific. The Hawaiian Islands and Guam becoming United States territory and forming convenient stopping places on the way across the sea, the necessity for speedy cable communication between the United States and all these Pacific islands has become imperative.

Such communication should be established in such a way as to be wholly under the control of the United States, whether in time of peace or of war. At present the Philippines can be reached only by cables which pass through many foreign countries, and the Hawaiian Islands and Guam can only be communicated with by steamers, involving delays in each instance of at least a week. The present conditions should not be allowed to continue for a moment longer than is absolutely necessary.

So long ago as 1885 reference was made in an Executive message to Congress to the necessity for cable communication between the United States and Hawaii. This necessity has greatly increased since then. The question has been discussed in the Fifty-second, Fifty-fourth, and Fifty-fifth Congresses, in each of which some effort has been made looking toward laying a cable at least as far as the Hawaiian Islands. The time has now arrived when a cable in the Pacific must extend at least as far as Manila, touching at the Hawaiian Islands and Guam on the way.

Two methods of establishing this cable communication at once suggest themselves: First, construction and maintenance of such a cable by and at the expense of the United States Government, and, second, construction and maintenance of such a cable by a private United States corporation, under such safeguards as Congress shall impose.

I do not make any recommendations to Congress as to which of these methods would be the more desirable. A cable of the length of that proposed requires so much time for construction and laying that it is estimated that at least two years must elapse after giving the order for the cable before the entire system could be successfully laid and put in operation. Further deep-sea soundings must be taken west of the Hawaiian Islands before the final route for the cable can be selected. Under these circumstances it becomes a paramount necessity that measures should be taken before the close of the present Congress to provide such means as may seem most suitable for the establishment of a cable system.

I commend the whole subject to the careful consideration of the Congress and to such prompt action as may seem advisable.

WILLIAM McKINLEY.

PROCLAMATIONS.

BY THE PRESIDENT OF THE UNITED STATES OF AMERICA.

A PROCLAMATION.

Whereas by a joint resolution passed by the Congress and approved April 20, 1898,* and communicated to the Government of Spain, it was demanded that said Government at once relinquish its authority and government in the island of Cuba and withdraw its land and naval forces from Cuba and Cuban waters, and the President of the United States was directed and empowered to use the entire land and naval forces of the United States and to call into the actual service of the United States the militia of the several States to such extent as might be necessary to carry said resolution into effect; and

Whereas in carrying into effect said resolution the President of the United States deems it necessary to set on foot and maintain a blockade of the north coast of Cuba, including all ports on said coast between Cardenas and Bahia Honda, and the port of Cienfuegos, on the south coast of Cuba:

Now, therefore, I, William McKinley, President of the United States, in order to enforce the said resolution, do hereby declare and proclaim that

* See p. 155.

the United States of America have instituted and will maintain a blockade of the north coast of Cuba, including ports on said coast between
Cardenas and Bahia Honda, and the port of Cienfuegos, on the south
coast of Cuba, aforesaid, in pursuance of the laws of the United States
and the law of nations applicable to such cases. An efficient force will
be posted so as to prevent the entrance and exit of vessels from the ports
aforesaid. Any neutral vessel approaching any of said ports or attempting to leave the same without notice or knowledge of the establishment
of such blockade will be duly warned by the commander of the blockading forces, who will indorse on her register the fact and the date of such
warning, where such indorsement was made; and if the same vessel shall
again attempt to enter any blockaded port she will be captured and sent
to the nearest convenient port for such proceedings against her and her
cargo as prize as may be deemed advisable.

Neutral vessels lying in any of said ports at the time of the establishment of such blockade will be allowed thirty days to issue therefrom.

In witness whereof I have hereunto set my hand and caused the seal
of the United States to be affixed.

[SEAL.] Done at the city of Washington, this 22d day of April, A. D.
1898, and of the Independence of the United States the one
hundred and twenty-second.

WILLIAM McKINLEY.

By the President:
JOHN SHERMAN,
Secretary of State.

BY THE PRESIDENT OF THE UNITED STATES.

A PROCLAMATION.

Whereas a joint resolution of Congress was approved on the 20th day
of April, 1898,* entitled "Joint resolution for the recognition of the independence of the people of Cuba, demanding that the Government of
Spain relinquish its authority and government in the island of Cuba
and to withdraw its land and naval forces from Cuba and Cuban waters,
and directing the President of the United States to use the land and naval
forces of the United States to carry these resolutions into effect;" and

Whereas by an act of Congress entitled "An act to provide for temporarily increasing the military establishment of the United States in time
of war, and for other purposes," approved April 22, 1898, the President
is authorized, in order to raise a volunteer army, to issue his proclamation calling for volunteers to serve in the Army of the United States:

Now, therefore, I, William McKinley, President of the United States,
by virtue of the power vested in me by the Constitution and the laws,
and deeming sufficient occasion to exist, have thought fit to call forth,

* See p. 155.

and hereby do call forth, volunteers to the aggregate number of 125,000 in order to carry into effect the purpose of the said resolutior, the same to be apportioned, as far as practicable, among the several States and Territories and the District of Columbia according to population and to serve for two years unless sooner discharged. The details for this object will be immediately communicated to the proper authorities through the War Department.

In witness whereof I have hereunto set my hand and caused the seal of the United States to be affixed.

[SEAL.]   Done at the city of Washington, this 23d day of April, A. D. 1898, and of the Independence of the United States the one hundred and twenty-second.

WILLIAM McKINLEY.

By the President:

JOHN SHERMAN,
   Secretary of State.

BY THE PRESIDENT OF THE UNITED STATES OF AMERICA.

A PROCLAMATION.

Whereas by an act of Congress approved April 25, 1898,* it is declared that war exists and that war has existed since the 21st day of April, A. D. 1898, including said day, between the United States of America and the Kingdom of Spain; and

Whereas, it being desirable that such war should be conducted upon principles in harmony with the present views of nations and sanctioned by their recent practice, it has already been announced that the policy of this Government will be not to resort to privateering, but to adhere to the rules of the Declaration of Paris:

Now, therefore, I, William McKinley, President of the United States of America, by virtue of the power vested in me by the Constitution and the laws, do hereby declare and proclaim:

1. The neutral flag covers enemy's goods with the exception of contraband of war.

2. Neutral goods not contraband of war are not liable to confiscation under the enemy's flag.

3. Blockades in order to be binding must be effective.

4. Spanish merchant vessels in any ports or places within the United States shall be allowed till May 21, 1898, inclusive, for loading their cargoes and departing from such ports or places; and such Spanish merchant vessels, if met at sea by any United States ship, shall be permitted to continue their voyage if on examination of their papers it shall appear that their cargoes were taken on board before the expiration of the above term: *Provided*, That nothing herein contained shall apply to

* See p. 201.

Spanish vessels having on board any officer in the military or naval service of the enemy, or any coal (except such as may be necessary for their voyage), or any other article prohibited or contraband of war, or any dispatch of or to the Spanish Government.

5. Any Spanish merchant vessel which prior to April 21, 1898, shall have sailed from any foreign port bound for any port or place in the United States shall be permitted to enter such port or place and to discharge her cargo, and afterwards forthwith to depart without molestation; and any such vessel, if met at sea by any United States ship, shall be permitted to continue her voyage to any port not blockaded.

6. The right of search is to be exercised with strict regard for the rights of neutrals, and the voyages of mail steamers are not to be interfered with except on the clearest grounds of suspicion of a violation of law in respect of contraband or blockade.

In witness whereof I have hereunto set my hand and caused the seal of the United States to be affixed.

[SEAL.]   ·Done at the city of Washington on the 26th day of April, A. D. 1898, and of the Independence of the United States the one hundred and twenty-second.

WILLIAM McKINLEY.

By the President:
> ALVEY A. ADEE,
> *Acting Secretary of State.*

BY THE PRESIDENT OF THE UNITED STATES.

A PROCLAMATION.

Whereas an act of Congress was approved on the 25th day of April, 1898,* entitled "An act declaring that war exists between the United States of America and the Kingdom of Spain;" and

Whereas by an act of Congress entitled "An act to provide for temporarily increasing the military establishment of the United States in time of war and for other purposes," approved April 22, 1898, the President is authorized, in order to raise a volunteer army, to issue his proclamation calling for volunteers to serve in the Army of the United States:

Now, therefore, I, William McKinley, President of the United States, by virtue of the power vested in me by the Constitution and the laws, and deeming sufficient occasion to exist, have thought fit to call forth, and hereby do call forth, volunteers to the aggregate number of 75,000 in addition to the volunteers called forth by my proclamation of the 23d of April, in the present year,† the same to be apportioned, as far as practicable, among the several States and Territories and the District of Columbia according to population and to serve for two years unless sooner

*See p. 201.   †See pp. 203–204.

discharged. The proportion of each arm and the details of enlistment and organization will be made known through the War Department.

In witness whereof I have hereunto set my hand and caused the seal of the United States to be affixed.

[SEAL.]   Done at the city of Washington, this 25th day of May, A. D. 1898, and of the Independence of the United States the one hundred and twenty-second.

WILLIAM McKINLEY.

By the President:

WILLIAM R. DAY *Secretary of State.*

By the President of the United States of America.

A PROCLAMATION.

Whereas, for the reasons set forth in my proclamation of April 22, 1898,* a blockade of the ports on the northern coast of Cuba from Cardenas to Bahia Honda, inclusive, and of the port of Cienfuegos, on the south coast of Cuba, was declared to have been instituted; and

Whereas it has become desirable to extend the blockade to other Spanish ports:

Now, therefore, I, William McKinley, President of the United States, do hereby declare and proclaim that in addition to the blockade of the ports specified in my proclamation of April 22, 1898, the United States of America has instituted and will maintain an effective blockade of all the ports on the south coast of Cuba from Cape Frances to Cape Cruz, inclusive, and also of the port of San Juan, in the island of Puerto Rico.

Neutral vessels lying in any of the ports to which the blockade is by the present proclamation extended will be allowed thirty days to issue therefrom with cargo.

In witness whereof I have hereunto set my hand and caused the seal of the United States to be affixed.

[SEAL.]   Done at the city of Washington, this 27th day of June, A. D. 1898, and of the Independence of the United States the one hundred and twenty-second.

WILLIAM McKINLEY.

By the President:

J. B. MOORE, *Acting Secretary of State.*

By the President of the United States of America.

A PROCLAMATION.

Whereas by a protocol concluded and signed August 12, 1898,† by William R. Day, Secretary of State of the United States, and His Excellency Jules Cambon, ambassador extraordinary and plenipotentiary of

* See pp. 202–203.   † See p. 174.

the Republic of France at Washington, respectively representing for this purpose the Government of the United States and the Government of Spain, the United States and Spain have formally agreed upon the terms on which negotiations for the establishment of peace between the two countries shall be undertaken; and

Whereas it is in said protocol agreed that upon its conclusion and signature hostilities between the two countries shall be suspended and that notice to that effect shall be given as soon as possible by each Government to the commanders of its military and naval forces:

Now, therefore, I, William McKinley, President of the United States, do, in accordance with the stipulations of the protocol, declare and proclaim on the part of the United States a suspension of hostilities and do hereby command that orders be immediately given through the proper channels to the commanders of the military and naval forces of the United States to abstain from all acts inconsistent with this proclamation.

In witness whereof I have hereunto set my hand and caused the seal of the United States to be affixed.

[SEAL.] Done at the city of Washington, this 12th day of August, A. D. 1898, and of the Independence of the United States the one hundred and twenty-third.

WILLIAM McKINLEY.

By the President:
WILLIAM R. DAY,
Secretary of State.

BY THE PRESIDENT OF THE UNITED STATES.

A PROCLAMATION.

The approaching November brings to mind the custom of our ancestors, hallowed by time and rooted in our most sacred traditions, of giving thanks to Almighty God for all the blessings He has vouchsafed to us during the year.

Few years in our history have afforded such cause for thanksgiving as this. We have been blessed by abundant harvests; our trade and commerce have wonderfully increased; our public credit has been improved and strengthened; all sections of our common country have been brought together and knitted into closer bonds of national purpose and unity.

The skies have been for a time darkened by the cloud of war, but as we were compelled to take up the sword in the cause of humanity we are permitted to rejoice that the conflict has been of brief duration and the losses we have had to mourn, though grievous and important, have been so few, considering the great results accomplished, as to inspire us with gratitude and praise to the Lord of Hosts. We may laud and magnify His holy name that the cessation of hostilities came so soon as to spare both sides the countless sorrows and disasters that attend protracted war.

I do therefore invite all my fellow-citizens, as well those who may be at sea or sojourning in foreign lands as those at home, to set apart and observe Thursday, the 24th day of November, as a day of national thanksgiving, to come together in their several places of worship for a service of praise and thanks to Almighty God for all the blessings of the year, for the mildness of the seasons and the fruitfulness of the soil, for the continued prosperity of the people, for the devotion and valor of our countrymen, for the glory of our victory and the hope of a righteous peace, and to pray that the divine guidance which has brought us heretofore to safety and honor may be graciously continued in the years to come.

In witness whereof I have hereunto set my hand and caused the seal of the United States to be affixed.

[SEAL.]   Done at the city of Washington, this 28th day of October, A. D. 1898, and of the Independence of the United States the one hundred and twenty-third.

WILLIAM McKINLEY.

By the President:

JOHN HAY,
Secretary of State.

EXECUTIVE ORDERS.

EXECUTIVE MANSION,
Washington, May 7, 1898.

DEWEY,
Care American Consul, Hongkong:

The President, in the name of the American people, thanks you and your officers and men for your splendid achievement and overwhelming victory.

In recognition he has appointed you acting rear-admiral and will recommend a vote of thanks to you by Congress as a foundation for further promotion.

LONG.

EXECUTIVE MANSION,
Washington, May 19, 1898.

The SECRETARY OF WAR.

SIR: The destruction of the Spanish fleet at Manila, followed by the taking of the naval station at Cavite, the paroling of the garrisons, and the acquisition of the control of the bay, has rendered it necessary, in the further prosecution of the measures adopted by this Government for the purpose of bringing about an honorable and durable peace with Spain, to send an army of occupation to the Philippines for the twofold purpose of completing the reduction of the Spanish power in that quarter and of giving order and security to the islands while in the possession of the United States. For the command of this expedition I have designated Major-General ·Wesley Merritt, and it now becomes my duty to give instructions as to the manner in which the movement shall be conducted.

The first effect of the military occupation of the enemy's territory is the severance of the former political relations of the inhabitants and the establishment of a new political power. Under this changed condition of things the inhabitants, so long as they perform their duties, are entitled to security in their persons and property and in all their private rights and relations. It is my desire that the people of the Philippines should be acquainted with the purpose of the United States to discharge to the fullest extent its obligations in this regard. It will therefore be the duty of the commander of the expedition, immediately upon his arrival in the islands, to publish a proclamation declaring that we come not to make war upon the people of the Philippines, nor upon any party or faction among them, but to protect them in their homes, in their employments, and in their personal and religious rights. All persons who, either by active aid or by honest submission, cooperate with the United States in its efforts to give effect to this beneficent purpose will receive the reward of its support and protection. Our occupation should be as free from severity as possible.

Though the powers of the military occupant are absolute and supreme and immediately operate upon the political condition of the inhabitants, the municipal laws of the conquered territory, such as affect private rights of person and property and provide for the punishment of crime, are considered as continuing in force, so far as they are compatible with the new order of things, until they are suspended or superseded by the occupying belligerent; and in practice they are not usually abrogated, but are allowed to remain in force and to be administered by the ordinary tribunals substantially as they were before the occupation. This enlightened practice is, so far as possible, to be adhered to on the present occasion. The judges and the other officials connected with the administration of justice may, if they accept the authority of the United States, continue to administer the ordinary law of the land as between man and man under the supervision of the American commander in chief. The native constabulary will, so far as may be practicable, be preserved. The freedom of the people to pursue their accustomed occupations will be abridged only when it may be necessary to do so.

While the rule of conduct of the American commander in chief will be such as has just been defined, it will be his duty to adopt measures of a different kind if, unfortunately, the course of the people should render such measures indispensable to the maintenance of law and order. He will then possess the power to replace or expel the native officials in part or altogether, to substitute new courts of his own constitution for those that now exist, or to create such new or supplementary tribunals as may be necessary. In the exercise of these high powers the commander must be guided by his judgment and his experience and a high sense of justice.

One of the most important and most practical problems with which the commander of the expedition will have to deal is that of the treatment of property and the collection and administration of the revenues. It is conceded that all public funds and securities belonging to the government of the country in its own right and all arms and supplies and other movable property of such government may be seized by the military occupant and converted to the use of this Government. The real property of the state he may hold and administer, at the same time enjoying the revenues thereof; but he is not to destroy it save in the case of military necessity. All public means of transportation, such as telegraph lines, cables, railways, and boats belonging to the state may be appropriated to his use, but unless in case of military necessity they are not to be destroyed. All churches and buildings devoted to religious worship and to the arts and sciences, all schoolhouses, are, so far as possible, to be protected, and all destruction or intentional defacement of such places, of historical monuments or archives, or of works of science or art is prohibited save when required by urgent military necessity.

Private property, whether belonging to individuals or corporations, is to be respected, and can be confiscated only as hereafter indicated. Means of transportation, such as telegraph lines and cables, railways, and boats, may, although they belong to private individuals or corporations, be seized by the military occupant, but unless destroyed under military necessity are not to be retained.

While it is held to be the right of a conqueror to levy contributions upon the enemy in their seaports, towns, or provinces which may be in his military possession by conquest, and to apply the proceeds to defray the expenses of the war, this right is to be exercised within such limitations that it may not savor of confiscation. As the result of military occupation the taxes and duties payable by the inhabitants to the former government become payable to the military occupant, unless he sees fit to substitute for them other rates or modes of contribution to the expenses of the government. The moneys so collected are to be used for the purpose of paying the expenses of government under the military occupation, such as the salaries of the judges and the police, and for the payment of the expenses of the army.

Private property taken for the use of the army is to be paid for when possible in cash at a fair valuation, and when payment in cash is not possible receipts are to be given.

In order that there may be no conflict of authority between the army and the navy in the administration of affairs in the Philippines, you are instructed to confer with the Secretary of the Navy so far as necessary for the purpose of devising measures to secure the harmonious action of those two branches of the public service.

I will give instructions to the Secretary of the Treasury to make a report to me upon the subject of the revenues of the Philippines, with a view to the formulation of such revenue measures as may seem expedient. All ports and places in the Philippines which may be in the actual possession of our land and naval forces will be opened, while our military occupation may continue, to the commerce of all neutral nations, as well as our own, in articles not contraband of war, and upon payment of the prescribed rates of duty which may be in force at the time of the importation.

WILLIAM McKINLEY.

EXECUTIVE MANSION,
Washington, May 19, 1898.

The SECRETARY OF THE TREASURY.

SIR: The destruction of the Spanish fleet at Manila, followed by the taking of the naval station at Cavite, the paroling of the garrisons, and the acquisition of the control of the bay, has rendered it necessary, in the further prosecution of the measures adopted by this Government for the purpose of bringing about an honorable and durable peace with Spain, to send an army of occupation to the Philippines for the twofold purpose of completing the reduction of the Spanish power in that quarter and of giving to the islands order and security while in the possession of the United States. For the command of this expedition I have designated Major-General Wesley Merritt, and it now becomes my duty to give instructions as to the manner in which the movement shall be conducted.

It is held to be the right to levy contributions upon the enemy in all places which may be in military possession by conquest, and to apply the proceeds to defray the cost of the war, including the expenses of government during the military occupation. It is desirable, however, and in accordance with the views of modern civilization, to confine the exercise of this power, so far as possible, to the collection of such contributions as are equivalent to the duties and taxes already established in the territory. I have determined to order that all ports or places in the Philippines which may be in the actual possession of our land and naval forces by conquest shall be opened, while our military occupation may continue, to the commerce of all neutral nations, as well as our own, in articles not contraband of war, upon payment of the rates of duty which may be in force at the time when the goods are imported. In the execution of this policy it may be advisable to substitute new rates of duty and new taxes for those now levied in the Philippines. You are therefore instructed to examine the existing Spanish laws in relation to duties and taxes, and to report to me such recommendations as you may deem it proper to make with respect either to the rates of duties and taxes or to the regulations which should be adopted for their imposition and collection.

As the levy of all contributions in territory occupied by a belligerent is a military right derived from the law of nations, the collection and distribution of duties and taxes in the Philippines during the military occupation of the United States will be made, under the orders of the Secretary of War and the Secretary of the Navy, by the military or naval commanders, as the case may be, of the ports or places which may be in the possession of our forces. Your report is desired in order that I may be able to give the proper directions to the Department of War and of the Navy.

WILLIAM McKINLEY.

Executive Mansion,
Washington, May 19, 1898.

The Secretary of the Navy.

Sir: The destruction of the Spanish fleet at Manila, followed by the taking of the naval station at Cavite, the paroling of the garrisons, and the acquisition of the control of the bay, has rendered it necessary, in the further prosecution of the measures adopted by this Government for the purpose of bringing about an honorable and durable peace with Spain, to send an army of occupation to the Philippines for the twofold purpose of completing the reduction of the Spanish power in that quarter and of giving to the islands order and security while in the possession of the United States. For the command of this expedition I have designated Major-General Wesley Merritt, and it now becomes my duty to give instructions as to the manner in which the movement shall be conducted.

I inclose herewith a copy of an order which I have this day addressed to the Secretary of War, setting forth the principles on which the occupation of the Philippines is to be carried out.* You are instructed to confer with the Secretary of War in order that measures may be devised by which any conflict of authority between the officers of our army and navy in the Philippines may be avoided.

I have given instructions to the Secretary of the Treasury to examine the subject of the duties and taxes imposed by Spain in the Philippines and to report to me any recommendations which he may deem it proper to make in regard to the revenues of the islands.† I have informed him, however, that the collection and disbursement of the duties and taxes collected there will, as a measure of military right derived from the law of nations, be made, under the orders of the Secretary of War and the Secretary of the Navy, by our military or naval commanders, as the case may be, at the ports or places which may be in possession of our forces.

WILLIAM McKINLEY.

* See pp. 208–211.　　　　　　　　† See pp. 211–212.

EXECUTIVE MANSION,
Washington, July 4, 1898.

Admiral SAMPSON,
Playa del Este, Cuba:

You have the gratitude and congratulations of the whole American people. Convey to your noble officers and crews, through whose valor new honors have been added to the American Navy, the grateful thanks and appreciation of the nation.

WILLIAM McKINLEY.

THE PRESIDENT'S ADDRESS TO THE PEOPLE FOR THANKSGIVING AND PRAYER.

EXECUTIVE MANSION,
Washington, July 6, 1898.

To the People of the United States of America:

At this time, when to the yet fresh remembrance of the unprecedented success which attended the operations of the United States fleet in the bay of Manila on the 1st day of May last are added the tidings of the no less glorious achievements of the naval and military arms of our beloved country at Santiago de Cuba, it is fitting that we should pause and, staying the feeling of exultation that too naturally attends great deeds wrought by our countrymen in our country's cause, should reverently bow before the throne of divine grace and give devout praise to God, who holdeth the nations in the hollow of His hands and worketh upon them the marvels of His high will, and who has thus far vouchsafed to us the light of His face and led our brave soldiers and seamen to victory.

I therefore ask the people of the United States, upon next assembling for divine worship in their respective places of meeting, to offer thanksgiving to Almighty God, who in His inscrutable ways, now leading our hosts upon the waters to unscathed triumph; now guiding them in a strange land, through the dread shadows of death, to success, even though at a fearful cost; now bearing them, without accident or loss, to far distant climes, has watched over our cause and brought nearer the success of the right and the attainment of just and honorable peace.

With the nation's thanks let there be mingled the nation's prayers that our gallant sons may be shielded from harm alike on the battlefield and in the clash of fleets, and be spared the scourge of suffering and disease while they are striving to uphold their country's honor; and withal let the nation's heart be stilled with holy awe at the thought of the noble men who have perished as heroes die, and be filled with compassionate sympathy for all those who suffer bereavement or endure sickness, wounds, and bonds by reason of the awful struggle. And above all, let us pray with earnest fervor that He, the Dispenser of All Good, may speedily remove from us the untold afflictions of war and bring to our dear land the blessings of restored peace and to all the domain now ravaged by the cruel strife the priceless boon of security and tranquillity.

WILLIAM McKINLEY.

WASHINGTON, D. C., *July 8, 1898.*

General SHAFTER,
    Playa, Cuba:

Telegram which it appears you did not receive read as follows:

The President directs me to say you have the gratitude and thanks of the nation for the brilliant and effective work of your noble army in the fight of July 1. The sturdy valor and heroism of officers and men fill the American people with pride. The country mourns the brave men who fell in battle. They have added new names to our roll of heroes.

R. A. ALGER, *Secretary of War.*

EXECUTIVE MANSION,
Washington, July 13, 1898.

The SECRETARY OF WAR.

SIR: The capitulation of the Spanish forces in Santiago de Cuba and in the eastern part of the Province of Santiago, and the occupation of the territory by the forces of the United States, render it necessary to instruct the military commander of the United States as to the conduct which he is to observe during the military occupation.

The first effect of the military occupation of the enemy's territory is the severance of the former political relations of the inhabitants and the establishment of a new political power. Under this changed condition of things the inhabitants, so long as they perform their duties, are entitled to security in their persons and property and in all their private rights and relations. It is my desire that the inhabitants of Cuba should be acquainted with the purpose of the United States to discharge to the fullest extent its obligations in this regard. It will therefore be the duty of the commander of the army of occupation to announce and proclaim in the most public manner that we come not to make war upon the inhabitants of Cuba, nor upon any party or faction among them, but to protect them in their homes, in their employments, and in their personal and religious rights. All persons who, either by active aid or by honest submission, cooperate with the United States in its efforts to give effect to this beneficent purpose will receive the reward of its support and protection. Our occupation should be as free from severity as possible.

Though the powers of the military occupant are absolute and supreme and immediately operate upon the political condition of the inhabitants, the municipal laws of the conquered territory, such as affect private rights of person and property and provide for the punishment of crime, are considered as continuing in force, so far as they are compatible with the new order of things, until they are suspended or superseded by the occupying belligerent; and in practice they are not usually abrogated, but are allowed to remain in force and to be administered by the ordinary tribunals substantially as they were before the occupation. This enlightened practice is, so far as possible, to be adhered to on the present occasion. The judges and the other officials connected with the administration of justice may, if they accept the supremacy of the United States, continue to administer the ordinary law of the land as between man and man under the supervision of the American commander in chief. The native constabulary will, so far as may be practicable, be preserved. The freedom of the people to pursue their accustomed occupations will be abridged only when it may be necessary to do so.

While the rule of conduct of the American commander in chief will be such as has just been defined, it will be his duty to adopt measures of a different kind if, unfortunately, the course of the people should render such measures indispensable to the maintenance of law and order. He will then possess the power to replace or expel the native officials in part or altogether, to substitute new courts of his own constitution for those that now exist, or to create such new or supplementary tribunals as may be necessary. In the exercise of these high powers the commander must be guided by his judgment and his experience and a high sense of justice.

One of the most important and most practical problems with which it will be necessary to deal is that of the treatment of property and the collection and administration of the revenues. It is conceded that all public funds and securities belonging to the government of the country in its own right and all arms and supplies and other movable property of such government may be seized by the military occupant and converted to his own use. The real property of the state he may hold and administer, at the same time enjoying the revenues thereof; but he is not to destroy it save in the case of military necessity. All public means of transportation, such as telegraph lines, cables, railways, and boats, belonging to the state may be appropriated to his use, but unless in case of military necessity they are not to be destroyed. All churches and buildings devoted to religious worship and to the arts and sciences, all schoolhouses, are, so far as possible, to be protected, and all destruction or intentional defacement of such places, of historical monuments or archives, or of works of science or art is prohibited save when required by urgent military necessity.

Private property, whether belonging to individuals or corporations, is to be respected, and can be confiscated only for cause. Means of transportation, such as telegraph lines and cables, railways, and boats, may, although they belong to private individuals or corporations, be seized by the military occupant, but unless destroyed under military necessity are not to be retained.

While it is held to be the right of the conqueror to levy contributions upon the enemy in their seaports, towns, or provinces which may be in his military possession by conquest, and to apply the proceeds to defray the expenses of the war, this right is to be exercised within such limitations that it may not savor of confiscation. As the result of military occupation the taxes and duties payable by the inhabitants to the former government become payable to the military occupant, unless he sees fit to substitute for them other rates or modes of contribution to the expenses of the government. The moneys so collected are to be used for the purpose of paying the expenses of government under the military occupation, such as the salaries of the judges and the police, and for the payment of the expenses of the army.

Private property taken for the use of the army is to be paid for when possible in cash at a fair valuation, and when payment in cash is not possible receipts are to be given.

All ports and places in Cuba which may be in the actual possession of our land and naval forces will be opened to the commerce of all neutral nations, as well as our own, in articles not contraband of war, upon payment of the prescribed rates of duty which may be in force at the time of the importation.

WILLIAM McKINLEY.

General SHAFTER,   WASHINGTON, D. C., *July 16, 1898.*
        Commanding United States Forces, Santiago, Playa:

The President of the United States sends to you and your brave army the profound thanks of the American people for the brilliant achievements at Santiago, resulting in the surrender of the city and all of the Spanish troops and territory under General Toral. Your splendid command has endured not only the hardships and sacrifices incident to campaign and battle, but in stress of heat and weather has triumphed over obstacles which would have overcome men less brave and determined. One and all have displayed the most conspicuous gallantry and earned the gratitude of the nation. The hearts of the people turn with tender sympathy to the sick and wounded. May the Father of Mercies protect and comfort them.

WILLIAM McKINLEY.

EXECUTIVE MANSION,
Washington, July 21, 1898.

In view of the occupation of Santiago de Cuba by the forces of the United States, it is ordered that postal communication between the United States and that port, which has been suspended since the opening of hostilities with Spain, may be resumed, subject to such military regulations as may be deemed necessary.

As other portions of the enemy's territory come into the possession of the land and naval forces of the United States, postal communication may be opened under the same conditions.

The domestic postal service within the territory thus occupied may be continued on the same principles already indicated for the continuance of the local municipal and judicial administration, and it may be extended as the local requirements may justify, under the supervision of the military commander.

The revenues derived from such service are to be applied to the expenses of conducting it, and the United States postage stamps are therefore to be used.

The Postmaster-General is charged with the execution of this order in cooperation with the military commander, to whom the Secretary of War will issue the necessary directions.   WILLIAM McKINLEY.

EXECUTIVE MANSION,
Washington, August 6, 1898.

Ordered, That the graves of our soldiers at Santiago shall be permanently marked. The present marking will last but a short time, and before its effacement occurs suitable and permanent markers should be put up.

The Secretary of War is charged with the execution of this order.
                WILLIAM McKINLEY.

ADJUTANT-GENERAL'S OFFICE,
Washington, August 17, 1898.

Major-General MERRITT,
      Manila, Philippines:

The President directs that there must be no joint occupation with the insurgents. The United States, in the possession of Manila City, Manila Bay and Harbor, must preserve the peace and protect persons and property within the territory occupied by their military and naval forces. The insurgents and all others must recognize the military occupation and authority of the United States and the cessation of hostilities proclaimed by the President. Use whatever means in your judgment are necessary to this end. All law-abiding people must be treated alike.

By order Secretary War: H. C. CORBIN,
                Adjutant-General.

EXECUTIVE MANSION,
Washington, August 21, 1898.

Major-General MERRITT,
      United States Army, Manila:

In my own behalf and for the nation I extend to you and the officers and men of your command sincere thanks and congratulations for the conspicuously gallant conduct displayed in your campaign.
                WILLIAM McKINLEY.

EXECUTIVE MANSION,
Washington, August 21, 1898.

Admiral DEWEY,
    Manila:

Receive for yourself and for the officers, sailors, and marines of your command my thanks and congratulations and those of the nation for the gallant conduct all have again so conspicuously displayed.

WILLIAM McKINLEY.

ADJUTANT-GENERAL'S OFFICE,
Washington, December 4, 1898.

General OTIS,
    Manila, Philippine Islands:

By direction of the Secretary of War, following from the President is sent you for your early consideration.

CORBIN.

The President desires that Admiral Dewey and General Otis shall have an early conference and advise him what force and equipment will be necessary in the Philippine Islands. The President would be glad to have suggestions from these commanders as to the government of the islands, which of necessity must be by the Army and the Navy for some time to come. When these islands shall be ceded to us, it is his desire that peace and tranquillity shall be restored and as kind and beneficent a government as possible given to the people, that they may be encouraged in their industries and made secure in life and property. The fullest suggestions are invited.

WILLIAM McKINLEY.

EXECUTIVE MANSION, *December 9, 1898.*

By virtue of the authority vested in me as Commander in Chief of the Army and Navy of the United States, I hereby order and direct that during the occupancy by the military authorities of the United States of the island of Cuba and all islands in the West Indies west of the seventy-fourth degree, west longitude, evacuated by Spain, said islands shall constitute a collection district for customs purposes. Havana shall be the chief port of entry. An officer of the Army shall be assigned to such port, who shall be the collector of customs of the islands and of the chief port and shall have general jurisdiction over the collection of customs in the islands.

The ports of Matanzas, Cardenas, Cienfuegos, Sagua, Caibarien, Santiago, Manzanillo, Nuevitas, Guantanamo, Gibara, and Baracoa, in said islands, are hereby declared to be subports of entry, and an officer of the Army will be assigned to each of the subports, who will be the collector of customs of a subport and shall have general jurisdiction of the collection of customs at such port. He shall make weekly reports to the collector of customs of the islands at the chief port of all transactions at the subport over which he has jurisdiction, with copies of all entries of merchandise, duly certified.

The Secretary of War shall appoint such civilian deputy collectors, inspectors, and other employees as may be found necessary.

The collectors of the subports shall deposit all moneys collected by them with the collector of the islands, and a receipt from the collector of the islands must be taken in duplicate for all such deposits.

There shall be appointed an auditor, who shall be stationed at the chief port, whose duty it shall be to examine all entries of merchandise and if found correct to certify to them. Such auditor shall on the first of each month make a full and complete report, duly certified, to the Secretary of War of all duties collected at each port, with an itemized report of all expenditures made therefrom, which shall be referred to the Auditor for the War Department for audit.

All questions arising in the administration of customs in the islands shall be referred to the collector of the islands at the chief port for decision, from which there shall be no appeal, except in such cases as may be referred by the collector of the islands to the Secretary of War for his decision.

WILLIAM McKINLEY.

EXECUTIVE MANSION,
Washington, December 21, 1898.

The SECRETARY OF WAR.

SIR: The destruction of the Spanish fleet in the harbor of Manila by the United States naval squadron commanded by Rear-Admiral Dewey, followed by the reduction of the city and the surrender of the Spanish forces, practically effected the conquest of the Philippine Islands and the suspension of Spanish sovereignty therein.

With the signature of the treaty of peace between the United States and Spain by their respective plenipotentiaries at Paris, on the 10th instant, and as the result of the victories of American arms, the future control, disposition, and government of the Philippine Islands are ceded to the United States. In fulfillment of the rights of sovereignty thus acquired and the responsible obligations of government thus assumed, the actual occupation and administration of the entire group of the Philippine Islands become immediately necessary, and the military government heretofore maintained by the United States in the city, harbor, and bay of Manila is to be extended with all possible dispatch to the whole of the ceded territory.

In performing this duty the military commander of the United States is enjoined to make known to the inhabitants of the Philippine Islands that in succeeding to the sovereignty of Spain, in severing the former political relations of the inhabitants, and in establishing a new political power the authority of the United States is to be exerted for the security of the persons and property of the people of the islands and for the confirmation of all their private rights and relations.

It will be the duty of the commander of the forces of occupation to announce and proclaim in the most public manner that we come, not as invaders or conquerors, but as friends, to protect the natives in their homes, in their employments, and in their personal and religious rights. All persons who, either by active aid or by honest submission, cooperate with the Government of the United States to give effect to these beneficent purposes will receive the reward of its support and protection. All others will be brought within the lawful rule we have assumed, with firmness if need be, but without severity so far as may be possible.

Within the absolute domain of military authority, which necessarily is and must remain supreme in the ceded territory until the legislation of the United States shall otherwise provide, the municipal laws of the territory in respect to private rights and property and the repression of crime are to be considered as continuing in force and to be administered by the ordinary tribunals so far as practicable. The operations of civil and municipal government are to be performed by such officers as may accept the supremacy of the United States by taking the oath of allegiance, or by officers chosen as far as may be practicable from the inhabitants of the islands.

While the control of all the public property and the revenues of the state passes with the cession, and while the use and management of all public means of transportation are necessarily reserved to the authority of the United States, private property, whether belonging to individuals or corporations, is to be respected, except for cause duly established. The taxes and duties heretofore payable by the inhabitants to the late government become payable to the authorities of the United States, unless it be seen fit to substitute for them other reasonable rates or modes of contribution to the expenses of government, whether general or local. If private property be taken for military use, it shall be paid for when possible in cash at a fair valuation, and when payment in cash is not practicable receipts are to be given.

All ports and places in the Philippine Islands in the actual possession of the land and naval forces of the United States will be opened to the commerce of all friendly nations. All goods and wares not prohibited for military reasons, by due announcement of the military authority, will be admitted upon payment of such duties and other charges as shall be in force at the time of their importation.

Finally, it should be the earnest and paramount aim of the military administration to win the confidence, respect, and affection of the inhabitants of the Philippines by assuring to them in every possible way that full measure of individual rights and liberties which is the heritage of free peoples, and by proving to them that the mission of the United States is one of benevolent assimilation, substituting the mild sway of justice and right for arbitrary rule. In the fulfillment of this high mission, supporting the temperate administration of affairs for the greatest good of the governed, there must be sedulously maintained the strong arm of authority to repress disturbance and to overcome all obstacles to the bestowal of the blessings of good and stable government upon the people of the Philippine Islands under the free flag of the United States.

WILLIAM McKINLEY.

ADJUTANT-GENERAL'S OFFICE,
Washington, December 21, 1898.

General OTIS,
  Manila:

Answering your message of December 14, the President directs that you send necessary troops to Iloilo to preserve the peace and protect life and property. It is most important that there should be no conflict with the insurgents. Be conciliatory, but firm.

By order of the Secretary War: CORBIN.

EXECUTIVE MANSION,
Washington, December 22, 1898.

Until otherwise ordered no grants or concessions of public or corporate rights or franchises for the construction of public or *quasi* public works, such as railroads, tramways, telegraph and telephone lines, water works, gas works, electric-light lines, etc., shall be made by any municipal or other local governmental authority or body in Cuba, except upon the approval of the major-general commanding the military forces of the United States in Cuba, who shall before approving any such grant or concession be so especially authorized by the Secretary of War.

WILLIAM McKINLEY.

[Similar orders applying to Puerto Rico and to the Philippines were issued.]

EXECUTIVE MANSION,
Washington, December 22, 1898.

The SECRETARY OF WAR:

*   *   *   *   *   *   *

The major-general commanding the United States forces in Cuba and the senior naval officer of the American fleet in the port of Havana are directed to observe such arrangements and ceremonies for the evacuation of Havana, to take place on January 1, 1899, as may be communicated to them by the United States commissioners on evacuation. They will aid in carrying out such arrangements.

WILLIAM McKINLEY.

ADJUTANT-GENERAL'S OFFICE,
General OTIS,   *Washington, January 1, 1899—4.30 p. m.*
 Manila:

The President considers it of first importance that a conflict brought on by you be avoided at this time, if possible. Can not Miller get into communication with insurgents, giving them President's proclamation and informing them of the purposes of the Government, assuring them that while it will assert its sovereignty its purpose is to give them a good government and security in their personal rights.

By order Secretary War:

CORBIN.

EXECUTIVE MANSION,
The SECRETARY OF STATE: *Washington, January 20, 1899.*

My communication to the Secretary of War dated December 21, 1898,* declares the necessity of extending the actual occupation and administration of the city, harbor, and bay of Manila to the whole of the territory which by the treaty of Paris, signed on December 10, 1898, passed from the sovereignty of Spain to the sovereignty of the United States and the consequent establishment of military government throughout the entire group of the Philippine Islands.

While the treaty has not yet been ratified, it is believed that it will be by the time of the arrival at Manila of the commissioners named below. In order to facilitate the most humane, specific, and effective extension of authority throughout these islands and to secure with the least possible delay the benefits of a wise and generous protection of life and property to the inhabitants, I have named Jacob G. Schurman, Rear-Admiral George Dewey, Major-General Elwell S. Otis, Charles Denby, and Dean C. Worcester to constitute a commission to aid in the accomplishment of these results.

In the performance of this duty the commissioners are enjoined to meet at the earliest possible day in the city of Manila and to announce by a public proclamation their presence and the mission intrusted to them, carefully setting forth that while the military government already proclaimed is to be maintained and continued so long as necessity may require, efforts will be made to alleviate the burdens of taxation, to establish industrial and commercial prosperity, and to provide for the safety of persons and of property by such means as may be found conducive to these ends.

The commissioners will endeavor, without interference with the military authorities of the United States now in control of the Philippines, to ascertain what amelioration in the condition of the inhabitants and what improvements in public order may be practicable, and for this purpose they will study attentively the existing social and political state

*See pp. 219-221.

of the various populations, particularly as regards the forms of local government, the administration of justice, the collection of customs and other taxes, the means of transportation, and the need of public improvements.

They will report through the State Department, according to the forms customary or hereafter prescribed for transmitting and preserving such communications, the results of their observations and reflections, and will recommend such executive action as may from time to time seem to them wise and useful.

The commissioners are hereby authorized to confer authoritatively with any persons resident in the islands from whom they may believe themselves able to derive information or suggestions valuable for the purposes of their commission, or whom they may choose to employ as agents, as may be necessary for this purpose.

The temporary government of the islands is intrusted to the military authorities, as already provided for by my instructions to the Secretary of War of December 21, 1898,* and will continue until Congress shall determine otherwise. The commission may render valuable services by examining with special care the legislative needs of the various groups of inhabitants and by reporting, with recommendations, the measures which should be instituted for the maintenance of order, peace, and public welfare, either as temporary steps to be taken immediately for the perfection of present administration or as suggestions for future legislation.

In so far as immediate personal changes in the civil administration may seem to be advisable, the commissioners are empowered to recommend suitable persons for appointment to these offices from among the inhabitants of the islands who have previously acknowledged their allegiance to this Government.

It is my desire that in all their relations with the inhabitants of the islands the commissioners exercise due respect for all the ideals, customs, and institutions of the tribes and races which compose the population, emphasizing upon all occasions the just and beneficent intentions of the Government of the United States.

It is also my wish and expectation that the commissioners may be received in a manner due to the honored and authorized representatives of the American Republic, duly commissioned, on account of their knowledge, skill, and integrity, as bearers of the good will, the protection, and the richest blessings of a liberating rather than a conquering nation.

WILLIAM McKINLEY.

* See pp. 219–221.

INDEX

ILLUSTRATIONS

INDEX

A.

A. B. Plot.—William H. Crawford, of Georgia, was a prominent Democratic-Republican candidate for the Presidency in 1824. During the early part of that year a series of letters signed "A. B." appeared in a Washington newspaper charging him with malfeasance in office as Secretary of the Treasury. They were written by Ninian Edwards, of Illinois, who had just been appointed minister to Mexico, and who acknowledged their authorship. Apr. 19, 1824, Edwards presented a memorial to the House of Representatives making specific charges. These he failed to sustain, and Crawford was exonerated.

Abaco Island, negotiations for cession of lands on, for erection of light-houses, II, 276.

Abandoned Lands. (See Freedmen's Bureau.)

Abbot, Henry L., member of Gun Foundry Board, VIII, 161.

Aberdeen, Lord, mentioned, IV, 229, 316.

Abert, James W., expedition of, on Arkansas River referred to, IV, 450.

Abert, John J., map of Texas compiled under direction of, IV, 313.

Ableman vs. Booth.—An important Supreme Court case maintaining the constitutionality of the fugitive-slave law of 1850. Booth was tried before a commissioner appointed by the United States district court of Wisconsin for violation of the fugitive-slave law, and ordered to appear before the district court. Failing to do so, he was imprisoned by Ableman, the United States marshal for the district, but was released by the supreme court of the State on a writ of *habeas corpus*. Later he was indicted before the United States district court, but was again released by the State supreme court. In 1858 the case came before the United States Supreme Court. Booth had pleaded the unconstitutionality of the law. The court upheld the law and reversed the decision of the State supreme court.

Abnaki or Tarrateen Indians.—A confederacy of tribes of the Algonquian stock of Indians, who originally inhabited the northeastern part of the United States, including the present State of Maine and parts of adjoining States, and a portion of Canada. The Abnaki included the Penobscot, the Passamaquoddy, and the Amali-
cite tribes. They assisted the French in their wars with the English and were expatriated by the latter. The name is interpreted as meaning "the whitening sky at daybreak"— i. e., Eastern people.

Abolition. (See Slavery.)

Abolitionists.—A term applied during and preceding the Civil War to the members of the New England Anti-Slavery Society and those who held with them that "immediate unconditional emancipation without expatriation was the right of every slave and could not be withheld by his master an hour without sin." Jan. 1, 1831, William Lloyd Garrison commenced the publication in Boston of a paper called The Liberator, which advocated the immediate liberation of slaves, regardless of all laws or constitutional provisions to the contrary. At the beginning of the following year he organized the above-named society, with the foregoing as its chief doctrine. Near the close of 1833 a similar society was formed in Philadelphia. From this time the question assumed national importance. In consequence of his uncompromising utterances Garrison was indicted by grand juries in several Southern States and rewards were offered for his conviction. The New York Weekly Emancipator was another organ of the Abolitionists. Some strong pamphlets on the subject were: Justice and Expediency; or, Slavery Considered with a View to its Rightful and Effectual Remedy—Abolition, by John G. Whittier, Haverhill, Mass.; Appeal in Behalf of that Class of Americans Called Africans, by Lydia Maria Child; and The Sin of Slavery and Its Remedy, by Elizur Wright, a professor in the Western Reserve College. Abolition sentiments were not confined solely to the Northern States.

Aborigines.—A word used to designate the earliest inhabitants of a country. In America the term is applied generally to the Indians found by the early settlers.

Absentee Shawnee Indians, agreement between Cherokee Commission and, IX, 79.

Proclaimed, IX, 156.

Academy, Military. (See Military Academy.)

Academy, Naval. (See Naval Academy.)

Academy of Sciences, National, commission from membership of, to formulate plans for forestry system, IX, 735.

229

Administration.—This term is generally applied to the President and his Cabinet. The President, as chief executive officer of the nation, may direct, without consultation, the acts of any departmental chief, guided solely by the Constitution. He is authorized, however, to consult the heads of Departments. Washington consulted with his Attorney-General and Secretaries of State, War, and the Treasury. When in 1798 the Navy Department was established, Benjamin Stoddert, its chief executive officer, was admitted to the President's council. The Postmasters-General were not called into council until 1829, during William T. Barry's incumbency. Secretaries of the Interior and Agriculture were invited to seats at the council table immediately upon the establishment of their Departments, in 1849 and 1889, respectively.

Admiral.—This term was introduced into Europe during the Crusades. The rank of admiral in the United States Navy, as distinguished from vice-admiral and rear-admiral, was established by act of Congress July 25, 1866. There have been only three admirals, the first of whom was David G. Farragut, commissioned in 1866, and the next David D. Porter, commissioned in 1870, after Farragut's death. On the death of Porter, in 1891, the rank became extinct. In 1899 the rank was revived and George Dewey commissioned.

Admission of States.—The Declaration of Independence declares "that these United Colonies are, and of right ought to be, free and independent States" (I, 6). Its adoption on July 4, 1776, created as such the original thirteen States of the Union. Shortly before this date several of the Colonies had modified their original charters and established independent local governments. Oct. 10, 1780, the Continental Congress passed a resolution providing that western territory to be ceded to the United States "shall be settled and formed into distinct republican States, which shall become members of the Federal Union." The steps by which a Territory may become a State are: (1) A petition to Congress expressing the desire of the people for admission; (2) an enabling act passed by Congress stating the conditions of admission; (3) the adoption of a constitution and a form of State government by a convention of delegates chosen by the people; (4) the ratification of the constitution and the election of State officers by the people; (5) a proclamation by the President announcing that the Territory has become a State. The date of a State's admission to the Union is the date on which the act takes effect.

Afognak Island, Alaska, lands in, set apart as public reservation by proclamation, IX, 360.

Africa.—One of the great divisions of the Eastern Hemisphere. It extends from lat. 37° 20′ north to 34° 50′ south and from long. 17° 31′ west to 51° 22′ east. It is bounded on the north by the Mediterranean Sea; on the east by the Isthmus of Suez, the Red Sea, and the Indian Ocean; on the south by the Southern Ocean, and on the west by the Atlantic Ocean. The countries bordering the Mediterranean have long been inhabited by nomadic tribes of Moors and Arabs. In Egypt are found traces of the most ancient civilization. Between the cultivated tract which borders the Mediterranean and the Soudan stretches the Great Desert of Sahara, 2,000 miles from east to west and 1,000 miles from north to south. Over a great part of this region rain never falls and it is everywhere rare. The inhabitants of Africa are chiefly of the negro race, with Kafirs, Hottentots, Copts, Arabs, Moors, Berbers, and some Europeans. The prevailing religions are Mohammedanism and various forms of paganism. The Coptic and Abyssinian churches have a large following. The missionaries of the Roman Catholic and of the various Protestant churches have in recent years made many converts in Africa. Much has been written by recent explorers concerning the interior of Africa, its people, and its peculiar fauna and flora. The writings of David Livingstone and Henry M. Stanley afford perhaps the best general idea of the country. Most of the "Dark Continent" has been subjugated by European nations and its dominions apportioned among themselves according to their ability to hold, France and England claiming the greatest area. The area of the entire continent is about 11,508,793 sq. miles, containing a population of 163,953,000, as estimated by Petermann. The western coast was for many years ravaged by European slave traders, who captured the natives and sold them into bondage in foreign lands. (See also African Slave Trade.)

Africa:

Agents sent to, to receive slaves taken from vessels, II, 64.

Citizens of United States must not violate rights of inhabitants of, I, 408.

Natives of, in slavery. (See African Slave Trade.)

Naval force of United States stationed on coast of, referred to, IV, 320; V, 540.

Protectorate proclaimed by France over districts of. (See Liberia.)

Slavery on coast of, VII, 206.

Vessels of United States seized on coast of, III, 640; V, 486.

Africa, The, attempted seizure of Mr. Fauchet by commander of, VI, 143.

African Slave Trade.—Prior to the discovery of America negroes, like other savage races, either enslaved or put to death the captives taken in war. The deportation of the cap-

tives to the mines and plantations of the New World increased the value of the African and made slavery rather than death the prisoner's fate. This disposition of captives also led many petty chiefs to wage war for the prospective gain in human chattels. The aborigines of America having proved too weak for the work required of them, the Portuguese, who possessed a large part of the African coast, began the exportation of negroes, in which they were imitated by other nations of the Old World. Sir John Hawkins was the first Englishman to engage in slave traffic. The first importation of negro slaves was authorized in 1517. Extreme cruelty and inhuman treatment characterized their transportation. They were landed at Haiti and Santo Domingo and placed in the mines. In 1619 a Dutch vessel brought a cargo of slaves into the James River. Twenty negroes were sold to Virginia settlers. In 1713, by the treaty of Utrecht, Great Britain obtained the contract for supplying slaves to the Spanish West Indies. This stimulated the slave trade generally. Several of the Colonies attempted to prohibit the importation of slaves, but Great Britain forced the trade upon them. Virginia passed several acts forbidding the traffic, but they were vetoed by the British Government, as were also those passed by Pennsylvania in 1712, 1714, and 1717 and by Massachusetts in 1774. It was prohibited by Rhode Island and Connecticut in 1774 and by all the Colonies under the nonimportation covenant of Oct. 24, 1774, and was forbidden by nearly all the States during the Revolution. The slave-trade question was an important one in the formation of the Constitution. The Southern States, except Virginia and Maryland, insisted that no restriction should be imposed upon the traffic. A compromise was finally effected allowing Congress to prohibit it after 1808. The act of Mar. 22, 1794, prohibited the carrying of slaves from one foreign country to another by American citizens; that of May 10, 1800, allowed United States war ships to seize vessels engaged in such traffic; that of Feb. 28, 1803, prohibited the introduction of slaves into States which had forbidden slavery. In 1808 the importation of slaves into the United States was forbidden. The acts of Apr. 20, 1818, and Mar. 3, 1819, authorized the President to send cruisers to the coast of Africa to stop the slave trade. As no restrictions were ever placed upon domestic slave trading before its abolition in 1865, the surreptitious trade in imported slaves was not entirely given up until that time.

African Slave Trade (see also Slavery):

Abuse of United States flag referred to, IV, 281.

Act for suppression of, referred to, IX, 186.

Agents sent to Africa to receive slaves, II, 64.

American citizens engaged in, IV, 362.

Information regarding, requested, V, 374.

Cargo of African negroes—

Captured on coast of Cuba, and return of, to Africa discussed, V, 527, 593, 595.

Alabama—Continued.

Railroads in, memorial from legislature of, asking extension of time to complete, VI, 381.

Alabama Claims.—During the Civil War in the United States the Queen of England issued a proclamation of neutrality, May 13, 1861, granting belligerent rights to both combatants and forbidding her subjects to take part with either. Great Britain's laws prohibited the equipment of any land or naval forces within her dominions to act against any friendly power. Notwithstanding this prohibition, the *Alabama, Florida, Georgia, Shenandoah,* and other vessels were built in Great Britain for the Confederate States, and, regardless of the remonstrances of the American minister, were allowed to escape from British ports fitted out as commerce destroyers. In less than 2 months the *Alabama* had taken 27 prizes. After a long cruise among islands of the East and West Indies and along the coast of Brazil the *Alabama* came to anchor at Cherbourg, France. Off this harbor she was sunk by the U. S. S. *Kearsarge,* after having destroyed 58 vessels and about $6,550,000 worth of property. After the war the United States pressed a claim for damages against Great Britain. After much discussion it was agreed to submit the matter to a court of arbitration composed of Charles Francis Adams, appointed by the President of the United States; Sir Alexander Cockburn, by the Queen of England; Count Federigo Sclopis, by the King of Italy; M. Jacques Staempfli, by the President of Switzerland, and Viscount d'Itajuba, by the Emperor of Brazil. The commissioners met at Geneva, Switzerland, Dec. 15, 1871, Count Sclopis presiding. The United States were awarded $15,500,000 in gold in satisfaction for all claims. All claims to indirect damages were rejected, and Great Britain was held culpable for not doing more to prevent the sailing and success of the cruisers. The award was paid.

Alabama Claims:

Arbitration of, proposed by United States, and reply of Great Britain discussed, VI, 367.

Commission to take proof on, recommended, VII, 102.

Correspondence regarding mode of settling, VII, 121.

Court of Commissioners of—
Discussed, VII, 290, 342, 402, 418.
Time of duration of, extended, VII, 324, 342.
Discussed, VI, 367, 457, 579; VII, 33, 102, 367.
Transfer of indemnity to United States referred to, VII, 358.
Tribunal at Geneva for settlement of—
Award of, VII, 184.
Commissioners to report on distribution of, appointment of, recommended, VII, 185, 236.
Payment of, VII, 236.
Case of United States and counter case referred to, VII, 161, 164, 165.
Differences of opinion regarding powers of, VII, 166, 168.
Discussed, VII, 143, 184.

Alabama Claims—Continued.

Tribunal at Geneva for settlement of—Continued.
Legislation in connection with, urged, VII, 210.
Referred to, VII, 207.

Alabama Indians encouraged to reduce themselves to fixed habitation, I, 458.

Alabama, The, destruction of, by the *Kearsarge* referred to, VI, 256. (See also Alabama Claims.)

Alaska.—A territorial possession of the United States lying in the extreme northwestern part of North America. Its area is about 530,000 sq. miles, or about the area of the United States east of the Mississippi River exclusive of the Gulf States. It is valuable for its extensive seal and salmon fisheries. Recent discoveries of rich and extensive gold deposits in the Klondike region of the Yukon River have added greatly to the wealth and population of the territory and to its importance to the United States. It is sparsely settled, though the climate on the coast is quite salubrious. As early as 1859 official communications passed between the United States and Russia concerning the purchase of Alaska, or, as it was then called, Russian America. Russia was desirous of parting with the territory, and the fishing and trading interests favored the change of sovereignty. It was not until 1867, however, that definite steps were taken toward the transfer. In March of that year the Russian minister at Washington reopened negotiations, and on the 23d of that month Secretary Seward made an offer of $7,200,000 for the peninsula. A week later the minister communicated the Czar's acceptance, and at 4 o'clock on the morning of the 30th the treaty was signed, and later ratified by the Senate, and on Oct. 18 following the formal transfer was made at Sitka, Gen. Rousseau taking possession for the United States. In 1884 Congress provided a civil and judicial government for Alaska, with a governor and other necessary officers. Population (1890), about 32,000.

Alaska:

Attempted occupation of portion of, by Great Britain and Canada, IX, 665.

Attempts of Great Britain and Canada to establish post routes in, IX, 665.

Boundary line with British possessions—
Commission to determine, recommended, VII, 187.
Discussed, VII, 187; VIII, 332, 400, 500, 781, 815; IX, 526, 631.
Report regarding, referred to, VIII, 400.

Cession of, to United States—
Discussed, VI, 580, 688.
Referred to, VI, 600.
Treaty regarding, referred to, VI, 521, 524.
Appropriation for payment under, recommended, VI, 521, 580.

Chinamen in, cruel treatment of, VIII, 498.

Collection district established at Sitka, VI, 667.

Education in, appropriation for, recommended, VIII, 80; IX, 48.

Albany Convention.—One of the important predecessors of the Continental Congress and among the first definite steps taken toward national union. Upon a call issued by the Lords of Trade, commissioners from the Colonies of New Hampshire, Massachusetts, Rhode Island, Connecticut, New York, Pennsylvania, and Maryland met at Albany, N. Y., on June 19, 1754, to arrange a treaty with the Six Nations of Indians. Benjamin Franklin proposed and the convention adopted a plan for colonial union. It provided for a president-general of all the Colonies, with veto power, and a grand council to be composed of from 2 to 7 delegates from each Colony, chosen by assembly for a term of 3 years each. This grand council was to be authorized to equip forces for the common defense of the Colonies and to levy taxes for their maintenance and have control of all Indian affairs. The plan was rejected by the Crown because it gave too much power to the Colonies.

Albany Regency.—A combination of politicians of the Democratic party. Prominent among these were Martin Van Buren, William L. Marcy, John A. Dix, and Silas Wright. This combination was, it was charged, organized to manage and control that party in New York State from about 1820 to 1855. Their organization was quite thorough and complete, and its success was mainly due to this fact. A ma-

jority of those in the combination resided in Albany or operated from that city. The name arose from this circumstance.

Albemarle, The.—A Confederate ironclad ram built on the Roanoke River, below Weldon, N. C., in 1863. She was destroyed with a torpedo by Lieut. W. B. Cushing on the night of Oct. 27, 1864 (VI, 256). Before her destruction she did much damage to vessels of the United States. In 1867 she was raised, towed to Norfolk, and sold.

Aleutian Islands.—A chain of about 150 islands extending from the western extremity of Alaska to near the continent of Asia. In appearance they are rough and craggy, apparently of volcanic origin. There are several active volcanoes on the islands. The inhabitants—about 2,000—are variously regarded as of Asiatic or American origin. Their trade is chiefly in fish and furs. The islands belong principally to the United States by reason of the acquisition of Alaska. They were discovered by the Russians about the middle of the eighteenth century.

Algeria.—A country on the north coast of Africa, 293,659 sq. miles in area and containing a population of about 4,000,000. Its capital and principal city is Algiers. It comprises the ancient country of Numidia and a portion of Mauritania. For many centuries it was a nest of corsairs, who haunted the coasts of the Mediterranean Sea and the Atlantic Ocean as far as the North Sea, preying upon the commerce of all nations which refused to pay them tribute. To pay this tribute was deemed wiser by many European powers than to wage war against them. Following the example of other nations, the United States signed a treaty in 1795 agreeing to pay the Dey $1,000,000 for the ransom of American captives and promising an annual tribute (I, 123, 182). Algeria made war against the United States in 1815. Commodore Decatur, with 10 vessels, sailed against the Dey and met with such success that he was enabled to exact indemnity from the Dey himself, and also a treaty renouncing all claim to tribute, presents, or ransom, and a promise not to reduce prisoners of war to slavery (I, 562). France has since reduced Algeria to the dominion of her Government, organizing it as a colonial possession in 1834.

Algeria:

Consuls of United States in, I, 177, 392, 521.

Banished, I, 518.

Change in pay of, III, 99.

Powers of, should be increased, I, 248.

Salary of, should be increased, I, 248.

Unjustifiable proceedings toward, by Dey of, I, 453.

Declaration of war against, recommended, I, 554.

Hostile attitude of, toward United States, I, 440, 554, 575.

Imprisonment of American citizens in, I, 88, 98, 123, 148, 177, 200, 205, 207, 554.

Reference to, I, 152, 153, 210.

Treaty of peace with, I, 569; II, 110.

Treaty with, transmitted and discussed, I, 123, 182, 186, 192, 205, 569; II, 110.

Annulled by Algeria, I, 575.

Payments made under, referred to, X, 50.

Tribute to be paid by United States to, I, 123, 182.

Payment of, I, 337.

Vessels sold to, I, 247.

War with United States. (See Algerine War.)

Algerine War (see also Algeria):

Declaration of war by Congress recommended, I, 554.

Dey of Algiers commences war against United States, I, 440.

Information of amicable settlement, I, 440.

Termination of, I, 562.

Threatened by Algiers, I, 575.

Treaty of peace concluded, I, 569; II, 110.

Algonquin Indians.—A tribe of the Algonquian stock of Indians. At the time of the advent of white settlers into America the Algonquian linguistic division occupied by far the largest area of any of the Indian nations. The name means "those on the other side of the river"—that is, the river St. Lawrence. They were spread over the territory from Labrador to the Rocky Mountains and from Hudsons Bay to Pamlico Sound. Though this territory was not exclusively peopled by Algonquian Indians, some of their tribes had wandered to the west and south through hostile nations and established their family beyond the limits of the present stock. The Cheyennes and Arapahoes had strayed westward to the Black Hills and finally into Colorado, and the Shawnees had penetrated into South Carolina and Tennessee. There were hundreds of divisions of these Indians into tribes and confederacies, the principal of which were the Abnaki, Illinois, Pennacook, Powhatan, and Siksika confederacies and the Cheyenne, Arapaho, Sac, Fox, Conoy, Cree, Delaware, Kickapoo, Mahican, Massachuset, Menominee, Miami, Micmac, Misisaga, Mohegan, Montagnais, Montauk, Munsee, Nanticoke, Narraganset, Nauset, Nipmuc, Ojibwa, Ottawa, Pamlico, Pequot, Piankishaw, Pottawotomi, Shawano, Wampanoag, Wappinger, and Algonquin tribes. The latter tribe, from which the stock takes its name, occupied the basin of the St. Lawrence and its northern tributaries in Canada. They allied themselves with the French in the early wars. About 5,000 of this tribe are now located in the Provinces of Quebec and Ontario. The Algonquian stock numbers about 95,000 at this time, of whom some 60,000 are in Canada and the remainder in the United States.

Alien and Sedition Laws.—Two important acts of Congress passed by the Federalists in 1798. Their importance consists not so much in their essential character and the fact that they largely caused the downfall of the Federalist party as in their position in American history as a landmark beyond which it is unsafe for the law-making power to go. During the French Revolution American feeling was high and bitter. Many public speakers and writers openly advocated intervention by the United States in favor of the one side or the other, denounced the neutral attitude of the Government as cowardly and ungrateful, and heaped invectives upon the Administration. The fact that many of the newspapers in which the Government was so bitterly assailed were in the hands of foreigners had much to do with the passage of the alien act. This law authorized the President to order out of this country all such aliens as he might judge to be dangerous to the peace and safety of the United States or engaged in plotting against them. The sedition act provided heavy fines and imprisonment for any person who should conspire to oppose the United States Government or laws, or who should print or publish any false, scandalous, or malicious writings against the Government, Congress, or the President intended to bring disrepute or hatred upon them or to stir up sedition. These laws were regarded by the Republican party of that day as unconstitutional and were denounced by the Kentucky and Virginia resolutions as subversive of the liberty of speech and the press. They expired in 1800 and 1801, respectively. (See also Kentucky and Virginia Resolutions.)

Alien Contract Law, amendment of, recommended, X, 201.

Alien Laborers discussed, IX, 633.

Aliens in United States (see also Naturalized Citizens):

Abduction of foreigners claiming protection of United States should be made a crime, V, 12.

tures of three fourths of the several States or by conventions in three fourths thereof, as the one or the other mode of ratification may be proposed by the Congress; provided," etc. (Article V: I, 31). Many amendments to the Constitution have been proposed, but only 15 have been ratified. They relate to (1) freedom of speech, the press, and religion (I, 34); (2) right to establish State militia (I, 34); (3) quartering of troops in private houses (I, 35); (4) security against unreasonable search and seizure (I, 35); (5) capital crime (I, 35); (6) criminal prosecutions (I, 35); (7) trial by jury under common law (I, 35); (8) forbidding excessive bail or fines and cruel and unusual punishment (I, 36); (9) relation of constitutional to natural rights (I, 36); (10) powers reserved to the States (I, 36); (11) suits of nonresidents against States in Federal courts (I, 36); (12) election of President and Vice-President (I, 36); (13) slavery (I, 37); (14 and 15) abridgment of the franchise, etc., by States (I, 37, 38). The first 10 of the amendments were submitted to the several State legislatures by a resolution of Congress which passed on Sept. 25, 1789, at the first session of the First Congress, and were ratified by a sufficient number of States on or before Dec. 15, 1791. The eleventh amendment was declared adopted Jan. 8, 1798; the twelfth Sept. 25, 1804; the thirteenth Dec. 18, 1865; the fourteenth July 28, 1868, and the fifteenth Mar. 30, 1870.

Amendments. (See Constitution.)

America.—The entire Western Continent or grand division of the world, including North, Central, and South America and the adjacent islands. It was named in honor of Amerigo Vespucci, an early explorer, whose accounts of the country received wide publicity. It was visited by Norse navigators as early as about 1000 A. D., and there are myths of Chinese and Irish discoveries, but it was not until after its discovery by Columbus in 1492 that it became generally known to Europeans. In a treatise on the new country published in 1507, called Cosmographiæ Introductio, by Waldseemüller, a teacher of geography in the college of St. Dié in the Vosges, the name of America was proposed. On the north the country includes the unexplored regions of the Arctic Ocean, and extending south all the land between the Atlantic and Pacific. The northern portion of America consists of a central basin divided by a watershed and marked by Hudsons Bay and its feeders on the north and drained by the Mississippi, Missouri, and Ohio rivers and their tributaries flowing into the Gulf of Mexico on the south. This great basin is separated from the ocean on each side by ranges of mountains in the general form of the letter V, having the Rocky Mountains for one arm and the Appalachian system for the other, the latter being shortened by the depression of the St. Lawrence River, which runs transversely to the general course of other rivers of the great basin. In South America the Andes—a continuation of the Rocky Mountain system—

skirts the Pacific coast, and the general course of the rivers is to the southeast, except those north of the valley of the Amazon, which run north to the Caribbean Sea, an arm of the Gulf of Mexico. All America, from the frigid zone of the north through the torrid Tropics to the icy extreme of the south, is rich in either mineral or vegetable products or the flesh and furs of native animals. The original inhabitants of the country, called Indians (q. v.), have now almost entirely disappeared in most regions before the advance of the Caucasian race. The several political divisions of America are treated under separate headings.

America, Four Hundredth Anniversary of Discovery of:
Celebration of. (See Madrid, Spain; World's Columbian Exposition.)
Observance of, enjoined by proclamation, IX, 289.

America, Russian. (See Alaska.)

American National Red Cross:
Aid furnished Cubans by, discussed, X, 142, 161.
Work accomplished by, in Spanish-American War, discussed, X, 173.

American Nations, Congress of. (See Panama, Isthmus of.)

American Protective Association.—While disclaiming to be a political party, the A. P. A. has influenced results in many localities. Its principles, as set forth in a platform adopted at Des Moines, Iowa, in 1894, are (1) protection of our nonsectarian free public-school system; (2) no public funds or property to be used for sectarian purposes; (3) preserving and maintaining the Constitution and Government of the United States; (4) restriction of immigration, and (5) extension of time required for naturalization. The association was organized in 1887, and soon had well-attended councils in nearly every State of the Union.

American Republics, Bureau of.—A bureau established upon the recommendation of the Pan-American Conference of October, 1889, for the prompt collection and distribution of information concerning the American Republics. The information so far obtained has been of much commercial value. Its first report was transmitted to Congress in 1891 (IX, 212).

American Republics, Bureau of:
Bulletins of, transmitted, IX, 243, 350.
Discussed, X, 191.
Report of, transmitted, IX, 212, 334, 475, 569, 667, 751.

American Seamen. (See Seamen, American.)

American Society of Mechanical Engineers, memorial of, relating to Ericsson transmitted, IX, 130.

American System.—In his annual message, December, 1848, President Polk discussed what its authors and advocates called the "American system" (IV, 654). He insisted that this so-called system was founded on a departure from the earliest policy of the Government; that it depended on an enlargement of the powers of the Federal Government by construction and was not warranted by a just interpretation of the Constitution. One branch of the new system, it was claimed, was the establishment of a large national bank. The next branch was a high protective tariff, levied not to raise the revenue needed, but for protection merely; the next was a comprehensive scheme of internal improvements, and finally a plan for the distribution of the proceeds of the sales of the public lands among the States. But the term "American system," as most generally understood, is used to denote the policy of protection to home industries by means of high duties on imports. The term was probably first used by Henry Clay in the debates which preceded the enactment of the tariff law of 1824, when he called his plan of protective duties and internal improvements the "American system."

American System discussed by President Polk, IV, 654.

American Wood Preserving Co., purchase of machinery from, referred to, VIII, 89.

Ames, Fisher:
Commissioner to treat with Indians, nomination of, I, 260.
On committee to conduct inaugural ceremony of President Washington, I, 47.

Amin Bey, visit of, to United States referred to, V, 119.

Amistad Case.—The case of the United States against the Spanish vessel *Amistad.* A cargo of kidnapped Africans, who had been landed near Havana, Cuba, by a Portuguese slaver, was shortly afterwards placed aboard the Spanish vessel *Amistad* for shipment to Puerto Principe. On the voyage the negroes took possession of the vessel and ordered the crew to return to Africa; but the sailors brought her into American waters, where, off the coast of Long Island, she was captured by a United States war vessel and carried into New London, Conn., Aug. 29, 1839. On a libel for salvage the Supreme Court of the United States held on appeal that the negroes, having been kidnapped from a foreign country, were free men, and not bound by treaties with Spain.

Amistad, The:
Appropriations for claimants in case of, recommended, IV, 551; V, 209, 446, 511, 561.
Claims arising out of, V, 98, 184.
Negroes taken on board, referred to, III, 639.
Reference to, IV, 275; V, 641.
Release of, demanded by Spanish minister, III, 588.
Salvage due on, referred to, IV, 232.

Ammunition. (See Arms and Ammunition.)

Amnesty.—An act of pardon for political offenses. The effect of it is that the crimes and offenses against the State specified in the act are so obliterated that they can never again be charged against the guilty parties. When amnesty is proclaimed without restriction as to persons or localities it is called absolute. Numerous instances of qualified amnesty are found in ancient and modern history. When Thrasybulus overthrew the oligarchy at Athens he proclaimed an amnesty, excepting 30 tyrants

and a few of their followers. President Lincoln's first amnesty proclamation excepted all officers or agents of the Confederate government, all army officers above the rank of colonel, all naval officers above the rank of lieutenant, all persons who left the service of the United States to participate in the insurrection, and all those who had resigned from the military or naval service and afterwards participated in rebellion; also all those who had treated colored persons or those in charge of them otherwise than as prisoners of war (VI, 213). Dec. 25, 1868, President Johnson proclaimed absolute amnesty (VI, 708).

Amnesty (see also Pardons):
Proclamation of President Lincoln, VI, 213.
Discussed, VI, 189, 254.
Persons entitled to benefits of, defined, VI, 218.
Referred to, VI, 310.
Proclamations of President Johnson, VI, 310, 547, 655, 708.
Authority for, discussed, VI, 697.
Circular regarding, VI, 341.
Persons worth more than $20,000 to whom special pardons issued, referred to, VI, 385.
Referred to, VI, 461, 471, 524, 581.
Recommendations of President Grant regarding, VII, 153, 255.

Amphitrite, The, mentioned, X, 171.

Amsterdam, Netherlands:
Accounts of bankers of United States in, rendered, I, 121.
Loan contracted by United States with, I, 128.

Anatolia College, partial destruction of, by mob in Turkey, and indemnity paid for, discussed, IX, 440.

Anderson, Edward C., lieutenant in Navy, resignation of, referred to, V, 74, 76.

Anderson, Mary, act granting pension to, vetoed, VIII, 445.

Anderson, Richard C., minister to Panama, nomination of, II, 320.

Anderson, Robert:
Commander of forts in Charleston Harbor, V, 658.
Dispatches of, while in command of Fort Sumter referred to, VI, 12, 21.
Empowered to receive volunteer troops, VI, 18.
Flag over Fort Sumter at evacuation of, to be raised on ruins of, by, VI, 283.

Anderson, Sarah C., act granting pension to, vetoed, VIII, 712.

Anderson, Willis, proclamation offering reward for, II, 377.

Anderson Case.—A negro named Anderson was found wandering around the plantation of Seneca Diggs, in Missouri. He had no pass, and was arrested by Mr. Diggs as a fugitive slave. The negro plunged a knife into his captor's heart and made his escape to Canada. Upon demand he was surrendered to the Government of the United States under the extradition treaty. He was tried, but was discharged on a technical point.

Anderson Case referred to, V, 668.

Anti-Federalists.—A political party which opposed the adoption and ratification of the Constitution. Its fundamental principle was opposition to the strengthening of the National Government at the expense of the States. George Clinton, George Mason, and Patrick Henry were its leaders. Their strength was shown in the First and Second Congresses. They opposed Hamilton and his followers and championed a strict construction of the Constitution as against monarchical federalism. They later became merged into the Republican party, under the leadership of Jefferson. There have been many political parties termed "antis." As their names imply, they have opposed some specific measure, organization, or person. Though acting as political parties, they are not such in the strict sense of the word, for they have no affirmative policy and their claims are negative. Organized with a specific purpose to oppose, they disappear with the issue. Prominent among quasi parties have been the Anti-Lecompton, Anti-Masonic, Anti-Monopoly, Anti-Nebraska, and Anti-Renters.

Anti-Masonic Party.—In 1826 William Morgan and David C. Miller, of Batavia, N. Y., announced that they were about to publish an exposé of Freemasonry. Before the book was produced Morgan was arrested for debt and confined in the jail at Canandaigua, whence he disappeared on the night of Sept. 12, 1826. It was charged, but never shown to be true, that he had been foully dealt with by members of the Masonic order, as all attempts to discover his whereabouts were unavailing. The oft-reiterated charges aroused a bitter opposition to the order, and Thurlow Weed began the publication of the Anti-Masonic Enquirer at Rochester. In 1827 a convention was held by the Anti-Masons of Genesee County at Le Roy, N. Y., and a political party organized. It was claimed that many of the State officials were Masons and regarded their fraternal obligations as more binding than their civil oaths. The Anti-Masonic feeling grew rapidly. The party cast 33,000 votes in New York State in 1828, 70,000 in 1829, and 128,000 in 1830, though many of the latter were anti-Jackson men regardless of Masonry. In September, 1830, a national convention met at Philadelphia, Francis Granger, of New York, presiding. In 1831 they nominated William Wirt for President, but carried only the State of Vermont. In 1835, through a Democratic split, they elected Joseph Ritner governor of Pennsylvania. After this date the Anti-Masonic party declined as rapidly as it had arisen.

Anti-Monopolists.—A political party organized in 1884 upon a platform demanding economical government, the enactment and enforcement of equitable laws, the establishment of labor bureaus, laws providing for industrial arbitration, a direct vote of the people for United States Senators, a graduated income tax, payment of the national debt as it matures, and "fostering care" for agriculture. The platform denounced a protective tariff and the granting of land to corporations. One of the reforms demanded was the passage of an interstate-commerce law, which was subsequently enacted. In May, 1884, the Anti-Monopolists held a national convention at Chicago and nominated Gen. B. F. Butler for President of the United States. He was later indorsed by the Greenback-Labor party, and the combination was known as the People's Party. It polled about 130,000 votes.

Antietam (Md.), Battle of.—After the severe engagement at South Mountain, Lee's army concentrated to the west of Antietam Creek, a small stream flowing into the Potomac River about 8 miles above Harpers Ferry. Here, near the town of Sharpsburg, between the Potomac and the creek, Lee awaited the return of Jackson, who had been sent to capture Harpers Ferry. According to Federal accounts, Lee had not more than 25,000 men until Jackson's two divisions came up. Later he was joined by D. H. Hill's, McLaw's, and Anderson's divisions. This raised the strength of Lee's command to over 45,000 combatants. Sept. 16, 1862, McClellan's army, about 70,000 strong, was assembled on the east bank of Antietam Creek. This command was reenforced to 87,164, of which 4,320 were cavalry. About 60,000 of this force bore the brunt of the battle. On the evening of the 16th Hooker's division crossed the creek and began an attack, which darkness ended. Fighting was resumed at daylight on the 17th and continued all day, with varying success and terrific slaughter. Darkness again put an end to the carnage. McClellan did not renew the attack on the 18th, but orders were issued to resume fighting on the 19th. During the night of the 18th, however, the Confederates withdrew to the west of the Potomac and proceeded toward Martinsburg. A few days later McClellan occupied Martinsburg. The total loss of the Union army was 12,469 (2,010 killed); of the Confederates, 25,899. Other estimates of the Confederate loss are 9,000 to 12,000. The official Confederate accounts claim that this was a drawn battle, and that the total effective force of Lee was a little more than 35,000. This was called by the Confederates the battle of Sharpsburg.

Antilles.—A term used to designate generally all of the West India Islands except the Bahamas. The Greater Antilles are Cuba, Jamaica, Haiti, and Puerto Rico. The Lesser Antilles consist of two chains, one trending in a southeasterly curve from Puerto Rico to the Gulf of Paria, on the northeast coast of Venezuela, and the other stretching westward north of Venezuela to the Gulf of Maracaibo. The Spanish called the latter chain the Leeward Islands and the former the Windward Islands, but strictly speaking the Leeward Islands are all those north of the fifteenth parallel north latitude, and the Windward are south of that line. (See also the several islands.)

Antwerp, Belgium:
Industrial exposition at, IX, 524.
Loan contracted with, I, 128.

Apache Indians.—A confederation of the Athapascan stock of North American Indians, consisting of a dozen or more tribes. In 1598 they inhabited northwestern New Mexico, and later spread over the valley of the Gila River. By 1800 their range extended from the Colorado River eastward to central Texas, and later they made incursions into Mexico as far south as Durango. They were the terror of the early Spanish settlers, and since the annexation of their territory to the United States they have given the Government much trouble under the leadership of such famous braves as Cochise, Mangus, Colorado, and Geronimo (III, 514). White settlers opposed the plan of the Government to remove the Apaches to a reservation in New Mexico, and on Apr. 30, 1871, over 100 of the Indians were massacred at Fort Grant, Ariz. The Apaches, numbering some 6,200, are now confined to reservations in Arizona, New Mexico, and Oklahoma.

Apache Indians:
Agreement between Cherokee Commission and, IX, 333.
Appropriation for support of, etc., recommended, VIII, 105.
Imprisonment of, recommendations regarding, VIII, 789; IX, 60, 66, 536.
Suppression of hostilities among, discussed, VII, 572; VIII, 50, 358, 514, 789.
Treaty with, V, 191, 229; VI, 193, 375, 598.
War with. (See Indian Wars.)

Apalachicola Indians, treaty with, III, 37.

Apollo, The, seizure of, by American Government referred to, II, 100.

Appeals, Courts of. (See Courts of Appeals.)

Appointing Power of President. (See Executive Nominations.)

Appointments to Office. (See Executive Nominations.)

Appomattox (Va.), Battle of.—After the battle of Farmville, Apr. 7, 1865, Lee moved off toward the west, closely followed by Meade on the north side of the Appomattox. Sheridan, learning of the arrival of supply trains for Lee's army at Appomattox Station, pushed forward for that place with all the cavalry. Lee's hopeless condition being now apparent, Grant sent him a note inviting surrender. Lee replied, asking for terms, and Grant insisted upon the unconditional surrender of the Confederate Army of Northern Virginia. On the night of Apr. 8 Custer, who was in Sheridan's advance, reached Appomattox Station, where the Confederate advance had just arrived. He attacked the forces and captured 25 guns and 4 supply trains, a hospital train, and a park of wagons. During the night Sheridan came up, and by daylight was joined by Gen. Ord's command and the Fifth Corps. Lee was now only 20 miles from Lynchburg, his objective point. At first, underestimating the opposing forces, he ordered Gen. Gordon to make a reconnoissance and attack. Sheridan's cavalry withdrew to one side and revealed the lines of Ord's and Griffin's commands in line of battle. Gordon sent forward a white flag. Gen. Lee

then dispatched a note to Gen. Grant requesting an interview, which being allowed closed with the signing of articles of surrender of Lee's army and camp followers, about 27,000 men. The officers and men were paroled Apr. 12 and allowed to return to their homes. All public property was turned over, but the officers were allowed to keep their side arms and both officers and men to retain their private horses and baggage.

Apportionment.—The distribution of representation in the Federal House of Representatives and in the general assemblies of the various States. In the Continental Congress each State had but one vote. Long contention over the matter of representation finally led to the establishment of two Houses of Congress—the Senate, wherein all States should have equal representation regardless of area or population, and the House, in which each State should have representation in proportion to its population. A census was taken and 1 Representative was allowed for every 30,000 inhabitants. This rule governed apportionments for 70 years, though the ratio was changed from time to time as the population increased. In order to keep the number of members of the House a fixed quantity, the Thirty-first Congress decided to divide the representative population by 233 after each census, and by the quotient thus obtained divide the representative population of each State. This gave the number of Representatives to which each State was entitled, and when the total number fell short of 233, Representatives were allowed the States having the largest fractions after division. The ratio at the present time is 173,901. Methods of legislative apportionment vary in different States. President Washington vetoed a bill on this subject (I, 124). (See also Gerrymander.)

Apportionment:
According to census of 1890 necessary, IX, 118.
Bill for—
Approved and reasons therefor, IV, 159.
Vetoed, I, 124.
Delay in making, V, 145.

Appropriations:
Acts making, vetoed. (See the several subjects.)
Appropriation bill, special session messages regarding failure to pass, V, 394; VII, 452, 520.
Appropriation bills failing to pass, effect of, discussed, V, 570.
General legislation in appropriation bills objected to, V, 462, 489; VIII, 778.
Power of Congress to designate officer to expend, discussed, V, 597.
Reference to, V, 385.
Should not be made unless necessary, III, 29.
Suspension of, referred to, III, 622.

Arapaho Indians.—A tribe of the Algonquian stock of Indians living on the head waters of the Platte and Arkansas rivers, but also ranging from the Yellowstone to the Rio Grande. The name is said to signify "tattooed people."

Arctic Expeditions.—There have been many expeditions into the arctic regions. One of the most noted was that of Sir John Franklin, who was sent out by the British Admiralty in search of a northwest passage in 1845. Henry Grinnell fitted out and sent an expedition in search of Franklin in 1850 under command of Lieut. E. J. De Haven. In 1853 Grinnell dispatched another expedition on the same mission under Dr. Elisha K. Kane. Still another, gotten up by subscription, in 1860 went, under command of Isaac I. Hayes, in search of an open polar sea. In 1860 Charles F. Hall led an expedition in search of Sir John Franklin. July 7, 1881, Lieut. (now Gen.) Adolphus W. Greely was sent by the United States Government to establish an arctic observing station. He established the station in Discovery Harbor. Three parties were sent to his relief, but only the third, under command of Commander Winfield S. Schley, reached him, at Cape Sabine, whither he had retreated, June 22, 1884 (VIII, 248). Greely attained in his explorations lat. 83° 24′ north, a higher latitude than any before reached. In 1891 Lieut. Robert E. Peary conducted an expedition to Greenland under the auspices of the Academy of Natural Sciences of Philadelphia. He returned in 1892 and made another expedition in 1893 with the intention of surveying the northeast coast of Greenland. Thirty-five relief expeditions, public and private, were sent out from England and America in search of the Franklin exploring party between 1847 and 1857.

Argentine Republic.—The largest of what are known as the Spanish-American Republics.

The Andes Mountains form its western boundary. The Atlantic Ocean, with Uruguay and Brazil, bound it on the east, Bolivia and Paraguay on the north, and on the south it extends to Tierra del Fuego. Its chief river system is that of the Rio de la Plata. The jurisdiction of the Argentine Republic extends over the whole South Atlantic coast, including all of Patagonia east of the watershed of the Andes and all of Tierra del Fuego east of the meridian of the mouth of the Strait of Magellan, a total area of about 1,118,000 sq. miles, divided into 14 self-governing provinces and several outlying territories dependent on the general Government. Argentina declared its independence of the mother country (Spain) in 1816. The constitution is modeled closely after that of the United States. Suffrage is limited to those who can read and write. The President is elected for a term of 6 years and can not be reelected. The population is about 5,000,000. The principal industry is stock raising. Roman Catholicism is the established religion, but all religions are tolerated.

they were governed in ancient times by independent kings, but afterwards became tributary to the Assyrians. After the Assyrian period Armenia became a dependency of Persia and Media. Subsequently it was conquered by Alexander the Great, and later it passed under the nominal supremacy of Parthia and Rome. Then it was ruled by Persian, Byzantine, and Arabic governors until the dynasty of the Bagratides, which came to an end in 1045. The last vestige of Armenian independence was destroyed by the Mamelukes in 1375. Since that date they have been without an independent state, their country being divided between Persia, Turkey, and Russia. They still have an independent church, with the seat of government at Constantinople. In 1894 the greatest cruelties were visited upon Armenians in Turkey, in part because they were Christians. These atrocities were so great as to shock the civilized world. It was claimed that some of those upon whom outrages were committed were persons who had declared their intention to become citizens of the United States. Our consuls were sent there to make investigation of these atrocities and cruelties, and important diplomatic correspondence followed. Ships were sent as far toward the point of actual disturbance as it was possible for them to go, that refuge might be offered our citizens and missionaries. Assurances were given by Turkey that our countrymen should be secured and protected in all their rights (IX, 557, 637, 663, 715).

Arms and Ammunition.—The use of firearms followed close upon the invention (about 1320) of gunpowder. The use of gunpowder in military operations in England dates from 1346. Gibbon writes of a cannon used at the siege of Adrianople by Mahomet II in 1543. During that year the first English cannon was cast at Uckfield, Sussex. The arquebuse and musket were evolved by successive improvements on the large guns. The Swiss are said to have had 10,000 arquebusiers in 1471. At the battle of Pavia, in 1525, the Spaniards, under Emperor Charles V, with a force of 2,000 arquebusiers and 800 musketeers, defeated Francis I of France, the effectiveness of the firearms turning the tide

of battle. The flintlock came into use in 1630, was introduced into England under William III, and was effectively used as late as 1840 in the British army. The Landgrave of Hesse armed his followers with rifles in 1631. The Fergusson breech-loading rifle was in use throughout the entire Revolutionary War, though the flintlock was the principal weapon used. The first practical breech-loading firearm made in the United States was that patented by Hall in 1811. About 10,000 were made for the Government, the inventor superintending their manufacture at the Harpers Ferry Arsenal until his death in 1844. In 1854 Congress made an appropriation for breech-loading rifles, and experiments in this arm were conducted until the breaking out of the Civil War, during the progress of which the Government manufactured and purchased at home and abroad over 4,000,000 small arms of between 25 and 30 different patterns. Among these were breech-loading rifles and carbines and a magazine gun—the Henry. In 1866, 1869, and 1872 boards of officers were appointed to report upon a desirable small arm, and their investigations led to the adoption in 1873 of the Springfield rifle, which remained in use for 20 years. The decade between 1880 and 1890 witnessed a further development in small arms in the substitution of magazines for the single breech-loading apparatus, a decrease in the caliber of the ball, and the adoption of smokeless powder. The different forms of gunpowder used in military operations in America as well as in foreign countries until within the last few years were essentially the same as those used a century or more ago. Ever since the invention of gun cotton by Schönbein in 1845 scientific attention has been directed to the manufacture of smokeless powder. The French seem to have been the first to compound a successful smokeless powder for use in small arms. The material used is a form of melinite and belongs to the nitrocellulose or nitro-gun-cotton preparations. The powder is not absolutely smokeless, but the film of smoke arising from individual rifle firing is not visible for more than 300 yards. Among the latest explosives produced in the United States are cannonite, fulgurite, progressite, Americanite, and Schnebelite. The Army has several depots for the storage of powder, the principal one of which is near Dover, N. J. Powder for both branches of the service is supplied by private firms. Projectiles for the naval guns are made at the Naval Gun Foundry at Washington, D.C. The armor-piercing shells are carefully machined and tempered, and are much more expensive to make than ordinary projectiles. In 1892 the United States adopted the Krag-Jörgensen cut-off model magazine rifle. It weighs 8.7 pounds. Its barrel is 30 inches long and has a caliber of 0.3 of an inch. The magazine holds 5 cartridges, and Wetterin smokeless powder gives an initial velocity of 2,000 feet per second to the bullet. (See also Arsenals; Artillery.)

Arms and Ammunition:
Contract for, referred to, VI, 597.
Delivery of, to—
State arsenals referred to, V, 306.
Territories and District of Columbia, VIII, 574; IX, 27.
Estimates of expenditures for purchase and fabrication of, X, 24.
Exportation of, order prohibiting, VI, 125.
Extended, VI, 235.
Modified, VI, 178.
Recommended, I, 385.
Rescinded, VI, 335.
Gunpowder manufactory, erection of, recommended, III, 391, 497.
Loans of, to private citizens inquired into, II, 67.
Manufactory for small arms recommended, III, 391, 497.
Manufacture of—
Progress made in, I, 311, 486.
Should be encouraged, I, 265, 307, 455.
Statement of, II, 28.
Patent rifle, expenditures relating to procurement and properties of, II, 370.
Statement of, II, 198, 201, 221.
Supply of, I, 476.

Armstrong, John:
Commissioner to settle questions with Spain, order respecting appropriation for use of, X, 100.
Mentioned, I, 446, 449.

Army.—The earliest American military establishment consisted of two parts, the Continental Army, organized by the Continental Congress June 15, 1775, and the militia, organized by the States, averaging between the years 1775 and 1781 about 60,000 men, though often not more than half that number were in active service. The War Department was established by act of Congress Aug. 7, 1789. Nov. 5, 1783, the Army was disbanded and 1,000 men retained until the peace establishment could be organized. Though temporarily increased by Indian wars and troubles with France, the Federal forces numbered only from 3,000 to 5,000 men at the outbreak of the War of 1812. During that war the number of regular troops was more than 30,000, and 470,000 militia were enlisted. Up to the time of the Mexican War the Army averaged 9,000 men. During that war the regular troops enrolled numbered 27,000 and the volunteers 74,000. With the return of peace the regular forces were reduced to 10,000, and later increased to 12,000. During the first year of the Civil War the Regular Army was increased to 35,000 by the addition of 11 regiments, viz: One of cavalry, 1,189 officers and men; 1 of artillery, 12 batteries, 6 pieces each, 1,909 men; 9 of infantry, consisting of 3 battalions of 8 companies each, 22,068 officers and men; but the number of militia and volunteers was very much larger. President Lincoln's first call, issued Apr. 15, 1861, was for 75,000 men for 3 months' service (VI, 13). Later enlistments were mostly for 3 years. At the beginning of 1862 the number of volunteers in the Army was 550,000, and during the next three years it was 900,000. At the close of the war the Federal Army numbered 1,000,000. The total number of enlistments was 2,688,523 (VII, 202). In 1867 the "peace est.blishment" of the Regular Army was fixed at 54,641 men. It was then reduced by successive enactments to 25,000 enlisted men in 1875. At the beginning of 1898 the peace establishment of the Army consisted of 10 regiments cavalry, 8,410; 5 regiments artillery, 2,900; 25 regiments infantry, 13,525; 1 engineer battalion, 216; total, 25,051. This did not include brigade and staff officers. At the outbreak of the Spanish-American War 2 additional regiments of artillery were added to the regular forces and the line of the Army was reorganized on the basis of 2 battalions of 4 companies each to the regiment, and 2 skeleton companies. In case of a declaration of war these skeleton companies are to be manned, and, with 2 other companies for which authority to raise is granted, are to form the third battalion in each infantry regiment. Under the provisions of a law approved Mar. 2, 1899, the Regular Army establishment was fixed at about 27,700 officers and men. To meet the exigencies of the service in the newly acquired possessions, the President was authorized to maintain the Regular Army at a strength of 65,000 enlisted men and to raise a force of 35,000 volunteers, to be recruited from the country at large or from the localities where their services are needed, "without restriction as to citizenship or educational qualifications." This act provided that from and after its approval the Army should consist of 3 major-generals, 6 brigadier-generals, 10 regiments of cavalry, 7 regiments of artillery, 25 regiments of infantry, an Adjutant-General's Department, an Inspector-General's Department, a Judge-Advocate-General's Department, a Quartermaster's Department, a Subsistence Department, a Medical Department, a Pay Department, a Corps of Engineers, an Ordnance Department, a Signal Corps, 30 chaplains to be assigned to regiments or posts in the discretion of the Secretary of War, the officers of the Record and Pension Office, the officers and enlisted men of the Army on the retired list, the professors, corps of cadets, an army service detachment and band at the United States Military Academy, and such other officers and enlisted men as might thereafter be provided for. The law further provided for the reduction of the Army to its normal strength not later than July 1, 1901. Following is a list of the commanders of the Army since 1775, together with their respective ranks and the period of command: Gen. George Washington, June 15, 1775, to Dec. 23, 1783; Maj. Gen. Henry Knox, Dec. 23, 1783, to June 20, 1784; Capt. John Doughty (artillery), June 20, 1784, to Aug. 12, 1784; Lieut. Col. Josiah Harmar (infantry), Aug. 12, 1784, to Mar. 4, 1791; Maj. Gen. Arthur St. Clair, Mar. 4, 1791, to Mar. 5, 1792;

Maj. Gen. Anthony Wayne, Apr. 13, 1792, to Dec. 15, 1796; Brig. Gen. James Wilkinson, Dec. 15, 1796, to July 13, 1798; Lieut. Gen. George Washington, July 13, 1798, to Dec. 14, 1799; Maj. Gen. Alexander Hamilton, Dec. 14, 1799, to June 15, 1800; Brig. Gen. James Wilkinson, June 15, 1800, to Jan. 27, 1812; Maj. Gen. Henry Dearborn, Jan. 27, 1812, to June 15, 1815; Maj. Gen. Jacob Brown, June 15, 1815, to Feb. 24, 1828; Maj. Gen. Alexander Macomb, May 29, 1828, to June 25, 1841; Maj. Gen. Winfield Scott, July 5, 1841, to Nov. 1, 1861; Maj. Gen. George Brinton McClellan, Nov. 1, 1861, to Mar. 11, 1862; Maj. Gen. Henry Wager Halleck, July 23, 1862, to Mar. 9, 1864; Gen. Ulysses Simpson Grant, Mar. 9, 1864, to Mar. 4, 1869; Gen. William Tecumseh Sherman, Mar. 8, 1869, to Nov. 1, 1883; Gen. Philip Henry Sheridan, Nov. 1, 1883, to Aug. 5, 1888; Lieut. Gen. John McAllister Schofield, Aug. 14, 1888, to Sept. 29, 1895; Maj. Gen. Nelson Appleton Miles, Oct. 5, 1895, to present time (1899).

Army (see also Militia; War Department):

Absence of soldiers of, orders and proclamation regarding, VI, 119, 163.

Act—

Depriving President of command of, discussed, VI, 472.

Repeal of, recommended, VI, 673.

Fixing military establishment vetoed, I, 211.

Making certain debts of soldiers, lien against pay recommended, VIII, 85.

Providing for additional medical officers in volunteer service vetoed, VI, 88.

Annuities for families of deceased soldiers recommended, VII, 473.

Appointments in, IV, 281.

Appropriations for. (See War Department.)

Artillery tactics for use of, prepared, II, 361.

Asylum for aged and disabled members of. (See Soldiers' Home.)

Barracks, permanent, for, recommended, III, 537.

Battalion formation in, recommendations regarding, IX, 196, 446, 535.

Brevet appointments in, referred to, VI, 384.

Brevet rank—

Conferred for services in Indian wars, IV, 155.

Discussed, II, 439; V, 21.

Cavalry tactics for use of, prepared, II, 361.

Certificate of merit granted enlisted men, additional pay to, recommended, VIII, 148.

Chaplains for hospitals, recommended, VI, 48.

Clothing accounts of enlisted men in, referred to, VIII, 73.

Clothing for—

Foreign and domestic articles consumed in, X, 49.

Manufactured in United States referred to, II, 66, 116.

Command and rank in. (See Officers of, *post.*)

Commanders of. (See Enc. Art., Army.)

Conduct of, in Mexican War discussed, IV, 631.

Courts-martial in. (See Courts-Martial; Courts, Military.)

Army—Continued.

Deserters from—

Pardons granted. (See Pardons.)

Shot, referred to, IV, 437.

Desertions in—

Discussed, VIII, 348.

Legislation regarding military statute of limitations as applied to, recommended, VII, 572.

Portion of pay withheld so as to prevent, II, 305.

Reduction in, IX, 115, 196.

Discussed by President—

Adams, J. Q., II, 305, 359, 387.

Arthur, VIII, 49, 137, 245.

Cleveland, VIII, 347, 514, 788; IX, 445, 534, 726.

Grant, VII, 108, 193, 248, 294, 350, 406.

Harrison, Benj., IX, 115, 196, 319.

Hayes, VII, 472, 499, 572, 617.

Jackson, II, 603; III, 32, 113, 168.

Jefferson, I, 329, 345, 385, 406.

Johnson, VI, 363, 451, 575, 683.

Lincoln, VI, 48.

McKinley, X, 194.

Madison, I, 476, 486, 494, 505, 528, 548, 553, 564, 566.

Monroe, II, 50, 111, 188, 211, 254.

Pierce, V, 215, 286, 408.

Polk, IV, 410, 426, 631.

Tyler, IV, 89, 268.

Van Buren, III, 390, 537.

Washington, I, 60, 65, 83, 122, 126, 184.

Education in, discussed, VII, 618; IX, 447.

Elections, interference in, by, inquired into, III, 96.

Prohibited, VI, 668.

Enlisted men in, orders establishing limits of punishment for, IX, 167, 602.

Executions in, contrary to law referred to, II, 66.

Expenditures of. (See War Department.)

Failure of, on northern frontier, X, 49.

Force and disposition of, in 1810 referred to, X, 35.

Imprisonment of American citizens by officers in, referred to, VII, 55.

Increase in, III, 497; V, 15.

Recommended, I, 441, 549, 553; III, 254, 389; IV, 426, 504; V, 21, 87, 130, 178, 215, 286, 297, 408, 456, 458; VI, 48; VII, 376, 472; VIII, 50; IX, 41; X, 194.

Indian campaigns. (See Indian Wars.)

Indians enlisted in, discussed, IX, 196.

Insane asylum for. (See Government Hospital for Insane.)

Inspector-General of. (See Inspector-General of Army.)

Intoxicating liquors, order prohibiting sale of, in, VII, 640.

Lands granted persons who have served in. (See Lands, Bounty.)

Large standing, unnecessary in time of peace, I, 329; III, 170, 390; IV, 48, 413; V, 200.

Legislation for, referred to, VI, 387.

Measures for efficiency of, recommended, VII, 194, 294, 350.

Medical corps for, recommended, VII, 194.

Army of the Potomac. (See War between the States.)

Army Officers. (See Army.)

Arner, Philip, act granting pension to, vetoed, VIII, 443.

Arnold, Gerrard, reward offered for murderer of, II, 377.

Arnold, Samuel, implicated in murder of President Lincoln, proceedings of trial and verdict of military commission, VI, 334, 335, 336, 342, 347, 348.

Arny, W. F. M., mentioned, VI, 468.

Aroostook, The, claim of owners of, for compensation in searching for bodies and property lost in steamer *Oneida*, VII, 165.

Aroostook War. — Between 1837 and 1839 the unsettled boundary between Maine and New Brunswick came near leading to active hostilities on the Aroostook River. The governor of Maine sent troops to drive off the intruders and erect fortifications, and Congress authorized the President to resist the encroachments of the British. President Van Buren sent Gen. Scott to the scene, who arranged a truce, and it was agreed that the country should be occupied jointly, as before, pending adjustment of the boundary, which was definitively settled Aug. 9, 1842, by the Ashburton treaty (III, 516, 521, 530).

Arsenals. — Armories and arsenals were not established in the United States until the beginning of the Revolutionary War. In 1776 powder was manufactured in Virginia and brass cannon were cast in Philadelphia. An arsenal was established at Carlisle, Pa., the same year. Washington in 1777 chose Springfield, Mass., as a suitable location for an arsenal, and small arms were manufactured there in 1787. The establishment now has a capacity of 1,000 rifles per day. The arsenal at Harpers Ferry, W. Va., was begun in 1795, and from that time the number was gradually increased until 1860, when there were 23 arsenals scattered over the country. The principal ones at present in use are at Allegheny, Pa.; Augusta, Ga.; Benicia, Cal.; Cheyenne, Wyo.; Columbia, Tenn.; Fort Leavenworth, Kans.; Fortress Monroe, Va.; Fort Snelling, Minn.; Frankford, Pa.; Indianapolis, Ind.; Augusta, Me.; Springfield, Mass.; Governors Island, N. Y.; Rock Island, Ill.; St. Louis, Mo.; San Antonio, Tex.; Dover, N. J.; Vancouver, Wash.; Washington, D. C.; Watertown, Mass., and Watervliet, N. Y. Ordnance, arms, ammunition, and accouterments are manufactured at many of these places, the idea being to devote each to a special line of fabrication. Thus the establishment at Watervliet is devoted to the manufacture of heavy ordnance. Casting and assembling of guns are carried on at Rock Island and Benicia, as well as the making of leather goods. Naval guns and projectiles are made at Washington, D. C.

Arsenals and Magazines (see also Arms and Ammunition; Gunpowder Manufactory; National Foundry):

Augusta, Ga., arsenal at, referred to, II, 327.

Arsenals and Magazines—Continued.

Erection of armories on Western waters referred to, II, 136, 212, 239; IV, 226; X, 67.

Establishment of, recommended, I, 107.

In the South, I, 335.

Estimates of expenditures for establishment of armories, X, 24.

Frankford, Pa., arsenal at, referred to, VIII, 74.

Location for magazines, referred to, VI, 646.

Replenishment of, recommended, I, 265.

Rock Island Arsenal, appropriation for, recommended, VIII, 93, 151.

Sale of, not used by Government recommended, VII, 40, 195, 408.

Schuylkill Arsenal, appropriation for, recommended, VIII, 198.

Sites for—

Appropriation for, II, 203.

Referred to, I, 186; V, 363; VII, 194.

Art. (See Science and Art.)

Art Exhibition. (See International Exhibition of Fine Arts.)

Arthur, Chester A. (twenty-first President United States):

Annual messages of, VIII, 37, 126, 170, 235.

Biographical sketch of, VIII, 31.

Bland-Allison Act discussed by, and recommendations regarding, VIII, 46, 133, 243.

Civil service discussed by, VIII, 60, 145, 161, 167, 186, 252, 276.

Collector of port of New York, suspension of, discussed, VII, 511.

Constitutional amendment regarding approval of separate items of bill and veto of others recommended by, VIII, 138, 187, 253.

Death of, announced and honors to be paid memory of, VIII, 496, 497.

Death of President Garfield—

Announced to, and reply of, VIII, 14.

Discussed by, VIII, 33, 37.

Finances discussed by, VIII, 45, 132, 176, 242.

Inaugural address of, VIII, 33.

Internal improvements discussed by, VIII, 59.

Oath of office administered to, VIII, 25.

Portrait of, VIII, 30.

Powers of Federal and State Governments discussed by, VIII, 120, 184, 221.

Proclamations of—

Day of mourning in memory of President Garfield, VIII, 34.

Discriminating duties on vessels from Cuba and Puerto Rico suspended, VIII, 223.

Duties on foreign vessels suspended, VIII, 284, 285.

Extraordinary session of Senate, VIII, 34, 286.

Hundredth anniversary of surrender by Washington of commission as Commander in Chief, VIII, 223.

Quarantine regulations, VIII, 225.

Thanksgiving, VIII, 36, 123, 159, 225.

Treaty with Great Britain, termination of, VIII, 280.

Unauthorized occupancy of lands in Indian Territory, VIII, 224.

Unlawful combinations in Utah, VIII, 122.

World's Industrial and Cotton Centennial Exposition, VIII, 159.

Arthur, Chester A.—Continued.

State of the Union discussed by, VIII, 235.

Tariff discussed by, VII, 49, 134, 252.

Thanksgiving proclamations of, VIII, 36, 123, 159, 225.

Veto messages of—

Chinese immigration, VIII, 112.

Passengers by sea, VIII, 118.

Relief of Fitz-John Porter, VIII, 221.

Rivers and harbors, VIII, 120.

Discussed, VIII, 137.

Articles of Confederation, I, 9.

Signers of, I, 17.

Artillery.—The history of artillery begins shortly after the invention of gunpowder. It was used by the Moors of Algeciras, in Spain, in 1343, and Edward III had 4 cannon at Crecy in 1346. During the sixteenth century brass guns and cast-iron projectiles were adopted throughout Europe. Gustavus Adolphus, Sweden's greatest warrior, introduced the battalion system and reduced the use of artillery to a science in Europe. Napoleon owed much of his military success to his skill in the manipulation of artillery. In his wars are seen the first important effects of the concentration of fire, which in those days could only be produced by the massing of guns. Napoleon III made a special study of the subject of artillery, and the treatise begun and mainly written by him is a standard work on the subject. During the Civil War Gen. William F. Barry did much to improve the organization of the artillery of the Union Army. The aggregate of field guns was about 15,000, with 40,000 horses and 48,000 men. The Regular Army of the United States at present (1899) includes 7 regiments of artillery, with full quota of officers and enlisted men. Each regiment consists of 12 batteries of heavy artillery, 2 batteries of field artillery, and a band. The regimental officers are colonel, lieutenant-colonel, 3 majors, 16 captains, 16 first lieutenants, 14 second lieutenants, sergeant-major, and quartermaster-sergeant. The personnel of the battery consists of a captain and first and second lieutenants, with full quota of noncommissioned officers and 52 privates. The matériel of a mounted battery of field artillery on a war footing is 6 guns and 6 caissons, battery wagon, traveling forge, and 112 horses. In time of peace the numbers of men and horses are reduced to 60 and 80, respectively. (See also Army.)

Artillery:

Increase in. (See Army, increase in.)

Organization of, discussed, V, 288.

Artillery School of Practice at Fortress Monroe, Va., II, 374.

Artists, Foreign, tariff discriminations against, VIII, 207, 237, 339, 506; IX, 66.

Arundel Manuscripts, copy of, placed in Library of Congress, III, 226.

Arve, The, seizure of, by Haitien authorities, V, 144.

Ashburton Treaty.—A treaty concluded at Washington Aug. 9, 1842, between Great Britain and the United States. It was negotiated by Lord Ashburton and Daniel Webster. It settled the long-disputed boundary line between the United States and Canada. The former secured about seven-twelfths of the territory which had been claimed by both countries. Provision was also made by the treaty for the suppression of the slave trade and the mutual extradition of fugitives from justice (IV, 162, 194, 229).

Ashburton Treaty:

Discussed, IV, 162, 194, 229.

Reference to, IV, 281, 423; V, 227, 540.

Asheville, N. C., act for erection of public building in, vetoed, VIII, 475.

Ashley, Gen., attacked by Indians, II, 212.

Ashton, J. Hubley, agent of United States before Mexican and United States Claims Commission, report of, transmitted, VII, 425.

Asia.—The largest grand division of the globe. It is generally regarded as the birthplace of the human family and the seat of the most ancient civilization. Its area, including adjacent islands, is (estimated) 17,255,890 sq. miles. Its population was estimated in 1891 to be 825,954,000. Asia lies in the northern division of the Eastern Hemisphere. The mass of the continent is more than four times that of Europe. Though it contains more than one-half the inhabitants of the globe, its area is so vast that the density of its population is only one-third that of Europe. The continent embraces in a general way all climates, physical features, grades of civilization, and forms of religion. In the southeast and north the people are Mongolians, the central and west central portions are peopled by Aryan races, while the Arabs, Hebrews, and Syrians of the southwest belong to the Semitic group of peoples. The countries of Asia are Siberia, China, Korea, Borneo, Sumatra, Annam, Siam, Burma, India, Tibet, Afghanistan, Baluchistan, Turkestan, Persia, Arabia, Asiatic Turkey, and the Japan and Philippine Islands.

Asia:

Commerce with, extension of, recommended, V, 88, 167.

Cooly trade with, referred to, VI, 60.

Asiatic Squadron. (See Manila Harbor, Battle of.)

Asphaltum, disposition of lands in Utah containing, discussed, IX, 736.

Aspinwall, United States of Colombia:

Claims arising out of destruction of, VIII, 327, 537.

Imprisonment of American citizens in, VIII, 211.

Maltreatment of passengers and seamen on ships plying between New York and, VI, 212.

Vessels from, duties on, suspended, VIII, 284.

Assassination of President Lincoln. (See Lincoln, Abraham.)

Assessments, Political.—In the conduct of a political campaign considerable expense is incurred for hall rent, printing, music, and the necessary and legitimate efforts of each party to present its claims to the voters and secure their attendance at the polls. This expense is paid out of the campaign funds of the various political parties, the money therefor being raised in part by assessments upon both candidates and officeholders, as well as by voluntary contributions. In order to properly apportion the contributions to the campaign funds, assessments are sometimes based upon the salary of the office held or asked for at the hands of the party. There is a limit to legitimate party assessments and party expenses, beyond which lies the criminal field of blackmail and bribery. The first legal knowledge of the system of levying political assessments is found in the testimony taken before the Swartwout investigating committee of the House in the Twenty-fifth Congress. A former deputy collector of the port of New York testified that he had frequently been called upon to contribute while in the custom-house. As far as can be ascertained, assessments have been pretty general since 1840. It is claimed by the advocates of civil-service reform that a proper execution of the civil-service laws will largely, if not entirely, destroy the plan of assessments of persons holding office when made without their consent.

Assumption of State Debts.—Early in the second session of the First Congress Alexander Hamilton, Secretary of the Treasury, recommended that in order to restore public credit the Federal Government should fund and pay the foreign debt of the Confederation ($13,000,000), the domestic debt ($42,000,000), and also that it assume and pay the unpaid war debt of the States. Massachusetts, Connecticut, New York, New Jersey, and South Carolina favored the plan. Virginia strongly opposed the latter clause. She was sustained in her opposition by Maryland, Georgia, and New Hampshire. The influence of North Carolina thrown against the measure defeated it for the time, but it was revived later, and passed Aug. 4, 1790, it was claimed, by a combination of its friends with those of the measure locating the Federal capital on the Potomac. The amount authorized to be assumed by the Government in the liquidation of the State debts was $21,500,000, but the amount actually assumed was $3,250,000 less than that sum.

Astronomical Observatory:
Establishment of, recommended, II, 313.
Report of Simon Newcomb on improvements for, VIII, 203.

Asylum, Military. (See Soldiers' Home.)
Asylum, Right of, discussed, VI, 685; IX, 529.
Atchison and Pikes Peak Railroad Co. referred to, VI, 460.
Atkinson, Edward, international arrangement fixing rates between gold and silver coinage, report of, on, VIII, 592.
Atkinson, Henry:
Mentioned, II, 132.
Treaty with Indians concluded by, II, 321.
Troops sent to suppress Indians, commanded by, II, 387, 603.
Atlanta, The. (See *Weehawken,* The.)
Atlanta, Ga.:
Capture of, and orders regarding celebration of, VI, 238.

Atlanta, Ga.—Continued.
Collection of remains of officers and soldiers around, referred to, VI, 383.
Cotton Exposition at, VIII, 44.
Atlanta (Ga.), Battle of.—On the night of July 21, 1864, Gen. Hood transferred his forces before Atlanta to a point near Decatur, about 5 miles east of Atlanta. Sherman came up and, finding the works on Peach Tree Creek abandoned, proceeded to invest the city. At 11 a. m. of the 22d Hood surprised the left wing of Sherman's army, under McPherson, by a sudden movement from Decatur. The whole line was soon engaged. Gen. McPherson was killed in the action, and the command of the Army of the Tennessee devolved upon Gen. Logan. After 4 hours of fighting the Confederates retired into their main works about Atlanta, leaving their dead and wounded on the field. The total Confederate loss was estimated at about 8,000. The Federal loss was 3,722 killed, wounded, and missing. Sherman now drew his lines closely around Atlanta and prepared for a siege, but was unable to cut off Confederate supplies from Macon. Aug. 25 he gave up the idea of a direct siege. Sept. 1, however, a part of Hood's forces under Hardee having been repulsed at Jonesboro, Hood blew up his magazines and evacuated the city.

Atlantic Ocean:
Canal from—
Great Lakes to, commission to consider construction of, IX, 747.
Gulf of Mexico to, discussed, II, 429.
Junction between Pacific and, referred to, IV, 275; V, 140.
Desired, V, 280, 457.
Atlantic Telegraph:
Discussed, VI, 455.
Referred to, VI, 128, 181, 244.
Atlixco (Mexico), Battle of.—Immediately after the battle of Huamantla Gen. Lane pressed forward to relieve the garrison at Puebla. Oct. 18, 1847, he learned that Rea, with a body of guerrillas, was at Atlixco, a town about 10 leagues from Perote. The enemy was encountered on the afternoon of the 19th outside of the city, driven into and through the city, and dispersed. The Mexican loss was very severe, no less than 519 having been killed and wounded, while the Americans lost only 2 men.
Attorney-General.—The early American Colonies had their attorneys-general. The judiciary act passed in 1789 under the new Constitution provided for an Attorney-General of the United States to act as Government counsel, at a salary of $1,500. His official duties, which were light, did not interfere with the regular practice of his profession. It was not until 1814 that he became a member of the Cabinet, and not until 1858 was he provided with an assistant. In 1861 he was given charge of the United States district attorneys and marshals. In 1870 the office was reorganized as the Department of Justice. The following is a list of Attorneys-General in the order of their appointment from 1789 to date: Edmund Randolph, Virginia;

Austria—Continued.

Imprisonment of American citizens by, V, 153, 209.

Minister of United States to be sent to, III, 375.

Relations opened with, III, 489.

Treaty with, transmitted and discussed, II, 409, 445, 463, 534, 542, 594; IV, 584; V, 378.

Correspondence regarding, referred to, V, 26.

Referred to, II, 507, 551.

Troops of, departing to Mexico referred to, VI, 390, 391.

Vessels of, discriminating duties on, suspended by proclamation, II, 440, 441.

War with Hungary, sympathy of American Government with latter, V, 12, 41.

Wines from, duties on. (See Wines.)

Austria-Hungary.—A bipartite State in the interior of Europe consisting of the Cisleithan Empire of Austria and the Transleithan Kingdom of Hungary. Each of the two countries has its own parliament, the connecting links between them being a hereditary sovereign, common army, navy, diplomatic corps, and a controlling body known as the Delegations. The Delegations form a parliament of 120 members, one half of whom is chosen by Austria and the other half by Hungary. On matters affecting the common welfare the Delegations have a decisive vote, their resolutions requiring neither approbation nor confirmation. The Austrian and Hungarian members usually sit in separate council, but if unable to agree they must meet as one body. Their jurisdiction is limited to foreign affairs, finance, and war. The country has a circumference of about 5,350 miles, about 500 miles of which is seacoast, bordering upon the Adriatic. Three-fourths of the surface is mountainous. The area is 265,189 sq. miles, containing a population of 43,720,729. The principal industries are mining, the cultivation of fruit, and wine making. The leading mineral products are coal, iron, salt, gold, and silver, though none of the useful minerals is wanting. Hungary is second only to France in the abundance and quality of the wine produced.

Austria-Hungary (see also Austria; Hungary):

Claims of, regarding subjects killed in conflict in Pennsylvania, X, 177.

Consular convention with, VII, 144.

Empress-Queen of, assassination of, referred to, X, 177.

Minister of, to United States received, VIII, 131.

Minister of United States to, appointment of A. M. Keiley as, and refusal to receive, discussed, VIII, 325.

Naturalization treaty with, VII, 115, 144, 188.

Tariff laws of, evidence of modifications of, proclaimed, IX, 283.

Discussed, IX, 312.

Trade-marks, treaty with, regarding, VII, 160.

Autonomous Government for Cuba discussed, IX, 720; X, 134, 142, 161.

Auttose Towns, Destruction of.—The news of the massacre of whites at Fort Mimms having spread into Georgia, Brig. Gen. John Floyd, at the head of 950 State militia and 400 friendly Indians, started on an expedition of chastisement. Between midnight and dawn of Nov. 29, 1813, the attack was made on two Auttose villages. The Indians fought fiercely, but were overwhelmed, driven to the woods and caves, and shot. Floyd lost 11 killed and 54 wounded.

Aux Canards (Canada), Battle of.—The first encounter between British and Americans in the War of 1812. Gen. William Hull, governor of the Northwest Territory, placed in command of forces in Ohio and ordered to begin the invasion of Canada, crossed the river July 12, 1812, and dispatched Col. Lewis Cass with 280 men toward Malden. Crossing the Rivière aux Canards, a tributary of the Detroit, he drove the outposts in and took 2 prisoners, from whom he learned that some of the enemy had been killed and 9 or 10 wounded. Cass did not lose a man.

Auxiliary Navy in Spanish-American War, X, 166.

Averysboro (N. C.), Battle of.—Mar. 16, 1865, Gen. Slocum, in the advance of the Union army, encountered the Confederates under Gen. Hardee near Averysboro, in the narrow swampy neck between Cape Fear and South rivers. Hardee hoped to hold Sherman in check until Johnston could concentrate his army at some point in his rear. Incessant rains had made the ground so soft that men and horses sank deep in the mud. A severe fight took place amid showers of rain and gusts of wind. The whole line advanced late in the afternoon and the Confederates retreated to Smithfield, leaving 108 dead upon the field. The Federal loss was 77 killed and 477 wounded.

Aves Islands.—A group of small islands in the Caribbean Sea, belonging to Venezuela.

Aves Islands:

Claims regarding, paid, VI, 244.

Convention with Venezuela regarding, V, 580, 663.

Reference to, V, 668.

Ayer, Ira, mentioned, IX, 307.

Ayers, Edward, act granting pension to, vetoed, VIII, 419.

Aztecas or Aztecs.—A branch of the Nahuatl stock of Indians, supposed to be the original inhabitants of Mexico. They appeared in the valley of Mexico about the middle of the thirteenth century, and are said to have been journeying southward for 600 years. The conquest of Mexico by Cortez in 1519 put an end to the power of the confederacy between the Aztecas, Tezcucans, and the Tecpanecans. From analogy of language it is probable that they crossed the Pacific Ocean by way of the Aleutian Islands from Asia. There are, however, various theories as to their origin. They founded Tenochtitlan on the present site of the City of Mexico in 1325, and ruled an empire of 30,000,000 people. They were well advanced in the arts and sciences, as is evidenced by the remains of their temples, roads, and waterways. Only about 2,000,000 pure-blooded Aztecas are left in the mountains of Mexico. In stature they are small and somewhat resemble the Egyptians.

B.

Bachelder, Elvira, act granting pension to, vetoed, IX, 679.

Bacon's Rebellion.—An insurrection in 1676 of the people of Virginia, led by Nathaniel Bacon. In 1673 the Crown assigned the entire Province of Virginia for 31 years to Lords Arlington and Culpeper, with power to collect for their own use all quit rents, escheats, and duties; to name sheriffs and other officers; to make new counties, and in general to exercise the authority of absolute rulers. Sir William Berkeley, the English governor of the Colony, was very unpopular on account of his opposition to free education and a free press. He seemed to think that the function of a governor was to get as much as possible from the colonists for himself and his masters at the least possible cost. He also proved inefficient in protecting the settlers against the ravages of the Indians. He laid heavy taxes upon the people and restricted the franchise. An Indian uprising having occurred in the State, a force of 500 men gathered to march against them. Berkeley ordered them to disband. The colonists chose Bacon, who was a popular lawyer, as their leader, and, despite the refusal of the governor to commission him, he led his men against and defeated the Indians. Berkeley thereupon proclaimed Bacon a rebel, notwithstanding which the people chose him a member of the new assembly. On his way to Jamestown he was arrested and tried by the governor and his council, but was released on parole and left the capital. He soon returned with 600 men and again demanded a commission, which was granted. While Bacon was successfully engaged in another campaign against the Indians Berkeley again proclaimed him a rebel and a traitor. Bacon then burned Jamestown, the governor taking refuge on an English vessel in the harbor. The rebellion was carried on in a desultory way until the death of Bacon in 1677, when it collapsed for want of a leader. The English executed 23 of the participants in this rebellion. It is notable as the first formidable resistance to colonial authority in British America. The significance of its occurrence just 100 years before Independence has often been remarked. One of Bacon's lieutenants, put to death for his part in the rebellion, was William Drummond, who had served for a few years as the first governor of North Carolina.

Baden, fugitive criminals, convention with, for surrender of, V, 365.

Bagley, Worth, ensign in Navy, killed while attempting to silence batteries at Cardenas, Cuba, X, 169. (See also X, 157.)

Bahama Banks, negotiations with Great Britain regarding cession of keys on, to United States, II, 347.

Bahama Islands, formerly Lucayos.—A chain of islands stretching from near the north coast of Haiti to the east coast of Florida. They are separated from Florida by the Gulf Stream and from Cuba by the Old Bahama channel. There are some 3,000 of these islands, but only about 30 of any size. The principal ones, beginning at the northwest, are Great Bahama, The Abacos, Eleuthera, New Providence, Andros, Guanahani or Cat Island or San Salvador, Watling Island, Exuma, Long Island, Crooked Islands, Mariguana, Inagua, Little Inagua, Caicos, and Turks Island. The climate of these islands is very mild and salubrious, even in winter. The soil is thin, but produces cotton, maize, pineapples, oranges, etc. The Bahamas were Columbus's earliest discovery, but there is some doubt as to which of the islands he called San Salvador. The islands were occupied by the English in 1629 and finally secured to them by the treaty of 1783. Area, about 5,450 sq. miles; population (1891), 47,565. The capital is Nassau, New Providence.

Bahama Islands, postal convention with, VIII, 792.

Bailey, Theodorus, thanks of Congress to, recommended, VI, 76.

Bainbridge, William:
Commander of the—
 Constitution, I, 522.
 Philadelphia, I, 364, 368.
Letter of, regarding—
 Hostile act of vessel of Morocco transmitted, I, 364.
 Wreck of the *Philadelphia* transmitted, I, 368.

Baker, Eugene M., engagement with Piegan Indians referred to, VII, 50.

Baker, John, imprisonment of, in New Brunswick, II, 397, 403, 424.
Claims arising out of, III, 470.

Baker, John M., act for relief of children of, vetoed, VII, 171.

Baker, Marcus, member of Board on Geographic Names, IX, 212.

Baldwin, Charles H., thanks of Congress to, recommended, VI, 76.

Baldwin, Leon, indemnity paid by Mexico for murder of, in Durango, IX, 527.

Balestier, Joseph:
Mentioned, V, 152.
Mission of, to eastern Asia referred to, V, 145.

Ball, Farnaren, act granting pension to, vetoed, VIII, 668.

Ballard, David W., governor of Idaho Territory, removal of, referred to, VI, 596.

Ballard, Henry E., commander of the *United States,* III, 54.

Ballier, J. F., act increasing pension of, vetoed, VIII, 690.

Ballot.—Literally a little ball. The term is applied to all methods of secret voting, because formerly all such votes were taken by black and white balls placed in the same box, or balls of only one color were deposited in different boxes so arranged that none but the voter could see which box received his ball. The Greeks used marked shells (*ostrakon*), whence the term ostracism. The Romans used tickets for secret voting as early as 139 B. C. The first use

Bank of United States:
Act to extend charter of, vetoed, II, 576.
Referred to, III, 6.
Act to incorporate, vetoed, I, 555.
Agent should be appointed to take charge of books of, III, 163.
Attempts to impair credit of Government, III, 13, 31.
Bills of exchange discounted at, for benefit of Senators inquired into, III, 127.
No report on subject of, III, 128.
Bills of, should not be received for taxes, III, 163.
Charter obtained by officers of, from Pennsylvania for new bank, III, 252.
Charter of, not to be renewed, III, 7, 31.
Expiration of, discussed, II, 462; IV, 44.
Chartered rights of, should be terminated, III, 31.
Claims of, and course pursued by, III, 110.
Constitutionality of law creating, questioned, II, 462, 529; III, 6.
Dangers from, apprehended, II, 528; III, 5, 30.
Deposits in, removal of, III, 30.
President Jackson's paper to Cabinet on, III, 5.
Refuses to transmit, to Senate, III, 36.
Recommended, II, 600; III, 17.
Referred to, III, 167.
Views of President Tyler on, IV, 44.
Directors of, nomination of, and reasons therefor, III, 41.
Discussed by President—
Jackson, II, 558; III, 163, 251.
Polk, IV, 654.
Tyler, IV, 44.
Distresses caused by, needlessly produced, III, 109.
Reference to, III, 164.
Flagrant misconduct of, commented on, III, 10, 30, 111.
Government must be separated from, III, 110.
Judicial power, attempts to usurp functions of, III, 40.
Money in, not accounted for, III, 40.
Notes of, can not be reissued after expiration of charter, III, 252.
Organization of, referred to, I, 579.
Panic, attempts to bring about, III, 31.
Papers and funds in possession of, refusal to deliver, III, 39.
Pension money retained by, III, 109.
Political power of, fund employed by, to sustain, III, 30.
President of, funds at disposal of, for electioneering purposes, III, 30.
Recharter of, a leading question in election of President, III, 6, 30.
Sound currency, failure of, to establish, II, 462.
Stock in—
Government should be notified regarding, III, 163.
Should be sold, III, 111.
Subscriptions to, I, 104.
Substitute for, must be adopted by Congress, III, 9.

Bank of United States—Continued.
Successor of, can not reissue notes of, III, 252, 383.
With limited powers, recommended, II, 529.
Bank of United States vs. Halstead.—An important Supreme Court case on appeal from the circuit court of Kentucky in 1825. Property, including real estate, was offered for sale for debt. The highest bid being less than three-fourths of its appraised value, the property was not sold. The Supreme Court held that it had jurisdiction in a case to which the Bank of the United States was a party, and that a law which forbade the sale of land under execution for less than three-fourths of its appraised value did not apply to writs of execution issued by Federal courts.
Bank of United States vs. Planters' Bank of Georgia.—A suit brought by the Bank of the United States for payment of a promissory note which had been indorsed to it by the Planters' Bank of Georgia. The State of Georgia had stock in this bank. The action was brought against the Planters' Bank and also against the State. The Supreme Court in 1824 decided that if a State became a party to a banking or a commercial enterprise the State could be sued in the course of business, on the principle that when a government becomes a partner in any trading company it divests itself, so far as concerns the transactions of that company, of its sovereign character and takes that of a private citizen. The State, said the court through Chief Justice Marshall, is not a party—that is, an entire party—in the cause. It was also held that the circuit court had jurisdiction in such matters.
Bankhead, Charles:
Correspondence regarding northeastern boundary. (See Northeastern Boundary.)
Correspondence relative to mediation offered by Great Britain in controversy between United States and France, III, 217.
Bankhead, James, correspondence regarding Dorr's Rebellion, IV, 299, 302, 304, 305.
Banking System. (See Banks and Banking.)
Bankruptcy.—The Constitution gives Congress the power to establish uniform bankruptcy laws throughout the United States. Bankruptcy is a state of inability to pay all debts. It is also the process by which an individual may secure a discharge of his indebtedness by surrendering his property and complying with the law. Apr. 4, 1800, a bankruptcy act was passed by Congress and was repealed in December, 1803. In May, 1837, a commercial crisis occurred in the United States, causing failures to the amount of some $100,000,000. On account of the heavy losses incurred during the financial panic which ensued, another act was passed Aug. 19, 1841, and repealed in 1843. Another financial panic occurred in 1857, and most of the banks suspended specie payments. A third (the Lowell) act was passed Mar. 2, 1867, and repealed in 1878 (VII, 250). The present law was passed in

deposit for the Federal moneys. Certain State banks were chosen, and the allegation was made that the selection was determined not so much on the ground of fitness as on that of party fidelity, a principle also much in vogue in the granting of bank charters before the system of free banking came into use. The banks selected by Jackson as public depositories were in derision called "pet banks."

Banks, Postal Savings.—Post-office savings banks were established in England in 1861 to meet the growing wants of the people for a secure place of deposit for savings, as well as to provide facilities for those who live in places remote from any regular savings institution. At first only certain post-offices were designated, but the system was later extended to include all the money-order offices in the United Kingdom. The depositor receives a pass book in which his deposit is entered, and the postmaster-general is immediately notified by the officer receiving the money, and the deposit is acknowledged by the department. The money is invested in Government funds. The Government is responsible for all money received, so that depositors are secured against the dishonesty of officials. A depositor may apply for repayment at any post-office savings bank in the Kingdom, and may direct payment to be made to him at that or any other post-office savings bank. His order is forwarded to the postmaster-general in London, and in due time he receives a warrant on the designated office, which he presents, together with his pass book, and receives the money. Deposits can be made of sums ranging from 1 shilling to £50 in one year, the total never to exceed £200, including interest, which is at the rate of 2½ per cent. The success of postal savings banks in England and other foreign countries has attracted the attention of economists in the United States. Several Postmasters-General have advocated their establishment in the United States, and from time to time their recommendations have been favorably indorsed by the Chief Executives.

Banks, Postal Savings, recommended by President—
Arthur, VIII, 52.
Grant, VII, 198, 250.
Hayes, VII, 622.

Banks, Savings.—The first savings bank in the United States was the Boston Provident Savings Institution, incorporated Dec. 13, 1816. The Philadelphia Savings Fund Society began business the same year, but was not incorporated until 1819. In 1818 banks for savings were incorporated in Baltimore, Md., and Salem, Mass., and in 1819 in New York, Hartford, Conn., and Newport and Providence, R. I. There are now (1898) 980 such banks throughout this country, with deposits aggregating $1,983,413,564. These institutions are for the encouragement of the practice of saving money among people of slender means and for the secure investment of savings, the profits thereof being paid as interest to the depositors.

Banks, State.—A State bank is an institution chartered by a State legislature for banking purposes. It performs similar functions to national banks. After the expiration of the charter of the Bank of the United States in 1836 and the refusal of Congress to recharter it, State banks sprang up in large numbers throughout the Union. Each State passed its own law for their government or control. In many States these laws were not carefully drawn and the holders of their circulating notes not sufficiently protected against loss from suspensions and failures. Between 1836 and 1863 there were no United States banks or national banks, and only State banks existed. Being allowed to issue notes to circulate as currency, they availed themselves of this privilege, and in many instances the privilege was much abused. By act of Congress passed Mar. 3, 1865, all circulating notes of banks other than national banks were taxed 10 per cent. The result of this law was to speedily cause the retirement of all such notes.

Banks, State:
Deposits in, should be regulated by law, III, 112, 166.
Discussed by President—
Buchanan, V, 437.
Cleveland, IX, 554.
Jackson, III, 250.
Tyler, IV, 46.
Van Buren, III, 324, 331, 494, 540.
Measures should be adopted to correct unlimited creation of, IV, 46.
Number of, IX, 725.
Practicability of, commented on, III, 17, 31, 111, 165.
Public deposits should be placed in, III, 17.
Order regarding, III, 30.
Paper to Cabinet concerning, III, 5.
President Jackson refuses to transmit, to Senate, III, 36.
Reference to, I, 566.

Bannock Indians:
Agreement with, for disposal of lands, VIII, 68, 192.
Treaty with, VI, 700.
War with. (See Indian Wars.)

Baptist Church in Mississippi Territory, act for relief of, vetoed, I, 490.

Bar Harbor, Me., acts for erection of public buildings at, vetoed, VIII, 672; IX, 136.

Barbados, or Barbadoes, Island.—An island of the British West Indies, near the Windward group, situated east of St. Vincent, in lat. 13° 4' north, long. 59° 37' west. It exports chiefly rum, sugar, and molasses. It has a governor, executive committee, legislative council, and house of assembly. It was colonized about 1625. Area, 166 sq. miles; population (1891), 182,000.

Barbados Island, postal convention with, VIII, 792.

Barbary States.—The region on the north coast of Africa bordering on the Mediterranean Sea. It is capable of high cultivation. In early times the soil was made to yield richly. Barbary was known in ancient times as Mauritania, Numidia, Africa Propria, and Cyrenaica. It now comprises the countries of Barca, Tripoli, Fezzan, Tunis, Algeria, and Morocco. Besides Europeans, 7 distinct races inhabit the Barbary States — Berbers, Moors, Bedouins, Jews, Turks, Kuluglis, and Negroes. The population is about 11,000,000 Mohammedans and a floating population of Jews and Christians not enumerated. The language of commerce is Arabic, except in Tunis and Tripoli, where the Turkish language and government dominate.

Barbary States (see also the several States):
Consuls of United States in, referred to, I, 177.
Disbursements in intercourse with, I, 479.
Expenditures in relation to, X, 50.
Friendly disposition of, toward United States, I, 407, 475, 484; II, 80, 108.
Friendly intercourse with, I, 427, 518; II, 80.
Reference to, I, 333, 336, 337.
Relations with, X, 53.
Unsatisfactory, I, 326.
Barberick, Catherine, act granting pension to, vetoed, VIII, 821.
Barcelona, Spain, International Exposition of Labor at, discussed, VIII, 592, 814.
Baring Brothers & Co., funds of United States on deposit with, VI, 630.
Barnburners.—A title at one time given to a faction of the Democratic party in New York. The election of President Polk in 1844 resulted in a division in the Democratic party in New York. The faction supporting Van Buren and opposing the extension of slavery in the Territories was called Barnburners, while the faction which supported the views of the Administration was called Hunkers. Most of the Barnburners joined the Free Soil party in 1848, but returned to the Democratic party in 1852.
Barnes, Rachel, acts granting pension to, vetoed, VIII, 479, 701.
Barnes, William, act granting pension to, vetoed, VIII, 833.
Barnwell, R. W., commissioner from South Carolina, mentioned, V, 658.
Barrataria, Island of, pardon granted lawless inhabitants of, who aided in defense of New Orleans, I, 558.
Barron, Samuel, correspondence regarding war with Tripoli transmitted, I, 391.
Barrundia, J. Martine, seizure and killing of, on the *Acapulco* and action of American minister discussed, IX, 109.
Conduct of Commander Reiter regarding, referred to, IX, 134.
Papers regarding, transmitted, IX, 130.
Barton, Clara, president American National Red Cross, work accomplished by, in Spanish-American War discussed, X, 173. (See also X, 142, 161.
Barton, Thomas P., chargé d'affaires to France: Correspondence regarding claims against France. (See France, claims against.)
Request of, for passports complied with, III, 197.
Bash, D. N., act for relief of, vetoed, VIII, 642.
Bashaw, Hamet, correspondence relating to Hamet Caramalli transmitted, I, 392, and X, 30.

Bass, H. V., act granting pension to, vetoed, VIII, 833.
Batchelder, J. M., mentioned, VII, 612.
Baton Rouge (La.), Battle of.—Early in May, 1862, after the fall of New Orleans, Admiral Farragut passed up the river and raised the American flag over the public buildings in Baton Rouge, the capital of Louisiana. Gen. Thomas Williams was placed in command of the place with a small garrison. Aug. 5, 1862, he was attacked by Gen. Breckenridge, who was to have been assisted by the ironclad gunboat *Arkansas*. The *Arkansas* exploded her boilers and failed to reach the scene of action. The Confederates were repulsed. The Union loss was 200, including Gen. Williams, who was killed.
Battle of July 3, 1898. (See Santiago Harbor, Cuba.)
Batture Cases.—Before the cession of Louisiana to the United States a man named Gravier had purchased a plantation on the Mississippi River near New Orleans. Part of it afterwards became the village of St. Mary. An alluvial deposit or river beach formed in front of the village and was used as a landing place for the citizens of St. Mary. Under the law it was a part of the Gravier estate, which was purchased by Edward Livingston, of New York, who began improving it for his own use. The people protested on the ground of an old French law giving alluvions to the government. President Jefferson dispossessed Livingston of the Batture, and the latter immediately began suit against Jefferson and the United States marshal. The Supreme Court refused to entertain the suit against the President, but decided to restore the Batture to Livingston.
Baumer, Julius, expulsion of, from German Empire referred to, VII, 508.
Bavaria.—A kingdom of southern Germany, the second in area and population of the States of the German Empire. It consists of two unequal and disconnected parts, the larger eastern and the smaller western. The country produces wheat, rye, oats, and other cereals, tobacco, potatoes, hops, flax, wine, etc. Its government is a constitutional hereditary monarchy, with a king, an upper house, and a chamber of 159 deputies. It made a treaty with the North German Confederation in 1870 and entered the German Empire in 1871. Area, 29,282 sq. miles; population (1895), 5,773,836.
Bavaria (see also Munich):
Convention with, IV, 365; V, 227.
Fugitive criminals, convention with, for surrender of, V, 227.
Immigration treaty with, VI, 636.
Naturalization treaty with, VI, 690.
Bayard, James A., jr., nomination of, as director of Bank of United States declined, III, 48.
Bayard, James A., sr.:
Minister to conclude treaty of peace with Great Britain, nomination of, X, 46.
Minister to conclude treaty with Russia, nomination of, X, 46.

Bayard, Thomas F.:
Ambassador to Great Britain, report relating to speeches of, transmitted, IX, 603.
Secretary of State, VIII, 304.
Treaty with Great Britain on subject of fisheries concluded by, VIII, 604.

Bayard vs. Singleton.—This is one of the earliest instances of a court passing upon the constitutionality of an act of the legislature. Suit was brought before the court of appeals of North Carolina in 1787 for the recovery of certain property that had been confiscated and sold to the defendant under an act of the legislature passed during the Revolution which authorized the confiscation of the property of aliens. Counsel for defendant moved the dismissal of the case in accordance with an act of the legislature passed in 1785, which "required the courts, in all cases where the defendant makes affidavit that he holds the disputed property under a sale from a commissioner of forfeited estates, to dismiss the case on motion." Judge Ashe refused to dismiss the case, declaring the act of the legislature "unconstitutional and void." Judgment was, however, found for the defendant on the ground that aliens can not hold land, and if they purchase it the land is forfeited to the sovereign.

Baylor, J. R., act granting pension to, vetoed, VIII, 548.

Baylor, Thomas G., member of Gun Foundry Board, VIII, 161.

Bayonne Decree.—Apr. 17, 1808, Napoleon decreed that all American vessels which should enter the ports of France, Italy, and the Hanse Towns should be seized, "because no vessels of the United States can now navigate the seas without violating the law of said States." In his attempts to subdue England Napoleon sought to destroy her commerce with all neutral powers, including the United States.

Beach, Lansing H., commissioner in marking boundary between Texas and Mexico, VIII, 317.

Beale, Edward F., superintendent of Indian affairs in California, accounts of, referred to, V, 425, 485.

Bear, The. (See Emory, W. H.)

Bear Flag War.—An insurrection against the Mexican Government in June, 1846, supposed to have been instigated by John C. Frémont, then a captain of United States troops in California. A body of American settlers seized some Mexican horses and then captured the town of Sonoma. They raised a flag having on it the figure of a bear. In July, the Mexican War having begun, the Stars and Stripes were raised at Monterey, and the Bear Flag War became a factor in the American conquest of California. A battalion called the Bear Flag battalion was active in expelling the Mexicans.

Beatty, Erkuries, captain of infantry, nomination of, I, 63.

Beaufort, N. C., blockade of, removed by proclamation, VI, 89.

Beaumarchais, Caron de, claims of, against United States, I, 418, 583; II, 22, 127; X, 57.

Beaver Dam (Canada), Battle of.—After the retreat of the American army from the Niagara River they rendezvoused near the western end of Lake Ontario. Gen. Dearborn sent Lieut. Col. Charles G. Boerstler with 540 men to capture Beaver Dam. A British lieutenant, on June 24, 1813, with 40 or 50 men, but claiming to be the advance guard of 1,500 troops and 700 Indians, demanded of him to surrender. Boerstler surrendered 542 men, one 12-pounder and one 6-pounder cannon, and a stand of colors.

Beck, W. H., act granting pension to, vetoed, VIII, 439.

Beckley, R. D., act for relief of, reasons for applying pocket veto to, VIII, 485.

Bedini, Gaetano, complimentary mission of, to United States referred to, V, 228.

Bedloes Island, Statue of Liberty Enlightening the World to be placed on. (See Liberty Enlightening the World.)

Beecher, Henry Ward, public address to be delivered by, at Fort Sumter, VII, 283.

Beef Products. (See Animals and Animal Products.)

Beet Sugar. (See Sugar-Beet Culture.)

Beezeley, Louisa C., act for relief of, vetoed, VIII, 446.

Behring Sea. (See Bering Sea.)

Belantse-Etva Indians. (See Minnetaree Indians.)

Belden, S. A., & Co., claim of, against Mexico, V, 151.
Distribution of award in case of, referred to, VIII, 403.

Belding, H. K., act for relief of, vetoed, VIII, 540.

Belgium.—One of the smallest of European States. It consists of the southern part of the former Kingdom of the Netherlands as created by the Congress of Vienna, and is divided into 9 provinces. It is the most densely populated country in Europe. Belgium's greatest length from north to south is 112 miles, its greatest width from northwest to southeast 173 miles. It contained a population in 1893 of 6,195,355 in an area of 11,373 sq miles. Agriculture and manufactures are extensively carried on. Coal and iron are abundant and all the useful metals are wrought. Belgium is chiefly noted, however, for the fine fabrics manufactured from linen, cotton, and wool. Brussels and Tournay have large carpet manufactories, and the lace of Bruges sometimes commands a price of $200 per yard. The intellectual progress of Belgium has not kept pace with its material prosperity. The population is of a mixed German and Celtic origin. The Government is a limited monarchy, established by the revolution of 1830. The constitution was re-formed in a democratic direction in 1893. The Kongo Free State was mortgaged to Belgium in 1890.

Belgium (see also Antwerp; Brussels):
Chargé d'affaires to, recommended, II, 567.
Claims of United States against, III, 237.
Commercial relations with, IV, 340.

Belgium—Continued.

Consular convention with, VI, 690,695; VII, 43, 587.

Referred to, VII, 609.

Consuls of, in United States, exequaturs to, re voked, VI, 219.

Convention with, for regulating right of inheriting and acquiring property, V, 161; VIII, 235, 254,277.

Convention with, regarding Scheldt dues, VI, 194.

Copyright privilege extended, IX, 147.

Referred to, IX, 190.

Differences of France and, with Venezuela, IX, 638.

Fugitive criminals, convention with, for surrender of, V, 188; VII, 170, 262, 293; VIII, 108, 128.

Importations of American products to, restrictions upon, discussed, IX, 524; X, 178.

Decrees regarding, referred to, IX, 668.

King of, arbiter in cases of the *Georgiana* and *Lizzie Thompson*, VI, 152.

Loan contracted by United States with Antwerp, I, 128.

Monetary convention of Latin Union, adhesion to, declared by, VIII, 372.

Naturalization treaty with, VI, 694.

Postal convention with, VI, 577,685; VII, 249.

Trade-marks, treaty with, regarding, VIII, 212, 235.

Treaty with, transmitted and discussed by President—

Arthur, VIII, 108, 128.

Buchanan, V, 532.

Fillmore, V, 161, 168.

Grant, VII, 170, 262, 293, 321, 342.

Jackson, II, 633.

Johnson, VI, 695.

Lincoln, VI, 194, 258.

Polk, IV, 422,629.

Van Buren, III, 604, 622.

Approbation of Belgian Chambers not received, IV, 79.

Delay in exchange of ratifications, III, 25; IV, 151.

Disavowal of, by Belgium discussed, III, 98.

Termination of, referred to, VII, 288.

Bell, Henry H., thanks of Congress to, recommended, VI, 76.

Bell, P. Hansboro, mentioned, V, 73.

Belligerent Rights.—Rights granted by neutral governments to nations at war with each other, as distinguished from the unrecognizable rebellious subjects of a friendly power. Belligerent rights were accorded the Confederate States by Great Britain in a proclamation by the Queen recognizing the existence of war between the United States and the Confederate States and the right of each to exercise belligerent powers on the ocean, but not recognizing the national independence of the latter. It also enjoined neutrality upon British subjects. Such recognition of rights was also made by France and other leading commercial powers of Europe and by Brazil.

Belligerent Rights:

Accordance of, to Cuban insurgents deemed unwise by President—

Cleveland, IX, 636, 719.

Grant, VII, 31, 64, 338.

McKinley, X, 131.

Accorded Confederate States by foreign powers discussed, VI, 58, 126, 367.

Recognition and aid of foreign powers invoked by Confederate States, VI, 20, 45.

Belmont (Mo.), Battle of.—Nov. 1, 1861, Gen. Grant, who had been in command of posts in eastern Missouri and southern Illinois under Frémont, had a force of 20,000 men at Cairo. A Confederate force under Gen. Polk held Columbus, Ky., on the east bank of the Mississippi River. This position commanded the navigation of the river and was eventually made very strong, being defended by more than 120 heavy guns. On the Missouri bank opposite Columbus the Confederates had established a camp at Belmont, under Gen. Pillow. Grant learned that reenforcements were to be sent by way of this camp in November to join Price. He thereupon left Cairo and, sending a force to occupy Paducah, Ky., conveyed 3,000 men down the river in transports, accompanied by gunboats, to attack Belmont. The battle was fought Nov. 7, 1861. Few of the men had been under fire before. Grant's men took the camp, but were compelled to abandon it and return to their transports. The Federal loss was 485 killed, wounded, and missing. The Confederate loss was 642, including prisoners.

Bemis Heights (N. Y.), Battles of.—Also called battles of Saratoga and Stillwater. In the autumn of 1777 the condition of Burgoyne's army in the Upper Hudson Valley began to grow serious. Provisions were running short and the likelihood of effecting a junction with Howe at New York was remote. Gen. Gates had been sent by Congress to succeed Schuyler in command. The American army was daily increasing. Sept. 19 the two armies met at Bemis Heights, between Saratoga Lake and the Hudson River. An engagement took place between about 3,000 British and 2,500 Americans. Of the British about 500 were killed, wounded, or captured; the Americans lost 319. This fight, sometimes called the battle of Freeman's Farm, was not decisive, as the British held their ground. The Americans showed, however, that Burgoyne could not break through their lines. The two armies remained almost within cannon shot of each other for some 3 weeks. Oct. 7 Burgoyne, despairing of reenforcements, made a second attack, but was forced to retire to the heights near Saratoga. The numerical strength of the Americans was now greater than that of the British. Burgoyne was completely surrounded by Gates's army, which refused to engage him, but held him until famine forced his capitulation Oct. 17, 1777. The number of troops surrendered was 5,791, of whom 2,412 were Riedesel's Hessians. The battle of Saratoga is often treated

Berlin Decree.—An edict issued from Berlin Nov. 21, 1806, by Napoleon I. It declared a blockade of the British islands and ordered all Englishmen in countries occupied by French troops to be treated as prisoners of war. All trade in English merchandise was forbidden, and no letters in the English language were to be allowed to pass through French post-offices. No vessel directly from England or the English colonies was to be admitted into any French port, and by a later interpretation all merchandise derived from England or her colonies, by whomsoever owned, was liable to seizure, even on board neutral vessels. The decree reserved for future consideration the question whether vessels carrying English merchandise might not themselves be liable to seizure and confiscation. The object of this decree was to destroy the foreign trade of England, as well as to retaliate against the British for an order in council issued May 16, 1806, declaring a blockade of the coasts of Germany, Holland, Belgium, and France, from Brest to the Elbe, a distance of about 800 miles. No condemnations took place under the Berlin Decree. (See Embargo; Milan Decree; Orders in Council.)

Bermudas.—A group of small islands belonging to Great Britain in the North Atlantic, about 600 miles east-southeast of Cape Hatteras, in lat. 32° 15' north and long. 64° 51' west. They are also called Somers Islands for Sir George Somers, who was shipwrecked there in 1609. This led to their settlement by the English in 1611. The group forms an important naval and strategic position and is a British Crown colony. It includes some 350 to 500 islets, the largest being St. George and Great Bermuda. The area is 20 sq. miles and the population (1891) 15,123. The islands were discovered about 1522 by Juan Bermudez, for whom they were named. Bishop Berkeley, the eminent English philosopher, author of the poem in which occurs the noted line "Westward the course of empire takes its way," resided for some time in the Bermudas, and earlier still Shakespeare sang of the "still vex'd Bermoothes."

Big Bethel (Va.), Battle of.—One of the preliminary skirmishes of the Civil War. In June, 1861, Maj. Gen. B. F. Butler, of Massachusetts, was placed in command of the Federal forces in eastern Virginia. He established headquarters at Fortress Monroe and was soon in command of 10,000 men. June 9 Butler sent Brig. Gen. E. W. Peirce with a detachment of 3,500 men (composed of New York, Massachusetts, and Vermont infantry and a battery of artillery) to dislodge the Confederates at Big and Little Bethel under Gen. J. B. Magruder's command. Magruder's force (1,400) had made frequent raids upon the Federal lines. The attack, which was intended as a surprise, was made by the Union forces on the morning of June 10 and was repulsed. The Union loss was 76. Among the killed was Maj. Theodore Winthrop. The Confederate loss was 1 killed and 4 wounded. Big Bethel was the first real battle of the war.

Big Black (Miss.), Battle of.—May 17, 1863, the day after the battle of Champion Hills, Grant's army pushed on toward Vicksburg. McClernand's corps, in advance, soon came upon Pemberton's army, strongly intrenched on both sides of the Big Black River. The Confederate batteries posted on the high bluffs were carried after a sharp engagement, the Federal assault being led by Lawler's brigade. The Confederates retreated. Seventeen pieces of artillery and about 1,200 prisoners were here taken. A portion of Pemberton's outposts crossed the river on temporary bridges, which they destroyed behind them, and joined the main body of the army in the retreat into the fortifications at Vicksburg. The Federal loss was 279.

Big Witchitaw River, exploration of, referred to, V, 364.

Bigamy. (See Mormon Church; Polygamy.)

Bill of Rights.—The earliest colonial or State declaration of American rights, after the "Body of Laws" of Massachusetts, in 1640, was that which accompanied the Virginia constitution of 1776. It was based upon the English Bill of Rights of 1689. The latter was an instrument signed by William and Mary when accepting the crown of England from the Convention Parliament. It asserted the right of subjects to petition, the right of Parliament to freedom of debate, the right of electors to choose representatives freely, and other privileges. This Bill of Rights, which contained the fundamental principles of political liberty, was not extended to the Colonies. Other State constitutions in defining the rights of the citizen as against the scope of the state largely followed the phraseology of this famous instrument. The National Constitution was harshly criticised on account of the omission of some such guaranty of personal rights, and might have failed of ratification had not the Federalists promised to incorporate such a set of statements. The first ten amendments stand as the partial fulfillment of their promises. (See also Amendments.)

Bills and Acts:

Acts to be published in certain newspapers, VII, 162.

Approved but not signed, whether in force, discussed, II, 287.

Consideration by President, time allowed for, discussed, V, 462, 529.

Constitutional amendment regarding approval of separate items of bill and veto of others recommended, VII, 242; VIII, 138, 187, 253.

Duly certified and approved which had not passed, discussed, III, 134.

Effect on, of adjournment of Congress before expiration of 10 days after presentation to President discussed, VI, 599.

List of acts transmitted, VII, 9.

Bimetallic Conference. (See International Monetary Conference.)

Bimetallism.—The use of two metals as money at relative values set by legislative enactment; the doctrine that two metals can and ought, at the same time and in the same country, to be adopted as standards of value and bear

to each other a fixed ratio established by the Government. As used in this country, the term usually refers to the use of gold and silver at a fixed relative value established by law. Monometallism is the doctrine that only one metal ought to be so used. (See also Coinage Laws.)

Bingham, D. J., act granting pension to, returned, VIII, 404.

Bingham, John A., special judge-advocate in trial of persons implicated in assassination of President Lincoln, VI, 336.

Biographical Sketches of President—

Adams, John, I, 227.

Adams, J. Q., II, 291.

Arthur, VIII, 31.

Buchanan, V, 429.

Cleveland, VIII, 297

Fillmore, V, 63.

Garfield, VIII, 3.

Grant, VII, 3.

Harrison, Benj., IX, 3.

Harrison, W. H., IV, 3.

Hayes, VII, 439.

Jackson, II, 435.

Jefferson, I, 319.

Johnson, VI, 301.

Lincoln, VI, 3.

McKinley, X, 125.

Madison, I, 465.

Monroe, II, 3.

Pierce, V, 195.

Polk, IV, 371.

Taylor, V, 3.

Tyler, IV, 35.

Van Buren, III, 311.

Washington, I, 41.

Bishop, Nathan, member of Indian commission, VII, 23.

Bishop, William, act for relief of, vetoed, VIII, 443.

Bismarck, Prince von, instructions of, to German minister respecting Samoa transmitted, VIII, 806.

Bissel, Russell, mentioned, I, 417.

Bissell, Daniel, colonel in Army, nomination of, discussed, II, 344.

Black, Jeremiah S.:

Counsel for President Johnson in impeachment proceedings, VII, 726.

Secretary of State, V, 672.

Black Cockades.—A badge first worn by the American soldiers during the Revolution and later, during the hostility toward France (about 1797) occasioned by the X. Y. Z. dispatches, adopted by the Federalists as a patriotic emblem and as a rejoinder to the tricolored cockade worn by the Republicans as a mark of affection toward France. Its significance in some degree lay in the fact that it had been a part of the Continental uniform.

Black Friday.—There have been several Black Fridays. The term is often used to designate a dark financial day. In England it has special reference to Friday, Dec. 6, 1745, the day on which news came to London that the young Pretender, Charles Edward, had reached

Derby; and also to Friday, May 11, 1866, which was the height of the commercial panic in London through the failure of Overend, Gurney & Co. Sept. 24, 1869, is sometimes referred to as Black Friday in the United States. On this day a syndicate of New York bankers advanced the price of gold to 162½, causing a panic. It sold at 143⅛ the previous evening. Another such day was Friday, Sept. 19, 1873, when Jay Cooke & Co., leading American bankers, failed. A great crash ensued in Wall Street, the center of financial operations in America, and the historic panic of 1873 began. Credit generally was impaired and many financial institutions were forced into bankruptcy.

Black Hawk War.—By a treaty signed at Prairie du Chien, Wis., July 15, 1830, the Sac and Fox Indians ceded all their lands in Illinois and Wisconsin to the United States. Black Hawk, a noted chief of the tribe, refused to abide by the treaty and made war upon the whites. He resisted the survey of the land at Rock Island, Ill., although most of the Sacs and Foxes were west of the Mississippi. In 1831 he attacked some Illinois villages, but was driven off by the militia under Gen. Gaines in June of that year. The next spring he returned with a strong force and began to massacre the whites. Gen. Scott was sent against him with a force of United States troops. Black Hawk was defeated at the Wisconsin River July 21, 1832, by a detachment of troops under Gen. Dodge, and again at Bad Axe River, Aug. 2 of the same year, by Gen. Atkinson. After these successive defeats Black Hawk was compelled to surrender.

Black Hawk War discussed, II, 603; III, 32.

Black Hills:
Emigration to, referred to, VII, 322, 352, 401.
Gold discovered in, referred to, VII, 352, 401.

Black Rock, N. Y., works at, referred to, III, 346.

Black Rock (N.Y.), Battles of.—Lieut. Col. Bishop, with about 400 men from the British camp at Lundys Lane, crossed the Niagara River July 11, 1813, and attacked the blockhouse at Black Rock, where the Americans had a considerable quantity of naval stores and ammunition. The blockhouse was in charge of Gen. Peter B. Porter, with less than a dozen artillerists. About 300 militia and a small band of Indians were scattered about in the neighborhood. The militia fled at Bishop's approach and Porter narrowly escaped capture. On his way to Buffalo, meeting reenforcements of 100 regulars, he returned and attacked the invaders. After a short struggle the British were driven with loss to their boats. Lieut. Col. Bishop was mortally wounded. In August, 1814, Black Rock was again attacked by the British and successfully defended by the Americans. After the battle of Lundys Lane the American army retired to Fort Erie and vicinity. Gen. Drummond, having received reenforcements, went in pursuit. As a preliminary step toward attacking Fort Erie, the British general resolved to take possession of Black Rock. About 1,200 men under Lieut.

Col. Tucker crossed the river on Aug. 3, 1814, and were met and driven back by 300 Americans under Lieutenants Ryan, Smith, and Armstrong. The British lost a considerable number; the American loss was slight.

Black Sea:
Navigation of, unlocked, II, 445.
Vessels of United States excluded from, discussed, II, 502.
Free passage for, secured by treaty with Turkey, II, 504, 594.

Black Warrior, The.—An American merchant vessel which was seized at Havana by Cuban customs officials Feb. 28, 1854, and with its cargo was declared confiscated. (V, 234, 245.) The proceeding aroused a bitter feeling against Spain, and a special messenger was dispatched instructing the American minister at Madrid to demand, as immediate redress, indemnification to the owners in the sum of $300,000. The reluctance of Spain to accede led to the Ostend manifesto (q. v.). Spain afterwards made compensation for the seizure (V, 336), but the incident was used as a pretext for later filibustering expeditions into Cuba.

Black Warrior, The, seizure of, by Spanish authorities discussed, V, 234, 245.
Disavowal of, by Spain, and payment of indemnity, V, 336.
Reparation for, refused, V, 246.

Blackfeet Indians.—A savage and warlike tribe of the Siksika Confederation of the Algonquian stock of Indians, now confined to their reservation in the State of Montana. When not fighting among themselves they are generally at war with their neighbors. They formerly belonged to the Kena tribe, but separated from them and wandered up the Missouri River. The Sihasapa, an independent tribe under the leadership of John Grass, was also known as the Blackfoot or Blackfeet Indians.

Blackfeet Indians, treaty with, V, 362; VI, 700.

Blackford, William, treaty with New Granada concluded by, IV, 315.

Blackstock's (S. C.), Battle of.—In November, 1780, Gen. Sumter started for Fort Ninety-Six to attempt its capture. He was pursued by Col. Tarleton. A skirmish took place Nov. 20 at Blackstock's plantation, on the Tyger River, Union District, S. C. Tarleton fled, leaving nearly 200 dead and wounded upon the field. The American loss was only 3 killed and 5 wounded.

Bladensburg (Md.), Battle of.—As early as January, 1814, intelligence was received at Washington that 4,000 British troops had landed at Bermuda, destined for the United States. The British Admiral Cockburn arrived at Lynnhaven Bay, Va., in March with 1 ship, 2 frigates, and 1 brig. Early in August he was joined by Vice-Admiral Cochrane, who took command, and was later joined in the Chesapeake by 4,000 veterans of Wellington's army, under Gen. Ross. The civil government at Washington was apathetic in the face of impending danger. Washington, with its public buildings and records, was entirely unprotected.

At the suggestion of Gen. Winder the President called a Cabinet council in July and proposed raising an army for the defense of the Federal capital. This comprehended a requisition on the States for militia aggregating 93,000 men. The naval defenses were intrusted to Commodore Barney, with a small flotilla of gunboats carrying 400 men. By Aug. 1 Gen. Winder, who was assigned to the defense of the capital, had 1,000 regulars and almost 4,000 militia under his command for the defense of Washington and Baltimore. The remainder of the army was on paper. The British moved up the Patuxent by land and water to Upper Marlboro. Barney destroyed his flotilla at Pig Point and crossed toward the Eastern Branch of the Potomac, forming a junction with Winder's advance, which had proceeded to Bladensburg, about 5 miles from Washington, on the post road to Baltimore. Here at noon Aug. 24, 1814, the two armies faced each other, the British, under Gen. Ross, nearly 5,000 strong, 4,000 of them seasoned by service in continental Europe, while the defenders of the capital consisted mainly of undisciplined, untried militia, many of them only 3 days from their homes. The battle lasted from about half-past 12 till 4 o'clock and resulted in the utter rout of the Americans. The British lost upward of 500 men in the engagement. The Americans had only 26 killed and 51 wounded. After this battle the invaders marched to the capital, seized it, and burned the public buildings.

Blaine, James G.:
Death of, announced and honors to be paid memory of, IX, 385.
Secretary of State, VIII, 13; IX, 15.
Correspondence regarding the *Baltimore* affair. (See *Baltimore*, The.)
Member of conference to discuss commercial relations with Canada, IX, 240, 243, 313.

Blaine, Walker, Third Assistant Secretary of State, mentioned, VIII, 107.

Blair, Frank P., jr.:
Commission of, as major-general discussed, VI, 203.
Correspondence regarding assignment of command to, VI, 206.
Letter and advice of President Lincoln as to accepting seat in Congress or remaining in command, VI, 205.
Resignation of, as major-general accepted, VI, 206.
Withdrawal of, VI, 208.

Blair, Frank P., sr., negotiations for and correspondence regarding restoration of peace, VI, 260.

Blair, Henry W., refusal of China to receive, as minister, IX, 186, 238, 244.

Blair, Montgomery, correspondence regarding resignation of Frank P. Blair, jr., as major-general, VI, 206.

Blakely, Johnston, British ship captured by vessel in command of, I, 549.

Blanco, Ramon, Captain-General of Cuba, directed by Spain to suspend hostilities, referred to, X, 150.

Bland, Theodorick:
Appointed on committee to meet President Washington, I, 45.
Reports of, on condition of South America, X, 58.

Bland-Allison Act:
Discussed by President—
Arthur, VIII, 46, 133, 243.
Cleveland, VIII, 342, 512, 788.
Harrison, Benj., IX, 40.
Hayes, VII, 559, 616.
Vetoed by President Hayes, VII, 486.

Bland Dollar.—A name sometimes applied to the silver dollar of the United States the coinage of which began in 1878. During that year Congress passed the act providing for such coinage. A bill was introduced in the House of Representatives by Richard P. Bland, of Missouri, July 25, 1876, providing for the free and unlimited coinage of silver, which had been suspended since 1873. Mr. Bland's bill passed the House providing for free coinage, but was modified in the Senate by the Allison amendment. As the bill became a law it provided that instead of free coinage the Secretary of the Treasury should purchase each month not less than $2,000,000 nor more than $4,000,000 worth of silver bullion to be coined into silver dollars of 412½ grains each. President Hayes returned the bill with his veto Feb. 28, 1878 (VII, 486), but on the same day both House and Senate passed the bill over his veto. The effects of the law were discussed by the Chief Executives from time to time. (See Bland-Allison Act.) This act was repealed in 1890 by the act of Congress known as the Sherman law.

Blatchford, Richard M., mentioned, VI, 78.

Blazer, Dolly, act granting pension to, vetoed, VIII, 676.

Blockade.—A well-defined principle of international law which secures to any nation the right in time of war to render intercourse with the enemy's ports unlawful, hazardous, or impossible on the part of neutrals. It was introduced by the Dutch about 1584. The principle recognized by European powers is that a blockade to be binding must be effective. It is carried into effect by a force of war ships, which patrol the sea outside the enemy's harbor and arrest any vessels of any power attempting to enter. Should any arrested vessel contain goods or persons contraband of war, it is condemned by a prize court and sold, the proceeds being divided among the blockading squadron. This right is incontrovertible, having its origin in the soundest principles of maritime jurisprudence, sanctioned by the practice of the best nations of enlightened times. The Elbe was blockaded by Great Britain in 1803; the Baltic by Denmark in 1848-49 and in 1864; the Gulf of Finland by the Allies in 1854. At the outbreak of the Civil War in America the Confederate government required every English vessel that entered its ports to bring arms and ammunition as part of its cargo. Plymouth, Newbern, Wilmington, and other North Carolina ports were much used by these vessels, as also the port of Charleston, S. C. United States cruisers blockaded these ports, and under the established rules of international law seized, searched, and confiscated foreign vessels attempting to run the blockade, as well as enemy's ships in transit. At the commencement of the Spanish-American War in 1898 the United States maintained a strict blockade of Cuban ports for several weeks under the direction of Acting Rear-Admiral Sampson, which finally resulted in the battle of July 3, when the American squadron under the immediate command of Commodore Schley entirely destroyed the Spanish fleet under Admiral Cervera.

Blockades:

Correspondence regarding, referred to, VI, 58.

During War of 1812 discussed, I, 501.

Established by—

Portugal, claims of United States growing out of, II, 535, 550; III, 24.

Spain, claims of United States growing out of, II, 549.

In order to be binding, must be effective, V, 412.

Maximilian's decrees declaring, proclaimed void, VI, 433.

Of Cuban ports proclaimed, X, 202, 206.

Discussed, X, 154, 165.

Removal of, referred to, X, 174.

Of Mexican ports, and effect of, on United States, III, 488, 516.

Of Southern ports proclaimed, VI, 14, 15, 280.

Claims of foreign powers arising out of, discussed, VI, 127.

Nonresident foreigners engaged in violating, order regarding, VI, 282.

Referred to, VI, 24, 184.

Removed, VI, 325.

From certain ports, VI, 89, 171, 216, 230, 281, 309.

Of Spanish coasts in South America by Spanish forces, X, 56.

Of Spanish Main referred to, II, 207.

Of Tripoli, questions between United States and Tunis growing out of, I, 400, 401.

Bloody Shirt.—A term used to describe the utterances of impassioned speakers and writers who after the close of the Civil War endeavored to revive its memories and to agitate the minds of their hearers for political effect. Reviving war animosities was said to be waving the bloody shirt.

Blount, James H., special commissioner to Hawaiian Islands, report of, discussed, IX, 441, 460.

Blow, Henry T., dispatch from, relative to commercial interests with South America transmitted, VII, 60.

Blue Book. (See Biennial Register.)

Blue Laws.—A name applied to the early laws of some of the American Colonies. The general court of New Haven, Conn., in April, 1644, ordered that the "judicial laws of God as they were delivered to Moses" should be binding on all offenders and a rule to all the courts of the jurisdiction "till they be branched out into particulars hereafter." New Haven's criminal code was developed along these lines. It is doubtful if some of the rigid rules of conduct often quoted as Blue Laws were ever enforced or even enacted. Here are a few specimens: "No one shall run on the Sabbath day, or walk in his garden or elsewhere, except reverently to and from meeting." "No woman shall kiss her child on the Sabbath or fasting day." "No one shall read common prayer, keep Christmas or saints' days, make minced pies, dance, play cards, or play on any instrument of music except the drum, trumpet, and jewsharp."

Blue Licks (Ky.), Battle of.—Aug. 19, 1782, a body of 182 Kentucky pioneers were drawn into an ambuscade at Blue Licks, Nicholas County, Ky., by Indians under Simon Girty. The settlers were defeated with the loss of 62, including a son of Daniel Boone.

Blue Lights.—During the summer and autumn of 1813, while the British commander, Sir Thomas Hardy, with his fleet, had the port of New London, Conn., blockaded, Commodore Decatur made several futile attempts to escape therefrom with his fleet, consisting of the frigates *United States* and *Macedonian* and the sloop-of-war *Hornet.* Decatur claimed that his failure was due to the fact that blue signal lights were flashed from the shore toward the British. The friends of the British and the opponents of the war became known as Blue-Light Federalists.

Bluefields. (See Mosquito Indian Strip.)

Blumer, Eliza Jane, act granting pension to, vetoed, VII, 384.

Board of Health. (See National Board of Health.)

Board of Trade and Plantations.—In 1660 Charles II established two separate councils, one for trade and the other for foreign plantations. For a time these were united (from 1672 to 1675). The charter of Rhode Island and Providence Plantations was secured from Charles II, July 8, 1663, by John Clarke, who acted as agent for the Colony. This charter continued in force 180 years. In 1695 the Board of Trade and Plantations was established and given charge of the English Colonies in America. In 1768 a secretary of state for America was established, and the duties of the board having been transferred to him, the board was abolished in 1782.

Board of War. (See War, Board of.)

Boats. (See Vessels.)

Boca del Toro, United States of Colombia, vessels from, tonnage duty on, suspended, VIII, 310.

Body of Liberties.—A bill of rights consisting of a code of 100 fundamental laws setting forth the sacredness of life, liberty, property, and reputation. The Body of Liberties was compiled by Nathaniel Ward, pastor of the church at Ipswich, Mass., from drafts submitted. A copy of these laws was sent to every town within the jurisdiction of Massachusetts, to be first considered by the magistrates and elders, and then to be published by the constables, "that if any man saw anything to be altered he might communicate his thoughts to some of the deputies." In December, 1641, the

General Court of Massachusetts adopted this fundamental code as the basis of common law, there having been up to that time no written law in the Colony. The Body of Liberties also prescribed some general rules for judicial proceedings.

Boggs, Charles S., thanks of Congress to, recommended, VI, 76.

Bogy, Lewis V., mentioned, VI, 521.

Bohemia Manor.—A tract of 5,000 acres of land in Maryland, along the Elk River, granted by Lord Baltimore in 1666 to a Bohemian surveyor named Augustine Herman. Herman obtained papers of denization and was naturalized with his family under the first act of the kind that passed in the Province.

Boilers. (See Steam Boilers.)

Bolivar, Simon:
Centennial celebration of birth of, at Caracas, referred to, VIII, 129, 173.
Delivered from assassins, medal offered President Jackson in commemoration of, declined, II, 466.

Bolivia.—A Republic in the western part of South America, named for Simon Bolivar. It extends from lat. 10° to 23° south and from long. 58° to 69° west. It is bounded on the north and east by Brazil, on the south by Argentina and Paraguay, and on the west by Chile and Peru. In the northern part of the country are the great plains of the Madeira. In the southeast is the Gran Chaco, a vaguely defined region imperfectly explored. The surface here is flat and subject to periodical inundation and inhabited by numerous bands of wild Indians. The western part is a plateau traversed by the Andes. Bolivia, though entirely within the tropical zone, boasts all the climates of the world, each with its peculiar vegetation. The country is remarkable for its mineral products. The silver mines of Potosi, after having produced $3,000,000,000, are still considered inexhaustible, while gold, lead, tin, salt, sulphur, niter, and copper are abundant. Bolivia was formerly a Spanish possession. It became independent in 1825 and united with Peru from 1836 to 1839. The country consists of 9 departments, governed by a President and two Houses of Congress, with a constitution modeled after that of the United States. Revolutions have frequently occurred. From 1879 to 1883 Bolivia and Peru were united in a war against Chile. The result was disastrous to the allies, and Chile became possessed of all the western seacoast, including the niter districts of Bolivia. The area of the Republic is about 597,271 sq. miles, with a population of 2,500,000, besides Indians. The capital is La Paz. A treaty of peace, friendship, commerce, and navigation was concluded with the United States May 13, 1858, in which the rights of neutrals were clearly outlined (V, 580).

Bolivia (see also Peru-Bolivian Confederation):
Controversy with Chile referred to, VI, 209.
Diplomatic relations with, IX, 33.
Resumed, VII, 497, 610.

Bolivia—Continued.
Earthquakes in, VI, 687.
Treaty with, V, 580.
Ratification of amendments to, recommendation regarding, VI, 59.
War between Chile, Peru, and, VII, 570, 611; VIII, 41, 130.
Claims of United States arising out of, VIII, 328, 498, 784; IX, 109.
Conditions of peace presented by Chile discussed, VIII, 75, 130, 173.
Efforts of United States to bring about peace discussed, VII, 570, 611, 630; VIII, 75, 130.
Negotiations for restoration of peace, VIII, 89.
Terminated, VIII, 235.
Treaty of peace discussed, VIII, 173.

Bollman, Erick, crimes charged against, I, 417.

Bollman Case.—An important Supreme Court case in which treason is defined and the authority of the Supreme Court to issue writs of *habeas corpus ad subjiciendum* is maintained. Bollman was charged with being implicated in a treasonable attempt to levy war upon the United States, in that he had joined Aaron Burr in a scheme to establish an independent state in the Southwest in 1805. It was decided that a mere conspiracy to subvert the Government by force is not treason, an actual levying of war being necessary. The court held that the crime with which the prisoners Bollman and Swartwout stood charged had not been committed, and they were discharged.

Bonds of United States (see also Debt, Public; Loans):
Authority vested in Secretary of Treasury to issue, recommendations regarding, IX, 445.
Discussed. (See Debt, Public, discussed.)
Issuance of, discussed and recommendations regarding, IX, 445, 553, 561, 567, 642, 644, 645, 743.
Purchase of, with Treasury surplus recommended, VII, 31.

Bonhomme Richard, The.—An old East India merchantman fitted up as a man-of-war by the French at L'Orient in 1779. It was one of five fitted out by the French at the suggestion of Benjamin Franklin, and christened in his honor *Bonhomme Richard*, or *Good-Man Richard*. She was commanded by John Paul Jones, an American officer, and carried American colors. She was accompanied by two French vessels. They attempted to enter the harbor of Leith, Scotland, but storms prevented. Off Flamborough Head, Sept. 23, 1779, the fleet encountered a British merchant fleet convoyed by the *Serapis* and *Countess of Scarborough*. The larger war ship, the *Serapis*, though much superior in every respect to the *Bonhomme Richard*, was fiercely attacked by the latter. The conflict took place by moonlight, in the presence of thousands of spectators. Jones lashed the *Serapis's* bowsprit to the *Richard's* mizzenmast and raked her deck with musketry. Broadside answered broadside in one of the most stubbornly contested battles in the history of naval warfare. The engagement lasted 3 hours. Finally a bucketful of **hand grenades thrown down the hatchway**

of the *Serapis* caused her commander to surrender. Jones transferred his crew to the conquered ship, and the *Bonhomme Richard* sank in a few hours.

Bonus Bill.—A bill introduced by John C. Calhoun Dec. 23, 1816, appropriating $1,500,000 for constructing roads and canals and improving the navigation of water courses. The bill was called the bonus bill. The intention was that the first work done under the appropriation should be the construction of a canal between Albany and the Lakes. The bill was strongly supported by New York and the South, and passed Congress, but was vetoed by President Madison, who held that the General Government could not give aid to internal improvements without a constitutional amendment (I, 584).

Boon, Clark, act increasing pension of, vetoed, VIII, 451.

Boone, William, act granting pension to, vetoed, VIII, 456.

Boonville (Mo.), Battle of.—When President Lincoln's call for troops, Apr. 15, 1861, reached Governor Jackson, of Missouri, he refused to furnish the 4 regiments forming the quota of the State. Francis P. Blair, jr., had, however, organized, under the military command of Nathaniel Lyon, 5 regiments, and these were mustered in immediately, Lyon being made brigadier-general. When another Missouri brigade had been formed, May 8, Lyon was put in command of the department. Meantime Governor Jackson ordered the State militia to camp at St. Louis. May 10 Gen. Lyon surrounded the camp, and on its surrender by Gen. Frost paroled the men, 700 in number. June 15 he occupied Jefferson City, the governor fleeing to Boonville. Lyon followed. On June 17 he dispersed the State troops collected there.

Booth, John Wilkes, persons claiming reward for apprehension of, directed to file claims, VI, 353.

Border States.—A designation for the several slave States of Delaware, Maryland, Virginia, Kentucky, and Missouri, lying next to the free States, and sometimes including Arkansas, North Carolina, and Tennessee. Many people of these States were anxious, both during and before the Civil War, for an amicable adjustment of the slavery question. They originated the Peace Conference of 1861.

Borneo.—Next to New Guinea, the largest island in the world, Australia being classed with the continents. It is about 800 miles long and 700 miles in width. It is situated in the Indian Archipelago, bounded on the east by the Sea of Celebes and the Macassar Strait, on the south by the Sea of Java, and on the west and north by the China Sea. Borneo has an area of about 285,000 sq. miles and a population of 1,750,000. Two chains of mountains traverse the island in a nearly parallel direction from northeast to southwest. Vegetation grows luxuriantly and choice woods and spices are exported. The fauna is peculiar to that quarter of the globe. It includes the elephant, rhinoceros, and tapir and many birds remarkable for their rich plumage. The inhabitants are Dyaks, Malays, Negritos, Bugis, and Chinese. The greater part of the island is ruled by the Dutch. It was first visited by Portuguese in 1518. The British have a preponderating influence on the north coast. A commercial treaty was concluded between the United States and Borneo in 1850.

Borneo, treaty with, V, 152.

Bosphorus, The, restrictions on passage of Straits of the Dardanelles and, by ships of other nations, VII, 124.

Boston:

Execution of laws for return of fugitive slaves forcibly resisted in, V, 101.

Proclamation regarding, V, 109.

Reference to, V, 137.

Fire in, referred to by President Grant, VII, 184.

Industrial exposition at, discussed, VIII, 186.

Navy-yard at, referred to, VIII, 89.

Title of United States to land occupied as, referred to, VIII, 111.

Unlawful assemblages in, and proclamation against, V, 101, 109.

Boston, The, mentioned, X, 88.

Boston, The, mentioned, X, 155.

Boston Case.—The case of a fugitive slave who escaped from his owner in Georgia and took passage on the *Boston*, a vessel bound for the coast of Maine. The governor of Georgia charged the captain of the ship with stealing the slave and demanded that the governor of Maine restore the fugitive. This was refused. The legislature of Georgia then called upon Congress to pass a law compelling the governor of Maine to comply with such demand. No action was taken by Congress.

Boston, Evacuation of.—During the winter of 1776 Washington, having received some ordnance captured at Ticonderoga and a supply of ammunition taken by privateers at sea, determined to attack Boston, then occupied by the British. In pursuance of this plan he occupied Nooks Hill (an eminence at the extremity of Dorchester Neck) and Dorchester Heights, which commanded Nooks Hill and the town itself. On the night of Mar. 4, 1776, the heights were covered with breastworks, and the British were forced to risk a general action to dislodge them or abandon the town. They chose the latter alternative, and on Mar. 17 the town and harbor were evacuated by the British army and navy without firing a gun.

Boston Fire referred to, VII, 184.

Boston Massacre.—The British navigation acts were a source of great annoyance and loss to the American colonists, and their execution was resisted at all points. Great Britain attempted to coerce the people into a compliance with the laws by sending Gen. Gage with 3 regiments to Boston in 1768. The presence of the troops further aggravated the people of Boston. During 1769 and the early part of 1770 numerous quarrels occurred between the citizens of Boston and British soldiers charged with the enforcement of the laws. In February, 1770, a press gang from the British frigate *Rose* boarded a ship belonging to a Mr. Hooper, of Marblehead, whereupon a riot ensued. On the night of Mar. 5 following a large crowd responded to the ringing of the fire bells and came into collision with the soldiers. The latter fired, killing 3 persons and wounding several others. The soldiers were tried and acquitted, but the news of the Boston massacre spread rapidly and did much to strengthen the spirit of revolution among the people.

Boston Port Act.—An act of Parliament introduced by Lord North and passed Mar. 7, 1774, in retaliation for the destruction of cargoes of tea in Boston Harbor. It provided for the discontinuance of landing and discharging, loading, or shipping of merchandise to or from the city of Boston or in Boston Harbor. Commerce was transferred to Salem and Marblehead, and Gen. Gage arrived in Boston June 1, 1774, to enforce the law. The Boston people were indignant. Much sympathy was expressed for them throughout the Colonies. In many places people refused to buy British goods. Oct. 20, 1774, the American Association was formed, pledging the members to nonconsumption and nonintercourse with Great Britain, Ireland, and the British West Indies. The association included 52 members of the Continental Congress.

Boston Tea Party.—In 1767 Great Britain imposed a duty on tea sold in the American Colonies. The East India Company prevailed upon the ministry in 1773 to amend the act so as to relieve the company from paying the duty, thereby forcing the consumers to pay it. The colonists were indignant at this transfer of the tax from the company to themselves, and adopted various methods to evade payment. Nov. 28, 1773, a ship arrived in Boston Harbor carrying 114 chests of tea, and early in December two others arrived. On the evening of Dec. 16 an enthusiastic meeting of citizens was held at Faneuil Hall, and at its close between 50 and 60 men disguised as Indians took possession of the 3 ships and threw overboard the cargoes of tea, amounting in all to 342 chests. Seventeen chests were also destroyed in New York Harbor about the same time. These events resulted in the passage of the Boston Port Act (q. v.) and were an important part of the train of causes of the American Revolution.

Boudinot, Elias:
Appointed on committee to meet President Washington, I, 45.
Invites President Washington to meet committee at his home, I, 46.
Director of Mint, report of, transmitted, I, 313, 315.

Boundaries.—The colonial boundaries of the United States were indefinite and often the subject of much dispute. The grants of territory in America were made by European rulers, who were careless or ignorant of the geography of the country. The boundaries

of the United States were agreed upon in 1783 at the treaty of Versailles (q. v.). Congress then took up the question of the border lines between States and provided an elaborate mode of procedure, modeled after the Grenville act of Great Britain. Since 1789 such cases, as well as all other matters between States, have been under the jurisdiction of the Supreme Court. In 1783 the northeast boundary of the United States was defined as extending from the source of the St. Croix River due north to the watershed between the St. Lawrence and the Atlantic, thence along the watershed to the northwesternmost head of the Connecticut River. After long and irritating disputes over the line, the Webster-Ashburton treaty was negotiated in 1842, fixing the boundary between the United States and British possessions on the present lines. The territory bounded on the north by latitude 54° 40', on the east by the Rocky Mountains, on the south by latitude 42°, and on the west by the Pacific Ocean has been variously claimed by Russia, Spain, and Great Britain. By treaty with Russia Jan. 11, 1825, the United States were to make no settlements north of 54° 40' and Russia none south of that line. By the treaty which ceded Florida in 1819 Spain relinquished all claims to anything north of latitude 42°. Though Great Britain had little claim to the territory, joint occupation was agreed upon by the treaty of Oct. 20, 1818, and this becoming unsatisfactory Great Britain was induced in 1846 to accept latitude 49° as the boundary between her possessions and the United States from the Rocky Mountains to the channel between Vancouver Island and the mainland.

Boundaries. (See Canada; Mexico; Northeastern Boundary; Northwestern Boundary; Spain; the several States.)

Bounty. (See Sugar Bounty.)

Bounty Lands. (See Lands, Bounty.)

Boutwell, E. B., report on operations of the *John Adams,* under command of, transmitted, V, 376.

Bowdoin, James, commissioner to settle questions with Spain, order respecting appropriation for use of, X, 100.

Bowell, MacKenzie, member of reciprocal-trade conference between United States and Canada, IX, 240.

Bowen, Henry, correspondence regarding Dorr's Rebellion, IV, 292.

Bowers, C. F., act for relief of:
Reasons for applying pocket veto to, VIII, 486.
Returned, IX, 73.

Bowlin, Mr., mentioned, VI, 70.

Boynton, Michael P., imprisonment of, by authorities of Great Britain, VIII, 12.

Boynton, Richard M., letter of Harriet M. Fisher and, to Secretary of Navy transmitted, VI, 471.

Brace, Charles L., imprisonment of, by Austrian authorities referred to, V, 153.

Bradford, T. C., mentioned, V, 527.

Bradley, Mr., commissioner to investigate affairs of New York custom-house, IV, 152.

Buckshot War.—The election in Philadelphia Oct. 9, 1838, was of considerable importance, because upon it hinged the control of the legislature which was to elect a United States Senator. The Democratic candidates for the legislature were elected by small majorities, but their Congressional candidate was defeated. The Democratic return judges thereupon cast out 5,000 Whig votes, claiming fraud. The Whig judges then issued certificates of election to both their Congressional and legislative candidates, and these returns were accepted by the Whig secretary of state. Dec. 4, 1838, the date for the meeting of the legislature, armed partisans of both sets of contestants met at Harrisburg. The senate, which was Whig, met and adjourned because of the mob. Two warring bodies met in the house. (III, 507, 508). The Whig governor called upon the militia and tried without effect to obtain Federal aid. The Democratic house was recognized Dec. 25. A remark made during the height of the excitement, that the mob would feel the effect of "ball and buckshot before night," gave the episode the name of the Buckshot War.

Bucktails.—A name applied to the Tammany Society of New York City from the fact that the members of the organization wore each a buck's tail in their hats as a badge instead of a feather. Between 1812 and 1828 the Bucktails were anti-Clintonian New York Democrats. They were the most vigorous opponents of Clinton's canal policy from its inception in 1817, and the name was later applied to all who opposed this policy throughout the State.

Buena Vista (Mexico), Battle of.—After part of his army had been sent to Gen. Scott, Gen. Taylor, with less than 5,000 men, mostly raw militia, was attacked at Buena Vista by Santa Anna's army of 21,000 Feb. 22, 1847. Taylor intrenched himself in the pass of Angostura, in the Sierra Madre Mountains, on the road leading to San Luis Potosí. The engagement began at 3 o'clock in the afternoon and was suspended at dark, the loss to the Americans being but 4 men wounded, while the enemy lost more than 300 killed and wounded. Fighting was renewed at dawn of the 23d and continued until sunset. The Mexicans retired during the night to Agua Nueva. The American loss in killed, wounded, and missing amounted to 740; that of the Mexicans upward of 2,000. Jefferson Davis in this battle commanded a Mississippi regiment as its colonel, and saved the army by receiving the charge of the Mexican lancers. His troops were formed in the shape of a V.

Buenos Ayres (see also Argentine Republic): Diplomatic relations with, discussed, IV, 263. Imprisonment of American citizens in, II, 63. Independence of, asserted, II, 43, 58. Minister of United States in, returns, II, 608. Revolution in, V, 166. War with Brazil—
Peace concluded, II, 411.
Questions between United States and Brazil growing out of, II, 363, 385.

Buétrago, Señor, mentioned, V, 34.

Buffalo (N. Y.), Destruction of.—During the winter of 1813 the British regained Forts George and Niagara. The British and Indians, under the command of Lieut. Gen. Drummond, Maj. Gen. Riall, and Col. Murray, overran and laid waste the valley of the Niagara and pressed hard upon Buffalo. Gen. Amos Hall succeeded Gen. McClure at Buffalo Dec. 26, in the command of 2,000 badly organized American troops. On the night of Dec. 29 Riall crossed the river at Black Rock with 1,450 men, largely regulars, and a body of Indians. At sight of the enemy 800 of Hall's troops deserted. He, however, made a gallant defense with the Chautauqua troops and Canadian refugees until he was forced to retreat, keeping the enemy in check and covering the flight of the inhabitants. The British and Indians took possession of Buffalo and proceeded to burn, plunder, and massacre. Only 4 buildings were left standing in the town and only 1 at Black Rock.

Building and Loan Associations.—Corporations organized primarily to enable persons of limited means to secure homes, and, secondarily, to enable such persons to put aside a certain fixed sum at stated intervals, so that the investment may be safe and remunerative. The original idea was pure cooperation and absolute mutuality. In the beginning the home-building or home-buying fund came entirely from the periodic payments of the members (shareholders). At present prepaid, full-paid, and permanent shares are sold by the association, payable in full or in large part on subscription. Special deposits in any amount are received. Shares partly paid are brought to their par value by adding to payments made dividends apportioned thereto. Special deposits are generally withdrawable by the depositor at pleasure. Installment shares and prepaid shares remain in until they reach their par value. Full-paid shares remain in a certain fixed time. Permanent shares remain in until the dissolution of the corporation. These associations came into existence in England nearly 100 years ago, but were not made the subject of legislative enactment until 1836. The first association established in the United States was the Oxford Provident Building Association, of Frankford,

Pa., organized in 1831. There are now in the United States over 6,000 associations, with assets of more than $650,000,000.

Building and Loan Associations, report on, transmitted, IX, 477.

Buildings, Public:
Acts for erection of, vetoed, discussed, IX, 118.
Architects for, authority for employing, referred to, V, 421.
At Washington destroyed by Great Britain, I, 545.
Commission appointed to determine extent of security of, against fire referred to, VII, 480.
Construction of—
Recommended, VII, 625.
Referred to, I, 411, 448; III, 264; IV, 58, 431.
Expenditures for, II, 419.
Discussed, VII, 243.
Reports on, transmitted, X, 27, 29, 31, 33, 34, 37, 39, 57, 59, 60, 61, 64, 65, 66, 68, 69.
Heating and ventilating, referred to, V, 579, 581.
Improvement of, recommended, II, 262.

Buildings, Public, Commissioner of, report of, transmitted, X, 57, 59, 60, 61, 64, 65, 66, 68, 69.

Buildings, Public, Surveyor of, report of, transmitted, X, 27, 29, 31, 33, 34, 37, 39.

Bulgaria.—An autonomous principality in the Balkan peninsula of Europe. It is bounded by Roumania (chiefly separated by the Danube) on the north, by the Black Sea on the east, Turkey on the south, and Servia on the west. The principality is composed of Bulgaria (as formed in 1878) and Eastern Roumelia, with Sofia as the capital. It is a constitutional monarchy, and has been the scene of many struggles in former Russo-Turkish wars. Bulgaria was constituted a principality by the treaty of San Stefano and the Congress of Berlin in 1878. It was made tributary to Turkey, and Prince Alexander of Battenberg was installed as its ruler in 1879. Union with Eastern Roumelia and war with Servia occurred in 1885. In 1886 Alexander was deposed through Russian intrigue and a regency was formed. In 1887 Prince Ferdinand of Coburg, in spite of Russian opposition, accepted the invitation of the regency to assume the throne. Bulgaria has an area of 37,860 sq. miles and a population of 3,309,816.

Bulgaria:
Diplomatic relations with, establishment of, recommended, VIII, 172.
Massacre by Turks in, referred to, VII, 422.

Bull Run (Va.), Battle of, or First Battle of Manassas.—For the double purpose of menacing Washington and preventing an advance of the Federal troops into Virginia, the Confederates during the summer of 1861 collected a large body of troops in the vicinity of Manassas Junction, Va. The position was 33 miles southwest of Washington. The troops here assembled numbered, including all reenforcements received during the battle, about 32,000, under command of Gen. Beauregard. The senior officer, Gen. J. E. Johnston, after his arrival on the field, did not take the actual command. The aggregate force of Union soldiers in and around Washington was 34,160 men. Both armies were composed mostly of undisciplined volunteers. July 16, 1861, Maj. Gen. McDowell began a general forward movement. Lieut. Gen. Scott advised postponement until the forces should be better prepared for service, but his warning was disregarded. The Federal army was divided into 5 divisions. Leaving 5,700 men under Brig. Gen. Runyon to guard the approaches to Washington, the other 4 divisions, aggregating 28,500 men, under Brigadier-Generals Tyler, Hunter, Heintzelman, and Miles, advanced to Bull Run, a tributary of the Potomac River, about 30 miles from Washington, on the way to Manassas Junction. Hunter's and Heintzelman's divisions crossed the run July 21 and attacked the Confederate left, slowly forcing it back. Beauregard's army, when the action began, consisted of about 24,000 available men. He was reenforced at intervals during the day by 8,000 men under Johnston, who had been encamped in the Shenandoah Valley and whose junction with the main army it was thought would be prevented by Gen. Patterson. The latter had been stationed at Martinsburg with 18,000 men. Between 3 and 4 o'clock in the afternoon, when everything seemed favorable to the Federals, the last 3,000 of Johnston's men, under Gen. Kirby Smith, arrived and fell upon the Federals, forcing a retreat. This attack was followed by another by Early's brigade, and the Federal retreat became a rout. Men threw away their arms and equipments; artillery horses were cut from their traces and guns abandoned on the road; soldiers, civilians, and camp followers fled panic-stricken toward Washington afoot, astride, and in carriages. The retreating army and followers reached Washington July 23. The casualties of the battle were: Federal losses—killed, 481; wounded, 1,011; missing, 1,216; total, 2,708. Confederate losses—killed, 387; wounded, 1,582; missing, 13; total, 1,982. This battle was the first very important engagement of the war. (See also Groveton (Va.), Battle of; Manassas (Va.), or Bull Run, Second Battle of.)

Bulwer, Sir Henry Lytton, treaty between United States and Great Britain concluded by John M. Clayton and, V, 42.

Buncombe.—To talk for buncombe is to speak for effect on persons at a distance, without regard to the audience present. The phrase originated near the close of the debate on the famous "Missouri Question," in the Sixteenth Congress. It was then used by Felix Walker, a naïve old mountaineer who resided at Waynesville, in Haywood, a western county of North Carolina, near the border of the adjacent county of Buncombe, which was in his district. The old gentleman rose to speak while the House was impatiently calling "Question," and several members gathered around him, begging him to desist. He persevered, however, for a while, declaring that the people of his district expected it, and that he was bound to make a speech for Buncombe.

Bundy, M. L., act for relief of, vetoed, VIII, 457.

Bunker Hill, or Breeds Hill (Mass.), Battle of.— After the battles of Lexington and Concord the British force under Gen. Gage was increased to 10,000 men by the arrival of Generals Howe, Clinton, and Burgoyne from England. These officers occupied the town of Boston, on a peninsula extending into the harbor. On the surrounding hills were encamped some 20,000 undisciplined Americans. On the night of June 16, 1775, 1,000 of them under Col. Prescott were sent to fortify Bunker Hill, on another peninsula lying north of Boston. Through some misapprehension they seized Breeds Hill, nearer Boston, and threw up a line of fortifications. On the morning of the 17th about 3,000 (possibly 3,500) British crossed the harbor in boats and charged the hill, which was defended by about half that number of raw recruits. After three bloody charges the Americans were driven from their position, having defended themselves with gunstocks and stones when their ammunition was exhausted. The British loss was about 1,050; that of the Americans about 450, including Gen. Warren. The statistics of this battle show the number of killed and wounded to have been more than 30 per cent of the number engaged, thus placing it among the bloodiest battles known to history. At Gettysburg, after 3 days' fighting, the Union army lost 25 per cent, while 30 per cent of those who fought at Bunker Hill fell in an hour and a half.

Burchard, Horatio C., Director of Mint, removal of, and reasons therefor, VIII, 367.

Bureaus. (See the several Bureaus.)

Burgess, Thomas M., correspondence regarding Dorr's Rebellion, IV, 302.

Burlingame, Anson, minister to China:
Appointment of, to mission by Emperor of China referred to, VI, 598, 627.
Dispatch from, transmitted, VI, 197, 583.

Burnet, Daniel, member of legislative council for Mississippi Territory, nomination of, I, 457.

Burnet, J., correspondence regarding removal of remains of the late President W. H. Harrison, IV, 53.

Burnett, John D., district attorney, nomination of, discussed, VIII, 375.

Burnham, Hiram, brigadier-general, nomination of, referred to, VI, 202.

Burnley, J. H., mentioned, VI, 259.

Burnside, Ambrose E.:
Brigadier-general, thanks of President tendered, VI, 104.
Major-general, ordered to assume command of Army of Potomac, VI, 124.

Burnt Corn Creek (Ala.), Battle of.—As a result of Tecumseh's efforts to induce all the Southern Indians to join in a war of extermination against the whites, the Creeks were divided into two factions—one for war, the other for peace. In 1813 Peter McQueen, a half-breed, of Tallahassee, one of the leaders of the war party, was furnished by British agents at Pensacola with large quantities of supplies, under sanction of the Spanish governor. On learning of this Col. James Caller, of Washington, set out July 25, 1813, to disperse the Indians McQueen had collected and intercept the supplies. On the morning of July 27 Caller's command, increased by reenforcements to 180 men, came upon McQueen's party at their camp on Burnt Corn Creek. The Indians were surprised and fled into the woods, leaving their pack horses to the whites. They soon returned, however, and fiercely attacked 100 of Caller's men. Overwhelming numbers compelled Caller's men to retreat after a brave resistance. Two of Caller's command were killed and 15 wounded.

Burr, Aaron:
Attempts made in Kentucky to bring, to justice, I, 415.
Boats of, with ammunition arrested by militia, I, 417.
Conspiracy of, letters regarding, not received by President, I, 449.
Military expedition against Union planned by, I, 412.
Passes Fort Massac with boats, I, 417.
Reaches Mississippi Territory, I, 419.
Surrenders to officers in Mississippi Territory, I, 421.
Trial of—
Acquittal of, referred to, I, 429.
Evidence against, presented at, I, 429, 431.
Expenses incident thereto, I, 433, 459.

Burr, Elizabeth, act granting pension to, vetoed, VIII, 677.

Burritt, Loren, act to increase pension of, vetoed, VIII, 562.

Burroughs, Marmaduke, consul at Vera Cruz, Mexico, charges preferred against, by Dr. Baldwin, III, 593.

Burt, Silas W., chief examiner of Civil Service Commission, nomination of, and reasons therefor, VIII, 158.

Burtch, Alexander, act for relief of, vetoed, VII, 319.

Burtram, B. A., act granting pension to, vetoed, VIII, 709.

Bussey, Catharine, act granting pension to, vetoed, VIII, 720.

Butler, Benjamin F., of Massachusetts:
Communication to, regarding employment for fugitive negroes, X, 108.
Swords of Gen. Twiggs forwarded by, recommendations regarding, VI, 145.

Butler, Benjamin F., of New York:
Correspondence regarding examination of affairs of New York custom-house referred to, IV, 154.
Secretary of War, nomination of, and reasons therefor, III, 281.

Butler, Col., mentioned, II, 133.

Butler, James, act granting pension to, vetoed, VIII, 422.

Butler, Matthew C.:
Member of military commission to Cuba, X, 175.
Statement of, regarding slaughter of American citizens in South Carolina referred to, VII, 375.

Butler, Pierce, mentioned, VI, 74.

Butter, act defining and imposing tax on, and regulating manufacture of oleomargarine approved, discussed, VIII, 407.

Butterfield, Anna, act granting pension to, vetoed, VIII, 698.

Butterfield, Carlos, & Co., claim of, against Denmark for seizure of the *Ben Franklin* and *Catherine Augusta*, VII, 510; VIII, 784.
Agreement to submit, to arbitration, VIII, 803.
Award of arbitrator, IX, 110.

By Chance, The, claim for, adjusted, IV, 263.

C.

Cabinet.—Specifically, a body of counselors, usually composed of heads of departments, meeting in a private room or cabinet. In the United States the term is applied to the council composed of the heads of the eight Executive Departments of the Government, with whom the President confers on matters of administrative policy. Their meeting as advisers of the President is unknown to law or the Constitution and their conclusions have no binding force. The Constitution does not provide for a Cabinet, but it authorizes the President to "require the opinion in writing of the principal officer in each of the Executive Departments upon any subject relating to the duties of their respective offices." Washington required such opinions frequently. Changes have taken place in the method pursued, and the Cabinet is now regarded as an advisory board with which the President holds regular consultations. From being merely the heads of the Executive Departments its members have come to be recognized as an essential part of the administrative branch of the Government; and a law passed in 1886 provides that in case of the death or inability of both the President and Vice-President the Executive office falls to the Cabinet officers in the order named in the act.

Cabinet:
Official conduct of, complimented, IV, 350.
Proceedings of, on conduct of French minister, X, 87.
Rules adopted by, for preservation of neutrality by United States, X, 86.

Cabinet, Confederate. (See Confederate Cabinet.)

Cables. (See French Cable Company; Ocean Cables.)

Caddo Indians:
Memorial from, regarding claims to lands in Oklahoma, IX, 236.
Treaty with, III, 188.

Cadet.—One who is under training for a commission in the Army or Navy of the United States by a course of instruction and discipline in the Military Academy at West Point or the Naval Academy at Annapolis. The several Congressional districts, the Territories, and the District of Columbia are each entitled to 1 cadet annually at each of the academies. There are also 10 appointments at large to each of the academies. The latter, together with those from the District of Columbia, are made by the President. The remainder are made by the Secretary of War and the Secretary of the Navy, respectively, at the request of the Representatives and Delegates from the several Congressional districts and Territories. Should the latter make no recommendation by July 1, the appointment is authorized to be made by the Secretaries. The person appointed must be an actual resident of the district or Territory from which the appointment is made. The cadets obligate themselves to serve the Government at least 8 years after graduation unless sooner discharged.

—In his expedition against the Creek Indians Gen. Floyd, with more than 1,200 Georgia volunteers, 1 company of cavalry, and 400 friendly Indians, arrived at Calebee Creek on the night of Jan. 26, 1814, and established a camp on the highland bordering on the swamp of that name in Macon County, Ala., 50 miles west of Fort Mitchell. Before dawn of the following morning the camp was suddenly attacked by Indians. The assailants were received with grapeshot, followed by a bayonet charge, and fled in dismay. They left 37 dead. The whites lost 17 killed and 132 wounded. Of the friendly Indians 5 were killed and 15 wounded. Floyd retired to Fort Mitchell, where most of his men were discharged. No other expedition against the Creeks was organized in Georgia.

—One of the United States; nickname, "The Golden State;" motto, "Eureka." California is named, it is said, after a fictitious island in the Spanish romance "Las Sergas de Esplandian." Other authorities derive the name from the Spanish words "caliente" (hot) and "fornalla" (furnace). The State extends from lat. 32° 30′ to 42° north and from long. 114° to 124° 25′ west. It is bounded on the north by Oregon, on the east by Nevada and Arizona, on the south by Lower California, and on the west by the Pacific Ocean. Its capital is Sacramento, and San Francisco is the chief city. The State is famous for its beautiful scenery, its salubrious climate, and its wealth of precious metals and choice fruits. It was admitted into the Union in 1850 as a result of the famous compromise of that year. It formed a part of the territory ceded to the United States by Mexico in 1848. Area, 158,360 sq. miles; population (1890), 1,208,130.

Caramalli, Hamet:
Appeals to United States to place him on throne of Tripoli, I, 392.
Correspondence regarding, transmitted, X, 29, 30.
Referred to, V, 418.
Cardenas Bay, Cuba, conflict in, discussed, X, 157, 169.
The *Winslow* rescued by the *Hudson* in, thanks of Congress, etc., to officers and men of latter recommended, X, 157.
Cardinal.—A prince of the Church of Rome, a member of the conclave or sacred college which is the council of the Pope. Since 1179 the cardinals have claimed the privilege of electing the Pope. The full college consists of 70 cardinals. Mar. 15, 1875, Archbishop John McCloskey, of New York, was made the first American cardinal. He died Oct. 10, 1885, and on June 7, 1886, Archbishop Gibbons, of Baltimore, was ordained cardinal.
Carib Indians.—A powerful and warlike tribe of Indians who occupied the northern part of South America and the Windward or Caribbee Islands. Columbus encountered them at Guadeloupe and had a battle with them at Santa Cruz in 1493. After many disastrous wars with the Europeans and becoming mixed with fugitive negro slaves, they were transported to the vicinity of Honduras, where their descendants, the Black Caribs, now live.
Carlin, Bernard, act granting pension to, vetoed, VIII, 707.
Carlisle Indian School, establishment of, discussed, VII, 577.
Carmanchee Indians, treaty with, referred to, III, 188.
Carmichael, William:
Commissioner to Spain, nomination of, I, 115.
Recall of, from Spain, I, 156.
Referred to, I, 192.
Carmick & Ramsey, claims of, referred to, V, 534.
Carnifex Ferry (W. Va.), Battle of.—After McClellan's promotion, July 22, 1861, to the command of the Army of the Potomac, Rosecrans succeeded him in command in West Virginia. Gen. Floyd took a position on the Gauley River, 8 miles south of Nicholas, W. Va., at Carnifex Ferry, with 2,000 Confederates, intending to cut off Cox's brigade from Rosecrans's army. Sept. 10 he was attacked in this position by Rosecrans with 10,000 men. Darkness terminated a sharp engagement, and the next morning Floyd was in the mountains 30 miles away. The Federal loss was 120 killed and wounded. Among the former was Col. Lowe, of the Twelfth Ohio, who fell at the head of his regiment.
Carnot, Marie François Sadi, President of France, assassination of, IX, 478.
Resolutions of Senate and House on, transmitted to widow of, IX, 525.
Caroline, The.—A steamer in the service of Canadian rebels which was seized on American soil by the British and burned. In 1836–37 a revolutionary spirit developed in Lower Canada. Dec. 12, 1837, the leaders of the insurrection, under one Mackenzie, seized the Canadian Navy Island, in the Niagara River, and set up a provisional government. Dec. 26 the Canadians, crossing the Niagara, after a fight in which several rebels were killed, burned the vessel (III, 401; IV, 76). The affair caused great indignation. President Van Buren issued proclamations demanding observance of the neutrality laws (III, 481, 482). The New York militia was called out and placed under command of Gen. Scott.
Caroline, The, attacked and destroyed by British forces, III, 401.
Correspondence regarding, III, 401, 459, 622, 623; IV, 163, 220.
Discussed, IV, 76.
Satisfaction demanded of Great Britain for destroying, III, 515.
Caroline, The (brig), claim on Brazil concerning, VII, 266.
Caroline Islands.—A Pacific archipelago extending from lat. 3° to 11° north and from long. 137° to 163° east. The principal islands are Yap, Ponape, Strong, Babelthouap, and Rouk. The name usually includes the Pelew Islands. The inhabitants are Polynesians. Germany and Spain both claimed Yap Island until 1885, when the dispute was settled in favor of Spain.
Caroline Islands:
Dispute between Germany and Spain relating to domination of, discussed, VIII, 331.
Questions with Spain touching rights of American citizens in, IX, 187, 316, 440.
Carondelet, Baron de:
Authority to dispose of lands of Spain in Louisiana referred to, II, 82.
Validity of grant made by, to Marquis de Maison Rouge to be tested, IV, 160.
Carpenter, W. S., act for relief of, vetoed, VIII, 714.
Carpenters' Hall.—Building owned by the guild or union of carpenters of Philadelphia. It was similar to the guild halls of London. The First and Second Continental Congresses held their sessions in this hall.
Carpetbaggers.—A term of reproach applied to certain Northern politicians who in the days of the reconstruction of the Southern States, shortly after the close of the Civil War, took up temporary residence in the South and sought election to Congress and various State offices. The name arose from the fact that only a few of them intended to settle permanently, and therefore carried, it was said, their effects in carpetbags. Some of them proved to be good and useful citizens, while many were unscrupulous adventurers who sought official positions for the purpose of enriching themselves.
Carr, Mary A., act granting pension to, vetoed, VIII, 739.
Carr, Mary G., act granting pension to, vetoed (pocket), IX, 761.
Carrington, Edward, district supervisor, nomination of, I, 99.

Cent.—Copper coins stamped with various designs were issued first by the States and later by the Federal Government. Vermont was the first State to issue copper cents, having granted permission in June, 1785, to Reuben Harmon, jr., to make money for the State for 2 years. In October, 1785, Connecticut granted the right to coin £10,000 in copper cents, known as the Connecticut cent of 1785. In 1786 Massachusetts established a mint and coined $60,000 in cents and half cents. In the same year New Jersey granted the right to coin £10,000 at 15 coppers to the shilling. In 1781 the Continental Congress directed Robert Morris to look into the matter of governmental coinage. He proposed a standard based on the Spanish dollar, 100 units to be called a cent. His plan was rejected, and in 1784 Jefferson proposed to Congress that the smallest coin should be of copper, of which 200 should pass for 1 dollar. In 1786, 100 was substituted. The act of Apr. 2, 1792, authorized the coinage of copper cents containing 264 grains and half cents in proportion. By the acts of Jan. 14, 1793, and Jan. 26, 1796, their weight was reduced (I, 191, and X, 78). Their coinage commenced in 1793. In 1857 the nickel cent was substituted and the half cent discontinued, and in 1864 the bronze cent was introduced, weighing 48 grains and consisting of 95 per cent of copper and the remainder of tin and zinc.

Cent. (See Copper Coins.)

Centennial Exposition at Philadelphia.—An international exhibition of arts, manufactures, and products of the soil and mines, held at Fairmount Park, Philadelphia, from May 19 to Nov. 10, 1876. It was the first international exhibition of the kind held in this country, and was intended to celebrate the completion of a century of the existence of the United States as an independent nation. The enterprise received President Grant's warmest support (VII, 204, 261, 300, 354). Citizens of Philadelphia subscribed $10,000,000 of capital stock. Congress appropriated $2,000,000 as a loan, Pennsylvania $1,000,000, and the city of Philadelphia $1,500,000. Eight million persons paid admission, and many foreign countries were represented by exhibits.

Central America.—A name applied collectively to the five Republics of Guatemala, Honduras, Salvador, Nicaragua, and Costa Rica. These States declared their independence Sept. 21, 1821, and seceded from the Mexican Confederation July 21, 1823. The Central American Confederation continued until 1839, when it was dissolved. The history of these States presents an almost continuous record of anarchy and civil war. Their union under one president was proposed at the Pan-American Congress, 1889-90. June 28, 1895, Nicaragua, Honduras, and Salvador united as a Central American Republic. By treaty signed June 15, 1897, the 5 States were united into a Republic, each, however, preserving its autonomy. Since that date important changes have occurred affecting the relations of these States to each other and to the central Government. At this date (1899) they are in a revolutionary and unsettled condition.

Cerro Gordo (Mexico), Battle of.—This battle was fought on Apr. 17 and 18, 1847. Ten days after the surrender of Vera Cruz the vanguard of Scott's army, under Brig. Gen. Twiggs, took up the march toward the Mexican capital. The distance to be covered was nearly 200 miles. Three days later they arrived at the foot of the Orizaba Mountains, 50 miles to the westward. Here Santa Anna, the Mexican President, had assembled a force of 15,000 men, intrenched on the heights of Cerro Gordo. The American force did not exceed 8,000 men.

By cutting a new road around the mountain to the flank of the enemy and simultaneously assaulting front and rear the Mexicans were forced to surrender. Santa Anna escaped with some 6,000 or 7,000 of his army down the road toward Jalapa. The loss to the Americans was 63 killed and 398 wounded. That of the enemy was estimated to be nearly 1,200 killed and wounded. The victors captured 3,000 prisoners (who were paroled), between 3,000 and 4,000 stand of arms, 43 pieces of heavy bronze cannon, and a large quantity of fixed ammunition.

Chalmette's Plantation (La.), Battle of.—One of the battles near New Orleans. After the indecisive engagement at Villere's plantation, Dec. 23, 1814, Sir Edward Pakenham joined the British army with reenforcements, which swelled the invading forces to 8,000. On the morning of the 28th the British advanced to Chalmette's plantation exposed to the deadly fire of the *Louisiana*. Jackson awaited the movement with 4,000 men and 20 pieces of artillery. The British were led into the engagement in 2 columns under Generals Keane and Gibbs. After facing the heavy fire of the American sharpshooters for a short time, Sir Edward Pakenham ordered a retreat. The British loss in the engagement was about 150. The loss of the Americans was 9 killed and 8 wounded. One man on board the *Louisiana* was killed. More than 800 shots were hurled from her guns with deadly effect. One of them is known to have killed and wounded 15 men.

Champion Hills (Miss.), Battle of.—Sherman was directed to remain at Jackson to destroy everything that could be of value to the Confederates. Grant himself turned toward the west. Pemberton, the Confederate general, with 25,000 men, had left Vicksburg hoping to cut off Grant from his supplies and form a junction with Johnston's forces. Learning the strength and position of the enemy, Grant ordered Sherman and McPherson to leave Jackson and hasten forward. May 16, 1863, Pemberton's army was encountered at Champion Hills, a precipitous, narrow, wooded ridge 25 miles west of Jackson and 20 miles east of Vicksburg. The Confederates were strongly posted, and it was necessary for the Federal troops to approach the position across open fields exposed to the fire of 10 batteries of artillery. Hovey's division and McPherson's corps, with the exception of Ramsey's division, which did not arrive till the battle was over, began the attack in front while Logan's division was working to the left and rear. The battle was hotly contested and the Confederates were driven back after they had sustained heavy loss. Grant's losses were 410 killed, 1,844 wounded, and 187 missing—total, 2,441. The Confederate losses were probably nearly the same, and in addition 2,000 prisoners.

Champlain, Lake. (See Lake Champlain.)

Chancellorsville (Va.), Battle of.—Jan. 26, 1863, Maj. Gen. Joseph Hooker succeeded Maj. Gen. Burnside in command of the Army of the Potomac. By Apr. 1 that army was in excellent condition, numbering at the beginning of the new operations over 100,000 infantry, 10,000 artillery, 12,000 or 13,000 cavalry, and more than 400 guns. Gen. Lee was at Fredericksburg, Va., with 57,000 Confederates. Apr. 28 (some authorities say the 29th) Hooker began a movement with Lee's left as his objective point. To cover his real design, however, he dispatched Gen. Stoneman with most of the cavalry on a raid to the rear of the Confederate army, stationed Gen. Sedgwick with 30,000 men opposite Fredericksburg, and moved with about 70,000 men toward the United States Ford, on the Rappahannock. By Apr. 30 Hooker had crossed the Rappahannock with the main body of the army and established his headquarters at Chancellorsville, 11 miles west of Fredericksburg. The Confederate accounts say he then had with him 91,000 men. Lee had 48,000. Fighting began May 1, a division of the Fifth Corps advancing on the road to Fredericksburg and engaging a Confederate advance. The result was the recall of Hooker's advance and a better position for the Confederates. May 2 Lee detached "Stonewall" Jackson, with about 25,000 men, to attack the Eleventh Corps, under Gen. O. O. Howard, at the Federal right. The attack culminated in the evening with a panic in the Federal lines. "Stonewall" Jackson was mortally wounded during the night by the fire of his own men, who in the darkness mistook him for an enemy. The next day, May 3, the contest was renewed, nearly 14,000 troops under Lee having made a junction with the forces under Stuart, Jackson's immediate successor. It resulted in general Confederate success. Sedgwick in the meantime had crossed the Rappahannock, forced Early out of the Fredericksburg Heights, and threatened

the Confederate rear at Chancellorsville. Lee, having defeated the greater wing of the Federal army and driven it away, reenforced on the 3d and 4th of May the troops in front of Sedgwick. The latter was pushed back and recrossed the river at night with a loss of 5,000 men. Hooker also recrossed the river during the night of the 4th. According to Federal accounts their loss was 17,197, of whom 5,000 were prisoners; 13 guns and 20,000 muskets also fell into the hands of the Confederates. Lee's loss was about 13,000, including prisoners. The battle of Chancellorsville was probably the most important victory won and the greatest disaster sustained by the Confederates up to that period. They here defeated the splendid Union Army which attacked them; but the death of Lieut. Gen. Jackson was a loss from which it was well-nigh impossible to recover.

Chandler, James C., act granting pension to, vetoed, VIII, 420.

Chandler, Zachariah, death of, announced and honors to be paid memory of, VII, 557.

Chantilly (Va.), Battle of.—Aug. 31, 1862, the day after the second battle of Bull Run, or Manassas, Lee sent Jackson northward for the purpose of turning Pope's right wing toward Washington. Pope's headquarters were at Centerville and he had been reenforced by Sumner's and Franklin's corps. Anticipating the movement of the Confederates, he disposed his forces in position to meet and frustrate it at Chantilly, just north of Centerville, on the evening of Sept. 1, by the troops under McDowell, Hooker, and Kearny. In the engagement Generals Kearny and Stevens were killed. Pope was forced to fall back upon the works at Washington. Federal loss, 1,300; Confederate, 800.

Chapultepec (Mexico), Battle of.—The reduction of El Molino del Rey and Casa de Mata by Gen. Scott's army left the City of Mexico still protected by the formidable citadel of Chapultepec. This was filled with troops and the approaches were guarded by mines. Sept. 12, 1847, a preliminary fire was opened on the outworks, and on the 13th a strategic assault was made and the walls scaled in the face of a terrible fire. The American force consisted of 7,180 men. Some 25,000 of Santa Anna's men were distributed between Churubusco and the City of Mexico and the causeways connecting them. Between Chapultepec and the City of Mexico proper were 2 causeways or elevated roads leading to the gates of Belen and San Cosmé. These were crossed under the enemy's fire and the divisions of Worth and Quitman entered the ancient seat of the Montezumas. During the fighting from Sept. 12 to 14 incident to the taking of Chapultepec and the occupation of the city the American loss was 862. The Mexican army, strongly fortified in the vicinity of its capital, numbering at first some 30,000, lost 10,743. Santa Anna, then President and commander in chief of the army, was a fugitive. The trophies included more than 20 colors and standards, 75 pieces of ordnance and 57 wall pieces, 20,000 small arms, and an immense quantity of ammunition.

Charleston, S. C., foreign vessels at, referred to, V, 661.

Charleston (S. C.), Surrender of.—After Sir Henry Clinton had learned of the failure of the attack on Savannah he sent an additional force of 8,500 men to the South under Maj. Gen. Leslie. The main body of the American army was in winter quarters at Morristown, and reenforcements were sent from there to join Gen. Lincoln, who had command of the Southern army. The entire garrison at Charleston was less than 4,000 regulars and militia. Mar. 20, 1780, the British squadron, having touched at Tybee Island, near Savannah, crossed the bar, and on Apr. 9 passed Fort Moultrie, with a loss of 27 men, and anchored off Fort Johnson, which had been abandoned by the Americans. Apr. 29 Admiral Arbuthnot, with 500 marines, forced the Americans to abandon L'Empries Point, with a loss of nearly 100 men, who were captured by the guard boats on the way to Charleston. May 4, 200 marines took Fort Moultrie, on Sullivans Island. May 12, 1780, Gen. Lincoln was compelled to surrender. The British casualties were 76 killed and 189 wounded. The American casualties were nearly the same; 5,618 men, which included all the male citizens of Charleston, were made prisoners, and 405 pieces of ordnance were captured.

Charlestown, Mass., docks constructed at, II, 419. Site for, II, 368.

Charter.—A name commonly applied to grants of land or special privileges made by governments or individual rulers to companies or bodies of men for a term of years. In American law a charter is a written grant from the sovereign power conferring rights or privileges upon a municipality or other corporation. The term is generally applied to the statute, letters patent, or articles of association sanctioned by statute creating a corporation, as a city, college, stock company, benevolent society, or social club. During the early settlement of America European potentates, claiming sovereignty by right of discovery, issued charters granting land for purposes of colonization. The principal charters granted for this purpose were those of the Virginia Company, 1606, 1609, and 1612; Plymouth, 1620; Massachusetts Bay, 1629; Providence Plantations, 1644; Connecticut, 1662; Rhode Island and Providence Plantations, 1663; Massachusetts, 1691, and Georgia, 1732. The same sort of charters were given to the Dutch West India Company by the States-General of the United Netherlands in 1621 and to the Swedish Company by Gustavus Adolphus in 1624.

Charter Oak.—A tree celebrated in American legend. According to tradition, in 1687 Edmund Andros, the colonial governor of Connecticut, demanded the return of the charter of the Colony. During a meeting held to deliberate upon the action to be taken the lights were suddenly extinguished. When they were relighted the charter was missing. It was said that Capt. Wadsworth prevented the confiscation of the charter by secreting it in the hollow of an oak tree near Hartford. The tree was long held in great veneration. Aug. 20, 1856, it was prostrated by a gale.

Chase, Charles A., act to pension, vetoed, VIII, 453.

Chase, Maj., *habeas corpus,* writ of, suspended in case of, VI, 19.

Chase, Nathaniel D., act granting pension to, vetoed, VIII, 687.

Chase, Ormond, shot by order of Mexican general, V, 566.

Chase, Salmon P.:

Chief Justice United States, death of, announced and honors to be paid memory of, VII, 229.

Regulations relating to trade with ports opened by proclamation signed by, VI, 90.

Chasta Indians, treaty with, V, 303.

Chatfield, Mr., mentioned, V, 45.

Chauncey, Isaac, naval talents of, commented on, I, 535.

Cheyenne Indians. (See Cheyenne Indians.)

Cheek, M. A., claim of, against Siam, IX, 752. Adjustment of, X, 189.

Chehalis Reservation, Wash., allotment of lands in severalty to Indians on, referred to, VIII, 192.

Chemulpo, Korea, agreement respecting foreign settlement at, VIII, 806.

Cherokee Commission:

Agreement with—

Cherokee Indians, IX, 236.

Cheyenne and Arapahoe Indians, IX, 130.

Comanche, Kiowa, and Apache Indians, IX, 333.

Indians of Pyramid Lake Reservation, Nev., IX, 214.

Iowa Indians, IX, 73, 77.

Proclaimed, IX, 156.

Kickapoo Indians, IX, 203, 214.

Pawnee Indians, IX, 333.

Pottawatomie and Absentee Shawnee Indians, IX, 79.

Proclaimed, IX, 156.

Sac and Fox Indians, IX, 73, 75.

Proclaimed, IX, 156.

Shoshone and Arapahoe Indians, IX, 214.

Tonkawa Indians, IX, 203, 214.

Wichita, Caddo, etc., Indians, memorial regarding, IX, 236.

Wichita Indians, IX, 203, 213.

Appointed and discussed, IX, 46, 71, 73, 203.

Lands acquired by, opened to settlement. (See Lands, Public, opened.)

Cherokee Indians.—An important tribe of the Iroquoian stock of Indians. The name means "upland field." When first known to Europeans they occupied the mountains of southern Virginia, North and South Carolina, Georgia, Alabama, and Tennessee. In 1755 they ceded lands to Governor Glen and permitted the erection of forts within their territory. As the country about them filled up with whites they made repeated cessions of their territory until

Ga. Longstreet having arrived from Virginia with reenforcements for Bragg, Rosecrans concentrated his army near Lee & Gordon's mill, on Chickamauga Creek, a tributary of the Tennessee. On the evening of Sept. 18 the two armies were on opposite sides of Chickamauga Creek. Rosecrans's army numbered between 55,000 and 60,000 men; Bragg's army, about 50,000. Bragg crossed the creek with a portion of his army during the night, and on the morning of the 19th Gen. Polk, in command of the Confederate right wing, attacked the Federal left under Thomas. The battle continued all day without definite results. On the morning of the 20th the Confederates renewed the attack. Longstreet penetrated the center of the Federal line and separated Rosecrans, McCook, and Crittenden from the rest of the army, and the brunt of the battle fell upon Thomas. The Federals retreated at night to Rossville, and on the night of the 21st to Chattanooga. The Federal losses in the battle were 1,687 killed, 9,394 wounded, and 5,255 missing; total, 16,336. The Confederate loss was 18,000.

Chickamauga Indians, depredations committed by, I, 126.

Chickasaw Case.—Through the efforts of Northern people in organizing vigilance committees to prevent kidnapping of free colored persons on the charge of being fugitive slaves, a writ of *habeas corpus* was served upon the captain of the brig *Chickasaw* demanding the delivery of 2 colored women whom, it was charged, he intended to carry South. On exhibiting their free papers the women were liberated.

Chickasaw Indians.—A tribe of the Muskhogean stock of Indians, originally inhabiting the southern portion of the United States, mostly in the present States of Mississippi and Tennessee. In the eighteenth century their villages were about Pontotoc County, Miss., and their principal landing place Memphis. The treaty of 1786 fixed their northern boundary at the Ohio River, and as early as 1800 a part of the tribe migrated to Arkansas. In the early colonial wars they took the part of the English against the French, and in 1739 entered into friendly relations with Gen. Oglethorpe. In 1765 they met the Choctaws and whites at Mobile and entered into friendly trade relations. During the Indian wars generally they continued peaceful, aiding the whites against the Creeks in 1793. By treaties of 1805, 1816, and 1818 they ceded all their lands east of the Mississippi. In 1832 and 1834 they ceded the remainder of their lands and went to live with the Choctaws, with whom they dwelt harmoniously until 1855, when they were separated. During the early days of the Civil War they sided with the South. They now number about 3,500.

Chickasaw Indians:

Agreement with Choctaws, V, 302.

Appropriation to pay claim of, for lands ceded, recommendations regarding, IX, 202, 229, 326.

Chickasaw Indians—Continued.

Boundary line with Choctaws, V, 305.

Claims of, referred to, IV, 436, 437.

Commissioners to treat with, for cession of lands discussed, X, 25.

Deed for release of lands by, discussed, IX, 202, 229, 326.

Funds of, to be invested, III, 187; V, 183, 190, 203, 275, 295, 360.

Lands—

Ceded to, I, 116.

Ceded to United States by, I, 387.

Of, sold, III, 593.

Removal of, III, 498.

Stock of, to be transferred to Choctaws, referred to, III, 620; IV, 421.

Subsistence to be granted, III, 508.

Treaty with, I, 332, 390, 397, 581, 582; II, 45, 47, 607, 609; III, 52, 280; V, 156, 352; VI, 385.

Proclamation regarding, I, 80.

Chief Magistrate. (See President of United States.)

Chief Signal Officer of Army, printing of report of, recommended, VIII, 71, 150, 191.

Childs, Thomas, gallantry of, at battle of Monterey, Mexico, IV, 518.

Chile.—A Republic of South America, lying between Peru on the north, the Pacific Ocean on the south and west, and the Andes Mountains on the east. It was invaded by Almagro in 1535, and was first settled by Valdivia in 1541. Independence was proclaimed in 1818, though the last stronghold of the Spaniards was not taken until 1826. It exports niter, copper, silver, wool, wheat, etc. It is governed by a President and a Congress consisting of a Senate and Chamber of Deputies. It has 24 provinces. During the seventeenth century the Government included some of the country east of the Andes. After the revolution conquests were extended into Patagonia, and that country was divided between Chile and Argentina, with the Andes as the boundary. Chile acquired Atacama and a portion of southern Peru by the war of 1879-1883 waged against Peru and Bolivia. Area, about 250,000 sq. miles; population (1895), 3,413,776.

Chile:

American sailors on the *Baltimore* assaulted at Valparaiso. (See *Baltimore,* The.)

American seamen impressed by, V, 239.

Boundary question with Argentine Republic, VIII, 42; X, 176.

Church of the Compañía at Santiago, destroyed by fire, VI, 197.

Claims of, against United States, commission to settle, discussed, IX, 430, 524, 626; X, 180.

Claims of United States against, III, 377; IV, 198, 340; VIII, 328, 498, 784; IX, 109. (See also *Baltimore,* The.)

Agreement regarding, referred to, III, 605.

Award of arbiter, King of Belgium, referred to, VI, 180.

Commission to settle, discussed, IX, 435, 524, 626; X, 180.

Convention providing for adjustment of, by arbiter, V, 533.

China—Continued.

Cooly trade, referred to, V, 374, 596; VI, 60, 639; VII, 37, 80, 236.

Difficulties with Japan discussed, VII, 288.

Emperor of, accession of, referred to, IX, 34.

Expenditures from appropriation for providing for intercourse with, referred to, IV, 418.

Immigration of Chinese. (See Chinese Immigration.)

Japanese citizens in, treatment of, and action of officers of United States regarding, inquired into, IX, 560.

Judicial tribunal in, for trial of American citizens recommended, IV, 550.

Maritime provinces of, passing under control of European powers discussed, X, 180.

Massacre of French and Russian residents in, discussed, VII, 101.

Military operations of Great Britain against, terminated by treaty, IV, 213.

Minister of, to United States—

Establishment of legation discussed, VII, 496.

Received, VIII, 131.

Minister of United States to—

Appointment of, to mission by Emperor referred to, VI, 598, 627.

Appropriation for support of American youths to serve as part of official family of, recommended, VII, 147, 191.

Instructions to, referred to, V, 582.

Letter of, transmitted, V, 533.

Reception of, discussed, V, 559; VII, 236.

Mr. Ward declines to submit to humiliating ceremonies attending, V, 559.

Referred to, IV, 365; V, 591.

Refusal to receive, IX, 186, 238, 244.

Return of, on account of illness, IV, 401.

Sent to, IV, 263; V, 446, 559.

Mission to, recommendation that it be raised to first class, VII, 37.

Missionaries in. (See American citizens in, *ante.*)

Opium traffic, treaty for repression of, referred to, VIII, 42, 401.

Legislation regarding, recommended, VIII, 498.

Outbreaks against foreigners in, IX, 186.

Political relations with, referred to, III, 628.

Population of, IV, 213.

Postal convention with, VI, 577.

Rebellion in, VI, 245.

Relations with, V, 446; VII, 37.

Revenue laws of, rules regarding fines for breaches of, etc., referred to, VI, 694.

Rules for seamen of American vessels in ports of, referred to, V, 146.

Slavery in, referred to, VII, 587.

Straw Shoe Channel, vessels sailing under American flag prohibited from passing through, VI, 698, 704.

Subjects of, in United States—

Outrages committed on, discussed, VIII, 329, 383, 498.

Indemnity to, recommended, VIII, 634.

Appropriation for, VIII, 782.

Registration of. (See Chinese Immigration.)

Troops sent to protect, VIII, 348.

China—Continued.

Swedish missionaries murdered in, IX, 436.

Treaty with, transmitted and discussed, IV, 352, 358, 401; V, 506, 530, 540, 558, 577; VI, 638; VIII, 42.

Modification of article of, VI, 197.

Proposed modification of, VI, 583.

Referred to, V, 74, 446, 559, 582.

Vessels of, discriminating duties on, repealed by proclamation, VII, 600.

War with—

France, VIII, 236.

Great Britain and France, neutrality preserved by United States in, V, 506, 558, 643.

Japan—

Action taken by United States regarding, IX, 525, 627.

Agents of United States requested to protect subjects of contestants, IX, 525, 627.

Women imported into United States from, for dishonorable purposes, VII, 355.

Chinese Immigration.—In 1844, under a treaty negotiated by Caleb Cushing, 5 Chinese ports were opened to American trade and protection of life and property was guaranteed American citizens. By the Burlingame treaty of 1868 the right of Chinese immigration was admitted, and the promise was made that the subjects of China should enjoy the same privileges, exemptions, and immunities respecting travel and residence as the subjects of the most favored nation. The census of 1880 showed 105,000 Chinese in the United States; that of 1890, 106,688. They were obnoxious to most Americans and occasioned considerable alarm on account of their increasing numbers and their habits of life, which render their assimilation with Americans impossible. Petty persecutions followed. In 1879 a bill restricting their immigration passed. Congress, but was vetoed by President Hayes (VII, 514). Several laws were made later restricting their immigration. In 1892 the Geary Act was passed, providing that any Chinaman not lawfully entitled to remain in the United States should be removed to China and all Chinese laborers should be obliged to procure certificates of residence from the collector of internal revenue, failure to do so within a year to be followed by deportation. This act was modified considerably by a law passed in 1893.

Chinese Immigration:

Act—

Regarding, vetoed, VII, 514; VIII, 112.

To execute certain treaty stipulations approved and discussed, VIII, 630.

Conventional regulation of passage of laborers across borders proposed to Mexico and Great Britain, IX, 109.

Conventions regarding. (See Treaty regarding, *post.*)

Discussed by President—

Arthur, VIII, 129.

Cleveland, VIII, 329, 383, 390, 498, 609, 630; IX, 436.

Grant, VII, 288, 355.

Choctaw Indians—Continued.

Claims of, referred to, III, 129, 134, 396; IV, 436; VII, 511.

Opinion of Attorney-General regarding, referred to, IV, 583.

Commissioners to treat with, for cession of lands discussed, X, 25.

Deed for release by, of lands discussed, IX, 202, 229, 326.

Lands of, proposition regarding cession of, I, 434.

Memorial from, regarding alleged violation of treaty by United States, IV, 150.

Proceeds of sales of lands to be invested for, III, 187.

Referred to, II, 562.

Removal of, III, 498.

Stock of Chickasaws to be transferred to, referred to, III, 620; IV, 421.

Treaty with, I, 338, 363, 438, 460, 581, 582; II, 81, 201, 283, 287, 370, 423, 529, 532, 542; III, 280; V, 352; VI, 385.

Advice of Senate regarding treaty for cession of lands east of Mississippi requested, II, 478.

President declines to appoint commission to conclude, II, 423.

Proclamation regarding, I, 80.

Referred to, II, 530.

Transmitted for exercise of powers for fulfilling, X, 32.

Choctaw Nation, Ind. T., right of way for railroads across lands of, VIII, 66, 68.

Cholera (see also Contagious Diseases; International Sanitary Conference; Quarantine Regulations):

Causes of, report on, referred to, VII, 305.

International conference on subject of, at Rome, VIII, 333.

International conference to be held at Constantinople upon subject of, referred to, VI, 378.

Representatives to foreign countries to report on progress, etc., of, appointed, VIII, 313, 317.

Report of, referred to, IX, 130.

Choteau, Auguste, treaty with Indians concluded by, II, 20.

Chouteau and Demun, depredations committed on property of, by Mexicans, III, 229.

Chouteau, Charles P., bills for relief of, vetoed, IX, 93, 686.

Christian Indians:

Claims of, against United States, II, 468.

Treaty with, V, 420, 579; VI, 199, 637.

Christiana Case.—In 1851 Edward Gorsuch and a party from Maryland attempted to seize a fugitive slave in Christiana, Pa. A riot ensued in which Gorsuch was killed. Castner Hanway, an invalid Quaker, was arrested and charged with treason, riot, and bloodshed for refusing to assist a marshal in quelling the disturbance. No indictments were found, but the case created much excitement.

Christians, massacre of. (See Armenians.)

Christie, Smith, treaty with Indians negotiated by, VI, 394.

Chrystler's Fields (Canada), Battle of.—Nov. 11, 1813, Gen. Wilkinson, with the main body of the American army, here fought a slightly superior force of British. The battle lasted 5 hours, victory alternately favoring one and then the other. Night ended the conflict, with the British in possession of the field. The Americans lost heavily, many officers being either killed or wounded. American loss, 339; British loss, 187 killed, wounded, and missing.

Church, George E., report of, upon Ecuador referred to, VIII, 157.

Church, Philip, death of Gen. Washington announced and honors to be paid memory of, X, 96.

Church and State.—The relation of the state to religious bodies in America differs from all previous relationships in Europe and the Colonies. Rhode Island, Pennsylvania, and Maryland provided for religious freedom early in their respective histories. Most of the Colonies established the Church of England, though Massachusetts and Connecticut maintained the Congregational. The Constitution guarantees religious freedom in all parts of the United States. Article VI declares that "no religious test shall ever be required as a qualification to any office or public trust under the United States." The first amendment provides that "Congress shall make no law respecting an establishment of religion or prohibiting the free exercise thereof."

Church of Latter-Day Saints. (See Mormon Church; Polygamy.)

Churches and Church Property. (See Religious Establishments.)

Churchwell, Mr., correspondence of, referred to, V, 583.

Churubusco (Mexico), Battle of.—Churubusco was a strongly fortified place near the City of Mexico. The American army, in 2 divisions, under Generals Worth and Twiggs, attacked the Mexicans under Gen. Santa Anna, Aug. 20, 1847, a few hours after the action at Contreras. The Americans numbered 8,000 and the Mexicans 25,000. Early in the engagement the garrison at San Antonio was routed. The hottest fighting took place along the Rio Churubusco, where for some time the Americans were threatened with defeat, but rallying they drove the Mexicans before them. Simultaneously were taken the tête-du-pont, or bridgehead (the key to Santa Anna's position), and the Pablo de Churubusco. The conflict lasted 3 hours. Including the casualties of Contreras, the Mexican loss was 5,877. The Americans lost 1,015.

Churubusco (Mexico), Battle of, referred to, IV, 536.

Cincinnati Industrial Exposition, board on behalf of Executive Departments designated, VIII, 232.

Instructions to, VIII, 233.

Cincinnati, Society of the.—A society originated in 1783 by Revolutionary officers. At the second general meeting in 1787 Washington was chosen president-general and was reelected every 3 years while he lived. The membership rolls were open only to the officers and their eldest sons, though a number of French officers were included. The hereditary principle aroused popular jealousy. It was denounced by the governor of South Carolina and the legislatures of Massachusetts, Pennsylvania, and Rhode Island. In 1784, at the solicitation of Washington, the society dropped the requirement of heredity. The chief immediate objects of the society were to raise a fund for the relief of the widows and orphans of those who fell in the Revolutionary War and to promote a closer political union between the States.

Cipher Dispatches.—The result of the Presidential election of 1876 was for several months in doubt. During this period of uncertainty numerous telegraphic dispatches passed between the friends of Samuel J. Tilden, Democratic candidate for the Presidency. The dispatches were in cipher and purported to be instructions to party workers in South Carolina, Oregon, and Florida. Charges of fraud having been made, these dispatches were ordered turned over to the Senate Committee on Privileges and Elections. A large number of them came into the possession of the New York Tribune, which caused a sensation by publishing transcripts of them. Mr. Tilden in a letter emphatically denied all knowledge of them.

Circuit Courts. (See Courts, Federal.)

Circuit Courts of Appeals. (See Courts, Federal.)

Circulating Medium. (See Medium of Exchange.)

Citizens of United States:

Aid furnished inhabitants of Cuba by, X, 142.

Appropriation for relief of, abroad in certain cases recommended, VII, 191.

Attacked by British forces, III, 401.

Militia called forth to protect, III, 403.

Captured by army of Mexico, IV, 91, 157.

Liberated, IV, 197.

Claims of, against—

Foreign powers. (See the several powers.)

United States. (See Private Claims; War Claims.)

Condemned to death in Cuba, VIII, 103.

Death of, in Cuba, IX, 746, 752.

Destitute, in—

Colombia, order for transportation of, to United States, VIII, 852.

Cuba, appropriation for, X, 136.

Recommended, X, 127.

Referred to, X, 129.

Emigration of, to Turkey for purpose of acquiring lands referred to, VI, 463.

Estates of deceased, in Cuba referred to, V, 360, 361.

Expelled from—

Jurisdiction of Mexico, IV, 327, 345; V, 513, 589.

Prussia, V, 592.

Forbidden to sell goods in Mexico, IV, 262.

Illegally taken from United States by the English, I, 500.

Citizens of United States—Continued.

Impressed into military service of foreign countries. (See Naturalized Citizens.)

Imprisonment of, abroad. (See Imprisonment.)

Imprisonment of, by army officers referred to, VII, 55.

Injuries inflicted upon, in Turkey discussed, IX, 658, 715.

Injuries sustained by, in Mexico, V, 336, 512, 563; VII, 189.

Interference of, in affairs of Great Britain, orders against, X, 106.

Legislation for protection of, VII, 52.

Marriages of, when abroad, recommendations regarding, VII, 292, 347, 406.

Murdered in—

Cuba, VII, 48, 50, 68, 69, 242; IX, 750.

Great Britain, retaliatory measures discussed, I, 537.

Mexico, V, 565.

Quallah Battoo, Sumatra, II, 575.

Naturalization discussed. (See Aliens; Naturalization.)

Of Hebrew persuasion discriminated against in Switzerland, V, 592.

Outrages on, in—

Costa Rica, V, 517.

Mexico, IV, 473, 533; V, 644.

New Granada, V, 415, 518.

Nicaragua, V, 517.

Pontifical States, V, 579.

Pardons granted. (See Pardons.)

Passports used by, in France referred to, VI, 704.

Presented at Court of France, VI, 64.

Privileges accorded, in Turkey discussed, VIII, 335.

Property of—

Confiscated in Cuba, VII, 65, 68, 69.

Destroyed by Spain, I, 384, 388; II, 113.

Destroyed in China, VIII, 236.

Seized by Sweden, X, 60.

Seized or destroyed in Mexico, IV, 473; V, 513, 565, 589.

Protection of, in China discussed, VII, 52, 101; IX, 109, 186, 627, 637.

Religious and educational establishments of, in Turkey, treatment of, discussed, IX, 317.

Rescued by Spanish brig, II, 560.

Compensation for services rendered recommended, II, 560.

Rights of—

Abroad discussed, VI, 180.

In Egypt discussed and proclaimed, VII, 390, 403.

Violated by Spanish authorities, V, 237.

Selected to serve in offices in Japanese Government, VII, 145.

Should not wage private war, I, 370, 404.

Slaughter of, in Hamburg, S. C., referred to, VII, 375.

Steps taken for protection of, in Turkey referred to, VII, 367.

Trading under false colors, I, 495.

Treatment of—

By Great Britain referred to, VI, 520.

In Cuba discussed, X, 129.

Civil-Rights Act.—A law passed by Congress Apr. 9, 1866, over President Johnson's veto, placing the negro on the same civil footing as the white man (VI, 405). It provided that all persons born in the United States and not subjects of any foreign power, excluding Indians not taxed, were to be recognized as citizens of the United States. The violation of the law was made a misdemeanor to be considered by the Federal courts alone. A long controversy ensued over the constitutionality of this law. The fourteenth amendment was framed in accordance with it (I, 37), and in 1875 more stringent measures were passed to secure the civil rights of the negro. In June, 1883, a number of cases were brought before the United States Supreme Court on certificates of division from the circuit courts of Kansas, California, Missouri, New York, and Tennessee. They were, respectively, United States *vs.* Stanley, United States *vs.* Ryan, United States *vs.* Nichols, United States *vs.* Singleton, and Robinson and Wife *vs.* Memphis and Charleston Railroad Co. The cases against Nichols and Stanley were on indictments for refusing the privileges of a hotel; against Singleton and Ryan for refusing admission to a theater. Robinson brought suit against the railroad company for refusing his wife, a colored woman, the privileges of the ladies' car on the Memphis and Charleston Railroad. In the latter case, as well as that of Ryan, judgment was given for the plaintiff on the ground of violation of the first and second sections of the fourteenth amendment to the Constitution. In the other cases the court declared certain provisions of the civil-rights act of 1875 null and void and judgment was rendered for the defendants.

Civil Service.—Jan. 16, 1883, Congress passed what is known as the civil-service law. This act established the United States Civil Service Commission, to be composed of 3 members, not more than 2 of whom should be adherents of the same political party. The act itself is a mere outline of its purposes, but for its amplification it provides for rules to be promulgated by the President, such rules to be equally binding with the statute upon the heads of Departments and offices, as well as upon the Commission. The fundamental purpose of the law and rules is to establish in the parts of the service within their provisions a merit system whereby selections for appointments shall be made upon the basis of demonstrated relative fitness without regard to political considerations. To carry out this purpose a plan of competitive examinations is prescribed. The term "classified service" indicates the parts of the service within the provisions of the civil-service law and rules requiring appointments therein to be made upon examination and certification by the Commission. The term "unclassified service" indicates the parts of the service which are not within those provisions, and therefore in which appointments may be made without examination and certification by the Commission. Under the terms of the law positions outside the executive branch of the Government, positions to which appointment is made by the President and confirmed by the Senate, and positions of mere unskilled manual labor are not required to be classified. With these limitations, the President is authorized to direct from time to time, in his discretion, the heads of Departments and offices to extend the classified service. Under this authority the classified service was gradually extended until it included about 83,000 individual positions. But by order of President McKinley May 29, 1899, about 5,000 of these positions were excepted and taken out of the service. The Commission has nothing to do with classifying any position except those in its own force. In the executive service not yet classified are the following: Consular service, post-offices without free delivery, governments of the District of Columbia and of Territories, Library of Congress, the Census Bureau, and some other parts of the service. A few positions which have been classified have afterwards been excepted from examination, and appointments to such positions may accordingly be made in the same manner as in the unclassified service. There are a few others to which appointments may be made upon noncompetitive examination. The civil-service law and rules do not give to the Commission any power of appointment and removal; that power is left where it was prior to such law, namely, in the President and heads of Departments. Upon requisition of an appointing officer the Commission provides eligibles secured as the result of competitive examination; from the eligibles thus provided the appointing officer makes selection and appointment. When the Commission certifies 3 eligibles for any particular position, the appointing officer has absolute discretion in making selection and appointment from such eligibles, except that the rules require that selection shall be made without regard to political considerations. When certification is made the Commission's duty ends so far as an appointment is concerned, except, of course, it is charged with investigating and reporting any irregularity of appointment or removal. A vacancy in the classified service may be filled either by original appointment upon examination and certification by the Commission, as explained, or by transfer or promotion from certain other positions in the classified service,

Commerce of the World, printing of special edition of, recommended, IX, 664, 751.

Commercial Law, Foreign, digest of, transmitted, X, 65, 66.

Commercial Relations, printing of special edition of, recommended, IX, 664, 751.

Commercial Relations with Foreign Powers. (See Commerce.)

Commercial Reports, publication and circulation of, referred to, VII, 587.

Commercial Rights of United States, decrees of belligerent powers of Europe affecting, referred to, I, 458.

Commercial Tariff. (See Foreign Import Duties; Import Duties.)

Commercial Treaties. (See treaties under the several powers.)

Commission of Labor. (See Labor, Commission of.)

Commissioners. (See the several commissioners.)

Commissioners, United States, jurisdiction to try misdemeanors recommended, VIII, 354; IX, 447, 536.

Commissions (see also Cherokee Commission; Mission Commission; Sioux Commission): To treat with Indians for cession of lands discussed, X, 25.

Committee.—One or more persons, elected or appointed, to whom any matter or business is referred, either by a legislative body or by a court or by any collective body of men acting together. It is the custom in all American legislative bodies to appoint committees for the transaction of their business. It is the duty of these committees to report to the central body their conclusions on all matters referred to them, thus presenting for discussion well-shaped or completed legislation, saving much valuable time and securing more concentrated effort. The committee system of conducting business was developed by the British House of Commons during Queen Elizabeth's reign and was in full operation during the Commonwealth. It has, however, been partially superseded in England by the system of cabinet government. During early colonial days Virginia, Maryland, New York, Pennsylvania, and North Carolina copied the system from England, and the familiarity of the members of the Continental Congress with its workings naturally led to its use in that body. After the adoption of the Constitution Congress made sparing use of the committee system, but by 1820, under Speaker Clay, the system of standing committees had reached full development. The Senate followed slowly. The Senate appoints its own committees. This was formerly the custom in the House, but soon their appointment was given to the Speaker, which adds greatly to his power.

Committee of the Whole.—It is the regular custom of legislative bodies, both in this country and in Europe, to intrust or commit all proposed legislation to committees appointed for the purpose of considering special subjects. These make reports and recommendations to the whole body. For the purpose of deliberating upon matters of general interest not comprehended in the scope of the regular committees, the entire legislative body sometimes resolves itself into a committee of the whole, under the chairmanship of some member other than the regular presiding officer. In the United States Congress the rules and practice of the House recognize two Committees of the Whole—namely, the Committee of the Whole House on the state of the Union, to which are referred public business and bills appropriating public money or property, and the Committee of the Whole House, to which are referred private bills and private business. The rules of proceeding in the House are observed in the Committee of the Whole so far as they are applicable. No legislation can be enacted by the Committee of the Whole.

Committees of Correspondence.—As early as 1744 the legislature of Pennsylvania had a committee of correspondence. The stated purpose of this committee was to keep up correspondence with the agents of the Colony in the mother country, but their real work consisted in uniting the Colonies in protest against the oppression of the parent Government. In a Boston town meeting in 1772 Samuel Adams moved that a committee be appointed to state the rights of the colonists and correspond with other Colonies and towns of New England. The system of secret correspondence thus established served to nourish the spirit of revolution in the Colonies. In the Virginia legislature similar committees were proposed in 1773 and advocated by Dabney Carr, Patrick Henry, and Richard Henry Lee. The Virginia resolutions tended more directly toward forming a confederacy than those of Massachusetts or any of the other Colonies.

Committees of Safety.—When organized opposition to the tyrannical acts of Parliament became a necessity, committees of safety were formed in each of the Colonies for the purpose of resisting the authority of the royal governors. A committee of 11 was appointed by the second provincial congress of Massachusetts in February, 1775, to resist the execution of the laws. It was empowered to muster the militia and seize army supplies. It communicated with similar committees in other Colonies. As the Revolution advanced these committees assumed the powers formerly held by the governors and continued to act as a sort of executive committee until the adoption of the State constitution.

Commodore.—Formerly a courtesy title given in the United States Navy to the senior officer of a squadron. By an act passed in 1857 the senior captain of a fleet was known as the flag officer. The grade of commodore was created in 1862, along with that of rear-admiral, and established as the grade next above that of captain. This grade had the relative rank of a brigadier-general in the Army. Until that year a captain was the highest naval officer recognized by law. A captain or flag officer who commanded more than one vessel at a time was by common consent called commodore, and the title, once applied, generally clung to him. The title of commodore was abolished, by the naval personnel act approved Mar. 3, 1899, and the number of rear-admirals was increased by the same act to 18.

Common Law.—Common law is defined to be those rules of action which have grown up from old usage and the decisions of judges. In the United States the term "common law" means that of England, including unwritten maxims and customs immemorial in that Kingdom and the statutes passed by the English Parliament before the first settlements in the colonial States were made. With the exception of Louisiana, this forms the basis of the jurisprudence of all the States. Under the first Constitution of the Colonies the people were declared entitled to the benefits of the common law of England, but it was left for the colonial courts to decide what common law was. The courts placed various constructions upon existing statutes and colonial legislatures modified the text in various ways. After the Constitution was adopted the strict constructionists maintained that there was no common law in respect to the jurisprudence of the Federal Government, the nationalists taking the opposite view.

Commons.—In early New England towns, on account of lack of facilities for fencing, part of the land, and in some instances all, was cultivated in common. Common cultivation was carried on in some of the towns on an extensive scale. No matter how large the area cultivated, all the people were interested in the work. Sometimes authority over such lands was given to the selectmen. The right of each freeman to a portion of the common lands was scrupulously maintained. The cultivators were known as proprietors, and were sometimes a separate body from the town organization proper. Common cultivation was derived from an English custom. (See Acre Right.)

Comonfort, Ignacio, President of Mexico, election of, discussed, V, 563.

Compensated Emancipation. (See Emancipation.)

Competitor, The, persons claiming American citizenship captured on, by Spanish authorities, IX, 748, 751.

Compromise, Missouri. (See Missouri Compromise.)

Compromise of 1833.—The high tariff of 1828 caused much dissatisfaction throughout the South. By the act of July 14, 1832, amending the tariff law of 1828, many of the revenue taxes were reduced and the first tax was laid on woolen yarn. The oppressive features of these laws were more bitterly opposed in South Carolina than elsewhere, and resulted in the nullification of the law by that State. This was done by a convention held at Columbia Nov. 19, 1832, which by ordinance declared the tariff acts of 1828 and 1832 null and void. Thus the

question of nullification in its fullest development was brought into national prominence. Mar. 1, 1833, Congress enacted a new tariff law in the nature of a compromise. It was practically the same bill as that introduced in the Senate by Henry Clay. It provided for the gradual scaling down of the high duties then existing until after 10 years a free-trade basis should be reached. This compromise took the place of a low-tariff measure then under consideration in the House. The latter provided for a gradual scaling down of all duties, so that 20 per cent should be the standard duty in 1842. (See also Nullification.)

Compromise of 1833, diminution of duties under, referred to, IV, 102.

Compromise of 1850.—On Jan. 29, 1850, Henry Clay introduced 6 resolutions in the Senate relating to (1) the admission of California as a free State; (2) Territorial governments for Utah and New Mexico without conditions as to slavery; (3) boundaries of Texas; (4) payment of Texas debt; (5) suppression of the slave trade in the District of Columbia; (6) fugitive-slave laws. A special committee of 13, with Clay as chairman, combined these resolutions into one omnibus bill, which failed of passage. After the defeat of this (Clay's omnibus) bill several separate bills, having practically the same purpose of compromising on the slavery question, were introduced and passed. Under the compromise Texas was allowed $10,000,000 for New Mexico, and the area of that Territory was reduced. Sept. 9, 1850, California was admitted to the Union with her free constitution. On the same day bills were passed for establishing Territorial governments in New Mexico and Utah. These laws contained Senator Soulé's slavery-option clause. Sept. 12 amendments to the fugitive-slave law of Feb. 12, 1793, was passed, denying arrested negroes trial by jury and prohibiting redress to free colored seamen imprisoned in Southern ports.

Compromise of 1850 (see also Slavery):
Adherence to, recommended, V, 92, 138.
Discussed, V, 222.

Compromises of the Constitution.—Three important compromises were made by the Constitutional Convention in 1787. The most important question that agitated the members was whether each State's influence should be equal to that of any other State, or whether representation should be based upon population. The plan proposed by Edmund Randolph, of Virginia, and called the "Virginia plan," favored representation in both Houses according to population; that of William Paterson, of New Jersey, an equal vote for all States and only one House. As a compromise, proposed by William Samuel Johnson, of Connecticut, and originally suggested by George Mason, of Virginia, the Convention agreed to have two Houses, with equal representation in the Senate and proportionate representation in the House. Secondly, it was proposed to tax both exports and imports at the discretion of Congress. Charles Cotesworth Pinckney, of South Carolina, declared that his State could not come into the Union under such a provision, as her wealth consisted mainly in one article of export—rice. It was therefore decided that no tax upon exports should be laid. Thirdly, North Carolina, South Carolina, and Georgia refused to enter the Union if the slave trade was to be prohibited; so the third compromise agreed to was that Congress should not prohibit traffic in slaves before 1808 and that a fugitive-slave law should be enacted.

Comptroller of Treasury referred to, II, 216.

Comstock, Cyrus B.:
Member of commission to try assassins of President Lincoln, etc., VI, 336.
Relieved from duty, VI, 336.
Mentioned, VI, 614.

Conard, John, memorial of, asking aid of Congress in discharge of judgment, II, 474.

Concord, The, mentioned, X, 155.

Concord (Mass.), Battle of.—One of the opening skirmishes of the Revolutionary War. A detachment of 800 British soldiers under Lieut. Col. Smith and Maj. Pitcairn had been sent from Boston to destroy or capture some military stores collected at Concord by the Americans. After a brief engagement at Lexington they reached Concord Apr. 19, 1775, where they were opposed by 300 minutemen under Col. Barrett and Maj. Buttrick. After a sharp conflict, in which several were lost on each side, the British fled to Boston under a harassing fire of the Americans. (See also Lexington (Mass.), Battle of.)

Confederate Cabinet.—The Confederate States had a cabinet composed of the heads of executive departments, similar to the United States Government and created for like purposes. The heads of the departments exercised similar powers and were clothed with duties and responsibilities corresponding to those of Cabinet officers in the United States. The President was empowered to remove members of his cabinet. Congress was authorized to provide for the admission of cabinet officers to a seat in either house, with the privilege of participating in debates pertaining to their departments. This provision remained inoperative, as the congress failed to provide the appropriate legislation. The secretaries of state were Robert Toombs, of Georgia, Robert M. T. Hunter, of Virginia, and Judah P. Benjamin, of Louisiana; of the treasury, Charles G. Memminger and George A. Trenholm, of South Carolina; of war, L. Pope Walker, of Alabama, Judah P. Benjamin, of Louisiana, George W. Randolph, of Virginia, James A. Seddon, of Virginia, and John C. Breckenridge, of Kentucky; of the navy, Stephen R. Mallory, of Florida; postmaster-general, John H. Reagan, of Texas; attorneys-general, Judah P. Benjamin, of Louisiana, Thomas Bragg, of North Carolina, Thomas H. Watts, of Alabama, and George Davis, of North Carolina. The sole surviving member (1899) of these cabinet officers is Mr. Reagan, of Texas.

Confederate Congress.—The provisional congress of the seceding Southern States met at Montgomery, Ala., Feb. 4, 1861. Two sessions were held here. The government removed to Richmond, Va., May 24, 1861. The last two sessions were held in the latter city, final adjournment taking place Feb. 17, 1862. The first Confederate congress held 4 sessions between Feb. 18, 1862, and Feb. 18, 1864, to organize the Confederacy, frame a constitution, and devise means for carrying on the war. It consisted of 24 senators and about 100 representatives. The second Confederate congress had 2 sessions between May 2, 1864, and Mar. 18, 1865.

Confederate Constitution.—The constitution adopted by the Confederate States of America at Montgomery, Ala. A provisional congress, composed of delegates from the seceding States, met in that city Feb. 4, 1861, and on the 8th of that month adopted a provisional or temporary constitution. Mar. 11 they agreed upon a permanent constitution, which was afterwards ratified by all the seceding States. It was based upon that of the United States, with the following chief exceptions: It recognized the principle of State sovereignty and the protection of slavery in all new territories; it prohibited internal improvements at federal expense and contained a prohibition against laying any duties on imports "to promote or foster any branch of industry;" new States were to be admitted by a vote of the States; State legislatures could impeach Confederate officers acting within their jurisdiction; the president was to be elected for a term of 6 years and was ineligible for reelection; the appropriating power of congress was limited, and the right of debate in congress was extended to heads of departments. (See also Confederate States.)

Confederate Flags:
Captured, to be presented to Congress, VI, 108.
Return of Union and, to respective States recommended, VIII, 578.
Proposition withdrawn, VIII, 579.

Confederate States.—A government formed in 1861 by the States of South Carolina, Mississippi, Florida, Alabama, Georgia, Louisiana, and Texas. Later Arkansas, North Carolina, Virginia, and Tennessee seceded from the Union and joined the Confederacy. The provisional congress met at Montgomery, Ala., Feb. 4, 1861, and adopted a provisional constitution Feb. 8. Jefferson Davis was elected provisional president and Alexander H. Stephens provisional vice-president. Later a permanent government was organized. A permanent constitution was adopted Mar. 11, 1861. Mr. Davis and Mr. Stephens were elected president and vice-president, respectively, and they were inaugurated Feb. 22, 1862, at Richmond, Va., which was made the permanent seat of government. The history of the Confederate States is almost entirely confined to a history of the Civil War. The United States Government denied the right of any State to secede from the Union, refused to recognize the Confederate States as anything more than rebellious members of the Union, and immediately took measures to bring them into subjection. The Confederate States were granted belligerent rights by most of the maritime nations, but their independence was recognized by none (VI, 126, 367). Money was obtained by the issue of treasury notes and by loans on cotton. After a war of 4 years the government of the Confederate States practically came to an end with the surrender of Gen. Lee at Appomattox, Apr. 9, 1865.

Confederate States (see also Confederate Constitution; Reconstruction; Restoration; Secession; Slavery; Southern States; War between the States):

Acts for admission of certain Southern States vetoed, VI, 648, 650.

Acts to provide for more efficient government of rebel States vetoed. (See Reconstruction.)

Agents of, abroad, suits instituted in English courts against, VI, 463.

Aid furnished to, by Great Britain. (See Alabama Claims.)

Belligerent rights accorded, by foreign powers discussed, VI, 58, 126, 367.

Recognition and aid from foreign powers invoked by, VI, 20, 45.

Blockade of ports of. (See Blockades.)

Circuit courts to be reestablished in, recommendations regarding, VI, 358.

Correspondence regarding, referred to, VI, 378.

Claims against citizens of, and means of collecting discussed, VI, 50.

Commercial intercourse with, prohibited, VI, 37, 165, 282.

Restrictions on, removed from certain ports, VI, 89, 109, 171, 174, 216, 230, 281, 309, 317, 326, 331, 333, 339.

Constitution of. (See Confederate Constitution.)

Courts of justice for, recommended by President Lincoln, VI, 50.

Direct tax, collection of, referred to, VI, 391.

Envoys of, sent to France and Great Britain. (See Mason and Slidell.)

Executive departments of, historical statement of Gen. Sherman concerning public policy of, referred to, VIII, 263.

Flags of—

Captured, to be presented to Congress, VI, 180.

Return of, to respective States recommended, VIII, 578.

Proposition withdrawn, VIII, 579.

Government employees assisting in rendition of public honors to rebel living or dead referred to, VI, 393.

Government of, first located at Montgomery, Ala., VI, 24.

Transfer of, to Richmond, Va., VI, 24.

Governments to be reestablished in—

Act to guarantee republican form of government to States whose governments have been overthrown, VI, 223.

Confederate States—Continued.

Governments to be reestablished in—Cont'd.

Discussed, VI, 189.

Proclamations regarding, VI, 213, 222.

In which insurrection exists proclaimed, VI, 37, 92, 157, 165.

Proclamations declaring insurrection at an end, VI, 429, 434.

Joint resolution declaring certain States not entitled to representation in electoral college discussed, VI, 260.

Joint resolution excluding electoral votes of States lately in rebellion vetoed, VI, 651.

Policy of President of United States toward, referred to, VI, 469.

President of. (See Davis, Jefferson.)

Products of, authority given to purchase, VI, 240.

Rebel debt referred to, VI, 385, 390.

Reconstruction of. (See Reconstruction.)

Restoration of. (See Restoration.)

Secretary of War of. (See Seddon, James A.)

Union and Confederate flags, return of, to respective States recommended, VIII, 578.

Proposition withdrawn, VIII, 579.

Confederate Veterans. (See United Confederate Veterans.)

Confederation, Articles of.—The Second Continental Congress appointed on June 11, 1776, a committee to draw up Articles of Confederation and Perpetual Union. This committee presented a draft to Congress July 12, 1776. Nov. 15, 1777, they were adopted with amendments as "Articles of Confederation and Perpetual Union between the States." July 9, 1778, the Articles were signed by delegates from 8 States. Mar. 1, 1781, the delegates from Maryland also signed, and on the same date the final ratification was ordered by Congress. The original is indorsed: "Act of Confederation of the United States of America." These Articles provided for a single House of Congress with power to raise money by requisitions on the States. Ratification of the Articles by all the States was necessary, and they could not be amended save by consent of every State. They did not operate on individuals and could not command respect abroad or enforce order at home. After numerous futile attempts to amend them a convention, following the suggestion of the Virginia and Maryland boundary commissioners, was called at Annapolis, Md., in 1786, which in turn called a convention at Philadelphia in 1787. The last-named body rejected the Articles of Confederation and framed instead the present Constitution, which, after its ratification by 9 States, became the supreme law of the land (I, 9).

Confederation, Articles of, I, 9.

Signers of, I, 17.

Conger, P. H., treaty with Indians concluded by, VI, 703.

Congo State. (See Kongo Free State.)

Congress.—A formal meeting or association of persons having a representative character for the enactment of laws, or the consideration of some special subject, or the promotion of some common interest. In the United States all legislative powers are granted by the Constitution to Congress. This body consists of the Senate and the House of Representatives. The powers of Congress are enumerated in the Constitution, Article I, section 8, and all the powers not delegated to the United States by the Constitution nor prohibited by it to the States are reserved to the States respectively or to the people. The power of Congress is absolute within the scope of its authority except as it may be restrained by the veto of the President. The Senate is composed of 2 members from each State, regardless of size or population. The members of the House are apportioned on the basis of Federal population. The Constitution provides (Article V) that "no State, without its consent, shall be deprived of its equal suffrage in the Senate." The Senate is presided over by the Vice-President of the United States, who is also President of the Senate, and the House of Representatives by a Speaker chosen by its members. The Vice-President has no vote except in cases where the Senate is equally divided. Congress is required to "assemble at least once in every year, and such meeting shall be on the first Monday in December unless they shall by law appoint a different day." Measures that have passed both Houses are sent to the President, who may either approve or veto them, or do neither, in which latter case the measure becomes a law after 10 days from the time it is presented to him, unless in the meantime Congress shall have adjourned. If he approve the bill and sign it, it becomes a law, but if he disapprove it he must return it with his objections to the House in which it shall have originated for reconsideration by them. In such a case, after reconsideration, it requires the affirmative vote of two-thirds of the members in each of the two bodies to pass the measure. Legislation which exceeds the constitutional power of Congress may be declared unconstitutional and void by the Supreme Court of the United States when that body is properly appealed to by either party to any controversy arising in an attempt to enforce such legislation. Each House is by the Constitution "the judge of the elections, returns, and qualifications of its own members" (I, 23). (See also Senate and House of Representatives.)

Congress:

Act appointing day for annual meeting of, vetoed, III, 231.

Act of—

Approved, but not signed, whether in force discussed, II, 287.

Duly certified and approved which had not passed discussed, III, 134.

Effect on, of adjournment of Congress before expiration of 10 days after presentation to President discussed, VI, 599.

Acts of, to be published in certain newspapers, VII, 162.

Address from committee of public safety of France transmitted to, I, 189, and X, 18.

Congress—Continued.

Adjournment of—

Postponement of recess requested, IX, 660.

Postponement of, recommended, V, 490; VI, 85; VII, 80.

Resolution authorizing, not approved, I, 267.

Appropriations, power to designate officer to expend, discussed, V, 597.

Appropriations should not be made by, unless necessary, III, 29.

Bills, time allowed for consideration of, discussed, V, 462, 529.

Building for temporary use of, lease of, referred to, X, 62.

Capitol prepared for. (See Capitol.)

Carpenter's painting of Lincoln and Cabinet at reading of Emancipation Proclamation presented to, VII, 483.

Constitution, copies of, printed for members of, II, 65, 109.

Constitutional amendments recommended to. (See Constitution.)

Contingent expenses of, discussed, V, 648.

Declaration of Independence, first copperplate of, bequeathed to, by Lafayette, letter of son presenting, III, 123.

Desk on which Declaration of Independence was written presented to United States by heirs of Joseph Coolidge, jr., VII, 588. Letter of Robert C. Winthrop regarding, VII, 589.

Discretionary authority which can be regulated by, should not be exercised by Executive, III, 168.

District of Columbia should be represented in, II, 528, 557; VI, 454.

Extraordinary sessions of, convened by proclamation of President—

Adams, John, I, 232.

Cleveland, IX, 396.

Harrison, W. H., IV, 21.

Hayes, VII, 447, 520.

Jefferson, I, 357, 424.

Lincoln, VI, 13.

Madison, I, 491, 524.

Pierce, V, 394.

Van Buren, III, 321.

(See also Senate, *post.*)

Information regarding foreign affairs requested by, refused, I, 194; IV, 382, 431, 566, 602; V, 154, 155, 159; IX, 669.

Joint resolution of—

Appropriating $50,000 for relief of American citizens in Cuba, X, 136.

Declaring freedom of Cuba and authorizing intervention, etc., X, 155.

Discussed, X, 164.

Regarded by Spain as "equivalent to an evident declaration of war," X, 165.

Loyal Senators and Representatives denied admission to seats in, discussed, VI, 446.

Mail, rates of transportation of, should be regulated by. (See Postal Service.)

Meeting of—

Act appointing day for annual, vetoed, III, 231.

Congress—Continued.

  Senate—Continued.

    Treaties, power to make, vested in President with consent of, I, 195.

Congress, Confederate. (See Confederate Congress.)

Congress, Continental. (See Continental Congress.)

Congress of Nations. (See Panama, Isthmus of.)

Congressional Elections:

  Federal supervision of, recommended, IX, 55, 127, 331.

  Gerrymander discussed, IX, 208.

Congressional Globe.—That part of the proceedings of Congress which was published between 1833 and 1873. The Globe was first issued as a newspaper. Later it succeeded the Register of Debates. It was succeeded by the Congressional Record. (See also Annals of Congress; Congressional Record; Register of Debates.)

Congressional Record.—A complete record of the debates and proceedings of Congress from December, 1873, to the present time. It is the successor to the Congressional Globe, and is printed and circulated by the Government. The Congressional Record is issued daily during the sessions of Congress. Each member of Congress is gratuitously supplied with a specified number for his constituents. It may also be obtained by subscription, the price being $8 for the long and $4 for the short session. (See also Annals of Congress; Congressional Globe; Register of Debates.)

Congressman at Large.—A member of the United States House of Representatives elected by the voters of an entire State, and not, as is customary, by those of a Congressional district. The election of a Congressman at large is a device adopted by a State to secure proper representation in Congress under a Federal apportionment act pending the passage of a State law redistricting the State in accordance with the Federal allowance of Representatives. The apportionment act of Feb. 7, 1891, provides that after Mar. 3, 1893, the House of Representatives shall be composed of 356 members, apportioned as follows: Alabama, 9; Arkansas, 6; California, 7; Colorado, 2; Connecticut, 4; Delaware, 1; Florida, 2; Georgia, 11; Idaho, 1; Illinois, 22; Indiana, 13; Iowa, 11; Kansas, 8; Kentucky, 11; Louisiana, 6; Maine, 4; Maryland, 6; Massachusetts, 13; Michigan, 12; Minnesota, 7; Mississippi, 7; Missouri, 15; Montana, 1; Nebraska, 6; Nevada, 1; New Hampshire, 2; New Jersey, 8; New York, 34; North Carolina, 9; North Dakota, 1; Ohio, 21; Oregon, 2; Pennsylvania, 30; Rhode Island, 2; South Carolina, 7; South Dakota, 2; Tennessee, 10; Texas, 13; Vermont, 2; Virginia, 10; Washington, 2; West Virginia, 4; Wisconsin, 10; Wyoming, 1. It also provided that Congressmen shall be elected from districts composed of contiguous territory and containing as nearly as possible an equal number of inhabitants, the number of such districts equaling the number of Representatives to which the State is entitled; but "in case of an increase in the number of Representatives which may be given to any State under this apportionment such additional Representative or Representatives shall be elected by the State at large and the other Representatives by the districts now prescribed by law until the legislature of such State, in the manner herein prescribed, shall redistrict such State." Since the census of 1890 Utah has been admitted to the Union, with 1 Representative, making the present membership of the House 357.

Conkling, Alfred, mentioned, V, 237.

Connecticut.—One of the thirteen original States of the American Union; nickname, "The Nutmeg State;" motto, "Qui transtulit sustinet" (He who transplanted still sustains). It lies between lat. 41° and 42° 3′ north and long. 71° 55′ and 73° 50′ west. It is bounded on the north by Massachusetts, on the east by Rhode Island, on the south by Long Island Sound, and on the west by New York. Its leading manufactures are hardware, firearms, silks, cotton and woolen goods, and clocks. Connecticut was settled by English colonists from Plymouth, Mass., about 1635, although the Dutch had been there somewhat earlier. Charles II granted a charter to the Connecticut and New Haven Colonies in 1662, and soon thereafter they united. The present constitution was adopted in 1818. Area, 4,990 sq. miles; population (1890), 746,258.

Connecticut:

  Ratification of amendment to Federal Constitution by, referred to, I, 259.

  Refusal of governor of, to furnish militia for defense of frontier, I, 516; X, 43.

Connecticut River, practicability of connecting Lake Memphremagog with, II, 307.

Connelly, Julia, act for relief of, vetoed, VIII, 448.

Conner, Capt., mentioned, IV, 321.

Conner, Lieut., court-martial of, II, 284.

Conservatives.—A faction of the Democratic party who from 1837 to 1840 voted with the Whigs against the subtreasury bill. On other questions the Conservatives acted with their party. The term is generally applied to those members of a political party who oppose radical measures of any kind.

Conspiracies, Unlawful. (See Illegal Combinations.)

Constantinople, Turkey:

  Expulsion of Greeks from, V, 241.

  International conference to be held at, upon subject of cholera referred to, VI, 378.

  Robert College at referred to, VI, 702.

Constellation, The.—The flagship of Commodore Thomas Truxtun of the squadron sent to protect American shipping in the West Indies during our troubles with France in 1799. The *Constellation* was built at Baltimore and commissioned in 1798. Feb. 9, 1799, she defeated and captured the French frigate *L'Insurgente*, of 40 guns. Feb. 1, 1800, she defeated *La Vengeance*, of 54 guns, which, after a fierce engagement, escaped, owing to a storm. Congress presented Truxtun with a gold medal and a vote of thanks for his bravery during this engagement.

Constitution.—Fundamental law in a limited or free government. As applied to the United States of America or to any State of the American Union, the constitution is a written statement of the powers of government. The people who hold the elective franchise are by prescribed forms called upon to establish their constitution, which they may subsequently amend in accordance with its provisions. When established the constitution is paramount to the government organized under it. If any department of the government exceeds its authorized powers, the act is irregular and void. Thus, if an act of Congress or of a State legislature does not conform in its terms to the constitution, which declares itself to be the supreme law of the land or of the State, as the case may be, the Federal or State Supreme Court, as the case may be, may decide the act in question to be unconstitutional and therefore of no effect. In Great Britain the constitution consists of customs, traditions, royal charters, statutes of Parliament, the common law, the Magna Charta, the Declaration of Rights, the Act of Settlement, the Reform Bill, etc. The British constitution has never had the direct sanction of the people; the Constitution of the United States and of each State of the Union has received such sanction. The Constitution of the United States was framed in a convention of the States, except Rhode Island, at Philadelphia in 1787, and went into effect Mar. 4, 1789, having been ratified by eleven of the thirteen States. North Carolina and Rhode Island ratified it Nov. 21, 1789, and May 29, 1790, respectively. (See also Amendments.)

Constitution:

Amendment to—

Fourteenth, recommendation that disabilities imposed under, be removed, VII, 153, 255.

Proclamation directing discontinuance of prosecutions, VII, 176.

Joint resolution proposing, VI, 643.

Joint resolution proposing fourteenth, opposed, VI, 391.

Question of Congress proposing, until after admission of loyal Senators and Representatives of unrepresented States referred to, VI, 391.

Ratification of. (See Ratification of, *post.*)

Referred to, II, 26, 217; VI, 524.

Relative to—

Abolishing slavery—

Defeated, VI, 252.

Recommended, VI, 358.

Ratification of, referred to, VI, 372, 446.

Approval of separate items of bill and veto of others recommended, VII, 242; VIII, 138, 187, 253.

Distribution of surplus revenue among States suggested, II, 452.

Expenditures for education suggested, I, 409, 456; II, 18.

Gradual emancipation of slaves recommended, VI, 136.

Constitution—Continued.

Amendment to—Continued.

Relative to—

Internal improvements suggested, I, 410, 568; II, 18, 191.

Legislation in extra session of Congress suggested, VII, 242.

Maintenance of free schools by States, VII, 334.

Mode of election of President and Vice-President suggested, II, 447, 518, 557, 605; III, 34, 117, 176, 259; VI, 639, 691; VII, 242.

Mode of election of United States Senators recommended, VI, 642, 691.

Postponement of meeting of Congress suggested, I, 250.

Selection of Presidential electors recommended, IX, 209.

Slavery recommended, V, 638.

Suability of States ratified, I, 260.

Successor to President in event of vacancy in Presidency and Vice-Presidency recommended, VI, 639, 691. (See also VIII, 365.)

Tenure of office by judiciary of United States recommended, VI, 643, 691.

Centennial anniversary of framing, proposition to celebrate, discussed, VIII, 533.

Journal of acts and proceedings of convention which formed, published, II, 65, 109.

Legislation to supplement guaranties afforded by fourteenth amendment recommended, VIII, 188.

Ratification of—

Fifteenth amendment referred to, VII, 44, 47, 53, 127.

Discussed, VII, 55.

Fourteenth amendment referred to, VI, 466, 467, 469, 524, 597, 638, 639, 645.

Proclamation regarding enforcement of, VII, 134.

Proclaimed, VI, 656, 657, 658, 659, 660.

Withdrawal of, by Ohio and New Jersey, VI, 638.

Thirteenth article of amendments to (citizens accepting titles from foreign powers), report regarding, X, 56.

Ratification of, by States. (See the several States.)

Referred to, I, 103, 109.

Right to make and alter, basis of our political system, I, 217.

Secret journal of Congress of Confederation published, II, 109.

Signers of, I, 32.

Constitution, The.—A famous American frigate, known also as "*Old Ironsides.*" She was built at Boston in 1797, and carried 44 guns. July 17, 1812, she encountered a fleet of 5 British frigates, but through the masterly seamanship of Capt. Hull eluded capture. Aug. 19 she was attacked by the British frigate *Guerrière*, carrying 38 guns. Within half an hour the latter was a wreck and 85 of her men killed and wounded (I, 517). Dec. 29, 1812, after a hard-fought battle of 2 hours, the British man-of-war *Java*, carrying 38 guns, surrendered to the *Constitution* (I, 522). The British loss was 161 in killed and wounded, while the American loss was only 34. Feb. 20, 1815, the *Constitution* captured the *Cyane*, 20 guns, and the *Levant*, 18 guns. British loss 77 and American loss 15.

Constitution, The:
British frigate *Guerrière* captured and destroyed by, I, 517.
British frigate *Java* captured and destroyed by, I, 522.
Capt. Bainbridge in command of, I, 522.
Capt. Hull in command of, I, 517.

Constitution, The (slave ship), proceedings of court regarding, II, 329.

Constitution, Confederate. (See Confederate Constitution.)

Constitutional Rights discussed. (See Powers of Federal and State Governments.)

Constitutional Treasury System:
Recommended by President Polk, IV, 406.
Successful operation of, discussed, IV, 556, 648.

Constitutional Union Party.—The issues of 1860 and the years immediately preceding disrupted the Whig party. May 9 of that year representatives of the party held a convention at Baltimore and nominated John Bell, of Tennessee, for President, and Edward Everett, of Massachusetts, for Vice-President. Delegates were present from about 20 States. They took the name of the Constitutional Union party. They denounced the platforms of the other parties as tending "to widen political divisions," and declared their principle to be "the Constitution of the country, the Union of the States, and the enforcement of the laws." In the election it carried 3 States—Kentucky, Tennessee, and Virginia.

Constitutionalists.—A political party in Pennsylvania which under the constitution of 1776–1790 favored the maintenance of that instrument as opposed to those who demanded a stronger government than could be had under it. They were the local forerunners of the Democrats and Anti-Federalists of later times. Between 1804 and 1808 a party arose which desired to amend the constitution. They were called Conventionalists and the party opposed to them Constitutionalists.

Constitutions, State.—At the time of the Declaration of Independence only a few of the Colonies had local governments of their own. These were only temporary organizations. Constitutions were first adopted by the 13 original States as follows: Maryland, New Hampshire, New Jersey, North Carolina, Pennsylvania, and Virginia in 1776; Georgia and New York in 1777; South Carolina in 1778; Massachusetts in 1780; Delaware in 1792; Connecticut in 1818; Rhode Island in 1842.

Consul-General, title of, should be abandoned, VIII, 338.

Consular and Diplomatic Service (see also Consular Reform):
Act making appropriations for—
Approved and reasons therefor, VII, 377.
Returned, VIII, 220.

Consular and Diplomatic Service—Continued.
Consular system referred to, III, 27; VI, 181, 192, 270, 394, 596, 639.
Costumes of persons in, referred to, V, 584; VI, 636.
Discussed, IX, 33, 112.
Elevation of missions, IX, 442; X, 188.
Recommended, IX, 33.
Inspector of consular offices discussed, IX, 723.
Organization of class of supernumerary secretaries of legation abroad recommended, VIII, 67.
Promotions, removals, and appointments in, VIII, 85.
Referred to, V, 536; VI, 192, 270, 394; VII, 115, 169; VIII, 208, 214, 262.
Reorganization of, recommended by President—
Arthur, VIII, 131, 242, 251.
Cleveland, VIII, 337, 506, 785; IX, 442.

Consular Conventions with—
Austria, VII, 69.
Belgium, VI, 690, 695; VII, 43, 587.
Referred to, VII, 609.
Chile, V, 424.
France, I, 57; V, 190.
Referred to, I, 83.
Germany, VII, 160, 188.
Italy, VI, 602; VII, 484, 496, 636; VIII, 39.
Expiration of, discussed, VII, 466.
Netherlands, VII, 485, 568.
Roumania, VIII, 35, 40.
Referred to, VIII, 170.
Salvador, VII, 116, 258, 293.
Servia, VIII, 40, 71.
Referred to, VIII, 170.

Consular Courts. (See Courts, Consular.)

Consular Laws discussed, I, 253; II, 554; V, 177.

Consular Offices, inspection of, discussed, IX, 723.

Consular Pupils referred to, VI, 146.

Consular Reform (see also Consular and Diplomatic Service):
Discussed, IX, 639, 722.
Order regarding examination for consular offices, IX, 624.

Consular Reports:
On production of and trade in coffee among Central and South American States referred to, VIII, 616.
On taxation referred to, VIII, 616.
On trade and industries of foreign powers referred to, VIII, 401, 537, 616.
Publication of, discussed, X, 191.
Recommended, VII, 612; VIII, 44, 506.
Value and importance of, discussed, VIII, 506.

Consuls.—In international law an agent appointed and commissioned by a sovereign state to reside in a foreign city or town to defend the personal rights and to protect the business interests of such of the citizens of his country as may reside therein, and to collect and forward to the home government information on industrial and economic matters. He is not a diplomatic agent. He must be formally recognized by the power within whose jurisdiction he serves before he can legally discharge the functions of his office. From the early days

September, when it adjourned to meet at Lancaster, Pa., Sept. 27, remaining there but 1 day. Oct. 1 it resumed its sessions at York, Pa. June 27, 1778, it adjourned to meet at Philadelphia, where it reassembled July 7, remaining there until June 21, 1783. Its next meeting was at Princeton, N. J., June 30, remaining in session at that place until Nov. 4, when it adjourned to meet at Annapolis, Md., Nov. 26, where its sessions were held until June 8, 1784. Adjourning, it next met at Trenton, N. J., Nov. 1. Dec. 24 it adjourned to meet at New York, where it remained in session until its final adjournment, Oct. 21, 1788. The several sessions here were as follows: Jan. 11 to Nov. 4, 1785; Nov. 7, 1785, to Nov. 3, 1786 (new officers being chosen at the commencement of this session); Nov. 6, 1786, to Oct. 30, 1787 (new officers again elected at beginning of session); Nov. 5, 1787, to final adjournment. It is a fact worthy of record that as the old Congress died, so the new was born, in the city of New York.

Continental Money.—On the authority of the Second Continental Congress an issue of paper money was begun in 1775 and continued till 1779. This "money" was in the nature of bills of credit and its value necessarily fluctuated with the fortunes of the Government which promised redemption. About $242,000,000 were put forth. At first the bills circulated on a par with gold, but later greatly depreciated. In 2 years they had become depressed to half the value of gold. In 1779 they were reduced to one-twentieth of their face value and afterwards to one-fortieth. Congress then ordered the notes bought up at their market value, replacing them by a new issue at the rate of 20 to 1, to bear interest at 5 per cent. The old notes sank as low as 1,000 to 1 and finally disappeared.

Continental Soldiers.—The regular troops of the American Revolutionary Army. They were under the command of Washington and were paid by the Government. In 1775 Congress appropriated £6,000 for their support and appointed Washington to the command. Ten companies of expert riflemen were enlisted in Pennsylvania and Virginia. Continental soldiers should not be confounded with guerrillas and militia.

Contraband of War.—A term said to have been first employed in the treaty of Southampton between England and Spain in 1625. The treaty of the Pyrenees between France and Spain, signed Nov. 7, 1659, modified the previously entertained notions of articles contraband of war, and a still more liberal construction was put upon the word by the Declaration of Paris, Apr. 26, 1856. All arms, ammunition, and supplies which may be of use in carrying on war or aiding in defense are by the laws of war contraband, and are liable to seizure by either belligerent should a neutral attempt to convey them to the other belligerent. Gen. B. F. Butler in 1861 pronounced slaves of persons in rebellion against the United States Government contraband.

Contraband of War:
On British vessels for insurgents, VI, 151.
Trade in, and protection for neutral vessels, order regarding, VI, 176.

Contracts, Government, recommendations regarding, V, 649.

Contreras (Mexico), Battle of.—Aug. 7, 1847, Gen. Twiggs's division began its march upon the City of Mexico. By the 18th the entire army was at San Augustine, 9 miles from the city. On the 19th a preliminary assault was made upon Contreras Hill, a fortified position about 4 miles from the city, held by Gen. Valencia with 6,000 men. Early the next morning Contreras Hill was taken by sudden assault, Valencia's army being completely routed, with a loss of 2,500 men. Among the prisoners were 4 generals. By this brilliant dash the Americans had gained one of the several strong positions by which the roads to the City of Mexico were guarded. The American loss was 50 men killed and wounded. The Mexicans lost heavily in cannon, muskets, and ammunition.

Contreras (Mexico), Battle of, referred to, IV, 536.

Convention, Diplomatic.—In the language of diplomacy, convention is usually synonymous with treaty, with the vague distinction that a convention relates to a few or unimportant or nonpolitical points. The protocol or informal treaty is sometimes referred to as a treaty. (See also Protocol.)

Convention, Nominating.—An assembly of delegates or representatives for consultation on important political concerns and the nomination of candidates for office. Early American candidates for office either made a public announcement of their candidacy or were placed in nomination by a caucus more or less select. Out of this custom grew the Congressional caucus of party leaders and, at a later period, the legislative caucus. This was defective in that parties having no legislative delegates had no caucus delegates. This was remedied by sending caucus delegates from those districts not represented by legislative delegates. This immediate step was succeeded by the nominating caucus or convention as at present conducted, both in the several States and in the nation, consisting of delegates from all parts of a State or of the nation chosen for the express purpose of making nominations. The first State convention of which we have any record was held at Harrisburg, Pa., in 1788. The first national nominating convention was that held at Baltimore in September, 1831, by the Anti-Masons. In December of the same year the National Republicans, who were the progenitors of the Whigs, held a national convention at Baltimore. In May, 1832, a Democratic national convention nominated Jackson for President and Van Buren for Vice-President. About 1840 both parties adopted this practice, since which time it has become universal.

Convention, Revolutionary.—Previous to and at the beginning of the Revolution the royal governors of the Colonies dissolved the legislative assemblies because of their opposition to the oppressive measures of the Crown and Parliament. These assemblies immediately met in what were called revolutionary conventions. In a short time these bodies acquired all authority over the people, to the exclusion of the parent Government.

Convention Troops.—A name applied to Gen. Burgoyne's army after the surrender at Saratoga, N. Y., Oct. 17, 1777. A convention was signed fixing the terms of surrender. Burgoyne's officers and men, numbering nearly 6,000, were allowed under the convention to march out bf camp with the honors of war, promising to refrain from further hostile acts against the States. Pending transportation to England they were quartered at Winter Hill and Prospect Hill, in Boston. Suspecting that the parole would be violated, Congress, after ratifying, revoked it. After a long delay Burgoyne and his staff were sent to England on parole and the troops were transferred to Rutland, Vt., and afterwards to Charlottesville, Va. There they remained till 1780, when the British were removed to Fort Frederick, Md., and the Germans to Winchester, Va. Later some of the convention troops were removed to Lancaster, Pa., and others to East Windsor, Conn. By the end of 1782 they had been dispersed by exchange or desertion.

Conventions. (See International Conventions; Treaties.)

Convicts, Foreign, involuntary deportation of paupers, idiots, insane persons, and, to United States, VII, 265.

Cooley, Dennis N., treaty with Indians concluded by, VI, 394.

Cooley, Lyman E., member of commission to consider construction of canal from Great Lakes to Atlantic Ocean, IX, 747.

Coolidge, Joseph, jr., desk on which Declaration of Independence was written presented to United States by heirs of, VII, 588.

Letter of Robert C. Winthrop regarding, VII, 589.

Cooly.—Originally the name of one of the aboriginal hill tribes of Hindustan. In a general sense the word is used to designate an Asiatic laborer not an artisan. In a more specific sense the term is applied to the common laborer of China or India who emigrates to a foreign country under contract. The name is applied by Europeans in Hindustan to porters and laborers in general. In the United States the word is almost restricted to Chinese laborers who come into the country either voluntarily or under contract. Cooly immigration began when slavery ceased. Their importation and immigration into the United States have caused loud and frequent protests from the American laboring classes, especially in those portions of the country where the coolies mainly settle. The principal objection to them is that they underbid white labor in the open market and live more cheaply and amid surroundings intolerable to native workingmen. Another objection to them is that they do not amalgamate with the Caucasian race

and do not become citizens of the country of their adoption.

Cooly Trade referred to, V, 374, 596; VI, 60, 639; VII, 37, 80, 236.

Cooper, Harriet E., act granting pension to, vetoed, VIII, 687.

Copper, act regulating duties on, vetoed, VI, 705.

Copper Coins, weight of, reduced, I, 191. Proclaimed, X, 78.

Copper Mines referred to, II, 195, 234.

Copperhead.—A term of opprobrium applied to citizens of the North who sympathized with the Southern Confederacy during the Civil War. The name was first used in a political sense in 1863 in reference to persons who favored peace on any terms. The epithet had its origin in the charge that those to whom it was applied were secret and insidious foes to the Union. The term has recently (1899) been applied to those who are not in sympathy with the prevalent ideas concerning the annexation of territory gained by the recent war with Spain, especially to those who are quietly endeavoring to foment discord among the people at home and the soldiers in the Philippines.

Copyright.—As defined by Drone, copyright is the exclusive right to multiply and dispose of copies of an intellectual production. Before the organization of the Federal Government the States issued copyrights. The Constitution authorized Congress to grant copyrights to authors and patents to inventors. Accordingly Congress passed a law in 1790 giving authors the exclusive right to their works for 14 years, with the privilege of renewal for 14 years. In 1831 the period was extended to 28 years, with the right of renewal for 14 years. The law of 1870 extends the right of renewal for 14 years to the widow or children of a deceased author who in his lifetime had been awarded a copyright for an original term of 28 years. Clerks of the district courts of the United States formerly issued copyrights, but they are now issued by the Librarian of Congress. In 1891 the international copyright law was passed, extending the privilege of American copyright to authors of such foreign countries as granted the same privilege to American authors. This reciprocal privilege, which is determined and effected by proclamation of the President, according to the terms of the law, has been availed of by several European and American nations. (See Copyright, *post*.)

Copyright:

Correspondence with—
Switzerland and France regarding international, referred to, VIII, 530.
Switzerland and Italy regarding international, referred to, VIII, 404.
Foreign holders of, to be privileged in United States discussed, VIII, 241; IX, 43, 126.
International law of—
Convention regarding, with—
Germany, IX, 191.
Great Britain, V, 189, 230.

Corinth (Miss.), Battle of.—Oct. 2, 1862, the Confederates under Generals Van Dorn and Price appeared in front of Corinth, and on the 3d fighting began. Grant directed Rosecrans to call in all his forces for the defense, and dispatched Brig. Gen. McPherson to his support from Jackson, Miss. Ord and Hurlbut were sent from Bolivar by way of Pocahontas to attack the flank of Van Dorn. Rosecrans's army advanced 5 miles beyond the town and fell back, fighting, upon Grant's fortifications. The battle was resumed on the morning of the 4th, and before noon the Confederate repulse was complete. The Confederates numbered 38,000. The Federal forces amounted to 19,000. The Federal loss was 315 killed, 1,812 wounded, and 232 missing. The Confederate losses were 1,423 killed, 5,962 wounded, and 2,225 prisoners. On the 5th, while in retreat, the Confederates were attacked by the divisions of Ord and Hurlbut at the crossing of the Hatchie River, 10 miles from Corinth. A battery and several hundred men were captured.

Corn Laws.—In English history a series of laws covering the period from 1436 to 1846 regulating the home and foreign grain trade of England. During this period the export and import grain trade was the subject of elaborate and varying legislation. Very high protective duties were levied, which amounted to a prohibition of imports of grain, and large bounties were granted to encourage its exportation. After a long and bitter agitation for the repeal of the corn laws throughout England, Parliament in 1846, under the ministry of Sir Robert Peel, who had become a free trader, passed an act largely reducing the duty on imported grain, to take effect immediately, and further providing for a merely nominal duty after 1849, which was later entirely removed.

Costa Rica.—One of the Central American Republics. The name is Spanish, and means "rich coast." It lies between lat. 8° and 11° 16' north and long. 82° and 86° west, and is bounded on the north by Nicaragua, on the east by the Caribbean Sea, on the south by Colombia, and on the west and southwest by the Pacific Ocean. The soil is remarkably fertile, especially on the table-lands and in the valleys. Coffee is the chief article of export. The country contains some rich gold mines. The Government consists of a President and a House of Deputies. The country was visited by Columbus in 1502. The first settlement was made by Francisco Hernandez in 1523. Independence from Spain was declared in 1821, and the territory formed part of the Federal Republic of Central America from 1823 to 1839. Area, 22,996 sq. miles; population (1892), 243,205.

which may not be diminished during their term of office. They have the privilege of retiring at the age of 70 if they have served 10 years and of drawing their salaries for the remainder of life. The jurisdiction of the Supreme Court extends to all cases in law and equity arising under the Constitution, the laws of the United States, and treaties which are made under their authority ; to all cases affecting ambassadors or other public ministers and consuls ; to all admiralty and maritime cases ; to controversies to which the United States is a party ; to controversies between 2 or more States, between citizens of different States, between citizens of the same State claiming lands under grants of different States, between a State and foreign States, and between citizens of a State and foreign States, citizens, or subjects. In all cases affecting ambassadors or other public ministers and consuls and those in which a State shall be a party the Supreme Court has original jurisdiction. In all the other cases aforementioned it has appellate jurisdiction both as to law and fact. The Supreme Court also has appellate jurisdiction over cases from the United States circuit courts where more than $2,500 is involved. The first session of the court was held in 1790.

Court, Supreme :

Courts.—In the United States courts are public tribunals for the administration of justice and the interpretation of law. Their functions include the protection of private rights, the punishment of crime, and the regulation of conflicting interests of individuals and States. In accordance with the provision of the Constitution establishing a Supreme Court and conferring upon Congress power to create inferior tribunals, a regular system of courts has been formed. The system at first adopted has not been changed in any essential manner. The Supreme Court is the highest tribunal of the United States. It consists of a Chief Justice and

8 associate justices. The court holds its sessions in the Capitol at Washington. It has both original and appellate jurisdiction, but in practice usually the latter. Its original jurisdiction is over all cases affecting representatives of foreign powers and cases in which a State is a party. In some cases its jurisdiction is not only original, but exclusive. In its appellate function it reviews and may affirm or reverse the judgments and decrees of the inferior United States courts, and, generally in civil cases, of the highest State courts. After the Supreme Court the most important Federal courts are, beginning with the lowest, the district courts, circuit courts, and circuit courts of appeals. All these exercise both law and equity jurisdiction, as prescribed by law. Final appeals are taken to the Supreme Court. United States district courts usually have jurisdiction over a single State, but some of the larger States have been divided into 2 or more districts by Congress. There are now 63 districts in the United States. Each district court consists of a single judge. Original jurisdiction is exercised in civil, criminal, and admiralty cases. The class of questions which may come before the district courts is modified by Congress from time to time. The district courts exercise concurrent jurisdiction with the circuit courts of all crimes and offenses against the United States the punishment of which is not capital. The United States is divided into 9 judicial circuits, each of which is presided over by a circuit judge. Each circuit judge is required to attend at least one term of such court to which he is appointed in each district of his circuit during every 2 years. Circuit courts have jurisdiction in patent cases, but they have no appellate jurisdiction. Their original jurisdiction extends concurrently with that of the State courts where the United States or an alien is plaintiff in certain cases or where the suit is between a citizen of the State in which it is brought and a citizen of another State. The circuit court of appeals was established by act of Mar. 3, 1891. This law created in each of the 9 judicial circuits a circuit court of appeals, consisting of 3 judges, 2 of whom constitute a quorum. An additional judge was appointed in each circuit. This judge and a Supreme Court associate justice assigned to the circuit, or the Chief Justice and any of the several district court judges within the circuit, are competent to sit as a circuit court of appeals. The judicial systems of the several States of the Union are in general modeled after the Federal system, but are diverse in many details. Besides the courts mentioned above, Congress in 1855 established the Court of Claims, of 5 judges, which sits in Washington City. The court has jurisdiction of claims against the United States. The District of Columbia has a supreme court and a court of appeals, over both of which the Supreme Court of the United States has appellate jurisdiction. Territorial courts are also provided, the judges of which

War of 1812. Tecumseh was defeated by Harrison at Tippecanoe and was killed in the battle of the Thames, Oct. 5, 1813, but his schemes agitated and divided the Creek Nation. Weathersford, or Red Eagle, became so troublesome as the leader of the war faction that bodies of militia were sent against him from Tennessee and Georgia. The first serious outbreak of the Creeks was the massacre of the garrison and refugees at Fort Mims, Aug. 30, 1813. As a result, Alabama was almost abandoned by whites. Self-protection and a desire for revenge took possession of the people of Georgia and Tennessee. Gen. Jackson entered the field at the head of the Tennessee militia. Gen. Floyd led the Georgians to avenge the massacre, and Gen. Claiborne was acting at the head of troops from Louisiana and Mississippi. The war received its death blow at the hands of Jackson at Horse Shoe Bend, Mar. 27, 1814. It lasted only 7 months. Taken alone it was of minor importance, but considered in connection with the War of 1812 it had an important bearing. With the subjugation of the Creeks perished all hope of Indian aid in the Southwest for the proposed occupation of the Mississippi Valley.

Creek Indians.—A powerful confederacy of the Muskhogean stock of Indians, which in the early days of American history inhabited Alabama, Georgia, and part of Florida. At the instigation of Spaniards the Yámasi tribe made several attacks upon the settlers during the eighteenth century. They aided the British in the War of the Revolution, attacking Gen. Wayne in 1782. In 1790 they signed a treaty of friendship, but broke it 2 years later. In 1802 and 1805 they ceded lands to the whites. They joined the British in the War of 1812, and Aug. 30, 1813, they attacked Fort Mims and massacred 400 people. Mar. 27, 1814, they were completely subjugated by Gen. Jackson and ceded the greater part of their land to the whites. The Seminoles, a renegade body of Creeks, made war upon the United States from 1835 to 1843. Part of the Creeks moved to Louisiana and part to Texas. Later Gen. Scott subjugated them, and they were removed to a reservation between the Canadian and Arkansas rivers. In 1866 they ceded a large tract of land to the Government. The Creeks now occupy lands in Indian Territory, are well organized, and have a population, including mixed bloods, of about 15,000.

Creek Indians:
Charges against United States agent for, II, 399.
Commerce with, I, 77.
Commissioners to treat with, for cession of lands discussed, X, 25.
Conflicting claims of Georgia and, to lands. (See Georgia.)
Convention with, I, 390.
Court of inquiry relative to campaign against, III, 289.
Opinion of, disapproved, III, 289.
Proceedings of, transmitted for action thereon, III, 291.

Creek Indians—Continued.
Difficulties of, with Seminoles, V, 295, 364.
Difficulties with, I, 151.
Frauds practiced upon, in land sales, III, 405, 480.
Hostilities of, ended, III, 253, 254.
Referred to, III, 280.
Lands—
Ceded to United States by, I, 343, 374, 387; II, 394; IX, 15.
Amount of cession, IX, 46.
Proposition regarding, VIII, 72, 807.
Opened to settlement by proclamation, IX, 15.
Purchased for Seminoles from, VIII, 199.
Additional proposition regarding, IX, 70.
Purchased from, title to, discussed, VIII, 266.
Murdered by outlaws, I, 151.
Protection for lands of, invoked, II, 370.
Removal of, discussed and referred to, III, 55, 113, 498.
Sales of reservations of deceased, III, 516.
Treaty with, transmitted and discussed, I, 70, 76, 78, 79, 111, 167, 175, 199, 210, 397, 554; II, 85, 287, 306, 324, 343, 345, 370, 394, 398, 399, 402, 509, 569; III, 37, 516; IV, 361; V, 242, 383; VI, 193, 393, 702; VIII, 807; X, 52, 57, 60.
Correspondence regarding, II, 320.
Proclamation regarding, I, 80.
Rights of, under, II, 370.
Spanish interference in execution of, X, 14.
War with. (See Indian Wars.)

Creole Case.—During the passage of the brig *Creole* from Hampton Roads to New Orleans with a cargo of slaves, in November, 1841, some of the negroes rose against the officers of the vessel, killed one of the owners, and ran the vessel into Nassau, New Providence. All were here set at liberty by the English authorities except those charged with murder. Great Britain refused to surrender them on demand of the United States (IV, 91), but the matter was finally settled by a treaty in 1842. During the negotiations for this treaty resolutions embodying the principles of the Anti-Slavery Party were offered in Congress by Joshua R. Giddings, of Ohio. He was censured by the House and thereupon resigned. Returning to Ohio, he was reelected by a large majority, with instructions to present the resolutions again.

Creole, The, liberation of cargo of slaves on, at Nassau, New Providence, IV, 91, 101.

Crescent City, The, not allowed to land passengers and mail at Havana, Cuba, V, 237.

Crete:
Resolution of Congress declaring sympathy for suffering people of, referred to, VI, 693.
Revolution in, referred to, VI, 462.

Cridler, Thomas W., special commissioner to Paris Exposition, report of, transmitted, X, 182.

Crime, international convention for suppression of, VII, 161.

Crimes and Misdemeanors:
Abduction of foreigners claiming protection of United States should be made a crime, V, 12.
Convictions, executions, and pardons for capital offenses referred to, II, 425.

Crimes and Misdemeanors—Continued.
Degrees in crime of murder should be recognized, IX, 320, 448, 536.
Limitation upon right in felony cases to review by Supreme Court recommended, IX, 197, 448.
Trial of misdemeanors by United States commissioners recommended, VIII, 354; IX, 447, 536.

Criminal Code, revision of, recommended, I, 576; V, 12, 136.

Criminal Law, abuse of administration of, referred to, VIII, 355; IX, 447.

Criminals. (See Fugitive Criminals.)

Criminals, Foreign, introduction of, into United States referred to, IV, 518; VII, 636.

Cristóbal Colón, The, mentioned, X, 170.

Crittenden, J. J., Acting Secretary of State, V, 112.

Crittenden Compromise.—This was one of the numerous schemes to compromise the slavery question on a peaceful basis. John J. Crittenden was a Senator from Kentucky and tried to harmonize North and South on the slavery question. He hoped to evade the impending war by proposing in 1860 a constitutional amendment which should divide the United States into slaveholding and nonslaveholding portions. He proposed dividing the two sections by the parallel of 36° 30′, the United States to pay the owner for every fugitive slave captured. The proposition, which included other compromise measures, was never submitted to the States.

Croker, Uriel, act for relief of, allowed to become law, VIII, 265.

Crook, George:
Member of—
Ponca Indian Commission, VII, 630.
Sioux Indian Commission, IX, 45.
Report of, regarding services of Apache Indians, IX, 60.

Crooks, James, claim of, against United States for seizure of schooner, VIII, 390; IX, 227.

Crosby, Pierce, thanks of Congress to, recommended, VI, 76.

Cross Keys (Va.), Battle of.—During Stonewall Jackson's movement up the Shenandoah Valley in the summer of 1862 Generals Frémont and Shields were both on the alert to capture him. Frémont reached Strasburg June 1, just after Jackson had passed through. At Port Republic the Shenandoah River divides, and on the larger of the two branches, at a village known as Cross Keys, Frémont brought Ewell's division of Jackson's army to bay June 8. A slight skirmish ensued and Ewell retired during the night. Jackson soon after effected a junction with Gen. Lee, and together they fought the battles around Richmond.

Crow Creek Indians. (See Umpqua Indians.)

Crow Creek Reservation. (See Sioux Reservation.)

Crow Indians:
Agreement with—
For sale of lands, IX, 132.
For use of railroad, VIII, 70.

Crow Indians—Continued.
Agreement with—Continued.
Regarding individual allotments, VIII, 372.
Appropriation for supplies for, recommended, VIII, 194.
Treaty with, II, 347; VI, 637.

Crow Reservation, Mont., opened to settlement by proclamation, IX, 292.

Crowell, John, treaty with Indians concluded by, II, 394.

Crown Lands. (See Lands, Crown.)

Crown Point (N. Y.), Capture of.—Immediately after the capture of Ticonderoga, May 12, 1775, Col. Seth Warner, with a small detachment of men, proceeded to Crown Point, on Lake Champlain, about 90 miles north of Albany. The place was strongly fortified and mounted 114 cannon, but was garrisoned by only 12 men. These were captured and the fort manned by Warner's men.

Crowninshield, A. S., report of, on lives lost by sinking of the *Maine*, X, 153.

Cruelties to Animals, national convention for prevention of, at Baltimore, VII, 506.

Cuartel Lot, survey and disposal of land known as, discussed, IX, 69.

Cuba.—The island of Cuba was discovered Oct. 28, 1492, by Christopher Columbus, who took possession of it in the name of Spain. The first attempt at a permanent settlement was made in 1511 by Don Diego Columbus, a son of Christopher Columbus, and Diego Velasquez, who landed at Baracoa with 300 men. The first settlement at Santiago de Cuba was made in 1514, and the following year a settlement was made at Trinidad. The island was first named Juana, then Fernandina, and later Ave Maria. It received its present name from the natives of the island, whom Columbus described as a peaceful, contented, and progressive race. It is called "The Gem of the Antilles," and is the largest of the West India Islands. Its length, following a curved line through its center, is 730 miles, and its average breadth is 60 miles. Its area is about 43,000 sq. miles. It is irregular, shaped somewhat like a half-moon, long and narrow, extending from east to west, its convex part facing the north. It has a coast line of about 2,000 miles, or, including all indentations, nearly 7,000 miles. The population of the island in 1894 was estimated at 1,723,000. It lies between long. 74° and 85° west and lat. 19° and 23° north. It is situated at the entrance to the Gulf of Mexico and divides that entrance into 2 passages. It is bounded on the north by the Florida, Ocanpo, and Old Bahama channels, on the east by the Strait of Maisi, on the south by the Strait of Colon and the Sea of the Antilles, and on the west by the Strait of Yucatan. Cuba is generally low and swampy along the coast. Especially is this true of the southern coast, while the interior of the island is high tableland. There are many mountain ranges in the interior, some reaching an elevation of over 6,000 feet above sea level. There are no known volcanoes in Cuba or in the Isle of Pines. On account of the peculiar shape of the island, being long and narrow, with its highlands in the interior, nearly all of the rivers flow to the north or to the south, and are therefore necessarily short. There are few navigable rivers, and these but for a short distance from their mouths and only for small coasters and canoes. In the interior there are many pretty lakes and bayous, and, while some of them are very picturesque, like the rivers they are of little importance commercially. Many of these lakes and bayous are salt-water bodies. Situated within and near the border of the northern tropical zone, the climate of the low coast lands of Cuba is that of the torrid zone, but the higher interior of the island enjoys a more temperate atmosphere. As in other lands on the border of the Tropics, the year is divided between a hot wet season, corresponding to the northern declination of the sun, and a cool dry period. From May to October is called the wet season, though rain falls in every month of the year. With May spring begins, rain and thunder are of almost daily occurrence, and the temperature rises high, with little variation. The period from November to April is called the dry season. For 7 years the mean annual rainfall at Havana in the wet season has been observed to be 27.8 inches and of the dry months 12.7, or 40.5 inches for the year. At Havana in the warmest months—those of July and August—the average temperature is 82° F., the maximum being 88° and the minimum 76°. In the cooler months—December and January—the thermometer averages 72°, the maximum being 78° and the minimum 58°. The average temperature of the year at Havana on a mean of 7 years is 77°; but in the interior, at elevations of over 300 feet above the sea, the thermometer occasionally falls to the freezing point in winter. Hoar frost is not uncommon, and during north winds thin ice may form, though snow is unknown in any part of the island. It hails frequently. The prevailing language is Spanish. Under Spanish rule the Roman Catholic was the only religion tolerated. There were no Jewish or Protestant places of worship. While a person complying with all the requirements was permitted to remain on the island, he was not allowed to promulgate doctrines at variance with those of the established church. Catholicism was supported by the general revenues of the island, and all the items of expense were determined at Madrid. The educational system of Cuba was under the direction of the Governor-General and the rector of the University of Havana, both being natives of Spain and appointed by the Crown. It is estimated that there are about 20,000,000 acres of wild and uncultivated land, 12,000,000 of which are virgin forest. These forests are to a great extent dense and almost impenetrable in some sections, especially the eastern portion of Santa Clara, Puerto Principe, and some parts of Santiago de Cuba provinces. The Isle of Pines, a dependency of

Cuba, is also heavily wooded. The forests preserve their verdure throughout the entire year. The palm is the most common of all the Cuban trees, and perhaps the most valuable. The lands most celebrated for their fertility are the districts of Sagua, Cienfuegos, Trinidad, Matanzas, and Mariel. The Valley of Guines owes its reputation to artificial irrigation. The principal agricultural products are sugar cane, coffee, tobacco, cocoa, cotton, sarsaparilla, vanilla, copal, china root, cassia, palma christi, mustard, pepper, ginger, licorice, balsam de Guatemala, india rubber, etc. The fruits are numerous and delicious. Among them are the pineapple, custard apple, cocoanut, plum, guava, banana, orange, citron, lemon, mango, etc. The island has a great variety of minerals, gold, silver, iron, copper, lead, asphaltum, antimony, platinum, petroleum, marble, jasper, etc., being found in greater or less quantity. As yet no coal has been found, although a substance resembling it is much used as fuel and generally called "coal" by the natives. Gold and silver have not been found in paying quantities, although the early settlers mined a considerable amount of each. The exports consist of sugar, tobacco, coffee, brandy, copper, wax, honey, cotton, leather, horn, cocoanut oil, timber, and fruit. Besides the cigar factories there are no manufacturing industries of importance in the island. The railroad systems of Cuba have been poorly developed. There are in all about 1,100 miles of trackage, not including the suburban roads, of which little information is obtainable. The telegraph system until recently has been notably poor. Havana was founded on its present site in 1519. It was totally destroyed in 1538 by French privateers, but was immediately rebuilt. The capital of the island was located at Santiago de Cuba until 1550, when it was moved to the city of Havana. During the latter part of the eighteenth and the early part of the nineteenth century a number of insurrections and revolts were instituted, but were successfully suppressed by the Spaniards. An important one of these occurred in 1827–1829, when Cuban refugees in Mexico and the United States planned an invasion of Cuba. They organized throughout Mexico, United States, and Colombia branches of a secret society known as the Black Eagle. On account of the antislavery sentiment, which was beginning to show itself in these countries, the scheme proved a failure. A more serious insurrection occurred in 1844, when the slaves on the sugar plantations, especially in the Province of Matanzas, revolted. They were finally subdued and over 1,300 persons convicted and punished. President Polk made a proposition in 1848 for the purchase of the island by the American Government for $100,000,000. In 1854 the Ostend Manifesto claimed the right of the United States, should Spain refuse to sell Cuba, to take and annex it. In the same year preparation was made in Cuba and the United States for another attempt at insurrection, but before the plans of the revolutionists were fully matured the leaders were betrayed, arrested, and executed. During the next 14 years the island enjoyed a period of comparative quiet and prosperity. In 1868 a revolution broke out in Spain, and in October the natives of Cuba took up arms and declared their independence. During this period many of the nations of the Western Hemisphere recognized the Cubans as belligerents. Spain did not succeed in putting down this rebellion until 1878. It was during this war that the American ship *Virginius* was captured by the Spaniards, her cargo confiscated, and many of her passengers executed as revolutionists. This act nearly brought on war between Spain and the United States. About this time Spain was engaged in wars, and for the purpose of keeping them up Cuba was called on to furnish the larger portion of the means. Revenues were raised and the Cubans taxed to the utmost, paying from $3 to $6 per capita. At one time the Cuban debt reached nearly $1,250,-000,000, and for the last 20 years of Spanish dominion the island paid an annual revenue to the Crown of from $25,000,000 to $40,000,000. In 1886 slavery was totally abolished. During the latter part of the year 1894 another revolution broke out. At first the Spaniards considered it nothing more serious than a riot, but they soon found the revolution to be general throughout the island and backed by the most influential of its citizens. It was a downtrodden people fighting for independence. Feb. 15, 1898, the United States battle ship *Maine* was blown up in the harbor of Havana. So much sympathy had been shown by the citizens of the United States for the Cubans and their cause that the Administration soon took a decisive step in the matter. By an act of Congress approved Apr. 25, 1898, it was declared that war did exist and had existed since Apr. 21, 1898, between the United States and the Kingdom of Spain (X, 201), whereupon the President, in a proclamation dated Apr. 26, 1898, declared the existence of war (X, 204). After an unprecedented campaign by the United States, Spain asked for terms of peace, and on Aug. 12 an agreement was signed by representatives of the two countries for a suspension of hostilities, and commissioners were appointed from each country to arrange the terms of peace. The treaty of peace, as concluded by the commission at Paris, provided, among other things, that Spain relinquish all claims of sovereignty over and title to Cuba. Soon after the termination of hostilities between the United States and Spain the former assumed control of the island, sent military forces there, and at this time (June, 1899) is directing the affairs of government.

D.

ence," the same State having previously (May 31, 1775), in her famous Mecklenburg resolutions, which were forwarded to the Continental Congress, declared the people of the Colonies "a free and independent people, under the control of no other power than that of our God and the general government of the Congress." The title of the document was suggested by Virginia in her resolution of May 17, 1776, directing her representatives to propose in Congress a "declaration of independence." Such a resolution was introduced by Richard Henry Lee and adopted June 11. The document was prepared by a committee composed of Thomas Jefferson, John Adams, Benjamin Franklin, Roger Sherman, and Robert R. Livingston. The draft was made by Jefferson. Congress made in the Declaration as presented by the committee 18 suppressions, 6 additions, and 10 alterations, many of them, however, not being important. The Declaration was adopted July 4, 1776, by the unanimous vote of 12 States, New York alone not voting. It was afterwards ratified by a convention of that State.

Declaration of Independence, I, 3.

Desk on which it was written presented to United States by heirs of Joseph Coolidge, jr., VII, 588.

Letter of Robert C. Winthrop regarding, VII, 589.

First copperplate of, bequeathed to Congress by Lafayette, letter of son presenting, III, 123.

Signers of, I, 6.

Declaration of Rights.—The earliest general declaration of rights of which we have any official record was that of the Stamp Act Congress in 1765, which published what it called a "Declaration of Rights and Grievances of the Colonists of America." In this document they vigorously protested against the Stamp Act and all other plans to tax them by a parliament in which they had no representation. They demanded all the rights of British subjects. In 1774 the Continental Congress made a similar declaration against later aggressions of Parliament. Declarations of the same character were incorporated in the Declaration of Independence. (See also Bill of Rights.)

Decoration Day.—The custom of strewing flowers on the graves of their dead soldiers early in the spring of each year originated among the women of the South before the close of the Civil War. In some parts of the North a similar custom grew up, but its observance was not universal. May 5, 1868, while Gen. John A. Logan was commander in chief of the Grand Army of the Republic, he issued an order fixing the 30th day of May of that year as a day for the general observance of the custom by members of the Grand Army and their friends. Since that time May 30 has been regularly observed as Decoration Day throughout the country. It is known as Memorial Day in the South. The principal dates observed there are Apr. 26 and May 10. In many States it is

a legal holiday. Congress has by law declared Decoration Day a holiday in the District of Columbia and the Territories.

Decoration Day. (See National Cemeteries.)

Defalcation of Public Officers:

Application of public money for private uses should be made a felony, III, 492.

Freedom from, discussed, IX, 107, 311.

Inquired into, V, 385; IX, 365.

Defenses, Public (see also Forts and Fortifications):

Board to examine and report upon, appointed, VIII, 314.

Correspondence regarding, referred to, VI, 60.

Provision for, recommended by President—

Adams, John, I, 236, 253, 265, 280, 291, 307, 311, 312.

Adams, J. Q., II, 389.

Arthur, VIII, 51, 137, 180, 211, 246.

Cleveland, VIII, 514; IX, 446, 534, 727.

Grant, VII, 248, 317.

Harrison, Benj., IX, 41, 115, 196, 320.

Hayes, VII, 619.

Jackson, III, 192, 214.

Jefferson, I, 385, 419, 428, 433, 459.

Lincoln, VI, 45.

Madison, I, 470, 486, 566.

Monroe, II, 194, 224.

Tyler, IV, 89, 90, 102, 202.

(See also Navy, vessels for.)

Referred to, I, 255, 257, 276, 279, 293, 296, 311; II, 231; III, 590.

De Fuca Explorations. (See San Juan de Fuca Explorations.)

De Haven, Lieut., expedition commanded by, in search of Sir John Franklin and companions, return of, V, 132.

De Kalb, Baron Johann, claims of representatives of, for services rendered United States in Revolutionary War, III, 51.

De Krafft, Elizabeth S., act granting pension to, vetoed, VIII, 436.

Delafield, Richard, member of board to examine quotas of States under call for troops, VI, 275.

Delagoa Bay Railway, seizure of, by Portuguese Government, IX, 35.

Claims regarding, submitted to arbitration, IX, 111.

Delaware.—One of the thirteen original States, and next to Rhode Island the smallest in the Union. Nickname, "The Diamond State;" motto, "Liberty and Independence." It is bounded on the north by Pennsylvania, on the east by New Jersey and the Atlantic Ocean (Delaware River and Bay separating it from New Jersey), and on the south and west by Maryland. Its principal productions are wheat, indian corn, and fruit. Delaware was originally settled by Swedes under Peter Minuit in 1638, passing under the rule of the Dutch in 1655 and of the English in 1664. In 1682 it was united with Pennsylvania. In 1703 it received a separate assembly, but had a governor in common with Pennsylvania until the Revolution. It was the first State to ratify the Federal Constitution, Dec. 7, 1787. Though a slave State, it remained in the Union throughout the Civil War. It has an area of 2,050 sq. miles and a population (1890) of 168,493. It is sometimes called the "Blue Hen State" and its citizens the "Blue Hen's Chickens."

Delaware Indians.—A confederacy of the Algonquian stock of Indians. They called themselves the Lenni-Lenape ("original men" or "preeminent men") and the French called them Loups (wolves). William Penn found them dwelling peaceably in the valley of the Delaware. He cultivated friendly relations with them and purchased much of their land. Their chief council fires blazed on the site of the present city of Philadelphia. In 1726 they refused to join the Iroquois in a war against the English and were stigmatized as "women." Later they became quite warlike, but were driven beyond the Alleghanies. Near the close of the Revolution a large number of Christian Delawares were massacred by Americans. The remnants of the tribe dwelt temporarily in Ohio, and in 1818 migrated to Missouri, in 1829 to Kansas, and in 1868 to the Indian Territory, where they live among the Cherokees and are well civilized. They number about 1,600.

Democratic Party.—Individual liberty rather than strict government is a paramount sentiment in many American hearts. Those who originally looked with apprehension on the possibility of the central Government's encroaching upon the personal liberties of the people or the rights of States formed the nucleus of the National Democratic party, which has now maintained a continuous existence for more than a hundred years. The chief tenets of the party are succinctly set forth by Mr. Jefferson in his first inaugural address. These tenets he characterized as essential principles of our Government. His definition of the principles of the party is thus expressed: "Equal and exact justice to all men, of whatever state or persuasion, religious or political; peace, commerce, and honest friendship with all nations, entangling alliances with none; the support of the State governments in all their rights, as the most competent administrations for our domestic concerns and the surest bulwarks against antirepublican tendencies; the preservation of the General Government in its whole constitutional vigor, as the sheet anchor of our peace at home and safety abroad; a jealous care of the right of election by the people—a mild and safe corrective of abuses which are lopped by the sword of revolution where peaceable remedies are unprovided; absolute acquiescence in the decisions of the majority, the vital principle of republics, from which is no appeal but to force, the vital principle and immediate parent of despotism; a well-disciplined militia, our best reliance in peace and for the first moments of war, till regulars may relieve them; the supremacy of the civil over the military authority; economy in the public expense, that labor may be lightly burthened; the honest payment of our debts and sacred preservation of the public faith; encouragement of agriculture, and of commerce as its handmaid; the diffusion of information and arraignment of all abuses at the bar of the public reason; freedom of religion; freedom of the press, and freedom of person under the protection of the *habeas corpus*, and trial by juries impartially selected" (I, 323). A strong sympathy with the French revolutionists in 1789 and a desire that the Government should aid France in her war with England drew a number of disciples to the party entertaining these sentiments. Under the leadership of Thomas Jefferson the party took the name of Democratic-Republican and opposed the Federalists. Since Monroe's time it has been commonly known as the Democratic party, though previously it was known as the Republican party. From its inception in 1792 to 1801 it was the party of opposition. When the party got control of the Government it lost sight of some of its tenets, and many of its members at certain times supported measures tending toward nationalization. After the War of 1812 the Democrats had a clear field of operations until the second election of Monroe in 1820. Subsequently dissensions began to appear. Adams and Clay and their followers advocated protection, national aid to internal improvements, and a broader construction of the Constitution. They were first known as National Republicans, and after drawing to themselves many of the opponents of Andrew Jackson were called Whigs. From the time of Jackson up to 1860 the Democrats by skillful party management won all the Presidential elections but two—those of 1840 and 1848. They carried the country through the war with Mexico, annexed Texas and the Californias, and abolished the United States Bank. With the introduction of the slavery question into politics the party began to lose strength in the North. The Democratic party was always strongest in the South, however. In 1860 the party split into two factions and the Republicans won the election. Then came the Civil War, and though many Democrats supported Lincoln and the Union the party lost power and prestige in the North generally, and the Republicans remained in control until 1884, when war issues had been superseded in the minds of many by economic questions. The party elected the President in 1884 and again in 1892 on a platform opposed to a high protective tariff. The Democratic party still holds in a general way to its original tenets, with a few important exceptions.

Democratic Societies.—Societies similar to the Jacobins of France were organized in 1793 in various parts of the United States to express sympathy with the French revolutionists and propagate extreme democratic views. Washington vigorously denounced them for their opposition to his efforts to suppress the Whisky Insurrection in western Pennsylvania in 1794. They soon became extinct.

Demonetization of Metal.—To demonetize a metal is to take from it its standard monetary value and thus make it merely a commodity.

Demun and Chouteau, depredations committed on property of, by Mexicans, III, 229.

Denby, Charles:
Member of commission to Philippine Islands, X, 222.
Minister to China, regulations for consular courts promulgated by, VIII, 803.

Denmark.—A Kingdom in northern Europe, comprising a part of the peninsula of Jutland and a group of islands, the principal ones being Zealand, Fünen, Laaland, Bornholm, Falster, Langeland, and Möen. The Government is a constitutional hereditary monarchy, with the legislature composed of 2 bodies. In the Middle Ages it was famous as the home of pirates. Christianity was introduced in the ninth century. Norway, Sweden, and Denmark were united in 1397. Sweden separated from Denmark in 1523. Norway was ceded to Sweden in 1814. An unsuccessful war, known as the Schleswig-Holstein War, in 1864 was waged by Denmark against Prussia and Austria, which resulted in the loss of territory to Denmark. The present constitution was adopted in 1866. Area, including islands, 15,289 sq. miles; population (1890), 2,185,335.

Denmark:
Cession of St. Thomas and St. John islands to United States, treaty regarding, VI, 579, 581, 598, 688.
Claims of, against United States, I, 356, 377; II, 65.
Claims of United States against, I, 484; II, 301, 343, 410, 445, 481, 505, 546, 594; III, 24; IV, 320; VII, 510; VIII, 784.

Denmark—Continued.
Claims of United States against—Continued.
Agreement to submit, to arbitration, VIII, 803.
Award of arbitrator, IX, 110.
Payment of, II, 410, 445, 505, 549, 594; III, 24.
Commercial relations with, II, 531; III, 25; V, 279, 411.
Consuls of United States in, I, 98, 117.
Convention with, VII, 42.
Convicts in, banished to United States, VI, 637.
Copyright privilege extended, by proclamation, IX, 395.
Referred to, IX, 442.
Fugitive criminals, failure to negotiate convention with, for surrender of, VII, 609.
Importation of American products into, decrees placing restrictions upon, IX, 668.
Minister of, to United States, grade of, raised, VIII, 131.
Naturalization treaty with, VII, 206, 239.
Privateers, regulations for, adopted by, transmitted, X, 34.
Sound dues, treaty regarding, V, 334, 463, 470.
Treaty with, transmitted and discussed by President—
Adams, J. Q., II, 345, 353.
Buchanan, V, 463, 470.
Grant, VII, 42.
Jackson, II, 481, 530, 574.
Johnson, VI, 581, 693.
Ratification of, by Denmark, VI, 621.
Vessels of, captured by American ships, VI, 70; X, 36.
Vessels of United States—
Seized or interfered with by, VIII, 803; X, 34.
Tolls levied on, discussed, V, 279, 334, 411.

Denniston, William H., act for relief of, vetoed, VII, 268.

Denny, Alfred, act granting pension to, vetoed, VIII, 439.

Departments, Executive. (See Executive Departments; the several Departments.)

Dependent-Pension Law discussed, IX, 117, 327, 451, 545.

De Poiery, Mr., captain by brevet, nomination of, and reasons therefor, I, 75.

Deposits, Public, Removal of.—In 1833 and prior thereto the public funds of the Government were deposited in the Bank of the United States. President Jackson determined to discontinue this practice and to deposit the funds collected in State banks, while those in the Bank of the United States should be withdrawn as needed. William J. Duane, the Secretary of the Treasury, was opposed to the removal of the funds, particularly before the meeting of Congress. After fruitless effort to have him change his opinion on the subject, the President requested his resignation. It was given, and on the same day, Sept. 23, 1833, Roger B. Taney, the Attorney-General, was appointed Secretary of the Treasury. He promptly made the necessary orders. The Senate passed a resolution of censure of the President and also rejected the nomination of Mr. Taney as Secretary of the Treasury. In a paper which he read to his Cabinet the President gave his reasons for removing the Government funds from the Bank of the United States (III, 5).

Deposits, Public, Removal of:
President Jackson's paper to Cabinet on, III, 5.
Refuses to transmit, to Senate, III, 36.
Recommended, II, 600; III, 17.
Referred to, III, 167.
Views of President Tyler on, IV, 44.

Depredations on Commerce. (See the several powers, claims against.)

Dermody, William, act granting pension to, vetoed, VIII, 463.

Derne Expedition.—Gen. William Eaton, United States consul at Tunis, in 1805 espoused the cause of Hamet, Pasha of Tripoli, against the latter's usurping brother. With the cooperation of the United States naval forces in the Mediterranean, they defeated the usurper at Derne Apr. 27, 1805. After this success a treaty highly favorable to the United States was negotiated with the Pasha.

Derrick, W. S., Acting Secretary of State, V, 77.

Desert Lands. (See Lands, Desert.)

Desertions in Army. (See Army; Pardons.)

Des Moines Rapids, act for continuing improvement of, vetoed, V, 388.

Des Moines River, acts to quiet title of settlers on lands on, vetoed, VIII, 411, 827.

De Stoeckl, Edward, mentioned, VI, 66.

Detroit, The, capture of, referred to, X, 45.

Detroit, Mich.:
Civil authority over, recommended, I, 198.
Lands—
Ceded for post of, I, 433, 438.
Lying near, referred to, I, 367.
Memorials for district of, I, 442.
Town and fort of, surrendered to the British, I, 515.
Recovery of, referred to, I, 539.

Detroit (Mich.), Surrender of.—In August, 1812, Col. Proctor, in command of the British troops in Canada, was joined by Gen. Brock with a body of militia and some Indians under Tecumseh. The forces at Sandwich amounted to 1,330 men, 600 of whom were Indians. Gen. Hull, in command at Fort Detroit, on the opposite side of the river, had 1,000 men available for duty. Aug. 16 the British sent a party of Indians and regulars across the river to assault the works. Hull surrendered the fort and the whole Territory of Michigan, of which he was governor, without the discharge of a gun. About 2,000 men in all became prisoners of war. During the firing by the British 7 Americans were killed and several wounded. Gen. Hull was afterwards convicted of cowardice by a court-martial and condemned to death, but was pardoned by President Madison in consideration of his age and his services in the Revolutionary War. Subsequent investigations greatly modified the blame attached to Gen. Hull.

Devils Lake Reservation, N. Dak., right of way for railroad through, bill for, VIII, 367, 592.

Dewey, George:
Attack of American land forces and capture of Manila assisted by squadron under, X, 172.
Thanks of President tendered, X, 218.
Member of Philippine Commission, X, 222.
Spanish fleet destroyed in Manila Bay by American squadron under, X, 155, 168.
Appointed acting rear-admiral, X, 155, 208.
Sword to be presented to, X, 157.
Thanks of Congress to, X, 156.
Recommended, X, 155.
Reply of, X, 157.
Thanks of President tendered, X, 208.
Referred to, X, 155.
Suggestions from, regarding force, etc., for Philippine Islands requested by President, X, 218.

De Witt, Hannah C., act granting pension to, vetoed, VIII, 645.

Dexter, John S., district supervisor, nomination of, I, 99.

Diaz, A. J., arrest and imprisonment of, by Cuban authorities, IX, 81.

Diaz, Porfirio, revolution in Mexico and installation of, as President discussed, VII, 467.

Dickens, William, act granting pension to, vetoed, VIII, 539.

Dickson, James C., receiver of public moneys, nomination of, withdrawn and reasons therefor, II, 477.

Dickson, Walter, outrages committed on family of, in Palestine, V, 484.

Dime.—The smallest piece of silver now coined by the United States. In value it is the tenth part of a dollar. The word is taken from the French dixième, one-tenth, and was spelled "disme" on some of the first coins. Authorized in 1792 with a weight of 41.6 grains, it was afterwards (in 1853) reduced to 38.4 grains. The first dimes were issued in 1796.

Dingle, W. B., arrest and maltreatment of, at Heidelberg, Baden, V, 239.

Dinsmore, Silas, commissioner to treat with Indians, I, 435.

Diplomatic Agents. (See Consuls; Ministers.)

Diplomatic Conventions. (See Conventions, Diplomatic.)

Diplomatic Service. (See Consular and Diplomatic Service.)

Direct Taxes. (See Taxation; Taxes.)

Disability-Pension Act discussed, IX, 117, 327, 451, 545.

Discretionary Powers of President. (See Executive Nominations; President; Removals from Office.)

Discriminating Duties. (See Vessels, Foreign, tonnage on.)

Diseases, Contagious. (See Cholera; Contagious Diseases; International Sanitary Conference; Plague; Quarantine Regulations; Yellow Fever.)

Diseases of Animals. (See Animals and Animal Products.)

Distilled Spirits:
Sale of, in Siam by American citizens, VII, 216.

Distilled Spirits—Continued.

Sale of, to Indians, recommendations regarding, I, 334; IX, 735.

Statement of quantity and value of, transmitted, X, 48.

Tax on—

Discussed by President—

Arthur, VIII, 136, 178, 244.

Harrison, Benj., IX, 39.

Washington, I, 99, 105, 112, 127, 130, 131, 133, 134, 150.

Division of United States into districts for collection of, I, 99, 105, 112, 134.

Laws for raising. (See Revenue, Public.)

Removal of, on spirits used in arts and manufactures discussed, IX, 39.

District.—A name applied in the United States to those portions of territory which are without elective or representative institutions—for instance, the District of Columbia. South Carolina counties were formerly called districts. From 1804 to 1812 that portion of the Louisiana Purchase lying north of the northern boundary of the present State was called the District of Louisiana. Before their admission as States Kentucky and Maine were called districts, respectively of Virginia and Massachusetts. The name "district" is also applied to those divisions of a State grouping certain counties or wards into separate Congressional districts for the election of Representatives in Congress.

District Attorneys. (See Attorneys, District.)

District Courts. (See Courts, Federal.)

District of Columbia.—Congress is authorized by the Constitution to "exercise exclusive legislation in all cases whatsoever over such district (not exceeding 10 miles square) as may, by cession of particular States and the acceptance of Congress, become the seat of the Government of the United States." July 16, 1790, after a long and bitter discussion, a district 10 miles square lying on both sides of the Potomac River was selected. Maryland ceded 64 sq. miles on the north bank of the river and Virginia 36 sq. miles on the south bank. The District was first called the Territory of Columbia. The seat of Government was removed thither in 1800. July 9, 1846, the portion south of the Potomac was ceded back to Virginia. For a time the superintendence of the District was in the hands of 3 commissioners, but in 1802 Washington was incorporated and its government was placed in the hands of the people, with a president and a council, the former appointed by the President. In 1820 a mayor, to be elected by the people, was substituted for the president. From 1871 to 1874 the District had a Territorial government, the upper house and the governor being appointed by the President and the lower house selected by the people. This was found to be unsatisfactory, and in 1874 Congress provided for a board of 3 commissioners to take charge of all matters pertaining to the District government. June 11, 1878, Congress provided for a permanent government, consisting of 3 commissioners, 2

to be appointed from civil life by the President, the third to be detailed by the President from the officers of the Engineer Corps of the Army. Area, 64 sq. miles; population (1890), 230,392.

District of Columbia (see also Washington City):

Act—

Fixing rate of interest on arrearages of taxes due in, returned, IX, 67.

For promotion of anatomical science and to prevent desecration of graves vetoed, VIII, 413.

Prescribing times for sales and for notice of sales of property in, for taxes returned, VIII, 627.

Prohibiting bookmaking and pool selling in, vetoed, IX, 93.

Referred to, IX, 116.

Providing for recording deeds, etc., in, vetoed, VII, 381.

Respecting circulation of bank notes in, vetoed, VI, 87.

To abolish board of commissioners of police in, etc., vetoed, VII, 430.

To authorize reassessment of water-main taxes or assessments in, returned, IX, 670.

To pay moneys collected under direct tax of 1861 to States, Territories, and, vetoed, VIII, 837.

To punish unlawful appropriation of property of another in, returned, IX, 237.

To regulate elective franchise in, vetoed, VI, 472.

To regulate practice of medicine and surgery in, etc., returned, IX, 670.

Appropriation for, recommended, VII, 154.

Armory of—

Damages to be incurred by repealing act providing for construction of, referred to, V, 368.

Location of, referred to, V, 378.

Site for, selected, V, 366.

Benevolent institutions in, deserve attention of Congress, VI, 187, 251; VII, 507, 627; VIII, 800.

Board of public works in, report of, referred to, VII, 165.

Work accomplished by, VII, 254.

Bonded indebtedness of, discussed and recommendations regarding, VII, 267.

Report on, VII, 302.

Boundaries of, referred to and proclaimed, I, 94, 100, 102.

Bridge over Rock Creek, construction of, referred to, III, 627.

Bridges over Potomac River in, construction and repair of, discussed, II, 608; III, 38; V, 174; VIII, 51, 92, 529.

Injuries sustained by, referred to, III, 229.

Buildings for offices of, recommended, VII, 626; VIII, 253, 365, 529.

Buildings, public, in, construction of, referred to, I, 190.

Ceded to Congress for permanent seat of Government, I, 100.

Congress assembles in, I, 271, 305, 308.

Contagious diseases, provisions against, recommended, II, 285.

Dix, John A.:

Applications to go south across military lines to be made to, VI, 101.

Authority given to, while commanding at Baltimore, VI, 112.

Commissioner to examine cases of state prisoners, VI, 109.

Mentioned, VI, 78.

Prisoners of war released to report to, VI, 102.

Dixie.—A term applied originally to New York City when slavery existed there. According to the myth or legend, a person named Dixie owned a tract of land on Manhattan Island and a large number of slaves. As Dixie's slaves increased beyond the requirements of the plantation many were sent to distant parts. Naturally the deported negroes looked upon their early home as a place of real and abiding happiness, as did those from the "Ole Virginny" of later days. Hence Dixie became the synonym for a locality where the negroes lived happy and contented lives. In the South Dixie is taken to mean the Southern States. There the word is supposed to have been derived from Mason and Dixon's line, formerly dividing the free and slave States. It is said to have first come into use there when Texas joined the Union, and the negroes sang of it as Dixie. It has been the subject of several popular songs, notably that of Albert Pike, "Southrons, hear your country call;" that of T. M. Cooley, "Away down South, where grows the cotton," and that of Dan Emmett, the refrain usually containing the word "Dixie" or the words "Dixie's Land." During the Civil War the tune of Dixie was to the Southern people what Yankee Doodle had always been to the people of the whole Union and what it continued in war times to be to the Northern people, the comic national air.

Dixie, The, mentioned, X, 171.

Doane, R. L., act granting pension to, vetoed, VIII, 718.

Dock Yards for construction of large vessels recommended, II, 31.'

Docks:

Appropriations for building, should be separated from those of naval service, V, 89, 134.

Construction of—

Appropriation for, recommended, II, 200; III, 116.

Discussed, I, 345, 347; V, 133.

Referred to, II, 200, 419; IV, 564.

Site for, II, 368.

Report of commission to select, transmitted, IX, 131, 215.

Spanish war vessels repaired at American, VII, 51.

Dodge, Henry, troops in Indian campaign under command of, III, 113.

Dodge, William E., member of Indian commission, VII, 23.

Dole, Sanford B.:

Member of commission to recommend legislation for Hawaiian Islands, X, 186.

Dole, Sanford B.—Continued.

Minister of foreign affairs of provisional government of Hawaii, letter from, transmitted, IX, 474, 475.

Sovereignty of Hawaiian Islands transferred to United States by, X, 185.

Dole, William P., treaty with Indians concluded by, VI, 192, 193, 194, 199, 201, 210, 212.

Dollar.—Derived from daler or thaler. The American silver dollar is modeled after the Spanish milled dollar. It was authorized by an act of Congress passed in 1792, which declared 371¼ grains of pure silver to be equal to 24¾ grains of pure gold and each equivalent to a dollar of account. It was made the unit of value. The silver dollar was first coined in 1794 and weighed 416 grains, 371¼ grains being of silver and the remainder alloy. In 1837 the weight was reduced to 412½ grains by decreasing the weight of alloy. In 1873 provision was made for a dollar of 420 grains for use in trade with China and Japan, known as the "trade dollar." The gold dollar was issued under the act of Mar. 3, 1849. Its coinage was discontinued in 1890. The coinage act of Feb. 12, 1873, tacitly suspended the coinage of silver dollars (except the trade dollar) and made the gold dollar the standard of value. The act of Feb. 28, 1878, authorized the Secretary of the Treasury to purchase each month, at market value, not less than $2,000,000 and not more than $4,000,000 worth of bullion, to be coined into silver dollars of 412½ grains each. This act was repealed by the act of June 14, 1890. (See Coinage Laws; Coins and Coinage.)

Dolphin, The (British cruiser), seizure of the *Catharine* by, discussed, IV, 217.

Dolphin, The (United States brig), seizure of the *Echo* by, discussed, V, 527.

Dolphin, The (United States dispatch boat), contract regarding construction of, discussed, VIII, 350.

Dominican Republic. (See Santo Domingo.)

Donaldson, Edward, thanks of Congress to, recommended, VI, 76.

Donaldson, Joseph, jr., treaty with Algiers concluded by, I, 192.

Donelson, Andrew J., minister to Germany, nomination of, IV, 605.

Recall of, referred to, V, 11.

Doorkeeper.—By an act of Mar. 3, 1805, the designation of Doorkeeper of the Senate was changed to Sergeant-at-Arms. He executes all orders relating to decorum and is officially charged with all matters relating to the keeping of the doors of the Senate. He orders persons into custody and makes arrests by direction of the Senate. The duties of the Doorkeeper of the House of Representatives are varied and complicated. Under the rules of the House he is required to enforce the rules relating to the privileges of the floor, and is responsible for the conduct of his employees—messengers, pages, laborers, etc. He also has charge of all the property of the House. He reports to Congress annually the amount of United States property in his pos-

Drexel, Joseph W., chairman of executive committee on pedestal of Statue of Liberty Enlightening the World, VIII, 397.

Driver, The, ordered from and forbidden to reenter waters of United States, I, 403.

Drum, Richard C., Adjutant-General:
Union and Confederate flags, return of, to respective States recommended by, VIII, 578.
Proposition withdrawn, VIII, 579.

Dry Docks. (See Docks.)

Dry Tortugas, survey of, for naval station, II, 475.

Duck Valley, Nev., payment of settlers for improvements on lands in, referred to, VIII, 77, 189.

Dudley, The, seizure of, and claims arising out of, VII, 160; VIII, 613; IX, 112, 238, 441, 530.
Award in case of, IX, 638.

Dullye, Eugene, expulsion of, from Prussia, V, 592.

Duluth, Minn., act for erection of public building at, vetoed, VIII, 469.

Dunbar, William, appointed to explore Washita River, I, 399.

Dunham, Aaron, district supervisor, nomination of, I, 99.

Dunkirk, N. Y., proclamation granting privileges of other ports to, V, 326.

Dunlap, Margaret, act granting pension to, vetoed, VIII, 542.

Dunlap, Robert P.:
Correspondence regarding imprisonment of Ebenezer S. Greely, III, 358, 405.
Correspondence regarding northeastern boundary. (See Northeastern Boundary.)

Dupont, Samuel F.:
Mentioned, VI, 78.
Thanks of Congress to, recommended, VI, 64, 70.

Durango, The, convention with Texas for adjustment of claims in case of, III, 469.

Duskin, George M., removal from office of, President declines to give reasons for, VIII, 375.

Dutch East Indies, discriminating duties on vessels of, suspended, VIII, 569.

Duties. (See Foreign Import Duties; Import Duties; Vessels, Foreign, tonnage on.)

Dwamish Indians, treaty with, V, 379.

E.

E Pluribus Unum.—A Latin phrase meaning "Out of many, one," or "One of many." It alludes to the formation of one Federal Government out of several independent States. It is the motto of the United States, having been selected by a committee composed of John Adams, Benjamin Franklin, and Thomas Jefferson. They made their report on a design for a motto and great seal Aug. 10, 1776. The phrase is probably derived from "Moretum," a Latin poem by Virgil. It was also the motto of the Gentleman's Magazine, which was quite popular in the Colonies at the time the selection was made. It first appeared on coin issued by New Jersey in 1786.

Eads, James B.:
Grants to, for construction of jetties in Mississippi River, order regarding, VII, 328.
Improvement of South Pass of Mississippi River under, discussed, VII, 408, 572.

Eagle.—The $10 gold coin of the United States. Its coinage was authorized in 1792. Coined first in 1794, it has since been legal tender to any amount. The first delivery was of 400 eagles Sept. 22, 1795. Coinage was suspended in 1805 and resumed in 1837. It takes its name from the figure of the national bird which is stamped on the reverse. (See also Coinage Laws; Coins and Coinage.)

Earthquakes in Peru, Ecuador, and Bolivia, VI, 687.

East Florida. (See Florida.)

East Florida Claims:
Discussed and payment of, recommended, III, 510; IV, 53; VII, 568, 584, 608.
Reports on, referred to, VII, 589.

East River, N. Y., appropriation for removal of Flood Rock in, recommended, VIII, 201.

East Tennessee University, act for relief of, vetoed, VII, 215.

Eastport, Me., proclamation granting privileges of other ports to, V, 326.

Eaton, Dorman B., chairman Civil Service Commission, report of, discussed, VII, 636.

Eaton, John, publication of second edition of Second Arctic Expedition suggested by, VIII, 79.

Eaton, John H., treaty with Indians concluded by, III, 52.

Eaton, Lydia A., act granting pension to, vetoed, VIII, 736.

Eaton, William:
Correspondence regarding war with Tripoli transmitted, I, 391.
Correspondence relating to Hamet B. Caramalli transmitted, X, 29.

Echo, The, captured with African negroes on board by U. S. brig *Dolphin*, V, 527.
Recommendations regarding removal of, V, 528.

Eckert, Jacob, act to remove charge of desertion from record of, vetoed, IX, 575.

Eckert, T. T., negotiations for and correspondence regarding restoration of peace, VI, 260.

Ecuador.—A Republic of South America. It is bounded on the north by Colombia, on the south by Peru, and on the west by the Pacific Ocean. Eastward its claims extend to the confines of Brazil, but the claim to the eastern base of the Andes is disputed by Colombia and Peru. The country is traversed from north to south by the Andes. Some of the highest peaks of South America are in Ecuador, and there are also numerous volcanoes. The principal products and exports are sugar, rubber, cacao, and hides. The inhabitants are whites (of Spanish descent), Indians, and mixed races. The President is elected for 4 years. The Congress consists of 2 chambers. Catholic is the prevailing religion, but the constitution of 1886 guarantees the free exercise of all religions. Ecuador was conquered by the Spaniards in 1533-34. With the aid of Bolivar the Spanish rulers were expelled (1822–23), and the country was united to the Colombian Confederation. In 1830 it seceded and adopted its present name. Political revolutions have been frequent in the country. Area, about 155,000 sq. miles; population (1892), 703,500.

Ecuador:
Civil war in, III, 100.
Claims of United States against, convention for adjustment of, VI, 147, 201.
   Failure of, to pay first installment of award under, VI, 386.
Commercial convention with, III, 534.
Convention with, respecting case of Emilio Santos, IX, 525.
Diplomatic relations with, discussed, VIII, 43; IX, 33.
Earthquakes in, VI, 687.
Fugitive criminals, convention with, for surrender of, VII, 206, 293.
Imprisonment of American citizens in, VIII, 269.
   Released, VIII, 330, 405.
   Treaty to settle claim regarding, VIII, 784.
Naturalization treaty with, VII, 165, 239.
Report of George E. Church upon, transmitted, VIII, 157.
Treaty with, transmitted and discussed, III, 567 IV, 198; VI, 147; VII, 206, 293.
   Expresses desire to negotiate, III, 477.
   Probably rendered abortive, IV, 80.

Edgcomb, Willard W., treaty with Orange Free State concluded by, VII, 162.

Education (see also Indian Schools; Military Academy; National University; Naval Academy):
Act donating lands for benefit of agricultural colleges vetoed, V, 543.
Appropriation of proceeds of sales of public lands for, recommended, VII, 152, 203, 606, 626; VIII, 58.
Constitutional amendment regarding, suggested, I, 409, 456; II, 18.
Constitutional amendment regarding maintenance of free schools by States, etc., recommended, VII, 334.
Government aid to, recommended by President—
   Arthur, VIII, 58, 143, 184, 253.
   Harrison, Benj., IX, 54.
In Alaska, appropriation for, recommended, VIII, 80; IX, 48.
In Army discussed, VII, 618; IX, 447.
In Indian Territory, recommendations regarding, X, 199.
Lands granted to States in aid of, II, 466, 482; VI, 389; VII, 252; IX, 542.
Recommended, I, 410, 485; VII, 111, 254.
Of freedmen discussed and referred to, VII, 41; IX, 54.
Recommendation that States be required to afford good common schools, VII, 356.
Recommendations regarding education in States, VII, 479, 506, 602, 626.
Sectarian tenets not to be taught in public schools, VII, 356.

Education, Bureau of.—An office established in 1867 to collect statistics showing the condition and progress of education throughout the country and to publish such information as will benefit the cause of education. It was made a bureau of the Interior Department in 1868.

Education, Bureau of:
Discussed by President—
   Grant, VII, 112, 253.
   Hayes, VII, 579, 626.
Establishment of, referred to, VII, 112.

Education, Commissioner of:
Duties of, respecting education of freedmen referred to, VII, 41.
Report of, referred to, VII, 506.

Education, Industrial, report on, transmitted, IX, 347.

Educational Land Grants.—Large tracts of land in the Northwest Territory were granted to the States formed therefrom, to be sold by the legislatures or by the Federal Government for educational purposes. As early as 1785 Congress, foreshadowing the permanent policy of the nation in encouraging education, enacted that one thirty-sixth of all the public lands should be set apart for and dedicated to the cause of education, and by the act of July 23, 1787, this reservation was made perpetual. (See also Agriculture.)

Educational Land Grants, II, 466, 482; VI, 389; VII, 252; IX, 542.
Recommended, I, 410, 485; VII, 111, 254.

Educational Requirements for Voters recommended by President Grant, VII, 356, 411.

Edwards, Arthur, et al., act for relief of, vetoed, V, 607.

Edwards, Ninian:
Minister to Mexico, examination of, by committee referred to, II, 239.
Treaty with Indians concluded by, II, 20.

Edwards, W. H., report of, transmitted, IX, 334.

Eel River Indians:
Payment to, in lieu of annuities, VIII, 530.
Treaty with, I, 363, 390, 397, 478, 479.

Egan, Patrick, minister to Chile. (See *Baltimore, The.*)

Egypt.—A country in northeastern Africa, now a dependency of Turkey. It is famous for the great antiquity and former splendor of its civilization. It is bounded on the north by the Mediterranean Sea, on the east by the Gulf of Suez and the Red Sea, and on the west by the African Desert. Its soil has been celebrated for its great productiveness, due to the inundations of the river Nile. Egypt has 14 provinces and is a hereditary vice-royalty ruled by a Khedive subordinate to Turkey. The prevailing language is Arabic. Area, 380,000 sq. miles; population, 6,817,265.

Egypt:
American citizens in, proclamation regarding rights of, VII, 277, 390.
   Discussed, VII, 290, 403.
American representative in, death of, referred to, VI, 245.
Ancient obelisk presented to New York City by Government of, VII, 568, 612.
Change of personal head of, VII, 568.

dent Lincoln, as he declared, to preserve the Union without freeing the slaves, if possible. Sept. 22, 1862, he issued a preliminary proclamation (VI, 96) as a war measure, calling upon all the people in rebellion against the United States to return to their allegiance, promising measures of relief in case of compliance, and threatening to free the slaves in those States and parts of States which should still be in rebellion on the 1st day of January next succeeding the proclamation. This had no effect. Accordingly, on Jan. 1, 1863, President Lincoln issued a supplementary proclamation (VI, 157) declaring the freedom of the slaves in all the States which had seceded except 48 counties in West Virginia, 7 counties in Virginia, including the cities of Norfolk and Portsmouth, and 13 parishes of Louisiana, including the city of New Orleans. The thirteenth amendment to the Constitution, in force Dec. 18, 1865, completed the work of emancipation, by which 3,895,172 slaves were made free.

Emancipation Proclamation, VI, 157.

Carpenter's painting of Lincoln and Cabinet at first reading of, presented to Congress, VII, 483.

Notice given that slaves would be emancipated on Jan. 1, 1863, VI, 96.

Embargo.—A prohibition imposed by a country to prevent its vessels or those of neutral or hostile powers leaving its ports. The United States Government laid embargoes at various times between 1794 and 1815. Upon the breaking out of war between France and Great Britain in 1793 each country ordered the seizure of neutral vessels bound for the ports of the other. In consequence of the depredations of England and France upon the commerce of the United States, an act was passed Apr. 18, 1806, prohibiting trade with Great Britain and her colonies. Dec. 22, 1807, Congress, at the suggestion of Jefferson, passed an embargo act prohibiting the sailing of any merchant vessel, save coasters, from any American port. Jan. 9, 1808, another and more stringent act was passed. These measures failed to bring either France or England to terms, and, though somewhat modified by the act of Mar. 12, 1808, they wrought much injury to the shipping and export trade of the United States. They were extensively evaded, and Mar. 1, 1809, were repealed and replaced by the nonintercourse law, which forbade French and English vessels entering American ports. Another embargo act was passed Dec. 10, 1813, during the second war with Great Britain.

Embargo:

On American vessels referred to, I, 439.

On foreign vessels—

For 60 days recommended, I, 499.

Governors requested to call forth militia if necessary to enforce, I, 152.

Imposed, I, 473.

Removed, I, 472, 481.

Embezzlement. (See Defalcation.)

Emerson, John B., petition of, regarding use of his invention referred to, IV, 678.

Emery, A. H., compensation to, for services in perfecting testing machine recommended, VII, 588.

Emigrants to United States. (See Immigration.)

Emigration of Negroes. (See Negroes.)

Eminent Domain.—The original or superior ownership retained by the people or State by which land or other private property may be taken for public use or benefit. This is the most definite principle of the fundamental power of the government with regard to property and the most exact idea of property remaining in the government or in the aggregate body of the people in their sovereign capacity, giving the right to resume original possession in the manner directed by law whenever its use is essential to the mutual advantage and welfare of society. If, for instance, the proper authorities deem it necessary for the general good to open a street, lay out a park, dig a canal, abate a nuisance, charter a railroad, etc., and the owners of the land on the route or space desired refuse to sell or demand an exorbitant price for their property, the State, by eminent domain, has the power of control, and the courts may compel the surrender of the property upon due compensation being determined by a board of appraisers. The Constitution of the United States limits the exercise of the right of eminent domain to cases where public good demands it and requires compensation to those from whom property is taken.

Emory, U. E., map of Texas compiled by, IV, 313.

Emory, W. H., report on survey of boundary between Mexico and United States transmitted, V, 382.

Emory, William H., commander of the *Bear* in Lady Franklin Bay Expedition, VIII, 248.

Employees. (See Government Employees; Officers, Public.)

Emucfau (Ala.), Battle of.—In January, 1814, Jackson, with 930 volunteers and 200 friendly Indians, again took the field against the hostiles. Jan. 21, with Gen. Coffee, he camped near Emucfau, on a bend in the Tallapoosa, in southern Alabama. Indications pointed to the presence of Indians, and the whites kept vigil all the night. At dawn of the 22d the savages made the attack. Gen. Coffee repulsed the Indians, driving them back 2 miles. The Indians then rallied, attacking a second time, but were again repulsed. Gen. Coffee was wounded. His aid-de-camp and 2 or 3 others were killed. Several privates were wounded. Jackson abandoned his excursion after this battle and retired toward Fort Strother.

Encomium, The, seizure of slaves on board, referred to, III, 280.

Compensation by Great Britain in case of, referred to, III, 515, 567.

Endicott, William C., Secretary of War:

Union and Confederate flags, return of, to respective States recommended, VIII, 578.

Proposition withdrawn, VIII, 579.

and the Kara River; on the south by the Mediterranean Sea, the Black Sea, and the Sea of Marmora, and on west by the Atlantic Ocean. It is the most highly civilized and populous of the three grand divisions of the Old World. In form it is a huge peninsula projecting from the northwest of Asia. Length northeast and southwest, 3,400 miles; breadth north and south, 2,400 miles. It lies within lat. 71° 11' and 35° 59' north and long. 9° 31' west and 66° east. Its area is estimated at about 3,850,000 sq. miles, and it has a coast line more extensive in proportion to its size than any other great natural division of the globe, estimated at about 19,500 miles. Population about 358,000,000, or about 94 for every square mile.

Europe, railway systems of, referred to, VI, 69.

European and West Virginia Land and Mining Co., agreement with agents of Mexico referred to, VI, 525.

Eustis, Abraham:
Correspondence regarding Dorr's Rebellion, IV, 300.
Troops under, in Seminole War, III, 617.

Eutaw Springs (S. C.), Battle of.—Lieut. Col. Stewart had succeeded Lord Rawdon in command of the southern division of the British army and established headquarters at Orangeburg, S. C. Gen. Greene, who had been resting the American army on the hills of the Santee River, had been reenforced by 700 North Carolina Continentals. His army thus increased to more than 2,500 men, Greene determined to attack Stewart, whose force did not exceed 2,000. Stewart fell back about 40 miles to Eutaw Springs, near the Santee River, in South Carolina. Here Sept. 8, 1781, a fierce but indecisive battle was fought. Stewart kept the field, but at night retired toward Charleston, and Greene took possession of the battle ground and sent detachments in pursuit of the British. The total American casualties as given by Gen. Greene were 408. The British loss was 693.

Evans, Fannie, act granting pension to, vetoed, VIII, 464.

Evans, John, geological survey of Oregon and Washington by, referred to, V, 485.

Evans, John:
Treaty with Indians concluded by, VI, 192.
United States Senator, mentioned, VI, 375.

Evans, Robley D. (See *Baltimore*, The.)

Evarts, William M.:
Counsel for President Johnson in impeachment proceedings, VI, 726.
Secretary of State, VII, 447.
Instructions to commission to Louisiana in 1877, X, 116.

Everett, Edward:
Mentioned, IV, 229, 316; V, 377.
Secretary of State, V, 191.

Ewell, Richard S., mentioned, V, 31.

Ewing, Thomas, Secretary of Treasury, mentioned, IV, 157.

Ex Post Facto Law.—A law passed after the commission of a crime or misdemeanor for which it provides punishment; a retroactive law. The Constitution of the United States prohibits the passage of such laws either by Congress or by any other legislative body. A law which renders an act punishable in a manner in which it was not punishable when it was committed has also been decided to be an *ex post facto* law. Various decisions of the courts specifically define an *ex post facto* law to be one which makes an innocent act done before its passage criminal; one which aggravates a crime and makes it legally greater than when committed; one which changes the punishment or makes it greater than that affixed to the crime by the law when committed; one that changes the legal rules of evidence applicable to an offense already committed, to the injury of the offender. The constitutional prohibition of *ex post facto* laws applies to criminal and penal statutes only, and not to those which affect property.

Exchange for Official Documents (see also International Bureau of Exchanges):
Agreement at Paris concerning, VIII, 131.
Convention concerning, VIII, 400.

Exchange, Medium of. (See Medium of Exchange.)

Exchequer, plan of, recommended, IV, 204, 266.

Excise Laws.—As early as 1790 a national excise law was passed. Alexander Hamilton, then Secretary of the Treasury, insisted that such a tax was necessary, but the law was not passed without a fierce debate. The tax imposed at first varied from 25 to 40 cents a gallon on imported spirits, from 9 to 25 cents on domestic distilled liquors, and from 11 to 30 cents when the material was molasses or other imported product. This tax was reduced in 1792. Opposition to it was strong throughout the country, culminating in the Whisky Insurrection in western Pennsylvania in 1794. Under Jefferson the excise tax was abolished. It was revived again in 1813, during the war with Great Britain. In 1817 it was again repealed and no excise tax was collected by the General Government until 1862, during the Civil War. Since that period this tax has been high on tobacco and liquors. The tax at present (1899) on whisky is $1.10 per gallon. (See also Revenue.)

Excise Tax. (See Taxation.)

Executive.—That branch of a government to which the execution of the laws is intrusted. The executive may be a king, an emperor, or a president, or a council or other body. From 1775 to 1789 the United States Government had no other executive than Congress, which, however, created a Board of War, Board of Treasury, etc. The Constitution invested the President with executive power, sharing only the powers of appointment and treaty making with the Senate. Executive Departments were established by the First Congress under the Constitution. Governors appointed by the Crown exercised the executive functions of the Colonies, except in Rhode Island, Connecticut, and for a short time in Massachusetts, whose governors were elected by the people. At the outbreak of the Revolution, when the royal governors had been deprived of their powers, and before the State constitutions had been adopted, executive power was invested in a committee of safety. In some Colonies an executive council, with a president or chairman, was chosen by the provincial congresses. Most of the State constitutions provided for governors. In the United States the executive is one of the three great departments of government, the other two being the legislative and the judicial. Historically the legislative branch is first, because it was placed first in order in both the work of the Convention and in the final draft of the Constitution. Practically the executive department is clearly prior in consideration so far as foreign powers are concerned. Under some Administrations executive power has been greatest in influence; under others perhaps smallest of the three. The weight of the Executive has steadily increased since the inauguration of the Government, not only on account of the appointing power, which is shared with the Senate and which grows with the expansion of the Republic, but for other reasons. The President's functions are constantly exercised when Congress and the judiciary are taking recess. Besides, he is the one person who represents to the average citizen the concrete majesty of law—the embodiment of authority in a democratic representative government.

Executive Cabinet:

Official conduct of, complimented, IV, 350; V, 178.

Proceedings of, on conduct of French minister, X, 87.

Rules adopted by, for preservation of neutrality by United States, X, 86.

Executive Departments.—The executive department of the United States Government comprises the following subordinate Departments: (1) State, which administers foreign affairs; (2) Treasury, which has charge of the finances; (3) Justice, which is the legal counsel of the Government; (4) War, which administers military affairs; (5) Post-Office, which has charge of mail service; (6) Navy, which has charge of naval affairs; (7) Interior, which has charge of matters pertaining to home affairs, including public lands, Indians, patents, pensions, education, railroads, and census; (8) Agriculture, which collects and disseminates information on agricultural subjects.

Executive Departments (see also the several Departments):

Accounts of condition of, requested by President Washington, X, 80.

Act regarding advertising of, vetoed, VII, 434.

Advertising in newspapers by, inquired into, V, 378.

Aliens employed in, report on number of, transmitted, IX, 670.

Applications to, should be in writing, VI, 348.

Appointments and promotions in, order regarding preference to be given veterans in, VI, 439.

Executive Departments—Continued.

Appointments in, having relation to civil service, VIII, 405. (See also Executive Nominations.)

Buildings occupied by, referred to, VI, 699.

Business of, order of President Jefferson regarding, X, 99.

Circulars asking for political contributions circulated in, VIII, 197.

Closed for Thanksgiving, VI, 44.

Communications to be transmitted to head of proper Department, order regarding, VI, 661; VII, 27.

Employees in—

Official conduct of, complimented, V, 178.

Order permitting—

To participate in decoration of graves of soldiers, VI, 664; VII, 164, 183, 230, 283, 328, 398, 450, 491, 556, 600; VIII, 13, 125, 166, 231, 314, 493, 765; IX, 28, 105, 174, 400, 517, 614.

To participate in dedication of Washington Monument, VIII, 292.

To witness inauguration of President Cleveland, VIII, 294.

Ordered to organize into companies for defense of Washington, VI, 122.

Partisan interference in elections by. (See Elections.)

Referred to, VI, 387.

Rendering honors to rebel living or dead inquired into, VI, 393.

Wages of, not to be affected by reduction in hours of labor, VII, 15, 175.

Examination of operations of, invited, IX, 626.

Extension of power to make temporary appointments of heads of, recommended, VI, 147. (See also IX, 133.)

Personal interviews with heads of, order regarding, VI, 348.

Postage accounts of, referred to, IV, 510.

Power of judiciary over, discussed, III, 503.

Record of efficiency of persons in, IX, 207.

Recommended, IX, 180.

Transfer of duties among, recommended, IV, 414; VII, 106.

Vacancy occasioned by death of head of, recommendations regarding filling, IX, 133. (See also VI, 147.)

Executive Mansion.—The President's official residence at Washington. It is built in the English Renaissance style of architecture, with a projecting columned and pedimented porch on the front entrance and a large semicircular projecting bay on the garden front opposite. The corner stone was laid by Washington in 1792, and it was first occupied by President John Adams in 1800. It stands on Pennsylvania avenue, slightly over a mile from the Capitol, and is surrounded by about 20 acres of handsomely laid out grounds. The Executive Mansion is 2 stories high, 176 feet long, 86 feet wide, and is built of freestone painted white. From this latter circumstance it is familiarly known as the White House. When the British captured Washington in 1814 the Executive Mansion, together with other buildings, was burned. Congress authorized its restoration in 1815, which was completed in 1818, and it has been occupied by each successive President since.

Executive Mansion:
Completion of, II, 26.
Furniture should be provided for, by Congress, II, 26.
Improvement of, II, 239.

Executive Nominations (see also Removals from Office):
Act—
    Prescribing oath of office to be taken by persons who participated in rebellion discussed, VII, 122.
    Regulating tenure of certain civil offices vetoed. (See Tenure-of-Office Act.)
Appointing power discussed by President—
    Buchanan, V, 659.
    Fillmore, V, 80.
    Jackson, III, 42, 53, 132.
    Johnson, VI, 492, 569, 622.
    Tyler, IV, 50, 105.
Appointments—
    During recess of Senate, X, 50.
    For limited period, II, 69.
    Referred to, VI, 464.
    Relation of members of Congress to, discussed, VII, 605.
Discussed, V, 531.
Errors in, arrangements for corrections of, recommended, II, 233.
In place of temporary appointments, X, 11.
Persons appointed or permitted to continue in office without consent of Senate inquired into, VI, 465.
President Madison declines to confer with Senate regarding, I, 530.
Rejections of, President Jackson's message asserting that Senate is not required to give reasons for, III, 42.
Renewal of, V, 110.
Request of—
    House for names of applicants for office refused by President Tyler, IV, 105.
    Senate for correspondence regarding, right to make, denied by President Jackson, III, 53.
    Senate for reasons for making, refused by President Jackson, III, 42, 132.
Resolution of Senate regarding, and reply of President Hayes, VII, 481.
Rules regulating interviews with President regarding, discussed, IX, 399.
Withdrawal of, by President—
    Harrison, W. H., not acted on by Senate, IV, 21.
    Jackson, not acted on by Senate, II, 439.

Executive Orders. (See the several subjects.)
Executive Salaries. (See Salaries, Executive.)
Executive Session.—The Constitution of the United States provides that the President "shall have power, by and with the advice and consent of the Senate, to make treaties, provided two-thirds of the Senators present concur; and he shall nominate and, by and with the advice and consent of the Senate, shall appoint ambassadors, other public ministers, and consuls, judges of the Supreme Court, and all other officers of the United States whose appointments are not herein otherwise provided for, and which shall be established by law." A rule of the Senate providing for the manner of advising and consenting to Executive recommendations requires that "when acting upon confidential or executive business, unless the same shall be considered in open executive session, the Senate Chamber shall be cleared of all persons except the Secretary, the Chief Clerk, the Principal Legislative Clerk, the Executive Clerk, the Minute and Journal Clerk, the Sergeant-at-Arms, the Assistant Doorkeeper, and such other officers as the Presiding Officer shall think necessary, and all such officers shall be sworn to secrecy." The Senate is then said to be in executive session. The House holds no executive sessions. It may go into secret session, however, whenever confidential communications are received from the President, or whenever the Speaker or any member shall inform the House that he has a communication which ought to be kept secret for a time.

Exequatur.—A Latin word meaning "Let him execute." In diplomatic usage the word is used to signify a document authorizing an official to act in the capacity of agent or representative. Usually a written recognition of a person in the character of consul or commercial agent issued by the government to which he is accredited and authorizing him to exercise his powers. The government from which an exequatur is asked has the right to refuse it either on political or personal grounds. The government may also withdraw it. When deprived of his exequatur a consul may withdraw with his records or delegate his powers to another, according to instructions.

Exequaturs:
Refusal of Turkey to grant exequaturs to consuls of United States referred to, IX, 660, 716.
Revoked—
    Consul of—
        Belgium, VI, 219.
        Chile, VI, 427.
        France, I, 270.
        Frankfort, VI, 511.
        Great Britain, V, 391, 392.
        Hanover, VI, 511.
        Hesse, VI, 511.
        Nassau, VI, 511.
        Oldenburg, VI, 512.
        Spain, V, 50.
        Sweden and Norway, VI, 428.
            Revocation annulled, VI, 432.
    Vice-consul of—
        Portugal, VII, 84.
        Sweden and Norway, VI, 429.
            Revocation annulled, VI, 432.

Exhibitions.—International and national exhibitions have been described as the milestones of commercial and industrial progress. They cultivate taste, afford material for comparison, and make people acquainted with the markets. Many branches of business have been called into existence or extended by their influence.

The first international exhibition held in America was that at New York City in 1853. On a very much larger scale was that held in Philadelphia in 1876, known as the Centennial Exposition. Then followed the International Cotton Exposition at Atlanta, Ga., in 1881; the Southern Exposition at Louisville, Ky., in 1883; the World's Columbian Exposition at Chicago, Ill., in 1893; the Midwinter Exhibition at San Francisco, Cal., in 1893–94; the International Cotton Exposition at Atlanta, Ga., in 1895; the Tennessee Centennial Exhibition at Nashville in 1897, and the Trans-Mississippi Exhibition at Omaha, Nebr., in 1898.

Expatriation.—The voluntary renunciation of the rights and liabilities of citizenship in one country to become the citizen or subject of another. The right of expatriation has been sanctioned by custom and usage in the United States. The Government has even in a number of instances refused protection to native-born and naturalized citizens on the ground that they had expatriated themselves. Notwithstanding this there has never been any statutory provision for expatriation other than is contained in the act of Congress of July 27, 1868, which declares it the natural and inherent right of all people, and that any denial or restriction thereof is contrary to the fundamental principles of government. Expatriation has been frequently pleaded before the Supreme Court, but the plea has always been overruled. Though the right be admitted, except in the case of persons subject to military service, holding public trusts, or charged with crime, the difficulty remains to give evidence of the mode of expatriation. British subjects cease to be such upon being naturalized in other countries, and such persons, in order to be again considered British subjects, must be renaturalized on their return to Great Britain. In France and Germany the somewhat indefinite claim of domicile in a foreign land is accepted as evidence of expatriation.

Expenditures, Public.—In 1794 the annual expenditures of the Federal Government amounted to only $6,300,000. In 1814 they ran up, on account of the war with Great Britain, to $34,700,000. They fell in 1834 to $18,600,000. In 1854 they were $55,000,000. During the last year of the Civil War (1865) they amounted to $1,295,000,000; but in 1878 they had declined to $237,000,000. For the following 10 years the expenditures averaged $260,000,000 per annum. For the fiscal year ending June 30, 1893, they were $459,400,000, made up largely of interest and pensions. In 1896 they were $434,678,654, and for the year ending Sept. 30, 1898, they had increased to $532,381,000.

Expenditures, Public (see also Foreign Intercourse):

Act making appropriations for—
Approved and reasons therefor, V, 597; VII 373.
Vetoed, VII, 536.

Act making appropriations to supply deficiencies vetoed, IX, 683.

Contingent fund, account of, rendered, I, 88, 135, 337, 355, 366, 378, 394, 417, 433, 459, 497; X, 14, 15, 17, 20, 22, 23, 24, 34, 37, 44, 48, 52, 55.

Discussed. (See Finances discussed.)

Economy in, recommended, IX, 458, 745.

Estimates, etc., of, referred to, I, 291, 307; VII, 259, 571; X, 70.

Failure of Congress to provide for, discussed and recommendations regarding, V, 542, 571; VII, 368, 452, 520.

Provision for, recommended by President—
Buchanan, V, 542.
Hayes, VII, 520.
Van Buren, III, 324.

Experiment Stations discussed, VIII, 799; IX, 456, 548; X, 200.

Exploring Expeditions (see also Arctic Expeditions; *Jeannette* Polar Expedition; Lady Franklin Bay Expedition; Pacific Ocean Exploring Expedition; South Sea Exploring Expedition; Wilkes Exploring Expedition):
Across continent recommended, I, 353; II, 320.
Naval expeditions referred to, VII, 497.

Explosives, order to prevent shipment of, VIII, 228.

Export Duties levied by foreign powers referred to, VIII, 157.

Exports.—The value of exports from the United States was, in round numbers, in 1790, $20,000,-000; in 1800, $32,000,000; in 1810, $42,000,000; in 1820, $52,000,000; in 1830, $58,500,000; in 1840, $112,000,000; in 1850, $135,000,000; in 1860, $356,-000,000; in 1870, $455,000,000; in 1880, $824,000,000; in 1890, $845,000,000; in 1892, $1,113,000,000, and in 1898, $1,231,700,000. These figures do not include exports of gold and silver.

Exports:

Aggregate of, to France referred to, II, 199.

Embargo on—
Modification of laws regarding, recommended, I, 542.
Recommended, I, 541.

Laws in regard to, I, 543; II, 300.

Prohibition on—
Recommended, I, 532.
Removal of, recommended, I, 542.

Value of, for year ending June—
1845, IV, 402.
1846, IV, 496.
1847, IV, 551.
1848, IV, 646.
1851, V, 122.
1852, V, 169.
1877, VII, 470.
1881, VIII, 46.
1884, VIII, 243.
1885, VIII, 340.

Exports—Continued.

Value of, for year ending June—
1886, VIII, 508.
1890, IX, 120.
1891, IX, 192.
1892, IX, 308.
1893, IX, 443, 455.
1894, IX, 532, 546.
1896, IX, 724, 739.

Value of, from commencement of Government, II, 482.

Expositions. (See Exhibitions.)

Express, The, American vessel attacked by, V, 139, 144.

Expunging Resolutions.—Mar. 28, 1834, the Senate passed a resolution censuring President Jackson and declaring that in removing the Federal deposits from the Bank of the United States he had assumed authority not conferred by the Constitution and the laws. Through the efforts of Senator Benton an "expunging resolution" was passed Jan. 16, 1837. A black line was drawn around the resolution of censure in the Journal and across it was written the words "Expunged by order of the Senate this 16th day of January, 1837." The expunging resolution was strenuously opposed by Webster, Clay, and Calhoun.

Extradition Conventions. (See Fugitive Criminals.)

Extradition, International.—Extradition treaties have been concluded by the Government of the United States with the principal governments of the world and many of the smaller ones. The first was that with Great Britain negotiated by John Jay in 1794. Congress, however, made no law for carrying out its provisions. Again, in 1842 a second treaty was negotiated. This was found to be inadequate in many ways. For instance, a criminal whose offense was not covered by the treaty was extradited on another charge and then tried for his real offense. This called forth a protest from Great Britain. By 1886 the treaty of 1842 was found to be entirely inadequate to existing conditions. The Phelps-Rosebery convention of that year offered a more satisfactory system, but was rejected by the Senate. That body, however, ratified the Blaine-Pauncefote convention of 1889, which accomplished the desired result. Extradition treaties were negotiated by this country with France in 1843; with Hawaii in 1849; with Switzerland in 1850; with Prussia in 1852; with Austria in 1856; with Sweden and Norway in 1860; with Mexico in 1861; with Italy in 1868; with Ecuador in 1872; with the Ottoman Empire in 1874; with Spain in 1877; with Japan in 1886; with the Netherlands in 1887, and with Russia in 1893.

Extraordinary Session Messages. (See Special Session Messages.)

Extraordinary Sessions of Congress, proclamations convening, by President—
Adams, John, I, 232.
Cleveland, IX, 396.
Harrison, W. H., IV, 21.

F.

following the Civil War in the United States. The Greenback party claimed that the fiat of the Government could itself give value to a circulating medium of no intrinsic value and not even containing a promise to pay, but issued by the State with the bare assertion of its identity with true money. The Latin word "fiat" means "Let it be done."

Field, Cyrus W., gold medal presented to, VI, 703.

Field, Stephen J., associate justice Supreme Court, assault upon, by David S. Terry, IX, 42.

Field Products. (See Agricultural Products.)

"Fifty-four Forty or Fight."—A campaign cry of the Democrats in 1844. This was during the northwestern boundary discussion. The treaty with Spain in 1819 fixed the parallel of 42° as the northern limit of that country's possessions in America. Between that parallel and 54° 40′ lay the Territory of Oregon, claimed by both America and England. Americans had made surveys as far north as 49° and settlements were springing up. English fur traders had passed south of that line, and for a time war seemed inevitable; but a treaty was arranged in 1846 fixing the boundary at lat. 49° north. It was during the Presidential campaign that the cry "Fifty-four Forty or Fight" originated. The supporters of Mr. Polk in that campaign vigorously proclaimed that the northwestern boundary line should be established as far north as 54° 40′ or the United States should fight. It was during his Administration that the line was established at 49°. When criticised by his political opponents for the failure to locate the line at 54° 40′, he excused and justified his Administration by stating that "all conflicting title to the Oregon Territory south of the forty-ninth degree of north latitude, being all that was insisted on by any of my predecessors, has been adjusted" (IV, 634). (See also Northwestern Boundary.)

Fiji, or Feejee, Islands.—An archipelago in the South Pacific Ocean belonging to Great Britain. The islands number over 200. The surface is generally mountainous. The inhabitants were formerly cannibals, but have been converted to Christianity. The leading export is sugar. Area, about 7,740 sq. miles; population, about 125,000.

Fiji Islands, report of agent to, for investigation of claim of B. H. Henry and others, IX, 666.

Filibuster.—From the Spanish word filibustero, meaning "freebooter" or "buccaneer." In 1849-1851 the term was applied by the Cubans to Narciso Lopez and his followers, and from that time became a common name for military adventurers who fitted out expeditions against the Spanish-American countries. The object of most of these filibusters has been to free the Spanish-American countries from their European rulers. After Lopez the most famous filibuster was Gen. William Walker, who invaded Sonora, Mexico, in 1853. In 1855 he took possession of Nicaragua and was elected President. He did not long enjoy this distinction, for he was soon compelled to surrender to the forces of the United States, but escaped punishment. In 1857 he organized a second expedition to Nicaragua, but was again compelled to surrender to the United States Government. Escaping punishment a second time, in 1860 he organized an expedition against the Government of Honduras, but was captured and by order of the President of Honduras shot. In the United States the term filibuster, when used in a legislative or political sense, means that method pursued by the members of the minority of a legislative body who seek to delay or defeat the adoption of measures obnoxious to them by obstructive and dilatory tactics, such as repeated motions to adjourn, for a recess, calls for the yeas and nays, or other dilatory motions.

Fillmore, Millard (thirteenth President United States):

Annual messages of, V, 77, 113, 163.

Appointing power of President discussed by, V, 80.

Biographical sketch of, V, 63.

Cuba—

Acquisition of, discussed by, V, 165.

Affairs of, discussed by, V, 113, 164.

Incorporation of, into Union not desired, V, 165.

Death of, announced, and honors to be paid memory of, VII, 282.

Death of President Taylor announced to, and reply of, V, 51.

Communication of, to Senate, V, 52.

Discussed by, V, 55, 64, 77.

Finances discussed by, V, 83, 122, 168.

Foreign policy discussed by, V, 78, 120, 165, 179.

Information regarding negotiations with Great Britain, Costa Rica, and Nicaragua refused by, V, 154.

Information regarding proposition to annex Hawaiian Islands refused by, V, 155, 159.

Internal improvements discussed by, V, 90.

Oath of office, time and place of taking, mentioned, V, 52.

Portrait of, V, 62.

Powers of Federal and State Governments discussed by, V, 90.

Proclamations of—

Discriminating duties on vessels of Chile suspended, V, 76.

Extraordinary session of Senate, V, 110, 191.

Military expedition to—

Cuba, V, 111.

Mexico, V, 112.

Texas boundary line, V, 107.

Unlawful combinations in Boston, V, 109.

State of the Union discussed by, V, 77.

System of government discussed by, V, 78.

Tariff discussed by, V, 83, 123, 125, 169.

Finances:

Act—

Directing coinage of silver bullion in Treasury vetoed, IX, 483.

Directing payment of surplus in Treasury on public debt, reasons for applying pocket veto to, VIII, 488.

Finances, Superintendent of.—Feb. 7, 1781, the Continental Congress passed an act establishing the office of Superintendent of Finance. Robert Morris was appointed to the position. Previous to this the Committee of Claims and the Treasury Office of Accounts were combined in what was called the Treasury Board, consisting of 5 members of Congress. This board expired with the appointment of Morris. He was authorized to examine into the state of the country's finances, report plans for improvement, direct the execution of orders respecting revenue and expenditure, and control the public accounts. Morris resigned in 1784 and the finances of the Government were placed under a board of 3 commissioners, where they continued until 1789, at which time the First Congress established the present Treasury Department.

instead of exercising this power, moved for a commission to amicably adjust the points of dispute under the convention of London. Thomas F. Bayard, William L. Putnam, and James B. Angell were selected to represent the United States, and Joseph Chamberlain, Sir Lionel Sackville-West, and Sir Charles Tupper represented Great Britain. Feb. 15, 1888, a treaty was signed and immediately laid before the two Governments for ratification. Great Britain abandoned her claim that the 3-mile limit extended from headland to headland, and agreed that, except in cases specially mentioned of bays more than 10 miles wide, the marine league should be measured outward from a line drawn across them, and also agreed that United States fishing vessels should have the same rights in Canadian ports as Canadian vessels, except that the purchase of bait was forbidden. The treaty also contained a reciprocity clause. It was rejected by the Senate. Aug. 21, 1888. Since that period good relations have been maintained by virtue of a *modus vivendi* terminable at will. At a meeting of conferees of the two powers held at Washington in May, 1898, it was agreed to submit the question of the fisheries, among others, to a joint high commission. This commission assembled at Quebec in August, 1898, and adjourned to Washington in the winter following, but arrived at no agreement thereon. Since then the matter has been under consideration by the Secretary of State and the British Government.

Fisheries (see also Bering Sea Fisheries; Fortune Bay Outrages; Geneva Tribunal; Halifax Commission; Halifax, Nova Scotia):

Capture and detention of American fishermen, II, 284, 286; VII, 114.

Commission on subject of, recommended, VIII, 170, 332, 529.

Commission to be organized, V, 334; VII, 121.

Correspondence regarding, with—
France, VI, 32.
Great Britain, VI, 32; VIII, 536, 608.

Discussed by President—
Adams, John, I, 251.
Jefferson, I, 346.
Washington, I, 85.

Joint commission between United States and Great Britain relating to preservation of, IX, 751.

Joint high commission between United States and Great Britain on subject of, to sit at Washington, VII, 121.

Outrages committed on American fishermen, VII, 590, 606.

Papers for protection of vessels engaged in, referred to, III, 557.

Questions growing out of, with Great Britain (see also Bering Sea Fisheries; Fortune Bay Outrages; Geneva Tribunal; Halifax Commission; Halifax, Nova Scotia)—

Discussed by President—
Cleveland, VIII, 331, 499, 529, 603, 620, 628, 779, 799.
Fillmore, V, 139, 158, 163, 188, 190.

Fisheries—Continued.
Questions growing out of, with Great Britain—Continued.

Discussed by President—
Grant, VII, 58, 102, 114, 121, 143, 187
Harrison, Benj., IX, 34.
Johnson, VI, 383, 690.
Pierce, V, 208, 228, 334.
Tyler, IV, 259.

Referred to, VI, 467, 703.

Regulations of Great Britain, France, and Germany respecting, referred to, II, 564.

Treaty with Great Britain regarding, V, 242, 247, 277, 411; VII, 210; VIII, 280, 603. (See also Geneva Tribunal.)

Acts passed to give effect to, passage of, proclaimed, VII, 225.

Meetings of commissioners referred to, VIII, 611.

Rejection of, discussed, VIII, 620, 779.

Termination of, discussed, VIII, 170, 331.
Proclaimed, VIII, 280.

Unfriendly treatment of American fishermen by Canadians, VII, 58, 102; VIII, 529.

Vessels sent to protect American fishermen, V, 158.

Fisheries Exhibition, International, at London, discussed, VIII, 101.

Fishermen, American:
Capture and detention of, II, 284, 286; VII, 114.
Outrages committed on, VII, 590, 606.
Unfriendly treatment of, by Canadians, VII, 58, 102; VIII, 529.
Vessels sent to protect, V, 158.

Fishers Hill (Va.), Battle of.—Early's retreat from the Opequan after the battle of Sept. 19, 1864, did not stop at Winchester, but continued to Fishers Hill, south of Winchester and about 12 miles from the scene of the battle of Opequan Creek. Here Early rallied his forces. To drive him from this position, Sheridan dispatched Torbert with 2 divisions of cavalry by a circuitous route to the Confederate rear, and on the evening of Sept. 22 the Sixth and Nineteenth corps engaged Early in front, while Torbert's forces fell upon his rear. The Confederates retreated and Sheridan followed them through Harrisonburg, Staunton, and the gaps in the Blue Ridge Mountains. Sheridan then devastated the valley so as to render it untenable for Confederate troops. At Fishers Hill he captured 1,100 prisoners and 16 guns.

Fishery Commissions. (See Fisheries.)

Fisk, Clinton B., mentioned, X, 111.

Fitz, Gideon, surveyor-general, removal of, from office, discussed, III, 132.

Fitzmorris, Mary, act for relief of, vetoed, VIII, 688.

Fitzpatrick, Thomas, treaty with Indians concluded by, V, 229.

Fitzsimons, Thomas, commissioner of United States under treaty with Great Britain, I, 196.

Five-Cent Piece.—In 1792 Congress authorized the coinage of a silver half dime of 20.8 grains in weight. This was the first coin struck by the United States Mint. In 1853 the weight was reduced to 19.2 grains. There were no issues of this coin in 1798, 1799, 1804, and from 1806 to 1828. In 1866 the nickel 5-cent piece was authorized and the legal-tender value reduced from $5 to 30 cents. Coinage of the silver half dime was discontinued in 1873.

Five Civilized Tribes:

Discussed, X, 199.

Relation of, to United States discussed, IX, 202, 735.

Representation of, in Congress recommended, IX, 202.

Five Forks (Va.), Battle of.—Mar. 27, 1865, Gen. Sheridan, with 10,000 cavalry, returned from his raid through the Shenandoah Valley and rejoined the Army of the Potomac before Richmond. On the 29th Grant began a movement to turn the Confederate right or destroy their line of retreat south. Sheridan, with the Fifth Corps, under Gen. Warren, and about 9,000 cavalry, crossed Hatchers Run and proceeded by way of the Boydton plank road toward Dinwiddie Court-House. Warren found the Confederates in force on the White Oak road. Sheridan, passing Dinwiddie, turned north. Lee had sent a strong force, chiefly the divisions of Johnson and Pickett, to meet the threatened attempt on the roads to his rear. Mar. 31 this column met and defeated Warren and then attacked Sheridan at Five Forks and drove him back toward Dinwiddie. The next morning, Apr. 1, Sheridan advanced with his cavalry and the Fifth Corps, about 12,000 strong. By 2 p. m. the Confederates had retired into their main works. Ayres, on the left of the Fifth Corps, made a charge, carrying all before him and taking 1,000 prisoners; Griffin captured the works in his front, taking 1,500 prisoners; Crawford seized the Ford road in the Confederate rear; Merritt's cavalry made a charge, and the day was won, but not without a desperate resistance. Lee's army was virtually overwhelmed. For 6 miles it fell back along the White Oak road. More than 5,000 prisoners were taken, with 6 guns and 13 colors. Sheridan's loss was about 1,000, of whom 634 were of Warren's corps.

Flag.—A banner or ensign, sometimes called colors. During the early days of the Revolution the colonists made use of various devices for flags, no less than half a dozen distinct banners being preserved. In three of these the combined crosses of St. George and St. Andrew form the union. The favorite in New England was the pine-tree flag, consisting of a green pine tree in a field of white. This was also used as the union of a flag with a red field. The rattlesnake flag consisted of 13 pieces of a rattlesnake marked with the initials of the Colonies and the legend "Join or die." Another snake standard consisted of alternate red and white bars with the design of a snake and the legend "Don't tread on me." In 1775 Congress adopted the stripes of a troop of Philadelphia light-horse cavalry. This still retained the British union. June 14, 1777, the flag of the United States had its statutory beginning in the following resolution: "*Re-*

solved, That the flag of the United States be 13 stripes, alternate red and white; that the union be 13 stars, white in a blue field, representing a new constellation." The stars (or mullets, heraldically speaking) are 5-pointed. They are arranged in a rectangular diagram. This flag was first displayed in the battle of Brandywine, Sept. 11, 1777. On the admission of Vermont and Kentucky in 1794 2 more stars and 2 more stripes were added. Apr. 4, 1818, the flag was reestablished with 13 stripes, representing the thirteen original States, and 20 stars, one star for each new State admitted to be added to the flag on the 4th of July succeeding such admission. As the stars represent the States, there are now (1899) 45 stars on the flag. The banner of the United States is commonly supposed to have been based upon the Washington coat of arms.

Flagler, Daniel W., mentioned, VIII, 151.

Flags:

Confederate, captured, to be presented to Congress, VI, 108.

Union and Confederate, return of, to respective States recommended, VIII, 578.

Proposition withdrawn, VIII, 579.

Flanagan, John, mentioned, IV, 365.

Flathead Indians:

Agreement with, for sale of lands, VIII, 153, 192. Treaty with, V, 380.

Fleming, Charles, lieutenant in Navy, court of inquiry in case of, referred to, VI, 74.

Fletcher, Thomas C., mentioned, IX, 231.

Flogging.—A chastisement by beating or whipping. It was a punishment inflicted in the United States Navy until 1850, when it was abolished. In 1861 it was prohibited in the Army.

Florida.—One of the United States; nickname, "The Everglade State;" motto, "In God We Trust." It lies between lat. 31° and 24° 30′ north and long. 79° 48′ and 87° 38′ west. It is bounded on the north by Georgia and Alabama, on the east by the Atlantic Ocean, on the south by Florida Strait and the Gulf of Mexico, and on the west by the Gulf of Mexico and Alabama (separated from the latter by the Perdido River). The leading products are corn, cotton, rice, tobacco, oranges and other tropical fruits, and timber. It is a favorite health resort for winter tourists. Florida was discovered by Juan Ponce de Leon on Easter Sunday in 1513. It was named, some say, from the profusion of flowers in bloom at the time of its discovery; others, from the day of its discovery, which in Spanish is called Pascua florida, or Flowery Easter. Expeditions fitted out at Cuba and Puerto Rico by Spaniards made futile attempts at settlement between 1516 and 1540. The French Admiral De Coligny sent 3 colonies of Huguenots from France to settle the country, but they were massacred by the Spaniards, and in 1565 St. Augustine was permanently established by the Spanish under Menendez. The territory was ceded to Great Britain in 1763 and returned to Spain in 1783. In February, 1819, East and

West Florida were ceded to the United States, Spain receiving therefor $5,000,000. The territory was the scene of the Seminole wars. It was admitted to the Union in 1845, seceded Jan. 10, 1861, and was readmitted by act of Congress June 25, 1868. The present constitution was adopted in the latter year. Area, 58,680 sq. miles; population (1890), 391,422. In 1811 Florida, then a Spanish possession, was claimed by Great Britain. During that year the President laid before Congress communications which showed that Great Britain had given orders for taking possession of a portion of the territory. While it is popularly understood that the first formal annunciation of the famous Monroe doctrine was made by President Monroe in his annual message of Dec. 2, 1823 (II, 218), yet it will be seen that as early as Jan. 3, 1811, in a special message of that date, President Madison substantially announced that doctrine, applying it specially to the efforts of Great Britain to acquire this territory from Spain. Discussing these communications and the attitude of Great Britain in this matter and her intention to take possession of this territory, President Madison used these words: "I recommend to the consideration of Congress the seasonableness of a declaration that the United States could not see without serious inquietude any part of a neighboring territory in which they have in different respects so deep and so just a concern pass from the hands of Spain into those of any other foreign power" (I, 488).

Florida (see also Confederate States):

Acquisition of, by United States—
Discussed, II, 55, 103, 363. (See also II, 390, 466.)
Effect of, discussed, V, 345.
Treaty regarding. (See Spain, treaty with, discussed by President Monroe.)

Archives of, to be delivered to United States, II, 593; III, 24, 98.
Contravention of treaty regarding, discussed, II, 103.
Portion of, delivered, III, 150.

Army in, called into action only on written requisition of officers of Territory, II, 127.

Bonds of, referred to, III, 590, 591, 627.

Boundary line with. (See Spain.)

Boundary line with Georgia discussed, II, 329, 395, 561; III, 41.

Canal routes in, survey of, III, 35.

Cession of, by Spain, correspondence regarding, transmitted, X, 56.

Change of possession of, from Spain to other power objected to, I, 488. (See also Monroe Doctrine.)

Claims arising out of invasion of. (See East Florida Claims.)

Constitution of, transmitted, VI, 634.

Courts of United States in, obstructions to execution of process of, IX, 104.

Demands of Spain for possession of, X, 53.

Expeditions against, II, 13, 21, 23, 32, 40, 51; X, 16. (See also Expeditions Against Foreign Powers.)

Fisheries on coast of, V, 189.

Florida—Continued.

Fourteenth amendment to Constitution ratified by, referred to, VI, 656.

Government should be established in, II, 105. Referred to, II, 127.

Governor and other officers appointed for, II, 104.

Inability of Spain to check Indian movements in, II, 31, 40.

Indian depredations in, III, 428; IV, 154, 199.

Indians in—
Authority to use certain funds in purchase of lands for, bill for, VIII, 612.
Hostile acts of, III, 214; IV, 154.
Referred to, IV, 275.
Removal of, discussed, V, 45, 171, 184. (See also Indians, removal of.)

Indian wars in (see also Indian Wars)—
Brevet nominations for army officers for services in, IV, 155.
Correspondence regarding, referred to, III, 579.
Discussed, IV, 154, 198.
Disposition of Indians to treat for peace, III, 430.
Referred to, II, 31; III, 537, 616; IV, 80, 154, 199.

Insurrection in, proclamation regarding, VI, 16.

Interference with collector of customs in Cedar Keys, and action of Government discussed, IX, 72.

Lands granted to, in aid of railroads referred to, VI, 382.

Lands in—
Claims to, II, 203, 427.
Titles to, II, 234, 427.
Treaty regarding security of, referred to, II, 363.

Legislative council of—
Memorial from, regarding government, etc., for, II, 200, and X, 121.
Resolutions of, referred to, IV, 220.

Maj. Gen. Jackson's entrance into, discussed, II, 42.
Courts-martial of Arbuthnot and Ambristie [Ambrister] referred to, II, 43.
Idea of hostility toward Spain not entertained, II, 43.
Not an encroachment upon rights of Spain, II, 42.

Orders to Gen. Matthews, Col. McKee, and Governor Mitchell regarding possession of, I, 506.

Ordinance of Spain respecting commerce of, X, 14.

Possession and occupancy of, measures authorized by President regarding, X, 52.

Progress in, checked by malady at Pensacola, II, 190.

Property owners in, should be compensated for losses sustained, III, 255.

Provisional governor for, appointed and restoration of, into Union discussed, VI, 329.

Report regarding, transmitted, X, 45.

Smuggling practiced by citizens of. (See Smuggling.)

Fort Brown (Tex.), Attack on.—In consequence of the annexation of Texas the War Department, apprehending trouble with Mexico, sent all the available troops in the South and West to the frontier. The territory between the Nueces and Rio Grande rivers was claimed by both Texas and Mexico. Gen. Zachary Taylor collected an army of 4,000 men at Corpus Christi, near the mouth of the Nueces, in November, 1845. Jan. 13, 1846, he was ordered to advance to a position on the Rio Grande, and on Mar. 25 he occupied Point Isabel, on the coast of the Gulf of Mexico, just north of the mouth of the river. During April Gen. Taylor had advanced his army up the Rio Grande to a point opposite Matamoros, which was occupied by the Mexican army under Gen. Arista. Here the Americans built a fort under the direction of Maj. Brown and named it in his honor. Learning that bodies of Mexicans had crossed the river both above and below him with the intention of cutting him off from his supplies at Point Isabel, Taylor fell back toward the latter place May 1. Learning of his departure, the Mexicans on May 3 began a heavy bombardment of Fort Brown, which was continued at intervals until the 10th. It was gallantly defended by Maj. Brown and Captains Hawkins and Mansfield. The former was killed during the engagement. The only other fatality was that of Sergt. Weigert. Thirteen privates were wounded.

Fort Cameron Reservation, Utah, disposal of, recommended, VIII, 153.

Fort Delaware, Del., title to island on which it stands referred to, II, 536, 562.

Fort Dodge Military Reservation, Iowa, disposal of, referred to, VIII, 103.

Fort Donelson (Tenn.), Capture of.—After the taking of Fort Henry the next logical move against the Confederate line of defense in the West was the reduction of Fort Donelson. This was a large fieldwork of 100 acres, on a bluff 100 feet high, near the town of Dover, Tenn., on the Cumberland River, about 63 miles from Nashville. It mounted 65 guns and was garrisoned by 21,000 men under Gen. Floyd. Feb. 12, 1862, Brig. Gen. Grant with 15,000 men moved upon the works by way of the roads leading from Fort Henry. While Grant was placing his forces in position Commodore Foote arrived in the river opposite the fort with a fleet of 6 gunboats, 4 of them ironclad. On the 14th he opened fire. In a desperate attack 2 of the vessels were disabled and the others withdrew after a loss of 54 men. The guns on the bluff were too high to be silenced from the water level. On the day of the unsuccessful attack by the gunboats Gen. Wallace arrived with reenforcements, swelling Grant's command to 27,000. On the 15th Floyd made an attempt to force his way through the surrounding Federal lines. Fighting continued all day during most intensely cold weather. When night fell upon Donelson the Confederates retired to their works. During the night Floyd surrendered the command to

Pillow and he to Buckner. The two former escaped by way of the river during the night, and next morning Buckner surrendered the fort unconditionally to Grant. Sixty-five guns, 17,600 small arms, and 14,623 prisoners fell into the hands of the victors. Grant's losses were 2,832 in killed, wounded, and missing. The Confederates lost 2,500 in killed and wounded.

Fort Erie (Canada), Battles at.—June 1, 1814, Maj. Gen. Brown established headquarters at Buffalo with the intention of retaking the lower peninsula of Canada. His army consisted of 2 brigades of infantry, commanded by Generals Scott and Ripley, respectively, and to each were added a train of artillery and a squad of cavalry. There was also a brigade of 1,100 New York and Pennsylvania volunteers and 500 Indians. July 3 the American army crossed the Niagara and demanded the surrender of Fort Erie, the first British post on the Canada side. Maj. Buck, with the garrison of 170 men, yielded without a struggle. Aug. 5 Gen. Gaines arrived at Fort Erie to take command of the American army of 2,500, which had retired to the southward after the battle of Lundys Lane. Here he was besieged by Lieut. Col. Drummond with 5,000 men. The latter subjected the fort to a heavy bombardment all day Aug. 14, and on the 15th, between midnight and dawn, made a series of desperate assaults, showing no quarter to Americans who fell into their power. The British were driven off, with a loss of 221 killed, 174 wounded, and 186 prisoners. The American loss was 17 killed, 56 wounded, and 11 missing. After this repulse the British kept up a constant bombardment of the fort for several weeks. Gen. Gaines was seriously injured, and Gen. Brown resumed command, though in ill health and suffering from wounds received at Lundys Lane. Sept. 17 a sortie was made by about 1,000 regulars and the same number of militia upon the British outposts, and all their batteries were captured or destroyed. This saved Buffalo and perhaps all of western New York and seriously crippled the enemy. The loss to the British during the sortie was 500 killed, wounded, and missing, and 385 prisoners. The American loss was 79 killed and 216 wounded. After this disaster Drummond retired precipitately and the Americans abandoned and destroyed Fort Erie.

Fort Erie, Canada, reduction of, by American arms, I, 539.

Fort Fisher (N. C.), Capture of.—In November, 1864, an expedition was planned against Fort Fisher, N. C. This fort occupies a peninsula on the south coast of North Carolina, between the mouth of the Cape Fear River and the Atlantic Ocean, about 18 miles from Wilmington. It formed the principal defense of that city, which was the most important seaport through which the Southern Confederacy received foreign supplies, and from which departed blockade runners laden with cotton and other products of the South. It was also deemed a point of considerable strategic importance. Fort Fisher and its connected works mounted 75 guns. The armament of the works guarding the approaches to Wilmington was about 150 guns, including some 150-pounder Armstrong guns. The garrison of the fort and outworks consisted of 2,300 men. Dec. 13, 1864, the expedition started. It was composed of a fleet of 73 vessels, carrying 655 guns, some of them of the largest caliber, and a land force of 6,500 men under Gen. Butler. The expedition was accompanied by a boat loaded with 215 tons of gunpowder, which it was designed to explode in the vicinity of the fort, with the object of igniting and exploding the magazines. This proved a failure. Dec. 24 the fort was bombarded by the fleet for an hour and a half. The next day, after a reconnoissance by the land troops, Butler ordered their reembarkation and return. Butler was relieved of the command and superseded by Gen. Terry, with the addition of 1,500 men and a small siege train. Jan. 13, 1865, the fort was again attacked. The troops were landed under protection of Porter's guns. On the 14th a small advance work was taken by the Federals. The ships reopened fire on the 15th. At 3 p. m. a general assault was made, and for 5 hours a desperate hand-to-hand encounter was maintained. Not until 10 p. m. was resistance ended and the garrison forced to surrender. Two thousand and eighty-three prisoners were taken, including Gen. Whiting and Col. Lamb. The Federal loss was 110 killed and 530 wounded. The Confederate loss in killed and wounded was about 500. The next morning by the accidental explosion of a magazine 200 men were killed and 100 wounded.

Fort Gaines (Ala.), Reduction of. (See Mobile Bay (Ala.), Battle of.)

Fort Gaines, Ala., reduction of, and orders regarding celebration of, VI, 238.

Fort George (Canada), Capture of.—After the occupation of Toronto, Apr. 27, 1813, the Americans turned their attention to the British forts along the Niagara River. On the west side of the river and near its mouth stood Fort George, which was held by about 1,800 regulars, 350 militia, and 50 Indians, under Brig. Gen. Vincent and Colonels Harvey and Meyers. Nearly opposite Fort George was the American Fort Niagara, in and about which had been collected some 4,000 troops under command of Gen. Dearborn. Acting under him were Maj. Gen. Morgan Lewis, Generals Boyd, Winder, and Chandler, and Col. Winfield Scott. May 27, 1813, an attack was made on Fort George. The army was transported to the Canadian soil by the fleet under Commodore Chauncey and Capt. Perry. After a severe battle of 20 minutes the British fled in confusion toward Beaver Dams, 18 miles distant, to rendezvous. At the end of 3 hours Fort George and its dependencies, with the village of Newark, were in the hands of the Americans. Their loss was about 40 killed and 100 wounded. The loss of the British regulars was 51 killed and 305 wounded, missing,

and prisoners. The number of Canadian militia made prisoners was 507, making the total British loss 863, as well as large quantities of ammunition and stores. July 8, 1813, a party of 40 Americans under Lieut. Eldridge, in attempting to drive off a small detachment of British and Indians who had approached to within a couple of miles of Fort George, were ambushed by Indians under Blackbird, and only 10 of the party escaped. The wounded and prisoners were massacred.

Fort George, Canada, reduction of, by American arms, I, 539.

Fort Griswold (Conn.), Capture of.—Sept. 6, 1781, after Arnold and the Tories had secured New London, they carried by assault Fort Griswold, on the opposite side of the river. The Americans offered a stubborn resistance. Out of the garrison of 150 men 73 were killed, including Col. Ledyard, the commander, and 30 were wounded, many after having surrendered.

Fort Hall Reservation, Idaho, agreement with Indians for disposal of lands on, for use of railroad, VIII, 68, 192, 602.

Fort Harrison (Ind.), Attack on.—Capt. (afterwards General and President) Zachary Taylor Sept. 4, 1812, held, until reenforcements reached him, a blockhouse on the Wabash River, Ind., with a garrison of 50 men, ill or convalescing from fever, against a fierce assault of Indians. The savages set fire to the blockhouse. Taylor's loss was 3 killed and 3 wounded.

Fort Henry (Tenn.), Capture of.—The main line of Confederate defense in the West in January, 1862, extended from Columbus, Ky., on the Mississippi River, to the Cumberland Mountains, in eastern Tennessee. On this line of defense were Forts Henry and Donelson, in the northern part of Tennessee, the former on the eastern bank of the Tennessee River and the latter on the western bank of the Cumberland, about 12 miles apart. Gen. Halleck, commander of the Department of Missouri, determined to make an attack on Fort Henry, which was near the center of the line. Jan. 30 an expedition was sent out from Cairo, consisting of 7 gunboats, 4 of them ironclad, under command of Commodore Foote, and a land force of 15,000 men commanded by Brig. Gen. Grant. On the night of Feb. 5 the infantry were landed 4 miles from the fort. The gunboats anchored abreast till 10 o'clock next morning, when they began to advance. Fort Henry mounted 17 guns and was garrisoned by 2,734 men, under command of Brig. Gen. Tilghman. The attack was to have been made by the gunboats, seconded by the land forces. Foote began the bombardment before the arrival of Gen. Grant, whose march was delayed by muddy roads and swollen streams. Tilghman answered the fire of the gunboats for 1 hour and 20 minutes and then surrendered unconditionally, the greater part of his garrison having already escaped to Fort Donelson. Grant arrived half an hour after the battle, and the fort was turned over to him. The part of the garrison that surrendered consisted of about 65 able-bodied men and 60 invalids. Tilghman's loss was 21 killed and wounded. The Federal loss was 48.

Fort Henry, Tenn., thanks of President to forces capturing, VI, 104.

Fort Jackson, Ala., treaty with Indians concluded at, II, 320.

Fort Leavenworth, Kans.:

Estimates for barracks at, referred to, VIII, 79, 87.

Military prison at, use of, as Government penitentiary discussed, IX, 729.

Recommended, IX, 537.

Fort Lewis, Colo, estimates for post at, VIII, 90.

Fort McAllister (Ga.), Capture of, and Fall of Savannah.—After the destruction of Atlanta and its railroad connections Gen. Sherman took up his march toward Savannah. His army was composed of the Fourteenth, Fifteenth, Seventeenth, and Twentieth corps. Gen. Howard commanded the right wing and Gen. Slocum the left. The cavalry was under the direction of Gen. Kilpatrick. Sherman passed down the peninsula between the Ogeechee and Savannah rivers and about the middle of December appeared before Savannah, held by the Confederate General Hardee with 15,000 men. To the south of Savannah, on the Ogeechee River, stands Fort McAllister, which had resisted many attacks from the sea and effectually prevented the ascent of the river by the Federal gunboats. The defenses of the fort were weak to the landward and a garrison of less than 300 men held the works. Fort McAllister mounted 23 guns in barbette and 1 mortar. Dec. 13, 1864, Gen. Hazen's division of the Fifteenth Corps crossed the river and assaulted the fort from the rear. The garrison was overpowered and in 15 minutes after the bugle sounded "Forward" the fort was taken. Communication was now open to Dahlgren's fleet, lying in the harbor. Siege guns were brought from Hilton Head, and when the investment of Savannah was completed Sherman demanded its surrender. Hardee refused, but on the night of Dec. 20, when all the arrangements for the assault had been completed, he evacuated the city. It was occupied next day by Sherman's army. Two hundred guns and 35,000 bales of cotton fell into Federal hands. Thus ended Sherman's march from Atlanta to the sea, a distance of more than 300 miles. Out of the entire army of 66,000 men 63 were killed, 245 were wounded, and 260 were captured on the march, which consumed 27 days.

Fort McHenry (Md.), Bombardment of.—In September, 1814, the British planned to take Baltimore by a combined land and sea attack. The night after the battle of North Point the British remained on the field. The following morning, Sept. 13, 1814, the British fleet, consisting of 16 heavy vessels, 5 of them bomb ships, began the attack on Fort McHenry, 3 miles southeast of the city. The fort was defended by Maj. Armistead with about 800 men. The bombardment continued 25 hours. The American loss was 4 killed and 24 wounded.

It was during this bombardment that Francis Scott Key wrote The Star-Spangled Banner. The British withdrew after losing 2 vessels and a large number of men.

Fort Mackinaw (Mich.), Capture of.—The War of 1812 was proclaimed June 19 (I, 512). The British in Canada learned of it sooner than their adversaries across the lakes. July 17 a force of 600 British and Indians under Capt. Roberts surprised and captured the garrison of 61 officers and men under Lieut. Hancks at Fort Michilimackinac, or Mackinaw. An attempt to recapture it in 1814 was unsuccessful.

Fort Mackinaw, Mich., attempted reduction of, referred to, I, 549.

Fort McKinney, Wyo., estimates for completion of post at, VIII, 93.

Fort Madison (Iowa), Defense of.—Sept. 5, 1812, about 200 Winnebago Indians attacked Fort Madison, on the Mississippi River above St. Louis, and were repulsed after 3 days' fighting. The garrison consisted of a small detachment under Lieutenants Hamilton and Vasques. The Americans lost 1 man.

Fort Maginnis, Mont., estimates for post at, VIII, 100.

Fort Malden, Canada, reduction of, by American arms, I, 539.

Fort Meigs (Ohio), Bombardment of.—In April, 1813, Col. Proctor, with a force of 1,000 British regulars and Canada militia and 1,500 Indians, set out on an expedition against Fort Meigs, on the Maumee River, about 12 miles from its mouth. Gen. Harrison was there with about 1,100 effective men. May 1 the British, having erected batteries at Maumee City, opposite the fort, opened fire, which they kept up for 5 days with slight injury to fort or garrison. Meantime Harrison was reenforced by Gen. Clay and 1,100 Kentuckians. Eight hundred of these, under Col. Dudley, were detached with orders to attack the British rear. They were successful at first, but instead of obeying the order to return they pursued the flying foe into the woods and fell into an Indian ambush. Of the 800 in Dudley's command only 170 escaped. After the fruitless bombardment, the Indians deserting Proctor, he abandoned the expedition.

Fort Meigs, Ohio, British attack on, repulsed, I, 539.

Fort Mercer (N. J.), Attack on.—Though the British forces under Gen. Howe had occupied Philadelphia in September, 1777, Washington's army in the immediate vicinity controlled the navigation of the Delaware and Schuylkill rivers. Just below the mouth of the latter stream, and on the opposite side of the Delaware, at Red Bank, N. J., was Fort Mercer, in command of Col. Greene, with a force of about 400 men. Admiral Lord Howe having arrived at Newcastle with his fleet early in October the necessity of opening the river to British navigation became urgent. Oct. 22 an attack was made on Fort Mercer by the British ships and some 1,200 Hessian troops. The assailants were repulsed with a loss of 400. One of the ships grounded and 2 others were burned. The American casualties were 35.

Fort Mifflin (Pa.), Attack on.—One of the principal defenses of the Delaware River after the occupation of Philadelphia in September, 1777, was Fort Mifflin, just below the mouth of the Schuylkill. On the arrival of Admiral Howe with his fleet off Newcastle, Del., early in October, it became necessary to open the river to British navigation. Fort Mifflin was in command of Lieut. Col. Smith, of Baltimore, with a garrison of about 400 men. Failing disastrously at Fort Mercer, the British turned to Fort Mifflin. A combined attack by the land and water batteries, begun on the 10th, resulted in the retreat of the American garrison to Fort Mercer on the night of Nov. 15, 1777, with the loss of 250 men. The next day the Royal Guards occupied the works. The British loss was 37.

Fort Mims (Ala.) Massacre.—In the summer of 1813 the inhabitants of Alabama, frightened by the hostile actions of the Creek Indians, took refuge at Fort Mims, near Montgomery, Ala., 10 miles above the junction of the Tombigbee and Alabama rivers. The place was garrisoned by 16 regulars and about 240 volunteers. At noon Aug. 30, 1813, about 1,000 Indians under Weathersford and the prophet Francis surprised the fort. Of the 550 persons (more than 300 of whom were women and children) who at the time were at Fort Mims, 400 were massacred, including all the women and children. The whites resisted desperately. The negroes were made slaves to the Indians. Twelve men of the garrison escaped into the swamp.

Fort Morgan (Ala.), Reduction of. (See Mobile Bay (Ala.), Battle of.)

Fort Morgan, Ala., reduction of, and orders regarding celebration of, VI, 238.

Fort Moultrie, Charleston (S. C.), Defense of.—In 1776 Clinton was charged with holding the Southern Colonies, and Cornwallis was sent to his aid with troops under convoy of Sir Peter Parker's fleet. Charles Lee commanded the Americans in the vicinity of Charleston. William Moultrie was in charge of a little fort of palmetto logs on Sullivans Island, S. C. June 4 the hostile fleet appeared and on the 28th bombarded Fort Moultrie. Clinton's troops had already landed on Long Island. The Americans fired with precision and effect, and one ship was abandoned. Clinton's forces failed to attack, and in a few days the British withdrew. The American loss was 12 killed and 24 wounded. The British loss was 205, and only 1 of their 10 vessels remained seaworthy. An incident of this battle was the replacing by Sergt. Jasper of a flag which had been shot from the bastion. This fort was abandoned by the Federals under Maj. Robert Anderson Dec. 26, 1860, and was seized by the Confederates, who served a battery from it during the bombardment of Fort Sumter, Apr. 12-14, 1861.

Fort Myer, Va., meteorological observatory at, establishment of, recommended, VIII, 205.

Fort Niagara (N. Y.), Bombardment of.—Nov. 21, 1812, Fort Niagara sustained a severe bombardment at the hands of the British artillery at Forts George and Newark, on the Canadian side of the Niagara River. The Americans returned the fire and silenced the batteries of the enemy. The loss to the Americans was 9; British loss not known.

Fort Omaha Military Reservation, Nebr., act to provide for lease of, to Nebraska, vetoed, IX, 687.

Fort Pillow (Tenn.), Capture of.—This fort was located on the Chickasaw Bluff, in the Mississippi River, 40 miles above Memphis. It was built by the Confederates during the Civil War. It was occupied by the Federal troops June 5, 1862, its evacuation having been compelled by the destruction of the Confederate flotilla on the previous day. The Federal forces not long afterwards abandoned it in consequence of operations on the Tennessee River. Apr. 12, 1864, the fort was garrisoned by 19 officers and 538 men of the Union Army, about one-half of whom were negro troops. On that day Gen. Forrest with Confederate cavalry assaulted and captured it.

Fort Polk, Tex., removal of, referred to, V, 67.

Fort Powell (Ala.), Reduction of. (See Mobile Bay (Ala.), Battle of.)

Fort Powell, Ala., reduction of, and orders regarding celebration of, VI, 238.

Fort Preble Military Reservation, Me., additional land for, recommended, VIII, 190.

Fort Riley, Kans., bridge over Republican River at, reconstruction of, recommended, VIII, 190.

Fort Ripley Military Reservation, Minn., Indian school at, establishment of, referred to, VIII, 96.

Fort St. Philip (La.), Bombardment of.—Jan. 9, 1815, while the British were burying their dead before New Orleans, a portion of the fleet attacked without success Fort St. Philip, at a bend in the Mississippi 65 miles below the city. It contained a garrison of 366 men under Maj. Overton. The bombardment was continued for 5 days. Two Americans were killed and 7 wounded.

Fort Selden, N. Mex., estimates for post at, referred to, VIII, 83.

Fort Smith, Paris and Dardanelle Railway, act granting right of way to, etc., vetoed, VIII, 693.

Fort Stedman (Va.), Assault on.—When, in March, 1865, it became apparent to Lee that he must evacuate Richmond, he planned an assault on Fort Stedman, on Grant's right. During the assault Longstreet and Hill were to retire to the south, followed by the assaulting column, and join Johnston. The assault took place Mar. 25. The batteries were carried and 500 prisoners captured. The Confederates were gathered in the works they had taken. Mar. 27 the surrounding artillery of the Union army was brought to bear on the position, and 1,900 of the Confederates surrendered. The Federal loss was 919.

Fort Stephenson (Ohio), Attack on.—In July, 1813, Maj. Croghan was sent with 160 men to garrison Fort Stephenson, or Lower Sandusky, now Fremont, Ohio, about 20 miles from Sandusky Bay. Here he was attacked Aug. 1, 1813, by Gen. Proctor, with 400 British regulars and several hundred Indians, while Tecumseh, with 2,000 Indians, held the roads leading to the fort, so as to cut off reenforcements. The firing was maintained all night from Proctor's gunboats and from howitzers landed by the British. Aug. 2 a general assault was made, which the garrison repulsed with the loss of 1 man killed and 7 slightly wounded. The British loss was 120. The Indians kept out of harm's way.

Fort Sullivan, Me., legislation to authorize sale of post at, recommended, VIII, 196.

Fort Sumter (S. C.) Fired on.—At 3.30 o'clock on the morning of Apr. 12, 1861, Gen. Beauregard, in command of the Confederate troops in and around Charleston, S. C., demanded the surrender of Fort Sumter, in Charleston Harbor, about 3½ miles from the city. The fort was garrisoned by Maj. Anderson with 70 men. Beauregard had a force of 7,000 men. Anderson having refused to surrender, at 4.30 a. m. the bombardment had begun. The firing was kept up until dark and renewed on the morning of the 13th. Buildings in the fort were several times set on fire. Anderson was only able to return a feeble fire, and it was impossible to furnish him with the number of reenforcements necessary to hold the fort. Accordingly, on Apr. 14 he evacuated the works, lowering the flag with a salute, and with the garrison sailed north. This was the first conflict of the Civil War. There were no casualties on either side.

Fort Sumter, S. C., assault upon, and reduction of, discussed, VI, 21, 77.

Flag floating over, at time of, to be raised on ruins of, by Gen. Anderson, VI, 283.

Fort Thornburg, Utah, estimates for construction of post at, referred to, VIII, 83.

Fort Wagner, S. C., Indian agency at, removal of, II, 401.

Fort Wagner (S. C.), Battle of.—In order to test the efficacy of monitors and ironclads as against land fortifications, Admiral Dupont attempted to force the defenses of Charleston Harbor with a fleet of such vessels. Apr. 7, 1863, he started to attack Fort Sumter. His fleet consisted of 7 Ericsson monitors, the frigate *Ironsides*, partially ironclad, and the *Keokuk*, a frailer ironclad. The opposing forts mounted 300 guns. The expedition signally failed. June 12 Gen. Gillmore was placed in command of an expedition against the same fort with 11,500 men, 66 guns, and 30 mortars. Admiral Dahlgren was to cooperate with him with the frigate *Ironsides* and 6 monitors. Gillmore's intention was to capture Fort Wagner, on Morris Island, and then proceed against Fort Sumter. July 10, 1863, a combined attack by sea and land was made on that fortification. He advanced within musket range of Fort Wagner, but delayed the assault till the next day, when it was repulsed. In these op-

erations Gillmore lost about 150 men, the Confederates 300. July 18 another attempt was made to reduce the place, but it was completely repulsed, with a loss of 1,200. Gillmore now determined to approach the fort by a series of parallel trenches. The first was opened July 24 and the third Aug. 9. Beauregard was in command of Fort Sumter. Aug. 17 Gillmore opened on that fort. By the 23d Sumter was battered to ruins. Additional parallels were opened toward Fort Wagner. Final operations began Sept. 5, with 17 siege and cohorn mortars, 13 Parrott rifles, and the 11-inch shells of the *Ironsides*. An assault was to have been made Sept. 7, but during the previous night the garrison evacuated the place. Though 122,300 pounds of metal were thrown against the work, the bombproofs were found intact.

Fort Wallace Military Reservation, Kans., act to provide for disposal of, vetoed, VIII, 723.

Fort Washington (N. Y.), Capture of.—One of the most serious disasters to the Americans of the early days of the Revolution. Howe sent an expedition to dislodge the Americans from Forts Lee and Washington, the principal defenses of the Hudson, which Congress had decided, against the advice of Washington, should be held. The garrison withdrew from Fort Lee in safety. Fort Washington was carried by storm Nov. 16, 1776, after a severe struggle, 2,600 men and all the munitions of war falling into the hands of the British. The American loss in killed and wounded did not exceed 130, while the loss of the combined British and Hessian troops amounted to about 450.

Fortress Monroe, Va. :

Artillery schools of practice at, II, 374.

Estimates for barracks and quarters at, referred to, VIII, 79.

Forts and Fortifications (see also Defenses, Public):

Appropriations for—

Bill for, defeated, III, 169.

Recommended, I, 407, 486; II, 45, 119, 361, 389; III, 169; V, 175, 362; VII, 39; VIII, 211, 246.

Armaments for, II, 201.

Appropriation for, recommended, V, 362; VIII, 211.

Recommended, VII, 317.

Board of Ordnance and Fortifications discussed, VIII, 788.

Ceded to United States, I, 110, 154, 396.

Constructed with view to permanence, II, 61.

Construction of, progress made in, II, 66, 78, 108, 119, 231, 417; III, 32.

Defense of, necessary, I, 447.

Expenditures for, II, 66, 341, 417.

In Lawrence, Kans., referred to, VI, 696.

Referred to, I, 107, 169, 186, 240, 307, 330; II, 45, 211, 328; III, 568, 590; IV, 416; X, 30.

Requisite on seacoasts, II, 17, 119; IV, 48.

Sale of, on Staten Island to United States proposed, II, 368.

Sites for, referred to, I, 447; X, 65.

Forts Clinton and Montgomery (N. Y.), Loss of.—Forts Clinton and Montgomery were situated on the west side of the Hudson River, about 6 miles below West Point. Fort Montgomery was a large unfinished work north of Poplopen Creek, its garrison consisting of 1 company of artillery, a few regulars, and some half-armed militia under Col. Lamb. Fort Clinton was south of the mouth of the creek, thoroughly built, and garrisoned by a few regulars and militia under Brig. Gen. James Clinton. Oct. 6, 1777, these forts were stormed and carried by the British under Gen. Henry Clinton. The Americans lost about 300 in killed, wounded, and missing, besides 100 cannon and large quantities of ammunition. The British loss was about 200 killed and wounded.

Fortune Bay Outrages.—The treaty of Washington, ratified in 1871, granted to American fishermen the right to take and cure fish on the Canadian coasts, and the Halifax Commission determined upon the compensation to be made for such privileges. In January, 1878, inhabitants of Fortune Bay, Newfoundland, attacked some Gloucester fishermen who were taking on cargoes of frozen herring, cut their nets, and drove away the crews. The Newfoundland people asserted that the local laws were being violated. The British Government, however, decided that these could not stand in conflict with the treaty. The injured fishermen claimed damages amounting to $105,305, of which the British Government paid about $73,000.

Fortune Bay Outrages discussed, VII, 566, 590, 606.
Claims arising out of, paid, VIII, 38.

Forward, Oliver, treaty with Indians concluded by, II, 374.

Forward, Walter, Secretary of Treasury, resignation of, mentioned, IV, 234.

Foster, C. W., member of board to examine quotas of States under call for troops, VI, 275.

Foster, Charles, member of Sioux Commission, IX, 45.

Foster, George E., member of reciprocal trade conference between United States and Canada, IX, 240.

Foster, Hugh, mentioned, VIII, 78.

Foster, John W.:
Counsel for United States in Bering Sea question, IX, 313.
Member of reciprocal trade conference between United States and Canada, IX, 240.
Secretary of State, IX, 289.
Treaty for annexation of Hawaiian Islands signed by, IX, 348.

Foster, Robert S., member of court to try assassins of President Lincoln, etc., VI, 336.

Foster, Stephen C., correspondence regarding northeastern boundary. (See Northeastern Boundary.)

Foulke, George C., claim of legal representatives of, against United States, IX, 668.

Foundries, estimates of expenditures for establishment of, X, 24.

Foundry, National, erection of, recommended, III, 390, 497.

Four Years' Law.—In May, 1820, Congress passed a law making the term of certain postmasters and revenue collectors 4 years. Though it was claimed that the only object of the bill was to have public accounts submitted for inspection every 4 years, its effect was to greatly increase the power of the President in making appointments.

Fourth of July Claims.—This name is given to a class of claims arising during the Civil War. The claims were for quartermaster and commissary stores and supplies taken from loyal citizens in certain territory named for the use of and actually used by the Union armies. The first act of Congress providing for the payment of these claims was passed July 4, 1864, from which fact the name arose.

Fourth of July Claims (see also War Claims):
Payment of, referred to, VII, 194.
Transfer of, to Southern Claims Commission recommended, VII, 407, 473.

Fox, Gustavus V., mentioned, VI, 460, 471.

Fox, Henry S., correspondence regarding—
Northeastern boundary. (See Northeastern Boundary.)
Outrages committed by Canadians on American frontiers, III, 401.

Fox Indians.—A tribe of the Algonquian stock of Indians. They followed the example of many other red men in joining the British forces during the Revolutionary War. In 1804 they made a treaty ceding valuable lands to the Government. They renewed their alliance with the British in 1812. In 1824 and 1830 they ceded large tracts of land, and after taking part in the Black Hawk War (q. v.) were compelled to cede more of their territory by a treaty made with Gen. Scott. They have been successively driven from one place to another until the remainder of the tribe now occupies a small part of Oklahoma. They were incorporated at an early date with the Sac tribe.

Fox Indians:
Agreement between Cherokee Commission and, IX, 75.
Proclaimed, IX, 156.
Hostile aggressions of, III, 32.
Treaty with, I, 375, 377, 569; II, 183, 322, 347, 542, 607; III, 265, 279, 395; IV, 210; V, 240, 578; VI, 73, 83, 194, 470, 702; X, 66.
Withdrawn, VII, 47.
War with. (See Indian Wars.)

Fox Reservation. (See Sac and Fox Reservation.)

Fox River, Wis., act regarding improvement of, vetoed, VII, 382.

F'peeksin Indians, treaty with, V, 303.

France.—A Republic of western Europe, bounded on the north by the English Channel, the Strait of Dover, and the North Sea; on the east by Belgium, Luxemburg, Germany, Switzerland, and Italy; on the south by Spain and the Mediterranean Sea, and on the west by the Bay of Biscay and the Atlantic Ocean. It extends from lat. 42° 25′ to 51° 5′ north, and from long. 7° 39′ east to 4° 50′ west. The surface in the south and east is mountainous, while in the north and west it is nearly level. Its frontier mountain ranges are the Pyrenees, Alps, Jura, and Vosges. The highest moun-

Franklin or Frankland.—The first constitution of North Carolina made provision for a future State within her limits on the western side of the Alleghany Mountains. In May, 1794, North Carolina ceded to the United States her territory west of the Alleghanies, provided Congress would accept it within 2 years. The general opinion among the settlers and people of that territory was that it would not be accepted by Congress, and in this they were correct. For a period of 2 years, not being under the protection of the Government of the United States nor of the State of North Carolina, they could not receive support from abroad and could not command their own resources at home, for the State had subjected them to the payment of taxes to the United States Government. During this period of uncertainty the Indians were committing frequent depredations, which added to the discontent among the settlers. Under these circumstances a majority of the people within the territory concluded to adopt a constitution and organize a State of their own. This they proceeded to do, and called a convention, which met at Jonesboro Aug. 23, 1784. Delegates assembled from portions of the territory and appointed a committee to consider their condition. The convention adjourned after issuing an address to the people. In the following November the delegates again assembled at Jonesboro. They did not adopt a constitution, but broke up in confusion because of the fact that in October of that year North Carolina repealed the act of cession. Dec. 14, 1784, another convention assembled at Jonesboro and adopted a constitution, which was to be ratified or rejected by a convention called to meet at Greenville Nov. 14, 1785. In the meantime a general assembly was elected, which met at Greenville early in 1785 and chose John Sevier for governor and other officers. The new State which they attempted thus to create was named in honor of Benjamin Franklin, and is therefore properly called Franklin and not Frankland. It is not perfectly clear that at first these people intended the new State to become part of the Union. One of the provisions in their proposed form of government was that "the inhabitants within the limits of the proposed State agree with each other to form themselves into a free, sovereign, and independent body politic or State by the name of the Commonwealth of Franklin." Later they concluded they would seek admission to the Union, and accordingly they made an effort to have Congress recognize the new State. The boundary lines of the proposed State show that it included what are now 15 counties of Virginia, 6 of West Virginia, one-third of Kentucky, one-half of Tennessee, two-thirds of Alabama, and at least one-fourth of Georgia. This territory is rich in mineral wealth. There is probably more iron and coal in it than can be found in the same area elsewhere in the United States. The convention met in Greenville in November, 1785, to adopt a constitution, but when the constitution proposed was submitted it was rejected and in lieu thereof the constitution of North Carolina was adopted. This was the beginning of the trouble which ended in the overthrow of the State. The assembly or legislature of the State continued to meet for several years, during which time dual governments existed in the territory. Courts were held in the same counties, one under the Franklin and the other under the North Carolina government; the same militia was called out by officers appointed by each government; laws were passed by assemblies of both States; taxes were laid by authority of both States, but as the people said they did not know which government had the right to receive their taxes, they adopted the easy solution of paying to neither. The people of the territory became divided, some adhering to Governor Sevier, while others yielded to the authority of North Carolina. Acts of violence were committed by one party against the other, the provocation on the one side being surpassed in the way of retaliation by a still greater provocation on the other. In October, 1788, Sevier was arrested and carried to North Carolina for trial, his property having been attached in January or February of that year. Soon after his arrest the government of Franklin collapsed and North Carolina passed an act of "pardon and oblivion," resuming her authority over these people. Later North Carolina passed a second act ceding the territory to the United States, and Aug. 7, 1790, President Washington appointed William Blount governor of the Territory. The State of Tennessee was soon thereafter organized out of this Territory.

Franklin (Tenn.), Battle of.—With the purpose of drawing Sherman's army out of Georgia, Gen. Hood evacuated Atlanta early in September, 1864, and marched north, threatening Sherman's communication with his base of supplies at Nashville. Oct. 29 Hood crossed the Tennessee River at Florence with about 35,000 infantry and 10,000 cavalry. (He stated his effective force at 40,000, Sept. 20.) His army was formed in 3 corps, under Cheatham, Stewart, and S. D. Lee; the cavalry under Forrest. Sherman had sent Gen. Thomas to Nashville and placed under his command Gen. Stanley with the Fourth Corps, Gen. Schofield with the Twenty-third, and most of Wilson's cavalry—a force aggregating, according to Federal accounts, 27,000 men. Schofield was in command of the field, and upon Hood's advance he fell back toward Nashville. By Nov. 30 Schofield's army had reached Franklin, on the south bank of the Harpeth River, about 18 miles south of Nashville. Hood here assailed him. His first blow fell upon two brigades of Wagner's division, which had been posted outside the hastily erected works. The Union troops lost 1,000 men in the attack. Schofield's line was broken and defeat seemed imminent, when Gen. Opdycke, commanding

one of Wagner's brigades, made a brilliant charge and saved the day. The Confederates made several assaults, each of which was repulsed with terrible loss. Schofield succeeded in getting his troops over Harpeth River in retreat, and by daylight he was well on his way to Nashville. The Federal statement of losses in this battle is as follows: Union, 189 killed, 1,033 wounded, and 1,104 missing, a total of 2,326; Confederates, 1,750 killed, 3,800 wounded, and 702 prisoners, a total of 6,252.

Fraser, Trenholm & Co., agents of Confederate Government, suits instituted in English courts against, VI, 463.

Frayser's Farm (Va.), Battle of.—One of the Seven Days' Battles before Richmond. June 30, 1862, Longstreet and A. P. Hill crossed the Chickahominy in pursuit of McClellan's retreating army. Huger and Magruder marched around the White Oak Swamp to operate on his flank, and a brigade was brought over the James River from Fort Darling. At 4 o'clock in the afternoon Longstreet and Hill made the attack. Huger and Magruder failed to arrive. The fighting was furious and the advantage with the Confederates. Nearly one-fourth of McCall's division, upon which the attack was made, were killed. Of the Confederate loss Gen. Pryor, of the Fifth Brigade of Longstreet's corps, reported the Fourteenth Alabama Regiment nearly annihilated. Of the 1,400 men with whom he crossed the Chickahominy June 26, 860 had been lost up to this time.

Frear, Walter F., member of commission to recommend legislation for Hawaiian Islands, X, 186.

Frear, William H., claim of, against France, VIII, 613.

Frederick III, Emperor of Germany, death of, referred to, VIII, 782.

Fredericksburg (Va.), Battle of.—After the battle of Antietam (or Sharpsburg) McClellan occupied Harpers Ferry Sept. 22, 1862. Nov. 7 he was relieved of his command by Gen. Burnside. Lee's army was at that time at Culpeper and westward of the Blue Ridge Mountains. Burnside divided the army, now numbering about 110,000 men, into 3 grand divisions of 2 corps each. By Nov. 17 he had moved this army down the left bank of the Rappahannock to Falmouth, opposite Fredericksburg. Here the advance was delayed, awaiting the pontoon train from Washington. In the meantime Lee had concentrated the Confederate army of about 80,000 in the hills behind Fredericksburg. Dec. 11, 1862, the pontoons were laid, and on the 12th Franklin's division crossed. The Union forces were formed with Franklin on the left, Hooker's division in the center, and Sumner's on the right. The battle was opened by Franklin on the morning of the 13th, and continued in a series of disconnected and unsuccessful attacks on the Confederate works until night. On the 14th and 15th a truce was obtained by the Federals for burying their dead. On the evening of the latter date they retired across the river and the Confederates again occupied Fredericksburg. The Federal losses were 1,284 killed, 9,600 wounded, and 1,769 missing—a total of 12,653. The Confederates lost 608 killed, 4,116 wounded, and 653 captured or missing—a total of 5,377. Later in the month the Federal army went into winter quarters at Falmouth, and Jan. 25, 1863, Burnside was relieved of the command at his own request. Gen. Burnside testified before the Committee on the Conduct of the War that he had 100,000 men in action at the battle of Fredericksburg. Col. Walter H. Taylor, late adjutant-general of the Army of Northern Virginia, stated that Gen. Lee had actively engaged in the battle less than 20,000 men.

Fredericksburg, Va., battle of, discussed, VI, 159.

Free Banking System.—Apr. 11, 1838, the New York legislature passed the free-bank act, under the provisions of which any person or persons might establish a bank by depositing stocks, bonds, and mortgages as security for its circulating notes. This law was afterwards amended, requiring at least half of the securities to be New York State stocks. Previous to the passage of the free banking law of New York charters were granted by special act of the legislatures of various States, and their circulating medium was often far in excess of their capital. This caused heavy losses to note holders. The action of the New York legislature was followed by that of many other States and was made the basis of the national banking act of 1863.

Free Coinage of Silver. (See Silver Coinage, under Coins and Coinage.)

Free-Delivery System:
Discussed and recommendations regarding, VII, 250; VIII, 182, 249, 352, 517, 791; IX, 321, 449, 539.
Extension of, to towns of 5,000 population recommended, IX, 198.
Inadequate facilities extended rural districts, IX, 198.

Free List. (See Import Duties.)

Free Negroes.—The first census taken in the United States showed nearly 60,000 free colored population. Of this number about half were in the Southern States. The fact that they were considered a dangerous element by many persons led to a movement for colonizing them in Liberia, and they were put under certain disabilities, especially in the Southern States. In the Dred Scott decision it was held that they were not citizens of the United States.

Free Negroes. (See Negroes.)

Free Ships, Free Goods.—The Declaration of Paris [1856] holds that "neutral goods in enemies' ships and enemies' goods in neutral ships, except contraband of war, are not liable to capture." As the United States refused to surrender the privilege of privateering, it could not subscribe to this declaration of the leading nations as to the conduct of war. The United States Government has always held to the doctrine that in time of war all goods, whether belonging to neutrals or to the belligerents, are if carried in neutral vessels thereby exempted from capture unless they are by nature contraband of war. During the war between England and France in 1793–1815 the United States contended for the recognition of this principle. England, on the other hand, always maintained that the ownership of the property itself should determine the question of seizure. This was a contributory cause of the War of 1812. The treaty of Ghent did not settle the question. The motive for privateering which once existed has been obviated by the addition of numerous cruisers to the Navy.

Free-Soilers.—That one of the anti-slavery political parties which came into existence in 1848. It was composed of the Liberty Party, the Barnburner Democrats of New York, and a number of Northern Whigs who favored the Wilmot Proviso to the appropriation bill to conclude the treaty of peace with Mexico. Wilmot's amendment provided that there should be no slavery in the territory acquired under the appropriation. It passed the House, but was defeated in the Senate. In the next session it failed to pass either House. Resolutions of the same import as the Wilmot Proviso were introduced in the Whig and Democratic conventions of 1846, but were rejected. Upon this many prominent men of New York, Massachusetts, and Ohio withdrew and formed the Free-Soil party. At Buffalo in 1848 they nominated Martin Van Buren and Charles Francis Adams for President and Vice-President. These candidates received no electoral votes and only 291,263 popular votes. At Pittsburg in 1852 they nominated John P. Hale and George W. Julian, but their vote only reached 156,149. In 1856 the Free-Soilers joined the Republican party.

Free Trade.—In politics this term is used to signify an exchange of merchandise between the people of different countries without the imposition of any tax by the government. A tariff tax imposed by the government for the protection of home manufactures is held by the advocates of free trade to be contrary to sound principles of political economy and unjust to the consumers of the articles so taxed.

Free Zone. (See *Zona Libre.*)

Freedman's Savings and Trust Co., affairs of, discussed and recommendations regarding, VIII, 528.

Freedmen (see also Civil Rights):
Act to protect all persons in United States in their civil rights and furnish means of vindication vetoed, VI, 405.
Violations of act referred to, VI, 468.
Appropriation for settlement under treaties of, and descendants upon lands in Oklahoma recommended, VIII, 198.
Colonization of. (See Negroes.)
Condition of, discussed, IX, 55.
Education of, recommendations regarding, VII, 41; IX, 54.

Army of the Northwest, resolved to regain what that unfortunate commander had lost. He dispatched Gen. Winchester with 2,000 men for Detroit, with orders to cross the river if opportunity offered and take Fort Malden. From his camp (at Presque Ile) Winchester on Jan. 17, 1813, detailed Col. Lewis with 660 men to advance to Frenchtown (now Monroe, Mich.), on the River Raisin. Lewis arrived on the 18th, and the British garrison, consisting of 200 Canadian militia and 400 Indians, were driven into the woods. The Americans lost 12 killed and 55 wounded. The loss to the enemy was considerable and occurred chiefly in the forest.

Friendly Islands. (See Tonga Islands.)

Friends, Society of. (See Society of Friends.)

Frigates. (See Vessels.)

Frolic, The, engagement with the *Wasp*, I, 521.

Fromentin, Eligius, misunderstanding of, with Andrew Jackson referred to, II, 113.

Frontiers (see also Indians; Militia):
Affairs on southeastern frontier, V, 376.
Posts should be established for protection of, II, 45.
Protection of—
Necessity of, I, 84, 94, 95, 104, 109, 141, 174, 566; III, 600; V, 286; VI, 246.
Sufficient, II, 79.
Referred to, I, 173, 410; II, 255.

Fruchier, John, impressed into military service of France, case of, referred to, VIII, 614.

Fruits, American, restrictions upon importation of, into Germany and Switzerland, X, 184.

Frye, William P., member of Spanish-American Peace Commission, X, 175.

Fugitive Criminals:
Laws regarding, amendment of, recommended, VIII, 505; X, 187.
Opinion of Attorney-General regarding right of Executive to surrender, when crime is committed out of United States, III, 591.
Reports of International American Conference on subject of, referred to, IX, 79.
Surrender of—
Ashburton treaty regarding, discussed, IV, 163.
By Costa Rica, IX, 436.
Convention regarding, with—
Austria, V, 378.
Baden, V, 365.
Bavaria, V, 227.
Belgium, V, 188; VII, 170, 262, 293; VIII, 108, 128.
Central America, VII, 101.
Chile, V, 379.
Colombia, VII, 635; VIII, 615.
Denmark, failure to negotiate, VII, 609.
Ecuador, VII, 206, 293.
France, IV, 272, 313, 366; V, 481.
Referred to, IX, 437.
Germany, V, 153.
Discussed, VIII, 237.
Great Britain, IV, 163; VIII, 404; IX, 35.
Demands made under, IV, 278, 360.
Discussed, VIII, 332.
Questions arising under, VII, 467.
Referred to, VIII, 215; IX, 110.
Refusal of, to comply with discussed, VII, 367, 370, 414.

Fugitive Criminals—Continued.
Surrender of—Continued.
Convention regarding, with—
Guatemala, VII, 113; VIII, 538, 594, 614.
Haiti, VI, 258.
Hanover, V, 301.
Honduras, VII, 207, 256.
Italy, VI, 630, 690, 698; VIII, 219.
Referred to, IX, 111, 527.
Japan, VIII, 402, 501.
Luxemburg, VIII, 195.
Mexico, V, 66; VI, 63; VIII, 280.
Demands made under, VIII, 204.
Extension of time of ratification of, recommended, VI, 73.
Questions arising under, VIII, 505; X, 186.
Report of Secretary of State regarding, V, 154.
Netherlands, V, 377, 419, 463; VII, 590, 610; VIII, 591, 812.
Withdrawn from Senate, V, 383.
Nicaragua, VII, 113, 146.
Peru, VII, 114, 293.
Termination of, referred to, VIII, 334.
Prussia, IV, 417; V, 153, 183.
Ratification of, refused, IV, 600.
Russia, VIII, 813; IX, 439.
Salvador, VII, 79, 258, 293.
Questions arising under, IX, 529.
Santo Domingo, VI, 471.
Sicily, V, 337.
Spain, VII, 422; VIII, 112, 151.
Referred to, VIII, 170.
Sweden and Norway, V, 583; IX, 439.
Swiss Confederation, IV, 506.
Turkey, VII, 304, 342.
Venezuela, V, 384, 654.
Discussed, IX, 530.
Conventions regarding, recommended, IX, 436.

Fugitive-Slave Laws.—Article IV, section 2, of the Constitution provides: "No person held to service or labour in one State, under the laws thereof, escaping into another, shall, in consequence of any law or regulation therein, be discharged from such service or labour, but shall be delivered up on claim of the party to whom such service or labour may be due." In pursuance of this provision Congress in 1793 passed the first fugitive-slave law, providing that on the owner's giving proof of ownership before a magistrate of the locality where the slave was found the magistrate should order the slave to be delivered to his owner without trial by jury. Hindering arrest or harboring a fugitive slave was punishable by a fine of $500. In 1850, as a part of the compromise measures of that year, a law was passed providing for United States commissioners to aid in the more strict enforcement of the law. Proof of identity and 2 witnesses to the fact of escape were all that were required in evidence. The negro could neither testify nor have jury trial. In all the Colonies laws had been passed providing for the return of fugitive slaves. The New England Confederation of

1643 had provided for mutual extradition of slaves. Extradition from British territory had been denied in the decision of the Somersett case in 1771. In the case of Prigg *vs.* Pennsylvania (1842) the Supreme Court held that the execution of the law of 1793 devolved upon Federal authorities alone; that State authorities could not be forced to act. Several States thereupon forbade action by their officials. The act of 1850 aroused much bitter feeling in the North, and "personal liberty" laws were passed in many of the States, some of them conflicting with Federal laws and some even with the Constitution itself. The Civil War ended the whole matter, and the laws were repealed.

Fugitive Slaves:

Acts passed to defeat laws regarding, discussed, V, 629.

Escaping into Mexico, return of, referred to, X, 69.

Execution of laws for return of, forcibly resisted at Boston, V, 101, 137.

Proclamation regarding, V, 109.

Legislation regarding restoration of, recommended, V, 137.

Negotiations with Great Britain regarding surrender of, II, 422; IV, 278.

State laws regarding, discussed, V, 341, 400.

Surrender of, referred to, II, 422.

Fulford, D., act for relief of heirs of, vetoed, IX, 572.

Fuller, Melville W., arbitrator in Venezuelan boundary dispute, X, 191.

Fundamental Constitutions of Carolina.—In 1669 John Locke, the celebrated English philosopher, drew up an elaborate constitution for the Colony of Carolina, providing for several orders of nobility. At the present day it is of interest only as a sample of early constitutions and an attempt to establish an American aristocracy. The scheme comprehended a grand court of proprietors and a parliament of landgraves and caciques having entailed estates.

Funding.—The process of funding a debt consists in dividing it into shares or bonds, with stated times of payment of interest and principal. Refunding a debt is the process of substituting bonds, usually at another rate of interest, for outstanding obligations. The first funding of the national debt was by the act of Congress of Aug. 4, 1790, at the suggestion of Alexander Hamilton, then Secretary of the Treasury. This act provided for the payment, by the issue of 6 per cent bonds, of all the floating foreign and domestic debts of the United States and such of the debts of the several States as were incurred in prosecuting the War for Independence. Since that time there have been numerous issues of bonds by the General, State, county, and municipal governments. It was not until July 14, 1870, that an attempt was made to refund the entire national debt, when Congress passed the Sherman Act, providing for the issue of $200,000,000 5 per cent bonds (later increased to $500,000,000), $300,000,000 4½

percents, and $1,000,000,000 4 percents. The 5 and 6 per cent bonds have been retired or extended at 3 and 3½ per cent interest, under agreements of 1881 and 1882, while nearly all the 4 and 4½ per cent bonds have been bought in the open market with the surplus cash in the Treasury.

Fur Seals. (See Bering Sea.)

Fur Trade, persons killed while engaged in, referred to, II, 565.

G.

Gadsden, James:

Mentioned, V, 237.

Rejection of nomination of, as colonel discussed, II, 126, 133.

Gadsden Purchase.—This term is applied to a tract of land consisting of 45,535 sq. miles in Arizona and New Mexico, extending from the Gila River to the Mexican boundary. It was acquired from Mexico by a treaty negotiated by James Gadsden Dec. 30, 1853. The United States paid Mexico $10,000,000 for the land, but Mexico relinquished claims against the United States for damages for Indian depredations amounting to from $15,000,000 to $30,000,000. For this transaction Santa Anna, President of Mexico, was banished as a traitor.

Gadsden Purchase, treaty with Mexico respecting, V, 229.

Gag Rule.—May 26, 1836, Congress passed a resolution providing that thenceforth all petitions, memorials, resolutions, propositions, or papers relating in any way to the subject of slavery or the abolition of slavery should lie upon the table without being printed or referred. John Quincy Adams led a strong and bitter opposition to this infringement upon the right of petition. The cry of "gag rule" was raised in the North and served to increase the spirit of petition in that section. Dec. 3, 1844, the rule was abolished.

Gaillard, John, letter of President Monroe to, referred to, II, 4.

Gaines, Edmund P.:

Calls of, for volunteers or militia discussed, IV, 448, 450.

Court of inquiry in case of, and opinion of, discussed, III, 292.

Inspection reports of, referred to, II, 429.

Mentioned, II, 128.

Requisition of, for volunteers in Indian war not sanctioned by President, III, 234.

Settlement of accounts of, referred to, IV, 277.

Victories of, over British troops, I, 548.

Gaines, John P., correspondence regarding seat of government of Oregon, V, 148.

Gaines Mill (Va.), Battle of.—One of the series of engagements which took place June 25 to July 1, 1862, before Richmond, commonly known as the Seven Days' Battles. June 27, the day after the battle of Mechanicsville, Fitz-John Porter retired to Gaines Mill Heights, about 5 miles east of his former position. Here he was attacked shortly after noon by A. P,

Hill's corps. Slocum's division was sent to reenforce Porter, increasing his army to 35,000. During the afternoon Jackson joined Hill and Longstreet, swelling the Confederate forces to about 60,000. Severe fighting was continued until dark. Porter succeeded in defending the bridges across the Chickahominy, allowing the heavy guns and wagon train to pass in safety on their way to the James. During the night he himself crossed over, destroying the bridges. The loss of the Confederates was reported at 3,284. Porter lost 894 men killed, 3,107 wounded, and 2,836 missing, a total of 6,837. He also lost 22 cannon.

Gainesville, McAlester and St. Louis Railroad Co., act regarding grant of right of way to, through Indian Territory returned, IX, 667.

Gale, George, district supervisor, nomination of, I, 99.

Gallatin, Albert:
Commissioner to settle boundary question with Georgia, I, 341.
Minister to conclude treaty of peace with Great Britain, nomination of, X, 46.
Minister to conclude treaty with Russia, nomination of, X, 46.
Secretary of Treasury—
Duties discharged by Secretary of Navy in absence of, X, 47.
Order to, respecting appropriation for use of commissioner to Spain, X, 100.
Order to, respecting loan, X, 101.

Galphin, George, claim of heirs of, referred to, III, 274.

Galveston, Tex.:
Equipment of privateers at, must be suppressed, II, 14.
Illicit introduction of slaves through, must be suppressed, II, 14.
Referred to, II, 21, 23.

Gannett, Henry, member of Board on Geographic Names, IX, 212.

Ganon, N., correspondence regarding unlawful expedition in New York, III, 399.

Garcia. (See Rey.)

Garcia, Manuel, act granting pension to, vetoed, VIII, 701.

Gardoqui, Don Diego, commercial relations with Spain, letter of, concerning, I, 121.

Garesché, J. P., assistant adjutant-general, order regarding Missouri militia, VI, 42.

Garfield, James A. (twentieth President United States):
Biographical sketch of, VIII, 3.
Civil service discussed by, VIII, 11. (See also Civil Service.)
Death of—
Action of Congress on, VIII, 25.
Action of Senators and Representatives in Washington on, VIII, 18.
Announcement of, to Vice-President and reply to, VIII, 14.
Announcements of, and honors to be paid memory of, VIII, 13, 14, 15, 16, 17.
Condolence on, of—
Guatemala, VIII, 40.
Russia, VIII, 39.

Garfield, James A.—Continued.
Death of—Continued.
Day of humiliation and mourning in memory of, appointed, VIII, 34.
Discussed, VIII, 33, 37.
Official bulletin of autopsy on body, VIII, 24.
Finances discussed by, VIII, 10.
Funeral of—
Announcement of, and arrangements for, VIII, 20.
Orders of heads of Executive Departments relating to, VIII, 18.
Inaugural address of, VIII, 6.
Portrait of, VIII, 2.
Statue of, to be erected in Washington, appropriation for, recommended, VIII, 208.
Unveiling ceremonies, order regarding, VIII, 577.

Garland, John, gallantry of, at battle of Monterey, Mexico, referred to, IV, 518.

Garland Case.—In 1860 Augustus H. Garland was admitted to practice in the United States Supreme Court. Not very long after the State of Arkansas had seceded from the Union in 1861 he was sent to the Confederate congress, where he served until the surrender of Gen. Lee in 1865. He was included in the general amnesty extended to citizens of the Southern States. July 2, 1862, Congress enacted a law requiring all candidates for office to take an oath that they had never engaged in hostilities against the United States, and on Jan. 24, 1865, this oath was required of persons admitted to the bar of any circuit or district court of the United States or Court of Claims. Garland refused to take the prescribed oath on the ground that it was unconstitutional and void as affecting his status in court, and that if it were constitutional his pardon released him from compliance with it. The court sustained him in his contention on the ground that the law was *ex post facto.* Justice Field, delivering the opinion, said: "It is not within the constitutional power of Congress thus to inflict punishment beyond the reach of Executive clemency." Chief Justice Chase and Justices Miller, Swayne, and Davis dissented.

Garrett, Eli, act granting pension to, vetoed, VIII, 823.

Garrett, William H., treaty with Indians concluded by, V, 242.

Garrieaux, Pierre, bill for relief of, VIII, 92.

Gates, William, major, United States Army:
Nomination of, discussed, III, 269.
Trial solicited by, III, 270.

Gaugers. (See Weighers and Gaugers.)

Gaven, Ester, act granting pension to, vetoed, VIII, 737.

Gayhead, Mass., land designated at, for lighthouse, proclamation concerning, II, 658.

Geary, John W., referred to, V, 449, 464.

Geary Law sustained by Supreme Court, discussed, IX, 436.

Geddes, Charles W., act for relief of, vetoed, VIII, 820.

Gedney, Lieut., mentioned, II, 475.

General.—The highest rank in the United States Army, conferred in recognition of distinguished military services. It was first created by act of Congress Mar. 2, 1799, and conferred upon George Washington; was abolished in 1802, but was revived July 25, 1866, for Ulysses S. Grant. William T. Sherman succeeded to the rank Mar. 4, 1869, Grant having become President, and held it until his retirement, Feb. 8, 1884. The grade was revived June 1, 1888, for Philip H. Sheridan, who held it until his death, Aug. 5 of that year. The rank of General was also the highest in the Confederate army.

General Armstrong, The:
Claims of owners of, against Portugal, IV, 418; V, 226.
Distribution of fund appropriated for relief of owners and crew of, referred to, VIII, 402.
President of France selected as arbiter in case of, V, 119.
Award of Emperor of France, V, 186.

General Land Office.—A bureau of the Interior Department, charged with the surveying and disposal of the public lands of the United States. Until 1812 the Secretary of the Treasury acted as agent for the sale of public lands. After the office of the Commissioner of the General Land Office was provided for, the Land Office remained a bureau of the Treasury Department until the creation of the Interior Department, Mar. 3, 1849, when it became a part of that Department.

General Land Office:
Appropriations for—
Estimates of, submitted, VIII, 90.
Recommended, III, 214.
Business of, suspension of, recommended, III, 214.
Creation of new offices in, recommended, VIII, 71.
Discussed, IX, 203.
Expenses of, statement of, transmitted, X, 70.
Improvements in, recommended, III, 162.
Increase in clerical force of, recommended, VIII, 76.
Surveyor-general's district for Missouri, Illinois, and Arkansas should be divided, II, 568.

General Land Office, Commissioner of:
Bill to increase salary of, referred to, VIII, 71.
Reports of, II, 420, 535; IV, 277.

General Urrea, The, capture of, by the *Na'chez* referred to, III, 400.

Genêt, E. C., mentioned, X, 87.

Geneva Convention.—An agreement entered into at Geneva, Switzerland, Aug. 22, 1864, by representatives of France, Belgium, Switzerland, Portugal, Holland, Italy, Spain, Denmark, Baden, and Prussia. It has since been agreed to by all the military powers of Europe and of America, except Brazil. Of Asiatic countries Persia has also consented to be governed by its provisions. The convention provides for the neutrality of ambulances, no distinction of nationality to be made in caring for the sick and wounded. Natives of an invaded country who bring aid to sick and wounded shall be free and respected. If they receive the wounded into their houses, they shall be exempt from military contributions and quartering of troops. Hospitals and their attachés, unless defended by a military force, shall be recognized as neutral. Nurses, surgeons, physicians, and those in charge of administration and transportation shall be marked by a distinctive flag or arm badge, consisting of a red cross on a white ground. The sick and wounded who fall into the hands of the enemy shall, when cured, be returned to their own country if incapable of service; otherwise they shall be paroled. In 1868 a second convention met at Geneva and extended the operations of the system to naval warfare so far as possible. Influenced by the agreement between nations, many Red Cross societies have been organized by humane civilians, whose work has done much to alleviate the horrors of war. The credit of originating the idea of neutralizing the sick and wounded is due to two Swiss gentlemen, Heinrich Dumont, a physician, and his friend, Gustave Moynier, chairman of the Society of Public Utility.

Geneva Convention for relief of wounded in war referred to, VIII, 44, 66, 83.

Geneva Tribunal.—A tribunal for the settlement of the claims of the United States against Great Britain for damages sustained by reason of the depredations of the *Alabama, Florida, Georgia, Shenandoah,* and other Confederate cruisers which had been fitted out in English ports. The treaty of Washington, concluded May 8, 1871, provided for the submission of these claims (known as "Alabama Claims") to a court of arbitration. The court met at Geneva, Switzerland, Dec. 15, 1871, and was composed of Charles Francis Adams, appointed by the President of the United States; Sir Alexander Cockburn, by the Queen of England; Count Federigo Sclopis, by the King of Italy; M. Jacques Staempfli, by the President of Switzerland, and Viscount d'Itajuba, by the Emperor of Brazil. The United States claimed the right to submit certain indirect claims—i. e., the cost of pursuing the privateers, compensation for increased rates of insurance, and the prolongation of the war by reason of the depredations—but these the board of arbitrators refused to entertain. Final judgment was rendered Sept. 14, 1872. The tribunal unanimously found Great Britain liable for the depredations of the *Alabama;* with the dissent of Sir Alexander Cockburn, the same finding was made in the case of the *Florida;* 3 of the arbitrators found against Great Britain in the case of the *Shenandoah.* In the other cases insufficient evidence was presented to justify a finding. The United States were awarded $15,500,000 in gold in satisfaction of all claims. Sir Alexander Cockburn, on the part of Great Britain, filed a long dissenting opinion. (See also Alabama Claims.)

Georgia—Continued.

Payment of amount due citizens of, under treaty with Creeks referred to, II, 402.

Payment of amount due, from United States recommended, I, 583.

Political and civil condition of, referred to, VII, 44.

Property owners in, should be compensated for losses sustained, III, 255.

Provisional governor for, appointed, and restoration of, into Union discussed, VI, 318.

Reconstruction of, referred to, VII, 48.

Georgia, The.—A Confederate cruiser built at Glasgow, Scotland, and sent out to prey upon the commerce of the United States during the Civil War. The *Georgia* sailed from Glasgow in April, 1863, under the name of the *Japan* and destroyed a number of Federal merchant vessels off the coast of France. Aug. 15, 1863, she was seized by the U. S. S. *Niagara*, Capt. Craven, and taken to England.

Georgiana, The, seizure of, by Spanish or Cuban authorities referred to, V, 143.

Claims arising out of, referred to, V, 185, 367.

Georgiana, The, convention with Peru regarding claims arising out of capture of, VI, 152.

Germanic Association of Customs and Commerce: Establishment and growth of, referred to, IV, 260.

Treaty with, regarding duty on agricultural products, IV, 314.

Germantown (Pa.), Battle of.—After the American defeat at Brandywine Creek and the British occupation of Philadelphia, Washington determined to attack the main body of Howe's army, which was quartered in Germantown, a suburb of Philadelphia. The American army was encamped at Skippock Creek, 20 miles from Philadelphia, and consisted of about 10,000 men. About two-thirds of these, under Generals Sullivan and Wayne, started for Germantown on the evening of Oct. 3, 1777. Washington accompanied Sullivan's division. The battle opened about 7 a. m. on the 4th. The attack failed on account of fog and a misunderstanding among the officers. After 3 hours of severe fighting the Americans were obliged to retreat with a loss of 673 killed and wounded and some 400 prisoners. The British loss was reported at 535, including Gen. Agnew and Lieut. Col. Bird, though 800 is claimed to be a more approximate figure. Washington retired to his former camp and Gen. Howe returned to Philadelphia.

Germany.—A country of Central Europe, bounded on the north by the North Sea, Denmark, and the Baltic Sea; on the east by Russia and Austria-Hungary; on the south by Austria-Hungary and Switzerland, and on the west by France, Luxemburg, Belgium, and the Netherlands. It extends from lat. 47° 16′ to 55° 54′ north, and from long. 5° 52′ to 22° 53′ east. The country is generally level in the north, but hilly and mountainous in the south. The principal mountains are the Alps, Vosges, Black Forest, etc. The chief products are grain, hemp, beets, wine, flax, etc. There are mines of iron, salt, coal, copper, lead, silver, etc., and valuable manufactures of cotton, woolen and linen goods, also of iron, steel, beer, etc. Germany comprises 26 States, and is a constitutional monarchy. The King of Prussia is hereditary German Emperor. The legislature consists of a Bundesrath of 58 members and Reichstag of 397 members. Germany has several foreign dependencies. The Empire as at present constituted replaced the North German Confederation, and is based on treaties between that body and the other German States. Area, 208,738 sq. miles; population (1890) 49,428,470.

Germany (see also Berlin; Hamburg):

Caroline Islands, dispute with Spain regarding, VIII, 331.

Commercial relations with, IX, 182, 629.

Compulsory insurance of workingmen in, referred to, IX, 347.

Consular convention with, VII, 160, 188.

Copyright privilege extended, by proclamation, IX, 278.

Referred to, IX, 317.

Diplomatic relations with, discussed, V, 11.

Emperor of—

Arbitrator in northwestern boundary dispute, VII, 143.

Award of, VII, 185.

Thanks of United States tendered, VII, 186.

Death of, VIII, 782.

Expulsion of Julius Baumer from, referred to, VII, 508.

Fruits, American, restrictions upon importation of, into, discussed, X, 184.

Fugitive criminals, convention with, for surrender of, V, 153.

Discussed, VIII, 237.

Government of united States of North Germany referred to, VI, 582.

Immigration treaty with, discussed, VII, 467.

Importation of American products into, restrictions upon, discussed, VIII, 171, 202, 331; IX, 525, 629; X, 183.

Decrees regarding, referred to, IX, 668.

Insurance companies, American, excluded from, IX, 629, 667, 751.

Minister of Hamburg, received in United States, II, 383.

Minister of, to United States, title of ambassador conferred upon, IX, 442.

Minister of United States to—

Recalled, V, 11.

Salary of, increase in, recommended, VII, 120.

Title of ambassador conferred upon, IX, 442.

Naturalization treaty with, VI, 630, 631, 632, 690.

Questions arising under, referred to, VII, 467, 568; VIII, 36, 331, 499; IX, 36, 437.

Political questions in, referred to, VII, 63.

Postal convention with, VI, 577, 685; VII, 249.

Samoan affairs discussed. (See Samoan Islands.)

Shipping interests of, report of consul-general on, referred to, VIII, 388.

Tariff laws of, evidence of modifications of, proclaimed, IX, 258.

Discussed, IX, 312.

Gerrymander.—An arbitrary arrangement of the legislative or Congressional districts of a State regardless of geographical contiguity and compactness, whereby a minority of the voters of one party may be so grouped as to elect all or a majority of the Representatives in Congress or a State legislature. The word was coined in 1811 from the name of Elbridge Gerry, who as governor of Massachusetts signed a bill passed by the Democratic majority of the legislature grouping the sections which gave Federalist majorities into one district, with a fancied resemblance to a salamander.

Gettysburg (Pa.), Battle of.—After the remarkable success of the Confederate arms at Chancellorsville, and in response to a general demand of the people of the Confederacy, Gen. Lee determined upon an invasion of the Northern States. In the early days of June, 1863, he started his army on the northward march into Pennsylvania. Passing up the Shenandoah Valley by way of Winchester (at which latter place he defeated Gen. Milroy, capturing 4,000 prisoners and 28 cannon), he crossed the Potomac at Williamsport and Shepherdstown, arriving in Hagerstown, Md., with a force of 68,352 effectives, according to Confederate accounts, or of 97,000 men and 280 guns, according to some Federal accounts. Hooker's army numbered about 80,000. By June 27 Lee had reached Chambersburg, Pa., with Longstreet's and Hill's corps, Ewell having pushed on as far as Carlisle and York. While the Confederates moved up the west side of the Blue Ridge Mountains Hooker marched along the east side, keeping always between his adversary and Washington. The movement of the Confederates toward the east through Chambersburg threatened Harrisburg and Columbia, and eventually Baltimore. Hooker asked to be relieved of command, which request was immediately granted, and he was succeeded by Gen. George G. Meade, who assumed command June 28. Meade was now reenforced by 15,000 men from Washington and 2,100 from the Middle Department and granted the privilege of calling upon the 11,000 at Harpers Ferry, making the two armies thus advancing to battle on Northern soil numerically equal, according to Northern statements. Lee, learning on June 28 that Meade was just across the South Mountain, and fearing the latter might attempt to cut off his communications with the Potomac by an advance through the mountain gaps in his rear, determined upon an eastward movement. Meade surmised that Lee would attempt a movement south on the east side of the South Mountain, and prepared to meet him and give battle at Pipe Creek, near Taneytown, Md., 15 miles southeast of Gettysburg. The left wing of the Federal army, consisting of the First, Eleventh, and Third corps, was sent forward to Gettysburg to mask the Pipe Creek movement. On the morning of July 1, 1863, Buford's cavalry, which had moved west of Gettysburg on the Chambersburg road, encountered the Confederate advance under Hill and Heth and were driven back to Seminary Ridge, west of the town. The corps were scarcely placed in line of battle when Gen. Reynolds was mortally wounded and the command of the field devolved upon Howard. He was later in the day superseded by Gen. Hancock. During the afternoon Ewell's corps and two-thirds of Hill's reenforced the Confederates and drove Reynolds's and Howard's corps to Cemetery Hill, south of the town, inflicting upon them a loss of nearly 10,000 men and 16 guns. Gen. Lee ordered Ewell to press forward and take the hill. Ewell failed to push on. On the advice of Hancock, Meade moved his whole army during the night and occupied Cemetery Hill. Lee's army was posted along Seminary Ridge, west of the town. July 2 the fighting of both armies was directed toward securing good positions, the Confederates gaining in two of three advance movements and capturing some trophies and prisoners. The attack on Cemetery Hill, while nearly successful, was disjointed, the Confederates retiring with their prisoners. The Union loss the second day was

10,000, Sickles losing half of his men. The Confederate losses were also great. July 3, the day of the decisive action, opened with slight skirmishing. After noon a heavy cannonade was kept up between the two armies for 2 hours. About 3 o'clock in the afternoon the Confederates, under Pickett, made a grand assault. They went forward in the face of a terrible fire and met with almost complete destruction. Hays's division took 2,000 prisoners and 15 colors; Gibbon's division took 2,500 prisoners and 12 colors. The charge on the left was under Pettigrew, and was made with the same desperate valor. The entire Federal losses at Gettysburg were 3,155 killed, 14,529 wounded, and 5,365 missing—a total of 23,049. The Confederate losses footed up, according to official reports, a total of 20,451, of whom 2,592 were killed, 12,709 wounded, and 5,150 taken prisoners. This report does not include the artillery losses. Gettysburg was probably the crucial battle of the Civil War.

Gettysburg Battlefield, work of locating and preserving lines of battle at, IX, 447.

Ghent, Treaty of.—A treaty of peace concluded by the United States and Great Britain at Ghent, Belgium, Dec. 24, 1814, and ratified Feb. 17, 1815. It brought to a close the War of 1812, leaving matters substantially as they were before the war. No mention was made of the right of search and the impressment of seamen by the British, though these were the chief causes of the war. Our seamen since that war have not been impressed by Great Britain. The treaty provided for the mutual restoration of territory, property, and archives, except certain islands in and near Passamaquoddy Bay, whose possession was to be determined by a commission; a cessation of hostilities; restoration of prisoners; an establishment of the disputed northeastern boundary by construction of the treaty of 1783, with possibly a final reference to some friendly power, other boundary questions to be disposed of in a similar manner, and a mutual promotion of measures for the abolition of the slave trade. The treaty was negotiated by John Quincy Adams, James A. Bayard, Henry Clay, Jonathan Russell, and Albert Gallatin on behalf of the United States, and by Lord James Gambier, Henry Goulburn, and William Adams on the part of Great Britain.

Ghent, Treaty of, between United States and Great Britain, I, 552; II, 250.

Commissioners—
Copy of journal of, transmitted, II, 463.
Disagree in opinions on, II, 208, 250.
Expenses of, referred to, II, 81.
To conclude, communications from and instructions to, I, 551, and X, 51; I, 552.
To make boundary in Passamaquoddy Bay according to description of, IX, 631.
Construction of first article of, regarding slaves, X, 59.
Construction of, referred to Emperor of Russia, II, 76, 103.
Decision of, II, 187.

Ghent, Treaty of, between United States and Great Britain—Continued.
Construction of, referred to Emperor of Russia—Continued.
Opinion of Attorney-General on, II, 400.
Ratification of, II, 198.
Convention for payment of claimants under, II, 393; X, 69.
Correspondence and protocols of conferences between envoys transmitted, X, 52, 63.
Expenses incurred under, referred to, X, 57.
Exportation of slaves by Great Britain in violation of, II, 60; X, 55.
Proclaimed, I, 560.
Referred to, II, 12, 22, 28, 60, 103, 187, 206, 244, 302, 329, 379, 429, 443.
Restitution of slaves referred to, II, 22, 48.
Settlement of boundaries under Article IV of, referred to, II, 12, 28.

Gibbon, Lardner, mentioned, V, 188, 229.

Gibbons vs. Ogden.—An important Supreme Court case denying the right of a State to grant the exclusive privilege of navigating the waters of a State extending to the coastwise traffic of another State. Aaron Ogden had obtained through assignment the exclusive right to navigate for 30 years, with boats propelled by fire or steam, the waters within the jurisdiction of the State of New York. In 1808 the New York court of chancery granted an injunction forbidding Thomas Gibbons from running steamboats between New York, Elizabethtown, and other places in New Jersey. Gibbons appealed, and the New York court of errors having sustained the chancery court, the Supreme Court rendered judgment for the appellant Gibbons on the ground that the granting of exclusive navigation of waters within the State of New York by the State's legislature, extending to coastwise traffic with another State, was repugnant to the clause of the Constitution of the United States authorizing Congress to regulate commerce, and was void. Ogden's bill was dismissed, the decree of the two New York courts having been annulled. The case occupies 240 pages of a large volume of the Supreme Court Reports. Daniel Webster appeared for the appellant. Chief Justice Marshall delivered the opinion.

Gibson, Walter M., held in duress by Dutch authorities at Batavia, V, 295, 298.

Gila Bend Reservation, Ariz., removal of Indians on, bill for, transmitted, IX, 64.

Gila Valley, Globe and Northern Railway, act granting right of way to, through San Carlos Reservation, Ariz., vetoed, IX, 571.

Gilbert, Henry C., treaty with Indians concluded by, V, 296, 351, 421.

Gillespie, Capt., dispatch to consul at Monterey forwarded and destroyed by, IV, 578.

Gillespie, G. L., mentioned, VIII, 157.

Gillis, James M.:
Mentioned, VI, 78.
Observations of, referred to, V, 243.

Gillmore, Quincy A., ceremonies at Fort Sumter to be conducted by, in absence of Gen. Sherman, VI, 283.

Gilmer, Thomas W., Secretary of Navy, death of, announced and honors to be paid memory of, IV, 279, 333.

Gilpin, Henry D., director of Bank of United States, nomination of, and reasons therefor, III, 41.

Gilsonite, disposition of lands in Utah containing, discussed, IX, 736.

Glamann, Charles, act granting pension to, vetoed, VIII, 680.

Glass, Eliza S., act granting pension to, vetoed, VIII, 739.

Glen, The, appropriation for illegal capture of, recommended, VI, 195.

Glendy, William M., captain in Navy, nomination for promotion withdrawn and reasons therefor, VII, 46.

Globe, Congressional. (See Congressional Globe.)

Gloucester, The, mentioned, X, 171.

Godfrey, Edwin J., act granting pension to, vetoed, VIII, 717.

Gold.—The most valuable of the metals in general use among civilized or barbarous nations, both in ancient and in modern times. Its earliest use was probably for personal adornment. It was extensively employed by the Oriental nations, such as the Hindus, Akkadians, Assyrians, Egyptians, and the Persians. Although it never was used to the same extent among the Greeks, they obtained it by their intercourse with the Phenicians and other navigators and merchants of the Mediterranean, and adorned their temples and made ornaments for their wealthier classes with it. Neither was gold in common use at an early day in Rome. Gold as money was not coined so early as silver. The Lydians made coins of this metal 860 B. C., but it had been in earlier use in the shape of rings, rods, etc., in the cities of the Chaldeans and in Assyria, and also among the Egyptians. The metal has been found most abundantly in South America, South Africa, and North America. Ancient gold mines of Russia were reopened in 1699 and those of the Ural Mountains have since been richly productive. Gold was discovered in Peru and Mexico in the sixteenth century by the Spaniards. It was found in Malacca in 1731, in Nueva Andalucía in 1785, in Ceylon in 1800, in New Zealand in 1842, in California in 1848, in Australia in 1851, in British Columbia in 1856, in Nova Scotia in 1861, in the Transvaal in 1868, in the Bendigo gold fields, Western Australia, in 1870, and in the Klondike region of the Yukon in 1896. The production of gold has been steadily increasing in recent years by reason not only of new discoveries but of the improved scientific methods of mining and of extracting the pure metal from the ore. The estimated value of all the gold in the world in 1848 was $2,500,000,000. In 1875 the amount had probably doubled. There was a large increase in the world's production of gold in 1897, the output for that year being twice that of 1890. More than 90 per cent of the supply was furnished by 7 countries, viz, the United States, the Transvaal, Australia, Russia (Siberia), British

India, Canada, and Mexico. The production of the Klondike region in 1897, according to Dr. Dawson, of the Dominion Geological Survey, was $2,500,000. In 1896 the total production of gold for the world was officially reported at $202,682,300, of which the United States produced $53,088,000; in 1897 the total production was $237,504,800, of which the United States produced $57,363,000, Australasia $55,684,200, and the Witwatersrand mines of South Africa $53,-567,414. During 1897 the United States coined $76,028,485 of gold. Russia alone exceeded this amount, with a coinage of $170,614,861. The nearest approach to it by any other nation was France, which coined $42,726,251. In 1898 the new gold added to the world's stock was $290,-000,000. The economic party in the world advocating the single gold standard has the example and practice of England, Germany, and most of the other commercial nations during a part of the present century to support their contention; but some of the most eminent of the economists in Europe, even in England, are bimetallists. In the United States the battle of the standards has been fiercely waging ever since the suspension of the coinage of silver in 1873.

Gold and Silver:

Adoption of, as standard of value discussed, III, 246.

Coinage of. (See Coins and Coinage.)

Depreciation in price of silver discussed, IX, 113, 193.

Discovery of—
Gold discussed, IV, 636; VI, 250; VII, 352, 401.
Silver discussed, VI, 250.

Export of, discussed, IX, 443, 532, 724.

Imports of, discussed, IX, 532.

International action for restoration of silver to full use as money referred to, VII, 635.

International agreement for free use of silver as a coin metal discussed, IX, 113.

International conference at Brussels, Belgium, in 1892 to consider enlarged use of silver, IX, 317.

Postponement of, discussed, IX, 444.
Report of, transmitted, IX, 349.

International conference for adopting ratio between, discussed, VII, 495, 512, 522, 558.

Appropriation for, recommended, VII, 486.

International conference to consider free coinage of silver, information regarding, refused, IX, 238.

International ratio of, establishment of, referred to, VIII, 344, 370.

Payments for public lands to be made in, order regarding, X, 104.

Production of, discussed, VI, 573, 681; IX, 444, 533, 724.

Production of gold in California discussed, V, 124.

Silver-purchase clause of act of 1890, repeal of, discussed, IX, 443, 641.
Recommended, IX, 401.

Use of, as medium of exchange. (See Medium of Exchange.)

Value of gold compared with national currency discussed, VII, 107, 148.

Governor.—The executive head of each of the States of the Union. When the first settlements were made in America the term governor was used in England to designate the head of large trading corporations like the East India Company, Massachusetts Bay Company, etc. In the Colonies, therefore, which operated under charters similar to the trading companies the executive head became known as the governor. In the royal Colonies he was appointed by the Crown, in the proprietary Colonies by the proprietors, and in Rhode Island, Connecticut, and most of the time in Massachusetts he was chosen by the people. After the Revolution the constitutions of the States provided for a single head, to be called the governor. Terms of the governors of the States vary from 1 to 4 years and the salaries from $1,000 to $10,000. To them is intrusted the execution of the laws, and they are usually invested with the veto and pardoning powers. In our early history the governors of many of the States were chosen by the legislatures thereof. At present the uniform practice is to elect the governor by popular vote.

Granby Token.—An unauthorized coin issued by John Higley, of Granby, Conn., in 1737. It was made of copper and on the obverse bore a deer with the words "Value me as you please," the Roman numerals III, and a crescent. The design on the reverse consisted of 3 hammers on a triangular field, each bearing a crown. The legend was, "I am good copper."

Grand Army of Republic.—A fraternal, charitable, and patriotic organization composed exclusively of ex-soldiers and ex-sailors of the Union Army, Navy, and Marine Corps who served during the Civil War and were honorably discharged. It was planned by Dr. B. F. Stephenson, ex-surgeon of the Fourteenth

Illinois Infantry. The first post was organized at Decatur, Ill., Apr. 6, 1866, and the first regular convention was held at Indianapolis, Ind., Nov. 20, 1866. Forty posts were represented, and Gen. S. A. Hurlbut, of Illinois, was chosen commander in chief. The organization now has branches in all parts of the Union. Its objects are to bring together in a spirit of friendship all former soldiers and sailors in the service of the Union during the Civil War, to care for the widows and orphans of their deceased comrades, to cultivate a spirit of devotion to the Union, and to perpetuate the memory of their dead. The membership in 1896 was 340,610.

Grand Jury.—A jury whose duty it is to inquire into charges for offenses and to determine whether indictments shall be brought against alleged criminals in any court. Provisions of the Federal and State constitutions prohibit the criminal prosecution of any person except upon presentment or indictment by a grand jury for any except the less serious crimes or misdemeanors or military or naval offenses. The custom is very ancient and has been scrupulously guarded as a safeguard of civil liberty since the time of Ethelred, an Anglo-Saxon king of the ninth century. At common law (and usually by statute) the grand jury consists of not less than 12 nor more than 23 members, and the concurrence of 12 is necessary to the finding of an indictment. They sit in absolute secrecy, and may either pass upon bills presented by the prosecuting officer of the State, or upon presentments made by one of their own number, or upon evidence laid before them of any violation of law. The proceedings are entirely *ex parte*. Witnesses for the prosecution only are examined. If the requisite number of jurors are satisfied, from the evidence presented, of the truth of the accusation, they write across the indictment the words "A true bill;" but if the evidence is unsatisfactory the indorsement is "Not a true bill." After all the indictments have been considered the work of the grand jury is ended and the cases are turned over to the court and petit jury for trial.

Grangers.—A common name for the Patrons of Husbandry, a secret association for the promotion of agricultural interests. The society had its origin in the depressed condition of agriculture immediately succeeding the Civil War. Its object was to redress the grievances of the farmers against the middlemen and railroad companies. The plan of organization embraces a secret ritual. It was organized in Washington Dec. 4, 1867, by employees of the Department of Agriculture. In a manifesto issued in 1874 the objects of the Grangers are declared to be "to develop a better and higher manhood and womanhood; to enhance the comforts of our homes; to buy less and produce more; to discountenance the credit system, the fashion system, and every other system that tends to prodigality and bankruptcy." Though nonpolitical, the order has exerted a strong influence in various State legislatures and in elections. In 1884 its membership exceeded 4,000,000. The organization has since lost many members and in some places has ceased to exist.

Grant, Ulysses S.—Continued.

Veto messages of—Continued.

Placing Daniel H. Kelly's name on muster roll, VII, 432.

Post-office statutes, VII, 385.

Recording conveyances in District of Columbia, VII, 381.

Relief of—

Best, J. Milton, VII, 172.

Brock, Michael W., VII, 382.

Burtch, Alexander, VII, 319.

Children of John M. Baker, VII, 171.

Contractors for war vessels, VII, 125.

Cooper, Charles, and other signers of bond, VII, 124.

Denniston, William H., VII, 268.

East Tennessee University, VII, 215.

Hanks, John F., estate of, VII, 170.

Hile, James A., VII, 379.

Johnston, James T., VII, 171.

Jussen, Edmund, VII, 214.

Leland, Edward A., VII, 435.

McCullah, James A., VII, 216.

Owners of salt works, VII, 216.

Spencer and Mead, VII, 271.

Tiffany, Nelson, VII, 383.

Turner, Junius T., VII, 389.

Objections to bill withdrawn, VII, 389.

Tyler and Luckett (assignees), VII, 380.

Wallace, Thomas B., VII, 173.

White, Rollin, VII, 80.

Willman, Henry, VII, 125.

Removal of charge of desertion from record of Alfred Rouland, VII, 433.

Restoration of Edward S. Meyer's name to army list, VII, 385.

Sale of Indian lands, VII, 387.

President requests that bill be returned for approval, VII, 388.

Request denied, VII, 388.

Union troops in Alabama and Florida, fixing status of, VII, 81.

United States notes and national-bank circulation, VII, 268.

Gray, George, member of Spanish-American Peace Commission, X, 175.

Gray, Samuel M., on committee to report upon sewerage system in District of Columbia, IX, 52, 79.

Gray, William E., refusal of Great Britain to surrender other fugitives and, discussed, VII, 414.

Great Britain.—In 1707, on the union with Scotland, Great Britain became the official name of the British Kingdom, and so continued until the union with Ireland in 1801. Since Jan. 1, 1801, the official name of that kingdom, including England, Wales, Ireland, and Scotland and the neighboring smaller islands is, The United Kingdom of Great Britain and Ireland. The government is a hereditary constitutional monarchy. The legislature consists of a Parliament, comprising the House of Lords and House of Commons, the former body having about 560 and the latter about 670 members. Great Britain has a larger number of colonies and foreign possessions than any other country. England is the wealthiest and most important portion, and with Wales forms the southern part of the island of Great Britain. England has important agriculture, but its chief interests are commercial, manufacturing, and mining. Great Britain has also by far the greatest, amounting almost to a monopoly, of the ocean carrying trade of the world. The chief manufactures are cotton and woolen goods, iron and steel, hardware, etc., while its mineral products are iron, coal, tin, copper, etc. The Anglican Church is established, and there are also many Protestant dissenting bodies and many Roman Catholics. Area of the United Kingdom, 121,483 sq. miles; population (1894), 38,779,031. Area of the British Empire, including colonies, protectorates, etc., 10,161,483 sq. miles; population (1891), about 350,000,000.

Great Britain (see also Canada, Dominion of; London):

Agency of—

In Canada in atrocities committed by Indians on frontiers, X, 42.

In hostile measures of Indians toward United States, X, 40.

American citizens—

Attacked by forces from, discussed, III, 401.

Militia called forth to protect, III, 403.

Illegally taken by, I, 500.

Treatment of, referred to, VI, 520.

Unlawfully put to death in, and retaliatory measures discussed, I, 537.

American interests in Spanish jurisdiction confided to consuls of, X, 184.

Arbitration, negotiations with United States for. (See Arbitration.)

Attempted occupation of portion of Alaska by Canada and, referred to, IX, 665.

Attempts of Canada and, to establish post routes in Alaska referred to, IX, 66.

Attempts of, to draw recruits from United States during war with Russia discussed, V, 331.

Attempts to draw United States into its contest with France, I, 449.

Bering Sea questions discussed. (See Bering Sea Fisheries.)

Blockade declared by, without presence of adequate force, I, 501.

Boundary dispute of, with Liberia, VIII, 129, 175.

Boundary dispute of, with Venezuela regarding British Guiana, VIII, 619; IX, 36, 181, 441, 526, 632, 655, 722.

Arbitration of—

Discussed, X, 190.

Recommended by President Cleveland, IX, 632.

Treaty regarding, IX, 722.

Monroe doctrine reasserted and attitude of United States respecting, discussed by President Cleveland, IX, 632, 655.

Boundary line with (see also Alaska; Ghent, Treaty of; Northeastern Boundary; Northwestern Boundary)—

Commission for determining, dissolved, VII, 35.

Commission to settle, recommended, VII, 102, 187.

from their neighbors. In 1824 they settled with the Blackfeet, near the Milk River. Their greatest chief was Sitting Squaw. Treaties were made with them in 1851, 1853, 1855, 1865, and 1868. In 1870 they were joined by their kindred, the Arapahoes, and are now occupying a portion of the Blackfeet Reservation in Montana. They number about 1,500.

Gros Ventre Indians:

Allotment of lands in severalty to, referred to, VIII, 196.

Treaty with, VI, 700.

Grosvenor, Charles H., brevet brigadier-general, acts and proceedings of, declared null and void, VI, 350.

Groveton (Va.), Battle of, or Second Battle of Manassas.—After eluding Pope's army and destroying the military stores at Bristow Station and Manassas, Stonewall Jackson retired across the battlefield of Bull Run and awaited reenforcements. Longstreet arrived on Aug. 29, swelling the numbers of the Confederate army to 49,000. Pope's army numbered about 40,000. On the evening of the 28th Kearny had driven the Confederate rear guard out of Centerville, and Pope, feeling sure of crushing Longstreet and Jackson, ordered an attack to be made at daylight next morning. Sigel began the attack, which soon became general. McDowell's corps arrived upon the scene of battle late in the afternoon. Fitz-John Porter never came into action, though ordered up by Pope. For alleged disobedience of orders in this connection charges were preferred against Porter by Pope. At night both armies rested on the field. The next day, Aug. 30, the battle was renewed. The fiercest fighting took place about 5 o'clock in the afternoon, and on the ground where the battle of Bull Run had been fought July 21, 1861. The result was a victory for the Confederates and the defeat of Pope's army. The loss of the Federals was about 15,000, that of the Confederates about 8,400. This battle is also called the Second Battle of Manassas.

Guadalupe Hidalgo, Treaty of.—Named from the Mexican village where Nicholas P. Trist, on behalf of the United States, Feb. 2, 1848, signed the treaty with Mexico (IV, 573) terminating the war and ceding territory now comprising Nevada, Utah, most of Arizona, a large part of New Mexico, parts of Colorado and Wyoming, and all of California to the United States and accepting the Rio Grande as the boundary between Mexico and Texas. The United States agreed to pay Mexico $15,000,000 (IV, 587) and to assume the claims of its citizens against Mexico arising before the treaty. Mexicans in the ceded territory were allowed to remain at their option and were assured protection as citizens.

Guadalupe Hidalgo, Treaty of:

Abrogation of eleventh article of, referred to, V, 238.

Amendments to, discussed, IV, 679.

Claims arising out of, V, 100, 238.

Discussed, IV, 573, 587, 679.

Guadalupe Hidalgo, Treaty of—Continued.

Fraudulent claims arising under, V, 147.

Proclamation regarding, IV, 627.

Ratifications of, exchanged at Querétaro, IV, 587.

Referred to, V, 7, 13, 27, 28, 42, 87, 100, 129, 169, 211, 232, 370, 393.

Guadeloupe:

Extraordinary commission of, apply to Congress for aid, I, 151, and X, 120.

Tonnage on American vessels at, referred to, II, 560.

Vessels of, duties on, suspended by proclamation, VIII, 742.

Guam, Island of, cable communication with, recommended, X, 201.

Guano:

Claim of American citizens to, on Alta Vela Island, VI, 629.

Deposits of, on Arcas Cays, IX, 244.

Discovery of, in Jarvis and Baker Islands referred to, V, 486.

Importation of, from Peru—

Desired, V, 83, 212, 231.

Negotiations regarding, V, 231.

Referred to, V, 487, 537.

Guantanamo (Cuba), Battle of.—As a preliminary step to the capture of Santiago, June 10, 1898, a force of 600 American marines, under the protecting fire of the *Oregon, Marblehead, Dolphin, Yankee, Yosemite, Porter,* and *Vixen,* was landed at Guantanamo Bay, on the south coast of Cuba, 35 miles east of Santiago, where it had been decided to establish a naval station. This important point was taken after a severe bombardment, and the position so won was held by the marines, assisted by 50 Cuban allies, despite desperate attempts to dislodge them. Seven Americans (including Surg. John B. Gibbs) were killed and 8 wounded, and 2 Cubans were killed and 4 wounded while holding Guantanamo prior to the arrival of Gen. Shafter's army. The enemy's loss was much greater, 40 of their dead being left on the field. Seventeen prisoners were taken. After several naval demonstrations on the north coasts of Cuba and Puerto Rico it became evident that well-ordered land operations were indispensable to the reduction of the forts. Accordingly a land force of 15,738 men, under Gen. W. R. Shafter, sailed from Tampa, Fla., June 14, and by the 24th had landed at Daiquiri, near Guantanamo. The landing was assisted by Cubans under Gen. Garcia. Little resistance was encountered from the Spaniards.

Guantanamo Bay, Cuba, landing of American marines and subsequent fighting at, discussed, X, 170.

Guatemala.—A Republic of Central America. It is bounded on the north by Mexico, on the east by Honduras, on the south and southeast by Salvador, and on the west and southwest by the Pacific Ocean. It is a mountainous country. The chief product is coffee. The country is divided into 22 departments. The executive is vested in a President and legislative in a

H.

Habeas Corpus.—In law a writ issued by a judge or court requiring the body of a person restrained of liberty to be brought before the judge or into the court, that the lawfulness of the restraint may be investigated and determined. The writ of *habeas corpus* is one of the chief bulwarks of civil liberty, being perhaps the best security against the grosser forms of tyranny ever devised. Its foundation is in the Magna Charta of England. The power to suspend it is naturally a subject of the gravest importance. The Constitution of the United States, Article I, section 9, provides: "The privilege of the writ of *habeas corpus* shall not be suspended unless when, in cases of rebellion or invasion, the public safety may require it." The writ has been suspended many times in England. It was suspended in Rhode Island by State authority during Dorr's Rebellion. July 5, 1861, Attorney-General Bates gave an opinion in favor of the President's power to suspend the writ. Mar. 3, 1863, Congress approved this opinion, and thereafter many arrests were made for disloyal practices. Sept. 24, 1862, the suspension of the writ was made general so far as it concerned persons arrested by military officers for disloyalty. In 1866, in the case of Milligan, arrested in Indiana in 1864 and sentenced to death by a military tribunal, the Supreme Court, having been appealed to, decided that the privilege of the writ could not be suspended in districts where the action of the civil courts was not interrupted, except that military commissioners might be given jurisdiction to try residents of rebellious States, prisoners of war, and persons in the military and naval services. Milligan, being a civilian, was exempt from the laws of war and could only be tried by a jury. (See also Merryman Case; Milligan Case.)

Harrison, William Henry—Continued.

Major-general, military talents of, commented on, I, 535.

Nominations of, unacted on withdrawn by, IV, 21.

Portrait of, IV, 2.

Proclamation of, convening extraordinary session of Congress, IV, 21.

Provision for family of, for expenses incurred in removing to Washington recommended, IV, 40.

Remains of, removal of, to North Bend, Ohio, for interment, IV, 54.

Correspondence regarding, IV, 53.

Hartford Convention.—Hartford, Conn., has been the scene of two historic conventions with almost opposite purposes. In the autumn of 1780 delegates from all the Northern States assembled there to devise means to strengthen the financial system of the Federal Government and to raise and equip troops for the prosecution of the War of Independence. A second convention was held there Dec. 15, 1814–Jan. 5, 1815, and had for its object the denunciation of the war with Great Britain. It consisted of delegates from Massachusetts, Connecticut, Rhode Island, New Hampshire, and Vermont, and was held behind closed doors. The New England Federalists were much opposed to the War of 1812, as it wrought great damage to their commercial interests. They denounced the policy of the Government in drafting men for the Army and demanded reforms in the direction of States' rights. Having been accused of an attempt to disrupt the Union, the convention denied "any present intention to dissolve the Union," but admitted that "if a dissolution should become necessary by reason of the multiplied abuses of bad administration it should, if possible, be the work of peaceable times and deliberate consent." It laid down the general principle that "it is as much the duty of the State authorities to watch over the rights reserved as of the United States to exercise the powers that are delegated." The resolutions of the convention were indorsed by the legislatures of Connecticut and Massachusetts and pressed upon Congress. No attention was there paid to them. They are of interest as showing that secession was contemplated in New England at an early date in our history. The strength of the Federalist party in the States where it had been strongest began to wane after the holding of this convention.

Hartmount, E. Hertzberg, Dominican consul-general in London, mentioned, VII, 63.

Hartranft, John F.:

Member of Cherokee Commission, death of, referred to, IX, 46.

Special provost-marshal in trial of persons implicated in assassination of President Lincoln, appointed, VI, 334.

Harvey, John, correspondence regarding—

Imprisonment of Ebenezer S. Greely, III, 358.

Northeastern boundary. (See Northeastern Boundary.)

Harvey, Thomas H., treaties with Indians concluded by, IV, 423, 454.

Hatch, Davis, imprisonment of, by Dominican Republic referred to, VII, 50, 59.

Hatch, Edward, brigadier-general, nomination of, referred to, VI, 202.

Hatchers Run (Va.), Battle of.—Oct. 27, 1864, in an attempt to seize the South Side Railroad and get nearer Richmond, the Second Army Corps, under Hancock, and 2 divisions of the Fifth Corps forced a passage of Hatchers Run, the termination of the Confederate works on the right, and moved up on the south side of it to the point where the run is crossed by the Boydton plank road. In support of the movement Butler made a demonstration on the north side of the James River and attacked the Confederates on both the Williamsburg and York River railroads. The Confederates moved across Hatchers Run and made a fierce attack upon Hancock, but were driven back into their works. During the night Hancock retired to his old position, having lost 1,900 men, one-third of whom were missing. Feb. 5, 1865, Grant made another attempt to turn the Confederate lines at Hatchers Run. The only gain was an extension to the westward of the Federal lines. The losses in the attempt were 2,000 on the Federal and about 1,000 on the Confederate side.

Hatteras Expedition.—Aug. 26, 1861, an expedition against forts Hatteras and Clark was sent out from Fortress Monroe under Commodore Stringham and Gen. Butler. The naval force consisted of the *Minnesota* and 4 other vessels and transports and the land force of about 900 men. Fort Clark was occupied on the 27th without serious opposition. On the morning of the 28th bombardment of Fort Hatteras began, and on the 29th at 11 o'clock the fort surrendered. Butler occupied the works with his land forces. Capt. Barron and 615 prisoners were sent north on the flagship *Minnesota*. Twenty-five pieces of artillery, 1,000 stand of arms, and a large quantity of ordnance stores, provisions, etc., fell into the hands of the victors.

Haupt, Herman, chief of construction and transportation in Department of Rappahannock, VI, 113.

Havana, Cuba (see also Cuba):

Destruction of the *Maine* in harbor of, X, 136, 148, 161.

Findings of court of inquiry discussed, X, 136, 148.

Number of lives lost in, report on, X, 153.

Proposition of Spain to investigate causes of, referred to, X, 148.

Hawaiian Islands.—A group of islands in the North Pacific Ocean. The principal islands are Hawaii, Maui, Oahu, Kauai, Lanai, Kahulaui, Molokai, and Niihau. They are mountainous and volcanic. The exports are sugar, rice, bananas, and wool. The inhabitants are about one-fourth Hawaiians, the remainder being Chinese, Japanese, and Portuguese, with a few Americans, British, and Germans. The islands were discovered in 1542. The government was a monarchy, with a king, cabinet, and legislature. David Kalakaua was made King in 1874, succeeding Lunalilo. He died in 1891 and was succeeded by Liliuokalani as Queen. She was deposed by a committee of public safety Jan. 17, 1893, and a provisional government was formed, headed by Sanford B. Dole. A treaty of annexation to the United States was then concluded and sent to the Senate by President Benj. Harrison, and it was pending when President Cleveland was inaugurated. He promptly withdrew it. The restoration of the Queen was attempted, but failed. July 4, 1894, a Republic was proclaimed, with Mr. Dole as President. After President McKinley's term began another treaty of annexation was sent to the Senate. Pending its consideration a joint resolution passed Congress annexing the islands. It was approved July 7, 1898. A government has not been (1899) provided for the islands. Area, 6,640 sq. miles; population, about 115,000.

Haymarket Riot.—A riot which took place at Haymarket Square, Chicago, May 4, 1886, involving the police and a number of anarchists. An open-air meeting, in which certain labor troubles were under discussion, was in progress. The police attempted to break up the meeting because of the inflammatory utterances of some of the speakers. In the fight which ensued a bomb was thrown and 7 policemen were killed and 60 wounded. Albert R. Parsons, August Spies, Adolph Fischer, George Engel, Michael Schwab, Louis Lingg, Samuel Fielden, and Oscar W. Neebe, prominent anarchists, were arrested and tried for complicity in the outrage. The case attracted universal attention and resulted in the hanging of the first four Nov. 11, 1887. Lingg escaped the gallows by committing suicide in prison. Fielden and Schwab were sentenced to imprisonment for life and Neebe for 15 years. They were pardoned by Governor Altgeld in 1893.

Helderberg War.—Demonstrations made at various times between 1839 and 1845 by the Anti-Renters of Albany, Rensselaer, Columbia, Greene, Delaware, Schoharie, and Otsego counties, N. Y., and the efforts of the State government to suppress them. Large tracts of land in these counties had been granted by the Government of Holland to the early Dutch settlers or patroons. The patroons sublet the land in perpetuity to tenants who agreed to pay the rent in produce. On the death of Stephen Van Rensselaer in 1839 his tenants, who had long been dissatisfied, refused to pay his successor the rent. Men disguised as Indians terrorized the region. A sheriff and posse who attempted to collect the rents were outnumbered and their efforts proved futile. In 1844 there was again armed opposition to the payment of rent. In 1845 an officer named Steele was shot while trying to collect rent in Delaware County. Governor Wright proclaimed the county in a state of insurrection. Two persons were convicted and sentenced to death for this murder, but they were afterwards pardoned. The court of appeals in 1852 rendered a decision which in the main sustained the tenants and practically ended the movement.

Helena (Ark.), Assault on.—To strengthen the army before Vicksburg, Grant had withdrawn troops from all the neighboring posts. Helena, Ark., was left in charge of 3,800 men under Gen. B. M. Prentiss. June 26 the Confederate Generals T. H. Holmes and Sterling Price left Little Rock with about 8,000 men to surprise and capture the place. July 4, 1863, the day Vicksburg surrendered, they made an assault on one of the batteries with 3,000 men. They were repulsed with a loss of 1,111 men. Four regiments then attacked a fort on Hindman Hill, but were defeated. A third assault was made by Marmaduke, with 1,750 men, upon a fort on the north side of the place, but was likewise repulsed with a loss of one-fifth of the assailants. The Confederate loss was officially reported as 173 killed, 687 wounded, and 776 missing—in all, 1,636. The Federal loss did not exceed 250 in all.

Hemp, Russian, import duties on, referred to, VII, 36.

Hempstead, Christopher, consul at Belize, British Honduras, mentioned, V, 36.

Hendricks, Thomas A., Vice-President, death of, announced and honors to be paid memory of, VIII, 319, 320, 324.

Henrick, The, indemnification for loss of, claimed, I, 356, 377; II, 65.

Henry, B. H., report of agent to Fiji Islands to investigate claim of, transmitted, IX, 666.

Henry, J. A., act for relief of, reasons for applying pocket veto to, VIII, 487.

Henry, John, alleged secret agent of Great Britain in United States for fomenting disaffection, I, 498, and X, 41.

Henry, Patrick, minister to France, nomination of, I, 284.

Henry Crosby, The, fired upon at Azua, Santo Domingo, IX, 663.

Hensley, Elijah P., act granting pension to, vetoed, VIII, 436.

Hepburn vs. Griswold.—One of the Supreme Court cases involving the constitutionality of the issue of United States legal-tender notes. June 20, 1860, Mrs. Hepburn promised to pay Mr. Griswold $11,250 on Feb. 20, 1862. At the time gold and silver only were legal tender. Feb. 25, 1862, the United States issued $150,-000,000 of its own notes, to be received as lawful money in payment of all debts, public and private, within the United States. This was 5 days after the note became due. Mrs. Hepburn in March, 1864, after suit had been brought, tendered these notes in payment, and

they were refused. The notes were then tendered and paid into court in Louisville, Ky. The Louisville court of chancery declared the debt absolved. The Kentucky court of errors and appeals reversed the chancellor's judgment, and the United States Supreme Court at the December term, 1867, affirmed the judgment of the court of errors and appeals. This ruling was afterwards reversed. (See Juilliard *vs.* Greenman.) Chief Justice Chase, in delivering the opinion of the court, said: "We can not doubt that a law not made in pursuance of an express power, which necessarily and in its direct operation impairs the obligation of contracts, is inconsistent with the spirit of the Constitution." "We are obliged to conclude," he continued, "that an act making mere promises to pay dollars a legal tender in payment of debts previously contracted * * * is inconsistent with the spirit of the Constitution, and that it is prohibited by the Constitution." Justices Miller, Swayne, and Davis dissented.

Hepner, George, treaty with Indians concluded by, V, 297.

Herbert, Michael H., Canadian canal tolls referred to, IX, 243. (See also IX, 240.)

Herbst, Theresa, act granting pension to, vetoed, VIII, 692.

Hering, Rudolph, on committee to report upon sewerage system in District of Columbia, IX, 52, 79.

Hermitage, The.—The name given by Andrew Jackson to his home, situated about 10 miles from Nashville, Tenn., near the Cumberland River. At this place President Jackson died and is buried. The premises and a portion of his farm have become the property of the State of Tennessee and have been converted into a State home for aged, indigent, or disabled ex-Confederate soldiers.

Hermitage, The, tendered to United States, V, 421.

Hermosa, The, slaves taken from wreck of, and liberated referred to, IV, 211.

Herndon, William L., report of, on exploration of valley of the Amazon transmitted, V, 188, 229.

Hero, The, seizure of, and claims arising out of, VII, 160; VIII, 613; IX, 112, 238, 441, 530.

Award in case of, IX, 638.

Herold, David E.:

Implicated in assassination of President Lincoln, proceedings of trial and verdict of military commission, VI, 334, 335, 336, 342, 347, 348.

Persons claiming reward for apprehension of, directed to file claims, VI, 353.

Herran, Pedro A., mentioned, VI, 67, 147.

Herschell, Lord, arbitrator in Venezuelan boundary dispute, X, 191.

Hesse, convention with, IV, 316, 357.

Hesse-Cassel:

Convention with, IV, 447.

Treaty of, with France, I, 193.

Hesse, Electorate of, exequatur issued consuls of, revoked, VI, 511.

Hester, William H., act granting pension to, vetoed, VIII, 667.

Honduras.—A Central American Republic. It is bounded on the north and northeast by the Caribbean Sea, on the southeast and south by Nicaragua, on the southwest by Salvador, and on the northwest by Guatemala. It was discovered by Columbus in 1502. The surface is varied by numerous mountain chains, especially in the west, and high open valleys and plateaus. The climate is temperate and healthful in the high altitudes and hot and miasmatic along portions of the coast. The plains support large herds of cattle. The principal exports are fruits, cabinet woods, hides, and indigo. Executive power is vested in a President, elected for 4 years, and the Congress consists of a single house. Honduras has been independent since 1839 and has suffered from frequent political revolutions and the wars of its neighbors, Salvador, Guatemala, and Nicaragua. Spanish is the prevailing language and the principal religion is the Roman Catholic. Area, 46,400 sq. miles; population (1893), 380,000.

Hornet, The.—An American sloop of war carrying 18 guns, commanded by Capt. Lawrence during the War of 1812. Feb. 24, 1813, near the mouth of the Demerara River, she attacked the British brig *Peacock*, of 18 guns. The *Peacock* was soon in a sinking condition, and struck her colors. Before the wounded could be removed she went down, carrying with her 9 British and 3 American seamen. Mar. 23, 1815, off the Cape of Good Hope, the *Hornet* captured and sunk the British brig *Penguin*, also of 18 guns, the latter losing her commander in the engagement. Shortly after this battle the *Hornet* was chased by the British frigate *Cornwallis*, 74 guns, and only escaped capture by throwing her guns and heavy stores overboard.

Horse Shoe Bend (Ala.), Battle of.—When Gen. Jackson was informed of the arrival of Creeks in considerable numbers in Tallapoosa County he resolved to strike a decisive blow. He sent his stores down the Coosa River from Fort Strother in flatboats and marched his army against the gathering Indians. Mar. 27, 1814, with 2,000 effective men, he halted within a few miles of the breastworks at the Horse Shoe Bend of the Tallapoosa River, where 1,200 Indians (one-fourth of whom were women and children) had intrenched themselves, with an ample supply of food. The whites and their Indian allies soon surrounded the camp. The Indians fought desperately. They were attacked in front with bayonet and ball, and the torch was applied to their camp in the rear. The battle lasted all day, and in the evening 557 Creek warriors were dead in the little peninsula and some 200 more were killed while trying to escape. The loss to the whites was 32 killed and 99 wounded. The Cherokees lost 18 killed and 36 wounded. Some 300 women and children were taken prisoners. The spirit of the Indians was broken by this battle. Weathersford, the chief, appeared personally before Gen. Jackson and offered to surrender. He was permitted to go free and counsel peace among his dejected followers.

I.

showed a steady increase up to 1854, when the number reached 427,833. Almost every year's figures show an increase over those of the preceding year. After 1854 there was a gradual falling off, until during the first year of the Civil War the number was reduced to 91,920— but little more than half the number of arrivals for the preceding year. The following year (1862) showed but 91,987, but this number was nearly doubled the next year, notwithstanding the result of the war was yet in doubt. After the war the tide of immigration again set toward our shores, and in 1882 the arrivals reached 788,992. The total immigration from Jan. 1, 1820, to the close of 1893 was more than 20,000,000. This large influx of foreigners so disturbed the existing social conditions that remedial legislation was demanded. By an act of Congress in 1882 a head tax was laid upon every immigrant by sea, and commissioners were appointed to inspect vessels entering American ports, who should have the power to prevent the landing of any "convict, lunatic, idiot, or person likely to become a public charge." Such persons were to be returned to the port whence they came at the cost of the owners of the vessels bringing them to this country. A further law, passed in 1885, makes it unlawful to pay the transportation or to encourage in any way the immigration of aliens under contract or agreement to perform labor or service in the United States. The penalties attached to this act are $1,000 fine upon the person so encouraging such immigrant and $500 upon the captain of a vessel who knowingly transports the laborers. The immigration laws were amended in 1887, 1888, 1891, and 1892 in the direction of protecting American workingmen from the ruinous competition with foreign pauper labor. These laws have served to reduce the number as well as improve the class of arrivals. The report for 1896 showed only 343,267 arrivals, against 603,322 in 1883.

Immigration :

Act to amend laws regarding, vetoed, IX, 757.

Chinese—

Act to execute certain treaty stipulations approved and discussed, VIII, 630.

Acts regarding, vetoed, VII, 514; VIII, 112.

Conventional regulation of passage of laborers across borders proposed to Mexico and Great Britain, IX, 109.

Discussed by President—

Arthur, VIII, 129.

Cleveland, VIII, 329, 383, 390, 498, 609, 630; IX, 436.

Grant, VII, 288, 355.

Harrison, Benj., IX, 34, 41, 197.

Hayes, VII, 569, 588.

Execution of acts regarding, referred to, IX, 60.

Head tax collected from Chinamen entering Canada, IX, 41, 197.

Registration of Chinese laborers required—

Extension of time for, IX, 406, 436.

Law regarding, sustained by Supreme Court, IX, 436.

Immigration—Continued.

Chinese—Continued.

Reports on, referred to, VIII, 388, 390.

Through Canada and Mexico discussed, IX, 41, 197.

Treaty regarding, VII, 609, 629; VIII, 610; IX, 476, 524.

Discussed, VIII, 42, 236, 609, 801.

Referred to, VIII, 104, 627, 630.

Rejected by China, discussed, VIII, 782, 801, 802; IX, 34.

Violation of laws restricting, discussed and recommendations regarding, VIII, 175; IX, 197.

Consular reports on emigration and, referred to, VIII, 536.

Convention for protection of emigrant passengers proposed, VII, 36.

Discussed by President—

Cleveland, VIII, 785; IX, 445, 725.

Lincoln, VI, 182, 246.

Inland passage tickets for emigrants referred to, V, 470.

Involuntary deportation of convicts, idiots, and paupers to United States discussed, VII, 265, 636.

Legislation for protection of immigrants recommended, VII, 154, 166; VIII, 63.

Measures for health and safety of immigrants discussed, V, 239, 242; VII, 166.

Of citizens of United States into Turkey referred to, VI, 463.

Dissatisfied citizens of United States into Mexico referred to, VI, 373.

Laborers, and *padroni* system discussed, IX, 633.

Mormons, laws to prevent, recommended, VIII, 362.

Pardons granted foreigners on condition of emigration to United States discussed, VI, 455.

Paupers introduced into United States discussed, III, 469; IV, 518.

Legislation respecting, recommended, VIII, 170.

Request of President to withdraw articles regarding, from consideration of House, III, 475.

Questions with Switzerland regarding, VII, 568; VIII, 40.

Treaties regarding, information respecting conflict of Senate bill with, transmitted, IX, 333.

Treaty regarding, with—

Bavaria, VI, 636.

China. (See Chinese, *ante.*)

Germany and claims arising under, discussed, VII, 467.

Prussia, VI, 629.

Immigration, Superintendent of, report of, discussed, IX, 445.

Impeachment.—The exhibition of charges of maladministration against a civil officer before a competent tribunal. In the United States the House of Representatives has the sole power of impeachment of the President, Vice-President, and all civil officers of the United States. The Senate has the sole power to try all impeachments. The Chief Justice presides at the trial of a President. A two-thirds vote is necessary to convict. Most States have similar regulations regarding impeachment. This mode of trial of public officials comes to us from England, where impeachments are made by the House of Commons and tried by the House of Lords. In the history of the Federal Government there have been only 7 cases of impeachment. Senator William Blount, of Tennessee, was impeached by the House in 1797 for treasonable negotiations with Great Britain for the transfer of New Orleans. The Senate acquitted him. Mar. 3, 1803, Judge John Pickering, of the Federal court of New Hampshire, was impeached and removed from the bench for drunkenness and profanity. Mar. 13, 1804, Judge Samuel Chase, of Maryland, an associate justice of the United States Supreme Court, was impeached for arbitrary conduct and the introduction of political matter into his charges to grand juries; acquitted Mar. 1, 1805. Dec. 13, 1804, Judge James H. Peck, of the Federal court of Missouri, was impeached for punishing as contempt of court a criticism of his opinions. He was acquitted. May 6, 1862, Judge West H. Humphreys, of the Federal district court of Tennessee, was impeached and afterwards removed upon the charge of aiding the rebellion. The vote of the Senate was unanimous. Feb. 24, 1868, the House impeached Andrew Johnson, President of the United States, for having removed Secretary of War Stanton in violation of the tenure-of-office act, for having appointed Gen. Lorenzo Thomas Secretary of War contrary to the same act, for conspiracy with Thomas and others for the intimidation of Stanton and the unlawful disbursement of the War Department's moneys, and for inducing Gen. Emory to disobey orders. The House adopted the impeachment resolution by a vote of 126 to 42. President Johnson was acquitted by the Senate by a vote of 35 to 19 (VI, 709). Mar. 2, 1876, Secretary of War W. W. Belknap was impeached on the charge of bribery in making appointments. He resigned a few hours before the impeachment resolution passed the House, and the President accepted his resignation. Aug. 1, 1876, he was acquitted by a vote of 36 for conviction to 25 for acquittal, the minority holding that, being out of office, he was not liable on impeachment proceedings.

Impeachment of President Johnson :
Articles of, exhibited by House of Representatives, VI, 709.
   Answer of President, VI, 728.
   Replication of House of Representatives, VI, 753.
Letter of Chief Justice Chase respecting proper mode of procedure, VI, 718.
Proceedings of Senate sitting for trial of, VI, 720.
Verdict of acquittal, VI, 757.

Imperial Mexican Express Co., organization of, referred to, VI, 377.

Imperialism. (See Expansion, Territorial.)

Import Duties (see also Revenue, Public):
Act—
In relation to immediate transportation of dutiable goods returned, IX, 67.
Regulating duties on copper, vetoed, VI, 705.
To extend for limited period present laws for laying and collecting, vetoed, IV, 180.
To provide revenue from imports, etc., vetoed, IV, 183.
Protest of President Tyler against action of House in adopting report assailing his conduct regarding, IV, 190.
Ad valorem duties—
Offer strong temptations to fraud, V, 84, 126, 170.
Recommended, IV, 406.
Amount of, and statement in regard to, II, 60, 98, 188, 304, 357, 386, 411, 596; III, 27; IV, 42; VIII, 46.
Collected by Great Britain and United States in contravention of treaty discussed, II, 27; IV, 424, 446.
Commercial tariff should be regulated, I, 485.
Commission to revise, recommended, VIII, 49, 135.
Complaints of Spain and Portugal against operations of revenue act, IV, 103.
Compromise act, diminution of duties under, referred to, IV, 102.
Constitutionality of tariff questioned, II, 523.
Correspondence with foreign governments regarding laws of, IV, 233.
Discussed by President—
Adams, J. Q., II, 413.
Arthur, VIII, 49, 134, 252.
Buchanan, V, 433, 521, 650.
Cleveland, VIII, 341, 508, 584, 774; IX, 458, 552, 741.
Fillmore, V, 83, 123, 125, 169.
Grant, VII, 30, 107, 148, 247, 293, 349.
Harrison, Benj., IX, 38, 121, 191, 309.
Hayes, VII, 470, 559.
Jackson, II, 449, 523, 556, 597; III, 28, 161, 251.
Jefferson, I, 409.
Johnson, VI, 575.
Madison, I, 485, 567.
Monroe, II, 106, 191, 215.
Pierce, V, 214, 338, 408.
Polk, IV, 403, 451, 498, 516, 553, 647, 656.
Taylor, V, 18.
Tyler, IV, 81, 102, 108, 180, 183, 200, 266.
Van Buren, III, 535.
Effect of, on treaties with foreign powers, IV, 233.
Frauds in importation of foreign merchandise discussed, II, 423; VIII, 210.
Free list—
Increase in, recommended, VII, 148, 293; VIII, 136; IX, 39.
Sugar placed on, discussed, IX, 191.
Imposition of, as war measure proposed, IV, 502, 516.
Increase in, recommended, II, 191; IV, 108.
Laws levying, repealed. (See Vessels, Foreign, tonnage on.)
Moderate schedule of, recommended, IV, 201; V, 84, 126.

Impressment.—The act of compelling persons to enter the public service, usually applied to the seizure of sailors for service on naval vessels. Great Britain has always claimed the right to levy land and naval forces in time of war by compulsory process. This method has been limited in the case of land forces to times of actual invasion; but that country still claims the right to impress British seamen into service wherever they may be found. The exercise of this claim was among the causes that led to the War of 1812. Great Britain refused to allow the right of her seamen to change their allegiance by naturalization and claimed the right to search neutral vessels and decide by her visiting officers who among the crew of such neutral vessels were British subjects. Many American sailors were in this way wrongfully impressed into the British navy. Although by the treaty of Ghent Great Britain did not relinquish this claim, it has been abandoned so far as United States vessels are concerned. She has acceded to the doctrine of Webster that in every regularly documented American vessel the crew who navigate it will find protection in the flag which is over them. (See also Ghent, Treaty of.)

Inauguration Day.—The choice of Mar. 4 as the
day for the inauguration of the President of the
United States dates back to 1788. After the ratification of the Constitution by the several States
the Congress of the old Confederation fixed
upon the first Wednesday in January, 1789, for
the choice of electors, the first Wednesday in
February for the voting by the electors, and the
first Wednesday in March for the inauguration of the President. The latter day fell on
the 4th in that year, and the twelfth amendment to the Constitution settled upon this as
the legal date. Bills have been frequently introduced in both Houses of Congress to change
Inauguration Day from Mar. 4 to Apr. 30.

Inauguration of President Cleveland, Government employees to witness, VIII, 294.

Income Tax.—A form of direct tax upon annual
incomes in excess of a specified sum. According to the doctrine of Adam Smith, "the subjects of every state ought to contribute to the
support of the government as nearly as possible in proportion to their respective abilities—
that is, in proportion to the revenues which
they respectively enjoy under the protection
of the state." In pursuance of this principle
all incomes should be taxed, but it is generally
conceded among the advocates of such a tax
that incomes below a certain amount should
be exempt. An income tax has been levied by
the United States Government but twice in its
history. Aug. 5, 1861, Congress authorized a
tax of 3 per cent on all incomes over $800 per
annum. July 1, 1862, an act was passed taxing
all incomes under $5,000 5 per cent, with an
exemption of $600 and house rent actually
paid. Incomes of more than $5,000 and less
than $10,000 were taxed 2½ per cent additional,
and on incomes of more than $10,000 5 per cent
additional with no exemptions. A tax of 5
per cent on incomes of Americans living
abroad and of 1½ per cent on incomes from
United States securities was levied, expiring
in 1865. In 1864 a special tax of 5 per cent was
imposed on all incomes between $600 and
$5,000 and 10 per cent on incomes of more than
$5,000. This law was repealed in 1872. The
amount collected under it was $346,911,760.48.
In August, 1894, the Wilson tariff law imposed
a tax of 2 per cent on all incomes in excess of

$4,000. The Supreme Court in 1895 declared this law unconstitutional. One-sixth of the revenue of Great Britain is derived from income-tax laws.

Income Tax:

Recommended by President Grant, VII, 30.

Upon certain corporate investments discussed, IX, 460.

Upon consuls to United States discussed, VI, 182.

Income-Tax Cases.—Famous cases involving the income-tax provision of the tariff law of Aug. 28, 1894. The first to come before the Supreme Court was that of Pollock *vs.* Farmers' Loan and Trust Co., on appeal from the circuit court of the United States for the southern district of New York, decided Apr. 8, 1895. The suit arose on a bill filed by Charles Pollock, a citizen of Massachusetts, on behalf of himself and all other stockholders of the defendant company similarly situated, against the Farmers' Loan and Trust Co., of the State of New York, and its directors. The syllabus shows both the argument and the opinion of the court as far as expressed. Omitting the mere technical points involved, the Supreme Court held that in the adjudicated cases referred to in the case, beginning with Hylton *vs.* United States, February, 1796, and ending with Springer *vs.* United States, October, 1880, taxes on land are conceded to be direct taxes, and in none of them is it determined that a tax on rent or income derived from land is not a tax on land. A tax on the rents or income of real estate is a direct tax within the meaning of the Constitution. A tax upon income derived from the interest of bonds issued by a municipal corporation is a tax upon the power of the State and its instrumentalities, and is consequently repugnant to the Constitution of the United States. So much of the act cited as provides for levying taxes upon rents or incomes derived from real estate or from the interest on municipal bonds is repugnant to the Constitution and is invalid. The justices who heard the argument were divided upon each of the other questions, as follows, and rendered no opinion as to them: (1) Whether the void provision as to rents and income from real estate invalidates the whole act; (2) whether as to the income from personal property as such the act is unconstitutional as levying direct taxes; and (3) whether any part of the tax, if not considered as a direct tax, is invalid for want of uniformity on either of the grounds suggested. Chief Justice Fuller delivered the opinion. Justice Field's opinion went further. He said: "The present assault upon capital is but the beginning. * * * Our political contests will become a war of the poor against the rich—a war constantly growing in intensity and bitterness. * * * I am of opinion that the whole law of 1894 should be declared void and without any binding force." Justices White and Harlan dissented. The former spoke of "the injustice and harm which must always result from overthrowing a long and settled practice sanctioned by the decisions of this court. Under the income-tax laws which prevailed in the past for many years, and which covered every conceivable source of income—rentals from real estate and everything else—vast sums were collected from the people of the United States. The decision here rendered announces that those sums were wrongfully taken, and thereby, it seems to me, creates a claim in equity and good conscience against the Government for an enormous amount of money." The Supreme Court made the same decree and the justices were aligned just as above in the case of Hyde *vs.* Continental Trust Co. This also was an appeal from the circuit court of the United States for the southern district of New York. This case with Pollock *vs.* Farmers' Loan and Trust Co. was accorded a rehearing and was decided May 20, 1895. In delivering the opinion of the court the Chief Justice alluded to the broadening of the field of inquiry. The whole case was reviewed, but the court did not retravel the entire ground covered in the former decision. It was held that taxes on rents or income of real estate are direct taxes. Taxes on personal property or on the income of personal property are likewise direct taxes. The tax imposed by sections 27 to 37, inclusive, of the act of 1894, so far as it falls on the income of real estate and of personal property, being a direct tax within the meaning of the Constitution, and therefore unconstitutional and void, because not apportioned according to representation, all those sections, constituting an entire scheme of taxation, are necessarily invalid. Dissenting opinions were rendered by Justices Harlan, Brown, Jackson, and White.

Independence Day, order regarding celebration of, VIII, 494.

Independence, Declaration of. (See Declaration of Independence.)

Independent State of Kongo. (See Kongo Free State.)

Independent Telegraph Co., military possession of, to be taken, order regarding, X, 109.

Independent Treasury. (See Subtreasury System.)

India.—An extensive region of southern Asia. The name India is and has been used with very different meanings. Passing over its ancient use and signification, the name is now ordinarily used to mean British India, or the Indian Empire, officially called India. This includes a large number of provinces, or minor divisions, having an area of about 964,992 sq. miles and a population (1891) of 221,172,952. In addition to the above there are the feudatory native states, with an area of about 595,000 sq. miles and a population of about 66,000,000. The most important exports of India are wheat, rice, cotton, opium, oil seeds, jute, hides, tea, and indigo. The government is vested in a secretary of state for India (in London), with a council of about 10 (also in London). The government is administered by a Governor General appointed by the Crown, a council, with a centralized system of governors for provinces, and commissioners and deputy commissioners for divisions and districts. The administration was transferred to the Crown in 1858, and Queen Victoria was proclaimed Empress of India in 1877.

India, coined silver and products of, referred to, IX, 476.

Indian Affairs, report on, transmitted, X, 62, 68.

Indian Affairs, Bureau of.—A bureau of the Department of the Interior. Previous to 1832 all matters relating to the Indians had been transacted by the clerks of the War Department. By this time, however, the business relations between the Government and the Indians had grown to such proportions that it became necessary to establish a Bureau of Indian Affairs. Accordingly Congress authorized the President to appoint a Commissioner who should have general superintendence, under the Secretary of War, of all Indian affairs. The first Commissioner was appointed July 9, 1832. In 1849 the Department of the Interior was created, and the Bureau of Indian Affairs was transferred to that Department.

Indian Affairs, Bureau of:
Appropriations for, recommended, V, 299; VIII, 69, 190.
Referred to, III, 428; VI, 392; VIII, 519; IX, 453, 545.
Commission to cooperate with, appointed and regulations for, VII, 23.
Contracts, purchases, etc., for, referred to, VII, 260.
Creation of new office in, recommended, VIII, 72.
Discussed by President—
Arthur, VIII, 54.
Cleveland, VIII, 518; IX, 545.
Harrison, Benj., IX, 326.
Employees in Indian service referred to, VII, 357, 360.
Expenditures of, referred to, II, 81, 113; VII, 260; VIII, 357.
Irregularities in, referred to, IV, 48.
Medical inspector for Indian service, bill creating office of, referred to, VIII, 69.
System of, recommendations regarding, VI, 132, 187, 250; VIII, 54, 357.

Indian Affairs, Commissioner of:
Bill to increase salary of, referred to, VIII, 72.
Commission to perform duties of Assistant Commissioner and, recommended, IX, 736.
Letter from, regarding salary of officers referred to, III, 590.

Indian Agencies:
Appointment and transfer of, V, 19.
Buildings for Mescalero Agency, N. Mex., recommended, VIII, 105.
Deficiency in supplies at Red Cloud Agency, Nebr., VII, 358, 359.
Discussed, VIII, 356, 519.
Removal of, from Fort Wayne, Ind., referred to, II, 401.

Indian Agents:
Appropriation for, recommended, V, 307.
Detail of army officers for, recommended, IX, 544.

M P--VOL X—27

Indian Agents—Continued.
Influence and disposition of, discussed, VIII, 356.
Term of office of, referred to, VIII, 90.

Indian Appropriation Bill, necessity of passing, discussed, VII, 79.

Indian Commission to perform duties of Assistant Commissioner and Commissioner of Indian Affairs recommended, IX, 736.

Indian Commissioners, appointment of 6, recommended, VIII, 357, 520.

Indian Commissioners, Board of:
Appropriation for defraying expenses of, recommended, VIII, 69.
Report of, referred to, VII, 122, 360; VIII, 79, 156, 387.

Indian Commissions. (See Commissions.)

Indian Corn, introduction of products of, into Europe discussed, IX, 329.

Indian Depredations (see also Indian Wars):
Abuses in prosecution of claims for, IX, 453.
Referred to, I, 82, 95, 104, 126, 130, 171; III, 428; IV, 560.

Indian Hostilities. (See Indian Wars.)

Indian Inspectors, term of office of, referred to, VIII, 90.

Indian Lands. (See Lands, Indian.)

Indian Reservations:
Allotment of lands in severalty to Indians—
Act providing for, etc., IX, 63.
Discussed, VIII, 796; IX, 45, 117, 202, 326, 544.
Recommended, I, 576; VII, 576, 624; VIII, 56, 143, 192, 196, 370, 521.
Remonstrances against, VIII, 82.
Survey necessary for, VIII, 358.
Crimes committed on, statute for punishment of, recommended, VIII, 250.
Disposition of damaged timber on, referred to, VIII, 76.
Establishment of, opposed, IX, 48.
Improvement of condition of Indians on, referred to, VIII, 69.
Proceeds of, bill providing for use of, for Indians, VIII, 388.
Reduction of—
Bill providing for, discussed, VIII, 595.
Discussed, IX, 117, 202.
Negotiations regarding, VIII, 595.
Restoration of, to public domain, order regarding, declared void, VIII, 305.
Discussed, VIII, 358.
Right of way for railroads through—
Acts regarding, vetoed, VIII, 472, 693; IX, 571, 576, 580, 582.
Compensation to be paid for, referred to, VIII, 593.
Referred to, VIII, 777.
Timber depredations on, referred to, VIII, 78, 188.
Unauthorized occupancy of, proclamation against, VIII, 307.
Chehalis, allotment of lands in severalty to Indians on, referred to, VIII, 192.
Cheyenne and Arapahoe—
Opened to settlement by proclamation, IX, 275.
Appropriation for, recommended, IX, 203.

Indians.—When Europeans first came to this hemisphere they called the natives Indians on the supposition that the land was India. This was soon found to be an error, but the name Indians has continued to be applied to the people of both North and South America. As the Indians were mostly barbarous, and as those who were partially civilized possessed no written records or reliable tradition, their origin and history became a problem for the ethnologist. Morton makes 2 grand divisions of the South American Indians—the Toltecan nations, who were civilized, and the barbarous tribes, the former embracing the ancient Mexicans and Peruvians and the latter all the uncivilized tribes. The Mayas of Yucatan built pyramids and had a literature. Some ethnologists claim that the American Indian is a distinct type of the human race, as indigenous to this continent as its fauna and flora, and as having subsisted as such from the earliest ages of the world. Others regard them as a branch of the Mongolian race which, at a remote period of their history, wandered from Asia to the American continent, and there remained for thousands of years separated from the rest of mankind and passing through various stages of progress or retrogression. Dr. Robert Brown says in his Races of Mankind : "Not only are the western Indians in appearance very like their nearest neighbors, the northeastern Asiatics, but in language and tradition it is confidently affirmed there is a blending of the people. The Eskimo on the American and the Tchuktchis on the Asiatic side understand each other perfectly." Anthropologists also admit that between the various tribes from the Arctic Sea to Cape Horn there is greater uniformity of physical structure and personal characteristics than is seen in any other quarter of the globe. Though the red men of Canada differ in many respects from the wandering Guranis of Paraguay and both from the Azteca of Mexico, all exhibit strong evidence of belonging to the same great branch of the human family, notwithstanding the wide diversity of language. Generally the physical characteristics are a low, broad forehead; full face; back of head flattened; powerful jaws; full lips; prominent cheek bones; dark, deeply set eyes; hair long and wavy; no beard; copper-colored skin; erect and slender figure; about the average in height. In Mexico and Peru the aboriginal inhabitants were a rich, powerful, and highly civilized people, dwelling in walled cities. They had fixed laws and were acquainted with some of the higher arts and the sciences. Taking similarity of language as a basis of grouping, the Indians of North America were divided into some 60 linguistic stocks. These stocks were composed of many tribes of varying dialects, and tribes sometimes united temporarily for purposes of offense or defense into confederations. The most important of these stocks were the Eskimaun, Athapascan, Algonquian, Siouan, Iroquoian, Salishan, Shoshonean, Muskhogean, Caddoan, Yuman, Piman, Sahaptian, Kiowa and Timuquanan. The different tribes wi which the United States have had dealings a mentioned under separate headings. T total number of _ndians in the United Stat at this time is about 300,000.

Innis, James, commissioner appointed by United States under treaty with Great Britain, I, 196.

Innocuous Desuetude.—This phrase occurs in a message of President Cleveland Mar. 1, 1886 (VIII, 381), when he was discussing laws on the subject of suspensions from office. The Senate had asked him for his reasons for suspending certain officials.

Insane Asylum. (See Government Hospital for Insane.)

Insane Persons, act making grant of lands to States for benefit of, vetoed, V, 247.

Insolvent Debtors. (See Bankruptcy; Debtors, Insolvent.)

Inspection, Sanitary. (See Animal Industry discussed.)

Inspector-General of Army, bill relative to department of, returned, VIII, 268.

Inspector, Revenue. (See Revenue Inspector.)

Institutions of Learning. (See Education; Military Academy; National University; Naval Academy; Seminaries of Learning.)

Insurance Companies, American:
Exclusion of, from Germany referred to, IX, 629, 667, 751.
Treatment of, in Russia discussed, IX, 529.

Insurrections. (See Illegal Combinations.)

Intercontinental Railroad:
Connection of Mexican railway system with, discussed, IX, 112.
Survey for, discussed, IX, 187.
To connect systems of North America with those of southern continent recommended, IX, 69.

Intercourse, Foreign:
Act providing for expenses of, approved, referred to, X, 30.
Appropriations for, I, 198, 460.
Reduction in, discussed, VII, 402.
Unexpended, VI, 630.
Contingent expenses—
Funds on deposit with Baring Brothers & Co. for, VI, 630.
Public interests demand that confidential items be not published, IV, 431.
Expenditures for, account of, transmitted, X, 15, 17.
Provision for, recommended, I, 66, 198.
Requests of House and Senate for information regarding, refused, I, 194; IV, 431, 566, 602; V, 154, 155, 159; IX, 669.
Referred to, IV, 679.

Interior Department Building:
Fire in, discussed and recommendations regarding, VII, 453, 455.
Fireproof roof for, recommended, VIII, 103.

Interior, Department of the.—One of the Executive Departments of the Government. It was created by act of Congress approved Mar. 3, 1849, and in the original law was called the Home Department. Its head is the Secretary of the Interior, who is appointed by the President and has a seat in the Cabinet. The Department has charge of all public business relating to pensions, patents, public lands, Indians, railroads, education, national parks, the Geological Survey, the census, certain public documents,

judicial accounts, mines and mining, etc. Heads of the Department since its organization have been: Thomas Ewing, Ohio; Alexander H. H. Stuart, Virginia; Robert McClelland, Michigan; Jacob Thompson, Mississippi; Caleb B. Smith, Indiana; John P. Usher, Indiana; James Harlan, Iowa; Orville H. Browning, Illinois; Jacob D. Cox, Ohio; Columbus Delano, Ohio; Zachariah Chandler, Michigan; Carl Schurz, Missouri; Samuel J. Kirkwood, Iowa; Henry M. Teller, Colorado; Lucius Q. C. Lamar, Mississippi; William F. Vilas, Wisconsin; John W. Noble, Missouri; Hoke Smith, Georgia; David R. Francis, Missouri; Cornelius N. Bliss, New York; Ethan A. Hitchcock, Missouri.

Interior, Department of the:
Additional room for clerical force in, recommended, VIII, 74.
Affairs of, discussed, IX, 325.
Appointments and removals in, referred to, VI, 471.
Establishment of, referred to, V, 168.
Increased number of law clerks in, recommended, VIII, 92.
Libraries in, consolidation of, referred to, VIII, 151.
Separation of Patent Office from, recommended, VII, 201, 252.
Transfer of—
Pension Bureau from, to War Department recommended, VII, 106.
Territorial affairs from State Department to, recommended, VII, 106, 191.

Internal Improvements.—There being no provision in the Constitution for internal improvements, the matter has always been a subject of dispute. Since Aug. 7, 1789, Congress has regularly appropriated money for such improvements as lie strictly within the Federal jurisdiction—harbors, beacons, buoys, light-houses, piers, etc. Mar. 29, 1806, Congress authorized the President to appoint 3 commissioners to lay out a national road from Cumberland, on the Potomac, to the Ohio River, and appropriated $30,000 for the expenses (I, 418). The road was to pass through several States. A national road was also projected through Georgia, with New Orleans as its proposed western terminus. Mar. 3, 1817, President Madison vetoed a bill to set apart the bonus and Government dividends of the national bank as a fund "for constructing roads and canals and improving the navigation of water courses," on the ground that Congress had no constitutional power to expend public revenues for such purposes (I, 584). May 4, 1822, President Monroe vetoed an appropriation for preserving and repairing the Cumberland road, on the same general ground (II, 142). President Jackson also vetoed several bills providing for internal improvements (II, 483, 493, 638; III, 118). Mar. 14, 1818, the House of Representatives passed a resolution declaring that Congress had the power to appropriate money for the construction of roads and canals and for the improvement of water courses. Mar. 3, 1823, the first appropriation for the improvement of rivers and harbors passed Congress. In April, 1824, $30,000 was appropriated for the survey of such roads and canals as the President should deem of national importance, and the act of Mar. 3, 1825, authorized the subscription of $300,000 to the stock of the Chesapeake and Delaware Canal. River and harbor bills have been vetoed by Presidents Tyler (IV, 330), Polk (IV, 460), Pierce (V, 256), Grant (VII, 382), Arthur (VIII, 120), and Cleveland (IX, 677). Appropriations for the improvement of rivers and harbors have sometimes been attached to general appropriation bills. Appropriations for rivers and harbors have increased from $2,000,000 in 1870 to nearly $30,000,000 in 1896. Not all of the latter sum was to be expended in one year.

Internal Improvements (see also Rivers and Harbors):
Acts on subject of, vetoed by President—
Arthur, VIII, 120.
  Discussed, VIII, 137.
Cleveland, IX, 677.
Grant, VII, 382.
Jackson, II, 483, 493, 508, 638; III, 118.
Madison, I, 584.
Monroe, II, 142.
Pierce, V, 256, 257, 386, 387, 388.
Polk, IV, 460, 610.
Tyler, IV, 330.
Aid for, should be by separate bills, VIII, 138.
Appropriations for, II, 483.
Applied, II, 306.
On the Lakes referred to, V, 424.
Recommended, II, 389; V, 91; VIII, 59.
Approval of bill for, explained, II, 483. (See also Rivers and Harbors.)
Board of Engineers for, examination made by, II, 284, 307.
Constitutional amendment relative to, suggested, I, 410, 568; II, 18, 190.
Referred to, II, 217.
Discussed by President—
Adams, J. Q., II, 388, 416.
Arthur, VIII, 59, 120, 137.
Buchanan, V, 599.
Cleveland, IX, 677.
Fillmore, V, 90.
Grant, VII, 382.
Jackson, II, 451, 483, 508, 601, 638; III, 118.
Madison, I, 584.
Monroe, II, 18, 142, 144.
Pierce, V, 218, 256, 257, 386, 387, 388.
Polk, IV, 460, 610, 656.
Tyler, IV, 330.
Expenditures for public works in States and Territories referred to, VI, 393.
Information regarding construction of roads transmitted, II, 25.
Lands granted in aid of, II, 466; VI, 453; VII, 111, 252; VIII, 795.
Referred to, II, 306, 311, 313, 343, 421, 427, 533; III, 559; V, 424.
Surveys for, transmitted, II, 464.

Internal Revenue.—That part of the revenue of a country which is derived from duties or taxes on articles manufactured or grown at home,

on licenses, stamps, incomes, etc.—in fact, all revenue not collected on exports or imports. The internal revenue of the United States is derived chiefly from taxes on liquors and tobacco and in cases of emergency upon commercial paper, bank circulation, and upon incomes. The receipts from these various sources have varied from $1,000,000, which figure was first reached in 1801, to $309,000,000, which was reached during the operation of the war tax in 1866. Later the taxes settled down to a normal basis of something like $150,000,000 a year. In 1892 $154,000,000 was collected and in 1896 $146,000,000. During the recent war with Spain this tax was much increased.

Internal Revenue. (See Revenue, Public; Taxation.)

Internal-Revenue Collection Districts, reduction in, VIII, 180.

Internal Revenue, Commissioner of, office of, discussed and recommendations regarding, VII, 31.

Internal-Revenue Stamps referred to, VI, 705.

Internal Taxation. (See Taxation.)

International African Association. (See Kongo Free State.)

International American Bank :
Charter for, recommended by President Benj. Harrison, IX, 125.
Establishment of, recommended by International American Conference, IX, 70.
Discussed, IX, 125.

International American Conference.—Oct. 2, 1889, on the invitation of the United States, an international conference of representatives from the United States and 17 States of Central and South America, also including Mexico and Haiti, assembled at Washington. This conference is known as the Pan-American Congress. The object was to adopt some plan of arbitration for the settlement of disputes and the improvement of business relations and means of communication between the countries. Santo Domingo was the only State to refuse the invitation. Before assembling as a congress the delegates were taken on a tour of the country, to give them an idea of the extent and resources of the United States. After traveling 6,000 miles they returned to Washington. The proceedings of the congress resulted in extending a knowledge of the commercial status of the various countries and the publication of an extensive series of proceedings, debates, and recommendations. The body adjourned Apr. 19, 1890. The Bureau of American Republics (q. v.) was established at the suggestion of this congress.

International American Conference at Washington:
Centennial celebration of discovery of America, resolution of, regarding, IX, 77.
Discussed, VIII, 784; IX, 32, 107.
Extradition, reports on subject of, adopted by, IX, 79.
Importations and exportations, recommendations of, regarding, IX, 71.
Intercontinental railroad, survey of route for, recommended by, IX, 69.

J.

Jackson (Miss.), Battle of.—After the engagement at Raymond, McPherson's column proceeded toward Jackson by way of Clinton, where it destroyed a portion of the railroad to prevent the sending of supplies from the east to Vicksburg. Sherman moved along the Raymond road. May 14, 1863, when within 2 miles of Jackson, both columns met the Confederates whom Gen. Joseph E. Johnston had been collecting in order to reenforce Pemberton at Vicksburg. The combined corps of Sherman and McPherson attacked the small force of Johnston and drove it through Jackson and toward Canton, taking some prisoners. The Union loss was 300. The Confederate loss was 845.

Jamestown (Va.), Battle of.—Early in 1781 Virginia became the chief theater of the operations of the British and American armies. Benedict Arnold, having turned traitor to his country, was sent by Clinton, with 1,600 men, to the James River with orders to lay waste the country and destroy the stores at Richmond. Washington ordered Lafayette, with 1,200 light infantry, to capture Arnold. Lafayette arrived at Richmond Apr. 29, just in time to witness the burning of the extensive tobacco warehouses at Manchester, on the opposite side of the river, by Gen. Philips, who had succeeded Arnold. Philips had 2,000 men. Cornwallis abandoned his unprofitable campaign in the Carolinas and reached Petersburg, Va., May 20, 1781, having nearly 8,000 men. Lafayette, realizing his inability to hold Richmond against this large force, returned northward to the Rappahannock. Here he was joined June 7 by Gen. Wayne with about 800 Continentals. Returning, Lafayette formed a juncture with Steuben June 18, augmenting his force to about 4,000 men. Eluding Tarleton's command, he pursued Cornwallis back toward Richmond, which place the latter evacuated June 20, retiring toward Jamestown. July 6 Lafayette attacked Cornwallis near Green Springs, within a few miles of Jamestown. Lafayette distinguished himself for personal bravery in the fight, but was forced to retire to Malvern Hill. The American casualties were reported as 118 killed, wounded, and missing. The British lost 75.

Japan.—"Land of the Rising Sun." An empire of Asia lying in the Pacific Ocean, east of China, Korea, and Siberia. It consists of 4 principal islands—the main island of Hondo or Nippon, Yezo, Shikoku, Kiushiu—and about 4,000 smaller islands, including the Loochoo and Kurile groups and the island of Formosa, which was acquired from China in 1895. The Japanese people are chiefly engaged in agriculture, but with growing industries of various kinds, Japan exporting largely silk, tea, rice, coal, copper, fish, lacquer, etc. The Government is a limited monarchy, with an Emperor, cabinet, and privy council and an Imperial Parliament consisting of 2 houses. Buddhism and Shintoism are the prevailing religions. The Emperor is called the Mikado, an enlightened sovereign, under whom Japan has made unexampled progress in the arts of Western civilization. Japan, like China, remained isolated from the rest of the world for many centuries. The dynasty of the Mikados, Japanese history informs us, has had a continuous existence since 660 B. C. Authentic history begins about 500 A. D. The Portuguese traded some with Japan between 1540 and 1638. With the exception of a limited trade with the Dutch, Japan held no commercial relations with the rest of the world till an American expedition under Perry, in 1853, forced a treaty upon her. This was followed by treaties with other countries. The area of the Empire is about 162,000 sq. miles, peopled by some 43,000,000 souls. In 1894, in a war with China, the latter was completely defeated on land and sea. The war ended in 1895 with the payment of indemnity by China, the cession of Formosa, and the independence of Korea.

Japan:
Advancement of, discussed, IX, 36, 527, 633.
American citizens in, legislation for protection of, VII, 52.
American citizens selected to serve in offices of importance in Government of, VII, 145.

Japan—Continued.
American interests in, measures for protection of, VII, 52.
American shipmasters warned by proclamation not to anchor at ports of, VI, 514.
Autonomy and independence, claims of, to, supported by United States, VIII, 501.
Cable communication with, recommended, VII, 613.
Citizens of, in China, treatment of, and action of United States officers regarding, inquired into, IX, 560.
Civil war in, neutrality of United States in, VI, 690.
    Proclaimed, VI, 514.
Claims of United States against, VI, 245; VII, 288.
    Indemnities received discussed and recommendations regarding, VI, 376; VII, 289, 568, 609; VIII, 43, 105, 128.
        Returned, VIII, 175.
    Propriety of applying indemnity to education of youths in Japanese language submitted, VII, 289.
Commercial relations with, V, 167, 210, 236; VII, 106, 288, 496.
Constitutional government, establishment of, contemplated by, VIII, 43.
    New constitution promulgated by, IX, 36.
Consular courts and jurisdiction thereof discussed, VII, 118; VIII, 43.
Consuls of United States in, claim of, to exercise judicial powers in certain cases referred to, VI, 694.
Difficulties of, with China discussed, VII, 288.
Fugitive criminals, convention with, for surrender of, VIII, 402, 501.
Legation of United States in, land for, offered by, recommendations regarding, VIII, 236, 275, 338.
Lew Chew Islands, controversy between China and, regarding, VII, 569.
Minister of, to United States received, VIII, 131.
Minister of United States to—
    Appropriation for support of American youths to serve as part of official family of, recommended, VII, 147, 191.
    Claim of, for loss of house by fire, VI, 181.
    Correspondence with, referred to, VII, 50.
    Fireproof building for use of legation recommended, VII, 609.
Naval expedition to, discussed, V, 167, 176, 210, 236, 300.
    Successful termination of, V, 279.
Postal convention with, VII, 249.
Questions with, settled, X, 186.
Referred to, VI, 634, 638.
Relations with, V, 149; VI, 181; IX, 527, 633.
Ships of war built in United States for, referred to, VI, 153.
    Orders regarding clearance of, VI, 242, 243.
        Prohibition of departure of, removed, VI, 341.
Shipwrecked seamen, convention with, for relief of, VII, 609.
Shipwrecks, convention regarding expenses incurred in consequence of, VII, 628.

Jonesboro (Ga.), Battle of.—On the night of Aug. 25, 1864, Gen. Sherman gave up the direct siege of Atlanta and attempted to gain possession of the Macon railroad to the southward. A part of his forces was moved back to the Chattahoochee to the northwest and others pushed southwest. The Army of the Tennessee, under Howard, having destroyed the roads southwest of Atlanta, moved east toward Jonesboro, 20 miles south of Atlanta. Hood, learning of this movement, sent Hardee's corps to defend Jonesboro. When Howard reached the town on the evening of Aug. 30 he found Hardee in possession. The latter attacked Howard on the 31st. After an engagement of 2 hours the Confederates retired with a loss of 1,400 killed and wounded. During the night Hardee retired to Lovejoy. Seeing his position in Atlanta indefensible, Hood on Sept. 1 blew up his magazines and evacuated the city, which was occupied by Gen. Slocum with the Twentieth Army Corps.

Jorgen Lorentzen, The, appropriation for seizure of, recommended, VI, 70.

Josephine, The, referred to, II, 467.

Journals of Congress.—The proceedings of Congress from 1774 to 1788 were first published at Philadelphia. They comprised 13 octavo volumes and were completed in 1788. This is the only record of the Continental Congress and that of the Confederation (except the "Secret Journals"), but contains no debates nor laws, that body being without legislative powers, although it adopted many resolutions, ordinances, and recommendations to the States. These journals were reprinted in Washington in 1823 in 4 octavo volumes. "The Journal, Acts, and Proceedings of the Convention Assembled at Philadelphia which Framed the Constitution of the United States" was published at Boston in 1819. There were also published in Boston in 1821 4 volumes of the "Secret Journals of the Acts and Proceedings of Congress from the First Meeting thereof to the Dissolution of the Confederation by the Adoption of the Constitution of the United States." According to the requirements of the Constitution, the Journals of Congress have been printed each session since its adoption.

Juarez, Benito P., President of Mexico:
Demonstration by Congress of United States of Colombia in honor of, referred to, VI, 377.
Government formed by, discussed, V, 564.
Referred to, V, 644; VI, 379.

Judge-Advocates, Corps of, recommendation regarding, VII, 618.

Judges, Circuit:
Increase in number of, recommended, VII, 501, 574, 622; VIII, 354, 518; IX, 536.
Inequality in amount of labor assigned each, discussed, III, 539.

Judges, District, increase recommended in—
Number of, VIII, 354, 518.
Salaries of, IX, 43, 126.

Judicial Salaries. (See Salaries, Judicial.)

Judiciary.—The Federal judiciary system was modeled after that of Great Britain. When at the beginning of the Revolution the States made their new constitutions they abolished their higher courts and gave their functions to the common-law courts, whose judges were usually appointed by the governors. The first steps toward a Federal judiciary were the commissions which decided land cases between the States. Commissioners of appeal decided prize cases, and in 1781, under the Articles of Confederation, these were erected into a court. The Constitution of 1787 provided for a Supreme Court and such inferior courts as Congress might establish. By the judiciary act of 1789 circuit and district courts were established. In 1891 the circuit court of appeals was added to this system. The Court of Claims, the Court of Private Land Claims, and a system of Territorial courts have also been established by Congress. The judiciary system of the several States is similar in a general way to that of the United States. (See also Courts.)

Judiciary System (see also Justice, Department of):
Act—
Making appropriation for certain judicial expenses vetoed, VII, 541.
Regarding judiciary act vetoed, VI, 646.
Constitutional amendment regarding tenure of office by judiciary of United States recommended, VI, 643, 691.
Extension and revision of, recommended by President—
Adams, John, I, 289, 306.
Adams, J. Q., II, 314, 392.
Arthur, VIII, 142.
Cleveland, VIII, 354, 518; IX, 447, 536.
Jackson, II, 461, 558, 605; III, 117, 177.
Jefferson, I, 331.
Lincoln, VI, 49.
Pierce, V, 217, 232, 292.
Washington, I, 127, 133, 151.
Judicial districts, increase in, recommended, VII, 299.
Misdemeanors, trial of, by United States commissioners recommended, VIII, 354; IX, 447.
Modifications in, recommended, VI, 49.
Witnesses' and jurors' fees referred to, VIII, 143, 183, 249.

Juilliard vs. Greenman.—One of several important legal-tender cases. Juilliard having contracted a sale of cotton for $5,122.90 to Greenman, the latter paid $22.90 in coin (which was accepted) and offered payment of the residue in United States notes. Juilliard refused to accept the notes, demanding gold or silver. The case came before the circuit court for the southern district of New York, which found a verdict for Greenman on the ground that notes issued by the United States are legal tender for payment of any debt. The Supreme Court, Mar. 3, 1884, the case having been appealed to that tribunal on a writ of error, affirmed this judgment, thus establishing the constitutionality of the legal-tender act of Mar. 31, 1862. George F. Edmunds and Benjamin F. Butler appeared as counsel in this cause, the former for plaintiff in error, the latter for defendant.

Justice Gray, in delivering the opinion, stated that the prohibition in the Constitution of the United States to the several States to coin money, emit bills of credit, or make anything but gold and silver coin a legal tender for debts does not deny to Congress either of these powers. These are powers incident to sovereignty, and the impressing upon Treasury notes the quality of being legal tender in payment of private debts is an appropriate means, conducive and plainly adapted to the execution of the undoubted powers of Congress, consistent with the letter and spirit, and therefore within the meaning, of the Constitution. The wisdom and expediency of such meaning is a political question to be determined by Congress, and not a judicial question to be afterwards passed upon by the courts. Justice Field filed a dissenting opinion.

Jules et Marie, The, collision with United States steamer *San Jacinto*, appropriation to former recommended, VI, 142.

Junket.—A word applied to any feast or merry-making, convivial entertainment, or picnic. Politically, any trip, excursion, or entertainment by an official at public expense under the guise of public service. The form of a junket is usually a legislative investigation requiring travel to various points and large hotel bills.

Jurors, fees of, referred to, VIII, 143, 183, 249.

Jury.—A certain number of men selected according to law and sworn to inquire into or to determine facts concerning a cause or an accusation submitted to them and to declare the truth according to the evidence adduced. The custom of trying accused persons before a jury as practiced in this country and England is the natural outgrowth of rudimentary forms of trial in vogue among our Anglo-Saxon ancestors. The ancient Romans also had a form of trial before a presiding judge and a body of *judices*. The right of trial by jury is guaranteed by the Constitution in all criminal cases and at common law in cases where the amount in dispute exceeds $20. A petit or trial jury consists of 12 men selected by lot from among all the citizens residing within the jurisdiction of the court. Their duty is to determine questions of fact in accordance with the weight of testimony presented and report their finding to the presiding judge. An impartial jury is assured by the practice of drawing by lot and then giving the accused the right to dismiss a certain number without reason and certain others for good cause. Each of the jurymen must meet certain legal requirements as to capacity in general and fitness for the particular case upon which he is to sit, and must take an oath to decide without prejudice and according to testimony presented. A coroner's jury or jury of inquest is usually composed of from 7 to 15 persons summoned to inquire into the cause of sudden or unexplained deaths. (See also Grand Jury.)

Jury System discussed, I, 331.

Jussen, Edmund, act for relief of, vetoed, VII, 214.

Justice, Department of.—One of the eight Executive Departments of the Government. Sept. 24, 1789, Congress created the office of Attorney-General, and 2 days later Edmund Randolph, of Virginia, was appointed to fill it. The duties of the Attorney-General were at first light, and it was not till 1858 that an assistant was appointed. All United States district attorneys and marshals were placed under the supervision of the Attorney-General in 1861. Second and third assistants were attached to the office in 1868 and 1871. June 22, 1870, the Department of Justice was created. (See also Attorney-General.)

Justice, Department of (see also Judiciary System):

Act making appropriation for certain judicial expenses vetoed, VII, 541.

Appropriations for, recommended, VII, 522, 573.

Building for, recommended, X, 196.

Discussed by President—

Cleveland, VIII, 353, 793; IX, 447, 536.

Grant, VII, 199.

Harrison, Benj., IX, 115, 197, 320.

Issuance of commissions to officials by Attorney-General recommended, VII, 109.

Legal business of Government, manner of conducting, referred to, V, 238, 292.

Recommendation that Attorney-General be placed on footing with heads of other Executive Departments, I, 577; II, 314, 453; IV, 415.

Transfer of Patent Office from State Department to, recommended, IV, 415.

K.

Kabler, James E., act granting pension to, vetoed, VIII, 711.

Kalakaua, David, King of Hawaiian Islands:

Coronation of, discussed, VIII, 174.

Death of, in United States discussed, IX, 188.

Visit of, to United States, VIII, 43.

Kane, Thomas L., mentioned, V, 505.

Kansas.—One of the United States; nicknames, "The Garden State," "The Sunflower State," etc.; motto, "Ad astra per aspera" ("To the stars through difficulties"). It is situated in the central part of the Union and extends from lat. 37° to 40° north and from long. 94° 38' to 102° west. Kansas is bounded on the north by Nebraska, on the east by Missouri (separated in part by the Missouri River), on the south by Oklahoma and the Indian Territory, and on the west by Colorado. It was a part of the Louisiana Purchase and was made a Territory in 1854. The Topeka constitution, prohibiting slavery, was framed in 1855 and the Lecompton constitution, which sanctioned slavery, in 1857. A civil war broke out between the adherents of these two constitutions. Finally, in 1859 the Wyandotte constitution, forbidding slavery, was adopted. The State was admitted to the Union Jan. 29, 1861. The soil is generally fertile. The chief mineral is coal and the leading industries agriculture and stock raising. Area, 82,080 sq. miles; population (1890), 1,427,096. (See also Lecompton Constitution; Topeka Constitution; Wyandotte Constitution.)

Kansas:

Act—

For sale of Indian reservation in, VIII, 69.

To provide for sale of New York Indian lands in, vetoed, VIII, 653.

Admission of, into Union discussed, V, 449, 471, 497.

Recommended, V, 360, 478.

Affairs of, referred to, V, 418, 464, 465.

Boundary line of, survey of, recommended, V, 340.

Chief justice of, functions of, referred to, V, 425.

Constitutional convention in, discussed, V, 471, 499.

Disorders and revolutions in, discussed, V, 340, 352, 382; V, 404, 449, 471, 497, 646.

Proclamation against, V, 390.

Election in, and qualifications for electors discussed, V, 352, 449, 471, 497, 646.

Expenditures for persons called into service of United States in, V, 420, 421.

Fortifications in Lawrence, referred to, VI, 696.

Governmental organization in, disturbed, V, 352, 361, 365, 404, 449, 471, 497, 646.

Proclamation against unlawful combinations, V, 390.

Indian refugees in, referred to, VI, 209.

Joint resolution authorizing grant of lands to, for benefit of agriculture, etc., vetoed, VIII, 723.

Meetings in, interfered with by Army, V, 382.

Memorial from citizens of, regarding creation of new territory, etc., V, 580.

Military forces of United States sent to, referred to, VII, 59.

Relief for suffering people in—

Recommended, V, 653.

Referred to, VII, 318.

Slavery in, discussed, V, 431, 450, 471, 497.

Soldiers employed in, to arrest violators of law referred to, V, 375.

Troops of, treatment of, captured by insurgents referred to, VI, 197.

Wea trust lands in, referred to, VI, 199.

Kansas Aid Society.—An organization to aid immigration into Kansas. Under the provisions of the Kansas-Nebraska act, passed by Congress in May, 1854, the question of slavery in Kansas was left to the residents of the State for settlement, on the principle of local option or "squatter sovereignty." An immigrant aid association, which had been already formed in Massachusetts for the purpose, began sending antislavery settlers into the new Territory to forestall its settlement by slaveholders. Similar societies were organized in July, 1854, in New York and Connecticut. The settlers were provided with ample funds and means of defense against the settlers from the slaveholding States of the South. Meantime slavery advocates from Missouri were passing over the line and preempting large tracts of fertile lands. For 4 years the conflict for supremacy raged between the two parties, the antislavery party finally prevailing.

Kansas City, Fort Scott and Gulf Railway Co., act to authorize construction of railway through Indian Territory by, returned, VIII, 401.

Kansas City, Oklahoma and Pacific Railway Co., act authorizing construction and operation of railway by, through Indian reservations vetoed, IX, 576.

Kansas Indians:

Lands of, accounts for advertising sale of, VIII, 77.

Treaty with, II, 317, 323, 346, 477; IV, 423; V, 578; VI, 76, 212, 519; VII, 11.

Withdrawn, VII, 47.

Kansas-Nebraska Act.—By the Missouri Compromise of 1820 slavery was prohibited in all the region lying north of lat. 36° 30' with the exception of that lying in the State of Missouri. As a result of the Mexican War the limits of the United States were extended from the one hundredth meridian westward to the Pacific and southward to lat. 32° 30' north. By the Kansas-Nebraska Act, passed by Congress in May, 1854, Kansas and Nebraska were separated and organized into 2 distinct Territories, and the question of slavery was left to the people for settlement. As both these States lie north of the line above which slavery was prohibited by the Missouri Compromise, the passage of the bill practically repealed that measure. The status of Nebraska as a free State was soon determined, but the struggle in Kansas was long and bitter. It disrupted the Whig party and led to the establishment of the Republican party, and was an important link in the chain of events that brought on the Civil War.

Kansas-Nebraska Act:

Discussed, V, 451.

Referred to, V, 499.

Kanso, Straits of, vessels of United States interfered with by British vessels in, referred to, VII, 114.

Karstetter, Mary, acts to pension, vetoed, VIII, 469, 821.

Kaskaskia Indians. (See Illinois Indians.)

Kaskaskia Indians:

Lands—

Ceded to, I, 365.

Ceded to United States by, I, 359, 363.

Treaty with, I, 359, 363, 365; II, 47; V, 242; VI, 69, 518.

Kasson, John A., report of, on commercial relations with Cuba, X, 152.

Ka-ta-ka Indians, treaty with, III, 395.

Kautz, August V., member of court to try assassins of President Lincoln, etc., VI, 336.

Kaw Indians. (See Kansas Indians.)

Kearny, Philip, major-general in Army, nomination of, and reasons therefor, VI, 161.

Kearsarge, The.—A United States corvette built at Portsmouth, N. H., in 1861. She carried 163 officers and men, four 32-pounder and one 28-pounder guns, and two 11-inch rifles. She was commanded by Capt. John A. Winslow. Her greatest service was the sinking of the Confederate cruiser *Alabama*, off Cherbourg, France, June 19, 1864. The *Alabama* had done much damage to United States commerce, and the *Kearsarge* had been sent to sink her. When the *Kearsarge* opened fire her superiority in point of management and gunnery was at once apparent. One of her shells cut off the *Alabama's* mizzenmast, and another exploded, killing half her crew. Feb. 2, 1894, the *Kearsarge* was wrecked on Roncador Reef, in the Caribbean Sea. (See also Alabama Claims.)

Kearsarge, The, destruction of the *Alabama* by, referred to, VI, 256.

Keiley, A. M. :

Minister to Austria-Hungary, appointment of, and refusal of Government to receive, discussed, VIII, 325.

Minister to Italy and Austria-Hungary, appointment of, referred to, VIII, 366.

Keim, D. B. R., report of, on consular affairs and amount paid to, referred to, VII, 169, 206, 207.

Keith, Charles B., treaty with Indians concluded by, VI, 83.

Kelley, Ellen, act granting pension to, vetoed, VIII, 738.

Kelley, Mr., commissioner to investigate affairs of New York custom-house, IV, 152.

Kellogg, William P. :

Candidate for governor of Louisiana, election disturbances discussed. (See Louisiana, elections in.)

Mentioned, VII, 223.

Kelly, Daniel H., act to place name of, upon muster roll of Second Tennessee Infantry vetoed, VII, 432.

Kenesaw Mountain (Ga.), Battle of.—Between the 1st and 6th of June, 1864, Sherman gradually moved his army so as to envelop Allatoona Pass. This compelled Johnston to withdraw his army from its strongly intrenched positions at New Hope Church and Acworth. Allatoona Pass was then made a depot of supplies, and June 8 Gen. Blair joined Sherman with 2 divisions of the Seventeenth Corps and a brigade of cavalry, raising his effective force to its original strength of 98,000. Johnston's force was 62,000. Sherman then advanced toward Kenesaw Mountain, and on June 14 an artillery duel took place in which the Confederate General Polk was killed. On the 15th and 17th of June the Confederates retired from Pine Mountain and Lost Mountain, and thoroughly intrenched themselves on Kenesaw Mountain. June 27 two assaults on the Confederate position were simultaneously made, one by Thomas and the other by McPherson. Both were repulsed. Nothing now remained for Sherman but to turn the position. July 2 the whole army was put in motion toward the Chattahoochee. The Confederates immediately abandoned their position on the mountain and retired to the river. Sherman's loss at the attacks on Kenesaw Mountain aggregated 3,000 men, including Generals Harker and McCook. The Confederate loss was 630.

Kennebec Purchase.—In 1628 the council for New England granted to William Bradford and other Plymouth colonists a tract of territory along the Kennebec and Cobbiseecontee rivers for fishing purposes. This was sold in 1661 to Tyng and others, and has since been known as the Kennebec Purchase.

Kennon, Beverly, court-martial of, referred to, D, 242.

Kent, Edward, correspondence regarding northeastern boundary. (See Northeastern Boundary.)

Kentucky.—One of the United States; nickname, "The Corn Cracker State;" motto, "United we stand, divided we fall." The name is said to mean in the language of the Indians "Dark and bloody ground." It lies between lat. 36° 30′ and 39° 6′ north and long. 82° and 89° 38′ west. It is bounded on the north by Ohio, Indiana, and Illinois (separated by the Ohio River), on the east by West Virginia (separated by the Big Sandy River) and Virginia, on the south by Tennessee, and on the west by Missouri (separated by the Mississippi River). A vast tract of land, including what is now Kentucky, was ceded to Great Britain by the Iroquois Indians in 1684. Kentucky was explored by Daniel Boone in 1769, and the first settlement was made at Harrodsburg in 1774. It was made a county of Virginia in 1776 and admitted to the Union June 1, 1792. It took a distinguished part in the War of 1812, the Mexican War, and the Civil War. Although a slave State, Kentucky wished to preserve neutrality in the latter war. It is the first State in the production of tobacco and hemp. Area, 40,400 sq. miles; population (1890), 1,858,635.

Kentucky (see also Louisville):

Admission of, into Union referred to, I, 81, 84, 86.

Amendment to Constitution, application to Congress to call convention for proposing, V, 663.

Arrests in, referred to, VI, 77.

Constitution adopted by, referred to, I, 128, 130, 132.

Digest of decisions of Supreme Court asked for, IV, 277.

Letter to governor of, respecting militia for suppression of troubles on Mississippi River, X, 101.

Martial law established in, and writ of *habeas corpus* suspended by proclamation, VI, 219.

Proclamation revoking, VI, 331.

Militia of, commended for Indian service, I, 104.

Officers of, attempt to bring Aaron Burr to justice, I, 415.

Ratification of amendment to Federal Constitution by, referred to, I, 259, 260.

Kentucky Resolutions.—Nine resolutions prepared by Thomas Jefferson and passed by the Kentucky legislature in 1798. These and the Virginia Resolutions were the outgrowth of a feeling that the Federal party, in passing the alien and sedition laws, was making an illegitimate use of the power granted to the Government by the Constitution. The resolutions declared that the Union was not based on the "principle of unlimited submission to the

General Government;" that the Constitution was a compact to which each State was a party as related to its fellow States, and that in all cases not specified in the compact each party had a right to judge for itself, as well of infractions as of the mode and measure of redress. They then proceeded to set forth the unconstitutionality of the alien and sedition laws and invited other States to join in declaring them void. A tenth resolution was passed the following year declaring that nullification of a Federal law by a State was the rightful remedy for Federal usurpation of authority. Upon these resolutions were based in part the doctrines of nullification and secession.

Kernan, John D., member of Strike Commission, IX, 551.

Kernstown (Va.), Battle of. (See Winchester (Va.), Battles of.)

Kerr, J. Bozman, chargé d'affaires in Nicaragua, mentioned, V, 151, 159.

Kerr, Joseph, commissioner for Cumberland road, I, 418.

Kerr, Michael C., Speaker of House of Representatives, death of, announced, VII, 398.

Kettle Creek (Ga.), Battle of.—Feb. 14, 1779, Col. Andrew Pickens, of South Carolina, and Col. Dooley, of Georgia, with 300 men, surprised Col. Boyd's provincials on the north side of Kettle Creek, in Wilkes County, Ga. A short skirmish ensued, in which Boyd's tories were routed with inconsiderable loss on either side.

Keweenaw, The. (See *Baltimore*, The.)

Key, Thomas M., interview with Gen. Cobb regarding exchanging of prisoners of war, VI, 258.

Key West, Fla.:
Blockade of port of, removed by proclamation, VI, 281.

Fever prevalent at, II, 213.

Fortifications and establishment of naval depot at, referred to, X, 64.

Health of squadron at, referred to, II, 258.

Keyes, Stephen, collector of port, nomination of, I, 99.

Keys, Crawford, trial and conviction of, for murder of Emory Smith, and subsequent release of, referred to, VI, 461.

Khedive. (See Egypt.)

Kickapoo Indians.—A tribe of the Algonquian stock of Indians, who early inhabited the valleys of the Ohio and Illinois rivers. The name was used by the Indians to describe smooth running rivers without rapids. In 1779 they allied themselves with the Americans against the British, but later turned and fought the new government until they were subjugated by Wayne in 1795, when they ceded part of their lands to the whites. In 1802, 1803, and 1804 the Kickapoos ceded more territory. They joined Tecumseh and fought against the whites at Tippecanoe in 1811. They united with the British in the War of 1812, but were badly defeated. By treaties made in 1815, 1816, and 1819 they ceded still more of their territory. Portions of them became roving bands. Some of them were removed to Kansas, and afterwards a portion of the tribe migrated to Mex-

ico, whence about 400 were in 1873 returned by the Government and placed upon a reservation in the Indian Territory. In 1894 their number in the United States and Mexico was estimated at 762.

Kickapoo Indians:
Agreement between Cherokee Commission and, IX, 203, 214.

Settlement of estates of deceased, referred to, VIII, 70, 189, 368.

Treaty with, I, 363, 479, 569, 581, 582; II, 66, 81, 85, 610; V, 240; VI, 83, 518.

Kidnapping of American child in Mexico referred to, VI, 374.

Kiel Canal, encomiums bestowed on American vessels at opening of, IX, 630.

Kik-ái-llus Indians, treaty with, V, 379.

Kilbourn vs. Thompson.—A case decided by the Supreme Court in 1880 denying the right of the Senate or House of Representatives to punish anyone except their own members for contempt of their orders. Kilbourn was summoned as a witness before the House in 1876 and required to answer questions as to his private business and to produce certain papers. He refused, whereupon Sergeant-at-Arms Thompson was ordered to imprison him in the jail of the District of Columbia. He remained in prison 45 days. He was then released on a writ of *habeas corpus.* He brought suit for false imprisonment against Thompson and the members of the committee who caused his arrest. The court decided that the House might punish its own members for disorderly conduct, but that the Constitution did not give either branch of Congress general authority to punish for contempt. It was held, Justice Miller delivering the opinion, that neither House of Congress is a part of any court of general jurisdiction. Judgment was given for Kilbourn, which was paid by an appropriation by Congress.

Kimball, James P., Director of Mint, nomination of, and reasons therefor, VIII, 367.

Kimberly, Lewis A., dispatched to Samoa, VIII, 805.

King, John H., acts and proceedings of, declared null and void, VI, 350.

King, Jonas, difficulties of, with Greece referred to, V, 240, 295.

King, Rufus, special minister plenipotentiary to negotiate treaty with Russia, nomination of, I, 282.

King, Sam. W., correspondence regarding Dorr's Rebellion, IV, 286, 290, 292, 293, 294, 298, 299, 303.

King, Thomas B., special agent to California, V, 27.
Report of, referred to, V, 41.

King, William R., Vice-President, death of, announced and honors to be paid memory of, V, 205.
Referred to, V, 225.

King Philip's War.—Philip, son of Massasoit, sachem of the Wampanoag Indians and a friend to the early settlers of Plymouth, determined to drive away or kill all the European settlers in his territory. His camp was **at**

Mount Hope, R. I., and his first blow was struck at Swansea, Mass., July 4, 1675. The settlers took up arms in defense and drove the Indians to the more remote settlements. Philip was reenforced by other tribes, but the Indians suffered many defeats and were finally subdued. Philip was shot in a swamp by a treacherous Indian and his head was carried in triumph to Plymouth. His son, the last of the line, was sold into slavery and sent to Bermuda.

Kings Mountain (S. C.), Battle of.—Early in October, 1780, Cornwallis sent Colonels Tarleton and Ferguson from Charleston, to invade North Carolina, enroll local militia, and compel the allegiance of the people. On the 6th Ferguson, finding himself hotly pursued by the Americans, took up a strong position on Kings Mountain, near the boundary line between North and South Carolina. The next day his army, about 1,500 strong, was attacked by about the same number of American militia under command of Colonels Shelby, Campbell, Cleveland, McDowell, Sevier, and Williams. After a desperate struggle, lasting an hour, in which Ferguson was killed, the British force surrendered. The casualties on the British side were 387 killed or so badly wounded as to be left upon the field and about 1,200 taken prisoners. The Americans lost 28 men killed and 60 wounded. Fifteen hundred muskets and other arms fell into the hands of the Americans.

Kinney, Ann, act granting pension to, vetoed, VIII, 480.

Kiowa Indians:

Agreement between Cherokee Commission and, IX, 333.

Claim of, discussed, IX, 327.

Treaty with, III, 395; V, 229; VI, 193, 598.

Kirby, Edmund, mentioned, III, 96.

Kirkpatrick, John S., act granting pension to, vetoed, VIII, 455.

Kitchen Cabinet.—A name applied to a group of intimate political friends of Andrew Jackson who, it was charged, had more influence over his official actions than his constitutional advisers. They were Gen. Duff Green, editor of the United States Telegraph, published at Washington as the organ of the Administration; Maj. William B. Lewis, of Nashville, Tenn., Second Auditor of the Treasury; Isaac Hill, editor of the New Hampshire Patriot, and Amos Kendall, of Kentucky, Fourth Auditor of the Treasury.

Kittery, Me., dry dock at, IV, 564.

Klamath Indians.—A tribe of Indians, numbering some 600, distributed among 11 settlements in the Klamath Reservation, in Oregon. They formerly occupied a part of California, but the influx of whites led to trouble in 1851. Peace was soon restored. In 1864 they ceded large tracts of land to the Government and settled on a reservation.

Klamath Indians, treaty with, VI, 269.

Knight, Richard R., act to pension, returned, IX, 566.

Knights of Labor.—A secret order of workingmen, founded by Uriah S. Stevens in Philadelphia in 1869, and formally organized as a national body, with district and local assemblies, in 1871. It was not until 1881 that the name of the order was made public. At that time nearly all the trades were represented. Each trade formed a district, as nearly as possible. The knights are governed by a general executive board, presided over by a general master workman, which has power to order strikes and boycotts. The membership is about 500,000. They have ordered many strikes among coal miners and railroad operatives. Perhaps the greatest strike ever undertaken by the general assembly of the order was that on the Missouri Pacific system, which failed. A general strike of the district composed of telegraphers also failed. The object of the order is the amelioration of the condition of workingmen.

Know-Nothings, or Know-Nothing Party.—A name applied to the American party, which advocated the control of the Government by native citizens. Its members received the name of "Know-Nothings" because from the time of the organization of the party, in 1853, till 1855 it was a secret fraternity, and when questioned as to its objects or workings its members professed to know nothing about it. The party was powerful for several years. In 1856 it nominated Millard Fillmore for the Presidency. In 1855 a society called the "Know-Somethings" was formed to oppose the Know-Nothings.

Knowlton, Harriet M., act to restore pension to, vetoed, IX, 756.

Knox, Henry:

Commissioner appointed by United States under treaty with Great Britain, I, 196.

Commissioner to treat with Indians, I, 78.

President attended by, meets and advises with Senate respecting treaty with Indians, I, 61, and X, 5.

Proceedings of Cabinet signed by, X, 87.

Knoxville (Tenn.), Siege of.—Sept. 3, 1863, Gen. Burnside, with the Army of the Ohio, occupied Knoxville, Tenn. Upon his advance the Confederate General Buckner evacuated eastern Tennessee and joined Bragg at Chattanooga. Early in November Longstreet, with 16,000 men, was detached from Bragg's army and sent to regain possession of Knoxville. Burnside, with a force of 12,000, met Longstreet at Campbells Station, Tenn., Nov. 16, and retarded his advance long enough to enable him to concentrate his forces at Knoxville. Longstreet then besieged that town. Nov. 18 and 20 he unsuccessfully assaulted the Federal works. Meantime Grant had defeated Bragg at Chattanooga, and Sherman, with 25,000 men, was sent to the relief of Burnside. Dec. 5, 1863, Longstreet, hearing of the approach of Sherman, raised the siege and retreated toward Virginia. Sherman thereupon returned to the line of the Hiawassee, leaving 2 divisions under Gen. Granger to sustain Burnside.

L.

Lafayette, Marquis de—Continued.
Writes concerning claims of—
Baron De Kalb, III, 51.
French citizens, II, 635.

Lafayette, Ind., act for erection of public building at, vetoed, VIII, 569.

Lafitte & Co., memorial from trustees of, presented; III, 431.

Lake Borgne (La.), Battle of.—The British army, repulsed at Baltimore, retired to the island of Jamaica. Being there reenforced by a sufficient number to make a total of above 7,000 men, it sailed from Jamaica Nov. 26, 1814, in Admiral Cochrane's ships, with the intention of capturing New Orleans, and thus securing possession of the Mississippi River and the Territory of Louisiana. Early in December Daniel T. Patterson, commanding the naval station at New Orleans, sent Lieut. Thomas A. C. Jones with 7 small vessels, mounting 23 guns and carrying 182 men, to intercept the British fleet. The British, Dec. 14, 1814, manned 60 barges with 1,200 volunteers from the fleet, under Capt. Lockyer, and sent them out to destroy the American gunboats. The battle took place on Lake Borgne, and lasted almost an hour. Several of the British barges were shattered and sunk and about 300 men killed and wounded. The Americans lost only 6 men killed and 35 wounded. The American gunboats were captured, which gave the British control of Lake Borgne.

Lake Champlain:
Act to authorize construction of bridge across portion of, vetoed, VIII, 475.
Insurgents on, proclamation against, I, 450.
Copy of, transmitted, X, 32.
Victory of American squadron on, I, 549.

Lake Champlain, Battle of.—After arriving at the head of Lake Champlain, Sept. 6, 1814, Governor-General Prevost awaited the cooperation of the British fleet on the lake. Sept. 11 Capt. Downie's squadron rounded Cumberland Head. It consisted of the frigate *Confidence*, brig *Linnet*, sloops *Chub* and *Finch*, and 12 gunboats—in all, 16 vessels, of about 2,402 tons, with 937 men and a total of 92 guns, throwing a broadside of 1,192 pounds. In Cumberland or Plattsburg Bay, awaiting the attack, lay the American squadron, under Capt. Thomas Macdonough, then only 28 years of age. It consisted of the ship *Saratoga*, brig *Eagle*, schooner *Ticonderoga*, sloop *Preble*, and 10 gunboats—in all, 14 vessels, of 2,244 tons and 882 men, with 86 guns, throwing a broadside of 1,194 pounds. Kneeling beside his heaviest gun, surrounded by his men, the young captain invoked divine protection and guidance. The first shot from the *Saratoga* was aimed by Macdonough and went entirely through the flagship of the British squadron, demolishing her wheel. The battle raged 2 hours and 20 minutes, when every British vessel struck her colors. Both squadrons were badly crippled. The British loss was more than 200, including Capt. Downie. The American loss was 110, of whom 52 were killed.

Lake Erie:
Rise of waters of, referred to, III, 346.
Victory of American squadron on, I, 534.

Lake Erie, Battle of.—In 1813 the Americans, under great difficulties, constructed a fleet of war vessels at Presque Isle, now Erie, Pa., for service on the Lakes. Aug. 12, 1813, the American squadron, consisting of the *Lawrence*, *Niagara*, *Caledonia*, *Ariel*, *Somers*, *Tigress*, *Scorpion*, *Porcupine*, *Ohio*, and *Trippe*, manned by less than 400 officers and men, under Capt. Oliver H. Perry, set forth in search of Barclay's British squadron of 6 vessels, manned by more than 500 men. Sept. 10 Perry's lookout sighted the enemy. At 10 o'clock in the morning the signal for action was run up to the masthead of the *Lawrence*. It bore the words of the dying Capt. Lawrence, of the *Chesapeake*: "Don't give up the ship." During the action the *Lawrence* was disabled and Perry transferred his flag to the *Niagara*. At 3 o'clock in the afternoon the flag of the British flagship was struck. The firing ceased. It was the first time an American fleet had met a British fleet in regular line of battle. The engagement was fairly fought, with the Americans at a disadvantage, and the British fleet surrendered. Perry sent word to Gen. Harrison: "We have met the enemy and they are ours." The British loss in the action was 135, 41 of whom were killed. The Americans lost 123, 27 of whom were killed.

Lake Memphremagog, practicability of connecting Connecticut River with, II, 307.

Lake Michigan, improvement of harbors and rivers on, V, 231.

Lake of the Woods, boundary line with Great Britain regarding, referred to, VII, 187, 237, 289, 402.
Final report of commissioners referred to, VII, 428.

Lake Ontario, movements of American squadron on, I, 535.

Lake Superior:
Copper mines on shores of, II, 195.
Mineral lands on, sale of, recommended, IV, 454.

Lake Traverse Reservation:
Agreement with Sioux for purchase of lands in, discussed, IX, 63.
Opened to settlement by proclamation, IX, 272.
Right of way for railroad through, VIII, 201, 369, 593.

Lakes, Great. (See Great Lakes; the several lakes.)

Lambert, William, astronomical observations by, II, 111, 119, 220.

Land Office. (See General Land Office.)

Land Offices, Public, act regarding fees of registers and receivers at, vetoed, IX, 675.

Land Sales. (See Lands, Public.)

Land Titles. (See Lands, Indian; Lands, Public.)

Lander, Frederick W., activity and enterprise manifested by, commended, VI, 104.

Landreau, John C., claim of, against Peru referred to, VII, 511.

Lawrence, Kans., fortifications at, referred to, VI, 696.

Laws of United States (see also Revised Statutes): Newspapers selected to publish, for Congress referred to, VII, 162.

Lawson, Thomas, Surgeon-General United States Army, directed to accompany ex-President Jackson home, III, 323.

Lazare, A. H., imprisonment of, in Haiti and claims arising out of, discussed, VIII, 333, 535, 538; IX, 667.

Lea, James, member of legislative council for Mississippi Territory, nomination of, I, 457.

Leach, D. C., treaty with Indians concluded by, VI, 259.

Lead Mines. (See Mines.)

League Island, Pa., bill accepting, for naval purposes referred to, VI, 451.

Leake, B. B., possession of property withheld from, order regarding, X, 111.

Leander, The.—A British war ship, which, while lying off Sandy Hook, Apr. 25, 1806, fired a shot which killed a sailor aboard an American coaster. The citizens of New York in mass meeting denounced the outrage and called upon the President for better protection. President Jefferson issued a proclamation ordering the arrest of the *Leander's* captain if found within the jurisdiction of the United States (I, 402).

Leander, The :

American citizen murdered by shot from, I, 402.

Ordered from and prohibited from reentering waters of United States, I, 402.

Lear, Tobias :

Consul to Algiers, mentioned, I, 392, 430, 440.

Letter of, announcing death of Washington, I, 297.

Secretary to President Washington, I, 70.

Learning, Institutions of. (See Education; Military Academy; National University; Naval Academy; Seminaries of Learning.)

Leary, John, act granting pension to widow of, vetoed, VIII, 708.

Leatherbury, P. A., act for relief of, vetoed, VIII, 695.

Leavenworth, Henry :

Attack upon Indians led by, II, 212.

Death of, referred to, III, 113.

Lecompte, Samuel D., judicial conduct of, referred to, V, 425.

Lecompton Constitution.—During the struggle in Kansas over the question of entering the Union as a free or a slave State, the proslavery party held a convention at Lecompton Sept. 5, 1857, and adopted a constitution sanctioning slavery and forbidding the enactment of emancipation laws. It was provided that the constitution as a whole should not be submitted to the people of the Territory, the vote being taken only on the main question of a constitution with slavery or a constitution without slavery. Free-State advocates refused to vote, and the constitution sanctioning slavery was adopted. Later the Territorial legislature ordered a vote on the constitution as a whole, and, the slave-State settlers abstaining

from voting, it failed of adoption. (See also Kansas; Topeka Constitution; Wyandotte Constitution.)

Lecompton Constitution. (See Kansas, government of.)

Lee, Col., commissioner, United States, II, 212.

Lee, Richard H., appointed on committee to conduct ceremonies of administration of oath to President Washington, I, 48.

Lee, Robert E., Gen. Grant directed not to have conference with, except for capitulation of army of, X, 111.

Lee, Samuel P., thanks of Congress to, recommended, VI, 76.

Lee, The, demand of Great Britain for surrender of mutineer in, referred to, III, 591.

Leese, Fred. J., act granting pension to, vetoed, VIII, 435.

Legal-Tender Acts, modifications in, recommended, VII, 348.

Legal-Tender Cases.—During the financial emergency caused by the Civil War Congress in 1862 issued $150,000,000 of Treasury notes, the law authorizing their issue making them legal tender for all private debts and public dues except duties on imports and interest on the public debt. The constitutionality of the act authorizing these notes was frequently disputed, especially as to its application to debts contracted prior to its passage, and the Supreme Court was called upon in several cases to decide the question. State courts generally maintained the constitutionality of the law. The Supreme Court in 1869 (Hepburn *vs.* Griswold, q. v.) maintained the validity of the law only in so far as it did not affect contracts made prior to its passage. A year later this decision was overruled, and the constitutionality of the law in its application to preexisting debts was maintained. The court in the meantime had undergone a change in its membership, 2 new judges having been appointed. (See also Juilliard *vs.* Greenman.)

Legal-Tender Notes, redemption of, recommended by President—

Grant, VII, 349, 425.

Hayes, VII, 559, 615.

Legation Asylum, action of American minister to Chile in harboring criminals discussed, IX, 435.

Legations :

Military and naval attachés at, recommended, VIII, 338.

Official residences for ambassadors and ministers recommended, IX, 640, 723.

Premises for, discussed, VIII, 236, 238, 275, 338.

Appropriation for erection of buildings on, recommended, IX, 59.

Public documents or libraries in, referred to, VII, 116.

Secretaries at large, appointment of, recommended, VIII, 338,

Leggett, Mortimer D., Commissioner of Patents, recommendation of, referred to, VII, 161.

Legislature.—The body of men in a state or kingdom invested with power to make and repeal laws. Colonial legislatures were generally modeled after the British Parliament, the King, Lords, and Commons having their counterparts in the governor, the council appointed by him, and the representatives of the people. Parliamentary procedure was also followed closely. The first representative legislature in America met at Jamestown, Va., in 1619. The first representatives were elected by voters having a property qualification. In 1776 Virginia substituted a senate for its upper council, and other States followed.

Leib, R. J., consul at Tangier, disposition of presents given, by Emperor of Morocco discussed, III, 37.

Leland, Edward A., act for relief of, vetoed, VII, 435.

Lemhi Reservation, Idaho, agreement with Indians for sale of lands on, VIII, 192.

Lenox, David, attacked while discharging duties of marshal, I, 159.

Leopard, The, attack of, on the *Chesapeake*. (See *Chesapeake*, The.)

Letcher, John, official acts of, in Virginia declared null and void, VI, 337.

Letters Rogatory, report regarding execution of, transmitted, IX, 135.

Levees of Mississippi River, preservation of, recommendations regarding, VI, 454; VIII, 95, 210.

Lew Chew Islands:
Compact with, for securing certain privileges to American vessels, V, 293.
Good offices of United States tendered China and Japan for settlement of controversy regarding, VII, 569.

Lewis and Clark Expedition.—A party of citizens and soldiers sent under command of Captains Meriwether Lewis and William Clark, by order of President Jefferson, to explore the country from the Missouri River to the Pacific Ocean. They ascended the Missouri River to its sources, crossed the Rocky Mountains, and, finding the source of the Columbia River, floated down that stream to its mouth. They explored nearly all of the territory lying south of the forty-ninth parallel. This expedition is important as for the basis of our claim to Oregon.

Lewis and Clark Expedition discussed, I, 39

Lewiston, N. Y., proclamation granting privileges of other ports to, IV, 469.

Lexington (Mass.), Battle of.—On the night of Apr. 18, 1775, a detachment of 800 British soldiers under Col. Smith left Boston to capture or destroy some military stores which the Americans had collected and stored at Concord. Maj. Pitcairn, who led the advance, was opposed at daybreak at Lexington Green, 11 miles northwest of Boston, by about 50 minutemen under Capt. Parker, who had been summoned by Paul Revere in his midnight ride. Pitcairn's men opened fire and 7 Americans were killed and 9 wounded. This was the first blood shed in the Revolutionary War. The Americans returned the fire and retreated, but rallied and pursued the British toward Concord, capturing 7 prisoners, the first taken in the war. On their return from Concord the British were reenforced at Lexington by

1,200 men under Lord Percy. The Americans had also been reenforced, and kept up a guerrilla fire upon the British, who fled to Boston in disorder. The loss for the day was 93 Americans killed, wounded, and missing, and 273 British. (See also Concord (Mass.), Battle of.)

Lexington (Mo.), Battle of.—Sept. 1, 1861, Col. Mulligan, in command of the "Irish Brigade," stationed at Jefferson City, Mo., was ordered by Gen. Frémont, who had recently been appointed to the command of the Western Department, to proceed up the Missouri River to Lexington, Mo., 160 miles to the northwest, and reenforce the garrison there. Mulligan's brigade reached Lexington Sept. 9, swelling the force to 2,780 men. After the battle of Wilsons Creek (q. v.) the Confederate General Price marched toward the northern part of the State with a constantly increasing force. He arrived in the vicinity of Lexington Sept. 11 with 28,000 men and 13 pieces of artillery. Mulligan's force was well intrenched and was constantly expecting reenforcements from St. Louis. Several unsuccessful efforts were made to dislodge them. The garrison suffered terribly from thirst and many of the horses and cattle perished. On the 20th Price advanced his artillery behind the shelter of bales of hemp, which the men rolled slowly before them as they approached Mulligan's redoubt. When this hempen breastwork was within 50 yards of his lines, no reenforcements having arrived, Mulligan surrendered unconditionally after a loss of 39 killed and 120 wounded. Two thousand six hundred men, including 500 home guards, laid down their arms. The Confederates lost 1,400 in killed and wounded. Col. Mulligan was twice wounded.

Libby Prison.—A famous Confederate military prison in Richmond, Va., during the War between the States. It was originally a tobacco warehouse and a ship chandlery and was named for its owner. It was taken down in 1888 and carried to Chicago and there set up as a war museum.

Libby Prison, rent for use of building known as, referred to, VI, 697.

Liberal Republican Party.—A defection from the regular Republican organization in 1870–1872. This party was opposed to the strict measures of coercion adopted by the Administration to maintain the newly granted rights of the freedmen, reconstruct the Southern States, and stamp out disorder in the South. Uniting with the Democrats in Missouri in 1870–71, it advocated universal suffrage, universal amnesty, a reform of the tariff, and a "cessation" of unconstitutional laws to cure Ku-Klux disorders." At a national convention held in Cincinnati in May, 1872, the Liberal Republicans nominated Horace Greeley for President and B. Gratz Brown, of Missouri, for Vice-President. The ticket was defeated.

Liberia.—A Republic on the west coast of Africa, extending from about 6° 40′ west about 400 or 500 miles along the coast to the northwest. The Republic was founded by the American

Colonization Society in 1822 and had for its object the settling in Africa of freedmen and recaptured slaves. The society sent some 18,000 persons to this colony. Liberia remained under the rule of the directors of the society until 1847, when the Republic was established. Its area is estimated at 14,360 sq. miles. The total population in 1891 was 1,068,000, mostly natives.

Liberia:

Liberty Bell.—The bell on the Pennsylvania statehouse at Philadelphia, which on July 4, 1776, was rung to announce the signing of the Declaration of Independence. It was cast in London and sent to Philadelphia in 1752. The bell was broken up and recast in April, and again in June, of the following year. It was cracked July 8, 1835, while being tolled in memory of Chief Justice Marshall. The Liberty Bell was placed on exhibition at the Centennial at Philadelphia in 1876, and at the Columbian Exposition in Chicago in 1893. It bears the motto "Proclaim liberty throughout the land unto all the inhabitants thereof." It is now in Independence Hall, Philadelphia.

Liberty Enlightening the World, statue of, erected in New York Harbor by citizens of France, VII, 427; VIII, 237, 498.

Libraries. (See Interior Department; Library of Congress; State Department.)

Library, Latin-American, establishment of, at Washington recommended by International American Conference, IX, 71.

Library of Congress.—When the seat of Government was removed to Washington in 1800, the idea of a Congressional library was conceived. In December, 1801, John Randolph made a report which formed the basis of an act of Congress of 1802 organizing the library. Some 3,000 books of reference were accumulated, when, in August, 1814, the British army burned the Capitol and the Library was consumed. In 1815 Congress purchased the private library of Thomas Jefferson, consisting of 6,700 volumes, for $23,950. An annual appropriation being made for the purchase of books, the Library continued to grow until in 1851 it numbered 55,000 volumes. Dec. 24 of that year a second conflagration destroyed 35,000 of these volumes. An appropriation of $72,000 was

made for repairs, and the Library grew apace. In 1866, 40,000 volumes were transferred from the Smithsonian Institution. The following year Congress purchased for $100,000 the historical collection of Peter Force, very rich in Americana. This library contained nearly 60,000 books, pamphlets, and manuscripts. In 1864 President Lincoln appointed Ainsworth R. Spofford to be Librarian, and he was succeeded in 1897 by John Russell Young, who died in 1899, and Herbert Putnam was appointed his successor. The Library now contains 840,000 volumes, besides very large collections of pamphlets, maps, engravings, etc. The present Library building was begun in 1886 and completed in 1895, at a cost of $6,360,000. No building in the United States equals the Library of Congress in artistic beauty. It has been resorted to by more than 600,000 visitors annually, since its opening in 1897. The hours are from 9 a. m. to 10 p. m. The public reading room occupies the rotunda. It consists of an octagonal hall 100 feet in diameter, sumptuously built of soft-tinted Numidian, Sienna, and Tennessee marbles of variegated hues. The reading desks are arranged in concentric circles about the Librarian's desk in the center, from which easy communication is had to all parts of the fireproof iron book stacks. The Library of Congress has been since 1870 the only office of record for copyrights, and its accessions from that source are very large.

Library of Congress:

Licenses for Vessels, prohibitory laws in regard to, I, 495, 519, 523.

Lieutenant-General.—In the United States Army the rank next below that of general and next above that of major-general. It was first authorized by Congress in 1798 and bestowed upon George Washington. It was abolished in 1799 and was not revived until 1855, when Winfield Scott was brevetted lieutenant-general. At his death it again lapsed. In 1864 it was revived by special act of Congress and conferred upon Ulysses S. Grant, on whose promotion to the grade of general, created in his behalf, William T. Sherman became lieutenant-general, and on his succession to the rank of general Philip H. Sheridan was promoted to be lieutenant-general. At his death in 1888 the office became extinct, but was revived in 1895 for John M. Schofield.

Lieutenant-General. (See Grant, Ulysses S.; Schofield, John M.; Scott, Winfield; Washington, George; Enc. Art., Lieutenant-General.)

Life-Insurance Companies, American:

Local Government.—Sometimes written local self-government. The regulation and administration of the local affairs of a city or district by the people of it, as distinguished from such regulation and administration by authority of the State or nation at large. The State was an institution of the Roman Empire, but the Teutonic tribes or nations developed a local government of their own, and gave the name "town" to language and the idea of "township" to constitutional law. As to whether the first English colonists in America derived the subdivision of the county known in England as town or township from the mother country there was no question until recently, when respectable authority was adduced for the statement that the Plymouth and Massachusetts Bay colonists, especially the former, who came directly from Holland, borrowed their local government system and several other institutions of high value from the Dutch Republic. Certain it is, nevertheless, that when the first settlements were made in this country England had well-developed forms of local government which served as a pattern, beyond doubt, for the Jamestown Colony, Va., and for some other colonies as well. The colony was subdivided into counties, the counties in some cases into hundreds, and the hundreds into parishes or townships. At the time of the colonization the parish in England had generally superseded the township. In the Southern Colonies, where the plantation system prevailed and the people were scattered over a large area, the colonists, on their separation from England, retained the county system as being best suited to their population. In the New England Colonies, where population was more compact, the township government was retained. Thus two distinct types of local government prevailed in the United States—the township system in New England and the county system in the South. In the middle Colonies a system of local government was instituted which combined the county and township systems. This is now generally in use in the Western States.

Local Option.—A principle of law established in some of the United States by which the determination as to whether or not any licenses to sell intoxicating liquors shall be granted is submitted to a vote of the people of a town or other minor political community. If the people of any locality decide upon prohibition, it becomes part of the State law for that community. Local option by States was suggested as a solution of the slavery question, and the Kansas-Nebraska law contained a provision to this effect.

Locke, Capt., mentioned, V, 35.

Lockrey, John J., act granting pension to, vetoed, VIII, 832.

Loco-Focos.—The radical faction of the Democratic party in New York in 1835-1837. The Equal Rights faction was opposed to the granting of bank charters and special privileges to favorites of the Government, and the Tammany men supported the Administration. At a meeting held in Tammany Hall, New York, Oct. 29, 1835, the regular Tammany Democrats tried to gain control, but finding themselves outnumbered they turned out the lights and left the hall. The Equal Rights men produced candles and lighted them by the aid of "loco-foco" matches and continued the meeting. The word, at first used in derision of this faction, was later adopted by the Democratic party as an emblem of promptitude in an emergency, and it was also applied to the party, sometimes in derision, by their opponents.

Lodges, Secret. (See Secret Lodges.)

Loewinger, Johanna, act granting pension to, vetoed, VIII, 674.

London, England:
Exhibition in, works illustrative of, referred to, V, 228.
Industrial exhibition to be held in, in 1862 discussed, VI, 32, 53.
Circulars, etc., regarding, VI, 60.
Vessel to transport American exhibits recommended, VI, 61.
International Fisheries Exhibition to be held in, VIII, 101.
International Inventions Exhibition to be held in, VIII, 240.
International Penitentiary Congress at, VII, 208.
Smoke Abatement Exhibition at, VIII, 108.

Long, John C., misunderstanding with Louis Kossuth referred to, V, 146.

Long, John D. :
Report of, on number of lives lost by sinking of the *Maine*, X, 153.
Thanks of President tendered Commodore Dewey by, X, 208.

Lookout Mountain (Tenn.), Battle of.—The arrival of the two corps under Hooker and the army of Sherman at Chattanooga increased the strength of Grant's command to 80,000 men. At this critical time Longstreet, with 16,000 men, was detached from the Confederate army and sent to besiege Burnside at Knoxville, leaving Bragg with only about 50,000 men to hold the position. Nov. 24, 1863, to cover Sherman's crossing the Tennessee River and securing a position, Hooker, with 10,000 men, made an attack on the western slope of Lookout Mountain. During a heavy mist he pressed up the mountain side and attacked the position in front and rear, capturing about 1,000 prisoners. The Confederates retired from the mountain to Missionary Ridge.

Loomis, Aretus F., act granting pension to, vetoed, VIII, 458.

Lopez, Segundo N., killing of, in Cuba referred to, IX, 750.

Lopez Expedition, pardon and release of members of, by Spain, V, 142.

Lord Nelson, The, claim of James Crooks against United States for seizure of, VIII, 390; IX, 227.

Lotteries, use of mails by, discussed and recommendations regarding, IX, 44, 80.
Passage of act regarding, discussed, IX, 116.

Lottery.—The Continental Congress tried to raise money by lottery in 1777. As early as 1612 the Virginia Company was authorized by its charter to hold lotteries for the benefit of its colonization schemes. In the eighteenth century lotteries were extremely popular in America. Legislatures authorized them for building churches, schools, and all sorts of public improvements. Faneuil Hall, in Boston, having been destroyed by fire in 1761, was rebuilt by lottery. The Louisiana State Lottery was the last authorized institution of the kind in the United States. Popular opinion has undergone a change regarding lotteries. They are now forbidden by act of Congress to use the mails. This act resulted in closing the Louisiana Lottery.

Loughery, Ardavan S., treaty with Indians concluded by, V, 66.

Louisa, The, proceedings of court regarding, II, 329.

Louisiana.—One of the United States; nickname, "The Pelican State;" motto, "Union, Justice, and Confidence." It extends from the Gulf of Mexico northward to the thirty-third parallel of north latitude and from the eighty-ninth to the ninety-fourth meridian west longitude. It is bounded on the north by Arkansas and Mississippi, on the east by Mississippi (separated by the Mississippi River) and the Gulf of Mexico, on the south by the Gulf of Mexico, and on the west by Texas (separated in part by the Sabine River). Louisiana is the leading sugar State of the Union, besides which is exported cotton, rice, and corn. It was explored by De Soto in 1541, by Marquette in 1673, and by La Salle in 1682. It was settled by the French under Iberville and Bienville about 1700, was ceded by France to Spain in 1763, retroceded to France in 1800, was purchased by the United States in 1803, and was made the Territory of New Orleans in 1804. The portion east of the Mississippi River was annexed in 1810. The State was admitted to the Union in 1812. Jan. 26, 1861, it seceded and joined the Southern Confederacy. It was readmitted by act of Congress June 25, 1868 (VI, 658). Louisiana contains an area of 48,720 sq. miles and a population (in 1890) of 1,118,587. (See also Louisiana Purchase.)

Louisiana (see also Confederate States; New Orleans):

Accession of, to United States discussed and referred to, I, 358, 360, 362; II, 100, 284, and X, 121; II, 363; VI, 54. (See also II, 391.)

Effect of, discussed, V, 345.

Appropriation for, I, 394.

Authority to grant or dispose of lands of Spain in, referred to, II, 82.

Boundaries of, I, 384, 389; II, 394.

Branch mint in, referred to, III, 164, 276; X, 73.

Cession of, to France referred to, I, 343, 350.

Colonel-commandant of, commissioned, I, 376.

Commission to, instructions of President Hayes to, X, 116.

Constitution of, referred to, VI, 633.

Division of, into subordinate districts, I, 375.

Louisiana—Continued.

Elections in, and complications growing out of, discussed, VII, 207, 212 296, 305.

Federal interference in, discussed, VII, 305.

Proclamations regarding, VII, 223, 276.

Electors in, letter of John Sherman and others regarding canvass of vote of, referred to, VII, 413.

Federal troops in, order for removal of, X, 119.

Fourteenth amendment to Constitution ratified by, VI, 639.

Proclaimed, VI, 658.

Government of—

Assumed by Governor Claiborne, I, 367.

Letter regarding, transmitted, 1, 367.

Referred to, I, 364, 371.

Governor of, letter from, I, 348.

Indians inhabiting, referred to, I, 398.

Lands granted to, in aid of railroads referred to, VI, 382.

Lands in—

Fraudulent practices of monopolizing, I, 368.

Proclamation regarding sale of, II, 495.

Treaty regarding security of titles to, discussed, II, 363.

Laws of, referred to, I, 364, 365, 418.

Lead mines in, I, 371.

Memorial from purchasers of land in, II, 466.

Mint at New Orleans seized by authorities of, referred to, V, 668.

Ordinance of Spain respecting commerce of, X, 14.

Possession of, commissioners appointed to receive, I, 367.

Private land claims in, recommendations regarding, VIII, 104.

Provisional court established in, order regarding, VI, 122.

Restoration of, into Union discussed, VI, 222, 251.

Slaves imported into, letter of Governor Claiborne regarding, transmitted, X, 27.

Support of, referred to, I, 394.

Title to, objections to validity of, withdrawn, I, 370.

Transfer of, to United States disagreeable to Spain, I, 388.

Unlawful combinations in, discussed and proclamations against, VII, 207, 212, 223, 276, 296, 305.

Louisiana, District of.—That part of the Louisiana Purchase which is not included in the present State of Louisiana. It was erected into a district and the capital was established at St. Louis in 1804. In 1805 it was given a separate government as the Territory of Louisiana. In 1812 the name of the Territory was changed to Missouri.

Louisiana Lottery Co. discussed, IX, 80.

Louisiana, Province of. (See Louisiana.)

Louisiana Purchase.—A name applied to the territory west of the Mississippi River purchased from France in 1803. It embraced all of the present State of Louisiana lying west of the Mississippi River, together with New Orleans and the adjacent district east, comprising Mississippi and Alabama below the thirty-first parallel; Arkansas, Missouri, Iowa, a portion of Idaho and Minnesota, all of the Dakotas, most of Kansas, all of Nebraska and Indian Territory, part of Colorado, most of Wyoming, and the whole of Montana. It is claimed by some that Oregon and Washington were included.

Louisiana Purchase:

Discussed and referred to, I, 358, 360, 362; II, 100, 284, and X, 121; II, 363; VI, 54. (See also II, 391.)

Effect of, discussed, V, 345.

Louisiana vs. Jumel.—An important Supreme Court case defining the liability of State officers. Jumel held bonds issued under an act of the Louisiana legislature of 1874 and the constitutional amendment adopted in that year. He demanded payment of these bonds in 1880. Payment was refused solely on the ground of obedience to the Louisiana State debt ordinance of the new constitution adopted July 23, 1879, and the law of 1880, carrying out provisions contained in this new constitution. This act, in the language and spirit of the ordinance, recited that coupons of consolidated bonds falling due in January, 1880, were remitted. Suit was brought against officers of the State. The circuit court of the State decided for the defendant, and its decision was affirmed by the United States Supreme Court on the ground that relief could not be awarded against officers obeying the supreme power of the State; that the money is the State's property, not held in trust by the officers except in the capacity of her servants. "The political power of the State," said Chief Justice Waite in the opinion of the court, "can not be ousted of its jurisdiction and the judiciary set in its place." Dissenting opinions were rendered by Justices Field and Harlan.

Louisville and Portland Canal Co., act for subscription of stock in, reasons for applying pocket veto to, II, 508.

Louisville, Ky., Southern Exposition at, discussed, VIII, 186.

Board on behalf of Executive Departments designated, VIII, 232.

Instructions to, VIII, 233.

Lounsberry, Clement A., act for relief of, vetoed, VIII, 715.

Lower Brulé Indians, selling and trading of annuity goods by, VIII, 84.

Loyalists.—Those of the American colonists who opposed the Revolutionary War and in some instances took up arms against their countrymen in the struggle for independence. They were also called Tories. As early as 1688 parties favorable to the Crown were exerting an influence in all the Colonies. As the revolutionary movement grew their opposition to it increased. In no Colony was there an overwhelming desire for independence, and in some the advocates of revolution were in the minority. Many of the most respected and eminent men of the middle Colonies were loyal to the Crown. During the progress of the war they were treated with great harshness. Their property was confiscated or destroyed; they suffered social ostracism, and some were tarred and feathered. Legislative assemblies banished them from some of the Colonies. When the British troops withdrew at the close of the war the Tories found life in the States unendurable and thousands retired to Canada, Nova Scotia, New Brunswick, the Bahamas and other West Indies. In the treaty of peace in 1783 the British asked to have provision made for recompensing the dispossessed Loyalists, but all they received was a promise to submit the matter to the States, and they refused relief.

Lubeck:

Minister of, received by United States, II, 383.

Treaty with, II, 422, 425; V, 150; X, 69.

Vessels of, discriminating duties on, suspended by proclamation, II, 73.

Luce, Elizabeth, act granting pension to, vetoed, VIII, 433.

Luckett and Tyler (assignees), act for relief of, vetoed, VII, 380.

Lumpkin, Wilson, mentioned, X, 106.

Lundys Lane (Canada), Battle of.—After his defeat at Chippewa in 1814 Gen. Riall retired by way of Queenston toward the head of Lake Ontario. He was soon reenforced, and returned to attack the Americans under Brown, who had pursued him as far as Queenston. Hearing of the British reenforcements, Brown retreated to the Chippewa River, and on July 24, 1814, encamped on the south bank, where he had defeated Riall on the 5th. On the 25th Gen. Scott, with about 1,200 men, went forward to reconnoiter and came upon the British army, 4,500 strong, near Niagara Falls, on Lundys Lane, a road leading from the Falls to the end of Lake Ontario. Soon the entire American force was engaged, the battle lasting from sunset till midnight. The American forces numbered about 2,500 men. During the engagement Gen. Scott and Lieut. Col. Miller distinguished themselves for daring and efficiency. The British were finally driven back and forced to abandon their artillery, ammunition, and baggage. Both armies claimed the victory, though both left the field. The American loss was 171 killed, 571 wounded, and 110 missing—a total of 852 out of an army of 2,500. The British lost 84 killed, 559 wounded, 193 missing, and 42 prisoners—a total of 878 out of an army of 4,500. Generals Brown and Scott were among the wounded.

Lüneburg, convention with, for acquiring and inheriting property, V, 293.

Lusk, Albert M. D. C., trial of, by military commission referred to, VI, 594.

Luther vs. Borden.—In 1841 a portion of the people of Rhode Island framed a new government and elected Thomas W. Dorr governor in opposition to the charter government. (See Dorr's Rebellion.) Governor King declared the State under martial law and Luther's house was searched, he being implicated in the armed conspiracy against the established government. Luther pleaded the constitutionality of the new government. The circuit court gave judgment against him, and the Supreme Court of the United States affirmed this decision in 1842. It was decided that under martial law suspected persons might legally be subjected to search and arrest by State authority, and that the question of the constitutionality of a State government was one with which Congress rather than the courts should deal.

Lutman, David H., act granting pension to, vetoed, VIII, 712.

Luxemburg, fugitive criminals, convention with, for surrender of, VIII, 195.

Lyman, Cornelius, proceedings of court-martial of, transmitted, X, 26.

Lynch, Robert B., arrest and trial of, by Great Britain, VI, 629.

Lynch, William, act granting pension to, vetoed, VIII, 543.

Lynch Law.—The practice of punishing alleged offenders, generally without trial, by unauthorized persons and without due process of law. Lynch law, it is said, took its name from Charles Lynch, a Virginia planter and Quaker, and his associates, who during Revolutionary days seized British sympathizers and hanged them by the thumbs till they shouted "Liberty forever."

Lynchings discussed, IX, 332.

Lynn, Mass., act for erection of post-office building at, vetoed, VIII, 565.

Lyon, Nathaniel, thanks of Congress tendered, VI, 99.

M.

McArthur, Duncan, treaty with Indians concluded by, II, 21.

McBlair, John H., act for relief of, vetoed, VIII, 409.

McCaleb, Sarah E., act for relief of, vetoed, VIII, 668.

McCall, E., & Co., agents to receive installments from Peru, V, 49.

McCalla, Bowman H., member of board to consider expedition to be sent for relief of Lady Franklin Bay Expedition, VIII, 226.

McCallum, D. C., military director and superintendent of railroads, appointed, VI, 101.

McCarty, Catherine, act granting pension to, vetoed, VIII, 470.

McCauley, Charles S., mentioned, V, 160.

McClellan, Capt., Florida volunteers under command of, referred to, IV, 580.

McClellan, George B.:
Command of Army of United States assumed by, VI, 40.
Plans of, approved, VI, 111.
Referred to, VI, 56.
Death of, announced and honors to be paid memory of, VIII, 319.
Negroes coming into Washington from Virginia arrested as fugitives, communication to, regarding, X, 108.
Relieved of command of Army of Potomac, VI, 124.
Relieved of command of other departments, retaining command of Department of Potomac, VI, 111.

McClellan, George B.—Continued.
Report of, on Dominican Republic transmitted, VII, 117.
Resignation of, as major-general accepted, VI, 242.

McConnell, H. W., act for relief of, vetoed, IX, 572.

McCook, Anson G., letter of, regarding statue of Gen Garfield to be erected in Washington transmitted, VIII, 208.

McCook, Edward M., brigadier-general in Army, nomination of, referred to, VI, 202.

McCool, John, act granting pension to, vetoed, VIII, 832.

McCord, Victor H., claim of, against Peru, IX, 556, 660; X, 188.

McCrary, George W., order to, for removal of Federal troops in Louisiana, X, 119.

McCrea, Lieut. (See *Baltimore*, The.)

McCullah, James A., act for relief of, vetoed, VII, 216.

McCulloch, Ben, sent to Utah during troubles with Mormons, V, 505.

McCulloch, Hugh, correspondence of, transmitted, VI, 606.

McCulloch vs. Maryland.—A case brought before the Supreme Court of the United States in 1819, in which the right of a State to interfere with the execution of Federal laws was denied. McCulloch was cashier of the Baltimore branch of the Bank of the United States, which had been incorporated by an act of Congress in 1816 and had headquarters in Philadelphia. The action brought by the State of Maryland against McCulloch was one of debt, he, it was averred, having refused to comply with an act of the Maryland general assembly of 1818 which imposed a tax upon all banks or branches of banks doing business in Maryland and not chartered by the State legislature. The court of appeals of Maryland decided against the plaintiff. The Supreme Court reversed this decision, declaring that the act under which the bank was chartered was constitutional, and that therefore the act of the Maryland legislature of 1818 was contrary to the Constitution of the United States, and therefore void, because States have no power, by taxation or otherwise, to impede or control the operations of constitutional laws enacted by Congress to carry into execution any of the powers of the Federal Government.

McDaniel, James, treaty with Indians concluded by, VI, 394.

Macdonald, Allan, abduction of, from Canada referred to, VI, 628.

Macdonough, Thomas, British ship captured on Lake Champlain by vessel under, I, 549.

McDuffie, George, referred to, III, 14.

McEldery, Hugh, director of Bank of United States, nomination of, and reasons therefor, III, 41.

McElvain, John, treaty with Indians concluded by, II, 466.

McEnery, Samuel D., candidate for governor of Louisiana, election disturbances discussed, VII, 307.

constituted by the State. It first became prominent in 1860. In 1874-75 the Italian Government made some fruitless efforts to suppress it. It is supposed to be the outgrowth of a pontifical bull of the fifteenth century which granted absolution to small malefactors for a money consideration. It depends upon community of sentiment rather than thorough organization for its strength, and its members are bound neither to seek redress at law nor give evidence in court. The boycott and blackmail are the usual means of offense, but violence is often resorted to. Members of the society emigrating to the United States have established branches in New York, New Orleans, and elsewhere. On the night of Oct. 15, 1890, David C. Hennessy, chief of police of New Orleans, was assassinated before his own house by members of the Maffia, to whose band he had traced a number of crimes. The officer received 6 wounds. Eleven Italians were arrested charged with the murder. By the 15th of the following March several of the prisoners had been acquitted, and, despairing of convicting any of them, on account of their disregard of oaths, a mob of enraged citizens, headed by a lawyer named Parkerson, broke into the jail and put to death the 11 prisoners, including those who had been acquitted. In consequence of the delay in bringing to justice the perpetrators of this deed the Italian Government made a protest against this violation of the rights of Italian citizens, and the United States arranged the matter amicably by paying an indemnity to the families of the murdered Italians.

Maine.—One of the United States; nickname, "The Pine Tree State;" motto, "Dirigo" ("I direct"). The most northeasterly State of the Union. It extends from lat. 43° 4′ to 47° 28′ north and from long. 66° 57′ to 71° 7′ west. It is bounded on the north by the Province of Quebec, on the east by New Brunswick, on the southeast and south by the Atlantic, and on the west by New Hampshire and Quebec. Agriculture, lumbering, and shipbuilding are the chief industries. It is the second State in the Union in fisheries. Settlements were made by the French under Du Monts in 1604 and by the English in 1607. The first permanent settlement dates from 1623. Maine was a part of the province of Massachusetts Bay in 1691 and became a separate State in 1820. The Webster-Ashburton treaty of 1842 settled the long-standing dispute regarding its northeastern boundary. The area of the State is 33,040 sq. miles and the population in 1890 was 661,086.

Maine, The.—One of the second-class battle ships of the United States Navy. This vessel was sent to Havana, Cuba, in January, 1898, on a peaceful mission. She was received by the Spanish forts and naval vessels in the harbor with the courtesies usually extended to visiting war ships of a friendly power. Her anchorage was selected by the Spanish authorities. On the night of Feb. 15, 1898, the *Maine* was destroyed by a submarine mine (X, 136). It was believed that the Spaniards, who at the time were very much incensed at the interest Americans were taking in the Cuban insurrection, had maliciously destroyed the vessel and crew. Two officers and 258 sailors and marines lost their lives by the explosion (X, 153). An investigation failed to place the responsibility for the catastrophe, and Spain hastened to send a message of regret at what she called an "incident." The blowing up of the *Maine* was among the causes of the war with Spain, begun soon afterwards.

Marine Hospitals:
Construction of, referred to, V, 214.
Plan for, referred to, III, 396.
Provision for, recommended, I, 336.
Sites for, referred to, III, 579, 618.
Appropriation for, recommended, IV, 100.

Marine, Secretary of.—Up to 1781 the Board of Admiralty had supervision of all naval affairs. Feb. 7 of that year the Continental Congress created the office of Secretary of Marine, whose duties corresponded with those of the present Secretary of the Navy. Before the end of that year, however, the duties of the office were transferred to the Treasury Department.

Marine Signals, international conference at Washington for adoption of system of, etc., IX, 33.

Marino, The, proceedings of court regarding, II, 329.

Marion, John H., act for relief of, vetoed, VIII, 674.

Maritime Canal Company referred to, IX, 188, 753; X, 179.

Maritime Law, declaration concerning, referred to, V, 384, 412.

Maritime Policy, adoption of, by United States recommended, X, 193.

Maritime Rights, correspondence with foreign powers regarding, referred to, VI, 33.

Maritime War, rights of neutrals and belligerents in, discussed, II, 252.
Uniform action of the powers regarding, II, 300.

Marks, I. D., contract alleged to have been made with Mexico by, referred to, V, 100.

Marmion Case.—The South Carolina legislature in 1822 passed a law providing that any free negroes entering the ports of that State on ships could be imprisoned until the departure of the vessels. This was done in the case of negroes on board the *Marmion*. The district court of the United States in 1823 decided that this law was contrary to the Constitution and incompatible with the international obligations of the United States. The Attorney-General rendered a similar opinion in 1824.

Marquez, Leonardo, American citizens murdered in Mexico by, V, 565, 645.

Marriages of American citizens abroad, recommendations regarding, VII, 292, 347, 406.

Marsden, George, imprisonment of, by Brazil, V, 246.

Marsden, Joseph, member of commission concluding treaty for annexation of Hawaiian Islands, IX, 348.

Marsh, George P., minister to Italy, death of, referred to, VIII, 128.

Marshall, Humphrey, correspondence of, referred to, V, 243.

Marshall, John:
Letter of Elbridge Gerry to, transmitted, I, 266.
Minister to France, nomination of, I, 245.
Secretary of State, I, 305.

Marshall, William, treaty with Indians concluded by, III, 135.

Marshals, United States:
Acts making appropriations to pay fees of, vetoed, VII, 541, 545, 591, 592.

Marshals, United States—Continued.
Appropriations for maintenance of service of, recommended, VII, 522, 573.
Necessity for, referred to, VII, 583.
Compensation to, discussed, V, 130, 178; VIII, 183, 249, 354, 518.
Referred to, I, 99.

Marthas Vineyard, Mass., lands designated by proclamation for light-houses on, II, 658.

Martial Law.—A system of government under the direction of military authority. It is an arbitrary kind of law, proceeding directly from the military power and having no immediate constitutional or legislative sanction. It is only justified by necessity and supersedes all civil government. Sir Matthew Hale said: "Martial law is built on no settled principle, but is arbitrary, and, in truth, no law, but sometimes indulged, rather than allowed, as law." Suspension of the writ of *habeas corpus* is essentially a declaration of martial law. "In this case," says Blackstone, "the nation parts with a portion of liberty to secure its permanent welfare, and suspected persons may then be arrested without cause assigned."

Martin, Alexander, legislative act of North Carolina received from, transmitted, I, 72.

Martin, Elijah, act for relief of, vetoed, VIII, 677.

Martin, Henry W., treaty with Indians concluded by, VI, 194.

Martin, Morgan L., treaty with Indians concluded by, IV, 679.

Martin vs. Hunter's Lessee.—In 1791 Martin brought suit of ejectment against the defendant in the district court of Virginia for the recovery of certain lands. The court decided for the defendant. The court of appeals of Virginia reversed this decision, and their judgment was reversed by the United States Supreme Court in 1816. The court of appeals of Virginia refused to execute this judgment, declaring that the "appellate power of the Supreme Court of the United States does not extend to this court under a sound construction of the Constitution of the United States," and that "the act of Congress to that effect is not in pursuance of said Constitution." The Supreme Court overruled this decision and thus established its jurisdiction upon such points.

Martinez, F. P., Mexican minister, mentioned, III, 573.

Martinique, tonnage on American vessels at, referred to, II, 560.

Marty, Martin, member of Chippewa Commission, IX, 65.

Marvin, William, provisional governor of Florida, appointed, VI, 329.

Mary, The, capture and sequestration of, by Netherlands, III, 395.
Claims arising out of, III, 476.

Mary Lowell, The, seizure of, by Spanish authorities referred to, VII, 32.

Maryland.—One of the thirteen original States of the Union; motto, "Fatti maschii; parole femine" ("Deeds are men; words are women"). It was founded by Lord Baltimore in 1634 and named in honor of Henrietta Maria,

Massachusetts, The (battle ship), mentioned, X, 171.

Massachusetts Bay Company.—A colonizing company chartered in England, Mar. 19, 1628, by John Humphrey, John Endicott, and others. The company grew out of the preexisting Dorchester Company, and was the result of imperiled political and religious rights in England under Charles I. The patentees received a grant of land extending from the Atlantic to the "Western Ocean," in width from a line running 3 miles north of the Merrimac to one running 3 miles south of the Charles. Endicott headed a colony which settled at Salem in September, 1628. Mar. 4, 1629, a new charter was granted to the governor and company of Massachusetts Bay, and the old officers were succeeded by John Winthrop as governor, with a deputy and 18 assistants. In 1630 Winthrop, at the head of a large body of settlers, transferred the company headquarters to America and founded Boston. Under this charter Massachusetts carried on her government for 55 years.

Massacre of Christians. (See Armenians.)

Mataafa, insurrection in Samoan Islands under, IX, 439, 531.

Arrangements for return of, and other exiles, X, 189.

Matanzas, Cuba, harbor and forts at, shelled by American squadron, X, 168.

Mather, Thomas, treaty with Indians concluded by, II, 323.

Mathews, John, district supervisor, nomination of, I, 99.

Matlock, Gideon C., treaty with Indians concluded by, IV, 454.

Matta, Mr. (See *Baltimore,* The.)

Matthews, Edmund O., member of Gun Foundry Board, VIII, 161.

Matthews, George, instructions to, regarding possession of Florida, I, 506.

Unauthorized conduct of, discussed and powers given, revoked, I, 507.

Matthews, James C., recorder of deeds, District of Columbia, nomination of, and reasons therefor, VIII, 531.

Maury, Matthew F.:

Immigration plans of, referred to, VI, 373.

Improvement in science of nautical affairs by, V, 134.

Maximilian (Ferdinand Maximilian Joseph):

Capture and execution of, referred to, VI, 527.

Decrees of—

Declaring blockade of ports proclaimed void, VI, 433.

Reestablishing slavery in Mexico referred to, VI, 371.

Organization for purpose of avenging death of, referred to, VI, 582.

Maxwell, Hugh, authority issued to, to arrest unlawful expedition, V, 161.

Maybrick, Florence E., imprisonment of, in Great Britain, IX, 669.

Mayflower Compact.—Before the landing of the Pilgrim Fathers the company gathered in the cabin of the *Mayflower,* in Provincetown Harbor, Nov. 11, 1620, and there bound themselves into a body politic and pledged themselves to abide individually and collectively by the laws they should make.

Mayson, F. G., lieutenant in Marine Corps, appointment of, referred to, IV, 423.

Maysville, Washington, Paris and Lexington Turnpike Road Co., act authorizing subscription of stock in, vetoed, II, 483.

Mazzei Letter.—A private letter written by Thomas Jefferson to an Italian named Mazzei in 1796. The letter was translated and published in an English paper. It aroused much animosity against Jefferson by its supposed allusion to Washington and others as those "Samsons in the field and Solomons in the council" who had formed an Anglican monarchical aristocratic party in America whose avowed object was "to draw over us the substance, as they had already done the forms, of the British Government."

Mead, Cowles:

Arrival of Aaron Burr in Mississippi announced by, I, 419.

Surrender of Aaron Burr announced by, I, 421.

Mead, James R., act for relief of, vetoed, VII, 271.

Meade, George G.:

Instructions to, referred to, VI, 628.

Order to, regarding suppression of military expedition, VI, 433.

Meade, Richard W., imprisonment of, by Spain and claim arising out of, II, 25; X, 61.

Meade, Richard W., United States Navy:

Agreement with great chief of Tutuila concluded by, VII, 168.

Mentioned, IX, 401.

Measures. (See Weights and Measures.)

Meat Products. (See Animals and Animal Products.)

Mechanicsville (Va.), Battle of.—One of the Seven Days' Battles before Richmond. On June 26, 1862, Lee massed his troops on his left, A. P. Hill crossing to the north side of the Chickahominy and being supported by Longstreet and D. H. Hill. Jackson joined the Confederate forces later. The Confederate attack on Fitz John Porter at dawn was repulsed, but the Federal army subsequently retired. According to Federal accounts, the Confederate loss was 1,500, the Union 361. This battle is also called the battle of Beaver Dam Creek.

Mecklenburg Declaration.—A series of resolutions purporting to have been adopted by the citizens of Mecklenburg County, N. C., May 20, 1775, declaring their independence of Great Britain, followed by a second series of resolutions, adopted on the 31st of May, providing for a local government. The independence resolutions were first published in 1819 and created much discussion as to their genuineness. They contained several phrases almost or quite identical with portions of the document adopted at Philadelphia July 4, 1776. Thomas Jefferson immediately declared them fraudulent. It was admitted that the original Mecklenburg resolutions were burned in 1800 and that those published in 1819 were reproduced from memory by a son of one of the secretaries of the meeting. The North Carolina legislature investigated the matter and secured enough evidence to warrant them in making May 20 a State holiday. The historians are divided in opinion. Hildreth, one of the most critical, admits the validity of the Declaration, but, curiously enough, says it was made May 31. Bancroft contends that only a provisional government was formed, and that on the date of the 31st. There is no dispute as to the fact that a government was organized. In North Carolina, among the Scotch-Irish people, there exists little doubt that the Mecklenburgers declared their independence on May 20, 1775. William A. Graham, Secretary of the Navy from 1850 to 1852 and candidate of the Whigs for Vice-President in 1852, was the son of Joseph Graham, who was present at the meeting in Charlotte which declared independence, and testified to the fact.

Mecklenburg-Schwerin.—A Grand Duchy and a State of the German Empire. It is bounded on the north by the Baltic Sea, on the east by Pomerania and Mecklenburg-Strelitz, on the south by Brandenburg and Hannover, and on the west by Lübeck, Ratzeburg, and Schleswig-Holstein. The chief occupation of the people is agriculture. The government is a constitutional hereditary monarchy, with 2 members in the Bundesrath and 6 members in the Reichstag. Prevailing religion is Protestant. It joined the new German Empire in 1871. Area, 5,135 sq. miles; population (1895), 578,342.

Mecklenburg-Schwerin:
Treaty with, IV, 567, 629.
Vessels of, discriminating duties on, suspended by proclamation, III, 146.

Medary, Samuel, mentioned in, V, 469.

Medical Museum, Army, building for, recommended, VII, 620; VIII, 193, 246.

Medill, William, treaty with Indians concluded by, IV, 671.

Mediterranean Sea:
Naval force in, should be increased, I, 345, 368; II, 257.
Piracies in, II, 363.
Trade with, I, 83, 85, 86.
Vessels sent to, for protection of commerce, I, 326, 359, 370; II, 62, 257, 308, 362, 445.

Mediterranean Squadron referred to, IV, 52, 100.

Medium of Exchange:
Augmentation of, discussed, II, 74.
Discussed by President—
Buchanan, V, 437.
Grant, VII, 29, 244, 285.
Johnson, VI, 571, 679.
Madison, I, 565, 578.
Monroe, II, 74.
Tyler, IV, 44, 82, 266.
Gold and silver—
Hope expressed that use of, for, will become general, III, 164.
To take place of bills below $20 recommended, III, 166.
Paper used as, discussed, IV, 44, 82.
Restoration of uniform system of, recommended, I, 578.

Mee-sée-qua-guilch Indians, treaty with, V, 379.

Meigs, Montgomery C.:
Act making appropriation for Government expenses, including work to be superintended by, discussed, V, 597.
Appointed on commission to examine subject of reorganization of Army, VII, 398.
Report of, on—
Extension of Capitol transmitted, V, 384, 579.
Error in, referred to, V, 385.
Water supply for Washington City, V, 189.

Meigs, Return J., treaty with Indians concluded by, II, 265.

Melbourne, Australia:
International exhibition at, to celebrate centenary of founding of New South Wales, VIII, 591.
International Exhibition of Arts and Industries at, discussed, VII, 567, 607; VIII, 38.

Melcher, Jacob, ensign in Navy, nomination of, I, 63.

Melcher, Louis, act granting pension to, vetoed, VIII, 418.

Melton, Miss, assailants of, in Turkey, conviction of, discussed, IX, 530.

Members of Congress. (See Representatives; Senators.)

Memphis (Tenn.), Capture of.—After the evacuation of Corinth, Miss., by Beauregard, Fort Pillow, 40 miles above Memphis, was useless, as the Union army could take it from the rear. The Confederates therefore spiked the guns, burned the barracks and what supplies they could not take away, and their gunboats dropped down the river to Memphis. The Confederate fleet consisted of 8 vessels, mounting 28 guns, commanded by Commodore Montgomery. On June 6, 1862, Commodore Davis, with 5 Union gunboats and 2 rams, appeared before the city, and Montgomery went forth to give him battle. After 1 hour and 20 minutes of fierce fighting the Confederate fleet was defeated. Col. Ellet, who built the rams, was the only person injured on the Federal side. The number of killed and wounded on the Confederate side is not known, but was probably between 80 and 100.

Memphis, Tenn., navy-yard to be established at, IV, 349.
Proposition of city authorities of, relative to, V, 296.

Memphremagog, Lake. (See Lake Memphremagog.)

Men-of-War. (See Vessels, United States.)

Menard, Pierre, treaty with Indians concluded by, II, 422, 423, 425, 466.

Mendenhall, Thomas C.:
Chairman of Board on Geographic Names, IX, 212.
Letter of, and memorial regarding preservation of forests transmitted, IX, 60.

Menocal, Anecito G., mentioned, VIII, 328.

Menominee Indians.—A tribe of the Algonquian family of Indians, which since it first became known to the whites has occupied lands in Wisconsin and upper Michigan, chiefly along the Menominee River and the west side of

Green Bay, and extending south to the Fox River and west to the Mississippi. The name means "wild rice men," from their principal article of food. The French translated the name into "Folles Avoines," by which the Menominees are sometimes known. They now number about 1,300 at the Green Bay (Wis.) Agency. In the early Indian wars they sided with the British.

Merchant Marine.—The British navigation acts, beginning in 1645, prohibited importations into the Colonies except in English or colonial built ships. Though seriously restricting commerce, these acts served to stimulate the shipbuilding interest. Between 1789 and 1797 the registered tonnage increased 384 per cent. From 1837 to 1857 the tonnage increased from 810,000 to 2,268,000, and in 1861 the aggregate tonnage of American registered vessels reached the highest point in its history—5,539,813. This nearly equaled the combined tonnage of all other nations excepting Great Britain, which alone was slightly in excess of it. For various reasons American shipping has fallen off since the Civil War, until it is quite insignificant.

Merrimac, The.—This vessel, a two-masted iron steamship of 5,000 tons, was used by the United States in the Spanish-American War as a collier. During the month of May, 1898, the Spanish fleet under Admiral Cervera took refuge in the harbor of Santiago. The city of San-tiago is well located within the harbor, about 5 miles from the ocean proper. The channel leading from the harbor out to the ocean is at certain points quite narrow and comparatively easy to obstruct. This channel was well covered by Spanish batteries on shore, so that it was deemed unwise on the part of the American officers to attempt to enter the harbor with war ships. The American commander decided to attempt to block the channel, and for this purpose concluded to sink the *Merrimac* at a narrow point. It follows necessarily that such an undertaking would be exceedingly dangerous to those who were to steer the unarmed vessel within the channel, and then at the proper moment sink it and endeavor to escape by swimming ashore or attempting to reach a lifeboat. Assistant Naval Constructor Richmond P. Hobson was chosen at his own request to execute the hazardous undertaking. Volunteers were called for to accompany and assist him. Fifteen hundred officers and men responded, gallantly tendering services, and begged that they be accepted. Six only were accepted, whose names are Daniel Montague, chief master-at-arms of the *New York;* George Charette, gunner's mate of the *New York;* John Murphy, cockswain of the *Iowa;* Francis Kelley, water tender; George F. Phillips, machinist, and Cockswain O. W. Deignan, the last three of the *Merrimac.* Randolph Clousen, cockswain of the *New York*, was during the delay of one day added to the company. On the morning of June 3, 1898, at about half past 3 o'clock, Hobson steered straight into the channel under a heavy fire from Spanish guns on both sides. As the *Merrimac* reached the spot that had been picked out for her sinking he gave orders to explode the torpedoes. Two of them only exploded. Amid the tremendous fire from the shore batteries, the firing of 8 electric mines in the channel, and torpedoes from 2 Spanish vessels the collier sank, her masts and smokestack showing above the water, obstructing but not blocking the fairway. As the ship went down the Spaniards sent up a cheer, believing they had sunk some large war vessel. Hobson and his men held on to a catamaran belonging to their sunken ship for about an hour. Just after sunrise a steam launch came down the harbor with Admiral Cervera on board. Hobson and his men were taken on board the launch, were courteously treated by their captors, and placed in prison. They were all exchanged July 6. The sinking of the *Merrimac* was an act of heroism which challenged the admiration of the world. The President, in a message to Congress, speaking of the incident, said: "This enterprise, demanding coolness, judgment, and bravery amounting to heroism, was carried into successful execution in the face of a persistent fire from the hostile fleet as well as from the fortifications on shore" (X, 158). Rear-Admiral Sampson said: "I can not myself too earnestly express my appreciation of the conduct of Mr. Hobson and his gallant crew. I venture to say that a more brave and daring thing has not been done since Cushing blew up the *Albemarle*" (X, 159). The President recommended that a vote of thanks be given Hobson by Congress. He and his crew were subsequently promoted.

Merrimac, The (United States collier), sinking of, in Santiago Harbor, Cuba, by Lieut. Richmond P. Hobson, X, 158, 169.

Naval Cadet Powell to be made ensign for attempting to rescue force of, X, 159.

Thanks of Congress to Lieut. Hobson and promotion of, recommended, X, 159.

Merritt, Edwin A., collector of the port of New York:

Congratulations of President on confirmation of, VII, 549.

Modifications of rules submitted by, VII, 550, 555.

Merritt, Wesley:

Directed to aid in executing laws in Indian Territory, IX, 48.

Expeditions to Philippine Islands under command of, X, 168.

Attack upon and surrender of Manila, X, 172.

Thanks of President tendered, X, 217.

Instructions of President regarding military occupation of islands, X, 208, 211, 212.

Joint occupancy with insurgents not to be permitted, X, 217.

Merryman Case.—Merryman, a citizen of Maryland, was arrested at his home in 1861 by order of an officer of the United States Army and charged with treason. He was imprisoned in Fort McHenry. Chief Justice Taney granted a writ of *habeas corpus*, which the officer in charge of the prisoner refused to execute on the ground that the President had suspended the writ. The case was taken before the Supreme Court of the United States. The court decided that power to suspend the writ of *habeas corpus* was not vested in the President, Congress alone having that privilege, and that a military officer has no right to arrest a person not subject to the Rules and Articles of War except in aid of judicial authority. (See also Habeas Corpus; Milligan Case.)

Mertz, Anna, act granting pension to, vetoed, VIII, 670.

Mescalero Agency, N. Mex., buildings at, recommended, VIII, 105.

Mescalero Reservation, N. Mex., improvements on, payment to settlers for, recommended, VIII, 397.

Meshouda, The, act for relief of captors of, returned, X, 27.

Messages and Papers of the Presidents, resolution authorizing compilation of, I, III.

Messages, Presidential.—A written communication by the President to Congress. At the beginning of each session an annual message is transmitted going into details of our standing as a nation and recommending such action by the House and Senate as may be deemed necessary to the progress of the country or the correction of abuses. Special messages are sent from time to time to either or both Houses, submitting treaties or correspondence, or in answer to a request from either branch for particular information, or to recommend specific or immediate legislation. Veto messages are sent with the returned bills which the President disapproves, in which he states his reasons for such disapproval. After pointing out wherein a bill fails to meet the requirements of the case he usually suggests the way to an effective measure that may receive Executive sanction. Article II, section 3, of the Constitution declares that the President "shall from time to time give to the Congress information of the state of the Union and recommend to their consideration such measures as he shall judge necessary and expedient." Washington and John Adams read their annual messages to Congress. Jefferson inaugurated the custom, since followed by all of his successors, of sending messages in writing to Congress (I, 325). They are carried by the private secretary of the President, who is received at the door of the Senate or House, and whose presence is formally announced by an officer of the body, whereupon he delivers the message to the clerks.

Messages, Presidential. (See Annual Messages; Special session messages; Veto messages, under the several Presidents.)

Metals, Precious. (See Gold and Silver.)

Meteor, The, seizure and detention of, referred to, VI, 382.

Meteorological Observatory, establishment of, at Fort Myer, Va., recommended, VIII, 205.

Metric Convention with certain foreign governments referred to, VII, 358, 608.

Metric System, obligatory use of, referred to, VII, 456. (See also Decimal System, etc.)

Mexican War.—The Mexican War grew out of the annexation of Texas by the United States. Mar. 2, 1836, Texas seceded from Mexico and declared her independence, which she maintained by the defeat of Santa Anna in the battle of San Jacinto, Apr. 21, 1836. The United States, England, France, and Belgium recognized the new Government as independent. Dec. 29, 1845, Texas was annexed to the United States. A dispute as to the boundary induced President Polk to order Gen. Taylor to take a position in the disputed territory on the left bank of the Rio Grande. Here (near Matamoros) he was attacked Apr. 23, 1846, by Mexicans under Arista, and a portion of his army was captured. Taylor advanced into the north of Mexico, leaving garrisons at Corpus Christi and at Fort Brown, opposite Matamoros, and after the battles of Palo Alto (May 8, 1846), Resaca de la Palma (May 9, 1846), Buena Vista (Feb. 22, 23, 1847), and a number of lesser fights, in which the Mexicans were defeated, he obtained control of all northern Mexico. Gen. Scott, landing at Vera Cruz, advanced to the City of Mexico, defeating Santa Anna at Cerro Gordo (Apr. 17, 18, 1847), Contreras (Aug. 19, 20, 1847), Churubusco (Aug. 20, 1847), and Molino del Rey (Sept. 7, 8, 1847), causing the surrender of the capital and the termination of the

the north by the United States, on the east by the Gulf of Mexico and the Caribbean Sea, on the south by British Honduras, Guatemala, and the Pacific Ocean, and on the west by the Pacific Ocean. The Republic includes Lower California and Yucatan. It has 27 States, 1 federal district, and 2 territories. Mining, agriculture, and cattle raising are extensively carried on. The Government is modeled after that of the United States. The language is Spanish, the religion Roman Catholic, and the people chiefly creoles, Indians, and mixed races. Mexico has an area of 751,664 sq. miles and a population (1894) of 12,080,725. The early inhabitants were Toltecs, Aztecs, and other native races. Some of the leading historical events of the country are: The invasion of Cortez, 1519; conquest of the capital, 1521; the country made a Spanish colony under the name of New Spain (a viceroyalty after 1535); revolution under Hidalgo, 1810; partially suppressed, 1815; revolution under Iturbide and Spanish viceroy deposed, 1821; Empire established, 1822; Texas seceded, 1836, which finally resulted in war with the United States, 1846–1848. There were frequent changes in its government until 1862, when war began with France. Maximilian established an Empire, which was upheld by French troops, in 1864, during the Civil War in the United States. The United States protested at the time against the establishment of the Empire because it was in violation of the Monroe doctrine. Shortly after the close of the American Civil War the French troops were withdrawn, and Maximilian, being left to his own resources, was unable to maintain the Empire. He was captured by the Republican forces, condemned to death, and shot in 1867. (See also Mexican War.)

Mexico:

Affairs of, referred to, VI, 77, 210, 527

Agent sent to, referred to, V, 583.

American citizens in—

Captured by army of, IV, 91, 157.

Liberated, IV, 197.

Expelled from jurisdiction of, IV, 327, 345; V, 513, 589.

Forbidden to sell goods, IV, 262.

Murdered, V, 565, 645.

Outrages on, and injuries sustained by, IV, 354, 437, 473, 533, 644; V, 336, 512, 563; VII, 189, 404.

Property of, seized or destroyed by, IV, 473; V, 513, 565, 589.

American flag insulted by, IV, 473.

American troops—

Occupying territory of, referred to, VI, 459, 462.

Sent to, for protection of citizens from Indian depredations, III, 238.

Act should not be considered as encroachment upon rights of, III, 238.

Referred to, III, 429.

To be sent to, for protection of citizens of United States in, recommendation regarding, V, 566, 645.

Mexico—Continued.

American troops—Continued.

Transit of, through territory of, in 1861 referred to, VI, 376.

Ample cause of war against, asserted, IV, 419, 533.

Armies of, in Texas defeated, III, 268.

Armistice between United States and, referred to, IV, 574.

Austin-Topolovampo Railroad survey across northern States of, referred to, VII, 523.

Austrian troops dispatched to, referred to, VI, 390, 391.

Blockade of coast of, referred to, III, 516.

Blockade of ports of, by France and injurious effect of, on United States discussed, III, 488.

Boundary dispute with Guatemala, VIII, 40, 129, 215.

Arbitration of, submitted to United States minister to, IX, 634.

Boundary line with United States—

Adjustment of, chief obstacle in settling difficulties, IV, 456, 459.

Appropriation for expenses of commission recommended, V, 13, 173; VIII, 215.

Commission engaged in marking, referred to, V, 13, 129, 173, 183, 280, 382.

Commissioners appointed, III, 99; IV, 644.

Convention regarding, VIII, 111, 129, 173, 254, 366, 372, 812, 815; IX, 187.

Matias Romero's note regarding, referred to, VIII, 372.

Proposed, VIII, 99.

Discussed, III, 26, 151; VIII, 99, 129, 333, 783; IX, 316.

International boundary commission discussed, IX, 187, 438, 634.

Proclamation regarding, V, 393.

Proposition regarding, submitted by United States commissioner unauthorized, IV, 569.

Recommendation that Executive be given power to advance money for settlement of, IV, 456, 459, 495, 538.

Referred to, III, 26, 371; V, 157, 367; VIII, 170; X, 69.

Settlement of, proclaimed, V, 393.

Treaty regarding transmitted and discussed, II, 567; III, 151, 187; IV, 482; V, 210; VIII, 99; IX, 187.

Legislative provision for execution of, recommended, III, 226, 238; VIII, 238.

Referred to, III, 26; VIII, 170.

Water-Boundary Commission discussed, X, 187.

Cession of California and New Mexico to United States by—

Area and value of, discussed, IV, 599, 634.

Discussed and recommendations regarding, IV, 456, 459, 494, 506, 536, 576, 587, 594, 634.

Treaty for, transmitted, IV, 587.

Cession of territory of, to United States—

Report on, transmitted, III, 371.

Treaty regarding, V, 229.

Charge that American army invaded territory of, refuted, IV, 482.

Chief of, captured, III, 268.

Michilimackinac. (See Mackinaw.)

Middle Creek (Ky.), Battle of.—Jan. 9, 1862, Col. James A. Garfield broke up his camp at Muddy Creek, Ky., and advanced with 1,800 men to attack Gen. Humphrey Marshall, who had some 2,500 troops, in Johnston County. Marshall, being advised of Garfield's approach, took up a position on the heights of Middle Creek, about 2 miles from Prestonburg. On the morning of the 10th Garfield began the attack. The battle lasted all day. Marshall retired from the field in the evening upon the arrival of Federal reenforcements and burned his stores to prevent their falling into Federal hands. Seventy-five of the Confederate dead were picked up on the field. The Union loss was less than 30, according to Federal accounts.

Middle States, armed neutrality in, discussed, VI, 24.

Midnight Appointments.—During the last days of his Presidential term John Adams, piqued at the success of Jefferson, whom he bitterly opposed for the Presidency, made a number of Federal appointments, in every instance of men opposed to Jefferson and his principles. Among the appointments were 16 circuit judges. Some of the commissions of these appointees were signed just before midnight of Mar. 3, 1801, and were called "midnight appointments."

Midway Island referred to, VIII, 602.

Mifflin, Thomas, letter of, referred to, I, 266.

Milan and Berlin Decrees discussed and referred to by President—
Jefferson, I, 421, 427, 442, 444, 446, 453, 458.
Madison, I, 482, 489, and X, 121; I, 491, 518, 528, 537; X, 35, 42, 45, 46, 47.
Proclamations regarding, I, 472, 481.

Milan Decree.—Nov. 11, 1807, France and England being then at war, the King of Great Britain and his privy council issued a decree forbidding trade between the United States and any European country under Napoleon's power. Napoleon thereupon, in retaliation, on Dec. 7, 1807, issued the Milan Decree, in which he declared "denationalized," whether found in continental ports or on the high seas, any vessel which should submit to search by a British vessel or should touch at or set sail to or from Great Britain or her Colonies. (See also Berlin Decree; Embargo; Orders in Council.)

Milan, Italy, Beneficence Congress at, VIII, 39.

Mileage.—Compensation for traveling expenses at a certain rate per mile. The First Congress passed a law allowing each member $6 for every 20 miles traveled in going to and from Congress. In 1818 this was raised to $8, and in 1856 mileage was limited to 2 sessions. Railway transportation having cheapened traveling expenses, Congress in 1866 reduced the mileage to 20 cents a mile.

Mileo, Nicolino, impressment of, into service of and punishment by Italy referred to, IX, 238.

Miles, Dixon S., court of inquiry in case of, referred to, VI, 59.

Miles, Nelson A. :
Member of Ponca Indian Commission, VII, 630.
Order to, for release of Clement C. Clay, jr., X, 113.
Outbreaks among Sioux suppressed by, IX, 201.
Puerto Rican campaign under command of, X, 171.
Surrender of Indians to, VIII, 514.

Miles, The, claims of owners of, against Portugal, IV, 603.

Military Academy.—As early as 1776 the idea of a national military academy had been advanced. A committee of the Continental Congress was appointed to "prepare and bring in a plan of a military academy of the army." Washington called the attention of Congress to the matter in 1793, and in 1796 recommended the institution of a military academy (I, 202). Mar. 16, 1802, Congress passed the law founding the Academy. The present high standard of the Academy is due largely to the efforts of Bvt. Maj. (afterwards Gen.) Sylvanus Thayer, of the Corps of Engineers, known as the "Father of the Academy." The General Commanding the Army has, under the War Department, supervision of the Academy. The immediate government consists of a Superintendent, commandant of cadets, and 7 commissioned professors. The Corps of Cadets consists of 1 from each Congressional district, 1 from each Territory, 1 from the District of Columbia, and 10 from the United States at large. Appointments from Congressional districts and from the Territories are made by the Secretary of War upon nomination by Members and Delegates. Those from the District of Columbia and from the United States at large are appointed by the President. Candidates must be between 17 and 22 years of age, at least 5 feet in height, of sound health and good moral character, and possessed of a common-school education. They take the oath of allegiance to the United States and serve 8 years unless sooner discharged. Graduates are commissioned second lieutenants by the President. The United States has also the Engineer School at Willets Point, N. Y., the Artillery School at Fort Monroe, Va., the Infantry and Cavalry School at Leavenworth, Kans., and the Light Artillery and Cavalry School at Fort Riley, Kans.

Military Academy :
Appropriations for, recommended, II, 389, 417.
Bequest of George W. Cullum for erection of memorial hall on grounds of, IX, 239.
Cadets in—
  Enlistment of, time of, should be extended, III, 390.
  Increase in corps of, recommended, VI, 48.
  Promotion of, referred to, IV, 572.
  Referred to, II, 52.
Discussed, II, 188, 212, 306, 417, 456; VII, 294; VIII, 349; IX, 447.
Enlargement of, necessary, I, 445, 486, 566.
Establishment of, recommended, I, 202, 205; II, 312.

Military Academy—Continued.
Expenditures of, VIII, 349.
Flags captured in Mexican War to be deposited in, X, 107.
Improvement in, recommended, VII, 194.
Military education in, recommendations regarding, III, 170.
Referred to, X, 120.
Regulations for, amended, VIII, 126.
Removal of, suggested, I, 445.
Rules for government of, II, 52.

Military Asylum. (See Soldiers' Home.)

Military Commanders (see also Military Districts and Divisions):
Anonymous letter filed with correspondence of, return of, requested, VII, 45.
Not vested with authority to interfere with contracts between individuals, order regarding, VI, 350.

Military Commissions to Cuba, Puerto Rico, and adjacent islands, X, 175.

Military Contributions. (See Mexico.)

Military Courts and Commissions (see also Lincoln, Abraham, military commission, etc.):
Order—
In relation to trials by, VI, 440.
Releasing certain persons undergoing sentences by, X, 114.
Sentences of imprisonment remitted, VI, 339.

Military Districts and Divisions:
Assignments to, VI, 551, 552, 556, 557, 661, 662, 663, 664, 665, 666, 668, 671; VII, 19, 21, 22, 93, 94; VIII, 166.
Orders regarding, rescinded, VII, 22, 94.
Creation of, VI, 662.
Authority for, referred to, VI, 632.
Dissolution of, VII, 94, 95, 666.
First, fourth, and fifth districts dissolved, VII, 94, 95.
Instructions relating to third district referred to, VI, 628.
Plans, etc., for barracks and quarters in Military Division of Potomac, VIII, 79.
Reports and recommendations of commanders of, VII, 40, 45.

Military Drafts. (See Drafts, Military.)

Military Encampment, International, to be held at Chicago during World's Fair discussed, IX, 234.
Foreign guests attending, not to pay duties on baggage, VIII, 579.

Military Establishment (see also Army):
Proposition of Czar of Russia for reduction of, discussed, X, 188.

Military Expeditions. (See Expeditions Against Foreign Powers.)

Military Governors. (See Provisional Governors.)

Military Information, Bureau of:
Discussed, IX, 447.
Reorganization of, IX, 320.

Military Justice, Bureau of, recommendations regarding, VII, 618.

Military Park. (See Chickamauga and Chattanooga National Military Park.)

Military Peace Establishment. (See Army.)

Military Posts:
Disposition of abandoned, recommended, VII, 572, 617.
Establishment of—
Lands donated by Indians for, I, 448.
Recommended, II, 262; III, 256; IV, 87, 25 337.
Estimates, plans, etc., for, VIII, 79, 83, 87, 90, 9 100.

Military Reservations:
Additional land for Fort Preble, Me., recommended, VIII, 190.
Indian school at, establishment of, recommended, VIII, 96.
Legislation to provide for disposal of, recommended, VIII, 73, 103, 150, 153, 195, 196.

Military Stores, provision for—
Discussed, I, 428.
Recommended, I, 329.

Military Tribunals. (See Military Courts an Commissions.)

Militia.—Citizens of a State enrolled as soldier for training and discipline, but called int active service only in emergencies, as distin guished from the regular soldiers, who are i constant service. The Constitution empower Congress "to provide for calling forth the mili tia to execute the laws of the Union, suppres insurrections, and repel invasions." In 1792 a act was passed to provide for the nationa defense by establishing a uniform militia throughout the United States by the enroll ment of every free able-bodied white male citizen between the ages of 18 and 45. An act of Mar. 2, 1867, permitted the enrollment of negroes. The militia was called out by Federal authority in 1794 to quell the Whisky Rebellion in western Pennsylvania, during the War of 1812, and in 1861, during the Civil War.

Militia (see also Army):
Arming and equipping of, recommended, VIII, 137, 181; IX, 727.
Artillery tactics for use of, prepared, II, 361.
Brigadier-generals of, appointed, X, 13.
Called out to prevent British invasion from Canada, III, 401.
Cavalry tactics for use of, prepared, II, 361.
Discharge of, directed, I, 470.
Discussed by President—
Adams, J. Q., II, 303, 392, 429.
Arthur, VIII, 181.
Cleveland, IX, 445, 536, 727.
Jackson, II, 603; III, 170, 255.
Jefferson, I, 329, 345, 385, 406.
Lincoln, VI, 48.
Madison, I, 476, 478, 486, 494, 349, 566, 576.
Monroe, II, 189, 212.
Polk, IV, 631.
Tyler, IV, 49, 268.
Van Buren, III, 537.
Washington, I, 65, 67, 86, 107, 140, 167, 169, 184, 204.
Distribution of arms, ordnance stores, etc., to District of Columbia and Territories, regulations regarding, VIII, 574; IX, 27.
Encampment of National Guard in coast works recommended, IX, 41.

Militia—Continued.

Encouragement of National Guard recommended, IX, 115.

General abstract of, transmitted, X, 60.

Increase in, recommended, I, 441.

Indian wars, campaigns of, in. (See Indian Wars.)

Insurrections suppressed by. (See Illegal Combinations.)

Laws for, revision of, recommended, I, 238, 240, 329, 519, 538; II, 303, 603.

Organization, arming, and disciplining, VII, 618.

Plan for, submitted, I, 71.

President can not call into service except by authority of Congress, V, 104.

Modification in laws regarding, recommended, V, 105.

Refusal of governors of Massachusetts and Connecticut to furnish quotas of, I, 516; X, 43.

Returns of, I, 350, 368, 378, 400, 421, 447, 461, 470; II, 15, 84, 118, 204, 212; X, 26, 36, 39, 46.

Rules and regulations for Army and, transmitted, X, 41.

Volunteer force should be enlisted, I, 441, 478, 494; IV, 268.

Young men should become members of, I, 385.

Mill Springs (Ky.), Battle of.—Early in the winter of 1861–62 the Confederate General Felix K. Zollicoffer, with a force of about 5,000 men, intrenched himself at Mill Springs, on the Cumberland River, in Wayne County, Ky. Jan. 17, 1862, Gen. George H. Thomas, with 8,000 Union troops, advanced to dislodge him. The Confederates set out to meet Thomas, and on Jan. 19, 1862, an engagement took place, begun by the advance guard of both armies. The Confederates were driven back to their camp, which they abandoned during the night. Twelve pieces of artillery, 156 wagons, 1,000 horses and mules, as well as large quantities of small arms, ammunition, and stores fell into the hands of the Union army. Crossing the Cumberland River, the retreating army burned their boats to prevent pursuit. The loss on the Confederate side was 350. The Unionists lost 246. Gen. Zollicoffer was among the Confederate dead.

Mill Springs, Ky., battle of, discussed, VI, 100.

Milledge, John, letter of President Madison to, regarding taking of oath, I, 466.

Miller, James, governor of Arkansas, legalization of official acts of, recommended, II, 232.

Miller, Joseph N., joint resolution annexing Hawaiian Islands delivered to President Dole by, X, 185.

Miller, Mary Ann, act granting pension to, vetoed, VIII, 445.

Miller, Samuel, act granting pension to, vetoed, VIII, 447.

Miller, Washington D., secretary to President Houston, of Texas, IV, 319.

Miller, William, refuge given to, by the *St. Louis*, II, 570.

Milligan Case.—A United States Supreme Court case involving the right of the President to suspend the rights of citizens under *habeas corpus* proceedings. Oct. 5, 1864, during the Civil War, Milligan was arrested by order of Gen. Hovey, and on Oct. 21 was brought before a military commission convened at Indianapolis, Ind., by the same officer. He was tried, found guilty, and sentenced to be hanged for participating in rebellious schemes. By the *habeas corpus* act of Congress in 1863 lists were to be furnished in each State of persons suspected of violating national laws. But any such persons arrested against whom no indictments should be found by the circuit or district court were to be freed on petition verified by oath. The Milligan indictment was not found by the circuit or district court. He objected to the authority of the military commission and sued for a writ of *habeas corpus* in the circuit court. The case coming before the Supreme Court in 1866, it was decided, Justice Davis reading the opinion, that the writ should be issued and the prisoner discharged. The court held that the power of erecting military jurisdiction in a State not invaded and not in rebellion was not vested in Congress and that it could not be exercised in this particular case; that the prisoner, a civilian, was exempt from the laws of war and could only be tried by a jury; that the writ of *habeas corpus* could not be suspended constitutionally, though the privilege of that writ might be. The Chief Justice and Justices Wayne, Swayne, and Miller, while concurring in the judgment, made through the first named a separate statement of reasons. The decision expressly stated that conspiracies to aid rebellion were enormous crimes and that Congress was obliged to enact severe laws to meet the crisis. (See also Habeas Corpus; Merryman Case.)

Millikens Bend (La.), Battle of.—During the operations before Vicksburg Grant had withdrawn troops from all the posts within his reach to strengthen his army. The fort at Millikens Bend, on the Mississippi River, in Louisiana, was left in charge of a small garrison, mostly negroes. June 6, 1863, the place was attacked by a party of Louisiana Confederates under Gen. Ben. McCulloch, who might have been successful in their assault but for the arrival of the gunboats *Choctaw* and *Lexington*. The Confederates were repulsed. The Federal loss was 404 killed and wounded.

Mills, Emily G., act for relief of, vetoed, VIII, 652.

Mills, Samuel M., mentioned, VIII, 191.

Milwaukee, Wis., proclamation granting privileges of other ports to, V, 326.

Mineral Lands. (See Lands, Mineral.)

Miners, act for protection of, in Territories discussed and recommendations regarding, IX, 228.

Mines (see also Lands, Mineral):

Copper, referred to, II, 195, 234.

Gold, discovered, VI, 250.

In Black Hills, VII, 352, 401.

In California, IV, 636.

Lead, referred to, I, 371; II, 141, 142, 190, 234, 326, 365.

Ministers of United States (see also Consular and Diplomatic Service; the several powers):

Accounts of, etc., transmitted, X, 50.

Minutemen.—At a session of the provincial congress of Massachusetts, Nov. 23, 1774, it was voted to enroll 12,000 minutemen. They were to be organized as militia and hold themselves ready for service at a minute's notice.

Miramon, Miguel:

President of Mexico, election of, discussed, V, 564, 644.

Property of American citizens confiscated by, V, 589.

Miranda Plot.—A joint scheme of citizens of the United States and Great Britain whereby, through the agitation of one Miranda, a citizen of Caracas, Venezuela, dissatisfaction was to be spread among the Spanish and French provinces. During the revolutions which it was hoped would ensue Great Britain was to obtain the West Indies and the United States Florida and Louisiana east of the Mississippi.

Mirboha, The:

Act for relief of captors of, returned, X, 27.

Indemnification to captors of, recommended, I, 366.

Miro District, brigadier-general for, appointed, X, 13.

Misdemeanors. (See Crimes and Misdemeanors.)

Mishouda, The, indemnification to captors of, recommended, I, 366.

Mission Commission, recommendations of, referred to, IX, 226.

Mission Indians:

Bill for relief of, VIII, 199, 369.

Commission to treat with, IX, 226.

Missionaries, American, treatment of, in Turkey discussed, VIII, 40, 505; IX, 440, 530, 637, 715.

Missionary Ridge, or Chattanooga (Tenn.), Battle of.—After retiring from Lookout Mountain Bragg's army concentrated on Missionary Ridge, across the Chattanooga Valley and southeast of the city. On the morning of Nov. 25, 1863, Sherman assailed the Confederate right wing at the extreme north end of the ridge. Hooker advanced from Lookout Mountain across the valley and attacked the left. The battle raged all day, but the Confederates held the position until late in the afternoon, when the center was weakened by withdrawals to support the left and right. It was then that Grant, watching the progress of the fight from Orchard Knob, ordered forward the Army of the Cumberland, under Thomas. Wood's and Sheridan's divisions charged the Confederate center. The brigades of Hazen and Willich were in advance. Darkness came on, when the Confederates retreated. Pursuit was stopped when the ridge was won. The Confederates lost more than 9,000, including 6,000 prisoners. Forty pieces of artillery and 7,000 stand of small arms fell into the hands of the victors. The Federal casualties in the Chattanooga campaign, between Nov. 24 and Nov. 29, were 753 killed, 4,722 wounded, and 349 missing—a total of 5,824.

Missions Boundary Dispute, evidence presented to President of United States as arbitrator by Argentine Republic and Brazil, IX, 435.

Award of, discussed, IX, 626.

M P—VOL X—31

Mississippi.—One of the United States; nickname, "The Bayou State." It is named for the river of that name and extends from lat. 30° 10′ to 35° north and from long. 88° 5′ to 91° 40′ west. It is bounded on the north by Tennessee, on the east by Alabama, on the south by the Gulf of Mexico and Louisiana, and on the west by Louisiana and Arkansas (separated by the Mississippi River). The chief industry is agriculture, cotton being the principal product. The region was visited by De Soto in 1540, and a settlement was attempted by the French under Iberville at Biloxi in 1699. The territory was ceded by France to Great Britain in 1763. Part was ceded to the United States in 1783 and the remainder was acquired in 1803. The Territory of Mississippi was organized in 1798 and admitted as a State in 1817. It seceded Jan. 9, 1861, and was readmitted Feb. 17, 1870. The State has an area of 46,810 sq. miles and a population (1890) of 1,289,600.

Mississippi (see also Confederate States):

Aaron Burr surrenders to officers in Territory of, I, 421.

Act endowing church in, vetoed, I, 490.

Act to authorize special term of circuit court of United States in, to be held in Scranton, vetoed, VII, 488.

Citizens of Territory of, must be protected, I, 384.

Colored troops to be recruited in, order regarding, X, 110.

Consolidation of Territory of, discussed, I, 438.

Elections in, and complications growing out of, proclamation regarding, VII, 322.

Fifteenth amendment, action of, on, referred to, VII, 47.

Lands granted to, in aid of railroads referred to, VI, 382.

Lands in Territory of, claimed by Great Britain, I, 450.

Laws of Territory of, referred to, I, 302, 313.

Legislative council for—

Dissolved by governor of, I, 457.

Nomination of, I, 457.

Letter to governor of, respecting militia for suppressing troubles on Mississippi River, X, 101.

Memorial from, regarding alleged violation of treaty by United States transmitted, IV, 150.

Offices in, President Jackson refuses to make further nominations for, II, 636.

Provisional governor for, appointed and restoration of, into Union discussed, VI, 314.

Reconstruction of—

Recommendations regarding, VII, 11.

Referred to, VII, 46.

Time for submitting constitution to voters proclaimed, VII, 16.

Referred to, VII, 29.

Survey of towns in, referred to, II, 28.

Unlawful combinations in, proclamation against, VII, 322.

Mississippi River:

Act to remove obstructions to navigation in mouth of, vetoed, V, 386.

kills to Lake Erie. Their villages were along the Mohawk River. They were known as one of the Five Nations, and were the first tribe of the region to obtain firearms. The Mohawks were allies of the English in their wars with the French and Americans. In 1784, under Brant, they retired to Upper Canada.

Mohawk Indians, treaty with, I, 265.

Mohegan Indians.—A tribe of the Algonquian family of Indians. They once lived chiefly on the Thames River, in Connecticut. The Mohegans claimed territory extending eastward into Massachusetts and Rhode Island. After the destruction of the Pequots, in 1637, they claimed the latter's lands. The death of King Philip, in 1676, left them the only important body of Indians in southern New England. They finally became scattered, some joining the Brotherton Indians in New York. The Mohegans are often confounded with the Mohicans and called River Indians.

Mohican Indians.—A tribe of the Algonquian family of Indians. The name is interpreted both as "wolf" and "seaside people." When first known to the whites they occupied both banks of the Hudson River, extending from near Albany to Lake Champlain. They were a distinct tribe from the Mohegans of the Connecticut River. The two tribes are generally confounded under the name of River Indians. The Mohicans were friendly to the English during the French and British struggles for supremacy in America. They assisted the colonists during the Revolution. Afterwards some of them became citizens.

Mo-lal-la-las Indians, treaty with, V, 381.

Mo-lel Indians. (See Mo-lal-la-las Indians.)

Molina, Luis, mentioned, V, 577.

Molino del Rey (Mexico), Battle of.—When the fortifications of Contreras and Churubusco had been passed, Gen. Scott took up his headquarters at Tacubaya, the bishop's castle, overlooking the western approaches to the City of Mexico, and 2½ miles distant. The first formidable obstruction was El Molino del Rey ("The King's Mill"). Gen. Worth's division of 3,100 men was detailed for attack upon this and its supporting fortification, Casa de Mata. These were stone buildings, strongly fortified and ably defended, the Mexicans contesting every foot of the ground. The attack was made on the morning of Sept. 8, 1847. After 2 hours' hard fighting the works were carried and the army of Santa Anna, 14,000 strong, driven back. The Mexican loss was 2,200 killed and wounded (among the former being Generals Valdarez and Leon) and more than 800 prisoners, including 52 commissioned officers. The American loss was 116 (including 9 officers) killed and 665 (including 49 officers) wounded and 18 missing. The magazine of Casa de Mata was blown up, and Worth returned to Tacubaya.

Monahan, Thomas R., arrest and imprisonment of, by Mexican authorities, VIII, 265.

Monetary Conference. (See International Monetary Conference.)

Monetary Convention of Latin Union, Belgium declares its adhesion to, VIII, 372.

Monetary Union, American. (See International American Monetary Union.)

Money, Continental. (See Continental Money.)

Money-Order System discussed, II, 419; VIII, 52, 352, 792; IX, 321, 449, 539.

Money Orders, International, discussed, IX, 449, 539.

Money, Public. (See Revenue, Public.)

Monitor, The. (See Hampton Roads (Va.), Battle of.)

Monitor, The, engagement with the *Merrimac* discussed, VI, 112.

Monmouth (N. J.), Battle of.—An important conflict of the Revolutionary War, fought during the afternoon of June 28, 1778, at Wenrock Creek, Monmouth County, N. J., Gen. Washington in command of the Americans and Sir Henry Clinton commanding the British. June 18 Clinton left Philadelphia for New York with 11,000 men and a large supply train. Washington pursued him with about 20,000 men. After some preliminary skirmishing, in which the Americans, led by Gen. Charles Lee, second in command, retreated, a general battle occurred. The British were defeated and drew off under cover of night, leaving about 300 dead upon the field. The Americans lost 228, less than 70 of whom were killed. An incident of the battle was Washington's severe reprimand of Gen. Charles Lee, which resulted in the latter's final dismissal. Lee had opposed bringing on the battle, but when his advice was rejected in the council of war asked and obtained the right to lead off in the engagement.

Monocacy (Md.), Battle of.—Gen. Hunter succeeded Gen. Sigel in command of the Federal forces in the Shenandoah Valley in June, 1864. Gen. Early was detached from Lee's army at Richmond and sent to reenforce Gen. Breckenridge, who commanded the Confederate forces in the valley. Hunter retired westward across the mountains, leaving Washington unprotected. Lee thereupon reenforced Early, increasing his strength to 20,000, and ordered him to threaten Washington, in the hope of compelling Grant to withdraw some of the troops before Richmond and Petersburg. The Sixth Corps, under Wright, was sent to defend Washington, with the Nineteenth Corps, which arrived from Hampton Roads. July 6 Early reached Hagerstown and moved a strong column toward Frederick, whereupon Gen. Lew. Wallace advanced from Baltimore with a force of 6,000 men. He encountered Early on the 9th at Monocacy, Md., and for 8 hours resisted his advance, but was finally defeated, with a loss of 98 killed, 579 wounded, and 1,282 missing. The Confederate loss was stated by Gen. Early at from 600 to 700, including the cavalry.

Monopolies, evils of trusts and, discussed and recommendations regarding, VIII, 773; IX, 43, 744.

Monroe, James (fifth President United States): Accounts and claims of, discussed by, II, 277. Referred to, II, 323.

Monroe Doctrine.—After the overthrow of Napoleon, France, Russia, Prussia, and Austria formed the so-called Holy Alliance in September, 1815, for the suppression of revolutions within each others' dominions and for perpetuating peace. The Spanish colonies in America having revolted, it was rumored that this alliance contemplated their subjugation, although the United States had acknowledged their independence. George Canning, English secretary of state, proposed that England and America unite to oppose such intervention. On consultation with Jefferson, Madison, John Quincy Adams, and Calhoun, Monroe, in his annual message to Congress in 1823 (II, 218), embodied the conclusions of these deliberations in what has since been known as the Monroe doctrine. Referring to the threatened intervention of the powers, the message declares: "We owe it, therefore, to candor and to the amicable relations existing between the United States and those powers to declare that we should consider any attempt on their part to extend their system to any portion of this hemisphere as dangerous to our peace and safety. With the existing colonies or dependencies of any European power we have not interfered and shall not interfere. But with the Governments who have declared their independence and maintained it, and whose independence we have, on great consideration and on just principles, acknowledged, we could not view any interposition for the purpose of oppressing them, or controlling in any other manner their destiny, by any European power in any other light than as the manifestation of an unfriendly disposition toward the United States." The promulgation of this doctrine is accredited to Mr. Monroe, but Jan. 3, 1811, the principle was substantially enunciated by Mr. Madison. In a message to Congress of that date (I, 488), while discussing a threat of Great Britain to take possession of a portion of Florida claimed by Spain, he used these words: "I recommend to the consideration of Congress the seasonableness of a declaration that the United States could not see, without serious inquietude, any part of a neighboring territory in which they have in different respects so deep and so just a concern pass from the hands of Spain into those of any other foreign power."

Monson, Sir Edmund, award of, as arbitrator in claim of Carlos Butterfield & Co. against Denmark, IX, 110.

Montana.—One of the United States; motto, "Oro y plata" ("Gold and silver"). It is included between lat. 45° and 49° north and long. 104°

Morgan's Raid.—In the summer of 1863 the Confederate General Buckner was in East Tennessee, near the borders of Kentucky, preparing for an expedition against Louisville. Gen. John H. Morgan was sent ahead with 2,460 cavalry to pave the way. He crossed the Cumberland River, and, having been joined by about 1,000 Kentuckians, passed over the Ohio River into Indiana. The advance of Rosecrans's army prevented Buckner from joining him. Morgan rode through southern Indiana toward Cincinnati, burning bridges, tearing up railroads, and fighting home guards. The whole State of Ohio became alarmed, and a strong Union force was soon in pursuit. Others were advancing upon his flanks, and gunboats were patrolling the Ohio River to prevent his recrossing into Kentucky. Passing around Cincinnati, he reached the river at Buffington Ford July 19. After a severe battle with various installments of Federal troops which had hotly pursued him, about 800 of the command surrendered, but Morgan, with the remainder, proceeded up the river to Belleville. About 300 succeeded in crossing the river here before the arrival of the gunboats. Many were drowned or shot in attempting to cross, and Morgan, with about 200 of his men, retreated farther up the river to New Lisbon, where he was surrounded and forced to surrender. In his raid Morgan traveled about 350 miles through Indiana and Ohio, making sometimes 50 miles a day. The amount of property destroyed scarcely exceeded $50,000. More than 2,000 of his men were killed or captured. Morgan and some of his officers were sent to Columbus and confined in the penitentiary, from which he and 6 others escaped. Immediately after his escape he planned another raid into the Union lines in Tennessee, but was surrounded and killed by Union troops under Gen. Gillem, near Greenville, Tenn.

Morhiser, William H., act for relief of, vetoed, VIII, 563.

Mormon Church (see also Polygamy):
Commissioners appointed under act in reference to bigamy, etc., referred to, VIII, 91, 144, 184, 214, 250, 361.
Letter of president of, advising Mormons to refrain from contracting marriage forbidden by law, IX, 118, 368, 510.
Suit instituted by Government for termination of, discussed, VIII, 794.

Mormons.—A religious sect calling themselves the "Church of Jesus Christ of Latter-Day Saints." They came into political prominence because of their practice and advocacy of polygamy. The sect was founded by Joseph Smith in 1830 on what they claim to have been a divine revelation. They organized first in New York and Vermont and later in Missouri and Illinois. Finally, about 1847, they settled at Salt Lake City, Utah. Their defiance and resistance of law caused many difficulties between them and the authorities. Their first armed resistance to Federal authority was in 1857. Special laws bearing upon the Mormons were passed by Congress in 1862, 1882, and 1887. The Supreme Court of the United States upheld these laws, which forbade polygamy and provided for its punishment by heavy fines and imprisonment, disincorporated the church and its societies, and confiscated their property.

Mormons, laws to prevent importation of, recommended, VIII, 362.

Morning Light, The, seizure of the *Jorgen Lorentzen* by, VI, 70.

Morocco.—A country in northwestern Africa. It is bounded on the north by the Mediterranean Sea, on the east by Algeria, on the south by the Sahara, and on the west by the Atlantic Ocean. The Atlas Mountains traverse the country from west to east. Its government is administered by a Sultan, who has despotic powers. The religion is largely Mohammedan. Area, exclusive of the Saharan tract and Tuat, about 170,000 sq. miles; population supposed to be about 8,000,000.

Morocco:
Consuls of United States in, I, 177.
Presents given to. (See Consuls.)
Differences with United States, communication from Commodore Morgan relative to adjustment of, referred to, IV, 210.
Emperor of—
Death of, I, 177.
Lion and horses presented to United States by, III, 37.
Legation of United States in, premises for, presented by Sultan of, VIII, 236, 338.
Moors in, conference regarding protection for, VII, 609.
Relations with, IV, 228.
Treaty regarding exercise of right of protection in, VII, 628.
Treaty with, transmitted and discussed, I, 98, 148, 182, 186, 189, 365 ; III, 239, 265, 279 ; VI, 384.
Expiration of first, near at hand, III, 99.
Vessels of United States seized or interfered with by, I, 364, 365.

Morrill, Ashley C., treaty with Indians concluded by, VI, 196.

Morris, Charles, correspondence relating to Hamet B. Caramalli transmitted, X, 29.

Morris, Edward J., mentioned, VI, 71.

Morris, George W., thanks of Congress to, recommended, VI, 144.

Morris, Gouverneur:
Minister to France, recall of, requested, I, 155.
Successor of, appointed, I, 156.
Treaty with Great Britain, appointed to conclude, I, 96.

Morris, Henry, thanks of Congress to, recommended, VI, 76.

Morris, Lewis R., United States marshal, nomination of, I, 99.

Morris, The, referred to, II, 467; IV, 263, 320, 353.

Morse, Freeman H., report of, on foreign maritime commerce of United States, etc., transmitted, VI, 633.

Morton, Joel B., act for relief of, vetoed, VIII, 681.

Morton, Oliver P., death of, announced and honors to be paid memory of, VII, 458.

Mosquito Indian Strip:

American citizens in—

Murdered, IX, 528.

Rights, etc., of, inquired into, IX, 559.

British troops landed at Bluefields, referred to, IX, 476.

Claims of Great Britain upon Nicaragua respecting treatment of citizens in, and action of United States, IX, 634.

Correspondence regarding, V, 31.

Insurrection in, and treatment of American citizens discussed, IX, 528.

Jurisdictional questions regarding, discussed, IX, 527, 634.

Mosquito Indians, correspondence regarding territory claimed by, referred to, V, 186, 361.

Mosquitos, Kingdom of. (See Mosquito Indian Strip.)

Motley, John L.:

Mentioned, VII, 60.

Minister to—

Austria—

Conversations and opinions of, referred to, VI, 466.

Removal of, referred to, VI, 582.

Resignation of, referred to, VI, 463.

Great Britain, recall of, referred to, VII, 116.

Mound Builders.—A prehistoric race of Americans who inhabited the valleys of the Ohio and Mississippi rivers. They are so named because the only traces of their existence are found in mounds of earth formed in regular geometrical shapes containing ashes, stone, and bronze implements and weapons. Some of these mounds seem to have been simply places of sepulture, while others show unmistakable evidences of having been erected as fortifications. The race probably became extinct only a few generations before the discovery of America, as De Soto found tribes of Southern Indians who built mounds and possessed other characteristics of the extinct race. They belonged distinctly to the Indian race and to the Stone Age. The mounds range from 2 or 3 feet in height to 132 feet high and 188 feet long, the latter being the dimensions of one at Marietta, Ohio, while one at Grave Creek, W. Va., measures 70 feet in height and 900 feet in circumference.

Mount Rainier Forest Reserve, Wash., establishment of, by proclamation, IX, 777.

Mountain Meadow (Utah) Massacre.—Efforts of the Federal Government to enforce the laws against polygamy incited the Mormons to bitter hatred of all opposed to their religion. Brigham Young made threats of turning the Indians loose upon west-bound immigrants unless what he considered the Mormons' rights were respected. Sept. 7, 1857, about 30 miles southwest of Cedar City, a body of about 120 non-Mormon immigrants were attacked by Indians and Mormons under the leadership of John D. Lee, and after a siege of 4 days were induced to surrender under promise of protection, but all were massacred except 17 children under 7 years of age.

Mountain Meadow Massacre referred to, V, 592.

Mowatt, Caroline D., act granting pension to, vetoed, IX, 673.

Mudd, Samuel A., implicated in assassination of President Lincoln, proceedings of trial and verdict of military commission, VI, 334, 335, 336, 342, 347, 348.

Mugwump.—A corruption of the Algonquian Indian word "mugquomp," which signifies a chief, ruler, or a person of importance. After long use in local politics the word came into national use in the Presidential campaign of 1884. The newspapers applied the term to those Republicans who refused to support James G. Blaine, the regular party nominee, and it has since been used to designate any person of independent politics or who is supposed to be lacking in loyalty to his political party.

Mulvihill, Thomas, petition of, for repossession of lands conveyed to United States by, VIII, 152.

Referred to, VIII, 191.

Mumfordville (Ky.), Battle of.—Here on Sept. 17, 1862, the Confederate army under Gen. Bragg attacked the Federals under Gen. J. T. Wilder. The post surrendered to the Confederates, the number of captured being about 4,000.

Munich, Bavaria, Third International Exhibition of Fine Arts to be held at, VIII, 608.

Munitions of War. (See Arms and Ammunition.)

Munn vs. Illinois.—One of the "elevator cases" decided by the Supreme Court of the United States. In 1872 Munn and another were found guilty of violating an article of the Illinois constitution in regard to grain warehouses. They had failed to take out a license and give bond and were charging higher rates for storage than the law allowed. The offenders were fined, and the supreme court of the State affirmed the action of the criminal court. The case was then appealed to the United States Supreme Court. That body affirmed the judgment on the ground that the act of the Illinois legislature was not repugnant to the Constitution of the United States, and that a State could lawfully determine how a man might use his own property when the good of other citizens was involved.

Munsee Indians, treaty with, I, 390, 397; III, 277, 429, 466, 556; V, 363; VI, 518, 637, 702.

Murat, Joachim, commerce of United States, depredations committed on, by, III, 50.

Murfreesboro (Tenn.), Battle of. (See Stone River (Tenn.), Battle of.)

Murray, Daniel, correspondence relating to Hamet B. Caramalli transmitted, X, 29.

Murray, William Vans, minister to France, nomination of, I, 282, 284.

Murrell, Mr., mentioned, I, 417.

Muscat:

Presents offered President Van Buren by Imaum of, declined, III, 592.

Offered United States, recommendations regarding, III, 592; IV, 316.

Treaty with, III, 53, 238, 376; VIII, 610.

Museum, National, appropriation for, recommended, VII, 479, 506.

Muskogee Indians. (See Creek Indians.)

N.

National Prison Congress at Baltimore referred to, VII, 208. (See also International Prison Congress.)

National Republican Party.—After the defeat of John Quincy Adams by Jackson in 1828 the broad-construction wing of the Democratic-Republican party organized and came out with a platform directly opposed to Jackson on the question of the tariff and the United States Bank. They opposed the spoils system in the public service, favored internal improvements at national expense, a bank of the United States, and the division of the proceeds of land sales among the States. In 1832 they supported Henry Clay for the Presidency and advocated a protective tariff. Clay was defeated, and in 1835 the party, reenforced by other elements, took the name of Whig.

National University.—Washington strongly disapproved of foreign education for American youth and early conceived the idea of establishing a national university in the central part of the United States. He bequeathed 50 shares of the Potomac Company toward the endowment of such an institution in the District of Columbia, but ultimately the stock of the company proved valueless. Several of the Presidents from time to time in their messages recommended the establishment of a national university or universities, or, as they sometimes called them, "seminaries of learning."

National University (see also Education; Seminaries of Learning):

Establishment of, recommended, I, 66, 202, 205, 410, 485, 568; II, 312; VII, 254.

Lands, donation of, to, recommended, I, 410, 485; VII, 254.

Nationality.—Federal and not State law determines the status of the nationality of persons in the United States. As the Constitution establishes no rules regarding the loss or acquisition of nationality, it is governed by the common law. All persons born in the United States are considered as endowed with nationality. The naturalization act of 1790 extended nationality to children born to American parents beyond the sea. In 1855 an act was passed restricting this to children whose fathers were citizens. The civil-rights act of 1866 declared "all persons born in the United States and not subject to any foreign power" to be citizens of the United States. The fourteenth amendment defines citizens as "all persons born or naturalized in the United States and subject to the jurisdiction thereof."

Nations, Congress of. (See under Panama, Isthmus of.)

Nations, Foreign. (See Powers, Foreign; the several powers.)

Naturalization.—The investment of an alien with the rights and privileges of citizenship. Section 8 of Article I of the Constitution empowered Congress "to establish a uniform rule of naturalization." Naturalization laws were passed by the colonial legislatures of Maryland, Virginia, New York, South Carolina, and Massachusetts between 1666 and 1715. In 1740 the British Parliament enacted a law regulating colonial naturalization. In 1790 Congress legislated for the first time so as to provide for uniformity of naturalization under the Constitution. The conditions of this law were that any free white alien might be admitted to citizenship by any court of record of the State in which he had resided for 1 year, having been a resident of the United States 2 years. An act of 1795 required 5 years' residence and application 3 years prior to naturalization; that of 1798 required 14 years' residence and application 5 years prior to naturalization. The act of Apr. 14, 1802, restored the conditions of the act of 1795 and required a proof of 5 years' residence in the United States and 1 in the State, good character, an oath of allegiance, and a renunciation of titles and prior allegiance. No alien may be naturalized if his country is at war with the United States. Conditions and procedure in naturalizing an alien are prescribed by sections 2163–2174 of the Revised Statutes of the United States. Naturalization of Chinamen is prohibited by section 14, chapter 126, laws of 1882. Naturalized citizens of the United States receive the same protection when abroad as native-born citizens. (See also Expatriation.)

Naturalization:

Act on subject of uniform rule of, vetoed, I, 523.

Discussed by President—

Adams, John, I, 258.

Arthur, VIII, 128, 241.

Buchanan, V, 640.

Cleveland, VIII, 336, 505, 781, 785.

Grant, VII, 36, 239, 291, 345, 405.

Harrison, Benj., IX, 37, 43, 116.

Jefferson, I, 331.

Johnson, VI, 517, 580.

Lincoln, VI, 180.

Madison, I, 523, 574.

Washington, I, 66.

Frauds in, discussed, VII, 291, 345, 405.

Questions regarding, with—

Germany, VII, 467, 568; VIII, 38, 331, 499; IX, 36, 437.

Russia, IX, 529.

Switzerland, VIII, 128; X, 190.

Turkey, VIII, 335, 504; IX, 440, 530; X, 190.

Treaty regarding, with—

Austria-Hungary, VII, 115, 144, 188.

Bavaria, VI, 690.

Belgium, VI, 694.

Denmark, VII, 206, 239.

Ecuador, VII, 165, 239.

Germany, VI, 630, 631, 632, 690.

Questions arising under, referred to, VII, 467, 568; VIII, 38, 331, 499; IX, 36, 437.

Great Britain, VI, 696, 758; VII, 60, 102, 123.

Prussia, VI, 629.

Sweden and Norway, VII, 79, 188.

Turkey, VII, 304; VIII, 813.

Questions arising out of, discussed, VIII, 335, 504; IX, 446, 530; X, 190.

Würtemberg, VII, 43.

Naturalization Laws:

Laws regarding expatriation and election of nationality discussed, VI, 458, 580; VII, 239, 291, 346, 405; VIII, 336. (See also Impressment; Naturalized Citizens.)

Revision of, recommended, I, 66, 68, 258, 331, 523, 574; VII, 405; VIII, 241, 336, 505, 785; IX, 43.

Naturalized Citizens (see also Aliens):

Allegiance of, to native government discussed, VI, 580.

Bureau of registration of. (See Registration Bureau.)

Distinctions not to be recognized between native citizens and, V, 641.

Duties of citizenship evaded by, discussed, VIII, 785.

Impressed into military service of foreign countries, V, 590; VI, 458.

By France discussed and referred to, V, 640; VI, 517; VIII, 614, 781.

Italy referred to, IX, 238.

Prussia discussed and referred to, V, 589, 592; VI, 517, 580.

Returning to native country and claiming citizenship in United States discussed, VI, 180; VII, 36, 239, 291, 345.

Navajo Indians.—An important tribe of the southern division of the Athapascan stock of Indians. From the time of their earliest discovery by the whites they have occupied the country along and south of the San Juan River, in northern New Mexico and Arizona, and extending into Colorado and Utah. They were surrounded by the Apache tribes except on the north, where the Shoshones were their neighbors. The Navajos are at present confined to the Navajo reservations in Utah, New Mexico, and Arizona.

Navajo Indians:

Practicability of restraining, within present reservations, etc., reports on, IX, 347.

Treaty with, V, 33; VI, 636.

Naval Academy.—An institution for the training of naval officers, founded at Annapolis, Md., in 1845, through the efforts of George Bancroft, then Secretary of the Navy. The Academy was not established by formal legislation of Congress, but was opened in October, 1845, under orders from the Secretary of the Navy. It was not until Aug. 10, 1846, that Congress took any action toward the encouragement of the enterprise. At that time $28,000 was appropriated for repairs, improvement, and instruction, and the following year a like sum was appropriated. In 1850 the school was reorganized and the name changed to the United States Naval Academy. At the outbreak of the Civil War the Academy was removed to Newport, R. I., where it remained until the summer of 1865, when it was reestablished at Annapolis. The Naval Academy is under the immediate control of an academic board, consisting of a superintendent, who is a naval officer; a commandant of cadets, and the heads of the different departments of study, who are, with one exception, naval officers. One naval cadet is allowed for each member of the House of Representatives, and, by appointment by the President, 1 for the District of Columbia and 10 from the country at large. The requirements for admission to the Academy are a robust constitution, freedom from physical defects, an age between 15 and 20 years, and a knowledge of the ordinary English branches. If admitted, cadets are obliged to sign an engagement to serve in the Navy 8 years and make a deposit of $200 to cover the cost of outfit. They receive $500 per year, but are required to pay for their subsistence, clothing, etc. The first three years all the cadets pursue the same course of study, but in the fourth the cadets destined for the line division pursue a course in seamanship, ordnance, gunnery, infantry tactics, navigation, surveying, compass deviation, and international law, while those who expect to serve in the engineer division take a course of instruction in marine boilers and engines and in designing machinery.

Naval Academy:

Appropriation for paving sidewalk at, recommended, VIII, 84.

Board of Visitors to, report of, referred to, VI, 389.

Discussed, V, 133; VI, 185.

Establishment of, recommended, II, 310.

Removal of, discussed, VI, 363.

Reorganization of, discussed, V, 177.

Naval Code, revision of, recommended, V, 89.

Naval Courts of Inquiry referred to, II, 326.

Naval Expeditions. (See Arctic Expeditions; Exploring Expeditions.)

Naval Militia.—In 1888 Congress passed an act authorizing the maritime States to organize a naval reserve, to be trained and fitted for operating the coast and harbor defense vessels, etc., in time of war, thus liberating the regular naval force to man the heavy seagoing war ships, etc. Massachusetts was the first State to pass laws providing for such organization. New York took similar action, and by 1898 most of the maritime States had regularly organized naval militia. The first appropriation for the equipment of the force was $25,000, made by Congress in 1891.

Naval Militia, development of, discussed, IX, 324, 734.

Naval Observatory.—A Government institution founded at Washington in 1842, and under the supervision of the Navy Department. It has published many volumes of astronomical observations, and an annual American Ephemeris or Nautical Almanac (issued some years in advance) ever since 1855. Important discoveries have been made by its 26-inch equatorial telescope, notably Asaph Hall's discovery of the satellites of Mars. It occupies a fine group of marble buildings on Georgetown Heights.

Naval Observatory:

Estimates for observation of transit of Venus referred to, VIII, 81.

Appropriation for, recommended, VIII, 101.

Referred to, VII, 295.

Removal of, recommended, VII, 573.

seized Monterey and Los Angeles, Cal. At the
outbreak of the Civil War the United States
had only about 40 vessels in commission. The
character of naval warfare at this time had
been changed by improved armament. The old
wooden vessels were useless when opposed by
the Whitworth and other modern guns of long
range and heavy caliber. The turreted ironclad was born of the emergency. A new navy
had to be constructed in order to maintain the
blockade of Southern ports, and by Jan. 1, 1864,
the National Government had over 600 vessels,
75 of them ironclads, with more than 4,600 guns
and 35,000 men. After the war the Navy was
reduced. Notwithstanding the appropriation
of large sums of money, 1882 found the United
States in possession of only 140 vessels, and
more than 100 of these were incapable of sea
service. Soon after this date a new policy regarding the Navy was inaugurated and has
since been pursued with credit and honor to
the nation. At present (1899) the Navy consists of 4 battle ships of the first class and 1 of
the second class, 2 first-rate armored cruisers, 3 first-rate and 12 second-rate protected cruisers, 9 unprotected cruisers, 1 first-
rate and 5 second-rate double-turret monitors
(including the *Monterey*, with barbette turret),
12 third-rate single-turret monitors, 16 third-
rate and 3 fourth-rate gunboats, 1 harbor-
defense ram, 1 dispatch boat, 1 dynamite
cruiser, 16 torpedo boats, 39 tugs, 1 training
ship, 6 receiving and 6 sailing ships—a total of
139 effective fighting vessels. There are at present under construction 8 first-class battle ships,
4 monitors, 20 torpedo boats, and 16 torpedo-
boat destroyers. Yachts, steamers, colliers,
etc., swell the total number of vessels in the
Navy to 242. By an act of Mar. 3, 1893, the
number of enlisted men and boys in the Navy
was limited to 9,000. The highest office in the
Navy is that of Admiral, which was established
by special act of Congress in consideration of
distinguished service, and corresponds to the
rank of general in the Army. (See Admiral.)
The Navy reorganization law of Mar. 3, 1899,
abolished the office of commodore and provided for 18 rear-admirals, 70 captains, 112 commanders, 170 lieutenant-commanders, 300 lieutenants, and not more than 350 lieutenants (ju-
nior grade) and ensigns. The pay of officers
ranges from $6,000 per year for a rear-admiral
at sea (the Admiral receiving $13,000) to $800 for
an ensign on waiting orders during his first 5
years of service. The principal navy-yards are
Brooklyn, N. Y.; Boston, Mass.; Norfolk, Va.;
Portsmouth, N. H.; League Island, Pa.; Mare
Island, Cal.; Pensacola, Fla., and Washington,
D. C.; and stations are maintained at Newport,
R. I.; New London, Conn.; Port Royal, S. C.;
Key West, Fla., and Bremerton, Wash.

Navy:

Admiral of, revival of grade of, recommended,
X, 198.

Appointments in, referred to, IV, 276, 281.

Apprentices, corps of, recommended, V, 177.

Appropriations for. (See Navy Department.)

Navy—Continued.

Auxiliary, in Spanish-American War, X, 166.

Boys, enlistment of, in, recommended, III, 173,
257; V, 177.

Canvas, etc., made of hemp grown in United
States used in equipment of vessels of, X, 67.

Clothing for, foreign and domestic articles consumed in, X, 49.

Code of, revision of, recommended, V, 89.

Condition of, report regarding, transmitted, X,
33.

Courts-martial in. (See Courts-Martial.)

Courts of inquiry in, referred to, II, 326.

Discipline of—

Discussed, IX, 734.

Flogging abolished, referred to, V, 97.

Punishment discussed, V, 133, 176, 178, 289.

Referred to, V, 97, 409.

Discussed by President—

Adams, John, I, 236, 273, 280, 307, 312.

Adams, J. Q., II, 310, 359, 389.

Arthur, VIII, 51, 84, 87, 139, 181, 209, 247, 261.

Buchanan, V, 459, 524, 531.

Cleveland, VIII, 350, 515, 790; IX, 450, 540, 732.

Fillmore, V, 88, 97, 132, 175, 178.

Grant, VII, 40, 55, 108, 149, 196, 248, 295, 350, 408.

Harrison, Benj., IX, 44, 116, 200, 323.

Hayes, VII, 453, 455, 473, 500, 573, 613, 621.

Jackson, II, 459, 604; III, 35, 50, 115, 173, 192,
225, 256.

Jefferson, I, 329, 345, 347, 372, 419, 428, 454.

Johnson, VI, 363, 451, 577, 684.

Lincoln, VI, 39, 48, 149, 184, 248.

McKinley, X, 197.

Madison, I, 470, 476, 478, 486, 519, 528, 534, 549,
553, 566.

Monroe, II, 16, 25, 31, 34, 46, 49, 62, 80, 108, 195,
214, 222, 231, 242.

Pierce, V, 215, 288, 339, 409.

Polk, IV, 412, 426, 505, 561, 651.

Taylor, IV, 49, 88, 202, 211, 269, 274, 276, 277,
278, 281; V, 21.

Van Buren, III, 392, 502, 537, 601, 618.

Washington, I, 193, 201.

Education in. (See Naval Academy.)

Elections, interference in, by, prohibited, VI,
668.

Establishment of, recommended, I, 201.

Expenditures of. (See Navy Department.)

Fighting force of, in Spanish-American War,
X, 166.

Foundry for making heavy guns for, recommended, VIII, 210, 246.

Gunboats. (See Vessels, United States.)

Increase in. (See Vessels for, *post.*)

Insane asylum for. (See Government Hospital
for Insane.)

Laws in relation to, III, 50.

Marine Corps. (See Marine Corps.)

Naval force abroad. (See Chile; Great Lakes;
Haiti; Mediterranean Sea; Peru; Squadrons;
West Indies.)

Naval force for protecting commerce indispensable, I, 201, 205, 236; III, 502.

Referred to, III, 618.

Naval parade to be held in New York Harbor,
IX, 325.

Navy Department.—One of the eight Executive Departments of the Government. It was created in 1798. It is officially denominated the Department of the Navy, and its head is a civil officer known as the Secretary of the Navy. He is appointed by the President by and with the advice and consent of the Senate. He receives a salary of $8,000 per annum. Under the Constitution the President is Commander in Chief of the Army and Navy, but the Secretary is his representative in the Department of the Navy, and the acts of the Secretary are regarded as having the full force and effect of Presidential acts. Prior to the establishment of the Department of the Navy the administration of naval affairs was intrusted to committees, boards, and agents appointed under various acts of the Continental and Federal Congresses. In 1789 all matters relating to the Navy were placed under the jurisdiction of the War Department, where they remained until by the act of Apr. 30, 1798, the separate Department was organized and the office of Secretary of the Navy created. It is the duty of the Secretary to execute such orders as he shall receive from the President relative to the procurement of naval stores and materials and the construction, armament, and equipment of vessels of war. Subsequent acts have provided methods of discharging the ministerial duties of the Department. June 8, 1880, an act was passed authorizing the appointment of a Judge-Advocate-General. He has special charge of all matters relating to courts-martial, and is in a great measure the law officer of the Department. By an act of Congress approved July 1, 1890, the office of Assistant Secretary was revived, having been abolished at a previous time. He is, under the Revised

Statutes, Acting Secretary of the Navy during the absence or incapacity of his superior. The Hydrographic Office was established in 1862 and added as a bureau to the Department of the Navy. Following is a list of the Secretaries of the Navy from the establishment of the office in 1798 to 1898: George Cabot, Massachusetts (appointed and declined); Benjamin Stoddert, Maryland; Robert Smith, Maryland; Jacob Crowninshield, Massachusetts; Paul Hamilton, South Carolina; William Jones, Pennsylvania; B. W. Crowninshield, Massachusetts; Smith Thompson, New York; John Rodgers (acting), Maryland; Samuel L. Southard, New Jersey; John Branch, North Carolina; Levi Woodbury, New Hampshire; Mahlon Dickerson, New Jersey; James K. Paulding, New York; George E. Badger, North Carolina; Abel P. Upshur, Virginia; David Henshaw, Massachusetts; Thomas W. Gilmer, Virginia; John Y. Mason, Virginia; George Bancroft, Massachusetts; William B. Preston, Virginia; William A. Graham, North Carolina; John P. Kennedy, Maryland; James C. Dobbin, North Carolina; Isaac Toucey, Connecticut; Gideon Welles, Connecticut; Adolph E. Borie, Pennsylvania; George M. Robeson, New Jersey; Richard W. Thompson, Indiana; Nathan Goff, jr., West Virginia; William H. Hunt, Louisiana; William E. Chandler, New Hampshire; William C. Whitney, New York; Benjamin F. Tracy, New York; Hilary A. Herbert, Alabama; John D. Long, Massachusetts.

Navy Department:
Accounts of, in Fourth Auditor's Office referred to, II, 533.
Amount charged to State Department for services rendered by naval vessels referred to, VI, 462.
Appointments in, referred to, IV, 112.
Appropriations for, II, 361; VII, 474.
　　Diverted to survey of Isthmus of Darien referred to, VII, 46.
　　Necessary to render efficient, III, 225.
　　Recommended, II, 389, 605; III, 257; IV, 202; V, 339; VII, 453; VIII, 87, 209.
　　Referred to, VII, 455.
　　Transfer of, referred to, III, 601; IV, 269.
　　　　Act authorizing, approved, IV, 278.
Appropriations for docks, etc., should be separated from those for naval service, V, 89, 134.
Board of Commissioners for, referred to, II, 34, 62.
Clerks in, referred to, VI, 387.
Deficiencies in, referred to, VII, 455.
Expenditures of, I, 347; II, 231; IV, 202, 211; V, 89, 134; VI, 249, 452, 577, 684; VII, 108, 455, 473, 500, 573, 621; VIII, 791; IX, 540.
Fireproof building for, recommended, IV, 431; V, 168.
Navy Board—
　　New organization of, III, 33.
　　Report of, referred to, IV, 458.
　　Should be dispensed with, II, 460.
Persons employed in, without express provision of law, IV, 111, 321.

Navy Department—Continued.
Transfer of—
　　Coast Survey to, recommended, VIII, 140, 347; IX, 541.
　　Light-House Service to, recommended, VIII 140.
Payment of naval pensions to, recommended, VII, 106.

Navy, Secretary of:
Letter of Boynton and Fisher to, referred to, VI, 471.
Report of, VI, 35; X, 152.
　　Discussed. (See Navy discussed.)
　　Transmitted, I, 347; II, 276, 428, 534; III, 225; IV, 211.

Navy-Yards:
At Boston, machinery at, for preserving wood, referred to, VIII, 89.
　　Title of United States to land occupied as, referred to, VIII, 111.
At New York, new boiler shop at, recommended, VIII, 94.
At Norfolk, employment at, referred to, VI, 462.
At Washington, manufacture of guns at, discussed, IX, 541.
Civil service in connection with, discussed, IX, 542.
　　Order regarding, IX, 714.
Defense of, demands attention of Congress, III, 537.
Discontinuance of, on Atlantic seaboard referred to, V, 425.
Establishment of—
　　At Memphis referred to, IV, 349; V, 296.
　　On Atlantic seaboard recommended, VI, 184, 249.
　　　　Mississippi River recommended, IV, 279.
　　　　San Francisco Bay recommended, V, 133.
　　　　Western river recommended, VI, 184.
　　Recommended, VI, 363.
Improvements in, recommended, VII, 108.
Labor at, secured through boards of labor employment discussed, IX, 734.
List of, transmitted, X, 63.
Officers and men in, referred to, II, 196; VI, 462.
Officers attached to, referred to, X, 63, 64.
Referred to, X, 30.

Nebraska.—One of the United States; motto, "Equality before the law." It extends from lat. 40° to 43° north and from long. 95° 25′ to 104° west. It is bounded on the north by South Dakota (partly separated by the Missouri River), on the east by Iowa and Missouri (separated from both by the Missouri River), on the south by Kansas and Colorado, and on the west by Colorado and Wyoming. The State is one of the first in the production of corn, being extremely fertile in the eastern part and along the Platte River. Its principal industries are agriculture and stock raising. Nebraska originally formed part of the Louisiana Purchase and was later made a part of the Territory of Missouri. It was made a Territory in 1854, and included portions of the Dakotas, Montana, Wyoming, and Colorado. Nebraska was ad-

Neutrality, Proclamation of.—Neutrality, in international law, is the attitude and condition of a nation or state which does not take part directly or indirectly in a war between other states, but maintains relations of friendship with all the contending parties. In ancient times war between any two nations was likely to involve any other, either through sympathy or by its being drawn unwillingly into the controversy on accusation of favoring one or the other of the belligerents. Modern civilization has made it possible for a peacefully inclined nation to avoid entanglements in quarrels not of its own making. The position which a state intends to take in case of war between its neighbors should be clearly defined. It is customary, therefore, on the breaking out of hostilities for every nation not participating therein to declare its position with reference to the belligerents. This is usually done by a proclamation by the chief ruler of a state proclaiming its neutrality and calling upon its citizens to refrain from any acts of hostility or special favor toward either of the parties to the strife. It is also customary for every nation to put on its statute books general laws regulating the acts of its citizens with reference to foreign wars. Upon the declaration of war between France and Great Britain in 1793 it was decided unanimously by Washington and his Cabinet that a proclamation of neutrality should issue and that a French minister should be received. The proclamation was drafted by John Jay and declared the intention of the United States to pursue a policy of friendship toward both nations, and enjoined upon all citizens to avoid a contravention of that disposition upon pain of prosecution. It is a curious fact that the word "neutrality" was omitted from this proclamation, but it was enforced with fairness.

Nevada.—One of the United States; nickname, "The Sage Brush State;" motto, "All for our country." Nevada extends from lat. 35° to 42° north and from long. 114° to 120° west. It is bounded on the north by Oregon and Idaho, on the east by Utah and Arizona, and on the west and southwest by California. The State is rich in the precious metals, the principal products being silver and gold. The territory was ceded by Mexico in 1848 and the first settlements were made in 1848 and 1850. Silver was discovered in 1859. Nevada Territory was organized in 1861 and was admitted to statehood in 1864. It has an area of 110,700 sq. miles and a population (1890) of 45,761.

Nevada:
Admission of, into Union proclaimed, VI, 229.
Referred to, VI, 249.
Condition of, referred to, VI, 204.
Creation and organization of, as Territory referred to, VI, 53.
Legislation in, recommended, VI, 71.
Payment of settlers for improvements on lands in Duck Valley in, referred to, VIII, 77, 189.

Nevil, William H., act granting pension to, vetoed, VIII, 463.

Neville, John, attacked while discharging duties as revenue inspector, I, 159.

New Brunswick:
Aggressions on rights of American citizens by citizens of, II, 397.
Imprisonment of American citizens by, II, 397, 403, 424; III, 358, 405, 470. (See also Great Britain.)

New England.—A name applied to the northeastern section of the United States by Capt. John Smith in his map of the New World published in 1616. Though composed of separate Colonies, there was always a similarity in the customs and habits of the people. New England formed part of North Virginia, granted to the Plymouth Company by James I in 1606. In 1643 most of the New England Colonies were united for defensive purposes into the New England Confederation. New England is now applied collectively to the States of Maine, New Hampshire, Vermont, Massachusetts, Rhode Island, and Connecticut.

New England, Council for.—On Nov. 3, 1620, Ferdinando Gorges and others incorporated in a reorganized form the old North Virginia Company of 1606. It was called the Council for New England, and had its headquarters at Plymouth, in the county of Devon. Its stated object was the "planting, ordering, ruling, and governing of New England, in America." The patent granted to this company gave them all the land lying between lat. 40° and 48° north and from the Atlantic to the Pacific Ocean. In 1621 Gorges obtained an additional grant of territory, covering the present States of Maine and New Hampshire, under the name of Laconia, most of which, however, seems to have been included in the original grant. The lands of this company were then divided among 20 noblemen. William Bradford obtained from this company a grant permitting the settlement of the Pilgrims, a sect of English separatists who had fled from England to Holland to escape religious persecution, and who sought in America an asylum where they might worship God according to the dictates of their own consciences.

New England Emigrant Company.—The passage of the Kansas-Nebraska law in 1854 made the institution of slavery in Kansas dependent upon the will of the majority of the people of the State. Proslavery advocates in Missouri set to work to establish slavery by assisting in the emigration of Southern families. In 1855 an association was formed in Boston to offset this movement by assisting New England farmers to establish homes in the debatable territory. This organization was known as the New England Emigrant Company, and did much toward making Kansas a free State.

New England Shilling.—The general court of Massachusetts on May 27, 1652, established a mint at Boston and installed John Hull as mint master. The first coins which were struck were but rude planchets stamped "N. E." near the border on the obverse and the denomination mark (XII) on the reverse, signifying the value of 12d. This was known as the New England shilling, and was valued at 18¼ cents.

New France.—A French expedition under Verazzano formed a settlement in America as early as 1524, on land discovered by John and Sebastian Cabot in 1497. In 1535 Jacques Cartier ascended the St. Lawrence River as far as the site of Montreal. The first permanent settlement in New France was founded at Quebec by Champlain in 1608. The colonists cultivated friendly relations with the Indians, and Jesuit missionaries extended the French influence through the region of the Great Lakes to the head waters of the Mississippi and down that stream to the French possessions in the South. The country was conquered by the English in 1629 and restored in 1632. At the beginning of the Seven Years' War New France was made the scene of a part of the struggle between France and England. By 1750 New France, with Louisiana added, comprised the St. Lawrence and Great Lakes basins and the Mississippi basin, though the settlements were scattered. In 1759 Canada was reconquered by the English and its possession confirmed to them by the treaty of Paris, Feb. 10, 1763. The result of this treaty was the cession of all the country east of the Mississippi to England and that west to Spain. The French laws were continued in force and religious liberty was extended to Roman Catholics.

New Granada (see also Colombia):

American citizens in, outrages on, V, 415, 518.

Claims of United States against, IV, 263, 340; V, 415, 518.

    Adjustment of, referred to, IV, 263; V, 644.

    Commission to settle, extension of time for, recommended, VI, 67.

    Convention for adjustment of, referred to, VI, 128.

Mail transported across Isthmus of Panama, complaints regarding, V, 14.

Minister of United States to, reasons for not presenting credentials discussed, VI, 147.

Postal convention with, IV, 315.

Relations with, discussed, V, 447.

Tonnage duties levied on American vessels by, in contravention of treaty discussed, V, 415, 518.

Treaty with, transmitted and discussed, IV, 364, 509, 511; V, 38, 39, 43, 44, 369, 532, 591, 643; VI, 148.

    Contravention of, by New Granada, V, 415, 518.

    Provisions of, discussed, IV, 511.

    Regarding Panama Canal. (See Panama Canal.)

    Right of passage over Isthmus of Panama guaranteed by, IV, 511; V, 17, 369, 517.

Wars in, discussed, VI, 148.

New Hampshire.—One of the thirteen original States; nickname, "The Granite State." It extends from lat. 42° 40′ to 45° 18′ north and from long. 70° 43′ to 72° 33′ west. It is bounded on the north by the Province of Quebec (Canada), on the east by Maine and the Atlantic Ocean, on the south by Massachusetts, and on the west by Vermont (separated by the Connecticut River) and Quebec. New Hampshire is called the "Switzerland of America," being noted for the grandeur of its mountain scenery and the beauty of its lakes. It is one of the leading States in the manufacture of cotton, woolen, and worsted goods. New Hampshire was visited by Pring in 1603 and by Capt. John Smith in 1614. It formed part of the territory granted to Gorges in 1621. It was settled by the English at Portsmouth and Dover in 1623. Between 1641 and 1679, and at various times thereafter, it was a part of Massachusetts. Its final separation was in 1741. Vermont was claimed as part of New Hampshire until 1764. Area, 9,305 sq. miles; population (1890), 376,530.

New Hampshire:

Claims of—

    For militia services in War of 1812, X, 55.

    Referred to, III, 279.

Constitution of United States, evidence of ratification of amendments to, by, I, 73, 175.

Light-houses ceded to United States by, I, 110.

Northeastern boundary, correspondence regarding. (See Northeastern Boundary.)

New Hope Church, or Pumpkin Vine Creek (Ga.), Battle of.—When Gen. Johnston withdrew the Confederate forces from Resaca, Ga., May 16, 1864, he retired by way of Cassville across the Etowah and occupied a strong position commanding Allatoona Pass. May 23 Sherman crossed the Etowah and moved toward Dallas. Hooker, with the Twentieth Army Corps, moving from Burnt Hickory toward Dallas, May 25 encountered a force of Confederate cavalry at Pumpkin Vine Creek. They were driven across the stream, and about 2 miles to the eastward the Federals encountered Johnston's entire army. Here a severe battle took place. The Confederates retired and occupied a strong position from Dallas to Marietta. The losses of each army in these operations were about 2,500 men killed and wounded.

New Ireland.—Jan. 12, 1779, Capt. Mowatt, with 3 British sloops of war, landed Gen. McLane and 900 troops on the peninsula of Biguyduce (now Castine), on the south coast of Maine. On the 25th of the following July an expedition of 19 armed vessels and 24 transports under Gurdon Saltonstall, a Connecticut sea captain, and 1,500 men from Massachusetts under Gen. Lovell, arrived at Penobscot for the purpose of dislodging the British. They delayed making the attack, however, and the arrival of 5 British ships from New York on the 13th of August forced them to burn their ships and disperse. As a result of their success the British during the next year attempted to erect Maine into a province under the name of New Ireland.

New Jersey.—One of the thirteen original States. It extends from lat. 38° 56′ to 41° 21′ north and from long. 73° 54′ to 75° 33′ west. It is bounded on the north by New York, on the east by New York (separated by the Hudson River, New York Bay, and Staten Island Sound) and the Atlantic Ocean, on the south by Delaware Bay, and on the west by Pennsylvania and Delaware (both separated by the Delaware River). It is the first State in the production of zinc, one of the leaders in the production of iron, and one of the chief manufacturing States, ranking first in the manufacture of silk and glass. Among its chief fabrications are leather, iron, hats, rubber, sugar, and steel. New Jersey was first settled by the Dutch at Bergen, probably about 1617. There were succeeding colonies there of Swedes, Finns, and English. In 1664 it was granted by the Duke of York to Sir George Carteret, lieutenant-governor of the isle of Jersey, to be a perpetual inheritance and to be called New Jersey. It was reconquered by the Dutch in 1673 and restored to England in 1674 and sold to the Quakers. Proprietary government ceased in 1702 and New Jersey was made a royal province. It was under the same governor as New York until 1738. The State has an area of 7,815 sq. miles and in 1890 the population was 1,444,933.

New Jersey:

New Jersey, The, interference by American minister to France in case of, I, 399.

New Jersey Plan.—At the convention held in Philadelphia in 1787 to amend the Articles of Confederation William Paterson, of New Jersey, proposed a constitution providing for a single house of Congress, with power to regulate taxation and commerce and choose the President; that requisitions from States should be continued as under the Articles of Confederation; that a judiciary should be established; that the Executive should coerce refractory States or individuals, and other matters of general but minor interest. The plan was unfavorably reported. The convention accepted the Virginia plan with extensive modifications.

New Jerseymen Foreigners.—The humorous reference to New Jersey as a foreign country had its origin in a special act of the legislature of that State permitting Joseph Bonaparte, former King of Spain and Naples, to hold real estate within its boundaries. After the downfall of Napoleon Joseph sought an asylum in America. The legislature of Pennsylvania refused to allow him, being an alien, to acquire land in that State, so he appealed to New Jersey. His request was granted and he established himself in princely magnificence at Bordentown. Hence the citizens of other States were accustomed to jestingly twit the Jerseymen with being foreigners under a foreign prince.

New London (Conn.), Capture of.—Sept. 6, 1781, Benedict Arnold's expedition against Connecticut arrived in the harbor of New London. The only defense of the town was the unfinished Fort Trumbull, manned by about 25 or 30 State militia under Capt. Shopley. About a third of these were lost while escaping in boats to Fort Griswold after firing one volley, disabling 4 or 5 of their assailants.

New Madrid (Mo.), Battle of.—On the surrender of Fort Donelson to Grant the Confederates abandoned Columbus, Ky., on the Mississippi, and fell back to New Madrid, Mo., about 80 miles below Cairo. It was defended by Fort Thompson and several batteries and by 6 gunboats mounting heavy guns, under Commodore Hollins. Mar. 4, 1862, Gen. Pope appeared before New Madrid with an army of 20,000, which he had been commanding in eastern Missouri. On the 14th, having received heavy guns from Cairo, he gave the place a severe cannonading, disabling several of the gunboats. Gen. McCown, unable to hold New Madrid, removed his garrison during the night and in the midst of a thunderstorm to Island No. 10. Pope lost 51 men killed and wounded. The Confederate loss is not known.

New Mexico.—An organized Territory of the United States; motto, "Crescit eundo" ("It increases as it goes"). It extends from lat. 31° 20' to 37° north and from long. 103° 2' to 109° 2' west. It is bounded on the north by Colorado, on the east by Texas and Oklahoma, on the south by Texas and Mexico, and on the west by Arizona. It was visited by Niza in 1539, and Francisco Vasquez de Coronado conducted an expedition consisting of 400 Spanish and 800 Indians as far north as the present city of Santa Fé in 1540. Near the close of the sixteenth century Spanish missionaries made settlements about the head waters of the Rio Grande, and in 1605 Santa Fé was founded. The Spanish were temporarily expelled by the Indians in 1680. In 1846 the region was conquered by the Americans under Gen. Kearny, who proclaimed himself provisional governor. By the treaty of Guadalupe Hidalgo, proclaimed in 1848, New Mexico became a part of the United States. A Territorial government was established by act of Congress approved Sept. 9, 1850. In 1853 a part of the Gadsden Purchase was added to New Mexico, making the present area 122,580 sq. miles. The population in 1890 was 153,593, engaged mostly in mining and stock raising.

New Mexico:

front. Only 800 of the latter were regulars. On the opposite side of the river was Gen. Morgan with 800 militia. This force of 5,800, indifferently armed and disciplined, was confronted by 10,000 of the finest soldiers in the world, most of them fresh from the continental campaign under Wellington. The Americans were intrenched behind their fortifications, which the British were compelled to approach across an open plain. In the conflict 2,600 were lost to the British, of whom 700 were killed, 1,400 wounded, and 500 taken prisoners. The Americans lost only 8 killed and 13 wounded. Probably no other battle in history presents this disparity in the number lost.

ew Orleans (La.), Capture of.—Feb. 20, 1862, Commodore Farragut, with his flagship, the sloop of war *Hartford*, arrived at Ship Island, 100 miles north-northeast of the mouth of the Mississippi. He was in command of the Western Coast Blockading Squadron, with directions to take possession of New Orleans. A military force to cooperate with Farragut arrived at Ship Island Mar. 25 under Gen. B. F. Butler. The defenses of New Orleans were Fort Jackson, on the right bank or south side of the river, near its last great bend before it separates into the Delta, and Fort St. Philip, a little farther upstream on the opposite side. The former, with its water battery, mounted 75 guns; the latter 40. Just above the forts was a fleet of 15 vessels, including the ironclad ram *Manassas* and a floating battery, covered with railroad iron, called the *Louisiana*. These were in command of Commodore J. K. Mitchell. A heavy chain was also stretched across the river below Fort Jackson. Farragut's fleet consisted of 6 sloops of war, 16 gunboats, 21 schooners, each carrying a 13-inch mortar, and 5 other vessels. The fleet carried more than 200 guns. Farragut bombarded the forts for 6 days with his mortar boats without much effect. The Confederate loss was 14 killed and 39 wounded. It was then decided to run by the forts. The obstructions were opened in the face of a heavy fire, and the fleet formed in 3 divisions and awaited the signal. It was given at half past 3 o'clock on the morning of Apr. 24, 1862. Capt. Bailey led off with his division of 8 vessels. Under the storm of shot and shell they passed the obstructions and ran by the forts against the current in a stream less than half a mile wide, escaping the blazing rafts only to be met at the end of their journey by the Confederate gunboats eager to begin the fight. The second division of the fleet was led through the fiery gantlet by the *Hartford*, with Farragut on board. The *Sciota*, carrying Fleet Captain Bell, led the third division. The *Kennebec*, *Itasca*, and *Winona* failed to pass the forts, becoming entangled in the rafts and floating débris and delayed beyond the dawn. The latter lost all but one man of her rifled-gun crew. Having passed the forts the fleet savagely attacked the small Confederate gunboats beyond and their destruction was speed-ily accomplished. May 1 New Orleans was formally occupied by United States troops. The Federals lost in the taking of New Orleans 37 killed and 147 wounded. The Confederate loss was stated at only 40 killed and wounded.

New Providence, slaves seized on board brigs by authorities of, III, 280.

New South Wales:

International exhibition at Melbourne to celebrate founding of, discussed, VIII, 591.

Postal convention with, VIII, 296.

New York.—One of the thirteen original States; nickname, "The Empire State;" motto, "Excelsior." It extends from lat. 40° 30′ to 45° 1′ north and from long. 71° 51′ to 79° 46′ west. It is bounded on the north and northwest by Ontario, Canada (separated for the most part by Lake Ontario and the St. Lawrence River); on the east by Vermont (partly separated by Lake Champlain), Massachusetts, and Connecticut; on the south by the Atlantic Ocean, New York Bay, New Jersey, and Pennsylvania (partly separated by the Delaware River), and on the west by Pennsylvania and Ontario (separated by Lake Erie and the Niagara River). Long Island, Staten Island, and several small islands are included in the State. It is mountainous in the eastern part, along the Hudson River. A beautiful rolling country constitutes the watershed separating the north and south drainage of the western and central parts of the State. To the north the surface descends in undulating terraces toward Lake Ontario. To the south the country is higher, in places reaching an altitude of 2,000 to 2,500 feet. The valley of the Mohawk extends westward from the Hudson for nearly 150 miles. New York is the first State of the Union in commerce, manufactures, population, and estimated value of property, and the second State in value of farms. The area of the State is 49,170 sq. miles and the population (1890) 5,997,853. (See also New Netherlands.)

New York (see also Hudson; New York City):

Boundary line with New Jersey referred to, III, 49.

Branch mint in. (See New York City.)

Canadian outrages on frontier of, discussed, III, 401, 459, 478, 623.

Canals in, recommendation regarding, VI, 133.

Colonial history of, referred to, IV, 101.

Constitution of United States, evidence of ratification of amendments to, by, I, 75, 172, 174.

Courts in—

Crowded condition of docket of, discussed, VIII, 534.

Recommendations regarding, VIII, 46.

Judge, additional, for southern district of, recommended, VIII, 513.

Judges of United States circuit court for district of, opinion of, regarding pensions, I, 123.

Sheriffs in, duties of, respecting prisoners, I, 75.

Statue of George Clinton presented to Congress by, VII, 260.

Unlawful expeditions in, III, 399; V, 161.

New York, The, mentioned, X, 166.

Newbern (N. C.), Capture of.—After securing Roanoke Island Burnside proceeded to the execution of another clause of his orders by advancing upon Newbern. Mar. 14, 1862, he landed a force of men on the banks of the Neuse River, 18 miles below the city. They advanced to within 5 miles of the place, when they encountered a redoubt, which was taken by assault. The bridge over the Trent, a tributary of the Neuse, was burned by the Confederates as they retreated. With the capture of Newbern 46 heavy guns, 3 batteries of light artillery, and a large amount of stores fell into Burnside's hands. The Federal loss was 90 killed and 466 wounded. The Confederate loss was 23 killed, 58 wounded, and about 2,500 prisoners.

Newburg Addresses.—There were many things to criticise and much to complain of in the conduct of the Revolutionary War, but heroic achievement and devotion to the cause of freedom, as a rule, overshadowed the jealousies of officers and the complaints of men. Gen. Horatio Gates had always been a rival of Washington for command of the Army, and frequently conspired against the latter's popularity. In 1783, while Washington's army was encamped at Newburg, two anonymous appeals were issued to the officers, urging them to hold a meeting to consider the question of the money due them by Congress. The appeals were written by Capt. Armstrong, of Pennsylvania, and were supposed to have been instigated by the Gates faction. Washington immediately denounced the meeting as subversive of discipline and called a regular meeting of the officers to consider the matter. Gates was placed in the chair. Washington's friends carried motions characterizing as "infamous proposals" the suggestions of the Newburg addresses, and furthermore declaring unshaken confidence in Congress.

Nez Percé Indians.—The leading tribe of the Shahaptian stock of Indians. They are also known as the Chopunnish, Nimapu, Shahaptan, and Sahaptin. They were found by Lewis and Clark in 1804 inhabiting the country now com-

Nicaragua Canal.—A proposed ship canal across the Republic of Nicaragua to connect the Atlantic and Pacific oceans. As early as 1522 Lake Nicaragua was entered from the western coast and explored by Spanish navigators. In 1550 Antonio Galvao, a Portuguese, proposed 4 routes for a ship canal across the Isthmus, one by way of Lake Nicaragua and the San Juan River. Later surveys were made by the Spanish and Central American Governments. In 1850 Col. O. W. Childs surveyed a canal route from Lake Nicaragua to the Pacific. More complete surveys were made for the United States in 1872–73 and 1885, and the cost of construction was variously estimated at from $40,000,000 to $140,000,000. The Nicaraguan Government made concessions to Americans for constructing a canal in 1849 and 1880 and to a Frenchman in 1858, but they all lapsed without results. In 1884 a treaty was signed for the construction of a canal by the United States, but the Senate refused to ratify it. In 1887 a new concession was granted by Nicaragua and confirmed by Costa Rica. The charter extends the concessions of the company 99 years, with privilege of renewal. The Nicaraguan Government binds itself not to make subsequent concessions to any other canal or railroad company. For this concession the Maritime Canal Co. of Nicaragua paid $100,000. The company obtained a charter from the United States and the State of Vermont. Its capital stock was placed at $80,000,000 and was all subscribed by private individuals. In November, 1889, the first surveying expedition under this company left New York for Greytown and began work immediately upon its arrival. It was estimated that 6 years would be required to complete the canal. The actual work was undertaken by the Nicaragua Construction Co., which laid part of a necessary railroad and improved the harbor of San Juan, when work ceased for lack of funds. In 1893 the company went into the hands of a receiver. Measures for organizing a new company were immediately begun, and provisional agreements between it and the Maritime Canal Co. were approved by Congress Nov. 1, 1898. The route decided upon is from San Juan del Norte or Greytown, on the Caribbean Sea, to Brito, on the Pacific, a distance of 169½ miles. Of this about 142 miles is through the lake and the San Juan River. Actual excavations will not exceed 27 miles. There are to be 2 canals proper, each with 3 locks, one from Ochoa, on the San Juan River, to the port of San Juan del Norte and the other from Lake Nicaragua to the Pacific. The summit level of the lake is 110 feet. The greatest excavation will be an average depth of 140 feet for 3 miles. A commission authorized by act June 4, 1897, reported Dec. 26, 1898, recommending a canal of greater dimensions, to cost by estimate $124,000,000. By a law approved Mar. 3, 1899, the President of the United States was authorized to make a complete investigation of the Isthmus of Panama with a view to securing all the concessions before granted and to ascertain the probable cost of constructing a canal at each of two or more of the most practicable and feasible routes, including that of Nicaragua. Section 1 of the Clayton-Bulwer treaty states: "The Governments of the United States and Great Britain hereby declare that neither the one nor the other will obtain or maintain for itself any exclusive control over the said canal." The canal is to be neutral in case of war, except that vessels of powers at war with any of the Central American Republics shall be refused transit.

Ninety-Six (S. C.), Siege of.—Immediately after the surrender of Charleston (May 12, 1780) Clinton sent Lieut. Conger up the Saluda to Ninety-Six, a village in South Carolina about 75 miles from Columbia. May 21, 1781, a part of Gen. Greene's army laid siege to the place. Kosciuszko planned the approaches and the condition of the garrison had become critical, when, on June 20, the siege was raised on the approach of Lord Rawdon with the flank companies of 3 regiments.

Nipmuc Indians.—A general name for the Indians of several tribes inhabiting in early colonial days south central Massachusetts and extending into Connecticut and Rhode Island. The majority of the Nipmucs did not at first join Philip in his war against the colonists, but were active against the English during the struggle in Connecticut in 1675. In January, 1676, the remnants of Philip's tribe, with the Narraganset, the Quaboag, and River Indians, joined the Nipmucs, and on the defeat of Philip fled north and west. Eliot's translation of the Bible is in the Natic dialect of the Nipmuc language. The word Nipmuc means "fresh-water fishing place."

Nipsic, The, disabled at Samoan Islands, IX, 44.

Niter, appropriation for improvement in manufacture of, recommended, V, 424.

No Man's Land.—A small island 3 miles southwest of Marthas Vineyard, Mass., to which it belongs. The term was also applied to a strip of land ceded by Texas to the United States in 1850. It lies between lat. 36° 30' and 37° north and long. 100° and 103° west. It was not included under any government, though often called part of the Indian Territory. In 1890 it became part of Oklahoma and is now known as Beaver County.

Noah, M. Mordecai, surveyor of customs, renomination of, II, 480.

Noland, N. B., claims of, against Peru, IX, 667.

Nominating Conventions. (See Conventions, Nominating.)

Nominations.—In politics, an act of designation to office, the ratification of which depends upon another person or body of persons. The President nominates to the Senate candidates for high Federal offices, and makes the appointment only after approval. The head of an Executive Department nominates to the President those whom he desires as his subordinates in the higher official positions. A national, State, city, county, or town convention of a political party nominates its candidates for office in anticipation of election.

Nominations. (See Executive Nominations.)

Nonimportation Agreement.—In 1765 the merchants of New York and Boston unanimously agreed to order no new merchandise from England and to countermand old orders. This was done in retaliation for the passage of the Stamp Act by Parliament. The agreement was strictly observed until 1770, when only tea was prohibited. The members of the Continental Congress signed a nonimportation agreement in 1775.

Nonintercourse Act.—In consequence of the interference with American commerce by vessels of France and England, who were then at war, Congress in 1807 passed the embargo act prohibiting foreign commerce. This was found to work unnecessary injury to American shipping interests, and in 1809 it was repealed and the nonintercourse act substituted. It forbade the entrance to American ports of public or private British or French vessels, all commercial intercourse with France or Great Britain, and the importation after May 20, 1809, of all goods grown or manufactured in the two countries or their colonies. The act was to continue until the next session of Congress, but was revived by acts of June 28, 1809, May 1, 1810, and Mar. 2, 1811.

Noo-whá-há Indians, treaty with, V, 379.

Nook-wa-cháh-mish Indians, treaty with, V, 379.

Norfolk, Va.:
Blockade of port of, removed by proclamation, VI, 230.
  Referred to, VI, 245.
British officers treated at hospital at, VI, 203.
Navy-yard at, referred to, IV, 462.
Surrender of, referred to, VI, 112, 114.
Vessels entering and leaving port of, order regarding, VI, 124.

Norfolk (Va.), Burning of.—Lord Dunmore, the royal governor of Virginia, assumed military control of Norfolk in November, 1775. He was defeated in an effort to dislodge some Virginia and Maryland militia who had taken up a position near the town. He thereupon embarked in a British vessel which lay in the Elizabeth River. Col. Woodford, with the Second Virginia Militia, and Col. Howe, with 1 regiment from North Carolina and 2 companies of Maryland militia, occupied the town. On Jan. 1, 1776, Dunmore began a bombardment, and sent ashore a party who set fire to the town. Its destruction was completed by the Americans to prevent its becoming a shelter for the British.

Norfolk (Va.), Surrender of.—The movement of the Federal Army up the peninsula of Virginia, in May, 1862, led to the withdrawal of the Confederate force from Norfolk and to the destruction of the ironclad *Merrimac*. This left the James River open to navigation. An expedition was sent out from Fortress Monroe, under Gen. Wool, May 10, to take possession of Norfolk. It was turned over by the mayor without a struggle.

Norman, Mary, act granting pension to, vetoed, VIII, 453.

Norris, P. W., petition of, for compensation for services rendered transmitted, VIII, 82.

Norsemen.—In the sagas or accounts of Scandinavian heroes the vikings of Norway are represented as having visited the coast of America as early as 861 A. D. The narratives of the early voyages of the Northmen to America are more or less intermingled with fiction. Enough has been verified, however, to warrant some reliable historians giving credence to the more likely part of their claims. We are told that Norsemen had established a settlement in America in 875 A. D. (probably in Iceland, visited by Nadodd 12 to 15 years previously), and that Gunnbiorn, a Norse navigator, sighted land farther west. Eric the Red discovered and named Greenland in 982, and 3 years later made a second voyage to the new country. During the same year an expedition under Bjarni sailed from Iceland for Greenland, but was driven south by a storm and sighted land at Newfoundland and at Cape Cod or Nantucket. Thence he returned to Greenland. In the year 1000 Leif, son of Eric the Red, sailed with one ship and 35 men in search of the land seen by Bjarni. He touched on the coast of Labrador and, journeying southward, stopped for the winter near the site of the present city of Boston. Leif called the place Vinland, from the abundance of grapes found. This seems to be the earliest authentic account of Norse discoveries in America. Thorvald, Leif's brother, visited Vinland in 1002, wintered near Mount Hope Bay, R. I., and in the spring of 1003 sent a party of his men to explore the coast, probably as far south as Cape May. In 1004 Thorvald was killed near Boston by Skraelings (the Icelandic name for the aboriginal Americans), and his companions returned to Greenland. About 1007 or 1008 Thorfinn Karlsefne sailed from Greenland with 3 ships and 160 persons. He landed at Rhode Island and spent 3 years in Vinland. Here a son was born to Thorvald, from whom

Albert Thorvaldsen, a Danish sculptor living at Copenhagen in the latter part of the eighteenth and the early part of the nineteenth century, was able to trace direct descent. A full account of these early voyages is preserved in the "Codex Flatöiensis," written in 1387-1395, and found in a monastery on the west coast of Iceland. The latest tidings of Vinland were received in 1347, and communication with Greenland ceased about 1400. Before Columbus was born European navigators had journeyed westward and touched land, and several maps of the Atlantic Ocean had been made. Prior to 1470 Columbus had visited Iceland, and it has been suggested that he there learned of the Western Continent from the Norse navigators.

North Anna Crossing (Va.), Battle of.—Proceeding southward after the battle of Spottsylvania, Grant's army arrived at the North Anna River May 23, 1864. Warren, whose corps was on the right, crossed the river at Jericho, Hancock at a point 4 miles below, and the Sixth Corps at Jericho. Lee meantime had retired to a position south of the North Anna, and his left wing rested on the river at a point between the two sections of Grant's army. Burnside's corps was unable to cross the river. Lee's position was impregnable, and Grant was compelled to withdraw his army to the north side of the river after a loss of 1,607 in killed and wounded. May 27, having been rejoined by Sheridan, the Army of the Potomac moved toward the Pamunky River.

North Carolina.—One of the thirteen original States; nicknames, "The Tar State," "The Tar-Heel State," and "The Old North State;" motto, "Esse quam videri" ("To be rather than to seem"). It extends from lat. 33° 50′ to 36° 33′ north and from long. 75° 27′ to 84° 20′ west. It is bounded on the north by Virginia, on the east and southeast by the Atlantic Ocean, on the south by South Carolina and Georgia, and on the west by Tennessee (separated by the Smoky and other ranges of mountains). The surface is mountainous in the west, rolling or gently undulating in the center, and toward the eastern coast or lands bordering on the Albemarle and Pamlico sounds generally level. The leading occupation is agriculture; the chief products corn, cotton, tobacco, rice, timber, etc. There are also mines of gold, mica, iron, and copper, and in certain counties manufactories of cotton, tobacco, etc. Unsuccessful attempts at colonization were made by Sir Walter Raleigh in 1584-1587. Scattering settlements were made prior to 1663, probably as early as 1653. The territory was granted to proprietors in 1663 by Charles II. The first two colonies are known in history as the Albemarle and the Clarendon. In 1669 a futile attempt was made to introduce a constitution modeled by Locke upon principles of a landed aristocracy. Citizens of North Carolina passed a set of resolutions in 1775 similar to the Declaration of Independence. (See Mecklenburg Declaration.) It was the first

Northwest Territory.—The portion of the United
States known in history as the Northwest
Territory comprised all the country lying between the Ohio River, the Mississippi River,
and the Great Lakes, immediately west of the
original States, and now forming the States of
Ohio, Indiana, Illinois, Michigan, and Wisconsin. The original States severally laid
claim to this territory by their charters, which
granted possession from ocean to ocean. New
York ceded her claims to this region to the
General Government in 1782, and was followed
by Virginia in 1784, Massachusetts in 1785, and
Connecticut in 1786. The latter State, however,
retained a small tract as the foundation
for her school fund. This became known as
the Western Reserve. Congress in July, 1787,
passed an ordinance for the government of
this territory, and to the wise measures incorporated into that law the States formed from
the territory are indebted for much that is
wise and judicious in their constitutions. It
is claimed by some that the foundations for
future national greatness were laid in the
manner in which Congress dealt with the
question of territorial government at this
time. A clause forbidding slavery after 1800
was at first voted down, but afterwards was
adopted. The ordinance provided that no land

should be taken up until it had been purchased
from the Indians and offered for sale by the
United States; no property qualification was
to be required of electors or elected; a temporary government might be established until
the male population of the territory reached
5,000, then a permanent representative government would be permitted, with a Representative in Congress entitled to debate but not to
vote. When the inhabitants of any one of the
five divisions of the territory reached 60,000 it
should be admitted as a State, these States to
remain forever a part of the United States, pay
their portion of the Federal debt, and in their
government uphold republican forms and prohibit slavery; but fugitive slaves were to be surrendered. Arthur St. Clair was governor from
1788 to 1802.

Northwestern Boundary.—The territory bounded
on the north by lat. 54° 40′, on the east by the
Rocky Mountains, on the south by lat. 42°, and
on the west by the Pacific Ocean has been variously claimed by Russia, Spain, Great Britain,
and the United States. Russia's claim rested
for the most part upon occupation by fur
traders, and was settled by a treaty of Jan. 11,
1825, under the terms of which the United
States were to make no settlements north of
lat. 54° 40′ and Russia none south of that latitude. England made a treaty with Russia on
the same terms. By the treaty which ceded
Florida in 1819 the Spanish claims were confined to the south of lat. 42°. This left the territory between 42° and 54° 40′ to the Americans
and English. Great Britain had no claim by
discovery. The claim of the United States
rested upon the voyage of Gray up the Columbia River in 1792 and the explorations of Lewis
and Clark through the Rocky Mountains and
the Oregon country in 1805 and 1806 under the
orders of Jefferson. By the treaty of Oct. 20,
1818, the entire country west of the Rocky
Mountains was to be opened to both countries
for 10 years, and at the end of this period
joint occupation for an indefinite time was
agreed upon. This arrangement produced
much dissatisfaction and was made a political
issue in the United States in 1844. After considerable negotiation lat. 49° was agreed upon
as the boundary from the Rocky Mountains to
the channel between Vancouver Island and the
mainland. (See also San Juan de Fuca Explorations.)

Norway.—The northernmost country of Europe, forming with Sweden the Scandinavian Peninsula. It is bounded on the north by the Arctic Ocean, on the east by Russia and Sweden, on the south by the Skager Rack, and on the west by the North Sea and the Atlantic and Arctic oceans. It forms the western part of the Scandinavian Peninsula, comprising also many islands. The coast line is deeply indented by fiords. The country generally is elevated and mountainous. Among the leading industries are fisheries and lumber manufacture and trade. There are mines of silver, copper, iron, and nickel. The Government is a limited hereditary monarchy. It is under the same sovereign with Sweden, with which it is united in foreign or diplomatic relations, but is otherwise independent. The King and a ministry form the executive council, and the legislative power is vested in the Storthing or Parliament, consisting of an upper and a lower house. The Kingdom was consolidated under Harold the Fair-Haired in the latter part of the ninth century. Christianity was introduced toward the close of the tenth century. The established religion is Lutheran. The country has an area of 124,445 sq. miles and a population in 1891 of 1,988,674.

Norway. (See Sweden and Norway.)

Nullification.—The general meaning of nullification is the act of invalidating or making void. In American politics it is almost exclusively applied to the doctrine set forth by John C. Calhoun and his friends in the South Carolina controversy with the Federal Government, 1828–1833. This doctrine asserted the right of any State to declare the unconstitutionality of any United States law, though it should have been enacted in the proper manner and held to be constitutional by the Supreme Court of the United States. It was further claimed that any attempt to enforce such law in a State which had refused to acknowledge its validity would justify it in at once leaving the Union. The immediate cause of this declaration of principles was that the existing tariff law bore unjustly, so it was claimed, on the nonmanufacturing and raw-material-producing States of the South. The arguments in favor of nullification were mainly based upon language used by Jefferson and Madison in the Kentucky and Virginia resolutions of 1798 and 1799 in regard to the alien and sedition laws. Here it was asserted that the General Government was not "the final or exclusive judge of the powers delegated to itself, but that, as in all other cases of compact among powers having no common judge, each party has an equal right to judge for itself, as well of infractions as of the mode and measure of redress." Senator Hayne, of South Carolina, was the first to advocate this doctrine in Congress. On the advice of Calhoun the governor of South Carolina called a convention, and an ordinance of nullification was passed on Nov. 19, 1832. This ordinance declared the Federal tariff law "null and void" and authorized the citizens to refuse payment of duties under it. It also denied the right of the Supreme Court of the United States to pass upon the nullification ordinance. The legislature was on the point of enacting a bill in accordance with this ordinance when the necessity was partly obviated by the passage of Clay's compromise measures (q.v.) in 1833. The attempt to interfere with the execution of Federal laws was met by President Jackson's prompt instructions to the revenue officers at Charleston, his proclamation of Dec. 10, 1832 (II, 640), and his special message to Congress on the subject (II, 610). Mar. 3, 1833, a new tariff bill was passed which gave satisfaction to the nullifiers, and on Mar. 16 a State convention of South Carolina repealed the ordinance of nullification.

O.

Ogdensburg (N. Y.), Capture of.—In September, 1812, Gen. Brown was sent to Ogdensburg, N. Y., at the mouth of the Oswegatchie River, to garrison Fort Presentation and attempt the capture of some British stores that were reported as being on the way up the St. Lawrence River. Oct. 2 about 40 British bateaux, escorted by a gunboat, were seen approaching. On the 4th 2 gunboats and 25 bateaux, containing 750 men, started for Ogdensburg. The American force amounted to about 1,200 effective men. After 2 hours of firing the invaders withdrew with a slight loss. No one was injured on the American side. Later Maj. Forsyth was placed in command of the garrison at Ogdensburg. With a party of citizens and militia he crossed over to Elizabethtown, Canada, Feb. 6, 1813, and rescued a number of prisoners held there. In retaliation for this exploit Lieut. Col. McDouell, with about 800 men, crossed the river on the ice Feb. 22, 1813, and after a short engagement gained possession of the town, which they gave over to plunderers.

Ohio.—One of the United States; nickname, "The Buckeye State." Ohio extends from lat. 38° 24' to 41° 57' north and from long. 80° 34' to 84° 49' west. It is bounded on the north by Michigan and Lake Erie, on the east by Pennsylvania and West Virginia (separated by the Ohio River), on the south by Kentucky (separated by the Ohio River), and on the west by Indiana. It is the fourth State in population, the first in value of farms, production of wool, and manufacture of agricultural machinery, and one of the chief manufacturing States. Its chief products are wheat, corn, wool, live stock, flour, pork, coal, iron, salt, butter, cheese, and petroleum. Ohio was first visited by the French under La Salle at the end of the seventeenth century. It was claimed by both the French and English. It was ceded to Great Britain in 1763 and to the United States in 1783. In 1787 it became part of the Northwest Territory. The first settlement was made at Marietta in 1788. The State was admitted to the Union in 1802. As Virginia was the mother of Presidents in the early period of United States history, so that honor seems to have fallen to Ohio in the later period. It has an area of 41,060 sq. miles and a population (1890) of 3,672,316.

Ohio (see also Columbus; Dayton; Portsmouth):
Boundary of—
  Act respecting, executed, II, 68.
  Controversy with Michigan regarding, III, 185, 188.
  Referred to, II, 610.
Lands in—
  Referred to, II, 264.
  Title of United Brethren to, II, 232.
Letter to governor of, respecting militia for suppression of troubles on Mississippi River, X, 101.
National Guard of, expiration of enlistment of, referred to and thanks of President tendered, VI, 239.

Ohio—Continued.
  Ratification of fourteenth amendment withdrawn by, VI, 638.

Ohio Companies.—In 1749 George II granted to a band of wealthy citizens of Virginia and Maryland, calling themselves the Ohio Company, a tract of land containing 500,000 acres, lying in the Ohio Valley south of Ohio River. Thomas Lee was the projector of the company, but it was later conducted by Lawrence Washington. The terms of the grant required that 100 families should be established upon the tract, a fort should be built, and a garrison maintained. A number of storehouses were also established. In 1783 the territory east of the Mississippi, north of the Ohio River, and west of Pennsylvania, which before the Revolution had been part of the Province of Quebec and afterwards had been claimed by Virginia, was ceded to the United States, with the proviso that it was to be settled and formed into States. Mar. 1, 1786, Rufus Putnam suggested a second Ohio Company, and 2 days later he and Messrs. Cutler, Brooks, Sargent, and Cushing formed an association and issued 1,000 shares at $1,000 each in Continental certificates or $125 in gold. A year afterwards Congress granted certain lots free of charge, and an enormous tract was bought at about 8 or 9 cents per acre in specie. Colonization was immediately begun. Slavery was prohibited. This company had large influence in shaping the ordinance for the government of the Northwest Territory, of which it became a part.

Ohio River:
Canal from Chesapeake Bay to. (See Chesapeake and Ohio Canal.)
Navigation on, II, 255, 343.
  Appropriation for, II, 368.
  Mode of improving, referred to, II, 633; V, 149.
Referred to, II, 541; III, 272.
Ship canal around Falls of, referred to, VI, 621.
Survey of, appropriation for, II, 199.

Ojibwa, or Chippewa, Indians.—A large tribe of the Algonquian stock of Indians. In the early history of the country their hunting grounds were along the shores of Lakes Huron and Superior and across the State of Minnesota into the mountains of Dakota. Their name means "A puckering up," and is variously contended to refer to a puckering of the lips in speaking or drinking, a peculiar seam in the moccasin, and the appearance of the flesh of roasted victims. They were known by the early French explorers as Saulteurs ("People of the falls"), having been first met with at Sault Ste. Marie. They were connected in a loose confederacy with the Ottawas and Pottawatomies and known as the Three Fires. After learning the use of firearms they greatly extended their territory by successful wars upon the Sioux, Foxes, and Iroquois. They joined Pontiac and were allies of England in the Revolution. They also participated in the Miami uprising. The Ojibwas ceded lands on Lake Erie in 1805. They again broke out into hostilities in 1812, and by the peace of 1816 relinquished all their lands in Ohio and retreated westward. By 1851 the remainder of the tribe in the United States was west of the Mississippi River. They now number about 30,000 in Canada and the United States, about one-half in each.

Oklahoma.—A Territory of the United States; motto, "Labor omnia vincit" ("Labor conquers everything"). It extends from lat. 34° to 37° north and from long. 96° to 103° west. It is bounded on the north by Kansas and Colorado, on the east by Indian Territory, on the south by Texas (separated by the Red River), and on the west by Texas and New Mexico. The Territory was formed in 1890 from the western part of Indian Territory and the public strip called No Man's Land (q. v.). An extensive scheme was organized in 1879 to take possession of that part of the Indian Territory not occupied by Indians, and parties from Missouri and Texas entered the territory, but were ordered out by proclamations of President Hayes (VII, 547, 598). Several subsequent invasions of the Territory were made in defiance of Federal law, but all expeditions of settlers were arrested and their towns broken up. Finally delegates of the Creek Nation met at Washington and sold the western half of their domain to the United States Government for $2,280,857. Congress ratified this agreement Mar. 1, 1889. By proclamation of President Harrison (IX, 15) Oklahoma was opened to settlement at noon Apr. 22, 1889, and during the afternoon of that day 50,000 settlers, who had been encamped on the border, rushed into the territory, formed a provisional government, and laid out town sites. One of the incidents of the afternoon was the establishment of a bank with a capital of $50,000, with a tent as a place of business. In 1893 the Cherokee Strip was ceded by the Indians to the Government for $8,300,000. The principal products of Oklahoma are wheat, corn, cotton, castor beans, oats, barley, sorghum, alfalfa, clover, timothy, flax, peanuts, and many varieties of fruit. The Territory has an area of 39,030 sq. miles and a population estimated in 1895 at 200,000.

Oklahoma:

Appropriation for settlement under treaties of freedmen, etc., upon lands in, recommended, VIII, 198.

Lands in—
Agreement for cession of, IX, 213, 214, 333.
Opened to settlement by proclamation, IX, 15, 156, 275, 406, 588.
Referred to, IX, 202.

Laws of Nebraska in force in, continuation of, recommended, IX, 131.

Memorial from Wichita and Caddo Indians regarding claims to lands in, IX, 236.

Organization of, discussed, VIII, 808.
Act regarding, returned, IX, 68.

Reservations in, ceded to United States, IX, 156.

Suffering among settlers in, recommendations regarding, IX, 81.

Memorial from legislature asking for relief, IX, 132.

Oklahoma—Continued.
Unauthorized occupancy of, VIII, 245, 358.
Proclamations against, VIII, 224, 303.

Oklahoma Central Railroad, act to authorize construction and operation of railway by, through Territories vetoed, IX, 582.

Oklahoma City, Okla., act authorizing issuance of bonds by, to provide right of way for railroad vetoed, IX, 136.

O'Laughlin, Michael, implicated in assassination of President Lincoln, proceedings of trial and verdict of military commission, VI, 334, 335, 336, 342, 347, 348.

Old Colony.—A popular name for Plymouth County, Mass. The territory was formerly included in the Plymouth Colony, but, being unable to obtain a charter from the British Crown on account of its outspoken opposition to the established church, was in 1692 absorbed into Massachusetts Bay Colony.

Old Dominion.—A name popularly applied to the State of Virginia. In colonial documents Virginia is frequently referred to as "His Majesty's Dominion of Virginia."

Old Point Comfort, Va., school for artillery instruction at, II, 255.

Old Settler Indians. (See Cherokee Indians.)

Old Winnebago Reservation, restoration of, to public domain, order regarding, declared void, VIII, 305.
Discussed, VIII, 358.

Oldenburg.—A Grand Duchy of northern Germany and a State of the German Empire. It is bounded on the north by the North Sea, on the east by Hannover and Bremen, and on the south and west by Hannover. Agriculture is the chief occupation of the people. The government is a hereditary constitutional monarchy. Oldenburg is represented in the Bundesrat by 1 and in the Reichstag by 3 members. The Protestant religion prevails. Oldenburg joined the North German Confederation in 1866. Area, 2,479 sq. miles; population (1895), 369,754.

Oldenburg:
Commercial relations with, II, 251.
Exequatur issued consul of, revoked, VI, 512.
Referred to, VI, 522.
Treaty with, IV, 629.
Vessels of, discriminating duties on, suspended by proclamation, II, 97, 496.

Oleomargarine, act defining butter and imposing tax on, approved and discussed, VIII, 407.

Olive Branch, The, condemnation of, indemnification asked for, III, 49.

Olmstead, Gideon:
Correspondence with governor of Pennsylvania in regard to case of, I, 477.
Resolutions of Pennsylvania legislature protesting against Supreme Court decision in case of, I, 471, and X, 121.

Olmstead et al. vs. Rittenhouse's Executrixes.—In 1778 Olmstead and other citizens of Connecticut were pressed into the service of the British aboard the sloop *Active*. They revolted and took possession of the vessel, and were in turn captured by the Pennsylvanian armed brig *Convention.* The State court of admiralty of Pennsylvania adjudged the *Active* lawful prize and awarded the proceeds of her sale to the State, the officers and crew of the *Convention*, and the owners, officers, and crew of *Le Gerard*, a privateer, which assisted in the capture. Olmstead and the others claimed the whole prize, but were awarded only one-fourth. They then appealed to the Federal commissioners of appeals and received a favorable verdict. The State court of admiralty of Pennsylvania set aside this verdict and ordered that the money be brought into court. May 1, 1779, the loan certificates for the prize money were deposited with State Treasurer Rittenhouse. In 1803 the district court of the United States for the State of Pennsylvania entered a final decree that the money be paid over to the libellants. The case having come before the United States Supreme Court, March, 1808, that court ordered a mandamus as against the district judge, and in 1809 judgment was executed in favor of the plaintiffs in spite of violent opposition from Pennsylvania, which opposition had prevented Judge Peters from carrying out his decree. The facts in the matter are all given in the Peters case. (See also I, 471, and X, 121; Peters *vs.* United States.)

Olney, Richard, Secretary of State, IX, 592.

Olustee (Fla.), Battle of.—In February, 1864, a Federal expedition was sent to Florida from Port Royal under command of Gen. Seymour. It was composed of 20 steamers, 8 schooners, and about 5,000 troops. Feb. 7 the land forces occupied Jacksonville. On the 18th they marched inland, encountering the Confederates on the 20th at Olustee, a railroad station about 50 miles west of Jacksonville. The battle was unexpected and was fiercely fought from 2 o'clock till dark, when the vanquished Federals retired 20 miles to Barbers. Seymour lost nearly 2,000 men, as well as 5 pieces of artillery, in this disastrous fight, and the expedition returned to Hilton Head.

Olympia, The, mentioned, X, 155.

Omaha, The. (See Ikisima Island.)

Omaha Indians.—A tribe of the Dhegiha division or confederacy of the Siouan stock of Indians. The name means "Those who went against the current." In 1815 and 1820 they ceded lands at Council Bluffs to the whites. In 1825 and 1830 they made similar treaties. In 1854 they gave up more of their lands and removed to a reservation in northeastern Nebraska. They number about 1,200.

Omaha Indians:

Act to extend time of payment to purchasers of land of, vetoed, IX, 90.

Claims of, against Winnebagoes, VIII, 264.

Relief of, bill for, VIII, 387.

Treaty with, III, 265, 478, 512; V, 235; VI, 376.

Omaha, Nebr., act to extend privileges to port of, vetoed, VIII, 414.

Omnibus Bill.—Early in the first session of the Thirty-first Congress Henry Clay introduced a series of 6 resolutions as a basis for the compromise of the slavery question. These reso-

lutions provided for the admission of Califo nia as a free State; Territorial governmen for New Mexico and Utah without conditio as to slavery; a territorial boundary line b tween Texas and New Mexico favorable the former; payment of the Texas debt; su pression of the slave trade in the District Columbia; a more effective fugitive-slave la and a denial of the power of Congress to inte fere with the slave trade between slave State On Feb. 5 and 6, 1850, Clay ably advocated th passage of his resolutions by the Senate. Th body was strongly Democratic, though the A ministration was Whig. Debate on Clay resolutions lasted 2 months and was partic pated in by Webster (Mass.), Calhoun (S. C Benton (Mo.), King (Ala.), Davis and Foo (Miss.), Hamlin (Me.), Cass (Mich.), Sewa and Dickinson (N. Y.), Chase and Corwi (Ohio), Douglas (Ill.), Frémont (Cal.), Sou (La.), Hale (N. H.), Mangum (N. C.), Hunt and Mason (Va.), Bell (Tenn.), and others note. On Apr. 19 the resolutions were referre to a committee of 13, with Clay as chairma and consisting of 6 other Whigs and 6 Dem crats. On May 8 this committee submitted a elaborate series of bills embodying the su stance of Clay's resolutions. These sever bills were known collectively as the "omnib bill," and the last was passed on Sept. 20. (S also Compromise of 1850.)

O'Neal, Charlotte, act granting pension to, v toed, VIII, 558.

Oneida, The. (See *Aroostook*, The.)

Oneida Indians.—A tribe of the Iroquois stock Indians. They formerly occupied lands ea of Oneida Lake, N. Y., and the head waters the Susquehanna River to the south. Th name means "Standing stone" or "People stone." They usually acted independently the other Iroquois and were not promine in the confederacy. The early French settler with whom they were generally friendl called them Oneiout. They took part with th Colonies in the Revolution. For this the Br ish destroyed their villages. By a treaty i 1794 the Government made compensation fe their losses. In 1785 and 1788 they ceded lan to New York State. In 1833 most of them r moved to Green Bay, Wis., where they sti remain, and others went to Canada. The number about 3,000.

Oneida Indians:

Lands of, proposition to sell, I, 266, 338.

Treaty with, I, 347; III, 467; X, 44.

Oneota, The, purchased for Peru, detention o VI, 633, 637.

Onis, Louis de, letter of, to captain-general Caracas transmitted, I, 488.

Onondaga Indians.—The leading tribe of the Ir quois stock of Indians. Their original hun ing grounds were along the shores of the cree and lake in New York which bear their nam They claimed all the country between Lak Ontario and the Susquehanna River. Th name is translated to mean "On the top the mountain." In the councils of the Iroquo

Original Package.—In the enforcement of the prohibitory liquor law in the State of Iowa the officers were frequently charged with exceeding the limits of the State's jurisdiction in interfering with the traffic in spirits. State officers seized and confiscated liquors which it was claimed by the owners were sent into the State for reshipment to points outside the jurisdiction of the State courts. State officers defended themselves under the prohibition amendment to the constitution. In 1890 the Supreme Court of the United States, in the case of Leisy & Co. *vs.* Hardin, held that the plaintiffs, brewers in Illinois, had the right to carry liquors into any State and sell them in the original package without reference to local prohibitory or restrictive laws. The decision of the court rested on the right of Congress to have exclusive control of interstate commerce. Congress thereupon passed a law giving States control of the liquors so imported, although in the original package.

Oriskany (N. Y.), Battle of.—In August, 1777, Gen. Burgoyne sent a detachment of his army, consisting of 200 regulars, Sir John Johnson's Royal Greens, and some Canadian rangers and Indians, under Col. St. Leger, to operate in western and central New York and ultimately to join the main army under Howe at New York. St. Leger proceeded by way of the St. Lawrence River, Lake Ontario, and the Oswego and Oneida rivers to within a few miles of Fort Stanwix (now Schuyler), near the present city of Rome, on the Mohawk River. The post was garrisoned by less than 1,000 men, under Colonels Gansevoort and Willet. Gen. Herkimer collected the militia of Tryon County and advanced to the assistance of the fort. On Aug. 6, when about 6 miles from the post, near Oriskany, he fell into an ambush and was fiercely assailed by the British and the Indians under Brant. By reason of a successful sally by Willet the assailants were repulsed, but not without the loss of 400, including many of the leading patriots of that region. St. Leger made no official report of his loss except that of his Indian allies. The fight lasted several hours and was one of the most fiercely contested conflicts of the war. St. Leger, deserted by his Indian allies, retired precipitately to Canada.

Orleans, Territory of.—The old name for the present State of Louisiana. In March, 1804, after the purchase of Louisiana from France, Congress divided the territory, cutting off that portion between Texas and the Mississippi River and from the Gulf of Mexico north to the parallel of lat. 33° north and establishing it as a Territory, with William C. C. Claiborne as governor. In 1810 the citizens of Baton Rouge, territory of St. Francisville, overcame the local Spanish garrison, shot the Spanish governor, and established the Territory of West Florida. After the people of West Florida had elected a governor and framed a constitution President Madison issued a proclamation (I, 480) directing Governor Claiborne, of the Territory of Orleans, to take possession of West Florida and annex it to Orleans. In February, 1811, an act was passed "to enable the people of the Territory of Orleans to form a constitution and State government." Apr. 12, 1812, an act was passed for the admission of the State of Louisiana into the Union, extending the limits to include all between the Mississippi and Pearl rivers south of lat. 31° north.

P.

Pacific Railroads.—In 1848 Asa Whitney, a New York merchant, zealously advocated the building of a railroad by the Federal Government to the Pacific Ocean from some point on the Missouri or Mississippi River. A bill providing for such a road was introduced in the Senate. It was opposed by Thomas H. Benton and finally tabled by a vote of 27 to 21. The next year Benton introduced a Pacific railroad measure of his own. In March, 1853, an act was passed providing for surveys. By 1855 Government surveyors had ascertained practicable passes through the Rocky Mountains. The rapid growth of the Pacific States in consequence of the "gold fever" and the difficulty of communication between the East and West on account of the vast extent of intervening plains made railroad communication more and more desirable. The hopelessness of undertaking so stupendous a work with private capital led many who otherwise were opposed to the principle of Federal aid to internal improvements to advocate the building of the Pacific railroads under Government subsidies. In 1860 both the leading political parties in their platforms declared in favor of building a road under national supervision. The outbreak of the Civil War and the necessity for closer military communication aided the movement. The bill providing for the Union Pacific and Central Pacific roads was approved July 2, 1862, and granted as subsidies 6 per cent gold bonds of the United States. It gave to the Union Pacific $16,000 per mile for the great plain west from Omaha, Nebr., $48,000 per mile for 150 miles over the Rocky Mountains, and $32,000 per mile for the remainder—in all, 1,034 miles, $27,236,512; to the Central Pacific $16,000, $48,000, and $32,000 per mile—in all, 883 miles, $27,855,562. Each company also received 12,800 acres of land per mile of road—25,000,000 acres in all—by a subsequent act, July 1, 1864. The companies were allowed to issue an equal amount of their own bonds, which were to be a first lien on the road, the Government bonds the second. The time fixed for opening was set at July 1, 1876, and the road was actually opened May 10,

1869. The general direction is nearly east and west on or about the fortieth degree of latitude. The total length of the road built by the two companies from Omaha to San Francisco is 1,917 miles. July 2, 1864, a charter with subsidies was granted to the Northern Pacific from Lake Superior to Puget Sound, a distance of 1,800 miles, and thence to the Columbia River, 200 miles. The land granted to this road amounted to 47,000,000 acres, or 73,000 sq. miles. The road was commenced in 1870 and was to have been finished in 1879, but in 1873 the company became embarrassed and ceased work. In 1875 the company was reorganized and the time for construction extended. On Sept. 9, 1883, the last spike was driven at a point 50 miles west of Helena, Mont. The Great Northern extension from Pacific Junction, Mont., to Lowell, on Puget Sound, was completed Jan. 6, 1893. July 27, 1866, the Atlantic and Pacific road was chartered to run from Springfield, Mo., to the Pacific on or near the thirty-fifth parallel of latitude, a distance of 2,000 miles, and subsidized with 42,000,000 acres of land. Mar. 3, 1871, the Southern Pacific road was chartered to run from Marshall to El Paso, Tex., thence through New Mexico and Arizona to Los Angeles, Cal., along the thirty-second parallel of latitude. The act granted the same amount of land per mile as the others had received.

Pacific Railroads:

Condition and obligations of, discussed, IX, 737.

Construction of, discussed by President—
Buchanan, V, 457, 526, 572, 650.
Fillmore, V, 86.
Johnson, VI, 362, 453.
Lincoln, VI, 132, 187, 250.
Taylor, V, 20.

Funding of debt of, recommended, VIII, 250.

Government aid to, recommended, V, 457, 526, 572, 650.

Indebtedness of—
Change of plan for payment of, suggested, VIII, 526.
Commission to report plan for settlement of, recommended, IX, 205.
Commission to settle, X, 196.
Discussed, IX, 737.
Order regarding, IX, 801.
Report of Commissioner of Railroads on, discussed, IX, 205.
Reports of commissioners on, discussed, VIII, 596, 799.

Lands granted in aid of, discussed, V, 290; VI, 453; VII, 111; VIII, 359, 799.
Forfeiture of, discussed, VIII, 250, 794.
Revocation of withdrawal of, referred to, VIII, 612.

Kansas Pacific, sale of, discussed, X, 195.

Northern Pacific, agreements with Indians for sale of lands for use of, VIII, 70, 153, 192, 277, 369, 593.

Southern Pacific, contracts and leases of, referred to, VIII, 373.

Pacific Railroads—Continued.

Union Pacific—
Bonds issued to, referred to, VI, 596.
Completion of section of, extension of time for, recommended, VI, 384.
Construction of—
Discussed by President—
Johnson, VI, 362, 453, 576.
Lincoln, VI, 132, 187, 250.
Referred to, VI, 693; VII, 49.
Discussed by President—
Cleveland, IX, 737.
Johnson, VI, 683.
Injunction restraining election of officers of, referred to, VII, 9.
Location of, referred to, VI, 380.
Points of commencement of, discussed and order regarding, VI, 200, 234.
Reorganization of, recommended, IX, 537.
Report of Attorney-General regarding, referred to, VII, 482.
Report of Government directors of, referred to, VIII, 74, 158, 202, 263, 373, 374.
Sale of, discussed, X, 195.
Subscriptions to capital stock of, order designating place for receiving, VI, 275.

Pacific Squadron. (See Manila Harbor (Philippine Islands), Battle of.)

Pacific Telegraph referred to, VI, 128, 181, 244, 366, 455.

Pactole, The, referred to, II, 609.

Padroni System discussed, IX, 633.

Paez, José Antonio, vessel to transport remains of, to Venezuela recommended, VIII, 608.

Page, Thomas J., claim of, against Argentina adjusted, X, 177.

Pageot, A., French chargé d'affaires:
Announces intention to return to France, III, 201.
Correspondence regarding claims against France. (See France, claims against.)

Painting presented to Congress, Lincoln and Cabinet at reading of Emancipation Proclamation, VII, 483.

Palatinate.—A name formerly applied to a German state under the dominion of a count, particularly to the States of the Rhine. The counts of the electoral or Rhenish palatinate were established in the hereditary possession of the territory of that name and of the lands attached to it as early as the eleventh century. A count palatine was, under the Merovingian Kings of France, a high judicial officer who had supreme authority in all causes that came under the immediate cognizance of the sovereign. After the time of Charlemagne a similar title was given to any powerful feudal lord to whom a province, generally near the frontier, was made over, with judicial powers similar to those the counts palatine had wielded in the palace. The district so governed was called a palatinate or county palatine. There were 3 counties palatine in England—Lancaster, Chester, and Durham. By virtue of their regal rights the counts palatine had their courts of law and appointed their judges and law officers. They could pardon treason, murder, and felonies, issue writs and judicial processes, and the King's writs were of no avail in the palatinate. Maryland was by its charter erected into a palatinate after the model of the palatinate of Durham, England, and so continued as long as it was under proprietary government. Carolina, too, was originally chartered as a palatinate.

Palestine.—A territory in southern Syria, bounded on the north by Phenicia, Lebanon, and Anti-Lebanon, on the east by the Syrian Desert, on the south by an indefinite line extending westward from the southern extremity of the Dead Sea, and on the west by the Mediterranean Sea. It is also called Canaan and the Holy Land. Its ancient inhabitants were the Canaanites. These were conquered by the Israelites, who divided the country among their several tribes. In the time of Christ the divisions west of the Jordan were Galilee in the north, Samaria in the center, and Judea in the south. Palestine formed successively a part of the Babylonian, Persian, Roman, and Byzantine Empires, and about the middle of the seventh century passed under Mohammedan rule. During the Crusades it was temporarily held by European Christians. Since 1516 it has been in the possession of the Turkish Government. The soil is naturally fertile. Area, between 10,000 and 11,000 sq. miles; population, about 400,000.

Palo Alto (Mexico), Battle of.—May 7, 1846, Gen. Taylor started from Point Isabel, with a force of 2,288 men, to relieve Fort Brown, 27 miles away. At noon on the following day, when about half way between Point Isabel and Fort Brown, Taylor's army sighted the enemy at the water hole of Palo Alto. The regular Mexican force under Arista numbered 6,000 men, and there were some irregular troops and 12 pieces of artillery. Battle was immediately begun and fiercely fought until sunset. By the light of the moon and the burning prairie grass the belligerents buried their dead. The Mexicans lost 200 killed and 400 wounded. The American loss was only 4 killed and 40 wounded.

Panama Canal.—The idea of constructing a ship canal between the Atlantic and Pacific oceans occurred to navigators as soon as the form of the continents of North and South America became known. As early as 1527 H. de la Serna surveyed a canal route from Chagres to Panama. Lopez de Gomarfa in 1851 proposed to the Spanish Government the building of a canal. In 1698, when William Paterson, an adventurous Scot, had established an English colony on the Isthmus of Darien which he called New Caledonia, he advocated constructing a canal across the narrow strip of land separating the two great oceans. Many surveys have been made of the Isthmus with the view of piercing it with an artificial waterway. The United States obtained some very complete maps of the country by the explorations of Col. Hughes in 1849, Lieut. Strain in 1854, Lieut. Michler in 1858, and Commodores Selfridge and Tull in 1870 and 1875. In 1877 the Colombian Government granted a concession to a Frenchman named Wyse for constructing a canal. At the invitation of Ferdinand de Lesseps, an International Scientific Congress met at Paris in 1879 and hastily decided upon the Panama route for a canal, the American members of the congress refraining from voting. A company was at once formed, and the Wyse concession was purchased. De Lesseps, as chief engineer, visited Panama and declared the Panama Canal practicable, and an "international technical committee" estimated the cost at $169,000,000. On the strength of these representations the shares of the company were taken by French citizens, many of them of the middle classes, to the amount of $260,000,000. Work was commenced in 1881. The route is close to the present line of the Panama Railroad, crosses the Chagres River 6 times, and contemplates a long and deep cut through the central Cordillera. After several temporary interruptions work was permanently suspended in 1889 by the failure of the company. Only 12 of the 54 miles of the route have been completed so far as to be navigable, and these do not include the more difficult portion. In 1892, after an investigation of the affairs of the company, De Lesseps, his son, the contractor Eiffel, and others in public life were arrested on charges of fraud in the management of the funds intrusted to them for use in the construction of the canal. At their trial it was shown that a large portion of the funds were used in subsidizing the French press and in bribing members of the French Chambers, etc. The works are now in ruins.

Panama Congress.—A congress called by the several South and Central American Republics to meet at Panama in June, 1826, to consider the rights of those States. The United States was invited to send delegates, and in response to this invitation President J. Q. Adams, with the consent of the Senate, appointed Richard C. Anderson, minister to Colombia, and John Sergeant, of Philadelphia, delegates, and Congress appropriated $40,000 for their expenses. They arrived too late for the preliminary meeting, and the adjourned session of the congress for 1827 never occurred. Among the objects of the proposed congress were the regulation of commercial intercourse, assent to the doctrine that free ships make free goods, and an agreement that "each will guard against the establishment of any future European colony within its borders." The failure of the congress demonstrated the inadvisability of an alliance between the United States and the smaller Republics. President Adams warmly favored the establishment of closer relations with the Central and South American Republics, and was supported in the Cabinet by Henry Clay, whose influence in Congress was considerable. In opposing the alliance of American Republics in a speech in the Senate in April, 1826, John Randolph referred to the coalition of Adams and Clay as a "coalition between the Puritan and the blackleg." This remark provoked a duel between Clay and Randolph.

Panchita, The, seizure of, on African coast, V, 486.

Panics.—A word formed from the name of the Greek god of shepherds, who is said to have had the power of inspiring sudden fright without apparent cause. It is now commonly used to describe a state of fear bordering on frenzy, from whatever cause induced. In history great commercial crises are spoken of as panics. England, Holland, and France have experienced them, and the United States has passed through several notable ones. Those most disastrous have usually followed general injudicious speculation in lands or inflated securities. The crisis of 1816-1819 in the United States, it is claimed, was due to the speculation and disorder following the War of 1812. The next occurred in 1825. A very memorable panic was that of 1837. The few years preceding had been marked by extraordinary speculation, carried on with an unsound banking system. Jackson's "specie circular" caused many banks to suspend, and credit was generally impaired throughout the country. Governmental aid was invoked by many financial institutions, but without avail, as Van Buren, who had succeeded to the Presidency, insisted upon individuals righting their own affairs. In 1857 another period of inflation was followed by another panic. Again in 1873 there was a severe monetary crisis. Just 20 years later occurred the last panic from which the country has suffered. (See also Black Friday.)

Paoli (Pa.) Massacre.—After the retreat from Brandywine Washington moved out on the Lancaster road as far as Warren's Tavern. Finding that Howe did not contemplate an attack upon Reading, Washington stationed Gen. Anthony Wayne with 1,500 men at Paoli, a retired and well-chosen position, to be ready to fall upon the rear of Howe's army. On the night of Sept. 20, 1777, Wayne was surprised, through the treachery of the people of the country, and 300 of his men were killed, wounded, or captured, with a loss of only an inconsiderable number of the enemy. Wayne saved his artillery and most of his baggage.

Papago Reservation. (See Gila Bend Reservation, Ariz.)

Papal States.—A former dominion of Italy, comprising the Romagna, the Marches, Umbria, and the present province of Rome, and governed directly by the Papal See. It was bounded on the north by the Lombardo-Venetian Kingdom, on the east by the Adriatic Sea, on the southeast by the Kingdom of Naples, on the southwest by the Mediterranean Sea, and on the west by Tuscany and the Duchy of Modena. In 1860 the larger part was annexed to Italy and the remainder in 1870.

Paper Currency. (See Currency; Finances discussed.)

Paraguay.—A Republic of South America. It is bounded on the north by Bolivia and Brazil, on the east by Brazil and a portion of Argentina, and on the south and west by Argentina. The capital is Asuncion. The main portion of the country is hilly or undulating. It has a semitropical climate. The Europeans found are mostly descended from Spaniards, by whom the country was first settled in 1536. The principal products are hides, fruits, tobacco, sugar, and Paraguay tea. Executive authority is vested in a President, elected for 4 years. The Congress consists of a Senate and a Chamber of Deputies. The country declared its independence in 1811, refusing to unite with the Argentine Confederation. In 1865 the Republic became involved in a war with Brazil, Argentina, and Uruguay, which resulted in impoverishing the country and almost depopulating it. The area of Paraguay is about 95,000 sq. miles. In 1886 the civilized population was estimated at 329,645, mostly Christianized Indians. The resident foreigners number about 17,000.

Paris, Monetary Conferences at.—There have been three important international monetary conferences held at Paris. The first assembled June 17, 1867, at the solicitation of France, to "consider the question of uniformity of coinage and seek for the basis of ulterior negotiations." The United States sent representatives, as did also nearly every European nation. The conference adjourned after about a month without having arrived at any definite conclusion. On Aug. 16, 1878, a second international monetary conference convened at Paris, this time at the instance of the United States, "to adopt a common ratio between gold and silver for the purpose of establishing internationally the use of bimetallic money and securing fixity of relative value between those metals." The collective decision of the European delegates was that this would be impossible, monetary questions being governed by the special situation of each state or group of states. With this as the final conclusion the conference adjourned Aug. 29. The conference of Apr. 8, 1881, assembled at the call of France and the United States to adopt a permanent relative value between gold and silver, but adjourned July 8 without arriving at an agreement. (See also Brussels, Belgium; Paris, France.)

Paris, Treaties of.—Paris has been the scene of numerous important diplomatic conferences, both between France and other powers and between neighboring nations, who found hospitable neutral ground at the French capital. Among the most important of the treaties of Paris is that of Feb. 10, 1763, between Great Britain on one side and France, Spain, and Portugal on the other. France ceded to Great Britain Canada, Prince Edward Island, Cape Breton, Mobile, all the territory east of the Mississippi, Dominica, Tobago, St. Vincent, and Grenada. England restored to France Guadeloupe, Martinique, St. Pierre and Miquelon, and Pondicherry, and ceded St. Lucia to her. Spain ceded Florida to Great Britain, England restored Havana to Spain, and France ceded Louisiana to Spain. The treaty of Paris of 1782–83 between Great Britain on one side and France, Spain, and the United States on the other was arranged in 1782 and formally ratified Sept. 3, 1783. John Jay, John Adams, Benjamin Franklin, and Henry Laurens formed the American commission. The absolute independence of the United States was recognized; Florida and Minorca were returned to Spain; navigation of the

Mississippi was made free to both Spain and the United States; the Americans relinquished their pretensions to the territory north of Lake Erie; the St. Lawrence River system from the western end of Lake Superior to the forty-fifth parallel was made the boundary between the United States and the British possessions (from the forty-fifth parallel to the sea the boundary followed the highlands after an uncertain fashion and was long a matter of dispute); loyalists and tories were to be protected in America; English troops were to be withdrawn without destroying any property or taking away any negro slaves belonging to Americans; the right of fishing on the Canadian and Newfoundland coasts was granted to Americans. The portion of the treaty which directly affected America was signed at Paris, but that between Great Britain, France, and Spain was signed at Versailles, by which name the entire treaty is sometimes called. At Versailles the region of Senegal was granted to France and mutual restitution of conquests in the West Indies was made. In 1898 commissioners were appointed by the Governments of the United States and Spain to meet at Paris and frame a treaty of peace in accordance with the terms of the protocol signed Aug. 12, 1898. The commissioners began their sessions Oct. 1 and ended with the signing of the treaty of peace, Dec. 10. (See also Spanish-American War.)

Paris Tribunal of Arbitration.—A treaty providing for the arbitration of the dispute between Great Britain and the United States as to the killing of seals in the Bering Sea was concluded on Feb. 29, 1892. The Tribunal of Arbitration met at Paris and made an award which was delivered to the agents of the respective governments Aug. 15, 1893. Congress passed an act, approved Apr. 6, 1894, to give effect to the award of the tribunal (IX, 494).

Paris Tribunal of Arbitration:

Acts to give effect to award of, proclaimed, IX, 494, 691.

Award of, discussed and recommendations regarding, IX, 526, 630.

Case of United States at, prepared by John W. Foster, IX, 313.

Convention for settlement of claims under, IX, 665.

Discussed, IX, 437.

Enforcement of regulations in accordance with decision of, referred to, IX, 568.

Failure of negotiations of, to protect fur seals of Alaska, IX, 750.

Reports of agent of United States to, transmitted, IX, 477.

Parish.—At the time of the settlement of America the parish was the unit of local government in England. In some of the Southern Colonies the name and institutions of the parish were imitated precisely. The Virginia parish was a subdivision of a county. Besides attending to its religious duties, the vestry of a parish had to choose church wardens and with them take charge of the poor, establish the

public bounds, count the tobacco, and attend to various other petty administrative matters. They also chose the clergyman and collected his salary. In New England the word parish had only an ecclesiastical significance. The colonists there divided the county into towns, which provided some of the institutions of the parish, and the others were left to the church to provide. In South Carolina the Colony was divided primarily into parishes, there being no counties at first. Louisiana still retains the parish instead of the county as the principal division of the State.

Parke, John G., negotiations for and correspondence regarding restoration of peace, VI, 260.

Parker, Foxhall A., commander of Home Squadron, mentioned, V, 140.

Parker, Newcomb, act granting pension to, vetoed, VIII, 456.

Parker, P. E., act for relief of, vetoed, VIII, 710.

Parker, Peter, commissioner to China, mentioned, V, 531, 582.

Parker, Willis W., inspector and collector, nomination of, I, 402.

Parks, Gorham, correspondence regarding African slave trade, IV, 688.

Parks. (See Chickamauga and Chattanooga National Military Park; National Parks.)

Parsons, Justin W., murder of, in Turkey, referred to, VIII, 40.

Parsons, Lewis E., provisional governor of Alabama, appointed, VI, 323.

Parsons, Marilla, act granting pension to, vetoed, VIII, 440.

Partridge, Frank C., mentioned, IX, 242.

Partridge, James R., mentioned, VI, 61.

Passamaquoddy Bay, commissioners to mark international boundary in, referred to, IX, 631.

Passamaquoddy Indians. (See Abnaki Indians.)

Passamaquoddy Indians:

Fought for liberty of American people, II, 463.

Memorial of, presented to Congress, II, 463.

Passport.—A document issued by competent civil authority granting permission to the person specified in it to travel or authenticating his right to protection. In some nations no person is allowed to leave the country without a passport from his government; but the regulations of different jurisdictions regarding the use of passports have greatly varied and of late years have exhibited a tendency toward a relaxation of stringency, extending in many countries to their total abolition. Passports of the United States, which are given under the seal of the Secretary of State, request that the person named therein be permitted to pass freely and safely, and in case of need that aid and protection be afforded him.

Passports:

Authentication of, denial of, by Russian consuls to Jews discussed, IX, 635.

Charge for, for citizens visiting foreign countries referred to, VIII, 400.

Laws regarding issue of, revision of, recommended, VIII, 785.

and Michael Pauw, who secured all the land on the west bank of the Hudson River from the Kills which separate Staten Island from the mainland of New Jersey to Hoboken. Livingston, Phillipse, Van Cortland, and others came afterwards. These wealthy grantees were called patroons and were privileged to rule their colonies in absolute feudal style, the colonists being bound to them for a stipulated number of years. This system proved faulty in that it debarred the poorer class of colonists; so in 1640 the charter of the Dutch Company was amended so as to extend the privileges of colonization to any good citizen of the Netherlands. In later years there were frequent quarrels between the patroons and the provincial government.

Patterson, Eliza W., act for relief of, permitted to become law and reasons therefor, VIII, 219.

Patterson, William, associate justice, Supreme Court, nomination of, void, I, 137.

Patton, Rachel, act granting pension to, vetoed, IX, 675.

Patuxent River, sites for fortifications on, referred to, X, 65.

Paul vs. Virginia.—An important case before the United States Supreme Court. The statutes of Virginia required the deposit in the State treasury of certain moneys in State bonds by insurance companies not incorporated under the State laws in return for licenses to do business in the State. This law was enacted Feb. 3, 1866, and later in the month a supplemental act was passed. In the same year Samuel Paul, a citizen of Virginia, acting as agent for a New York insurance company, was indicted before the circuit court of Petersburg and sentenced to pay a fine of $50 for refusing to comply with the above law. The court of appeals of Virginia affirmed the decree of the circuit court, and, the case having been taken to the Supreme Court of the United States, that tribunal affirmed the judgment of the State court of appeals on the ground that the State law in question did not conflict with that clause of the National Constitution which declares that "the citizens of each State shall be entitled to all privileges and immunities of citizens in the several States," nor with the power of Congress to "regulate commerce with foreign nations and among the several States." Justice Field, for the court, held that issuing a policy of insurance is not a transaction of commerce. The policies are local transactions and are governed by the local law. Justice Field stated that corporations are not citizens within the meaning of the Constitution.

Paulding, Hiram, arrest of William Walker and associates in Nicaragua by, V, 466.
Referred to, V, 470, 486.

Pauls, George, death of, referred to and appropriation to widow of, recommended, IX, 59.

Paulus Hook (N. J.), Capture of.—In the summer of 1779 the British had a garrison of 383 men stationed at Paulus Hook, N. J., opposite New York City. At 3 o'clock on the morning of Aug. 19 Maj. Harry Lee with a force of 300 picked men, made a descent upon the fort and in a short engagement killed 30 men and took 160 prisoners. The British having retired to a small circular redoubt too strong for Lee's men, he returned to camp with his prisoners. Congress rewarded Lee with thanks and a gold medal.

Pauncefote, Sir Julian, British ambassador:
Agreement between United States and Great Britain for *modus vivendi* regarding Bering Sea fisheries signed by, IX, 146.
Communications in regard to Venezuelan boundary transmitted by, IX, 655.

Paupers, Foreign:
Introduction of, into United States, III, 469; IV, 518.
Legislation respecting, recommended, VIII, 170.
Request of President to withdraw articles regarding, from consideration of House, III, 475.
Involuntary deportation of convicts, idiots, insane persons, and, to United States referred to, VII, 265, 636.

Pawnee Indians.—A confederacy of tribes of the Caddoan stock of Indians. They formerly inhabited the plains of Kansas and Nebraska and the banks of the Platte and Republican rivers. This confederation has always been friendly to the Americans. By a treaty in 1833 they sold their lands south of the Nebraska. They were afterwards attacked by the Sioux and the remainder of their hunting grounds was devastated. In 1857 the Pawnees sold more of their lands, and, the depredations of the Sioux continuing, the remnants of the Pawnee Confederation were removed to a reservation in Oklahoma. There are now some 800 individuals, divided into 4 tribes—the Tcawi or Grand Pawnee, Pitahauerat or Tapage, the Republican Pawnee, and the Skidi or Pawnee Loup.

Pawnee Indians:
Agreement between Cherokee Commission and, IX, 333.
Aid for, recommended, VII, 360.
Treaty with, II, 47, 322, 347; III, 37; IV, 671; V, 464.

Pawnee Reservation, Ind. T., enlargement of, bill for, VIII, 108.

Payne, John Howard, minister to Tunis, nomination of, referred to, V, 75.

Payne, Lewis:
Implicated in assassination of President Lincoln, proceedings of trial and verdict of military commission, VI, 334, 335, 336, 342, 347, 348.
Persons claiming reward for apprehension of, directed to file claims, VI, 353.

Pazos, Mr., mentioned, II, 32.

Pea Patch Island:
Fortifications for, II, 475; III, 508.
Jurisdiction of, should be secured by Government, III, 508.
Private claims to, II, 126, 230.
Proceedings to try title to, referred to, III, 592.

Pea Ridge (Ark.), Battle of.—Called by the Confederates the battle of Elk Horn. In December, 1861, Gen. Samuel R. Curtis took command of the 12,000 Federal troops at Rolla, Mo., and advanced against Gen. Sterling Price, who retreated before him into Arkansas. Gen. Price was joined by Gen. Ben. McCulloch. In January Gen. Earl Van Dorn assumed command of the combined Confederate forces, estimated at 16,000, including some 5,000 Cherokee Indians recruited for the service by Albert Pike. Curtis had about 10,000 men in line and 48 pieces of artillery. Mar. 7, 1862, Van Dorn attacked Curtis in his position on Pea Ridge, a line of bluffs along Sugar Creek, in Benton County, Ark. Skillful manipulation of the artillery in Sigel's division did much toward determining the result. Fighting continued all day, and during the night both armies changed positions. The battle was renewed at sunrise on the 8th, and after 2 hours Van Dorn's forces retreated. The Confederate Generals McCulloch and McIntosh were killed and Price and Slack were wounded. The Confederate losses were about 1,300. The Union army lost 1,351 in killed, wounded, and missing.

Peabody, Charles A., provisional judge for Louisiana, appointed, VI, 122.

Peabody, George, medal presented to, referred to, VI, 699.

Peace Commission.—In May, 1778, Lord North sent a peace commission to the Colonies. It consisted of the Earl of Carlisle, George Johnstone, and William Eden. They arrived at Philadelphia June 4. The commission offered many conciliatory terms, including an extension of the privileges of trade, an abolition of the quartering act, a representation of the Colonies in Parliament, an arrangement for sustaining continental bills of credit, and an almost independent colonial administration. As the commissioners had no power to acknowledge the independence of the Colonies, Congress declined to appoint commissioners to meet them.

Peace Commission:
Of 1867, treaties concluded by, VII, 51.
Spanish-American, at Paris, X, 174, 175.

Peace Conference.—In January, 1861, a resolution was passed by the legislature of Virginia inviting the various States to appoint delegates to meet at Washington to devise means to avert, if possible, the impending war. The conference, at which 21 States were represented, met Feb. 4 and adjourned two weeks later. It proposed a constitutional amendment which prohibited slavery north of lat. 36° 30′ north. South of this line it was not to be interfered with. The proposed amendment denied the right of Congress to pass laws giving freedom to slaves temporarily in free States or to fugitive slaves. It also forbade Congress controlling slavery in the Southern States, but prohibited the slave trade. The amendment was brought up in the Senate, but was not introduced in the House. In July, 1864, President Lincoln sent Horace Greeley to confer with representatives of the Confederates in the interest of peace. Clement C. Clay, jr., of Alabama, James P.

Holcombe, of Virginia, and others met Mr. Greeley at the Clifton House, Niagara Falls, but the conference was without result. About the same time Rev. James F. Jaques, of the Seventy-third Illinois Regiment, and J. R. Gillmore visited Richmond and held a fruitless peace conference with Jefferson Davis. Another conference was brought about by Francis P. Blair, sr., at Hampton Roads, Feb. 3, 1865, between Alexander H. Stephens, John A. Campbell, and R. M. T. Hunter, on the part of the Confederates, and President Lincoln and Secretary Seward, on behalf of the Federal Government. This was also without result.

Peace Congress, International, at Washington, VIII, 97, 130.
Invitation extended American nations to attend, VIII, 98.
Postponement of, referred to, VIII, 130.

Peace Establishment of Navy. (See Navy.)

Peach Tree Creek (Ga.), Battle of.—July 17, 1864, Sherman's army advanced across the Chattahoochee River and Johnston fell back toward Atlanta. Just at this time Johnston was superseded in command of the Southern army by Gen. John B. Hood. Before the Federal forces could be brought into line of battle before Atlanta they were attacked by Hood's army near Peach Tree Creek, July 20, 1864. The attack fell mainly upon Newton's division of the Fourth Corps, the Twentieth Corps, and Johnson's division of the Fourteenth Corps. After a severe battle the Confederates retired into their intrenchments, leaving upon the field 500 dead, 1,000 wounded, 7 stand of colors, and many prisoners. The Federal loss in killed, wounded, and missing was 1,500. Gen. Hood censured Hardee for the reverse.

Peacock, The.—A United States sloop of war, carrying 18 guns, commanded by Capt. Lewis Warrington. On Apr. 29, 1814, when off the coast of Florida, this vessel attacked the British brig *Épervier*, also mounting 18 guns. After a battle lasting 40 minutes, in which 22 of her men were killed or wounded, the *Épervier* surrendered. It proved a rich prize, as it had on board $118,000 in specie. On June 30, 1815, the *Peacock* attacked and captured the *Nautilus*, of 14 guns. This capture took place after the treaty of peace. Next day, on ascertaining this fact, Capt. Warrington released the *Nautilus* and returned home.

Pearce, Samuel, ensign in Navy, nomination of, and reasons therefor, VI, 156.

Pearl River, Hawaiian Islands, improvement of harbor of, and establishment of naval station at, recommended, IX, 188.

Peck, Ferdinand W., commissioner-general to Paris Exposition, X, 183.

Peck, Mr., labor commissioner of New York, mentioned, IX, 307.

Pedersen, Peder, Danish minister, mentioned, II, 345.

Peirpoint, Francis H., governor, to be aided in restoring Virginia into Union, VI, 337.

Pensions.—The word "pension" is derived from the Latin word *pensio*, a payment, and refers to allowances of money paid in fixed amounts at certain intervals by a government to such persons as have rendered some valuable public service, or to the dependent relatives of such. In England pensions are granted to those "who by their useful discoveries in science and attainments in literature and the arts have merited the gracious consideration of their sovereign and the gratitude of their country." Aug. 26, 1776, the Continental Congress passed an act to provide by pension for the disabled soldiers of the Revolution. It was also resolved during the same year that all the officers who should continue in the service until the end of the war should receive half pay for 7 years after peace had been established. A few years later the widows and orphans of those who had died were included in the provisions of this act. In 1785 Congress recommended that the several States provide for invalid soldiers. By laws passed in 1789 and 1808 the United States assumed the pension obligations of the several States. Officers and seamen of the Navy disabled in service were placed on the pension lists by act of July 1, 1797, and by acts passed in 1799 and 1800 money accruing from prizes was made to constitute a fund for the payment of naval pensions. By an act passed Apr. 24, 1816, the rate of pension for total disability was fixed at $17 per month for first lieutenants, $15 for second lieutenants, and $8 for noncommissioned officers and privates. In 1818 an act was passed granting pensions to all who had served 9 months or more in the Revolutionary Army and were in indigent circumstances. More claimants applied than could possibly have survived from Washington's army. The amount required to be paid the first year was eleven times what had been estimated, and the second year seventeen times the estimate. In 1868, when all the Revolutionary pensioners had died, there remained 888 widows of such soldiers. There yet remain on the pension rolls (1898) 5 widows of Revolutionary soldiers. Acts of July 14, 1862, and subsequent dates provided pensions for soldiers and sailors disabled in the Civil War and for the dependent relatives of those who had died. Under these acts expenditures for pensions reached $34,443,895 in 1871, and then declined until, on Jan. 25, 1879, the arrears act was passed, allowing back pay on all claims theretofore allowed. In 2 years this act doubled the total annual sum paid for pensions. Meanwhile, in 1871, another act had pensioned all who had served a certain time in the War of 1812, and their widows if married before the treaty of Ghent. In 1898 there were 3 of the former and 2,407 of the latter. The act of June 27, 1890, pensioned all who served 90 days in the Civil War and were honorably discharged, and who were incapacitated for manual labor, and the widows, children, and dependent parents of such. This act has nearly doubled the number of pensioners and increased the annual expenditures for pensions to more than $160,000,000—nearly twice the ordinary annual expenditure for the German army. The total number of pensioners reported June 30, 1898, was 1,001,328. The disbursements were: Pensions on account of Army and Navy, $144,651,880; cost of disbursement and fees of examining surgeons, $1,207,515; salaries and per diem expenses of the Pension Bureau, $2,683,213; total, $148,542,608. June 30, 1898, there were 635,059 claims for pensions pending. Of these some 200,000 are called original claims, while the other 435,000 are for increase, rerating, etc.

Of the 200,000 original claims the Commissioner of Pensions estimates that about 125,000 are made under the general law by persons now drawing pensions under the act of June 27, 1890. Should an original claim be allowed by the provisions of one law the claimant is dropped from the rolls under any other law by the terms of which he may have received benefits.

Peru—Continued.

Vessels purchased for, from United States detained, VI, 633, 637.

Vice-President of, refuge given to, by the *St. Louis*, II, 570.

War between Chile, Bolivia, and, VII, 570, 611; VIII, 41, 130.

Claims of United States arising out of, VIII, 328, 498, 784; IX, 109.

Conditions of peace proposed by Chile discussed, VIII, 75, 130, 173.

Efforts of United States to bring about peace discussed, VII, 570, 611, 630; VIII, 75, 130.

Stable government restored in Peru, VIII, 503.

Terminated, VIII, 235.

Treaty of peace discussed, VIII, 173.

Peru-Bolivian Confederation (see also Bolivia· Peru):

Dissolution of, referred to, III, 534.

Treaty with, III, 346, 377, 489.

Pet Banks. (See Banks, Pet.)

Petersburg, Va., explosion of mine in front of, referred to, VI, 270.

Petersburg (Va.), Siege of.—When Grant crossed the Rapidan, May 4, 1864, with the Army of the Potomac to operate against Lee, he ordered Gen. Butler, with the Army of the James, to proceed up the James River toward Richmond. Butler's army consisted of the Tenth and Eighteenth army corps, under Generals Gillmore and W. F. Smith, and numbered 38,648 officers and men and 90 guns. May 5 he occupied City Point and Bermuda Hundred, 18 miles southeast of Richmond. On the evening of May 13 and the morning of the 14th he carried a portion of the first line of defenses of Richmond at Fort Darling, on Drurys Bluff. On the 16th Butler was attacked and driven back to Bermuda Hundred. June 10 he sent a force under Gillmore and Kautz against Petersburg. The cavalry entered the town, but were driven back, and the expedition returned to Bermuda Hundred. June 15, after a march of 55 miles from Cold Harbor in 2 days, Grant was ready to cross the James. The army of 130,000 men crossed by pontoon bridge in 3 days. The two armies were now united and prepared for final operations against Richmond. The first step toward taking Richmond seemed to be the occupation of Petersburg, 22 miles to the south, on the Richmond and Petersburg Railroad. June 16, 1864, after the junction of the Army of the James and the Army of the Potomac, an attack was made on Petersburg by W. F. Smith's corps. The assaults were continued for 4 days. Reenforcements were sent from Richmond to defend the place, and the attempts cost Grant 7,881 men. During parts of June and July a powder mine was dug beneath portions of the Petersburg intrenchments. It was intended to explode this and make an assault through the breach thus made. The mine, known as "the Crater," was charged with 8,000 pounds of powder, and at 4 o'clock a. m. July 30, 1864, was exploded. A Confederate battery and most of a regiment

were blown up. The assault, which was made by 50,000 men under Burnside, Warren, and Ord, was a total failure, and 4,000 men were lost in it. Gen. Mahone commanded the Confederate force that recovered the line broken by the explosion. During this siege a number of brilliant sorties were made. The losses in Lee's army are not fully reported. Elliott's brigade lost 677 men. Petersburg was not surrendered until Apr. 3, 1865, nearly a year afterwards.

Petition.—The Constitution prohibits Congress from making any law to abridge "the right of the people peaceably to assemble and to petition the Government for a redress of grievances." Feb. 11, 1790, a petition signed by Benjamin Franklin was offered to Congress praying for the abolition of slavery, but no notice was taken of it. Between 1830 and 1844 numerous petitions from Abolitionists poured into Congress. May 26, 1836, the House resolved, by a vote of 117 to 68, that "all petitions, memorials, resolutions, propositions, or papers relating in any way to the subject of slavery or the abolition of slavery shall, without being printed or referred, be laid on the table, and that no further action be taken thereon." This was the first of the famous "gag rules" of Congress. John Quincy Adams championed the cause of the Abolitionists and opposed the gag rules for 10 years, finally securing their repeal. In 1837 he presented a petition to Congress purporting to come from slaves. This was the first of the kind ever offered, though in 1800 Congress was thrown into an uproar of debate by a petition from freed negroes. In his annual message to Congress Dec. 2, 1835, President Jackson asserted that publications addressed to the passions of slaves and stimulating them to insurrection were being circulated through the mails, and suggested laws to prohibit, under severe penalties, such circulation (III, 175). One of the most noted laws under this recommendation was the Atherton gag, introduced by C. G. Atherton, of New Hampshire. It was rescinded in 1845. The rules of Congress now provide that petitions, when presented, shall be indorsed with the name of the member presenting them and the committee to which they are referred. They are entered by the Clerk on the Journal and then transmitted to the proper committee. The notice of their introduction appears in the Congressional Record.

Petrel, The, mentioned, X, 155.

Petroleum, taxation of, in Holland, etc., referred to, VIII, 394, 401.

Pettaquamscut Purchasers.—In 1660 John Hull, who had become well known through his coinage of pine-tree money (q. v.), organized a company and purchased a tract of land from the Narraganset Indians, about Pettaquamscut Rock, on the south shore of Rhode Island, between Point Judith and Wickford. About the same time lands near Wickford had been purchased by a company headed by Humphrey Atherton, of Massachusetts, the two companies claiming the same territory. When the boundary line between Connecticut and Rhode Island was settled, in 1662, the Atherton Company had its region placed under the government of Connecticut. In 1665 the royal commission ordered the Indians to return the price paid by the Atherton Company and that the lands be returned to them. The disputed territory became the King's province. It was later made part of Rhode Island and was known as King's County until the Revolution, when the name was changed to Washington County. It was a subject of contention between Connecticut and Rhode Island for 50 years.

Pewter Muggers.—A faction of the Democratic party in New York City which in 1828 bolted the Tammany candidates. These dissatisfied Democrats held their meetings over a resort in Frankfort street, New York, locally famous for its refreshments served in pewter mugs; hence the name.

Philippine Islands.—The Philippine Islands form a great part of the vast archipelago lying southeast of Asia. They were discovered by Magellan in 1521, but it was not until 1564 that the group received its present name, in honor of Philip II of Spain. In many respects these islands were Spain's best possessions, due to the abundance and variety of products, numerous and good ports, character of inhabitants, and on account of the vicinity of certain countries of eastern Asia which are now entering upon a stage of civilization and commerce. From the year of discovery until 1542 several expeditions from Spain attempted to gain possession of the islands, but all failed. In 1564 another expedition, commanded by Miguel de Legaspi, was dispatched and a footing established in Cebu. Headquarters were later transferred to Luzon, and in 1571 the city of Manila was founded. Various attempts to drive out the Spaniards were made during the following years by the Portuguese, Dutch, and Chinese. In 1762 Manila was taken and held by the English for a ransom of £1,000,000. This, however, was never paid, and the islands were finally returned to Spain. The archipelago extends from lat. 5° 32′ to 19° 38′ north and from long. 117° to 126° east. It thus covers about 1,000 miles north and south and 600 east and west. On the north and northwest the islands are separated from China by the China Sea and the Indo-Chinese Peninsula. Toward the east is the Pacific. On the north a number of small islands stretch out toward Formosa. On the south, while a double connection is formed with Borneo by the lines of the Palawan, Balabac, and Sulu islands, the basin of the Celebes Sea extends for a distance of 300 miles between the southernmost island (Mindanao) and the Celebes. The number of islands is not definitely known, but it is variously estimated at from 1,200 to 2,000. New ones are being continually added to the maps. Some members of the vast archipelago, as well as the more remote districts in the larger islands, lying beyond the direct control of the Spanish, have remained unexplored. The principal islands are Luzon, Mindanao, Palawan, Samar, Panay, Mindoro, Leyte, Negros, Cebu, Masbate, Bohol, Catanduanes, Polillo, Marinduque, Tablas, Burias, and Ticao. The coast line of all the islands is very irregular and broken, the ocean cutting in and forming many gulfs, bays, isthmuses, and peninsulas. There are long stretches of canals and passages between the islands, but these are not always navigable. The whole surface of the Philippines is essentially mountainous, the only plains that occur being alluvial districts at the river mouths and the spaces left by the intersection of the ranges. The principal ranges have a tendency to run north and south, with a certain amount of deflection east and west, as the case may be, so that the orographic diagram of the archipelago as a whole has a similarity to a fan, with northern Luzon as its center of radiation. The three lines of partially submerged ridges stretching from Indonesia toward the Philippines, running north and south, continue their main axis and strike the southern part of the same region at the Saragani Volcano. East of this range is found a broad chain, occupying all the eastern section of Mindanao, which borders on the Pacific. While none of the mountain peaks greatly exceeds 8,000 feet in height, Apo, in Mindanao, is over 9,000 feet; Halson, in Mindoro, is over 8,900 feet, and Mayón, in Luzon, over 8,200. The latter is an active volcano, which has been the scene of several eruptions during the present century. Extinct or active craters are relatively as numerous in the Philippines as in the eastern archipelago, and as a consequence of these subterranean forces earthquakes are frequent and violent. In 1627 one of the most elevated mountains of Cagayan disappeared, and on the island of Mindanao, in 1675, a passage was opened to the sea and a vast plain emerged. The more recent of the convulsions occurred in 1863 and in 1880. The destruction of property was great, especially in Manila. The general belief is that the Philippines once formed a part of an enormous continent, from which they were separated by some cataclysm. This continent probably extended from Celebes to the farthest Polynesian islands on the east, to New Zealand on the south, and to the Ladrone and Sandwich islands on the north. The immense coast line of the islands contains a great number of good harbors, but as a consequence of the exclusive policy of the Spanish Government in closing them to foreign commerce very little is known except to coastwise navigators. Trade is confined chiefly to Manila, Iloilo, Cebu, and Sual. Zamboanga, on the island of Mindanao, is also an open port. The bay of Manila, one of the finest in the world, is about 120 miles in circumference, with very few dangers to navigation. Of the interior roads little can be said, and of those running along the coast positive information is not available. The extreme length of the Philippine group from north to south, their northern extremity reaching to the northern limit of the tropical zone, causes a considerable variety of climate. However, the general characteristics are tropical. In the region of Manila the hottest season is from March to June, the greatest heat being in May, before the rains set in, when the maximum temperature ranges from 80° to 100° in the shade. The coolest weather occurs in December and January, when the temperature falls at night to 60° or 65° and seldom rises in the day above 75°. From November to February the sky is bright, the atmosphere cool and dry, and the weather in every way delightful. The gales of the Philippines occur chiefly in the northern islands, and their direction is from the northward. Typhoons have their origin to the east or to the southeast of the Philippines, whence their course is westward, with a slight divergence to the north or south, the average direction appearing to be west by north. They occur in all months of the year, but the greater number take place about the time of the equinoxes. Among the Philippine Islands when the sun has north declination the higher tides about spring occur during the day, and when it has south declination during the night. The population has been estimated at about 8,000,000, of which the bulk is of Malay origin. On their first arrival the Spaniards found a part of the natives somewhat civilized, but while they had a written language, of which some specimens have been preserved, it was of no value in throwing light upon their early history, and their traditions are very few. The soil is most fertile, but agriculture almost wholly undeveloped. The people are skillful weavers of cotton and silk. They tan leather and make rude wagons and carts. The islands are very rich in woods, ebony, cedar, ironwood, sapanwood, logwood, and gum trees being plentiful. Gutta-percha is found in certain localities. The cocoa palm is of great value, trunk, branches, leaves, fruit, shell, and husk all being used. Bamboo and areca palm are abundant and of great utility. Two woods—the "banava" and the "malave"—resist the destructive action of water for centuries. Many plants have medicinal value. Mangoes, plantains, jack fruits, and the Malayan fruits are met with. Rice is the staple food, but often not enough is raised to supply the demand. Potatoes, pease, and even wheat are raised in the higher localities. Deer abound in the thickets of all the islands. There are also many buffalo ("caravaos") and wild horses. The buffalo, called "karbo" by the Malays, is the great beast of burden. It is very strong and docile if domesticated, but dangerous in the wild state. The Philippine horse is small and of poor appearance, but it is a strong and sturdy animal. The bull (of Spanish origin) has propagated his species very numerously, and is found wild. There are various kinds of monkeys, mountain cats, and the "nasigan," a small quadruped that is an enemy to rats. Among reptiles are found the "boa" or "culebra casera," the python, and the terrible "dehenpalay." The bite of the latter is almost instantly fatal. Of birds there are many species. Fish are plentiful and sharks and alligators are found in the seas. Swampy and damp localities swarm with insects, the mosquito being conspicuous. The "anay," a sort of ant, destroys all wood except the "molane" with astonishing rapidity. From what is known of the mineralogy of the islands there is no doubt that a scientific geological survey would prove that they are rich in ore deposits of many kinds. Gold is found, especially in the mountainous districts of Luzon and on the islands of Mindanao and Mindoro. It is not believed that true coal is to be found in large deposits. Iron ore of excellent quality is abundant, but from lack of means of transportation and machinery it has so far been found cheaper to depend upon importation. Rich deposits of copper exist, and galena and zinc blendes have been found. Sulphur is found in the vicinity of many of the ancient volcanoes. Early commerce with the world was greatly restricted by the efforts of Spain to secure a monopoly for her subjects. It was not until 1809 that the first English firm obtained permission to establish a business house in Manila. In 1814 this permission was more general. It is, however, only since 1834 that greater freedom of intercourse and larger introduction of foreign capital and methods have materially affected the development of natural resources. Internal commerce as well as foreign trade suffer from lack of facilities for transportation. But one railroad (123 miles in length) has been built, running from Manila to Pangasinán. A single-track road, it is of substantial construction and connects the capital with the rice-growing districts. The principal staples of export are tobacco, manila hemp, sugar cane, coffee, and cacao. The principal manufactures consist of a variety of textile fabrics, hats, mats, baskets, ropes, coarse pottery, and musical instruments. The chief imports are rice, flour, dress goods, wines, coal, and petroleum. The public revenue is about $12,000,000 per annum, of which the larger part is raised from direct taxation, customs, monopolies, and lotteries. For the imposition and collection of taxes Spanish ingenuity was exercised to the utmost, but the basis of the financial system in the Philippines was the poll tax, which every adult under 60 years of age, male or female, had to pay. There was no export duty on tobacco, but almost every article of import was heavily taxed. On muslin and petroleum the duty was about 100 per cent of cost. Manila is connected with Hongkong by cable. There are also many lines of steamers. The Roman Catholic was the established church in the Philippines. Most of the ecclesiastical authority was in the hands of the various religious orders—Dominicans, Augustines, Franciscans, etc.—who were the real rulers of the country, as their power among the natives far exceeded that of the various civil and military authorities. This power caused a great deal of jealousy, as is evidenced by the long record in the history of the islands of bitter controversies between the church and civil authorities. The religious affairs on the islands are far behind the age, and it would be of great benefit to the people, who are naturally devout, if they were infused with more modern ideas and methods. Education is much neglected, and both the institutions for higher and primary instruction are antiquated in their methods and far behind the times. Although in nearly every town and village under the control of the Government a school might be found, neither the quality nor quantity of the instruction given was satisfactory. In Madrid there was a council of state for the Philippines, which had in charge the interests of the colony and acted as an advisory board to the minister for the colonies. At Manila the administration of the government had for its head and chief a governor-general. At the close of the Spanish-American War the treaty of peace provided, among other things, for the cession of the entire Philippine group to the United States. The natives of the island are at this time (June, 1899) in insurrection, and reports are received daily of conflicts between them and the American land and naval forces in the islands.

Pine-Tree Money.—On May 27, 1652, the general court of Massachusetts passed an act establishing a mint at Boston. John Hull was appointed mint master, and he began the coinage of shillings, 6d. pieces, and 3d. pieces. This was called pine-tree money from a design on the obverse of a pine tree encircled by a grained ring, with the legend "Masathusets. In." The coinage was discontinued on the death of the mint master, Oct. 1, 1683.

Piracy.—Robbery on the high seas. In the law of nations the essential element of piracy is the intention of preying indiscriminately on the human race, and not a desire to interfere with the trade of some distinct power. As the high seas are not under the jurisdiction of any one state, the crime of piracy is triable in any court. The difference between a pirate and a privateer consists in these facts, that whereas the former is a sea rover who preys on the vessels and goods of any nation he may chance to run across, or who makes descents upon land for purposes of plunder, a privateer, on the other hand, has for his purpose the preying upon the commerce of a hostile nation only; he is under bond to the state whose flag he flies and of which he carries the commission or letter of marque granting him a share in the prizes taken. A privateer exceeding his commission might not be considered a pirate, but one with commissions from two opposite belligerents would be, for it would be apparent that his motive would be plunder of both. A vessel of a part of a country organized for rebellion has been held to be piratical because, although it may have a commission, such commission issued by an unknown and unrecognized power can not be admitted as valid, as it offers no guaranty of legal belligerent behavior. Piracy, in the international sense of the word, however, is a crime against all nations; but any nation may class other crimes under this head. The United States in 1820 made the slave trade piracy for any of its citizens on any ship and for persons not citizens on any of its vessels. Notwithstanding this law passed by the United States, slave trading was not piracy in the international sense of the word. Search of a vessel by a public ship of another state is a war right only, but the right to search on suspicion of piracy exists at all times. The usual penalty for piracy is the confiscation of the vessel and hanging of the crew, while the penalty for privateering is at most imprisonment. (See also Privateering.)

Plague, The (see also Contagious Diseases; International Sanitary Conference; Quarantine Regulations):
Regulations to prevent introduction of, into United States, VII, 549.
Revoked, VII, 557.

Plaster of Paris, restriction on importation of, removed by proclamation, II, 34, 36.

Platforms.—In politics the platform of a party is the public declaration of the principles that the party represents. In May, 1832, a national assembly of young men was held in Washington, D. C., to indorse the nomination of Henry Clay by the National Republican party. They agreed to the first platform ever adopted by a national convention. In 1844 both the Whigs and Democrats drew up platforms, but in 1848 the Whigs refused to commit themselves by a platform. After this time the adoption of party platforms by national conventions became general.

Plattsburg, The, surrender of persons charged with murder on board of, referred to, III, 591.

Plattsburg (N. Y.), Battle of.—The overthrow of Napoleon by the allied powers in 1814 released many British soldiers from service in Europe, and several thousand of them were sent to reenforce the little army in Canada. By Aug. 1 Governor-General Prevost had 15,000 troops under his command at Quebec, most of them hardened veterans from the Peninsula. One brigade was sent west. The remainder were held for a contemplated invasion of New York. Wilkinson and Hampton had been retired from the American Army and Gen. George Izard was placed in command of the right wing of the Army of the North May 4, 1814, with headquarters at Plattsburg, N. Y., near the head of Lake Champlain. Notwithstanding it was evident that the British contemplated a descent upon New York by way of Lake Champlain and the Hudson, Izard was detached from his command and sent with 4,000 men to the Niagara frontier, leaving Gen. Macomb in command with about 3,500 men. Sept. 6, 1814, the British army, fully 14,000 strong, already upon American soil, marched toward Plattsburg. Maj. Wool, with a body of about 300 regulars, met the invading army at Beekmantown, about 4 miles north of Plattsburg, and subjected it to a harassing fire all the way to the Saranac River. Wool's retreating column crossed the stream to South Plattsburg and destroyed the bridges. Though in overwhelming force, the British army was checked, with a loss in killed and wounded of more than 200 men. The American loss was 45. From Sept. 7 to 11 Prevost's army rested, preparatory to acting in conjunction with the fleet on Lake Champlain. On the 11th, while the forces of Macomb and Prevost contended on land, a desperate naval battle was fought on Lake Champlain between the American and British fleets, the former under Macdonough and the latter under Downie. This battle lasted for 2 hours, resulting in victory for the Americans. The British lost 200 men and the commodore of the fleet. The news of the naval victory reached the contending armies at a critical point of the battle and turned the tide in favor of the Americans. Prevost fled with his army to Champlain, leaving behind his sick and wounded and large quantities of stores. Sept. 24 the British returned to Canada, having lost in the expedition about 2,000 men.

Plattsburg, N. Y., battle of, British troops defeated in, I, 549.

Pleasant Hill (La.), Battle of.—After the defeat of the Federal army under Gen. Banks at Sabine Cross Roads, Apr. 8, 1864, it retreated by way of Pleasant Grove to Pleasant Hill, about 18 miles south, where Banks was joined by Gen. A. J. Smith with 10,000 men. Occupying a strong position here, the Federals awaited the pursuing force under Kirby Smith and Dick Taylor. Apr. 9, about 4 o'clock in the afternoon, the Confederates came up and began the attack. In the battle which ensued they were checked and some of the guns they had taken the day before at Sabine Cross Roads were retaken. Banks now returned to the Red River at Grand Ecore, having lost in the campaign 18 guns, 5,000 men, 130 wagons, 1,200 horses, and many small arms.

Pleuro-Pneumonia among cattle discussed, VII, 626, 628; VIII, 184, 527, 798; IX, 329, 455.

Plymouth Colony.—The earliest settlement in Massachusetts. It was founded by a party of English Separatists who arrived in this country Dec. 21, 1620, and landed for permanent settlement in the following January. These Separatists were dissenters from the Church of England. Unlike the Puritans, who sought to purify the church, they regarded such purification as hopeless, and therefore advocated and practiced separation. The Plymouth colonists came to America from Delft, Holland, whither they had emigrated from Plymouth, England. One of the chief objects in coming to America was to enjoy their religion without molestation. The company named their settlement Plymouth, partly because it had been so called by Capt. John Smith, who had previously surveyed the harbor, and partly because the people of Plymouth, England, had treated them kindly. Miles Standish was made captain, with military authority, soon after landing, and John Carver was chosen the first governor of the colony. They entered into a treaty with Massasoit, chief of the Wampanoags, which was faithfully kept for 55 years. No royal charter was ever granted. With the arrival of the ship *Fortune* and 29 immigrants in 1621 came a land patent from the Council for New England. The patent did not fix territorial limits, but allowed 100 acres of land to each immigrant and 1,500 for public buildings, and empowered the grantees to make laws and set up a government. After enduring many hardships and privations the first colonists were joined by others from England and material prosperity followed. Plymouth Colony became a member of the New England Confederation in 1643. By the Massachusetts charter of 1691 it was united with the Colony of Massachusetts Bay.

Plymouth Company.—In 1606 a company of merchants of Bristol and Plymouth, England, were incorporated under a charter granted by James I and called the North Virginia Company. They became a rival of the London Company. In 1607, having obtained a grant of land between Long Island and Passamaquoddy Bay, they sent out 2 ships carrying a company of colonists commanded by George Popham. A settlement was attempted on the Kennebec, but Popham died and the other colonists returned home. The company continued to exist till 1620, when it was reorganized as the New England Company or Council for New England.

Plymouth, N. C., capture of, referred to, VI, 257.

Pocket, The, convention with Texas for adjustment of claims in case of, III, 469.

Pocket Vetoes. (See the several Presidents; the several messages.)

Poindexter, George:
Commissioner to investigate affairs of New York custom-house, IV, 152.
Notes and bills discounted at Bank of United States for benefit of, inquired into, III, 127.

Poinsett, Joel R.:
Correspondence regarding Canadian outrages on American frontier, III, 401.

Pontiac's War.—A war between the English garrisons and settlers on the western frontier and a confederacy of the Delaware, Shawnee, Mingo, Ottawa, Chippewa, and other Indian tribes, led by Pontiac, an Ottawa chief. Pontiac assembled a great council of Indians near Detroit Apr. 27, 1763, and unfolded his plans for retarding or preventing white settlers locating west of Pittsburg. To capture Detroit was Pontiac's special task, and May 7 was the date selected, but the commander of the post was warned of the plot by an Indian girl, and the attempt was not made. The town was surrounded, however, and July 31 the garrison made a night attack on the Indians, in which 59 English were killed or wounded. Oct. 12 Pontiac raised the siege and retired. Forts Sandusky, St. Joseph, Miami, Ouatanon, Mackinaw, Presque Ile, Le Bœuf, and Venango were taken and their garrisons massacred by the Indians in this war. A treaty of peace was made in 1766. Pontiac was murdered by a Kaskaskia Indian in 1769.

Pontifical States. (See Italy; Papal States.)

Poor Richard's Almanac.—In 1732 Benjamin Franklin began the publication of Poor Richard's Almanac. It contained many homely but very striking maxims, and for this reason became famous.

Pope, Benjamin F., assistant surgeon in Army, nomination of, and reasons therefor, VII, 321.

Pope, John:

Directed to assume command of Military Division of Pacific and Department of California, VIII, 167.

Instructions to, referred to, VI, 628.

Mentioned, VI, 144.

Pope of Rome, sentiments of regard for President conveyed, referred to, V, 228.

Popular Sovereignty.—This was the name applied to the doctrine that the principle of slavery "should be kept out of the National Legislature and left to the people in their respective local governments." In 1847 the doctrine was thus stated substantially by Lewis Cass. Many of the Northern Democrats indorsed it. On the other hand, Mr. Calhoun contended that a man's right to his property, even if it was in slaves, should everywhere be maintained, and that a man could take his slaves into any Territory regardless of the wishes of the inhabitants thereof. Mr. Douglas was the chief supporter of the former doctrine. He maintained that it was the basis of the compromise of 1850. Another effort was made to apply it in the Kansas-Nebraska bill. Calhoun nicknamed the doctrine "squatter" sovereignty. It was charged that the inhabitants of some of the Territories had become citizens thereof for political purposes only and were only "squatters," or temporary tenants, on the lands of others.

Population.—The first United States census having been taken in 1790, all population figures previous to that date are based upon estimates. Figures obtained from the best possible sources place the population of New Hampshire in 1700 at about 5,000; Massachusetts and Maine, 70,000; Rhode Island, 6,000; Connecticut, 25,000; New York, 25,000; New Jersey, 14,000; Pennsylvania and Delaware, 20,000; Maryland, 30,000; Virginia, 80,000, and the Carolinas, 15,000. By 1750 the thirteen Colonies are thought to have contained nearly 1,500,000 inhabitants, and at the breaking out of the Revolutionary War something less than 3,000,000. The population of New England was almost purely English; that of New York largely Dutch. Pennsylvania and the Colonies to the southward contained many German, Scotch-Irish, and a few Huguenot settlers, and South Carolina many of the last named. The census of 1790 showed a total population of 3,929,214; that of 1800, 5,308,483; 1810, 7,239,881; 1820, 9,633,822; 1830, 12,866,020; 1840, 17,069,453; 1850, 23,191,876; 1860, 31,443,321; 1870, 38,558,371; 1880, 50,155,783; 1890, 62,622,250.

Population. (See Census.)

Population, Center of.—At the time of the First Census, in 1790, the center of population in the United States lay some 23 miles to the east of Baltimore. In 1800 it was about the same distance west of Baltimore; in 1810, about 40 miles west-northwest of Washington; in 1820, 16 miles north of Woodstock, Va.; in 1830, 19 miles west-southwest of Moorfield, W. Va.; in 1840, 16 miles south of Clarksburg, W. Va.; in 1850, 23 miles southeast of Parkersburg, W. Va.; in 1860, 20 miles south of Chillicothe, Ohio; in 1870, 48 miles east by north of Cincinnati, Ohio; in 1880, in Kentucky, 8 miles west by south of Cincinnati; in 1890, in southern Indiana.

Pork Products. (See Animals and Animal Products.)

Port Gibson (Miss.), Battle of.—On the night of Apr. 16, 1863, the Federal gunboats under Admiral Porter succeeded in running past the batteries at Vicksburg. Grant ordered Sherman to make a feint on the Confederate batteries at Haines Bluff, above Vicksburg, while Porter covered the landing of McClernand's and McPherson's corps at Bruinsburg, a few miles below Grand Gulf. Immediately upon landing McClernand pushed forward toward Port Gibson. A march of 8 miles brought him in sight of the Confederates, whom he forced back until dark. The next day (May 2) the Confederates held a strong position, which they stubbornly defended. That night the troops slept on their arms. During the night the Confederate forces retired across the Bayou Pierre, pursued next day by McPherson's corps. The Federal loss was 131 killed, 719 wounded, and 25 missing—a total of 875. One thousand prisoners and 5 cannon were taken from the Confederates.

Port Hudson (La.), Surrender of.—As early as August, 1862, the Confederates began to fortify Port Hudson, a point on the Mississippi River in Louisiana, at the terminus of the Clinton and Port Hudson Railroad, 25 miles above Baton Rouge and 147 above New Orleans.

Dec. 14, 1862, Maj. Gen. N. P. Banks took command of the Department of the Gulf, and in March, 1863, made a demonstration against Port Hudson while Farragut's fleet attempted to run the batteries to assist Porter in the naval investment of Vicksburg. The attempt was a failure. May 26, 1863, Banks again invested Port Hudson, and was reenforced by Maj. Gen. Augur, Brig. Gen. T. W. Sherman, and Gen. Weitzel, increasing his forces to 12,000 men. An unsuccessful assault was made on the 27th, which showed the place to be strongly fortified. Banks lost 2,000 men in the assault. June 14 a second assault was made after a bombardment of several days by Farragut's fleet. This was also repulsed, with a loss of 700 in killed and wounded. Banks now invested the place by a series of approaches. July 6 the news of the surrender of Vicksburg reached Port Hudson, and 3 days later Gardner surrendered, with 6,340 men and 51 guns. Besides, the garrison lost about 500 prisoners or deserters before surrender, and about 700 killed and wounded.

Port Republic (Va.), Battle of.—June 9, 1862, the morning after the skirmish between the forces of Ewell and Frémont at Cross Keys, Jackson drew in Ewell, crossed the branch of the Shenandoah, and, destroying the bridges, cut off 2 brigades of Shields's advance from Frémont, defeated them in battle, and captured some 450 prisoners and 800 muskets.

Port Royal, S. C., blockade of, removed by proclamation, VI, 89.

Port Royal (S. C.) Expedition.—Oct. 29, 1861, a strong naval and military expedition left Hampton Roads under command of Commodore Samuel F. Du Pont and Gen. Thomas W. Sherman. The fleet was composed of the steam frigate *Wabash*, 14 gunboats, 22 first-class and 12 smaller steamers, and 26 sailing vessels. The land forces under Sherman consisted of 13 regiments of volunteers, forming 3 brigades and numbering 10,000 men. After a tempestuous voyage the fleet arrived off Port Royal, S. C., Nov. 3. Upon each side of the mouth of the Broad River is an island on which the Confederates had built forts. On Bay Point Fort Beauregard mounted 23 guns and on Hilton Head, opposite, Fort Walker had 6, some of them of the largest caliber. A fleet of 8 steamers lay inside the harbor. The guns of the forts were fully manned by 1,700 South Carolinians, and a field battery with 500 men supported one of them. On the 7th Du Pont brought his gunboats into action. He maneuvered his fleet in a circle around the harbor between the forts, firing broadsides as he passed the Confederate batteries. His shells wrought havoc in the works, but the moving ships were little damaged. For 4 hours the battle raged, when the garrison retreated, leaving everything behind. Forty-three guns were captured. Hilton Head was made the center of later naval operations.

Portage Lake, Mich., act authorizing establishment of new harbor lines in, returned, IX, 71.

Porter, David:
Frigate in command of, surrenders to British, I, 549.
Mentioned, II, 276.
Naval talents of, commented on, II, 213.

Porter, David D.:
Admiral of Navy, death of, announced and honors to be paid memory of, IX, 134, 165.
Captain in Navy, nomination of, VI, 155.
Rear-admiral in Navy, nomination of, VI, 192.
Thanks of Congress to, recommended, VI, 76, 83, 151.

Porter, Fitz John:
Act for relief of, vetoed, VIII, 221.
Appeal of, referred to, VIII, 270.
Proceedings and report of board in case of, referred to, VII, 522.
Relieved from command of corps, VI, 124.
Sentence of court-martial in case of, in part remitted, VIII, 125.

Porter, Horace, member of court to try assassins of President Lincoln, etc., VI, 336.
Relieved from duty, VI, 336.

Porter, Moses, mentioned, II, 132.

Portland Company, bill for relief of, vetoed, IX, 92.

Portland, Oreg., proclaimed port of delivery, V, 50.

Porto Rico. (See Puerto Rico.)

Ports. (See Rivers and Harbors.)

Portsmouth, N. H., dry dock at, about completed, V, 133.
Site for, II, 368.

Portsmouth, Ohio, act to erect public building at, vetoed, VIII, 567.

Portugal.—A Kingdom of western Europe. It extends from lat. 36° 58′ to 42° 10′ north and from long. 6° 10′ to 9° 30′ west. It is bounded by Spain on the north and east and by the Atlantic Ocean on the south and west. The principal exports are wine, cork, fish, live stock, and copper. The trade is mostly with Great Britain, Brazil, the United States, and France. Portugal is a hereditary constitutional monarchy, the legislative power being vested in the Cortes. The territory was partly included in the ancient Lusitania. Portugal became a Kingdom under Alfonso I in 1139, and was a great maritime power in the fifteenth and sixteenth centuries. It has an area of 36,038 sq. miles; population (1890), 5,049,729.

Portugal (see also Lisbon; Oporto):
Blockade established by, claims of United States growing out of, II, 535, 550; III, 24.
Brazil, questions with, respecting escape of insurgent Admiral Da Gama, IX, 524.
Citizens of, effort made to improve condition of, II, 193, 217.
Claims of United States against, II, 508, 550, 594; III, 24, 98; IV, 418, 603; V, 12, 82, 144, 226. (See also *General Armstrong*, The; *Miles*, The.)
Admitted, but payment of, delayed, III, 237.
Convention for adjustment of, referred to, V, 82, 106, 119.
Payment of, II, 594; III, 24, 149, 532; V, 119.

Portugal—Continued.

Commercial relations with, II, 242.

Vessel sent to protect American interests, II, 536.

Copyright privilege extended, by proclamation, IX, 398.

Cotton culture in African possessions of, referred to, VI, 66.

Diplomatic relations with, resumed, II, 445.

Duties on rice reduced by, III, 24.

Friendly disposition of, toward United States, II, 353.

Government of, removed to Lisbon, II, 105.

Internal tranquillity restored to, III, 98.

Minister of United States in, I, 98.

Salary of, referred to, VI, 469.

Railroad in, operated by American citizens seized by Government of, IX, 35.

Claim regarding, submitted to arbitration, IX, 111.

Relations with, I, 97, 176; II, 251.

Revenue laws of United States, complaints of, against, referred to, IV, 103.

Slavery in colonies of, abolition of, discussed, VII, 335.

Treaty with, referred to, III, 604, 622; IV, 41, 274.

Vessels of—

Discriminating duties on, suspended by proclamation, VII, 126.

Report regarding, II, 572; III, 224.

Requested by Portugal, III, 223.

Duties on, II, 572.

Proclamation levying duties on, III, 372.

Referred to, III, 375.

Vessels of United States seized or interfered with by, II, 507, 535, 550; III, 24.

Vice-consul of, to United States, exequatur of, revoked, VII, 84.

Wines of, duties on, referred to, IV, 274, 400.

Post-Office.—The post-office has existed in America from almost the earliest settlement. In the more thickly settled Colonies of the North some meager arrangements for postal communication were made previous to 1692. Feb. 17 of that year King William and Queen Mary granted to Thomas Neale a patent making him postmaster-general for the Colonies. Before this time letters had been deposited in coffee houses to be taken by those to whom they were addressed or carried to them by their neighbors. The first legislation on the subject is found in the records of the general court of Massachusetts for 1639, and the next in the colonial law of Virginia in 1657. Gradually a postal service was established between the several Colonies along the coast, and in 1672 there was a monthly post between New York and Boston. One of the first acts of the Continental Congress was the establishment of post-offices and post routes from Falmouth, Me., to Savannah, Ga. Benjamin Franklin was the first Postmaster-General, and under his practical management the postal service was soon extended throughout the Colonies. Newspapers were generally published by the postmasters of the several cities, and their papers had not only been

sent free through the mails, but all others had been excluded. Franklin was the first to give equal privilege to all publishers. Subsequently a small sum was charged as postage, which seems to have been a perquisite of the postmaster, but no regular postage was charged under the law until 1792.

Post-Office Building:

Destruction of, by fire referred to, III, 264.

Erection of—

Appropriation for, recommended, III, 264; IV, 58.

Recommended, III, 258, 503.

Erection of, for joint use of Washington City post-office and Post-Office Department recommended, IX, 44.

Extension of, referred to, V, 382, 384.

Heating and ventilating of, referred to, V, 579, 581.

Referred to, III, 581.

Uniform standard in amount of gross receipts to fix right of community to, recommendations regarding, VIII, 792.

Post-Office Department.—One of the eight Executive Departments of the Government. The head of this Department is called the Postmaster-General. In 1774, when Benjamin Franklin was deprived of his office as postmaster-general of the American Colonies by the King because of his opposition to the course of Parliament in dealing with the colonists, William Goddard planned a constitutional post-office. This was laid before Congress and adopted July 26, 1775, and Franklin was made Postmaster-General. The Articles of Confederation and the Constitution both gave Congress power over the matter. Congress in 1790 continued the post-office with little substantial change. There were several temporary enactments, but in 1794 the Department was permanently established. The plan to conduct the post-office system merely on the expense-paying basis originated about 1840. In 1820 a 4-year term for postmasters was instituted. The Postmaster-General was not made a member of the Cabinet until 1829, during President Jackson's Administration. The following gentlemen have been Postmasters-General under the Constitution: Samuel Osgood, Massachusetts; Timothy Pickering, Pennsylvania; Joseph Habersham, Georgia; Gideon Granger, Connecticut; Return J. Meigs, jr., Ohio; John McLean, Ohio; William T. Barry, Kentucky; Amos Kendall, Kentucky; John M. Niles, Connecticut; Francis Granger, New York; Charles A. Wickliffe, Kentucky; Cave Johnson, Tennessee; Jacob Collamer, Vermont; Nathan K. Hall, New York; Samuel D. Hubbard, Connecticut; James Campbell, Pennsylvania; Aaron V. Brown, Tennessee; Joseph Holt, Kentucky; Horatio King, Maine; Montgomery Blair, District of Columbia; William Dennison, Ohio; Alexander W. Randall, Wisconsin; John A. J. Creswell, Maryland; J. W. Marshall, Virginia; Marshall Jewell, Connecticut; James N. Tyner, Indiana; David M. Key, Tennessee; Horace Maynard, Tennessee;

Thomas L. James, New York; Timothy O. Howe, Wisconsin; Walter Q. Gresham, Indiana; Frank Hatton, Iowa; William F. Vilas, Wisconsin; Don M. Dickinson, Michigan; John Wanamaker, Pennsylvania; Wilson S. Bissell, New York; William L. Wilson, West Virginia; James A. Gary, Maryland, and Charles Emory Smith, Pennsylvania.

Post-Office Department:

Act regarding post-office statutes vetoed, VII, 385.

Assistant for, recommended, VIII, 353, 517.

Building for. (See Post-Office Building.)

Clerks in, referred to, VI, 387.

Discussed. (See Postal Service discussed.)

Funds of, deficit in, III, 116; V, 410, 576.

Issuance of commissions to officials by Postmaster-General recommended, VII, 109, 239.

Laws of, recommendations regarding, II, 215.

Reforms in, recommended, IX, 731.

Revenues and expenditures of—

Appropriation for, IV, 349; V, 461.

Bill providing for, failure of, to pass, V, 571.

Discussed by President—

Adams, J. Q., II, 311, 363, 390, 419.

Arthur, VIII, 52, 141, 182.

Buchanan, V, 461, 523, 525, 576.

Cleveland, VIII, 352, 516, 792; IX, 448, 537, 729.

Fillmore, V, 89, 134.

Grant, VII, 40, 197, 249, 296, 409.

Harrison, Benj., IX, 116, 198, 321.

Hayes, VII, 474, 500, 574, 622.

Jackson, II, 460, 527; III, 34, 116, 174, 257.

Johnson, VI, 363, 452, 577, 684.

Lincoln, VI, 51, 131, 185, 249.

McKinley, X, 197.

Monroe, II, 215, 258.

Pierce, V, 215, 289, 339, 410.

Polk, IV, 414, 505, 652.

Tyler, IV, 49, 203, 349.

Van Buren, III, 393, 502, 538, 619.

Treasurer for, should be appointed III, 117.

Post-Offices:

Classification of fourth-class, recommended, IX, 740.

Clerks in, legislation regarding classification of, recommended, VIII, 793.

Consolidation of, recommended, IX, 732, 740.

Number of, II, 215; X, 197.

Increase in, II, 311, 367, 390, 419; III, 393, 502, 538; IV, 505; V, 89, 134, 461; VII, 249, 622; VIII, 182, 791; IX, 321, 449, 539.

Report on, transmitted, X, 53.

Post Roads. (See Mail Routes.)

Postage.—The price established by law to be paid for the conveyance of a letter or other mailable matter by a public post. Rates of postage were fixed by the Continental Congress in 1789 as follows: Single letters under 60 miles, 7.4 cents; between 60 and 100 miles, 11.1 cents; between 100 and 200 miles, 14.8 cents, and 3.4 cents for each additional 100 miles. As early as 1794 a delivery system was inaugurated, a fee of 2 cents being required for each letter delivered. In 1814 the rates of postage were increased by 50 per cent, but the old rate was restored in 1816. Mails were first carried

on horseback, later by stage coach, and in 1834 by railway. July 7, 1838, Congress declared every railroad to be a mail route. In 1847 and 1848 post-offices were established at Astoria, San Diego, Monterey, and San Francisco. The rate of postage between the Atlantic and Pacific coasts was fixed at 40 cents. Mar. 3, 1851, letter postage was reduced to 3 cents per half ounce for distances under 3,000 miles, postage prepaid. In 1857 prepayment of postage was required on all transient printed matter. By act of Mar. 3, 1883, postage on all first-class mail matter was reduced to 2 cents per ounce. Merchandise was first admitted to the mails in 1861. Registration was begun in 1855, and postal money orders were first issued in 1864. The free-delivery system was established in 1872 in cities of 50,000 population or over, and in 1887 the system was extended.

Postage (see also Franking Privilege):

Amount of, report on, transmitted, X, 53.

Increase in, recommended, V, 525.

On census papers discussed, II, 85.

Reduction in—

Discussed, IV, 349, 414, 562; V, 22, 135, 177, 410; VIII, 248, 352, 516.

Recommended, III, 257, 619; IV, 653; V, 22, 89; VIII, 141, 182, 249.

Revenue derived from. (See Post-Office Department, revenues, etc., of.)

Postage Stamps.—An official mark or stamp affixed to or embossed on letters sent through the mails as evidence of the prepayment of postage. Adhesive stamps were made as an experiment by James Chalmers in his printing office in Dundee in 1834, but they were not made public till November, 1837. In February, 1837, Sir Rowland Hill proposed a postage stamp for prepayment of letter postage. In 1840 Mulready's envelope was introduced, bearing an allegorical design of England attracting the commerce of the world, but this was soon superseded by the adhesive stamp. Local stamps were in use in various cities in the United States as early as 1842—in New York, St. Louis, Baltimore, and Brattleboro. By act of Mar. 3, 1847, the use of postage stamps was authorized, and issues of 5 and 10 cent stamps were made by the Government, bearing, respectively, designs of the heads of Franklin and Washington. In 1851 three new values were added—1, 3, and 12 cents. From this time till 1860 a complete series was issued in values from 5 to 90 cents. In 1869 a new series was brought out in various designs, such as a horseman, a locomotive, eagle, steamship, landing of Columbus, Declaration of Independence, heads of Franklin, Washington, and Lincoln. The series of 1870-1872 bore heads of Franklin, after Rupricht's bust; Jackson, after Powers; Washington, after the bust by Houdon; Lincoln, after Volk; Stanton, from a photograph; Jefferson, after Powers's statue; Clay, after the bust by Hart; Webster, after the Clevenger bust; Scott, after the bust by Coffee; Hamilton, after Cerrachi; and Perry, from Wolcott's statue. At the International Postal

Conference held at Berne, Switzerland, in 1874, the Universal Postal Union was formed, with rates of 5 cents per half ounce on all letters passing between the countries composing the union. In 1875 a 5-cent stamp was issued for this foreign service, bearing the head of Jackson, taken from a photograph, and in 1882 another of the same value with the head of Garfield. Stamped envelopes were issued in 1852 and postal cards in 1872.

Postal Currency.—During the Civil War, when silver became very scarce, a substitute for fractional currency was invented by Gen. Spinner, United States Treasurer under President Lincoln. It consisted of postage stamps pasted upon paper used for Government securities and representing different sums. These pieces of paper were circulated among the clerks of the Department and became for a while the medium of exchange in a small way.

Pottawatomie Indians.—A tribe of the Algonquian stock of Indians. When first known (about 1670) they lived on the Noquet Islands, in Green Bay, Wis. At the close of the seventeenth century they were established on the Milwaukee River, at Chicago, and on the St. Joseph River. At the beginning of the nineteenth century they possessed the country around the head of Lake Michigan from the Milwaukee River, Wis., to the Grand River, Mich., extending south into Illinois and in Indiana to the Wabash River. They took a prominent part in Pontiac's War and in the War of the Revolution, when they fought on

Prairie Grove (Ark.), Battle of.—Sept. 19, 1862, President Lincoln directed that Missouri, Arkansas, Kansas, and the eastern portion of Indian Territory should constitute the Department of the Missouri, to be commanded by Brig. Gen. Samuel R. Curtis. The only important engagement that occurred in this department while Curtis was in command was at Prairie Grove, Ark. The Confederate General Thomas C. Hindman was on his way north into Missouri with a large force when, on Dec. 7, 1862, he encountered the united forces of Generals James G. Blunt and Francis J. Herron. During the engagement which ensued the Federals lost 1,148 and the Confederates 1,317. The latter retired during the night.

Preble, Edward:
Energy and judgment displayed by, I, 377.
Medal presented to, referred to, X, 44.
Mentioned, I, 364.

Preble, George H.:
Commander in Navy, nomination of, and reasons therefor, VI, 153.
Thanks of Congress to, recommended, VI, 76.

Preble, William P., mentioned, II, 559.

Precious Metals. (See Coins and Coinage; Gold and Silver.)

Preemption Laws.—The first law regulating the preemption of and payment for public lands was passed Mar. 3, 1801. It was a special act affecting the Symmes colonization scheme on the Miami River. A number of preemption laws were passed, most of them of a more or less special nature. The first general law was passed in 1830. The law of 1841 granted, in consideration of residence and improvement, freedom of entry upon 160 acres of public lands to any person over 21 years of age; 12 to 33 months were allowed for payment, and the amount to be paid varied with the situation and value of the tract preempted. The law of 1841 was repealed in 1891, since which time there has been no legislation on the subject.

Preemption Laws:
Discussed, III, 496, 536; VI, 453; VII, 110; IX, 49.
Recommended, III, 389; IV, 409.
    Amendments to law recommended, IV, 558, 650.
Repeal of preemption act recommended, VIII, 183, 250, 522.

President, The.—Previous to the War of 1812 American commerce had suffered considerably at the hands of British cruisers, which hovered about our coasts and captured many United States vessels bound for France. These cruisers also made many impressments of sailors. In May, 1811, Commodore John Rodgers, commanding the American frigate *President*, was ordered to put to sea from Chesapeake Bay and protect our commerce. When 30 miles off Cape Charles, May 16, Rodgers gave chase to the *Little Belt*, a British frigate. The latter fired upon the *President*, attempted flight, and failed to show her colors. The fire was returned by the *President*, and in 18 minutes the *Little Belt* was disabled. A dispute arose as to which of the commanders was at fault, but it was never decided, as the discussion was dropped by mutual agreement. In September, 1814, the *President*, under Decatur, was captured by the *Endymion* and other British vessels.

President of a State.—Some of the earlier organized States provided for a president as the executive head. To avoid misunderstanding and confusion, this was afterwards changed to governor. The first constitutions of Pennsylvania and New Hampshire, adopted in 1776, provided for an executive council, of which one member was president. Delaware, South Carolina, and the New Hampshire constitution of 1784 provided for a single head, but called him president. South Carolina in 1778, Pennsylvania in 1790, and Delaware and New Hampshire in 1792 altered the title to governor.

President of United States.—The title of the Chief Executive of the United States. In 1696 William Penn proposed a plan for a general government for the Colonies in America. This plan comprehended a chief executive with the title of president. The Albany Convention proposed that of president-general. The Continental Congress had its president. In the Convention of 1787 it was decided that there should be a single executive, to whom the title of President was given. In order to be eligible, the President must be 35 years of age, a native-born citizen of the United States, and a resident within the United States for 14 years. He is elected for a term of 4 years by electors chosen by the different States. These electors are chosen by direct vote of the people, on ballot tickets usually headed by the names of the candidates voted for as President and Vice-President, followed by the names of the electors, who are pledged to vote for these candidates only. (See Electoral College.) The President's duties and powers under the Constitution are to approve or veto bills; to grant reprieves and pardons for offenses against the United States, except in case of impeachment; to make treaties; to nominate ambassadors and other public ministers, consuls, judges of the Federal courts, etc., and, by and with the consent of the Senate, appoint such officers; to fill vacancies that may occur during the recess of the Senate by granting commissions which shall expire at the end of the next session; to convene one or both Houses of Congress, and to adjourn Congress to such a time as he may deem proper in case it can not agree upon an adjournment. He is also commander in chief of the Army and Navy and of the militia of the several States when called into the service of the United States. He is required to give information to Congress from time to time regarding the state of the Union and recommend to its consideration such measures as he shall judge necessary and expedient; receive ambassadors and other public ministers; see that the laws are faithfully executed, etc. He receives a salary of $50,000 per annum. Up to the time of the ratification of the twelfth amendment (1804) the President and Vice-President were not separately voted for, but the candidate for President who received next to the highest number of votes was made Vice-President. Jefferson and J. Q. Adams were elected by the House of Representatives, as provided by

President of United States—Continued.

Oath of, and ceremonies attending administration of. (See the several Presidents.)

Personal interviews with, respecting—
Appointments to office, rules regulating, discussed, IX, 399.
Business transactions unnecessary, order regarding, VI, 348.

Pocket vetoes of. (See the several Presidents; the several messages.)

Power should be given, to prevent injuries to citizens of neighboring nations, III, 399.

Presents offered, by Imaum of Muscat, recommendations regarding, III, 592; IV, 316.

Provisions and laws respecting election of, etc., VI, 668.

Public money, authority of, over, discussed, III, 324.

Removals from office discussed. (See Removals from Office.)

Right of, to make public confidential information of predecessors discussed, IV, 433.

Successor to, in event of vacancy in Presidency and Vice-Presidency discussed, VI, 639, 691; VIII, 365.
Act regarding, returned, IX, 239.

Term of, recommendations regarding limitation of, II, 448; III, 117; VII, 445.

Thanks of, tendered. (See Thanks of President.)

Treaties—
Power to make, vested in President with consent of Senate, I, 195.
Request of House for correspondence regarding, declined, I, 194.

Vacancies, power of, to make provisional appointments to fill, discussed, V, 659.

Veto messages of. (See the several Presidents; the several messages.)

Veto power of, discussed, IV, 662; V, 23.

War, power to declare, discussed, V, 569.
Executive authority to furnish instant redress recommended, V, 569.

Presidential Electors:

Constitutional amendment regarding selection of, recommended, IX, 209.

Method of appointment of, and effect of gerrymander discussed, IX, 208.

Presidential Succession.—The Constitution provides for the succession of the Vice-President in case of the death, removal, resignation, or disability of the President, and gives Congress power to provide what officer shall succeed in case of the death, removal, etc., of the Vice-President. In 1793 Congress enacted that in such case the President of the Senate should succeed, and then the Speaker of the House of Representatives. This was attended with some inconvenience and danger and there was some doubt of its constitutionality. An act of Congress approved Jan. 19, 1886, provided that the succession should pass to the members of the Cabinet in the following order: Secretary of State, Secretary of the Treasury, Secretary of War, Attorney-General, Postmaster-General, Secretary of the Navy, and Secretary of the Interior. The following Vice-Presidents

have succeeded to the Presidency on account of the death of the President: John Tyler, Millard Fillmore, Andrew Johnson, and Chester A. Arthur.

Presque Isle, Pa.:

Obstructions to entrance of harbor of port of, II, 217.

Title to, proffered by marine hospital of Pennsylvania, VIII, 148.

Press, Freedom of.—The first amendment to the Constitution, introduced in the First Congress, established freedom of speech, religion, and the press. Though the Federal Constitution was originally silent upon the subject, nearly all of the States inserted in their constitutions clauses permitting freedom of speech and publication to every citizen. Abuses of this liberty were punishable under the common law. New York and New Jersey made no provision in their first constitutions, but clauses were later embodied insuring the widest liberty of expression. During British rule of the Colonies this freedom was much restricted by the star chamber press censorship regulation of 1637, which was confirmed by Parliament in 1643.

Pretoria, Republic of, joint resolution relating to congratulations from, vetoed, VII, 430.

Prince of Wales, visit of, to United States, V, 640.

Princeton, The, construction of, referred to, IV, 277.

Princeton (N. J.), Battle of.—The beginning of the year 1777 found the British army of 7,000 or 8,000 men encamped at Princeton, N. J. On Christmas night, 1776, Washington had turned back his retreating army, recrossed the Delaware, overcome the Hessians at Trenton, and again crossed the Delaware into Pennsylvania. To relieve Cadwalader he again crossed the river and was ready to march upon Princeton. Cornwallis, who had been sent by Howe from New York, advanced to meet him with most of his army. Washington skillfully passed around the left wing of Cornwallis's army, and on Jan. 3, 1777, encountered the British rear guard, consisting of 3 regiments and 3 troops. These were scattered, with the loss of about 500. The American loss was 25 or 30, besides officers. Cornwallis retreated to New Brunswick and Washington occupied a strong position at Morristown, remaining there until the latter part of May.

Printing executed by authority of the several Departments referred to, V, 378.

Printing Office. (See Government Printing Office.)

Prioleau, Samuel, claim of representatives of, refused and reasons therefor, V, 293.

Prison Congress, International, at—
St. Petersburg, VIII, 532.
Stockholm, VII, 454, 512.

Prison Congress, National, at Baltimore, VII, 208.

Prisoners. (See Imprisonment.)

Prisoners of War. (See War between the States; War of 1812.)

Prisons. (See Penitentiaries.)

Privateers.—Armed vessels owned and officered by private persons, but acting under commissions from the government known as letters of marque. It was formerly the custom of all nations in time of war to legalize private vessels to assist the regular navy in blockading the ports of an enemy, intercepting supplies, and capturing prizes. Vessels so employed are called privateers and are supplied with letters of marque on condition of their conforming to the rules and usages of war. Herein lies the difference between privateers and pirates (q.v.). These vessels and crews may be hired or impressed by the government or they may be owned, officered, and sent to sea at private expense under government commission. The latter has been a favorite way of employing sailors and merchant ships when commerce has been hampered by war, and to a nation with a small navy it affords protection against formidable naval foes. The practice of privateering has long been looked upon as an evil by the most advanced nations. At the Declaration of Paris in 1856 (q. v.) one of the rules of warfare subscribed to was that "privateering is and remains abolished." The United States refused to agree to this clause of the declaration on the ground that without privateers it would have no adequate sea force in time of war. As the agreement was only binding on parties thereto, American commerce was left a prey to the ships of all other nations. In 1861 Secretary Seward, on behalf of the United States, made an offer to England and France to come under the operation of the rules of war subscribed to in the Declaration of Paris, but the offer was refused on the ground that it would impose an international rule of warfare upon the Confederate States then in rebellion. In the colonial wars Great Britain derived much support from colonial privateers. Upward of 400 were fitted out and ravaged the French West Indies and made numerous captures along the coast of France. In March, 1776, the Continental Congress accorded permission to citizens to fit out privateers against the British. During that year 342 British vessels fell a prey to privateers fitted out at Salem, Cape Ann, Newburyport, Bristol, and other seaports. This sort of warfare became so lucrative that sailors could hardly be induced to enter the regular service. Jan. 28, 1778, an American privateer surprised and captured the British fort of New Providence, in the Bahamas, and a 16-gun man-of-war. During the War of 1812 some 500 privateers were fitted out. They were mostly schooners or brigs of 200 or 300 tons and carried from 80 to 100 men. Of 400 British vessels captured in 1813 four-fifths were taken by privateers. Later in this war larger vessels, like the *Reindeer*, *Avon*, and *Blakeley*, were built. They did not confine themselves to merchant vessels, but attacked and frequently captured British war ships. They hung about the coasts of Great Britain, Ireland, and the Canary and West Indian Islands, and greatly aided the American cause.

Prize Agents, accounts of, referred to, II, 204, 247.

Prize Courts.—Courts which adjudicate the property in vessels captured at sea from a belligerent. The general rule is that when a captor brings home a prize the tribunal of his own country has sole jurisdiction over it and the decision rendered is binding everywhere. A prize court differs from other courts in that the property of foreigners is brought within its jurisdiction, not voluntarily, as in ordinary courts, but by force. During the colonial wars prize cases were adjudged by the admiralty courts held by colonial governors as vice-admirals, or by judges whom they appointed, with appeal to commissioners in England. With the outbreak of the Revolution the States established admiralty courts to hear prize cases. The Continental Congress established a court of appeals for such cases when in dispute between the States. Under the judiciary act of 1789 the United States district courts were made prize courts, with appeal to the Supreme Court.

Prize Money.—A dividend from the proceeds of a captured vessel and her cargo, etc., paid to the captors. Prior to Mar. 3, 1899, prize money in the United States was distributed according to an act of June 30, 1864. If the prize was equal or superior to the captor, it became the sole property of the latter. If inferior, the United States took half and the captors divided the remainder. Privateers with letters of marque kept the whole of the prize unless otherwise stipulated in their commissions. By the Navy personnel act of Mar. 3, 1899, the law authorizing the distribution of prize money among the captors of vessels was repealed.

Prize Money referred to, V, 32.

Probert, Anna A., act granting pension to, vetoed, VIII, 450.

Proclamations. (See the several Presidents or the several subjects.)

Proctor, Col., mentioned, I, 111.

Proctor, Redfield, resignation of, as Secretary of War and appointment as United States Senator from Vermont referred to, IX, 195.

Products. (See Agricultural Products; Animals and Animal Products.)

Progressive Labor Party.—At the annual session of the United Labor Party held at Syracuse, N. Y., Aug. 19, 1886, the radical or socialistic element withdrew and formed the Progressive Labor Party. They advocated a common inheritance of land, wealth, and industries and upheld all the tenets of extreme socialism.

Prohibition.—The prohibition of the manufacture and sale of alcoholic drinks has long been a subject of political discussion in America. Long before the Revolution the liquor traffic was taxed, and the Continental Congress advised the States to pass laws prohibiting the distillation of grain. Prohibition became a purely State political issue first in the Maine legislature in 1837, when a prohibitory bill was introduced and defeated. In 1846 a bill with the same purpose became a law, but did not serve the purpose and was succeeded in 1851 by a more effective measure drafted by Neal Dow. This law provided for search and seizure; but the Prohibitionists lost their majority and the law was repealed. Later a second law was passed and is still in force. Following the example of Maine, prohibitory laws were enacted between 1850 and 1856 in Rhode Island, Massachusetts, Vermont, Michigan, New York, Iowa, and Connecticut. Prohibition amendments to the constitutions of several States have been passed, but in none except Kansas has the Supreme Court upheld them. Most of the States have restrictive laws and a few give to each county the option of permitting liquor traffic within their limits. Prohibition first appeared as a national issue in 1869. Since 1872 the Prohibitionists have placed Presidential tickets in the field, with an ever-increasing vote.

Prometheus, The, firing into and seizure of, by British vessel, V, 139, 144.

Property at Sea:

International agreement to regard, as exempt from capture by belligerent powers recommended, X, 191.

International conference at Washington for security of life and, IX, 33, 58, 63.

Maritime powers invited to attend, VIII, 785.

Recommended, VIII, 595.

Treaty with Italy regarding, VII, 144.

Property, Captured:

Cotton captured and forfeited referred to, VI, 468.

Should not be adjudged without regular investigation, I, 500.

Property, Industrial, international convention at Paris for protection of, VII, 608; VIII, 207, 270, 533.

Property, Private:

Seizure and confiscation of, referred to, VI, 633.

Shall not be taken for public use without just compensation, I, 447.

Proprietaries.—American territory was parceled out by the various crowned heads of Europe to personal friends or favorites or in recognition of some useful service to the sovereign. Persons to whom these grants were made established what were known as proprietary governments. The proprietor appointed the governor, and in general performed all those acts of government which are usually the prerogative of the Crown. New York, New Jersey, Pennsylvania, the Carolinas, Delaware, and Maryland were proprietary governments. The laws of Pennsylvania and Delaware were subject to the supervision of the Crown, but those of Maryland were not.

Protection.—In political economy the principle or system of imposing such duties on imported goods as will protect or foster domestic industries. Tariffs are either chiefly to produce revenue or to afford protection. Nearly all American tariffs previous to that of 1824 come under the former head. But the principle of protection was ably advocated by Secretary Hamilton, in his elaborate report on manufactures, in 1791 and by many members of Congress from that time to the present. The tariff of 1816 was claimed as protective and opposed as such by Northern members, while Calhoun and other Southerners advocated it. Later the relative views of North and South were radically changed, and the North became protectionist, while Southern members (except Clay and his Whig followers) were for a low tariff for revenue only. The first protective tariff bill *per se* was introduced in the House of Representatives in 1820 by Representative Baldwin, of Pennsylvania, from the Committee on Manufactures. It did not pass, but in 1824 a tariff bill became a law with average duties of 37 per cent. This was not enough for the protection advocates, and in 1828, after a prolonged commercial depression, a high protective tariff, denounced as "a bill of abominations," became a law. It was the chief cause of the nullification movement (q. v.). The Clay-Calhoun tariff of 1833, known as the "Compromise of 1833," gradually reduced duties to a revenue basis. The act of 1842 was protective; that of 1846 (the Walker tariff) was strictly a revenue tariff. The Morrill tariff of 1861 and all subsequent tariff acts have been protective. The duties have been high, running from an average of 18 per cent to 48 per cent *ad valorem* on all dutiable articles.

Public Buildings, Commissioner of. (See Buildings, Public, Commissioner of.)

Public Buildings, Surveyor of. (See Buildings, Public, Surveyor of.)

Public Credit. (See Credit, Public.)

Public Debt. (See Debt, Public.)

Public Defenses. (See Defenses, Public.)

Public Deposits. (See Deposits, Public.)

Public Documents. (See Records and Documents.)

Public Health. (See Quarantine Regulations.)

Public Land Laws. (See Lands, Public.)

Public Land Offices. (See Land Offices, Public.)

Public Lands. (See Lands, Public.)

Public Lands Commission, report of, referred to, VII, 583.

Public Money. (See Revenue, Public.)

Public Officers. (See Officers, Public.)

Public Records. (See Records and Documents.)

Public Reservations. (See Reservations, Public.)

Public Revenue. (See Revenue, Public.)

Public Roads. (See Mail Routes.)

Public Statutes of United States. (See Revised Statutes.)

Public Supplies. (See Supplies, Public.)

Public Works. (See Internal Improvements.)

Publications, Official. (See Records and Documents.)

Puebla (Mexico), Battle of.—After Gen. Scott had proceeded on his march to the City of Mexico Gen. Rea, a guerrilla chief, was joined by Santa Anna. Col. Childs, commandant of the Puebla garrison left by Scott, sent Capt. Blanchard with 33 men to capture a band of guerrillas. Blanchard and 22 men were ambuscaded and killed the latter part of August, 1847. Sept. 25 Santa Anna demanded the surrender of the forts at Puebla. Childs, who had only about 360 men, refused and maintained his position, in spite of an almost continuous fire of the Mexicans, until relieved by reenforcements under Gen. Lane, Oct. 12.

Pueblo Indians.—A common name for several distinct tribes and nations of Indians occupying western New Mexico, Arizona, Chihuahua, Texas and the valleys of the Rio Grande and Colorado rivers. The Zuñis inhabit the largest pueblos or villages. They are distinct nations. When discovered by the Spaniards they occupied 7 villages, known as the Seven Cities of Cibola, on the site of one of which stands the present pueblo of Zuñi. The Tañoan are also a distinct stock of Indians and comprise several tribes of closely allied dialects. The Tusayan is a confederacy of tribes inhabiting northeastern Arizona. The Pueblo Indians have always been friendly. The Supreme Court declared them citizens in 1857. The name was also applied by Spaniards to the early colonies established in California by authority of Philip II. Pueblo lands were vested either by proprietary right in the individual or in companies reserving to them certain rights as citizens and colonists. The first settlers were also allowed money and supplies and permitted to elect their own magistrates, of whom the chief was the alcalde.

They were allowed common use of the pasture lands reserved to the Crown outside the pueblo grants.

Puerto Rico.—The easternmost island of the Greater Antilles, lying between lat. 17° 54' and 18° 30' 40'' north and long. 9° 45' and 11° 25' east from Washington. It is bounded on the north by the Atlantic, on the east and south by the Sea of the Antilles, and on the west by the Mona Channel. It is the fourth in size of the Greater Antilles and has an extent of about 3,688 sq. miles—43 miles broad and 108 miles long. It is of an oblong form, extending from east to west. Puerto Rico was discovered by Columbus in 1493, and the inhabitants were conquered by Ponce de Leon in 1508-1520. It is the first among the Greater Antilles in density of population and in prosperity. The population in 1887 was 813,937 (now estimated at 900,000 or upward), over 300,000 being mulattoes and negroes, this being one of the few countries of tropical America where the number of whites exceeds that of other races. The eastern portion of the island is less populous than the western. The ground is very fertile, being suitable for the cultivation of cane, coffee, rice, and other products raised in Cuba, which island Puerto Rico resembles in richness and fertility. The climate is hot and moist, the maximum temperature often reaching 104°. Constant rains and winds from the east cool the heavy atmosphere of the low regions. On the heights of Central Cordillera the temperature is healthy and agreeable. Iron rusts and becomes consumed, so that nothing can be constructed of this metal. Even bronze artillery has to be covered with a strong varnish to protect it from the damp winds. Although one would suppose that all the large islands in the Tropics enjoyed the same climate, yet from the greater mortality observed in Jamaica, Santo Domingo, and Cuba, as compared with Puerto Rico, one is inclined to believe that the latter island is much more congenial than any of the former to the health of Europeans. The heat, the rains, and the seasons are, with very trifling variations, the same in all; but the number of mountains and running streams, which are everywhere in view in Puerto Rico, and the general cultivation of the land may powerfully contribute to purify the atmosphere and render it salubrious to man. The only difference of temperature to be observed throughout the island is due to altitude—a change which is common to every country under the influence of the Tropics. In the mountains the inhabitants enjoy the coolness of spring, while the valleys would be uninhabitable were it not for the daily breeze, which blows generally from the northeast and east. At one place the thermometer is as high as 90°, while in another it is sometimes under 60°. Although the seasons are not so distinctly marked in this climate as they are in Europe (the trees being always green), yet there is a distinction to be made between them. The division into wet and dry seasons (winter and summer) does not give a proper idea of the seasons in this island, for on the north coast it sometimes rains almost the whole year, while sometimes for 12 or 14 months not a drop of rain falls on the south coast. However, in the mountains at the south there are daily showers. As in all tropical countries, the year is divided into two seasons—the dry and the rainy. In general, the rainy season commences in August and ends the last of December, southerly and westerly winds prevailing during this period. The rainfall is excessive, often inundating fields and forming extensive lagoons. The exhalations from these lagoons give rise to a number of diseases, but nevertheless Puerto Rico is one of the healthiest islands of the West Indies. In the month of May the rains commence, not with the fury of a deluge, as in the months of August and September, but heavier than any rain experienced in Europe. Peals of thunder reverberating through the mountains give a warning of their approach, and the sun breaking through the clouds promotes the prolific vegetation of the field with its vivifying heat. The heat at this season is equal to the summer of Europe, and the nights are cool and pleasant, but the dews are heavy and pernicious to health. The nights are delightfully clear and serene at this season. Objects may be clearly distinguished at the distance of several hundred yards, so that one may even shoot by moonlight. The months of June and July offer very little variation in the weather or temperature. In August a suffocating heat reigns throughout the day, and at night it is useless to seek for coolness; a faint zephyr is succeeded by a calm of several hours. The atmosphere is heavy and oppressive, and the body, weakened by perspiration, becomes languid; the appetite fails, and the mosquitoes perplex and annoy by their sting, while the fevers of the Tropics attack Europeans with sudden and irresistible violence. This is the most sickly season for the European. The thermometer frequently exceeds 90°. The clouds exhibit a menacing appearance, portending the approach of the heavy autumnal rains, which pour down like a deluge. About the middle of September it appears as if all the vapors of the ocean had accumulated in one point of the heavens. The rain comes down like an immense quantity of water poured through a sieve; it excludes from the view every surrounding object, and in half an hour the whole surface of the earth becomes an immense sheet of water. The rivers are swollen and overflow their banks, the low lands are completely inundated, and the smallest brooks become deep and rapid torrents. In the month of October the weather becomes sensibly cooler than during the preceding months, and in November the north and northeast winds generally set in, diffusing an agreeable coolness through the surrounding atmosphere, which exerts a bracing and genial influence on body and mind of the convalescent. The north wind is accompanied, with few exceptions, by heavy showers of rain on the north coast, and the sea rolls on that coast with tempestuous violence, while the south coast remains perfectly calm. When the fury of the north wind abates it is succeeded by fine weather and a clear sky. This is considered to be the healthiest season of the year, when a European may visit the Tropics without fear. The land breeze is an advantage which the large islands derive from the inequality of their surface, for as soon as the sea breeze dies away the hot air of the valleys, being rarefied, ascends toward the top of the mountains and is there condensed by cold, which makes it specifically heavier than it was before, and it descends back to the valleys on both sides of the ridge. Hence a night wind (blowing on all sides from the land toward the shore) is felt in all the mountainous countries in the torrid zone. On the north shore the wind comes from the south and on the south shore from the north. The hurricanes that visit the island, and which obey the general laws of tropical cyclones, are one of the worst scourges of the country. For hours before the appearance of this terrible phenomenon the sea appears calm. The waves come from a long distance very gently until near the shore, when they suddenly rise as if impelled by a superior force, dashing against the land with extraordinary violence and fearful noise. Together with this sign the air is noticed to be disturbed, the sun red, and the stars obscured by a vapor which seems to magnify them. The sea emits a strong odor, the waters of the rivers become sulphurous, and there are sudden changes in the wind. These omens, together with the signs of uneasiness manifested by various animals, foretell the proximity of a hurricane. Earthquakes are somewhat frequent, but not of much consequence. The shocks are sometimes violent and are usually repeated, but, owing to the special construction of the houses, they cause no damage. The tide for 7 hours runs rapidly in a northwest direction, returning in the opposite direction with equal rapidity for 5 hours. The general relief of Puerto Rico is much inferior in altitude to that of the rest of the Great Antilles, and even some of the Lesser Antilles have mountain summits which rival it. A great chain of mountains divides the island into two parts, northern and southern, which are called by the natives Banda del Norte and Banda del Sur. The whole island may be said to form a continuous network of sierras, hills, and heights. Few countries of the extent of Puerto Rico are watered by so many streams. Seventeen rivers, taking their rise in the mountains, cross the valleys of the north coast and empty into the sea. Some of these are navigable 2 or 3 leagues from their mouths for schooners and small coasting vessels. The rivers of the north coast have a decided advantage over those of the south coast, where the climate is drier and the rains less frequent. Nevertheless the south, west, and east coasts are well supplied with water; and although in some seasons it does not rain for 10 and sometimes 12 months on the south coast the rivers are never entirely dried up. On the west coast 3 rivers, 5 rivulets, and several fresh-water lakes communicate with the sea. In the small extent of 330 leagues of area there are 46 rivers, besides a countless number of rivulets and branches of navigable water. There are few roads or ways of communication which are worthy of mention, with the exception of the broad pike which starts from the capital and runs along the coast. Navigation is very active, but the part the inhabitants take in the commercial fleet is small. The Puerto Ricans are not sea-going people. The eastern part of the island offers less advantage to commerce than the western, being to the windward and affording less shelter to vessels. In 1887 only one-seventh of the population could read and write, but of late years progress in public instruction has been rapid. While Puerto Rico was under the dominion of Spain it was not considered as a colony, but as a province assimilated to the remaining provinces. The Governor-General, representing the Monarchy, was at the same time captain-general of the armed forces. In each chief town there resided a military commander, and each town had its alcalde or mayor, appointed by the central power. At the termination of the Spanish-American War the treaty of peace provided, among other things, for the cession of Puerto Rico and adjacent islands to the United States. Nearly all the island is cultivated, the soil fertile, and coffee exports in 1897 were $8,789,788, and sugar $3,747,891. Three million cocoanuts and 200,-000,000 bananas are exported annually. Exports in 1896 were $17,295,595, and imports $18,945,793, the latter mainly flour, provisions, wines, textiles, and machinery. Spain had no less than 72 per cent of this whole trade. There are 307 miles of railway finished or in progress and 470 miles of telegraph. San Juan, the capital city, was settled in 1511. Population now about 40,000. Ponce had 37,545 inhabitants in 1887.

Puerto Rico:

American citizens in, unlawfully punished, II, 214.

Campaign against, under command of Maj. Gen. Miles, X, 171.

Commercial relations with, III, 41, 128; VIII, 239, 336, 504; IX, 35, 637.

Treaty regarding, VIII, 255, 260, 261.

Expeditions against, referred to, V, 208.

Grants of public or corporate rights in, order regarding, X, 221.

Military commission to superintend Spanish evacuation of, X, 175.

Piracies from, suppressed, II, 214.

Privateering in ports of, IV, 495.

Sanitary problems connected with, referred to, X, 194.

Slavery in, discussed, VII, 146.

Release of persons held in, discussed, VII, 240.

Puerto Rico—Continued.

Tariff laws of, evidence of modifications of, proclaimed, IX, 148.

Referred to, IX, 180, 312.

Vessels from certain ports of, duties on, suspended by proclamation, VIII, 284.

Vessels of Spain from, discriminating duties on, suspended by proclamation, VIII, 223, 490, 570.

Discussed, VIII, 504.

Suspension revoked, VIII, 489.

Vessels of United States, discriminating duties and fines on, in, VIII, 39, 127, 176, 199, 201; IX, 529.

Abolished, VIII, 223, 570.

Retaliatory measures discussed, VIII, 176.

Visit of American naval officer to, referred to, II, 276.

Puget Sound.—An arm of the Pacific extending into the State of Washington southward from the Strait of San Juan de Fuca, by which it is connected with the Pacific. The sound is divided into two parts—Puget Sound proper and Admiralty Inlet. The latter is to the north and the former to the south. Fine harbors are found along the sound, the water generally being quite deep. It is about 80 miles long.

Puget Sound Agricultural Co.:

Claims of, against United States referred to, VI, 690.

Treaty with Great Britain regarding, VI, 194, 200.

Commissioners appointed under, VI, 246.

Award of, and appropriation for, recommended, VII, 35.

Value of possessory rights of, referred to, V, 333.

Pulaski, Count Casimir, brigadier-general in Army, service rendered by and compensation to, referred to, VIII, 539.

Pumpkin Vine Creek (Ga.), Battle of. (See New Hope Church (Ga.), Battle of.)

Puritan, The, mentioned, X, 171.

Purvis, H. W., report of, on slaughter of American citizens in South Carolina, VII, 375.

Putman, Eunice, act to pension, vetoed, IX, 579.

Putman, Charles F., mentioned, VIII, 139.

Putnam, Rufus, treaty with Indians concluded by, I, 135.

Putnam, William L., treaty with Great Britain on subject of fisheries concluded by, VIII, 604.

Puyallup Commission, report of, transmitted, IX, 228.

Puyallup Indians:

Commission to treat with, IX, 228.

Treaty with, V, 303.

Pyramid Lake Reservation, Nev., agreement for cession of portion of, IX, 214.

Q.

Quallah Battoo, Sumatra, American citizens murdered in, II, 575.

Quapaw Indians, treaty with, II, 47, 279, 286; V, 296; VI, 518.

Quarantine.—A term derived from the French word "quarantaine" (m. Lat. quarantena), meaning "forty days." Passengers on vessels arriving at Venice from the Levant were formerly required to remain 40 days in the House of St. Lazarus, or the Lazaretto. This regulation was afterwards adopted by other ports in southern Europe, and, with various changes in the period of detention, extended to travelers from all ports whence contagion might be carried. In the United States quarantine enactments were passed by the colonial legislatures and subsequently for many years by the States. The first national quarantine act was passed Feb. 23, 1799, and required Federal officers to aid in the execution of State or municipal quarantine regulations. In 1878, however, a national quarantine law was passed authorizing the establishment, in certain contingencies, of national quarantines. In March, 1883, $100,000 was appropriated by the Federal Government for maintaining quarantine stations along the coasts, and the authority for declaring quarantine was conferred upon the President. Most of the quarantine stations are under State supervision. The mode of procedure is as follows: On the arrival of a vessel she is visited by the health officer, who examines her bill of health, musters the passengers and crew, and inspects the vessel in every part. If free from contagious disease, and if she does not hail from an infected port, she is allowed to proceed without further detention. If she hail from an infected port, she is detained until the expiration of the period of incubation of the disease prevalent at the port whence she sailed. If disease is found on board, or if the vessel is in an insanitary condition, the diseased persons are removed to a quarantine hospital and the vessel allowed to proceed after a thorough purification.

Quarantine Regulations (see also Contagious Diseases; International Sanitary Conference):
Proclamation regarding, VIII, 225.
Referred to, VIII, 253.
Recommendations regarding, by President—
Adams, John, I, 271.
Arthur, VIII, 85, 253.
Cleveland, IX, 445.
Harrison, Benj., IX, 330.
Hayes, VII, 492.
Jefferson, I, 383.
Monroe, II, 285.

Quarter Dollar.—In 1786 the Continental Congress decided upon certain coins. Among these was a quarter dollar, to be made of silver. The United States Mint was established in 1792 and began coinage in 1793. It was not until 1796, however, that the silver quarter was issued. Its weight was fixed at 104 grains. It was reduced to 93 grains in 1853, and by the coinage act of 1873 was raised to 96.45 grains, or 0.200 of an ounce, the present weight, and 900 fine. The coin is legal tender to the amount of $5. The quarter dollar of 1827 is one of the rare coins of the United States. There were no issues of this coin during the years 1798 to 1803, 1808 to 1815, nor during 1817, 1824, 1826, and 1830.

Quarter Eagle.—A gold coin of the United States authorized in 1792 and first coined in 1796. It is legal tender in any sum. The present weight of the coin is 0.134 ounce, or 64.5 grains, and the fineness 900. It is coined under an act of Congress of June 28, 1834.

Quartering Acts.—Certain acts of the British Parliament distasteful to the American colonists. The first was passed in 1765 and compelled the Colonies to provide the garrisons in America with fire, candles, vinegar, salt, bedding, cooking utensils, and liquors. This was the first act requiring the colonists to tax themselves for imperial objects. In 1774 an act was passed legalizing the quartering of imperial troops in Boston.

Quartermaster-General of Army, fireproof building for records in office of, recommended, VII, 572.

Quebec (Canada), Battle of.—After taking Montreal Gen. Montgomery proceeded down the St. Lawrence River to Quebec, where, on Dec. 5, 1775, he joined the expedition which had been sent by way of the Kennebec and Chaudière rivers under Benedict Arnold. Their combined forces amounted to about 3,000 men, supported by about a dozen light guns. Carleton had for the defense of Quebec one company of regulars, a sloop of war, and a few marines, together with as many of the citizens as could be induced to enlist—in all something like 1,600 men. On the night of Dec. 31 the city was attacked. Montgomery was killed, Arnold was wounded, and the troops retired in confusion. Three thousand troops were sent to reenforce Arnold, and 4,000 occupied Montreal, St. Johns, and Chambly. May 6, 1776, 3 brigades of infantry, besides artillery, stores, ammunition, transports, and men-of-war, arrived from England and the Americans retired, leaving Canada as it was before the invasion. (See also Montreal (Canada), Capture and Loss of.)

Queen, Walter W., thanks of Congress to, recommended, VI, 76.

Queen Anne's War.—The name by which the War of the Spanish Succession was known in America. It broke out in 1702 and was ended with the treaty of Utrecht in 1713. The New England Colonies suffered from frequent inroads of French and Indians from Canada, but the New York Colony was protected by the barrier of the Six Nations of Indians, then at peace with the English. Aug. 10, 1703, Indians under French leaders attacked Wells, Cape Porpoise, Saco, Casco, Scarboro, Spurwink, and Purpooduck, completely destroying the last two. In 1704 and 1705 James Moore, of South Carolina, with 50 whites and about 1,000 Creek Indians, attacked and destroyed several Spanish settlements in Florida. Col. Church organized an expedition in Maine in 1704 and proceeded up the coast as far as the Bay of Fundy, destroying all the settlements and taking 106 prisoners, with the loss of only 6 men. Feb. 28, 1704, about 350 French Canadians and Indians burned the town of Deerfield, Mass., massacring 40 persons and taking 100 prisoners. After three attempts by the New England troops Acadia was finally captured. July 30, 1711, Gen. Nicholson left Albany with an army of 4,000 men and Hovenden Walker sailed from Boston with a fleet and 7,000 men, as well as a fine train of artillery, to attack Quebec and Montreal. The fleet was driven upon the rocks at the mouth of the St. Lawrence, losing 8 transports and more than 1,000 men. The survivors sailed for England and the army disbanded.

Queenston Heights (Canada), Battle of.—Early in October, 1812, Gen. Van Rensselaer resolved to invade Canada from western New York. His headquarters were at Lewiston, opposite Queenston, Canada. The American army consisted of 3,650 regulars and 2,650 militia. The British force on the western bank of the Niagara River numbered about 1,500, including about 250 Indians under John Brant. Maj. Gen. Brock, who had taken Detroit in August, had returned to the east and established his headquarters at Fort George. He posted batteries every mile along the river from there to Queenston. On the morning of Oct. 13, 1812, the invasion was begun prematurely, insufficient boats having been provided for transportation. Reenforcements came so slowly that the advance guard was forced to surrender. Gen. Brock was mortally wounded, Van Rensselaer was disabled, and the American command fell upon Capt. Wool. British reenforcements and Indians pressing hard upon the Americans, they were forced to surrender. About 900 Americans were taken prisoners, 90 were killed, and about 100 wounded. The British lost in killed, wounded, and captured about 130. The number of Indians killed is not known.

Querétaro, Treaty of. (See Guadalupe Hidalgo, Treaty of.)

Qui-nai-elt Indians, treaty with, V, 380.

Quids.—A name applied to the anti-Madison faction of the Republican party, led by John Randolph from 1805 to 1811. Jefferson strongly favored the succession of Madison and the Quids declared war upon the Administration, charging "backstairs" influence. They opposed the restrictive system and nominated Monroe in 1808.

Quiggle, Chloe, act granting pension to, vetoed, VIII, 648.

Quil-leh-ute Indians, treaty with, V, 380.

Quint.—One of the silver coins presented by Robert Morris to the Continental Congress in 1783 for consideration as a national coin. It weighed 5 pennyweights and 15 grains and was equal to about 35 cents. On the obverse was an eye, 13 points crossing (equidistant) a circle of as many stars, and the legend "Nova Constellatio;" on the reverse, "U.S. 500," surrounded by a wreath and the legend "Libertas, Justitia." This coin was not accepted and afterwards, with the mark, became known as the Nova Constellatio coinage.

Quitman, John A., mentioned, IV, 565.

Quorum.—A word adopted from the Latin, meaning in the original tongue "of whom." Legally it denotes a certain specified number out of a larger number necessary to act for certain purposes. Business in charge of trustees or committees might often be retarded on account of the absence of one or more members if the actions of a quorum were not legal. Unless otherwise stipulated, a majority of the members of any body is considered a quorum. In parliamentary usage a quorum is the number that must be present in order that business may be transacted. It is sometimes less than 1 per cent of the members, as in the case of the British House of Lords, where 3 out of 450 members constitute a quorum. According to the Constitution, a majority of either branch of Congress constitutes a quorum. For the first fifty Congresses the presence of a constitutional quorum in the House was determined by a count of votes. No matter how many members were present, unless a majority voted it was considered there was not a quorum present. This sometimes led to obstructive tactics. In 1890, during the first session of the Fifty-first Congress, the Speaker of the House ruled that a quorum was present when enough members were visible to constitute a quorum, whether they voted or not. The Senate enforces the rule which requires a majority of the body to vote in order that a quorum may be counted.

R.

Rabun, William, mentioned, X, 58.

Railroad Commission:

Recommended, IX, 205, 328.

Report of, on indebtedness of Pacific railroads discussed and recommendations regarding, VIII, 596, 799.

Railroad Employees, legislation for increased safety in use of couplers and brakes recommended, IX, 51, 126, 207, 331.

Railroad Transportation:

Bill authorizing payment of, transmitted, VIII, 87.

Discussed, IX, 740.

State laws regulating rates of, adjudged inoperative by Supreme Court, VIII, 526.

Railroad, Underground. (See Underground Railroad.)

Railroads (see also the several railroads; Interstate Commerce; Interstate Commerce Commission; Railroad Commission; Railroads, Commissioner of; Strike Commission):

Between United States and Mexico, VII, 610.

Construction of, as military measure recommended, VI, 46.

Couplers and brakes upon freight trains, legislation for increased safety in use of, recommended, IX, 51, 126, 207, 331.

From—

Atlantic to Pacific States recommended, V, 457.

Missouri River to Pacific Ocean, uniform gauge for, VI, 160.

Railroads—Continued.

From—

Omaha, Nebr., to Sacramento, Cal., discussed, VI, 683.

Government aid to, under Constitution discussed, V, 220.

Grant to American citizens for lines of, through Mexico, VI, 467.

In Europe, VI, 69.

Lands granted in aid of, discussed, V, 216, 290; VI, 382, 453; VII, 111; VIII, 359, 799.

Forfeiture of, discussed, VIII, 250, 794.

Revocation of withdrawal of, referred to, VIII, 612.

Military possession of, taken by United States, VI, 113, 178.

Referred to, VI, 278.

Right of way for, through reservations. (See Indian Reservations.)

Strikes discussed. (See Strike Commission.)

Subsidies to—

Discussed, VII, 110.

Information regarding, transmitted, VIII, 373.

Survey for, across continent discussed, V, 220.

Recommended, V, 20.

Taxation of, discussed, VIII, 143.

Total mileage of, discussed, IX, 306.

Transportation rates. (See Railroad Transportation.)

Railroads, Commissioner of, report of, discussed, IX, 205, 328.

Railway Mail Service:

Classification of employees in, VIII, 844.

Amendments to rules regarding, IX, 30, 31, 107, 175, 516, 522, 523, 608.

Discussed, IX, 450.

Recommended, VII, 575.

Time for, extended, IX, 27.

Discussed, IX, 53.

Discussed, IX, 450.

Railway Postal Service. (See Postal Service; Railway Mail Service.)

Raleigh, The, mentioned, X, 155.

Rambouillet Decree.—Mar. 23, 1810, after the American Congress had repealed the non-intercourse act of Mar. 1, 1810, Napoleon ordered the immediate seizure and sale of all American vessels in the ports of France or the ports of her territories occupied by French armies. In this decree Napoleon avowed his determination to prohibit any commercial intercourse with the enemies of France which was not enjoyed by that country also. Under this decree 132 vessels, with their cargoes, valued at $8,000,000, were ordered sold. (See also Berlin Decree; Embargo; Milan Decree; Nonintercourse Acts.)

Ramsay, David, arrest and maltreatment of, at Heidelberg, Baden, V, 239.

Ramsden, Fred. W., British consul at Santiago, Cuba, services of, to United States and subsequent death of, referred to, X, 184.

Ramsey, Alexander:

Superintendent of Indian affairs in Minnesota, misconduct of, referred to, V, 227.

Treaty with Indians concluded by, VI, 196.

M P—VOL X—36

Ramsey & Carmick, claims of, referred to, V, 534.

Randall, A. F., mentioned, VI, 611.

Randall, Alex. W., correspondence of, transmitted, VI, 606.

Randall, Sally A., act granting pension to, vetoed, VIII, 664.

Randolph, Edmund, Attorney-General, proceedings of Cabinet signed by, X, 87.

Randolph, John, jr., letter of, demanding that officers insulting, be punished, I, 301, and X, 120.

Ranger, The, referred to, II, 467.

Ransom, George M., thanks of Congress to, recommended, VI, 76.

Raritan, The, postponement of sailing of, referred to, IV, 276.

Ratification of Constitution.—The Constitution, by its terms, was not to become binding until ratified by nine of the thirteen States. It was signed by the delegates in convention Sept. 17, 1787, and by them submitted to Congress. Congress immediately ordered copies sent to all the States. Hamilton, Jay, and Madison took leading parts in bringing about the ratification by the States. Gen. Washington's great influence was also thrown into the scale. The commercial classes in most of the States favored its adoption, but there was much opposition to it on all sides. Delaware was the first State to ratify the new document, taking favorable action thereon Dec. 7, 1787. It was then ratified by the other States in the following order: Pennsylvania, Dec. 12; New Jersey, Dec. 18; Georgia, Jan. 2, 1788; Connecticut, Jan. 9; Massachusetts, Feb. 6; Maryland, Apr. 28; South Carolina, May 23; New Hampshire, June 21; Virginia, June 25; New York, July 26; North Carolina, Nov. 21, 1789, and Rhode Island, May 29, 1790. The Constitution went into effect Mar. 4, 1789, before North Carolina and Rhode Island had ratified it.

Ratification of Constitution. (See Constitution.)

Rawlins, John A.:

Secretary of War, death of, announced and honors to be paid memory of, VII, 24.

Statue of, recommendations regarding erection of, VII, 170.

Ray, James B., treaty with Indians concluded by, II, 365.

Raymond, Charles H., mentioned, IV, 357.

Raymond (Miss.), Battle of.—May 7, 1863, Sherman effected a junction with Grant, swelling the force about to proceed to the siege of Vicksburg to 50,000 men, including infantry, cavalry, and artillery. Grant immediately ordered a general movement on two parallel roads on the southeast of the Big Black River. McPherson, advancing on the road nearest the river, met two brigades of the enemy, under Gregg and Walker, at Raymond, 15 miles southwest of Jackson, on May 12, and after a sharp engagement defeated them. The Confederate loss was 103 killed and 720 wounded and missing. McPherson lost 69 killed, 341 wounded, and 32 missing.

Read, John, agent of United States, referred to, I, 340.

Readjusters.—A faction of the Democratic party in Virginia in 1878. Its formation was due to the passage of a bill by the State legislature in the early part of that year providing for the refunding of the State debt. The party was led by William Mahone and was violently opposed to the payment of the entire debt, holding that the State of West Virginia should share in the payment of the debt, as that State enjoyed some of the benefits of the original loan. In 1879 and 1881, by combining with the Republicans, they gained control of the State government and elected Mahone to the United States Senate, and later elected H. H. Riddleberger to the same position.

Real Estate, liens and incumbrances on property of United States referred to, III, 567.

Rear-Admiral.—This is a naval grade created by act of Congress in 1862. This grade in the Navy ranks with that of major-general in the Army. Until the special acts creating the grades of admiral and vice-admiral, that of rear-admiral was the highest naval office. There are now (1899) 18 rear-admirals in the Navy.

Rear-Admiral, rank of acting, conferred upon certain officers inquired into, VIII, 261.

Rebecca, The, seizure and sale of, at Tampico, VIII, 538; IX, 67.

Rebellion Records. (See War of Rebellion, Official Records of.)

Rebellion, War of. (See War between the States.)

Rebellions. (See Illegal Combinations.)

Rebello, Vicenzo, seizure of, at New Orleans, VIII, 66.

Reciprocal Trade Agreements. (See Foreign Import Duties.)

Reciprocity.—Reciprocity is the granting by one nation of certain commercial privileges to another, whereby the citizens of both are placed upon an equal basis in certain branches of commerce. A reciprocity agreement between the United States and Canada was concluded in 1854 and terminated in 1866. A similar one was made with Hawaii in 1875. Other treaty arrangements of a reciprocal character were made from time to time. The subject derived the greatest interest from attention directed to it in 1888 and the final incorporation of the principle in the tariff act of 1890. For many years previous to this time the anti-protection or tariff-reform party had attacked the existing tariff regulations on the ground that by levying high duties on the products of South American Republics those countries had not only to send their products elsewhere for sale, but, as a natural consequence, to purchase their goods in other markets than those of the United States; in other words, that a vast trade was diverted from us to Europe because of the restrictions imposed upon commerce by our tariff. This discussion led to the adoption of a reciprocity arrangement with Central and South American countries. The first step toward this end was the calling of the Pan-American Congress (q. v.). Among the numerous subjects of mutual interest discussed at this congress was a recommendation for reciprocity treaties. The Secretary of State of the United States sent a letter to the President for transmission to Congress calling attention to the proposed scheme. He suggested a practical and prompt test of the reciprocity principle by an amendment to the pending tariff bill authorizing the President to declare the ports of the United States free to all the products of any nation of the American hemisphere upon which no export duties are imposed whenever and so long as such nation shall admit to its ports, free of all national, provincial, municipal, and other taxes, certain specified articles from the United States. The "reciprocity section" was incorporated in the tariff law approved Oct. 1, 1890. The first practical operation of the law was made by a proclamation of President Benj. Harrison, Feb. 5, 1891 (IX, 141). The passage of the tariff law of 1894 practically annulled the reciprocity arrangements.

Reconcentrados.—The name given the agricultural inhabitants of Cuba who were by the edict of Feb. 16, 1896, of Captain-General Weyler concentrated within the lines of the Spanish armies and cities of that island. This resulted in great suffering to the persons thus herded together, many of them dying of disease and from starvation. The mortality was so frightful and their suffering so intense that their condition excited universal pity. On the suggestion of the President, the United States Congress made an appropriation for their relief.

Reconcentrados:

Appropriation for, recommended, X, 150.

Policy of Gen. Weyler regarding, discussed, X, 129, 141, 142, 161.

Revoked, X, 143.

Reconstruction.—In American politics a term signifying the restoration to those States which had seceded of local self-government and normal relations with the Union. The period of reconstruction embraced the Administrations of Johnson and Grant and presented some perplexing problems to the statesmen of the reunited country: Were the States still in the Union, with no other disability than that of having no legal governments, or had their act of secession reduced them to the condition of territories subject to the Union? Did reconstruction mean their erection into new States or their restoration with their old names and boundaries? Did the power to reconstruct lie in the States themselves or in the General Government; and if in the General Government, did it lie with Congress or with the Executive? If it lay with the people of the disorganized State, who or what defined that people and decided who might and might not vote in the reorganization? If it lay with Congress, could the Executive, without the authority of Congress, proceed to reconstruct, simply leaving it to Congress to accept or reject the States so reconstructed? President Lincoln had proceeded upon the theory that

nothing more was necessary than that a sufficient number of loyal citizens should form a
State government of which the officials were
loyally desirous of maintaining constitutional
relations with the Union (VI, 222). President
Johnson proceeded upon nearly the same
theory. The view held by the majority in
Congress was that the Southern States could be
readmitted only on such terms as that body
should impose. The ground taken in support
of this view was that the substantial results of
the war respecting the civil rights of the negro
could not be secured in any other way, because
of the reluctance of some legislatures to accept
these results. Before Congress met in December, 1865, President Johnson had recognized
provisional governments in all the Southern
States except one, on their acceptance of the
thirteenth amendment. Congress then proposed the fourteenth amendment and insisted
upon its acceptance as a prerequisite to read-
mission to the Union. The same body, on
Mar. 2, 1867, passed, over President Johnson's
veto, the military reconstruction bill introduced in the House by Thaddeus Stevens.
Under this law the South was divided into five
military districts under the command of generals of the Army, who were to effect a registration of voters, including negroes and excluding those persons who had been disqualified
by the fourteenth amendment. These voters
were to make and ratify a constitution and
submit it to Congress, and if it was acceptable
the State should be reinstated whenever its
legislature had ratified the fourteenth amendment. Tennessee was readmitted to the Union
in 1866, Alabama, Arkansas, Florida, Georgia,
Louisiana, North Carolina, and South Carolina
in 1868, and Mississippi, Texas, and Virginia
in 1870. (See also Restoration.)

Reconstruction Acts:
Interpretation of, VI, 552.
Proceedings of President and Cabinet re-
garding, as set forth in National Intelli-
gencer, discussed, VI, 527.
Repeal of, recommended, VI, 562, 672.
Vetoed. (See Reconstruction.)

Reconstruction of Southern States (see also Res-
toration):
Act providing for more efficient government
of rebel States vetoed, VI, 498.
Acts supplementary to, vetoed, VI, 531, 536.
Assignments under, VI, 551, 552, 556, 557, 661,
662, 663, 664, 665, 666, 668, 671.
Expenses of carrying act into effect dis-
cussed, VI, 521, 525, 566.
Joint resolution to carry act into effect ap-
proved and reasons therefor, VI, 521.
Joint resolution to carry acts into effect ve-
toed, VI, 545.
Acts to admit certain Southern States into
Union vetoed, VI, 648, 650.
Discussed by President—
Grant, VII, 11, 28, 96.
Referred to, VII, 400.
Hayes, VII, 442, 458, 493.
Johnson. (See Restoration.)

Reconstruction of Southern States—Continued.
Government for Tennessee, order of Presi-
dent to Governor Johnson regarding, X, 109.
Ratification of fourteenth amendment pro-
claimed—
Alabama, VI, 659.
Georgia, VI, 660.
Louisiana, VI, 658.
North Carolina, VI, 656.
South Carolina, VI, 657.
Record, Congressional. (See Congressional Rec-
ord.)
Records and Documents (see also Exchanges for
Official Documents; International Bureau of
Exchanges):
Building for, recommended, VII, 500; VIII, 194.
Documents in care of legations referred to,
VII, 116.
Laws for punishing persons abstracting or
mutilating, recommended, V, 147, 177, 408.
Rector, Wharton:
Conviction of, for crimes committed referred
to, II, 476.
Indian agent, renomination of, and reasons
therefor, II, 482.
Red Cloud Agency, Nebr., deficiency in supplies
at, VII, 358, 359.
Red Cross, American National:
Aid furnished Cubans by, discussed, X, 142, 161.
Work accomplished by, in Spanish-American
War discussed, X, 173.
Red Cross Association, international conference
of:
Held at Carlsruhe, Baden, referred to, VIII, 620.
Report of, referred to, VIII, 269.
Red Cross, International, proposition of Switzerland to extend compact of, in Spanish-Ameri-
can War discussed, X, 189.
Red-Line Map.—An early map of part of North
America, discovered by Jared Sparks in the
archives of Paris and sent to Daniel Webster
during treaty negotiations with Great Britain
over the northeastern boundary question. It
had been executed in 1746 by D'Anville, and
later (1782) sent to the French minister, Ver-
gennes, by Franklin. A strong red line drawn
near the ridge in which the Kennebec and
Penobscot rivers rise more than favored the
English claims respecting the northeastern
boundary of the United States. The map was
displayed in a secret session of the Senate and
before the Maine commissioners, and was, in
part at least, the ground on which the Webster-
Ashburton treaty was signed.
Red River:
Exploration of, I, 398.
Unsuccessful, I, 408.
Improvement of, progress made in, III, 223.
Redemptioners.—A name applied to a class of
indentured servants who came to the American Colonies under bond for a certain number
of years in payment for their passage hither.
Many were kidnapped and placed in forced
slavery for a term of years. They usually
served from 4 to 7 years. On their release
these redemptioners were awarded 50 acres of
land and became free citizens. The system was

introduced into Virginia with the first colony in 1607 and in Massachusetts in 1631. It obtained also in Maryland, New York, Connecticut, and Pennsylvania, but was discontinued in 1750.

Redstone, Albert, act for relief of, returned, IX, 479.

Reed, Catharine, act granting pension to, vetoed, VIII, 721.

Reed, John, sr., act granting pension to, vetoed, VIII, 559.

Reed, Marinda W., act granting pension to, vetoed, VIII, 835.

Reed, Silas, surveyor of Missouri and Illinois:
Nomination of, and reasons therefor, IV, 103.
Error in, corrected, IV, 104.
Official conduct of, referred to, IV, 359, 361.

Reed, William B.:
Commissioner to China, instructions to, referred to, V, 484.
Dispatches of, regarding convention with China referred to, V, 540.

Reeves, Benjamin H., treaty with Indians concluded by, II, 323.

Reform Schools. (See District of Columbia.)

Refunding.—The process of substituting a series of low-interest-bearing bonds for those of a higher rate or for a floating debt not funded. Aug. 31, 1865, the debt of the United States amounted to $2,845,907,626, of which sum only $1,109,568,192 was funded. By December, 1867, the floating debt, compound-interest notes, seven-thirties, and United States notes had been converted into a funded debt of nearly $700,000,000. The refunding act of 1870 authorized the issue of certain amounts of 5, 4½, and 4 per cent bonds to take the place of the existing bonds, most of which were bearing 6 per cent interest. During the next 10 years this substitution was carried to an extent that decreased the annual interest charges from $82,000,000 to $62,000,000. In 1881 the annual interest was decreased nearly $20,000,000 more by the Windom refunding scheme, which converted $460,000,000 5 and 6 per cent bonds into bonds bearing 3 and 3½ per cent interest.

Register of Debates.—A record of the Congressional debates and proceedings from December, 1824, to October, 1837. It is a continuation of the Annals of Congress and contains many valuable state papers as well as the routine Congressional work. The Register of Debates was succeeded by the Congressional Globe. (See also Annals of Congress; Congressional Globe; Congressional Record.)

Registration.—A precaution taken in certain States to prevent frauds in elections. It consists of the preparation of lists of the electors of every precinct, voters being required to present themselves before the registrar on specified days prior to election to have their names recorded and to answer questions as to their qualifications as electors. These lists are open to inspection and scrutiny by the public.

Registration Bureau of naturalized citizens recommended, VIII, 241, 336, 505, 785.

Registry, American, repeal of law denying, to ships built abroad and owned by Americans recommended, IX, 553.

Regulators.—In 1768 the people of Orange County, N. C., oppressed by the unjust acts of Edmund Fanning, clerk of the court of Orange, formed an association, headed by Herman Husbands and William Hunter, for regulating public grievances and abuse of power. They sent messengers to the governor with a statement of their grievances. The governor and council decided that the course of the Regulators tended to high treason, and on their reassembling in July to hear the report of the messengers, the governor, at the head of a body of troops, compelled them to take the oath of allegiance to the Crown and disperse. Some of the leaders of the Regulators were held to answer in the courts for their actions. The following year another petition was rejected. The Regulators offered an organized resistance to the troops under Governor Tryon, and at Alamance, on the Haw River, they were routed by the governor and their leaders arrested. Some of these leaders were executed. Martin, the next governor, compromised with the Regulators.

Reid, Samuel C., battle sword of father offered to United States by, VIII, 534.

Reid, Whitelaw, member of Spanish-American Peace Commission, X, 175.

Reiter, George C., conduct of, in connection with arrest and killing of Gen. Barrundia referred to, IX, 134.

Relations, Foreign. (See the several powers.)

Relief Party.—A political faction in Kentucky politics between 1820 and 1826. The party was composed of debtors and included a majority of the voters. It advocated relief of delinquent debtors and disputed the constitutionality of the replevin act. In 1823 the supreme court decided the replevin act to be unconstitutional, and in 1824 the legislature of the State repealed the court of appeals act and organized a new court. The Relief Party then became known as the New Court Party. The Anti-Relief or Old Court Party, securing a majority in the legislature in 1827, restored the old court, and the issue was not renewed.

Religious Establishments:
Baptist church in Mississippi Territory, act for relief of, vetoed, I, 490.
Protestant church at American embassy at Rome, removal of, referred to, VI, 464, 519.
Protestant Episcopal church in Alexandria, Va., act incorporating, vetoed, I, 489.
Separation of church and state, recommendation to declare, VII, 356.
Value of church property discussed and taxation of, recommended, VII, 334, 356.

Removals from Office.—The Constitution gives the President power to make appointments to civil office by and with the advice and consent of the Senate, but is silent on the subject of removals. Debate on this point arose in Congress in 1789, and it was concluded to allow the power of removal to rest with the President alone. This continued to be the policy of the Government until 1867. In this year charges were preferred in the House of Representatives against President Johnson, alleging corrupt use of the appointing, pardoning, and veto powers, corrupt disposition of public property, and interference in elections. The charges were referred to the Judiciary Committee and a bill was prepared and passed over the President's veto providing that, with certain exceptions, every officer appointed by the President with the concurrence of the Senate should retain his office until a successor should in like manner be appointed. This is known as the tenure-of-office act (q.v.). Johnson's suspension of Secretary Stanton in violation of this act led to his impeachment in 1868. The law was repealed in 1887.

Removals from Office (see also Executive Nominations):

Act regulating tenure of certain civil offices vetoed. (See Tenure-of-Office Act.)

Discretionary authority of President regarding, discussed by President—

Cleveland, VIII, 375.

Grant, VII, 38.

Jackson, III, 132.

Johnson, VI, 492, 569, 622.

Tyler, IV, 88. (See also IV, 52.)

For partisan purposes discouraged, IV, 88.

Partisan interference in elections cause of removal, IV, 52.

Referred to, III, 579; IV, 58, 59.

Resolution of Senate regarding, and reply of President Hayes, VII, 481.

Rennels, Hiram G., receiver of public money, nomination of, II, 477.

Reno, Jesse L., major-general in Army, nomination of, and reasons therefor, VI, 161.

Renshaw, William B., thanks of Congress to, recommended, VI, 76.

Renwick, James, report of, as commissioner on northeastern boundary. (See Northeastern Boundary.)

Representatives.—The constitutional designation of the members of the House of Representatives. They are elected by direct vote of the people, in representative districts fixed by State law, according to the apportionment made every 10 years by Congress as to the quota of each State. Representatives must be at least 25 years of age, residents of the State in which chosen, and citizens of the United States for 7 years previous to their election. (See also Congress.)

Representatives:

Appointment of, by President in whose election they have been officially concerned discussed, II, 448, 557.

Appointments to office, relation of, to. (See Executive Nominations.)

Apportionment of—

According to census of 1890 necessary, IX, 118.

Bill for—

Approved and reasons therefor, IV, 159.

Vetoed, I, 124.

Delay in making, referred to, V, 145.

Representatives—Continued.

Election of—

Federal supervision of, recommended, IX, 55, 127, 331.

Gerrymander discussed, IX, 208.

Law appointing day for, recommended, V, 572, 650.

List of, appointed to office referred to, II, 22, 345, 633; IV, 510.

Loyal Senators and, denied admission to seats in Congress discussed, VI, 446.

President declines to give names of, applying for office, IV, 105.

Representatives at Large.—Representatives in Congress elected on general tickets, as distinguished from those elected on district tickets, in cases where the State has failed to redistrict after it has become entitled to additional representation in Congress.

Representatives, House of. (See Congress.)

Republican Party.—In the early days of the Republic Thomas Jefferson became the leader of a party opposed to the monarchical ideas of the Federalists. This party was first known as the Democratic-Republican, and the adherents were called both Democrats and Republicans, usually the latter, until the Jackson-Adams contest. The Republican party of later days was formed in 1854, with opposition to slavery as its chief tenet. The compromise of 1850 (q. v.) had disrupted the Whig party. The passage of the Kansas-Nebraska act materially influenced the general coalition that followed of Whigs, Free Soilers, Abolitionists, and Know-Nothings. They assumed the name of Republicans and at once won a plurality in the House of Representatives. In 1856 they held their first national convention in Philadelphia and nominated Frémont and Dayton for President and Vice-President. At the election which followed they were defeated, but in 1859 again came into control of the House. In 1860 they elected Mr. Lincoln to the Presidency. For the next 14 years the party was supreme. It enlarged the powers of Congress by a broad construction of the Constitution, carried on the Civil War, abolished slavery, reconstructed the governments of the seceding States, maintained a protective tariff, and refunded the national debt. The party has elected 6 Presidents—Lincoln, Grant, Hayes, Garfield, Harrison, and McKinley—besides 2 Vice-Presidents who served as Chief Executive. Johnson succeeded to the Presidency on the death of Lincoln, and Arthur on the death of Garfield. Besides the suppression of slavery the Republican party has favored full citizenship to emancipated slaves, prompt payment of the national debt, tariff for protection as well as revenue, free ballot, generous pension legislation, increase of the Navy and the strengthening of the coast defenses, a system of national-bank currency based on United States bonds deposited with the Secretary of the Treasury, and a national circulating medium based on a gold standard. It has also taken advanced ground on questions of civil-service reform, temperance legislation, etc. There was a serious defection from the party in 1872, when a large number of those who had theretofore supported its measures united in the formation of the Liberal Republican party (q. v.). This latter party was opposed to the extreme reconstruction policy of the Republicans.

Republican Party in Pennsylvania.—A party organized in that State in the period before the adoption of the Constitution of the United States to advocate a stronger form of Federal government than that comprehended by the Articles of Confederation. It formed the germ of the Federal party in Pennsylvania. The Republicans were opposed by the Constitutionalists.

Republican River, bridge over, reconstruction of, recommended, VIII, 190.

Republican Valley Railroad, right of way across Otoe and Missouria Reservation, Nebr., for, bill for, VIII, 94.

Repudiation.—The refusal of a state or government to pay or to be bound by debts contracted by a previous administration. In 1790 the debts of all the States of the Union were assumed by the National Government, partly on the ground of justice, because they had been contracted in the prosecution of the Revolutionary War, and partly on the ground of expediency, as this action tended to strengthen the credit of the States. For 40 years thereafter the States remained almost free from debt. Bonds of the several States were easily disposed of abroad, and by 1840 an aggregate of $200,000,000 had been sold. In that year Indiana found it impossible to pay the interest on her outstanding bonds, and it was only by strong efforts that Ohio managed to meet her obligations. In 1842 the Bank of Pennsylvania failed, and soon afterwards Pennsylvania, Maryland, Mississippi, Michigan, Louisiana, Indiana, and Illinois found themselves almost bankrupt. They all suspended payment of interest on their debts, but Mississippi, Michigan, and Louisiana felt constrained to repudiate the capital as well as interest. It was in Mississippi that the word "repudiation" originated in this connection. Governor McNutt, in a message to the legislature, suggested a plan for "repudiating the sale of certain of the State bonds on account of fraud and illegality." The bonds fell into default and an appropriation for their payment was overwhelmingly defeated at the polls in 1852. Michigan repudiated certain canal bonds. The Southern States came out of the Civil War with heavy indebtedness and diminished resources, and were in some instances almost bankrupt. In the years immediately following the close of the Civil War most of the Southern States compromised or readjusted their bonded indebtedness, and in some States the legislature declared certain bond issues fraudulent, illegal, and void. During the depression following the panic of 1873 some cities, towns, and counties endeavored to repudiate their bonds, but the Supreme Court of

the United States gave judgments against them. The eleventh amendment forbids suits against the States. Some European countries have also at times repudiated their obligations.

Requisitions.—Under the Articles of Confederation the Continental Congress had only one means of raising money—by requisitions upon the States. Between 1782 and 1786 requisitions amounting to more than $6,000,000 had been made. Only one-sixth of this had been paid by March, 1787. Under the Constitution the President may make requisitions upon the States for men to assist the National Government in time of war, but there is no provision for requisitions of money. Instead that instrument provides for the expenditures of the Government by duties on imports and taxes collected from the citizens.

Resaca (Ga.), Battle of.—Mar. 14, 1864, Gen. Sherman was placed in command of the Military Division of the Mississippi, which was composed of the Army of the Cumberland, under Maj. Gen. Thomas; the Army of the Tennessee, under Maj. Gen. McPherson, and the Army of the Ohio, under Maj. Gen. Schofield, and numbered a total of 98,797 men and 254 guns. The Confederate forces under Gen. Johnston were estimated at 60,000. After the battle of Chattanooga the Confederates had retreated to Dalton, Ga., 39 miles southeast of Chattanooga and 99 miles northwest of Atlanta. May 4 Sherman made a demonstration in front of the Confederate position on Rocky Face Mountain, northeast of Dalton, while McPherson, with some 40,000 men, attempted to turn the Confederate left and occupy Resaca. Johnston thereupon, on May 13, evacuated Dalton and fell back upon Resaca. Polk was posted on Johnston's left, resting on the Oostanaula River, Hardee in the center, and Hood on the right. Sherman laid a pontoon bridge across the Oostanaula and sent a division across to threaten Johnston's connections with Rome, while the main body of the army pressed Resaca in front. May 14 an attack by a portion of Sherman's force was repulsed with a loss of 1,000 men. Johnston attempted to turn Sherman's left flank, which gave McPherson a good position, to recover which the Confederates fought stubbornly till 10 o'clock that night. Skirmishing was renewed the next morning and continued all day. During the night of the 15th Johnston again retreated. Sherman's losses during the two days were between 4,000 and 5,000 in killed, wounded, and missing. Johnston's losses aggregated 2,500.

Resaca de la Palma (Tex.), Battle of.—On May 9, 1846, the day following the battle of Palo Alto, Gen. Taylor's army of 2,200 proceeded on the way toward Fort Brown. When about 3 miles from the Rio Grande River Arista's army of 5,000, which had been slowly retreating before the advancing Americans, halted in the valley of Resaca de la Palma (dry river bed of the palm) and prepared to give battle. At 3 o'clock in the afternoon the action began. Before dark the Mexicans were completely routed. They fled in disorder across the river to Matamoros. Eight pieces of artillery, large quantities of ammunition, 3 standards, and about 100 prisoners, including Gen. La Vega and other officers, fell into the hands of the Americans. The total casualties in the Mexican army were 755. The American loss was 107.

1830, which exiled Charles X and elevated Louis Philippe to the throne; the uprising of the French people in 1848, which deposed Louis; the Italian Revolution of 1859–60, whereby the various minor sovereigns of the peninsula were driven into exile and the whole territory came under the dominion of King Victor Emmanuel; the insurrections which established the third French Republic in 1870 and the Republic of Brazil in 1889.

Revolutionary Convention. (See Convention, Revolutionary.)

Revolutionary Pensions. (See Pensions.)

Revolutionary War.—The war for redress of grievances, and later for independence, waged by the thirteen American Colonies against the mother country, Great Britain. The Revolution had several causes. Increase of population in America naturally caused a desire for independence, especially after the expulsion of the French. In 1763 the Government of George III resolved to enforce more strictly the navigation act and other laws restricting American trade in the interest of England, to station garrisons in America, and to pay a part of the expense by a stamp tax. The Stamp Act aroused violent opposition, expressed through the Stamp Act Congress of 1765. Taxation without representation in Parliament was declared illegal and tyrannous. The British Government persisted in the principle, taxing various imports from 1767 to 1770 and tea thereafter. The Boston Tea Party led Parliament to pass acts retaliating on that city and altering the charter of Massachusetts. The Colonies were by this time united, through their committees of correspondence, in opposition to the Crown. Sept. 5, 1774, the First Continental Congress was convened in Philadelphia. It published a declaration of rights, protested to the King and Parliament, and entered into a nonimportation agreement. Apr. 19, 1775, Gen. Gage, the British commander in Boston, met with the first armed resistance at Lexington and Concord, and war was begun. The colonists were assisted by France, Spain, and, in the latter years of the struggle, by the Netherlands. Following are the principal events of the Revolution: Boston Massacre, Mar. 5, 1770; Boston Tea Party, Dec. 16, 1773; First Continental Congress, Sept. 5, 1774; battles of Lexington and Concord, Apr. 19, 1775; meeting of the Second Continental Congress and capture of Ticonderoga, May 10; Mecklenburg Declaration of Independence, May 20; battle of Bunker Hill, June 16 and 17; evacuation of Boston, Mar. 17, 1776; British repulse off Charleston, June 28; Declaration of Independence, July 4; battle of Long Island, Aug. 27; battle of White Plains, Oct. 28; loss of Forts Washington and Lee, retreat through New Jersey, and battle of Trenton, end of 1776; battle of Princeton, Jan. 3, 1777; battle of Bennington, Aug. 16; battle of Brandywine, Sept. 11; battle of Stillwater, Sept. 19; battle of Germantown, Oct. 4; battle of Saratoga, Oct. 7; Burgoyne's surrender, Oct. 17; adoption of the Articles of Confederation, Nov. 15; treaty with France, Feb. 6, 1778; battle of Monmouth, June 28; storming of Stony Point, July 16, 1779; victory of Paul Jones, Sept. 23; British capture Charleston, May 12, 1780; battle of Camden, Aug. 16; Arnold's treachery exposed, Sept. 23; battle of Kings Mountain, Oct. 7; battle of the Cowpens, Jan. 17, 1781; Articles of Confederation ratified by the last of the States, Mar. 1; battle of Guilford Court-House, Mar. 15; battle of Eutaw, Sept. 8; surrender of Cornwallis at Yorktown, Oct. 19; peace of Paris, Sept. 3, 1783; evacuation of New York, Nov. 25, 1783. The United States then comprised the territory from Canada to Florida and from the Atlantic Ocean to the Mississippi River. The total number of enlistments in the American Army during the war was 368,410; the total cost was $135,193,703.

Revolutionary War:
Allowances to officers in, referred to, II, 340.
Pensioners of. (See Pensions.)
Referred to, V, 222.
Soldiers of, land warrants issued to, II, 323.

Revolutions. (See Illegal Combinations; the several powers.)

Reward offered for arrest of—
Alleged instigators of assassination of President Lincoln, VI, 307.
Distribution of, referred to, VI, 379.
Persons claiming, directed to file claims, VI, 353.
Revoked as to certain persons, VI, 353.
Persons from foreign countries committing depredations in United States, VI, 283.
Willis Anderson, II, 377.

Rey, abduction of, referred to, V, 26.

Reynolds, Alexander W., assistant quartermaster, nomination of, and reasons therefor, V, 465.

Reynolds, John C., directed to accompany ex-President Jackson home, III, 323.

Reynolds, John W., act granting pension to, vetoed, VIII, 713.

Reynolds, Thomas C., report of, on commerce of Nicaragua, Honduras, and Salvador, VIII, 531.

Rhea, Hiram R., act to pension, vetoed, IX, 578.

Rhind, Charles:
Arabian horses received by, from Turkey referred to, II, 536.
Treaty with Turkey concluded by, II, 530.

Rhine, The, French steamer, referred to, VI, 259.

Rhode Island.—One of the thirteen original States of the Union and the smallest of the United States; nickname, "Little Rhody;" motto, "Hope." It lies between lat. 41° 18' and 42° 1' north (not including Block Island) and long. 71° 8' and 71° 53' west. It is bounded on the north and east by Massachusetts, on the south by the Atlantic Ocean, and on the west by Connecticut. It is an important manufacturing State, being first in proportion to its population in the manufacture of cotton, woolen, worsted, etc., and second only to Massachusetts in the production of cotton goods. Among its other manufactures are jewelry, machinery, screws, rubber, etc. It was visited by Verrazano in 1524 and probably by Norse navigators in the twelfth century. Roger Williams made the first permanent settlement at Providence in 1636. The first charter was granted in 1643 and a more liberal one in 1663. Rhode Island ratified the Federal Constitution in 1790. The official name of the State is, "The State of Rhode Island and Providence Plantations." Its dual origin is also indicated by its two capitals—Providence and Newport. Area, 1,250 sq. miles; population (1890), 345,506. (See also Providence Plantations.)

Rhode Island:
Accession of, to Union, I, 75.
Claims of, for militia services in War of 1812, X, 55.
Constitution of United States—
Convention for consideration of, I, 72.
Evidence of ratification of amendments to, I, 76, 190.
Dorr's Rebellion in—
Correspondence regarding, IV, 286.
Discussed, IV, 283.
Free constitution in, attempts of people to establish. (See Dorr's Rebellion.)
Lands in, United States empowered to hold, I, 154.
Letter of governor of, declaring friendship for sister States, X, 10.

Ricara Indians:
Treaty with, II, 322, 347.
War with. (See Indian Wars.)

Rice, Francis W., arrest and imprisonment of, at Acapulco, Mexico, V, 301, 304.

Rice, Henry M., member of Chippewa Commission, IX, 65.

Rice. (See Agricultural Products.)

Rich Mountain (W. Va.), Battle of.—Soon after the ordinance of secession had been ratified by the State of Virginia Maj. Gen. George B. McClellan, who had been assigned to the command of the Federal forces in the Department of the Ohio, issued an address to the loyal citizens of western Virginia. Many enlistments from that State followed, and he determined to occupy at least a part of it with Federal troops. Accordingly, May 23, 1861, the First Virginia Regiment, 1,100 strong, which had been organized in Cincinnati by Virginians, crossed the Ohio with the Fourteenth and Sixteenth Ohio regiments and took possession of Parkersburg. The Confederates, commanded by Governor Wise and under the immediate direction of Col. Porterfield, retired after several skirmishes to the base of Rich Mountain, near Beverly, in Randolph County. McClellan's forces in the neighborhood amounted to more than 30,000 men on July 4, while the Confederates could scarcely muster 10,000. July 11 Gen. Rosecrans made a detour of the mountain and forced the surrender of 600 men under Col. Pegram, and Gen. McClellan defeated the main body of the Confederates under Gen. Garnett. The Union losses in the actions at Rich Mountain were 11 killed and 35 wounded. The loss to the Confederates was 200 killed and 1,000 prisoners. Seven pieces of artillery also fell into the hands of the Union forces.

Richards, Mary K., act granting pension to, vetoed, VIII, 731.

Richardson, Aurelia C., act for relief of, vetoed, VIII, 484.

Richardson, Israel B., major-general in Army, nomination of, and reasons therefor, VI, 161.

Richardson, James D., resolution authorizing compilation of Messages and Papers of the Presidents by, I, III.

Richmond, James C., application of, for redress of wrongs, V, 239.

Richmond (Ky.), Battle of.—After the Confederates had evacuated Corinth, Miss., in the summer of 1862, they began to concentrate in the vicinity of Chattanooga, Tenn. By the middle of August they had collected an army estimated at from 55,000 to 65,000 under Gen. Braxton Bragg. Gen. E. Kirby Smith, with about 20,000 men, passed up the Cumberland Mountains on the east and, going through the gaps, invaded Kentucky. At Richmond he encountered Gen. Manson (Aug. 30), who was defending the place with a garrison of Buell's army. Manson was defeated and Smith proceeded to Frankfort. Loss, about 5,000 on each side.

Richmond, Va., Government of Confederate States transferred to, VI, 24.

Riddells, Bennett, consul to Chihuahua, Mexico, nomination of, and reasons therefor, V, 49.

Riddle, William P., act granting pension to, vetoed, VIII, 705.

Riders.—Objectionable legislative measures likely to be vetoed if passed as separate bills, but which are made part of important bills, such as appropriations for current expenses, etc., in order to insure Executive sanction. The rider is an encroachment on the independence of the Executive. In many of the States a rider has been made an impossibility by confining each bill to a single subject or by permitting the veto of single clauses of appropriation bills. It has never been prohibited in Congress. Riders were numerous during the anti-slavery contest, the Civil War, and the conflict with President Johnson. A number of important bills have been passed as riders, among them the bill increasing salaries in 1873. The first use of the rider of national importance was the joining in 1820 of the bill for the admission of Maine to that permitting slavery in Missouri, so as to compel the acceptance of both or neither. These were afterwards separated. The Army appropriation bill of 1856 had a rider prohibiting the employment of Federal troops for the enforcement of Territorial law in Kansas. The President signed the measure, but protested against the rider.

Riel, Louis, trial and execution of, by authorities of British North America, report regarding, transmitted, IX, 14.

Rifle Clubs in South Carolina, proclamation against, VII, 396. (See also Ku-Klux Klans.)

Rifle, Magazine, for use of infantry service selected, IX, 446.

Right of Asylum discussed by President—
Cleveland, IX, 529.
Johnson, VI, 685.

Right of Search.—Great Britain has always claimed the right to search vessels of other powers upon the high seas for deserting English sailors and for contraband goods in time of war. This right has not been exercised with regard to the vessels of the United States since the War of 1812, though nothing was said in the treaty of Ghent about search and impressment of sailors. Before that war this right was exercised and search was made for deserting English sailors, and many American seamen were impressed as deserters from the English navy, and search was made for such goods as were declared subject to confiscation in accordance with the paper blockade of the Continent and the orders in council. This was one of the grievances that brought on the War of 1812. The right of search for the purpose of suppressing the slave trade was carefully regulated by several treaties between Great Britain and the United States.

Right of Search:
Discussed by President—
Buchanan, V, 507, 639.
Madison, I, 499, 520.
Tyler, IV, 77, 195, 229.
Proposition regarding mutual, referred to, V, 90.
Questions regarding, with—
Cuba, VII, 32.
Great Britain, I, 499, 520; IV, 77, 195, 229.
Claim of Great Britain abandoned, V, 507, 640.
Mutual right of search referred to, IV, 90.
Referred to, IV, 436, 447.

Right of Suffrage. (See Elective Franchise.)

Right of Way. (See Indian Reservations.)

Rights, Bill of. (See Bill of Rights.)

Rights of Federal and State Governments. (See Powers of Federal and State Governments.)

Rigny, M. de, correspondence regarding claims against France. (See France, claims against.)

Riley, Bennett:
Correspondence regarding affairs in California referred to, V, 46.
Mentioned, V, 32.

Riley, Frank B., American sailor, alleged killing of, in Genoa, Italy, IX, 334.

Riley, Patrick, deputy United States marshal, assaulted in Boston, V, 101.
Proclamation regarding, V, 109.

Rio Grande River:
Construction of dams in, opposite El Paso, Tex., referred to, VIII, 815.
Disorders on, discussed by President—
Arthur, VIII, 40, 129.
Buchanan, V, 582, 584.
Fillmore, V, 152.
Grant, VII, 189, 207, 266, 290, 341, 404.
Harrison, Benj., IX, 316.
Hayes, VII, 455, 472, 497, 569, 160.
Neutrality violated by army on, referred to, VI, 376.
Storage and use of waters of, for irrigation discussed, IX, 527.

Riots at Chicago, proclamation regarding, IX, 499.

S.

Sabine Cross-Roads (La.), Battle of.—Gen. N. P. Banks's army, which had been concentrated at Alexandria, La., advanced up the Red River Mar. 25, 1864, by way of Natchitoches, Pleasant Hill, and Mansfield, toward Shreveport. Apr. 8, arriving at Sabine Cross-Roads, on the Sabine River, the Federals encountered a part of the Confederate army under Gen. Kirby Smith, commanded by Gen. Richard Taylor. The Confederates attacked and Banks was badly defeated, losing 3,000 in killed, wounded, and missing. The Confederates captured 19 guns and an immense amount of ammunition and stores. The Confederate loss was reported by Gen. E. Kirby Smith as over 2,000 killed and wounded.

Sac Indians.—A tribe of the Algonquian stock of Indians who formerly lived near the mouth of the Ottawa River and along the Detroit River. They were driven thence by the Iro-

gress, justices of the Supreme Court, and other Federal officials were materially increased. The provisions for the increase were introduced by Benjamin F. Butler, of Massachusetts, and made a rider to the appropriation bill. By this law the President's salary was increased from $25,000 to $50,000 per year; that of the Chief Justice from $8,500 to $10,500; those of the Vice-President, Cabinet officers, associate justices, and Speaker of the House from $8,000 to $10,000, and of Senators and Representatives from $5,000 to $7,500. Another act, passed the next day, made that part of the law relating to salaries of members of Congress retroactive, thus giving themselves $7,500 instead of $5,000 a year from Mar. 4, 1871, to Mar. 4, 1873, and following years. This excited the indignation of the people to such an extent that the laws were repealed the following year, except such provisions as related to the President and justices of the Supreme Court.

Salcedo, Manuel de, governor-general of Louisiana, letter of, to W. C. C. Claiborne, I, 348.

Salinas, Sebastian, mentioned, V, 35.

Salmon, D. E., chief of Bureau of Animal Industry, mentioned, IX, 548.

Saloman, Louis E. F., President of Haiti, death of, referred to, VIII, 783.

Salt, duties on, discussed, I, 409; III, 251.

Salt Springs:
Cession of, to United States, I, 354.
Referred to, II, 234, 326.

Salt Works in Kentucky, act for relief of owners of, vetoed, VII, 216.

Salter, William D., captain in Navy, nomination of, withdrawn, III, 528.

Salvador.—The smallest but most thickly populated of the Central American Republics. It is often incorrectly referred to as San Salvador, which is the name of its capital. It is bounded on the north and east by Honduras, on the south and southwest by the Pacific Ocean, and on the northwest by Guatemala; the Gulf of Fonseca separates it from Nicaragua on the southeast. The main cordillera of Central America runs along the northern frontier. Parallel to this and about 30 miles farther south another mountain chain crosses from east to west. This is a volcanic range and contains about 30 craters, some of which are active. Between these two mountain ranges is an irregular plateau 2,000 feet in elevation. This is the main settled portion of the Republic. South of the volcanic range a strip of lowland skirts the Pacific coast for 200 miles. Volcanic and seismic disturbances are so common as hardly to be noticed. San Salvador has been destroyed 8 times by earthquakes. Most of the inhabitants are engaged in agriculture, the principal products being coffee, indigo, sugar, and balsam of Peru. There is little mining or manufacture. The government is administered by a President, elected every 4 years, and a Congress consisting of one house, elected annually. Independence was proclaimed in 1821. There have been many wars

and revolutions. The present constitution dates from 1886. The area of Salvador is 7,225 sq. miles; population (1894), 803,534.

Salvador:
Commercial relations with, IX, 228.
Consular convention with, VII, 116, 258; VIII, 293.
Difficulties of, with Great Britain, V, 107.
Fugitive criminals, convention with, for surrender of, VII, 79, 258, 293.
Questions arising under, discussed, IX, 529.
Insurrection in, and refuge on board American vessel sought by insurgents discussed, IX, 529.
President of, confirmed, IX, 109.
Report of Thomas C. Reynolds on, transmitted, VIII, 531.
Tariff laws of, evidence of modifications of, proclaimed, IX, 249, 365.
Discussed, IX, 312.
Treaty with, transmitted and discussed, V, 34, 158; VI, 79; VII, 79, 116, 258, 293.
Vessel condemned by, subsequently presented to United States, recommendations regarding, VIII, 403.
War with Guatemala, IX, 108.

Sam-áhmish Indians, treaty with, V, 379.

Samana Bay:
Convention with Dominican Republic for—
Lease of, VII, 45.
Transfer of, VI, 601.
Possession of, desired by European power, VII, 61.
Proposition of foreign power to purchase right to, referred to, VII, 63.

Samoan Islands.—A group of 14 islands in the South Pacific Ocean. The principal islands are Savaii, Upolu, and Tutuila. They export mainly cotton, coffee, and copra. The United States has a coaling station in the harbor of Pago-Pago, granted in 1872. The neutrality of the islands was guaranteed by the United States, Great Britain, and Germany in 1889 by treaty. This convention or treaty between the three countries provided for a foreign court of justice, a municipal council for the district of Apia, the chief town, with a foreign president thereof, authorized to advise the King; a tribunal for the settlement of native and foreign land titles, and a revenue system for the Kingdom. It entailed upon the three powers that part of the cost of the new government not met by the revenues of the islands. The agreement binds the United States jointly with Great Britain and Germany to so interfere with the government and control of Samoa as in effect to assume the management of its affairs. Area, 1,100 sq. miles, population (1887), 35,565 native Polynesians and 450 whites.

Samoan Islands:
Affairs of, and policy of United States regarding—
Discussed by President—
Cleveland, VIII, 503, 804, 806, 812; IX, 439, 531, 635.
Harrison, Benj., IX, 34, 110.
McKinley, X, 189.
Reports on, transmitted, VIII, 612, 782, 800, 807, 810, 812; IX, 477, 479, 569.

the landing. The debarkation was attended with serious difficulties, as there was no harbor there. With the aid of the small boats of the fleet and transports the landing was made, but not until after the surf had dashed to pieces several of the boats. Upon landing at Daiquiri, Gen. Wheeler's command of cavalry was ordered to take position on the road to Siboney. Gen. Young's brigade (about 964 men), during the night of June 23-24, passed Gen. Lawton's division, which was on the road from Siboney to Santiago. About 3 miles from the former place, near Las Guasimas, June 24, they encountered the enemy posted in a strong natural position. The Spanish forces occupied a range of hills in the form of obtuse angles, with the salient toward Siboney. The attack, says Gen. Young, of both wings was simultaneous, and the junction of the two lines occurred near the apex of the angle, on the ridge, which had been fortified with stone breastworks flanked by blockhouses. The Spanish were driven from their position and fled precipitately toward Santiago. The American forces numbered about 965, the Spanish 2,000 to 2,500. American losses, 1 officer and 15 men killed; 6 officers and 46 men wounded. Forty-two dead Spanish soldiers were found on the field, while the Santiago (Spanish) papers the day after the battle gave their loss as 77 killed. Gen. Wheeler says in his report: "This engagement inspirited our troops and had a bad effect upon the spirits of the enemy." After this battle the Spaniards retired to the outer defenses of Santiago. These were the village of El Caney to the northeast, and the San Juan Hill extending south from that village and forming a natural barrier to the eastward of the city. July 1 these defenses were attacked by forces under Gen. Lawton, who was expected to take El Caney and then move toward Santiago and support the attack of Wheeler's and Kent's divisions upon the main Spanish army. The battle began at 6 a. m. and soon became general. The enemy fought with much obstinacy, but were slowly driven back. After Lawton had become well engaged, Grimes's battery, from the heights of El Poso, opened fire on the San Juan blockhouses, and Wheeler's and Kent's divisions moved forward, crossed the river, and formed for attack on San Juan Hill. During this formation Col. Wikoff was killed. The command of the Second Brigade then devolved upon Lieut. Col. Worth, who was soon severely wounded, and then upon Lieut. Col. Liscum, who fell a few minutes later, and Lieut. Col. Ewers took command. The enemy were strongly intrenched upon the hills in front of the American forces, San Juan Hill and Fort San Juan, the latter position being a few hundred yards nearer Santiago. The American forces charged up San Juan Hill in the face of a heavy fire, captured this point, crossed the plain below, and charged Fort San Juan, driving the enemy before them, and the battle of July 1 was won. At midnight

of July 1 Gen. Bates arrived with reenforcements, and at daylight on the 2d his brigade was placed on the ridge to the left of the American lines. Gen. Lawton's forces were placed on the right. July 2 a brisk and almost continuous fire was kept up by the two armies throughout the day, part of the time in a drenching rain. At nightfall the firing ceased, but at 9 p. m. a vigorous assault was made all along the lines, which was repulsed, the Spaniards retiring to their trenches. The following morning firing was resumed and continued until near noon, when a white flag was displayed by the enemy and the firing ceased. The total losses of the American forces during the 3 days' fighting (July 1, 2, and 3) were: Officers killed, 13; men, 87; officers wounded, 36; men, 561; missing, 62. The entire strength of the command which fought the battle of San Juan was 362 officers and 7,391 men. The defenses of Santiago were constructed with much engineering skill, as were also the batteries in the harbor. The city was at once surrounded by the American army, so that the Spaniards could not escape. The ridge upon which the Americans were stationed was favorably located and overlooked the city. The fortifications and barbedwire fences could easily be seen. The Spaniards seemed to realize that their condition was hopeless, and on Sunday morning, July 3, their fleet steamed out of the harbor. The destruction of this fleet was complete. (See Santiago Harbor (Cuba), Battle of.) July 5 the Spanish commander, Gen. Toral, in reply to a demand of Gen. Shafter for the surrender of the Spanish army and of the city, proposed to withdraw all his forces from the eastern province of Santiago, provided it was stipulated that he should not be molested until he had reached the city of Holguin, about 70 miles to the northwest. This proposition was declined at Washington. From the 5th to the 10th the time was divided between flags of truce and some skirmishing along the entire line. The losses, however, were small. On the 13th Gen. Miles, commander of the United States Army, arrived. Generals Miles, Shafter, and Wheeler then had an interview with Gen. Toral on the subject of the surrender. Another interview was had the next day between the same officers. Some misunderstanding occurred at this interview as to terms of surrender, etc., so that other meetings were necessary; but on the 15th the agreement for capitulation was duly signed. On the 16th Gen. Toral informed the American commander that the Spanish Government at Madrid had authorized the surrender, and thereupon final terms of absolute capitulation were duly signed. The conditions of surrender included all forces and war material in the division of Santiago. The United States agreed to transport, without unnecessary delay, all the Spanish troops in the district to Spain. Officers were to retain their side arms and officers and men their personal property.

The Spanish commander was authorized to take the military archives of the district. All Spanish forces known as volunteers, mobilizados, and guerrillas wishing to remain in Cuba were to be allowed to do so, under parole during the war. The Spanish forces were to march out of Santiago with honors of war and deposit their arms at a point to be mutually agreed upon, to await the disposition of the United States Government, etc. The troops surrendered and returned to Spain were about 24,000.

Santiago, Cuba:

American army under Maj. Gen. W. R. Shafter lands near, X, 170.

American interests in, confided to British consul, X, 184.

Movement against and subsequent capitulation of, discussed, X, 170.

Thanks of President tendered commander and men, X, 214, 216.

Postal communication with, order regarding, X, 216.

Santiago Harbor (Cuba), Battle of.—This engagement, which is also known as the battle of July 3, was the decisive naval combat of the Spanish-American War. For 6 weeks the Spanish fleet under Rear-Admiral Pascual Cervera had been imprisoned in the harbor of Santiago by the American blockading squadron in command of Acting Rear-Admiral Sampson. On the morning of July 3, 1898, at about 9.30 o'clock, while the men of the American vessels were at Sunday quarters for inspection, the Spanish fleet, consisting of the *Infanta Maria Teresa*, *Vizcaya*, *Cristobal Colon*, *Almirante Oquendo*, *Pluton*, and *Furor*, attempted to escape. The ships, coming out of the harbor at the rate of 8 or 10 knots an hour, passed without difficulty the collier *Merrimac* which had been sunk in the channel by Lieut. Hobson. Signals were at once made from the United States vessels, "Enemy's ships escaping," and general quarters was sounded. Rear-Admiral Sampson being about 7 miles from the scene of battle, the command of the American vessels during the engagement devolved upon Commodore Schley. Under his direction the squadron closed in on the fleeing vessels, and in about 2 hours the entire Spanish fleet was destroyed. The Spanish losses were 600 killed and about 1,400 prisoners, including the admiral. The loss on the American side was 1 killed and 1 wounded, while not a vessel was materially damaged. From this crushing defeat Spain was unable to recover, and her effort upon the ocean ceased.

Santiago Harbor, Cuba:

Forts at mouth of, shelled by American squadron, X, 169.

Spanish fleet in, X, 169.

Attempting to escape, destroyed by American squadron, X, 170. (See also Enc. Art., Santiago Harbor, Battle of.)

Thanks of President tendered officers and men of American squadron, X, 213.

Santiago Harbor, Cuba—Continued.

The *Merrimac* sunk in, by Lieut. Hobson, X, 158, 169.

Naval Cadet Powell to be made ensign for attempting to rescue force of, X, 159.

Thanks of President to Lieut. Hobson and promotion of, recommended, X, 159.

Santo Domingo, or Dominican Republic.—A Republic occupying the eastern portion of the island of Haiti. It is often called San Domingo and sometimes the Black Republic. The surface is irregularly broken by mountains, and in the center is an extensive elevated plain. The inhabitants are of mixed Spanish, Indian, and negro blood, with some pure Africans. The language is principally Spanish, though French and English are spoken. The principal religion is the Roman Catholic, but other sects are tolerated. The principal industries are agriculture, stock raising, and timber cutting. Sugar, coffee, hides, and fine-grained woods are exported. It was separated from the remainder of Haiti by a revolution which ended with the establishment of the Republic in 1844. Between 1861 and 1865 it was under the dominion of Spain. The present constitution dates from 1887. Executive authority is vested in a President, who is elected every 4 years, and the Congress is composed of 22 members elected by restricted suffrage. The Republic claims an area of 18,045 sq. miles, and the population is estimated at 610,000. The desirability of a coaling station for United States vessels at Santo Domingo led to a movement in 1869 looking toward the annexation of that Republic to the United States. President Grant sent Gen. Babcock to make an investigation into the condition of the Republic and the American interests there. Upon his making a favorable report a treaty was concluded Nov. 29, 1869, providing for annexation of the island and the leasing of Samana Bay and peninsula. The Senate rejected the treaty June 30, 1870. Grant persisted in spite of the unpopularity of the scheme and Congress concurred in sending a second commission to examine the matter in 1871. They also reported favorably, but Congress still disapproved of annexation, and President Grant abandoned the enterprise in a special message, Apr. 5, 1871 (VII, 128).

Santo Domingo:

Annexation of, to United States—

Discussed by President—

Grant, VII, 52, 61, 99, 128, 222, 411.

Johnson, VI, 688.

Report of Secretary of State on, transmitted, VII, 118.

Treaty for, submitted, VII, 46, 61.

Failure of ratification of, discussed, VII, 99, 222, 411.

President declines to communicate privileges relating to, VII, 58.

Referred to, VII, 52, 128.

Views of Cabral on, communicated to Senate, VII, 117.

Application of, to United States to exercise protectorate over, referred to, VII, 239.

River Railroad. After destroying the supplies there Heintzelman moved south across the swamp. Magruder, in pursuit, finding Fair Oaks abandoned, advanced to Savages Station and made an attack on Sumner's corps in the afternoon. The latter maintained his ground till dark. During the night he retreated into the White Oak Swamp, leaving 2,500 sick and wounded in the hospital at the station.

Savannah (Ga.), British Occupation of.—Nov. 27, 1778, Commodore Hyde Parker convoyed a fleet of transports to Savannah which carried about 3,500 British soldiers. The troops landed at Tybee Island, 15 miles from Savannah, and captured the city Dec. 29. The American force under Gen. Robert Howe consisted of about 800 Continentals and 400 militia. The British loss was officially reported as 3 killed and 10 wounded. Eighty-three American dead and 11 wounded were found on the field. Some 450 were taken prisoners, while the others retreated up the Savannah River and reached South Carolina. Forty-eight cannon, 23 mortars, 94 barrels of powder, and a large quantity of provisions fell into the hands of the British.

Savannah (Ga.), Fall of. (See Fort McAllister, Ga.)

Savannah (Ga.), Siege of.—In 1779 Washington sent Gen. Lincoln to take command of the army in the South, and requested Count d'Estaing, in command of the French fleet in American waters, to cooperate in an effort to retake Savannah, Ga. Sept. 16, 1779, the latter appeared off Savannah with 33 vessels and 6,000 men. After the capture of 2 frigates and 2 storeships a regular siege was commenced by the allies. The city was defended by a force of about 3,000 British troops under Gen. Prevost. On the morning of Oct. 9, 1779, about 3,500 French and 850 Americans advanced to the attack. The fighting was fierce for nearly an hour, when the assailants gave way after a loss of nearly 1,000 men. Count Pulaski was killed and Count d'Estaing was wounded. The loss to the garrison was only 55 in killed and wounded. Next to Bunker Hill this fight was the bloodiest of the war.

Savannah River, survey of, referred to, II, 565.

Savings Banks. (See Banks, Savings.)

Saxberry, Edson, act for relief of, vetoed, VIII, 707.

Saxony.—A Kingdom of the German Empire, bounded on the north and east by Prussia, on the south by Bohemia, and on the west by Saxe-Altenburg, Saxe-Weimar-Eisenach, and Reuss. It is noted for its rich mines of coal, silver, tin, lead, iron, etc. It manufactures extensively machinery, tools, porcelain, glass, etc. The government is a hereditary constitutional monarchy, administered by a King, an upper chamber, and a lower chamber of 82 deputies. Saxony sends 4 representatives to the Bundesrath and 23 to the Reichstag. It entered the North German Confederation in 1866 and became a State of the German Empire in 1871. Area, 5,787 sq. miles; population (1895), 3,787,688,

of Philadelphia, was appointed to submit designs. Sir John Prestwich, an English antiquarian, suggested a design to John Adams in 1779. It was not until June 20, 1782, however, that a seal was adopted. This was by the Congress of the Confederation. It was a combination of the various designs of Barton and Prestwich, and consisted of: Arms—Paleways of 13 pieces argent and gules; a chief azure; the escutcheon on the breast of the American eagle displayed proper, holding in his dexter talon an olive branch and in his sinister a bundle of 13 arrows and in his beak a scroll with the motto *E Pluribus Unum* (out of many, one). Crest—A glory *or* (gold) breaking through a cloud proper and surrounding 13 stars, forming a constellation *argent* (silver) on an azure field. Reverse—A pyramid unfinished, symbolizing the strength and growth of the States; in the zenith an eye in a triangle surrounded with a glory proper; over the eye, around the rim, the words *Annuis coeptis* (God has favored the undertaking); beneath the pyramid MDCCLXXVI and the words *Novus ordo sæclorum* (a new order of things). This seal has never been changed, and is in charge of the Secretary of State. Accompanying the report, and adopted by Congress, was the following remarks and explanation: "The escutcheon is composed of the chief and pale, the two most honorable ordinaries. The pieces pales represent the several States all joined in one solid compact entire, supporting a chief, which unites the whole and represents Congress. The motto alludes to this union. The pales in the arms are kept closely united by the chief, and the chief depends on that union and the strength resulting from it for its support, to denote the confederacy of the United States of America and the preservation of their union through Congress. The colors of the pales are those used in the flag of the United States of America; white signifies purity and innocence; red, hardiness and valor; and blue, the color of the chief, signifies vigilant perseverance and justice. The olive branch and arrows denote the power of peace and war, which is exclusively vested in Congress. The constellation denotes a new State taking its place and rank among other sovereign powers. The escutcheon is borne on the breast of an American eagle without any other supporters, to denote that the United States of America ought to rely on their own virtue. The pyramid on the reverse signifies strength and duration. The eye over it and the motto allude to the many signal interpositions of Providence in favor of the American cause. The date underneath is that of the Declaration of Independence, and the words under it signify the beginning of the new American era which commences from that date."

Seamen, American:
Captured by Tripolitans, I, 368.
Impressment of, by—
    Chile, V, 239.
    Foreign powers, X, 40.

Seamen, American—Continued.
Impressment of, by—
    Great Britain, I, 395, 442, 510; II, 368; IV, 163; X, 36, 42, 55.
        Account of J. B. Cutting for expenditures incurred in liberating, I, 116, and X, 120.
        Refusal to deliver up, referred to, X, 51.
        Transferred from British ships to Dartmoor prison referred to, X, 55.
    Maltreatment of, on ships plying between New York and Aspinwall, VI, 212.
    Number of, on vessels referred to, I, 386.
    Outrages committed upon, by pirates in West Indies and Gulf of Mexico, II, 196.
    Protection for, measure providing, proposed, X, 201.
    Relief of—
        Agent appointed for, I, 200.
        Appropriation for, recommended, I, 487.
        Convention with Japan regarding shipwrecked seamen, VII, 609.
        In foreign ports, report on, transmitted, X, 61.
        Provision for, I, 355.
            Recommended, X, 186.
        When discharged abroad recommended, I, 343.
    Shipment and discharge of, or payment of extra wages to, referred to, VIII, 153.
Seamew, The, satisfaction due for detention of, admitted by Great Britain, IV, 258.
Seaport Towns, protection for. (See Defenses, Public, provision for.)
Search, Right of. (See Right of Search.)
Seat of Government:
    Boundaries of, referred to and proclaimed, I, 94, 200, 202.
    Removal of, from Philadelphia to Washington, I, 291, 305, 308, 309, 310.
Seaver, William, proclamation offering reward for murderer of, II, 94.
Seavey, Stephen A., act granting pension to, vetoed, VIII, 699.
Seawell, Washington, major in Army, nomination of, and reasons therefor, IV, 517.
Sebois River referred to, II, 565.
Secession.—The act of going aside or withdrawing, as from a religious or political organization. The word has received world-wide notoriety from its use in connection with the secession of certain of the United States from the Union in 1860 and 1861. After the adoption of the Constitution of 1787 the idea of the sovereignty of the individual States remained familiar to the minds of many Americans. The Federalists of New England made threats of secession in 1811 and 1814, and secession was generally looked upon as an available remedy for Federal aggression. This claim has been advanced, directly or indirectly, by many of the States in turn, and has on such occasions usually been condemned by the others as treasonable. It was involved in or explicitly put forward by the Kentucky Resolutions, the Hartford Convention, and the South Carolina Nullification Ordinance (q. v.). While Jefferson condemned "scission," some of his writings admitted it to be a remedy of

Index

the last resort. As agitation against slavery became more intense secession was looked upon as the right and destiny of the Southern States. South Carolina was ready to secede in 1850. The Nullification Ordinance of 1832 and other measures passed by that State were early steps in that direction. Gen. Jackson, then President, felt that such a power lodged in a State would be fatal to the Union and altogether unconstitutional. His emphatic opposition, as expressed in his military preparations, as well as in his strong message and proclamation on nullification in 1833 (II, 610, 640), checked this feeling for a time, but the postponement to a final test was perhaps chiefly due to the unpopularity of the nullification doctrine among the States-rights people themselves. Another reason why the South Carolina nullification movement was stopped was the adoption by Congress of the Clay-Calhoun compromise tariff bill, which gave satisfaction to the nullifiers and their States-rights friends in the South who did not accept nullification as a rightful or expedient remedy. The secession doctrine was revived on the election of Lincoln in 1860. Many of the Southern people felt that the triumph of the Republican party meant the adoption of a policy of such interference with the institution of slavery as to make it impossible for the Southern States any longer to secure and enjoy their constitutional rights within the Union. Accordingly, Dec. 20, 1860, after the election of Lincoln, South Carolina, by convention, passed an ordinance repealing her adoption of the Constitution in 1788 and reviving her independence. Mississippi seceded Jan. 9, 1861; Florida, Jan. 10; Alabama, Jan. 11; Georgia, Jan. 19; Louisiana, Jan. 26; Texas, Feb. 1; Virginia, Apr. 17; Arkansas, May 6; North Carolina, May 20; Tennessee, June 8, all by conventions. Opposition to secession in many States was based rather upon the ground of inexpediency than unconstitutionality. The National Government never recognized the validity of the ordinances of secession adopted by the Southern States.

Secession, right of States regarding, discussed by President—
Buchanan, V, 628, 655.
Lincoln, VI, 5, 20.

Secret Lodges, proclamation against lawless incursions of, on northern frontier, IV, 72.

Secretaries.—By a series of acts passed in the early part of 1781 Congress organized the Government under several Departments, at the head of which were placed secretaries with duties similar to those of the secretaries of the British Government. The Secretary of the Navy was originally the Secretary of the Marine. The Secretary of the Treasury was originally the Superintendent of Finance. Now all the heads of Departments, 8 in number, are denominated secretaries, except the Attorney-General and the Postmaster-General.

Secretaries. (See the several Department Secretaries.)

Seddon, James A., secretary of war of Confederate States, mentioned, VI, 599.

Sedition Law.—In 1798, when war between the United States and France was imminent, there were in the United States by estimate 30,000 Frenchmen organized into clubs, and 50,000 sympathizers with France who had been English subjects. Many of the newspapers of the country at the time were controlled by aliens, mostly French, English, Irish, and Scotch refugees. Those alien residents who sympathized with France—the larger number—attacked the Government fiercely through the press for its attitude toward that country. In order to restrain this feeling, which excited bitter animosity among those Americans who resented the French attitude toward the United States, the Federalists in control of Congress passed the famous alien and sedition acts. The sedition act of July 14, 1798, was modeled on two English acts of 1795. It provided heavy fines and imprisonment for any who should combine or conspire against the operations of the Government, or should write, print, or publish any "false, scandalous, and malicious writings" against it or either House of Congress or the President, with intent to bring contempt upon them or to stir up sedition. This, as well as the alien act, was regarded by the Republican party as unconstitutional and subversive of the liberty of press and speech. They called forth the Virginia and Kentucky resolutions (q.v.). The sedition act expired in 1801. (See also Alien and Sedition Laws.)

Seed Distribution:
Act making special, in drought-stricken counties in Texas vetoed, VIII, 557.
Recommendations regarding, IX, 456, 550, 739.

Seigniorage:
Act for coinage of, vetoed, IX, 483.
Discussed, IX, 443.

Seizures. (See Vessels, United States.)

Selbach, Mary A., act granting pension to, vetoed, VIII, 836.

Selden, Withers & Co., reimbursement of Indians on account of failure of, recommended, V, 303.

Selfridge, Thomas O., jr., report of, on condition of Dominican Republic transmitted, VII, 55.

Sells, Elijah, treaty with Indians concluded by, VI, 394.

Seminaries of Learning (see also Education; National University):
Establishment of, discussed and recommended, I, 485; II, 312.
Power to establish, should be conferred upon Congress, II, 18.

Seminole Indians.—A tribe of the Muskhogean stock of Indians. The tribal name is translated to mean "renegade" or "separatist," and refers to their having separated from the Creek confederacy during the latter part of the eighteenth and the early part of the nineteenth centuries and settled in Florida. During the War of 1812 the British were materially aided by the Seminoles, and in 1817-18 they made many depredations on the settlements of Georgia and Alabama. By a treaty ratified in 1834 they ceded all their lands in the eastern part of the United States to the General Government and agreed to move to the Indian Territory. Their refusal to comply with the terms of this treaty led to a long and bloody war. (See Seminole Wars.) The number of Seminoles finally removed in 1843 was officially reported as 3,824. They became one of the five civilized nations of the Indian Territory. In 1898, including negroes and adopted whites, they numbered some 3,000.

Seminole Wars.—After the War of 1812 the combined British and Indian stronghold known as the Negro Fort, on the Appalachicola River, was a constant menace to the Georgia settlers. During 1817 there were several massacres of whites. Gen. E. P. Gaines was intrusted with the task of subjugating the Indians. He destroyed an Indian village on the refusal of the inhabitants to surrender certain murderers, and the Indians retaliated by waylaying a boat ascending the Appalachicola with supplies for Fort Scott and killing 34 men and a number of women. Gen. Jackson took the field against the Indians in January, 1818, and in a sharp campaign of 6 months defeated them completely, destroying their villages and driving them from every stronghold. Among the prisoners taken were two English subjects, Arbuthnot and Ambrister, who were charged with inciting the Indians to hostilities. These were tried by court-martial and hanged. Jackson pursued the Indians into Florida, which was then Spanish territory, captured Pensacola and St. Marks, deposed the Spanish government, and set up an American administration. This territory was later returned to Spain, but the outgrowth of the incident was the cession of Florida to the United States in satisfaction of the latter's claims, and the payment to Spain besides of $5,000,000. The second Seminole war was the most stubborn and bloody of all the Indian wars. It originated in the refusal of part of the tribe to cede their lands to the whites and remove to the Indian Territory. Osceola, one of the chiefs opposed to immigration, was placed in irons by Gen. Thompson, an agent of the United States. Osceola regained his liberty, killed Thompson and others at Fort King, and cut to pieces a body of troops. Operations against Osceola and his warriors were conducted with great severity, but with varying success, under Scott, Call, Jesup, Taylor, and others. The Indians were supposed to be subjugated in 1837, but Osceola fled and renewed the struggle. He was taken by treachery in 1842, and the war ended.

Senate.—The name "senate" was first applied to a branch of the American legislative system by the Virginia constitution of 1776. It was later adopted by all those States whose legislatures were organized in two branches. In some States senates were elected by voters having a higher property qualification than the electors of the lower house. In the deliberations of the Convention of 1787 the Federal upper house was at first designated as the "second branch." The name "senate" first appears in the report of the committee of detail on Aug. 6. One of the most important compromises in the Constitution was that proposed by Dr. Franklin, which harmonized the conflicting interests of large and small States by arranging that while Representatives should be apportioned according to population each State should have 2 Senators, chosen by the State legislature for a term of 6 years. In 1789 the Senate was divided by lot into three classes, one class retiring every 2 years. Until 1794 the Senate sat with closed doors. The executive of a State has the power to make a temporary appointment of a Senator if a vacancy should occur in that State during the recess of its legislature. Senators must be at least 30 years of age and be for 9 years citizens of the United States. The Vice-President of the United States is President of the Senate, but has no vote except in case of a tie. Besides its legislative function the Senate exercises the powers of a high court of impeachment. It ratifies or rejects all treaties made by the President with foreign powers, a two-thirds vote of the Senate being necessary for ratification. The consent of the Senate is necessary to appointments to the higher Federal offices. The election of Senators was not governed by any Federal law until 1866, when an act was passed providing for the present mode of election. In case the electors fail to make a choice the Senate elects the Vice-President of the United States from the two highest on the list of those voted for.

Senate. (See Congress.)

Senatorial Courtesy.—In order that the dignity of the body may be preserved, the Senate gives considerable attention to the personal wishes of its members. In addition to the observance of courteous address, polite language, and the exercise of those acts of kindness which tend to lighten official duties and render social life a pleasure, there is a tacit understanding as to the conventional privileges to be accorded each in the official deliberations. Should the name of any former member of the Senate be presented to that body by the President for their advice as to his appointment to a Federal office, Senatorial courtesy requires immediate confirmation without reference to a committee. The privilege of speaking as long as he may choose on any question before the Senate is a courtesy granted each Senator, and though it is charged that undue advantage has sometimes been taken of this privilege it has never been abridged. There is no previous question provided in the rules of the Senate.

Senators of United States:

Appointments to office, relation of, to. (See Executive Nominations.)

Constitutional amendment regarding election of, recommended, VI, 642, 691.

Loyal Representatives and, denial of seats in Congress to, discussed, VI, 446.

Seneca Indians.—A tribe of the Iroquois confederacy of Indians. The name is foreign to the language of the tribe, and is probably a corruption of a word meaning "red paint." They called themselves by a name meaning "people of the mountain." When first known they occupied lands in western New York between Seneca Lake and the Genesee River. They allied themselves with Pontiac, destroyed Venango, attacked Fort Niagara, and cut off an army train near Devils Hole in 1763. They were conspicuous in the wars west of Lake Erie. On the defeat of the Erie and Neuter tribes they took possession of the territory westward to Lake Erie and southward along the Allegheny River into Pennsylvania, receiving by adoption many of the conquered tribes, which act made them the largest tribe of the Iroquois confederacy. They sided with the British in the Revolutionary War, and their territory was devastated by the Americans. Peace was made with them in 1784. In the War of 1812 the tribe divided, those in New York taking part with the Americans and those in Ohio joining the hostile Western tribes. These were removed to the Indian Territory in 1831, the friendly tribes remaining in New York. In 1893 they numbered about 3,000.

Seneca Indians:

Conveyance made by, II, 374.

Memorial from, referred to, IV, 428.

Money held in trust for, II, 456.

Portion of, opposed to treaty of Buffalo, III, 567.

Remonstrance of, against allotment of lands in severalty to, VIII, 81.

Treaty with, I, 211, 259, 347, 554, 569; II, 21, 47, 542, 561, 634; IV, 157; V, 296; VI, 518; VII, 47; X, 51.

Serbia. (See Servia.)

Sergeant, John, nomination of, as minister to Panama, II, 320.

Sérurier, M., correspondence regarding claims against France. (See France, claims against.)

Servia.—A Kingdom of the Balkan Peninsula, in southeastern Europe. It is bounded on the north by Austria-Hungary (separated by the Save and Danube), on the east by Roumania (separated by the Danube) and Bulgaria, on the south by Turkey and Bosnia, and on the west by Bosnia (separated in part by the Drina). The surface is mountainous. Agriculture is the chief industry. The government is a constitutional hereditary monarchy. The Byzantine governors were expelled and the title of king assumed in the eleventh century. After being twice under Turkish dominion, Servia became practically independent in 1817. By uniting with Russia against Turkey in 1877-78 the territory of the Kingdom was extended. It has now an area of 19,050 sq. miles and a population (1895) of 2,312,484.

Servia:

Consular convention with, VIII, 40, 71.

Referred to, VIII, 170.

Diplomatic relations with, referred to, VII, 570; VIII, 131.

Treaty with, VIII, 71.

Servis, David A., act granting pension to, vetoed, VIII, 670.

Sessions of Congress. (See Extraordinary Sessions of Congress.)

Seven Days' Battles.—A series of battles fought in the Peninsular campaign, in the vicinity of Richmond, Va., between the Army of the Potomac, under McClellan, and the Confederate army under Lee. The first conflict occurred on June 25, 1862, and a battle was fought each succeeding day but one to July 1. June 25 McClellan's army before Richmond, numbering 115,102, received orders to advance. Lee's army on both sides of the Chickahominy aggregated 80,835. Hooker advanced beyond Fair Oaks and secured his ground. Meantime the Confederates had placed Richmond in a state of security and determined upon aggressive movements. Lee had succeeded Johnston in command, and it was determined to bring the mass of the army down the Chickahominy and threaten McClellan's communications with the York River. Jackson had moved out of the Shenandoah Valley and was at Hanover Court-House, ready to render what assistance might be required. Some Federal historians say that McClellan determined to change his base of operations to the

James River, 17 miles south of Fair Oaks. The writers on the Southern side deny this. The retreat was accomplished with a loss to the Federal Army of 15,249 men. The operations of the two armies are described under the headings Mechanicsville, Gaines Mill, Savages Station, Frayser's Farm, and Malvern Hill. A few weeks later the Federal army was withdrawn from the James and the Peninsular campaign was ended.

Seven Nations. (See Cohnawaga Indians.)

Seven Pines and Fair Oaks (Va.), Battle of.— From Williamsburg to Richmond, Va., the distance is about 50 miles. By May 30, 1862, Casey's and Couch's divisions of Keyes's corps of McClellan's army had crossed the Chickahominy and advanced respectively to Fair Oaks and Seven Pines, 6 and 7 miles, respectively, from Richmond. Heintzelman's corps had also crossed and was encamped several miles to the rear of Couch on the Williamsburg road, and Sumner was ready to make the passage of the stream when a heavy rain, which occurred on the night of May 30, rendered this impracticable. Joseph E. Johnston, who was in command of the Confederate forces, sent Generals Longstreet, Huger, D. H. Hill, and Gustavus W. Smith to attack this advance guard of the invading army. The fighting began at 1 p. m. May 31. The Federals gradually fell back. At 4.30 the arrival of Sedgwick's division of Sumner's corps turned the tide of battle. At sunset Gen. Johnston was severely wounded by a piece of shell, and the command devolved upon Gen. Smith. In the morning the Confederates renewed the attack. They were finally repulsed about noon. The Confederates lost 4,233. The Federals lost 5,739, of whom 890 were killed. Gen. Lee assumed command of the Confederate army the day following the battle.

Sevier, Ambrose H., commissioner of United States to Mexico:
Illness prevents departure of, IV, 577.
Instructions to, referred to, IV, 687.
President declines to transmit instructions to, to House, IV, 602.

Sevier, John, brigadier-general of militia, nomination of, X, 13.

Sewall, Thomas, consul to Santiago, Cuba, nomination of, withdrawn and reasons therefor, V, 46.

Seward, Frederick W., Acting Secretary of State, VI, 708; VII, 448.

Seward, George F.:
Decree prohibiting steamers sailing under American flag from using channel on Yangtse River promulgated by, VI, 698, 704.
Minister to China, charges against, referred to, VII, 359.
Instructions to, concerning immigration referred to, VIII, 104.

Seward, William H.:
Correspondence regarding Dorr's Rebellion, IV, 298.
Death of, announced and honors to be paid memory of, VII, 183.

Seward, William H.—Continued.
Letters addressed by, to governors of certain States referred to, VIII, 615.
Negroes coming into Washington from Virginia arrested as fugitives, communication regarding, X, 108.
Secretary of State, VI, 14, 312.
Wounding of, by assassins announced, VI, 284, 285, 286.
Military commission to try persons implicated in, and proceedings of, VI, 334, 335, 336, 342, 347, 348.
Report on, referred to, VI, 594.
Reward offered for alleged instigators of, VI, 307.

Sewells Point, Va., evacuation of batteries on, referred to, VI, 112.

Sexton, Ellen, act granting pension to, vetoed, VIII, 680.

Seyfforth, Caroline, act granting pension to, vetoed, VIII, 705.

Shackerly, Peter, claims of orphan child of, III, 476.

Shadrach Case.— One of many exciting fugitive-slave cases of ante-bellum days. In May, 1850, Frederic Wilkins, a Virginia slave, made his escape and found his way to Boston, where he obtained employment under the name of Shadrach. Subsequently he was arrested and imprisoned in the United States court-house, pending trial. He was liberated by a body of colored people and assisted to Canada. Intense excitement prevailed in Boston, which spread over the entire country when Congress turned its attention to the infringement of the law. Clay introduced a resolution requesting the President to inform Congress of the facts in the case. President Fillmore issued a proclamation (V, 109) announcing the facts and calling upon the people to prevent future disturbances.

Shafter, William R.:
Army under, lands near Santiago, Cuba, X, 170.
Operations of, around and subsequent capitulation of Santiago, Cuba, X, 170.
Thanks of President tendered, X, 214, 216.

Shakespeare, N. O., appointed representative to foreign countries to investigate causes, cure, etc., of cholera, VIII, 317.
Report of, referred to, IX, 130.

Shannon, Thomas, act granting pension to, vetoed, VIII, 690.

Shannon, Wilson, mentioned, IV, 353.

Sharkey, William L., provisional governor of Mississippi, appointed, VI, 314.

Sharp, Solomon, authority to accept present from British officers referred to, VI, 203.

Sharpe, George H., report of, on assassination of President Lincoln and attempted assassination of Secretary Seward transmitted, VI, 594.

Sharpsburg (Md.), Battle of. (See Antietam (Md.), Battle of.)

Shawanese Indians, treaty with, X, 51.

Shawnee Indians.— A tribe of the Algonquian stock of Indians. From their wanderings and the difficulties of identification their real habitat is uncertain. They seem to have wandered

Sherman, William T.—Continued.

Confederate States, historical statement concerning public policy of executive departments of, filed by, VIII, 263.

Death of, announced and honors to be paid memory of, IX, 135, 165.

Increase in Army recommended by, VII, 376.

Lands set apart by, for refugees and freedmen referred to, VI, 351.

Mentioned, VI, 614, 618.

Report of, on conditions in Southern States, VI, 378.

Requested to proceed to Mexican frontier and communicate with American minister, VI, 443.

Referred to, VI, 456.

Thanks of President tendered, VI, 238.

Treaty with Indians concluded by, VI, 636.

Sherman Act.—A compromise financial measure introduced into Congress by Senator John Sherman, of Ohio, and passed July 14, 1890. It repealed the Bland-Allison Act of 1878 and directed the Secretary of the Treasury to purchase silver bullion to the amount of 4,500,000 ounces per month, at the market rate, issuing Treasury notes in payment therefor. These notes were to be redeemed in coin at the Treasury on demand. The act also directed the coinage each month of 2,000,000 ounces of the bullion into standard silver dollars. The repeal of the Sherman Act was frequently urged. In the summer of 1893 the law was claimed to be a leading cause of the business depression, and President Cleveland summoned Congress to meet in special session Aug. 7. Congress, after a long debate, passed Nov. 1 the Voorhees bill, repealing the silver-purchasing clause of the Sherman Act, but affirming bimetallism as a national policy.

Sherman Act:

Discussed, IX, 113, 193.

Repeal of purchasing clause of, discussed, IX, 443, 641, 642.

Recommended, IX, 401.

Shields, Thomas, arrest and imprisonment of, in Mexico, VIII, 85, 91, 105, 109.

Shilling.—The name of a coin in use in several European States, varying in its value. The English shilling is one-twentieth of a pound sterling, the Danish copper shilling is one ninety-sixth of a rixdaler, and equal to one-fourth of a penny of English money. The Swedish shilling is twice the value of the Danish. In some parts of Germany the shilling is used as a fractional coin of the value of 1 penny sterling. In America this coin was first issued from the mint at Boston. The first struck were known as the New England shilling, Willow Tree, Oak Tree, and Pine Tree coins. One of the earliest coins used in America was the Bermuda shilling. Lord Baltimore had shillings coined in London for use in Maryland. As money of account the shilling varied greatly in the Colonies.

Shiloh, or Pittsburg Landing (Tenn.), Battle of.—One of the most hotly contested battles of the Civil War. After the first line of Confederate defenses in the West had been broken by Grant, Gen. Beauregard was sent to establish another. He selected the line of the Memphis and Charleston Railroad. The Confederate army to the number of 45,000 was concentrated at Corinth, Miss., under command of Albert Sidney Johnston. Polk, Bragg, Hardee, and Breckenridge were there with their corps, and Van Dorn and Price were on the way from Arkansas with 30,000 more. After taking Fort Donelson, the Federal army under Grant proceeded up the Tennessee River to Pittsburg Landing, a point 219 miles from its mouth, on the west bank, near the intersection of the State lines of Alabama, Mississippi, and Tennessee, and about 20 miles from the Confederate camp at Corinth. Five divisions of Grant's army, under Generals W. T. Sherman, Hurlbut, W. H. L. Wallace, McClernand, and Prentiss, were here encamped, and, including Gen. Lew. Wallace's division, about 7 miles down the river, numbered 40,000 men. Buell's army of 40,000 was expected to reenforce them here, and it was the intention upon his arrival to proceed against Johnston at Corinth. The latter, however, without waiting for his own reenforcements, resolved to attack Grant before the arrival of Buell's forces. Apr. 3, 1862, Johnston marched his army from Corinth and on the 6th attacked the Federal army. After a day's hard fighting Grant's army was driven back from the vicinity of Shiloh Church nearly to the river, a distance of 3 miles. A part of the expected reenforcements arrived just in time to help to check the last charge of the victorious Confederates. The battle was reopened on the morning of the 7th by Buell, who had arrived during the night with 20,000 men. The second day's fighting was as stubborn as the first had been, but the Confederates were outnumbered. At 2 p.m. Beauregard ordered preparations made for the retreat, which by 4 o'clock was under way. He was not pursued. The casualties were: Confederates—killed, 1,728; wounded, 8,012; prisoners, 959; total, 10,699. Federals—killed, 1,735; wounded, 7,882; prisoners, 3,956; total, 13,573. Gen. Albert Sidney Johnston was killed on the first day of the battle and was succeeded by Gen. Beauregard in the command of the Confederate army.

Ship Canals. (See Canals.)

Ship Island, utility of forts on, for protection of Mississippi coast, IV, 416, 443.

Shipbuilding:

Consular returns on, in foreign countries referred to, V, 422.

Decline in American, discussed, VII, 246.

Encouragement to American, recommended, VII, 106, 301; VIII, 140; IX, 552.

Shipping, American. (See Commerce discussed.)

Ships of War. (See Vessels, United States.)

Shire.—A division of the Kingdom of Great Britain, dating back to the time of the Saxon invasion. It is now taken to mean almost the same as county, as most of the English county names terminate in the word shire. The shire

in the land of Canaan, bought a field for sepulture and paid for it in silver. But the best authorities state that the first regular coinage of either gold or silver was in Asia Minor, in Phrygia or Lydia. The Egyptians did not have coins in the earliest times, although otherwise their civilization was advanced. In ancient times silver was plentiful in Spain. Hannibal, it is stated, obtained 300 pounds per day from the mines there during the Carthagenian occupation of that country. At a much earlier day the Athenians had valuable silver mines at Laurium, in the territory of Attica. Silver, as well as gold, was employed by Hiram, King of Tyre, in the erection of Solomon's Temple at Jerusalem. Silver drinking cups and silver ornaments on horn or ivory drinking cups were in use among the Vikings. In fact, all the civilized and semicivilized nations and tribes of antiquity made free use of this metal. It was more common even then than gold, and therefore less precious. At a later period the Incas in Peru, the Toltecs and Aztecas in Mexico, and the Mayas in Yucatan employed it for ornamental purposes and for objects of utility, both in their temples and palaces. Among modern civilized and enlightened peoples its use is so common as to require no special remark. The metal itself is found in almost every part of the globe, usually in combination with other metals. Take the whole historical period and it is found that the South American mines are the richest. Mulhall is authority for the statement that Mexico has produced more silver since 1523 than any other country within the last 500 years. He values the total output there for the period at $3,050,000,000. Peru, he says, comes next with nearly $3,000,000,000 and is followed by the United States with $1,000,000,000 since 1849. The United States led the world in production in 1890 with $70,000,000, Mexico coming next with $50,000,000. Large masses have been found in nuggets, as one of 370 pounds at La Paz, Bolivia, in 1749; another of 560 pounds at Konigsberg, Norway, and still another of 800 pounds at Huantaya, Peru. Sonora, Mexico, however, claims to have extracted a huge lump of silver weighing 2,700 pounds. The ratio of silver to gold has varied greatly. 1000 B. C. it was 12 to 1, if the best figures obtainable are to be relied upon. At the Christian era it was 9 to 1. 500 A. D., just 24 years after the downfall of the Western Empire of Rome, the ratio was 18 to 1, but in 1100 A. D. it had fallen to 8 to 1. At the close of the seventeenth century it was 10 to 1, and at the end of the last century 15 to 1. In 1850 the ratio was 15.4 to 1; in 1879, 18.40 to 1; in 1893, 25.77 to 1. The subject has entered into American politics, the Democratic party in 1896 having declared for the free coinage of the metals at the former ratio of 16 to 1. The French ratio was at 15½ to 1. The repeal in 1873 of the law providing for the free and unlimited coinage of silver was the beginning of an agitation for the restoration of bimetallism, which has continued until the present day. (See also Bland-Allison Act; Coinage Laws; Sherman Act.)

Silver. (See Gold and Silver.)

Silver Certificates:
Discussed, IX, 39.
Repeal of act for issuance of, recommended, VIII, 46, 133.
Suspension of issuance of, recommended, VIII, 243.

Silver Coinage. (See Coins and Coinage.)

Simmons, James F., correspondence regarding Dorr's Rebellion, IV, 305.

Simpson, Edward, member of Gun Foundry Board, VIII, 161.

Simpson, Slingsby, vessel under, ordered from and forbidden to reenter waters of United States, I, 403.

Single Standard. (See Monometallism.)

Singletary, G. E., dismissal of, from volunteer regiment referred to, IV, 605.

Sinking Fund.—An account or fund set aside for the payment of a debt or obligation. It is formed by successively appropriating or setting aside sums for the designated purpose. Alexander Hamilton made an unsuccessful attempt under the Confederation to establish a sinking fund for the liquidation of the national debt. The first national sinking fund in this country was created by act of Congress Aug. 2, 1790. The present sinking fund to retire the national debt was established by an act of Feb. 25, 1862, and amended by later acts. It sets apart annually a special fund for the payment of interest on and for the purchase of a given per cent of the national debt. Bonds so redeemed are to be canceled and deducted from the outstanding indebtedness of the Government. In addition there is to be purchased annually an amount of Government bonds equal to the annual interest on bonds previously bought for the sinking fund. The sinking fund is thus, as far as interest is concerned, in the position of any other holder of the Government's obligations receiving interest on the bonds that have been purchased for its account, except that the bonds belonging to it have been canceled and the debt is considered reduced by that amount. An act of Apr. 17, 1876, provides that fractional currency redeemed by the Treasury shall constitute a part of the sinking fund.

Sinking Fund, repeal of law recommended, IX. 319.

Sioune Indians, treaty with, II, 346.

Sioux City, Iowa, acts for erection of public building at, vetoed, VIII, 430, 716.

Sioux Commission:
Discussed, IX, 45.
Report of, discussed, IX, 61.

Sioux, or Dakota, Indians.—The principal division of the Siouan stock of Indians. The name is translated to mean "The snakelike ones." The early habitat of the Siouan family included parts of British America and the following States and Territories: Montana, Wyoming, the Dakotas, Minnesota, Iowa, Wisconsin, Nebraska, Kansas, Missouri, Oklahoma, Indian

Territory, Mississippi, Kentucky, the Carolinas, and Virginia. The Dakotas, generally known as the Sioux, have always been the most warlike of the stock. They have been hostile not only to whites and to Indians of other stocks, but also to tribes of their own stock. The principal divisions of the family are the Dakota, Dhegiha, Tciwere, Winnebago, Mandan, Hidatsa, Tutelo, Biloxi, and Kataba. The present number of the Siouan stock is nearly 45,000, about 2,000 of whom are in British America. The Sioux proper, or Dakotas, are divided into 7 council fires, and they are sometimes known by an Indian name signifying that fact. They aided the English in 1812. In 1837 they ceded all their lands east of the Mississippi to the Government and in 1851 made further grants. In 1854 they engaged in war against the whites, but were subjugated in 1855. In 1862 a general Sioux uprising occurred, in which many whites and Indians were killed. They were defeated and scattered by Government troops, and a treaty was made with them by Gen. Sherman in 1868. Nevertheless, Sitting Bull and some of the other chieftains were unreconciled. June 25, 1876, Gen. Custer and 276 men were surprised by a force of 9,000 Sioux on the Little Big Horn River, Montana, and massacred. (See also Custer Massacre.)

Sioux Indians:
Agreement with, for purchase of lands discussed, IX, 63.
  Proclaimed, IX, 272.
Commission to treat with, for—
  Cession of lands, IX, 45, 61.
  Modifications of treaties, VIII, 155.
Concessions obtained from, referred to, VII, 414.
Hostile demonstrations of, referred to, VII, 373.
Lands of—
  Opening of, to settlement refused by, VIII, 796.
  Relinquished to United States, IX, 45.
Outbreak among, discussed, IX, 201.
Pursuit of hostile bands of, into Hudsons Bay territories referred to, VI, 198.
Removal of, to—
  Indian Territory, VII, 413.
  Nebraska, VI, 389.
Report on condition of, transmitted, VI, 699.
Right of way for railroad through reservation of, VIII, 188, 193.
Sioux expedition referred to, V, 379.
Treaty with, II, 321, 322, 347; III, 265, 280, 395; IV, 59, 152; V, 26, 171, 485, 533; VI, 375, 700, 703.
  Reasons for concluding, IV, 59.
War with. (See Sioux Wars.)

Sioux Reservation:
Division of portion of, into separate reservations proclaimed, IX, 94.
Compensation to, for losses sustained in, referred to, IX, 133.
Lands granted to Chicago, Milwaukee and St. Paul Railway Co. declared forfeited by proclamation, IX, 512.
Purchase of portion of, recommended, VIII, 250.

M P—VOL X—38

Sioux Reservation—Continued.
Restoration of, to public domain, order regarding, declared void, VIII, 305.
  Discussed, VIII, 358.
Right of way for railroad through, VIII, 188, 193.
Sioux Wars discussed, VI, 132; VII, 406; IX, 201.
Sir Robert Peel, The, outrages committed on, III, 478.
Sisseton Indians, VI, 470.
Sitgreave, Samuel, commissioner of United States, nomination of, I, 300.
Sitka, Alaska, port of entry, order regarding, VI, 667.
Sitting Bull:
Disturbances caused by, discussed, VII, 624.
Surrender of, discussed, VIII, 38, 50.
Six Nations of Indians.—A confederation of the Indian tribes of the Huron-Iroquois family. They originally occupied the territory now included in New York State and southern Canada. The five original nations were the Mohawks, Senecas, Cayugas, Oneidas, and Onondagas. In 1712 the Tuscaroras, a branch of the Iroquois living in North Carolina, returned northward after their defeat by the white colonists, and joined their kindred. The confederation then became known as the Six Nations.

Six Nations of Indians:
Conference with, I, 111, 174; II, 82.
Depredations of, I, 65, 68, 69, 82, 84, 86.
Negotiations with, I, 338.
Opinion of Senate concerning treaty with, requested, I, 62.
Referred to, I, 155.
Treaty with, I, 62, 106, 167.
Skagit Indians, treaty with, V, 379.
Skai-wha-mish Indians, treaty with, V, 379.
Skerrett, Joseph S., mentioned, IX, 466.
Skipwith, Fulwar, consul-general to France, nomination of, and reasons therefor, I, 178.
S'Klallams Indians, treaty with, V, 380.
Skope-áhmish Indians, treaty with, V, 379.
Sk-táh-le-jum Indians, treaty with, V, 379.
Sk-táhl-mish Indians, treaty with, V, 379.
Slacum, George W., report of, relating to African slave trade transmitted, IV, 418.
Slaughter, William B., mentioned, III, 51.
Slaughterhouse Cases.—A series of 5 cases bearing upon the creation of monopolies or trusts and defining the scope of the fourteenth amendment. The Crescent City Live Stock, Landing and Slaughterhouse Co. was incorporated by the Louisiana legislature Mar. 8, 1869. The Butchers' Benevolent Association protested against this act of the legislature on the ground that it created a monopoly. Suit was brought against the State by Paul Esteben and others on the ground that their business was injured. It was claimed by the plaintiffs that the creation of a monopoly of this sort by the State legislature was in violation of the fourteenth amendment to the Constitution, which prohibits State legislatures from enforcing laws "which shall abridge the privileges or immunities of the citizens of the United

States." The supreme court of Louisiana decided that the law did not conflict with the amendment to the Constitution. The Supreme Court of the United States, Apr. 14, 1873, and Jan. 24, 1887, affirmed the decision. In these celebrated cases the Supreme Court likewise decided that the fundamental character of the Government had not been changed in any way by the Civil War. The judgment of the supreme court of Louisiana was not entirely affirmed in the last case mentioned—that of the Crescent Live Stock Co. *vs.* Butchers' Union. That part which constituted a judgment against the Crescent City Live Stock, Landing and Slaughterhouse Co. solely, for damages for the malicious prosecution, was reversed and the case remanded for further proceedings. In that case Justice Matthews delivered the opinion, and there was no dissenting opinion. In the other cases Justice Miller rendered the court's judgment. Justice Field, for himself and Justices Swayne and Bradley, delivered a dissenting opinion.

Slave Representation.— One of the most difficult problems encountered by the framers of the Constitution was the representation to be accorded in Congress to those portions of the country whose population consisted partly of slaves. It was contended, on the one hand, that, being persons, they should be represented, and, on the other hand, that, being property, they should be made the object of taxation. A compromise was finally reached providing that for purposes of reckoning a State's proportion of Representatives, as well as its direct taxes, its population should be "determined by adding to the whole number of free persons, including those bound to service for a term of years, and excluding Indians not taxed, three-fifths of all other persons"— i. e., slaves. This method of computing population was first suggested in 1783 by the Continental Congress as a basis for the apportionment of contributions from the States, to be agreed upon as an amendment to the Articles of Confederation. It remained in force until the abolition of slavery.

Slave Trade. (See African Slave Trade.)

Slavery.—A slave is defined as a person who is the chattel or property of another and is wholly subject to his will. Slavery probably originated at an early period of the world's history in the accident of capture in war. It existed in all the ancient Oriental nations of which we have any record. In the Homeric poems it was the ordinary destiny of prisoners of war. The prevalence of Christianity tended to ameliorate the condition of the slave. Laws respecting the sale of slaves in England were made by Alfred the Great. The English peasantry were commonly sold for slaves in Saxon and Norman times; children were sold in Bristol market like cattle for exportation, many being sent to Ireland and Scotland. In 1574 Queen Elizabeth ordered her bondsmen in the western counties made free at easy rates, and in 1660 serfdom was finally extinguished in England. By the decision of Lord Mansfield, of the court of King's bench, in the Sommersett case (q. v.) slavery was declared illegal in England. In Scotland bondage to the soil was not gotten rid of until the close of the last century. Parliament abolished trade in negro slaves in 1807, and in 1833 an act was passed abolishing slavery throughout the British colonies. In pursuance of this act 770,280 negroes became free Aug. 1, 1834. About the time of the American Revolution societies of prominent men were formed for the purpose of ameliorating the condition of the negro slaves. Pennsylvania was the first State to organize such a society, in 1787, with Benjamin Franklin as president. New York followed with a similar society, John Jay as its first president and Alexander Hamilton as its second. Immediately after came Rhode Island and Maryland, in 1789, with such members as Samuel Chase and Luther Martin; Delaware, with James A. Bayard and C. A. Rodney; Connecticut, in 1790; Virginia, 1791, and New Jersey in 1792. The most that was accomplished by these societies was the suppression of the slave trade in 1808. Pennsylvania provided for the gradual emancipation of her slaves in 1780; Massachusetts, by a bill of rights prefixed to her constitution, the same year; New Hampshire, by her constitution, and Connecticut and Rhode Island by enactment, in 1784; Vermont, by her constitution, and New York and New Jersey by gradual abolition, the former in 1799 and the latter in 1804. In 1817 New York enacted further legislation, decreeing total abolition on July 4, 1827. By this law 10,000 slaves were freed. Following are some of the important steps leading to the Civil War in America, by which the institution of slavery was finally abolished: Passage of the ordinance for the government of the territory northwest of the Ohio containing the unalterable article forbidding slavery, 1787; Quakers present a petition to Congress praying for the abolition of slavery, 1794; important debate in Congress on the abolition of the slave trade, 1806; slave trade abolished, 1808; American Colonization Society organized at Washington to aid emigration to Africa, 1816; Missouri Compromise passed by Congress, 1820; antislavery societies organized in New York and Pennsylvania, 1833; passage of fugitive-slave law and compromise measures, 1850; negroes seized at Boston under fugitive-slave law, 1851; passage of Kansas-Nebraska bill, 1854; repealing of the Missouri Compromise; Kansas war, 1854; Dred Scott decision, 1857; John Brown's insurrection, 1859; election of Lincoln to the Presidency, 1860; secession of South Carolina, December, 1860, followed by other States in 1861; President Lincoln proclaims the abolition of slavery in all parts of the country in rebellion, Jan. 1, 1863 (VI, 157); submission of the Southern armies in April, 1865, and official announcement of the final abolition of slavery Dec. 18, 1865.

court of chancery of Great Britain $515,169, which was increased by investment to $703,000. After the discussion of numerous plans, Congress in 1846 created the present establishment. The Institution has devoted itself to the two lines of work marked out in the terms of the bequest—the prosecution of original research and the publication and distribution of memoirs on subjects relating to science. During its existence it has originated many important scientific undertakings, which have later been taken up by the Government and prosecuted on broader lines under the control of special bureaus, some under the direction of the Institution, others independently. Out of its meteorological service the Weather Bureau has grown; in connection with its work in ichthyology the Fish Commission was established. Under the direction of the Institution are the National Museum, which is the legal custodian of all Government collections, the Bureau of International Exchanges, the Bureau of American Ethnology, the Astro-Physical Observatory, and the Zoological Park. The Institution has a library of 150,000 volumes. The direction of the affairs of the Institution is vested in a Board of Regents, consisting of the Chief Justice, the Vice-President, 3 Senators, 3 Representatives, and 6 other citizens, 2 of whom shall reside in Washington. The President of the United States and his Cabinet are members of the Institution. The Secretary is elected by the Board of Regents. Joseph Henry, the first Secretary, served from the founding of the Institution, in 1846, till his death, in 1878; he was succeeded by Spencer F. Baird, and upon the latter's death, in 1887, Samuel P. Langley was placed in charge of the work. The Institution is located in Washington City, and occupies an ornate building of Seneca brown stone, situated in a prominent place in the Mall, which extends from the Capitol to the Washington Monument.

Smithsonian Institution:

Bequest to United States by James Smithson for founding, III, 187.

    Fulfillment of objects of, suggested, III, 506; IV, 89, 271.

    Prosecution of claim to, referred to, III, 430, 506.

    Referred to, III, 271.

Medium for interchange of official publications, VIII, 131.

Organization of, recommended, V, 218.

Request of regents of, for appropriation for National Museum commended, VII, 479, 506.

Smoke Abatement Exhibition at London referred to, VIII, 108.

Smuggling.—In the United States the offense of smuggling is defined as "the act, with intent to defraud, of bringing into the United States, or, with like intent, attempting to bring into the United States, dutiable articles without passing the same, or the package containing the same, through the custom-house or submitting them to the officers of the revenue for examination." The penalties which may be

enforced are a fine of not less than $50 nor more than $5,000, or imprisonment for not more than 2 years, or both, seizure and condemnation of the vessel or vehicle used, and various other special penalties. The British navigation laws of the latter part of the seventeenth and the first half of the eighteenth centuries induced bold and extensive smuggling into the Colonies. Merchants and prominent public men otherwise respectable felt no hesitation about cheating the revenue by illicit trade with pirates and West Indian merchants. New York was the principal port for smugglers, though Boston, Philadelphia, and Charleston were also enriched by smuggled goods. This led the British Government to enforce the acts of trade which did much to precipitate the Revolution.

Smuggling:

Pernicious practice of, should be prevented, II, 75.

Practice of, criminal in free governments, I, 495.

Snake Indians, treaty with, VI, 381.

Sno-ho-mish Indians, treaty with, V, 379.

Snoquálmoo Indians, treaty with, V, 379.

Soc Indians, treaty with, II, 322; X, 66.

Socialistic Labor Party.—In 1883 a congress of socialists met in Baltimore and organized a national party. A manifesto was issued, setting forth their demands and principles. They held their first national convention in New York City Aug. 28, 1892, and nominated Simon Wing, of Massachusetts, for President and Charles H. Matchett, of New York, for Vice-President. In 1896 the party polled only 36,274 votes for Matchett, its Presidential candidate.

Society of American Florists, act incorporating, vetoed, IX, 578.

Society of Army of the Cumberland, statue of Gen. Garfield to be erected in Washington by, VIII, 208.

    Unveiling ceremonies, order regarding, VIII, 577.

Society of Friends:

Management of Indians committed to, VII, 38, 109, 152, 200, 252, 300, 353.

Paper to President from, on Indian affairs, referred to, VII, 121.

Society of the Cincinnati. (See Cincinnati, Society of the.)

Soldiers' Home:

Erection of, recommended, V, 21, 88.

Recommendations of board of commissioners regarding, VIII, 190.

Site for, selected, V, 132.

Solicitor of the Treasury, office of, established, II, 527.

Operations of, referred to, IV, 689.

Somerlat, Maria, act granting pension to, vetoed, IX, 754.

Sommersett Case.—A negro slave named Sommersett accompanied his master from Boston to London in October, 1769. He became ill and was turned adrift by his master. His condition aroused the compassion of Granville

Sharp, who cared for him until he was re-stored to health. He was then claimed by his master and taken before Lord Mansfield, of the court of King's bench. Here he was discharged on the ground that in England slavery could exist only by positive law, and in the absence of such a law a person could not be deprived of liberty on the ground that he was a slave. This decision determined the future course of England in the delivery of fugitives

Sons of American Revolution.—A patriotic society composed of lineal descendants of soldiers, sailors, and conspicuous patriots of Revolutionary times. The society was organized in California July 4, 1876. It has now over 30 State branches.

Sons of Liberty.—A society organized by the younger and more ardent patriots of Connecticut in 1755 to advance colonial liberty. They advocated nonimportation, aided in the hanging in effigy of the stamp distributer Oliver in 1765, and in 1774 proposed the organization of a continental congress. The appellation is sometimes applied to the whole body of American patriots. Another organization calling themselves "Sons of Liberty" existed in 1862-1864 in Indiana and other States and actively opposed the efforts of the United States Government in the prosecution of the war for the preservation of the Union, and several leaders were tried and condemned by a military commission. (See also Milligan Case.)

Sons of the Revolution.—A society of the same nature as the Sons of the American Revolution. It was established in New York in 1875, and has now about 20 State branches. The principal point of difference between the Sons of the Revolution and the Sons of the American Revolution is in the matter of eligibility, which in both is dependent on hereditary descent. In the latter society membership is contingent upon lineal descent from patriots of the Revolution, while in the former it is extended to collaterals.

Sound Dues. (See Baltic Sea.)

South America (see also South American Provinces, South American Republics; the several States)·

Blockade of Spanish coast in, by Spanish forces, X, 56.

Commercial relations with, VII, 60; VIII, 239; IX, 74.

Commission to Central America and, for improving commercial relations discussed, VIII, 239, 276, 277, 330, 370, 531.

Condition of, reports on, transmitted, X, 58.

International American Conference at Washington. (See International American Conference.)

Monarchical government in, establishment of, referred to, VI, 201.

Negotiations for restoration of peace in, referred to, VIII, 89.

Policy of United States toward, discussed, IX, 315.

South American Provinces (see also South American Republics):

Independence and political condition of, referred to, II, 32.

Independence of—

Achieved by, before recognized by United States, II, 260.

Asserted, II, 43.

Emperor of Russia intervenes for recognition of, II, 326.

Not recognized until danger of subjugation had passed, III, 267.

Should be recognized by United States, II, 116.

To be recommended by United States, II, 105.

Recognition of, referred to, II, 137, 192.

Supplies sent to, II, 242.

War with Spain. (See Wars, Foreign.)

South American Republics (see also South American Provinces; the several Republics):

Commercial relations with—

Discussed by President—

Hayes, VII, 508.

Pierce, V, 336.

Report of Hamilton Fish on, VII, 70.

Condition of, discussed, II, 446.

Congress of, referred to, II, 344.

Differences existing among, referred to, IV, 402.

Friendly disposition of United States toward, II, 384; VI, 686.

Independence of—

Achieved by, before recognized by United States, II, 260.

Asserted, II, 43.

Emperor of Russia intervenes for recognition of, II, 326.

Not recognized until danger of subjugation had passed, III, 267.

Should be recognized by United States, II, 116.

To be recommended by United States, II, 105.

Mediation of United States offered in wars among, VI, 578, 686.

Minister for, requested, II, 51.

Peace conference between Spain and, held in Washington, VII, 98, 145.

Pledge of United States to, against foreign interference with, referred to, II, 341.

Policy of United States toward, discussed, IX, 315.

Political condition of, discussed, V, 371.

Recognition of, referred to, II, 137, 192.

Treaty of, with Spain discussed, III, 150.

Treaty with, II, 302.

War of, with Spain—

Armistice referred to, VII, 190.

Good offices of United States tendered, VI, 578, 686.

Accepted, VII, 33, 98.

Vessels being built in New York for Spain forbidden to depart, VII, 33.

South American Republics, Recognition of.—In 1817 Henry Clay endeavored to secure an appropriation from Congress for sending an accredited minister to Buenos Ayres, which had become a free and independent Republic. Congress, however, refused. Mar. 8, 1822,

President Monroe in a special message to Congress (II, 116) recommended the recognition of Buenos Ayres, Chile, Colombia, and other Republics, and the establishment of international relations with them. This Congress agreed to. The commercial relations between the United States and these Republics have steadily improved since this action. A conference, known as the International American Conference (q. v.), representing the United States and these Republics, met in Washington in 1889 to encourage closer business relations. This resulted in the establishment of the Bureau of American Republics (q. v.).

South American Revolution. (See Wars, Foreign.)

South Carolina.—One of the thirteen original States; nickname, "The Palmetto State;" motto, "Animis opibusque parati" ("Prepared in mind and resources"). It lies between lat. 32° 4′ 30″ and 35° 13′ 2″ north and long. 78° 28′ and 83° 18′ west. It is bounded on the north and northeast by North Carolina, on the southeast by the Atlantic Ocean, and on the southwest and west by Georgia (separated for most of the distance by the Savannah River). The surface is level near the coast, undulating in the interior, and mountainous in the northwest. The State produces gold, porcelain, clay, phosphates, and other minerals, and is especially noted for the production of rice and sea-island cotton. It was partially explored by the Spaniards in 1525, who named it Chicora. An unsuccessful attempt to colonize was made by the French under Ribault in 1562. The first permanent settlement was made by the English in 1670. Charleston was founded in 1680. Charles II gave the territory between lat. 29° and 36° 30′ north to eight of his favorites in 1663, and 2 years later he issued a charter placing the control of the colony in their hands. They employed John Locke, the philosopher, to draw up a constitution which should provide an ideal government. This "grand model" proved to be an attempt to set up the feudal system in America, and was abandoned by the proprietors in 1693. South Carolina became a royal colony in 1729. The first constitution was adopted in 1776. The Federal Constitution was ratified May 23, 1788. The State protested against the inequality of the tariff of 1828, and though the act was modified the legislature passed the ordinance of nullification in 1832. Early the next year it was repealed on the adoption of the compromise tariff. Dec. 20, 1860, an ordinance of secession was passed. The State was readmitted by act of Congress June 25, 1868. South Carolina has an area of 30,570 sq. miles and a population (1890) of 1,151,149.

South Carolina (see also Confederate States):
Amendment to Federal Constitution referred to, II, 29.
Census of—
　Referred to, I, 116.
　Return of, delay in, I, 112.
Claims of, for advances made during War of 1812, II, 464.

South Carolina—Continued.
Commissioners from, to President Buchanan, V, 658.
　Correspondence of, referred to, V, 664.
Constitution of, referred to, VI, 632.
Enlistments in, for service of France, X, 15.
Forts and fortifications ceded to United States by, I, 396.
Fourteenth amendment to Constitution ratified by, VI, 639.
　Proclaimed, VI, 657.
Imprisonment of free negroes in ports of, referred to, IV, 101.
Ku-Klux Klans, etc., in, discussed, VII, 150, 163.
　Proclamations against, VII, 132, 134, 135, 136, 139, 396.
Provisional governor for, appointed and restoration of, into Union discussed, VI, 326.
Railroad in, survey of, II, 464.
Ratification of amendment to Federal Constitution by, referred to, I, 74, 259.
Revenue laws for—
　Act of Congress in regard to, declared void by, II, 610.
　　Referred to, II, 632.
　Deliberations of convention in regard to, made known to President Jackson, II, 611.
　Military operations in, growing out of opposition to, II, 634, 640.
　Nullification message, II, 610.
　Nullification proclamation, II, 640.
　Opposition to, from citizens of, II, 611.
　Proclamation regarding, II, 640.
Rifle clubs in, proclamation against, VII, 396.
Slaughter of American citizens in Hamburg, referred to, VII, 375.
Unlawful combinations in, discussed and proclamations against, II, 610, 640; VI, 545; VII, 132, 134, 135, 136, 139, 150, 163, 396.
　Copies of proclamations for executive clerks, VI, 558.
Habeas corpus, writ of, suspended in certain counties, VII, 136, 139.
　Revoked as to Marion County, VII, 138.

South Dakota.—One of the United States; motto, "Under God the people rule." It lies a little north of the center of the continent, between lat. 45° 57′ and 42° 28′ north (extreme southeast point; west of the Missouri the southern boundary is 43° north) and long. 96° 26′ and 104° 3′ west. It is bounded on the north by North Dakota, on the east by Minnesota and Iowa, on the south by Nebraska, and on the west by Montana and Wyoming. The Missouri River divides the State into two nearly equal portions. The eastern part is generally smooth and rolling. West of the river the country rises more rapidly and culminates in the Black Hills, an elevated region some 60 by 100 miles in extent, the central point of which is Harneys Peak, 9,700 feet high. The Bad Lands, in the southeastern part, is an interesting geological formation, consisting of a desert region abounding in canyons, depressions, walls, and castles of white earth, rich in soil-making chemicals and interesting fossils. Gold, silver, tin, and building materials are produced in paying quanti-

portion of this territory into a new State to be called Franklin (q. v.). With the admission of Tennessee and Kentucky and the organization of a Territorial government in Mississippi this territory went out of existence.

Spain.—A Kingdom of southwestern Europe. It is the Iberia and Hispania of the ancients. The earliest settlers are supposed to have been the progeny of Tubal, fifth son of Japhet. The Phenicians and Carthaginians successively planted colonies on the coasts as early as 350 B. C. The Romans conquered the whole country 206 B. C. The present Kingdom is bounded on the north by the Bay of Biscay and France (separated by the Pyrenees Mountains), on the east and south by the Mediterranean Sea, and on the west by Portugal and the Atlantic Ocean. The southern coast terminates in the promontory of Gibraltar, separated from the north coast of Africa by the Strait of Gibraltar, 15 miles in width. Spain has very valuable mineral resources, especially quicksilver, lead, copper, silver, salt, zinc, etc. The leading productions are wine, grapes, raisins, olive oil, cork, and fruits. Christian kingdoms were founded in the eighth, ninth, and tenth centuries. Castile and Aragon were united in 1479, and Granada was taken from the Moors in 1492. Spain reached its greatest power in the sixteenth century. The Hapsburg dynasty ruled from 1516 to 1700, when the Bourbons succeeded them. The throne was given to Joseph Bonaparte in 1808. The Peninsular War lasted from 1808 to 1814. The first Carlist war was carried on from 1833 to 1840. A republic which had been formed in 1873 was overthrown in 1875, and the Bourbon dynasty restored. A second Carlist war was carried on from 1872 to 1876. War with the United States in 1898 resulted in the loss of Spain's West Indian possessions, the Philippine Islands, and an island in the Ladrones. The area of continental Spain is 197,670 sq. miles, and the population in 1887 was 17,565,632. Spain was an ally of the United States from 1778 to 1782.

Spanish-American War.—In February, 1895, the natives of Cuba, being dissatisfied with the treatment accorded them by Spain and discontented with the government afforded them, determined to throw off the yoke of oppression, with all the unreasonable burdens which it imposed. They took up arms against the mother country, and quickly the entire island was in a state of insurrection. This insurrection, like previous revolutions which had occurred in the island, was not at first considered of sufficient importance to warrant interference or recognition on the part of the United States. A similar outbreak in the island occurred in 1868, during the Administration of President Grant. In his message to Congress Dec. 6, 1869, President Grant said: "The contest [in the island] has at no time assumed the conditions which amount to a war in the sense of international law, or which would show the existence of a *de facto* political organization of the insurgents sufficient to justify a recognition of belligerency" (VII, 31). In a message of June 13, 1870, describing the conditions in the island, he said: "The insurrection itself, although not subdued, exhibits no signs of advance, but seems to be confined to an irregular system of hostilities, carried on by small and illy armed bands of men, roaming without concentration through the woods and the sparsely populated regions of the island, attacking from ambush convoys and small bands of troops, burning plantations and the estates of those not sympathizing with their cause" (VII, 64). Again, Dec. 7, 1875, in a message to Congress he used the following language in respect to conditions in the island: "Considered as a question of expediency, I regard the accordance of belligerent rights still to be as unwise and premature as I regard it to be, at present, indefensible as a measure of right" (VII, 339). President Cleveland entertained an opinion in regard to the insurrection in Cuba arising in 1895 similar to those expressed by President Grant in regard to the insurrection of 1868, and in his message of Dec. 2 of that year he said: "Whatever may be the traditional sympathy of our countrymen as individuals with a people who seem to be struggling for larger autonomy and greater freedom, deepened, as such sympathy naturally must be, in behalf of our neighbors, yet the plain duty of their Government is to observe in good faith the recognized obligations of international relationship" (IX, 636). He insisted that belligerent rights should not be accorded to the insurgents, because of peril and injury to our own interests. He said in his message of Dec. 7, 1896: "Imperfect and restricted as the Spanish government of the island may be, no other exists there, unless the will of the military officer in temporary command of a particular district can be dignified as a species of government" (IX, 719). The foregoing expressions of opinion prove unmistakably that there was no reaching out on the part of the United States to interfere with the Spanish rule in Cuba. When President McKinley was inaugurated the insurrection described by his immediate predecessor still existed, and the grave questions which had confronted the latter were now presented for his consideration. He declined to interfere in the troubles in the island in any way and expressly refused to recognize the independence of Cuba. He announced that Spain would be given reasonable time in which to apply the reforms promised. In pursuance of Spain's promise autonomous administrations were established in some of the larger cities, but subsequent developments demonstrated the futility of such action and the failure of the newly formed governments. The revolution dragged on, sapping the substance of the people as it progressed and rendering destitute the poorer classes. Crimes were committed on every hand, while desolation and disorder reigned. To add to the horrors and atrocities of the struggle, the Captain-General of the island, Valeriano Weyler, Feb. 16, 1896, issued an edict initiating a cruel policy called "reconcentration." By this edict the agricultural inhabitants were herded into the cities, their lands laid waste, and their homes destroyed. The results in suffering and cruelty have been unprecedented in modern times. The mortality among the reconcentrados was frightful and distressing. Crowded within the cities and lines of the Spanish armies, the noncombatant men, women, and children, with scarcely any protection from the weather, poorly fed and clad, died from disease and starvation in untold numbers. The shocking cruelties thus practiced and the indescribable horrors of the situation attracted the attention of the civilized world and excited universal pity. Reports of the conditions in Cuba were from time to time brought to the United States, and the public mind throughout the country was greatly stirred. While this state of affairs existed the second-class battle ship *Maine*, which had been dispatched to Cuban waters on a friendly mission, was on the night of Feb. 15, 1898, blown up in the harbor of Havana. In this catastrophe 2 officers and 258 sailors and marines perished (X, 153). A thorough investigation of this disaster was immediately instituted, and at its close a report was made to the effect that the destruction of the ship had been wrought by an explosion from without, produced by a submarine mine (X, 139). The tension of the public mind, already great, was increased by this report and by the suspicion in the minds of many as to the cause of the disaster. The people could not much longer be held in check, and to those who were even casually observant it was apparent that a crisis in our affairs with Spain was imminent. Conservatism became unpopular, the feeling that war was necessary grew rapidly, and forbearance could not longer be tolerated. Congress was in session and unanimously appropriated $50,000,000 for the national defense. This provision was timely. The coasts of the United States were poorly defended, the Navy needed ammunition and supplies and an increase in vessels, while the Army required enlargement in men and munitions. Apr. 6 the continental powers, through their envoys in Washington, gave expression to the hope that an amicable adjustment of the impending troubles might be reached. The President replied to their representations, and with them shared the hope that peace might be preserved. Negotiations with Spain continued for a brief period, but were barren of results. The President in his message of Apr. 11, 1898, announced the failure of diplomacy to bring about a satisfactory settlement of the difficulties and recommended to Congress forcible intervention (X, 139). Apr. 19, after refusing to recognize the government of Cuba, Congress with much unanimity declared the island independent of Spain and authorized forcible intervention (X, 155). The resolutions met with the approval of the Executive, and he signed them the next day. Spain regarded this act on the part of the United States as "equivalent to an evident declaration of war." The ministers of the two countries were recalled and diplomatic relations terminated. Apr. 22 a blockade of Cuban ports was proclaimed (X, 202), and the following day a call was made for 125,000 volunteers (X, 203). A formal declaration of war was recommended by the President, and Apr. 25 Congress declared the existence of war from and including Apr. 21. Due notification of the existence of war was given to the various governments Apr. 25, nearly all of which immediately responded with proclamations of neutrality. May 25 there was a second call for volunteers, 75,000 in number (X, 205). Like the initial call for 125,000, this was responded to without delay. The Regular Army was largely increased, as was the enlisted force of the Navy. Over 100 vessels were added to the Navy by purchase. The coast defenses were rapidly strengthened, additional guns placed in position, and an auxiliary navy was created. About 1,500 submarine mines were placed at the most exposed points on the coast. Cable, telegraph, and telephone lines were constructed in many places. In addition to the national-defense fund of $50,000,000, which was expended in large part by the Army and Navy, Congress provided further means for prosecuting hostilities by the war-revenue act of June 13, authorizing a 3 per cent popular loan not to exceed $400,000,000 and levying additional imposts and taxes. Of the authorized loan $200,000,000 was offered and promptly taken, the subscriptions far exceeding the call. The first encounter occurred Apr. 27, when a detachment of the blockading squadron made a reconnoissance in force at Matanzas, Cuba, shelled the harbor forts, and demolished several new works in course of construction. The next engagement occurred May 1, at Manila, in the Philippine Islands. The American squadron at Hongkong, under Commodore George Dewey, had been instructed to proceed to the Philippine Islands and to capture or destroy the formidable Spanish fleet assembled at Manila. At daybreak of May 1 Dewey's fleet, successfully passing over the submarine mines, entered Manila Bay and after a few hours' engagement destroyed the entire fleet of 10 warships and 1 transport, captured the naval station and forts at Cavite, and completely controlled the bay of Manila, with the ability to take the city at will. On the American side not a life was lost, the wounded numbering only 7, and not a vessel was materially injured. The Spanish loss in killed and wounded exceeded 400. Thus the first great battle of the war was a victory for the United States magnificent in effect and extraordinary in detail, standing unequaled in the achievements of naval warfare. The effect of this remarkable victory gave a prestige of invincibility to the United States which, though long deserved, had never been appreciated by the great naval powers of the earth. Reenforcements, under Maj. Gen. Wesley Merritt, were hurried to the Philippine Islands and firmly established within sight of Manila, which lay helpless before the American guns. The first expedition sailed from San Francisco May 25 and arrived off Manila June 30. Other expeditions soon followed, until the total force landed at Manila consisted of over 15,000 officers and men. In the meantime large forces were assembled at various points along the coast of the United States to invade Cuba and Puerto Rico. San Juan, Puerto Rico, and the forts at the entrance to Santiago Harbor, Cuba, were shelled by the American squadrons, but none of the attacks had any appreciable result. On the night of June 3, in an attempt to blockade the mouth of Santiago Harbor, Assistant Naval Constructor Richmond P. Hobson, accompanied by 7 men from the American squadron, sank the collier *Merrimac* across the narrow channel. This unparalleled act of heroism thrilled not only the hearts of the American people, but challenged the admiration of the world. Under the protection of a portion of the American fleet a landing of 600 marines was effected at Guantanamo Bay on June 10. This port was taken and held after severe fighting by the marines, who were the first organized forces of the United States to land in Cuba. By June 16 additional forces had been landed. June 22 the advance of the American army under Maj. Gen.

William R. Shafter landed at Daiquiri, about 1 miles east of Santiago, and the next day began the movement against the city. The first serious engagement in which the American troops lost heavily occurred at Las Guasimas June 24. By nightfall of that day ground within 5 miles of Santiago was won. The outworks of Santiago were taken July 1 after a severe battle, and on the next day El Caney and San Juan were captured after a desperate struggle. The investment of the city was now complete. The naval forces cooperated, shelling the town and the coast forts. On the following day, July 3, occurred the decisive naval combat of the war. The Spanish fleet, under Rear-Admiral Pascual Cervera, which had been confined in the harbor of Santiago for 6 weeks by the blockading squadron under Acting Rear-Admiral William T. Sampson, attempted to escape. The Spanish vessels were intercepted and utterly destroyed by the American fleet, under the immediate direction of Commodore Winfield S. Schley, who assumed command during the temporary absence of Rear-Admiral Sampson. The Spanish loss was 600 killed and about 1,400 prisoners, including the admiral. Spain was unable to recover from the catastrophe, and her efforts upon the ocean virtually ceased. The capitulation of Santiago, which embraced the entire eastern end of Cuba, soon followed. July 17 the American army occupied the city. The number of Spanish soldiers surrendered was 22,000. An expedition against Puerto Rico, consisting of about 3,500 men, under the command of Maj. Gen. Nelson A. Miles, was immediately fitted out, and landed at Guanica July 25. Gen. Miles's force was subsequently increased to about 17,000. With the exception of a few slight engagements there was no serious resistance, and the middle of August found much of the island in the possession of the American troops. As early as July 26 Spain made overtures for peace through M. Jules Cambon, the French ambassador at Washington. Aug. 12 the peace protocol was signed, by which hostilities were brought to an end. Aug. 15, the news of the signing of the protocol not having reached the Philippines, the battle of Manila was fought, and the last scene of the war was enacted when, after a brief assault by the American land and naval forces, the city was compelled to surrender. The total casualties in killed and wounded during the war were: Army, officers killed, 23; enlisted men killed, 257—total, 280; officers wounded, 113; enlisted men wounded, 1,464—total, 1,577. Navy, killed, 17; wounded, 67; died as result of wounds, 1; invalided from service, 6—total, 91. In the entire campaign by land and sea the United States did not lose a flag, gun, ship, or transport, and, with the exception of the crew of the *Merrimac*, not a soldier or sailor was taken prisoner. Aug. 7 the American troops in Cuba began to embark for home, and the entire force was returned to the United States by Aug. 24, after an absence of only 2 months.

A treaty of peace was signed at Paris by the commissioners of the two countries Dec. 10, 1898. It was ratified on the part of the United States Feb. 6, and on the part of Spain Mar. 19, 1899. By the treaty it was provided that Spain relinquish all claim of sovereignty over and title to Cuba; that Puerto Rico and other West Indian islands of Spain, one island in the Ladrones, and the entire Philippine group be ceded to the United States, and that Spain be paid $20,000,000. The ratifications of the two Governments were exchanged in Washington Apr. 11, 1899, and on the same day President McKinley issued the following proclamation: "Whereas a treaty of peace between the United States of America and Her Majesty the Queen Regent of Spain, in the name of her august son, Don Alfonso XIII, was concluded and signed by their respective plenipotentiaries at Paris on the 10th day of December, 1898, the original of which, being in the English and Spanish languages, is word for word as follows: [Here the full text of the treaty is inserted.] And whereas the said convention has been duly ratified on both parts and the ratifications of the two Governments were exchanged in the city of Washington on the 11th day of April, 1899: Now, therefore, be it known that I, William McKinley, President of the United States of America, have caused the said convention to be made public, to the end that the same and every article and clause thereof may be observed and fulfilled with good faith by the United States and the citizens thereof."

Spanish-American War:

Almodóvar, Duke of, communication from, regarding peace negotiations, X, 173.

Auxiliary Navy of United States in, referred to, X, 166.

Bagley, Worth, killed while attempting to silence batteries at Cardenas, X, 169. (See also X, 157.)

Barton, Clara, president Red Cross, work accomplished by, in, X, 173. (See also X, 142, 161.)

Battle of July 3 discussed, X, 170. (See also Enc. Art., Santiago Harbor, Battle of.)

Blockade of Cuban ports proclaimed, X, 202, 206.

Discussed, X, 154, 165.

Removal of, referred to, X, 174.

Brooke, John R.—

Member of military commission to Puerto Rico, X, 175.

Puerto Rican expedition reenforced by corps of, X, 171.

Butler, Matthew C., member of military commission to Cuba, X, 175.

Cambon, Jules, French minister, representative of Spain in preliminary peace negotiations, X, 173, 206.

Cardenas Bay, conflict in, discussed, X, 157, 169.

The *Winslow* rescued by the *Hudson* in, thanks of Congress, etc., to officers and men of latter recommended, X, 157.

Casualties on American side in, X, 172.

Spanish-American War—Continued.

Causes leading up to, discussed and reviewed, X, 127, 136, 139, 160.

Cavite, water batteries at, silenced by American squadron, X, 155, 168.

Cervera, Pascual, Spanish fleet under command of, in Santiago Harbor, X, 169.

Destroyed by American squadron while attempting to escape, X, 170. (See also Enc. Art., Santiago Harbor, Battle of.)

Corbin, H. C.—

Directs Gen. Otis to avoid conflict with Philippine insurgents, X, 222.

Dispatch to Gen. Otis regarding force, etc., for Philippine Islands, X, 218.

Instructions to Gen. Merritt regarding joint occupancy of Philippine Islands with insurgents, X, 217.

Order of, to send troops to Iloilo, X, 221.

Crowninshield, A. S., report of, on number of lives lost by sinking of the *Maine*, X, 153.

Cuban insurrection and policy of United States regarding, discussed, X, 127, 139, 160.

Davis, Cushman K., peace commissioner on part of United States, X, 175.

Day, William R., peace commissioner on part of United States, X, 175.

Dewey, George—

Attack of American land forces and capture of Manila assisted by squadron under, X, 172.

Thanks of President tendered, X, 218.

Member of Philippine Commission, X, 222.

Spanish fleet destroyed in Manila Bay by American squadron under, X, 155, 168.

Appointed acting rear-admiral, X, 155, 208.

Sword to be presented to, X, 157.

Thanks of Congress to, X, 156.

Recommended, X, 155.

Reply of, X, 157.

Thanks of President tendered, X, 208.

Referred to, X, 155.

Suggestions from, regarding force, etc., for Philippine Islands requested by President, X, 218.

Diplomatic relations broken off, X, 153, 164.

Discussed, X, 153, 155, 156, 157, 158, 160.

Efforts of foreign governments to preserve peace discussed, X, 162.

El Caney captured by American troops, X, 170.

Enlisted force of American Navy in, X, 166.

Evacuation of—

Cuba, Puerto Rico, and adjacent islands, military commissions to superintend, X, 175.

Havana, order regarding, X, 221.

Executive orders regarding, X, 208.

Existence of, act declaring, X, 201.

Recommended, X, 153.

Referred to, X, 165.

Fighting force of American Navy in, X, 166.

Frye, William P., peace commissioner on part of United States, X, 175.

Gordon, William W., member of military commission to Puerto Rico, X, 175.

Spencer, John C.:
Associate justice Supreme Court, nomination of, and reasons therefor, IV, 328.
Correspondence regarding Dorr's Rebellion, IV, 299, 300, 302, 304.

Spirits. (See Distilled Spirits.)

Spitzer, Solomon, act for relief of heirs of, returned, VIII, 615.

Spoils System.—The policy of bestowing public offices upon members of the party in power as rewards for political services. These official rewards once secured, the beneficiaries found it incumbent upon them to assist in keeping in power the party to which they owed their positions, not only by a strict attention to the duties of their offices, but also by making friends and votes for their superior officer. Under the spoils system, it is charged, official duties are often made secondary to partisan obligations. This system is not confined to American politics, but is carried on in England, where Parliament has created a patronage secretary, who takes charge of the apportionment and keeps regular accounts with the members of Parliament of the positions which have been filled upon their recommendation. In the United States the system developed first in New York and Pennsylvania. Tammany Hall made effective use of the system in its fight against the Clintons in the first quarter of the present century. It was extended to State politics by the "Albany Regency," established by Martin Van Buren in 1818. It was not until Jackson's time, however, that it became a feature of Federal politics. The spoils system derived the name commonly applied to it from a sentence used in a speech made by Senator William L. Marcy, of New York, while urging the Senate to confirm the nomination of Martin Van Buren as minister to England. In defense of the charge against Van Buren that he had introduced the custom of removal from office for opinion's sake, Mr. Marcy, speaking for the Democrats of New York, Jan. 25, 1832, declared that "they see nothing wrong in the rule that to the victor belongs the spoils of the enemy." It has since been a regular feature of American politics in every Administration, tempered of late by the provisions of the civil-service act of 1883. (See also Civil Service.)

Spoliation Claims (see also France, claims against discussed):
Act providing for—
Ascertainment and satisfaction of, vetoed, IV, 466.
Ascertainment of, vetoed, V, 307.

Spoliations (see also Alabama Claims; the several powers, claims against; Vessels, United States, seized):
Discussed by President—
Adams, John, I, 247.
Jefferson, I, 383, 395, 425.
Monroe, II, 196.
Washington, I, 146.

Spottsylvania Court-House (Va.), Battle of.—After 2 days' fighting in the Wilderness, south

of the Rapidan River, in Virginia, Grant attempted to turn Lee's right flank and advance toward Richmond by way of Spottsylvania Court-House. This resulted in a series of battles. Lee discovered the movement of Grant's army and reached Spottsylvania first. By May 9, 1864, Grant had his army concentrated near Spottsylvania. Hancock commanded the right, Warren the center, and Sedgwick the left. The latter was killed while placing his artillery on the 9th, and Wright succeeded him in command of the Sixth Army Corps. May 10 and 11 there was desultory fighting, skirmishing, and maneuvering for positions. Grant's losses during the 10th are supposed to have exceeded 10,000 men, and Lee's are also supposed to have been severe. The morning of May 12 opened with an advance by Hancock's column, which surrounded and captured with the salient an entire division (Gen. Edward Johnson's) of 3,000 Confederates, including 2 generals and between 30 and 40 guns. The fighting of this day was as severe as any during the war. Lee made 5 furious assaults in quick succession, with the view of dislodging Hancock and Wright from the captured salient. From dawn till dusk the battle raged. The Federal assault on the Confederate line was checked. It was renewed without success on the 18th. After several days of maneuvering, and having received reenforcements enough to make up for his losses, Grant, on the 20th and 21st of May, moved southward toward the North Anna River. The Federal losses in the battle of Spottsylvania Court-House, including the conflicts at Todd's Tavern, Corbin's Bridge, Alsop's Farm, Laurel Hill, Po River, Ny River, the angle of the salient, Piney Branch Church, Harris's Farm, and Guineys Station, between May 8 and 21, 1864, were officially reported as 2,725 killed, 13,416 wounded, and 2,258 missing, a total of 18,399. The Confederate losses, only partially reported, were (Ewell's, Johnson's, and McGowan's divisions) 4,001 killed and wounded.

Sprague, William, correspondence regarding Dorr's Rebellion, IV, 305.

Springfield, Mo., act for erection of public building at, vetoed, VIII, 476.

Springfield (N. J.), Battle of.—June 6, 1780, Generals Sterling, Knyphausen, Mathews, and Tryon left Staten Island with 5,000 men to attack Washington's army at Morristown, N. J. Sterling was killed and Knyphausen took command. He advanced to within half a mile of Springfield, harassed all the way by the settlers and militia. Sir Henry Clinton returned to New York on June 17 from Charleston, S. C., and prepared to join Knyphausen. On June 23 the British advance was made in two columns. The American outposts were forced back upon Springfield, which the British burned, and then retreated to Staten Island. The British loss amounted to about 150, the American to 83.

Springfield, Ohio, act to establish port of delivery at, vetoed, VIII, 417.

Squadron:

African, instructions to officers of, referred to IV, 320; V, 540.

Asiatic. (See Manila Harbor, Battle of.)

Home, proposed extension of duties of, referred to, IV, 276.

Mediterranean, referred to, IV, 52, 100.

Pacific. (See Manila Harbor, Battle of.)

Squawksin Indians, treaty with, V, 303.

Squi-aitl Indians, treaty with, V, 303.

Squier, E. George, treaties with Nicaragua and San Salvador concluded by, V, 34.

Squin-áh-mish Indians, treaty with, V, 379.

Staff of Army. (See Army.)

Stamford Harbor, Conn., survey of, referred to, II, 480.

Stamp Act.—An act of the British Parliament passed in 1765 and put into effect in the American Colonies Nov. 1 of that year. It levied on British subjects in America specific sums for each of the common transactions of business. Deeds, bonds, notes of hand, indentures, insurance policies, leases, contracts of sale, etc., were not to be enforced by courts unless written on stamped paper bought of the officers of the Crown. Without stamped wills testamentary dispositions would be void; without stamped receipts debts could not be acquitted; vessels at sea without clearances written on stamped paper were liable to seizure and confiscation if they fell in with one of the King's ships; only stamped newspapers could be exposed for sale; without stamped certificates marriages could not lawfully be contracted; unstamped writs and executions had no force or effect; in short, the American citizen must have been daily paying money into the British treasury at its stamp office or in respect to much of the protection which society undertakes to afford he was an outlaw. Under this act business was suspended. The people absolutely refused to use the stamps. Benjamin Franklin presented a petition of the colonists to the House of Commons, and on Mar. 18, 1766, the stamp act was repealed. The agitation resulting from the act was one of the leading causes in effecting the Revolution.

Stamp-Act Congress.—A body which met at New York Oct. 7, 1765, composed of delegates from all the Colonies except Virginia, North Carolina, New Hampshire, and Georgia. There were 26 members, including 4 from New York, 2 each from Rhode Island and Delaware, and 3 each from Massachusetts, Connecticut, New Jersey, Pennsylvania, Maryland, and South Carolina. Timothy Ruggles, of Massachusetts, was chosen president. The manifestoes issued by this congress were "A Declaration of the Rights and Grievances of the Colonists of America," an address to the King, a memorial to the House of Lords, and a petition to the House of Commons, all of a loyal and respectful tone. The congress adjourned Oct. 25.

Stanbery, Henry:

Counsel for President Johnson in impeachment proceedings, VI, 726.

Stanbery, Henry—Continued.

Special commissioner to investigate administration in military division on Mississippi River, VI, 273.

Standefer, Mr., mentioned, X, 105.

Standley, John S., mentioned, IX, 233.

Stanly, Edward, military governor of North Carolina, authority and action of, referred to, VI, 80.

Stanly, Fabius, mentioned, V, 595.

Stanton, Edwin M.:

Communication of, regarding employment for fugitive negroes, X, 108.

Death of, announced and honors to be paid memory of, VII, 93.

Gen. Grant directed by, not to hold conference with Gen. Lee except for capitulation of latter's army, X, 111.

Negotiations for and correspondence regarding restoration of peace, VI, 260.

Secretary of War—

Removal of, discussed and orders regarding, VI, 621, 622, 663.

Suspension of, discussed and orders regarding, VI, 556, 583. (See also VI, 603.)

Stapleton, Robert H., act granting pension to, vetoed, VIII, 468.

Star Routes. (See Postal Service.)

Star Spangled Banner.—A patriotic song written by Francis Scott Key, of Baltimore, on the night of Sept. 13, 1814, during the bombardment of Fort McHenry by the British. Key had gone under a flag of truce to solicit the release of some friends who had been seized by the English Admiral Cochrane during the attack on the city of Washington. Upon Key's arrival the British fleet was about to begin the attack on Fort McHenry, and, though his request for the release of his friends was granted, Admiral Cochrane refused to allow him or his friends to leave the ship before the battle. During the excitement of the bombardment Key wrote the famous song on the back of a letter. It was published and sung at the theaters to the tune of "Anacreon in Heaven."

Starr, William H., act granting pension to, vetoed, VIII, 454.

Stars and Bars.—The flag of the Confederate States of America. The first provisional Senate recommended that "the flag of the Confederate States shall consist of a red field with a white space extending horizontally through the center and equal in width to one-third the width of the flag." The union was a blue square extending across the upper red and the white stripe. In the blue square 9 stars were arranged in a circle. The bars were by their colors, red and white, intended to express the qualities of courage and purity. The blue field of the union expressed fortitude and the 9 stars represented the number of States in the confederacy. It was first displayed Mar. 4, 1861, simultaneously with the inauguration of Lincoln, being unfurled over the statehouse at Montgomery, Ala. In 1863, the Stars and Bars too closely resembling the Stars and Stripes, he Confederate congress adopted a white flag with 1 blue star in the center. Another variation commonly used was a white field with blue diagonal stripes and white stars, and a piece of fringe at the outer edge. Some of the army corps adopted a battle flag with a red ground, blue diagonal cross, and white stars.

ars and Stripes. (See Flag.)

ate Banks. (See Banks, State.)

ate Constitutions. (See Constitutions, State.)

ate Courts. (See Courts, State.)

ate Debts:

Contracted abroad discussed, IV, 87.

Guaranty of, by General Government discussed, IV, 211.

Injure public credit, IV, 208.

Referred to, III, 552.

Repudiation of contracts referred to, IV, 109.

ate, Department of.—One of the eight Executive Departments of the Government. This Department has charge of the relations of the United States with foreign powers. Its head is the Secretary of State, who ranks as the first of the Cabinet officers. He is charged, under the President, not only with all negotiations relating to foreign affairs, but is the medium of correspondence between the President and the chief executives of foreign governments, is custodian of the great seal of the United States, and publishes the laws and resolutions of Congress and proclamations of the President. He is also required to make annual reports to Congress. Under the Continental Congress foreign affairs were at first managed by a committee. Jan. 10, 1781, the office of Secretary of Foreign Affairs was created and placed in charge of Robert R. Livingston, who was succeeded by John Jay in 1784. July 27, 1789, the two departments of Home and Foreign Affairs were combined in the Department of State. The following have been Secretaries of State under the Constitution: Thomas Jefferson, Virginia; Edmund Randolph, Virginia; Timothy Pickering, Pennsylvania; John Marshall, Virginia; James Madison, Virginia; Robert Smith, Maryland; James Monroe, Virginia; John Quincy Adams, Massachusetts; Henry Clay, Kentucky; Martin Van Buren, New York; Edward Livingston, Louisiana; Louis McLane, Delaware; John Forsyth, Georgia; Daniel Webster, Massachusetts; Hugh S. Legaré, South Carolina; Abel P. Upshur, Virginia; John C. Calhoun, South Carolina; James Buchanan, Pennsylvania; John M. Clayton, Delaware; Edward Everett, Massachusetts; William L. Marcy, New York; Lewis Cass, Michigan; Jeremiah S. Black, Pennsylvania; William H. Seward, New York; Elihu B. Washburne, Illinois; Hamilton Fish, New York; William M. Evarts, New York; James G. Blaine, Maine; Frederick T. Frelinghuysen, New Jersey; Thomas F. Bayard, Delaware; John W. Foster, Indiana; Walter Q. Gresham, Indiana; Richard Olney, Massachusetts; John Sherman, Ohio; William R. Day, Ohio, and John Hay, District of Columbia.

State, Department of:

Agents employed by, without express provision of law, IV, 151, 281.

Amount charged to, for service rendered by naval vessels referred to, VI, 462.

Appropriations and expenditures of, referred to, VII, 427.

Building for—

Completed and possession taken by, VII, 347.

Recommended, V, 168; VII, 106.

Change in laws regulating management of, referred to, VII, 635.

Changes made in force of, referred to, IX, 746.

Clerks in, referred to, VI, 387, 601; VIII, 67.

Contingent fund of bureaus in, estimates for, referred to, VIII, 535.

Historical archives in, referred to, IX, 669.

Historical manuscripts in, plan for publishing, referred to, VIII, 613.

Legal services, amounts paid for, by, referred to, VI, 630.

Library in, referred to, VIII, 153.

Officers commissioned by, referred to, VII, 49.

Officers in, referred to, VII, 378.

Public records in, means for preservation of, referred to, VII, 159.

Salaries and expenses of, referred to, VI, 694.

Substitutes in, employment of, referred to, VIII, 390.

Transfer of—

Patent Office from, to Attorney-General recommended, IV, 415.

Portion of business of, recommended, II, 461; V, 168.

Territorial affairs from, to Interior Department recommended, VII, 106, 191.

State of the Union discussed by President—

Adams, J. Q., II, 299, 350, 378, 412.

Arthur, VIII, 235.

Buchanan, V, 436, 497, 520, 552, 626, 661, 669.

Cleveland, VIII, 324, 773; IX, 714.

Fillmore, V, 77.

Grant, VII, 27, 96, 153, 184, 284, 305, 332, 399.

Harrison, Benj., IX, 32, 107, 306.

Hayes, VI·, 458, 492, 557, 601.

Jackson, II, 442, 500, 544, 591; III, 147, 292.

Jefferson, I, 328, 346, 361, 385.

Johnson, VI, 353, 372, 391, 395, 445, 558, 639, 673.

Lincoln, VI, 44, 54, 133, 188, 251.

McKinley, X, 160.

Madison, I, 539, 567, 573.

Monroe, II, 54, 73, 98, 207, 222, 248.

Pierce, V, 207, 273, 341, 397.

Polk, IV, 471, 532, 629.

Taylor, V, 9.

Tyler, IV, 74, 194, 257, 334.

Van Buren, III, 373, 483, 529, 602.

Washington, I, 103, 183, 213.

State, Secretary of:

Appointments by, referred to, IV, 112.

Letter of Don Joaquin de Anduaga to, II, 140.

Letter to, regarding Louisiana province, I, 348.

Report of, I, 34, 346, and X, 120; I, 396, 442; II, 68, 83, and X, 121; II, 568.

State, War, and Navy Building, construction of, discussed, VII, 347, 572; VIII, 51.

raiders started out Apr. 12 and were captured May 3, 1863, near Rome, Ga., having accomplished nothing. The capture was made by Forrest's cavalry.

Stricklett, Georgia A., act for relief of, vetoed, VIII, 659.

Strike Commission:
Discussed, IX, 551.
Report of, transmitted, IX, 556.

Stringham, Silas H., thanks of Congress to, recommended, VI, 83.

Stryker, Cyrenius G., act granting pension to, vetoed, VIII, 665.

Stuart, Charles B., report on waterway referred to, VI, 201.

Stuart, George H., member of Indian commission, VII, 23.

Subconstitutional Centennial Commission, memorial of, proposing to celebrate centennial anniversary of framing Constitution discussed, VIII, 533.

Submarine Cables. (See Ocean Cables.)

Subsidies to Railroads:
Discussed, VII, 110.
Information regarding, transmitted, VIII, 373.

Subsidies to Steamships:
Discussed, VII, 197, 352; VIII, 353.
Views of Postmaster-General regarding, VI, 363.

Subsidy.—Derived from the Latin *subsidium*, originally the troops stationed in reserve in the third line of battle, from *subsidere*, to sit down. In Europe, after the period of its first use, it meant a sum of money paid to an ally to aid in carrying on war. In England it was a special tax levied upon persons and not upon property. It has now come to mean money paid by a government to individuals or companies, such as steamship or railway, in excess of the value of services rendered and in aid of individual enterprise. Railways in the United States have been assisted by State and municipal subscriptions to their bonds. National aid to railways, with the exception of the Union and Central Pacific, has been in the form of land grants. In the case of the Pacific roads, in addition to 33,000,000 acres of land, the company was granted a money subsidy of more than $25,000 a mile. The first subsidized steamships were those of the Cunard Line, which in 1838 were allowed an annual subsidy of £81,000 by Great Britain. Two years later agitation was begun in the United States to have steamship mail lines established on the subsidy plan, and in 1845 the Postmaster-General was authorized to make contracts for carrying foreign mail in steamships sailing under the American flag. In 1847 an act was passed requiring the Secretary of the Navy to arrange for United States steamships to carry the mail from New York to Liverpool, to the West Indies and Gulf ports, and from Panama up the Pacific coast. By 1852 the Government was paying $2,000,000 a year for foreign mail service, but Congress soon after put an end to all mail subsidies. An act of Mar. 3, 1891, directed the Postmaster-General to pay $4 a mile run for first-class vessels for carrying foreign mails and in consideration of their use as auxiliary naval vessels. In 1892 the International Navigation Company made an arrangement for first-class European service in connection with the American registry of the *Paris* and *New York*. Other acts granting subsidies have since been passed by Congress.

Subtreasury System.—The subtreasury system of the United States is an outgrowth of the panic of 1837. In his special session message to Congress that year President Van Buren strongly recommended such a system (III, 324). Silas Wright, of New York, introduced a bill in Congress in accordance with the President's recommendations. It prohibited Government agents from receiving anything but gold and silver. In 1840 the bill became a law and subtreasuries were established at New York, Boston, Charleston, and St. Louis, the mint at Philadelphia and the branch mint at New Orleans having been also made places of deposit. The law was repealed in 1841 and reenacted in 1846.

Subtreasury System:
Condemnation of, referred to, IV, 45.
Discussed by President—
Taylor, V, 18.
Tyler, IV, 45, 207.
Van Buren, III, 324, 379, 489, 534, 546, 610.
Modifications in, recommended, V, 18.

Suffrage.—The privilege of participating in the government of a state or nation by voting at an election of officers or on a change in the fundamental law. Suffrage under the Constitution of the United States is exercised by such electors in each State as have the qualifications necessary for electors of the most numerous branch of the State legislature (I, 21). The Constitution does not guarantee the suffrage to any citizen, but by the fourteenth and fifteenth amendments the States are forbidden to abridge the privileges or immunities of United States citizens or to deny or abridge the right of suffrage on account of race, color, or previous condition of servitude. The age of 21 is universally fixed upon as that when suffrage may be exercised. In some States ability to read and write is required, and in some a small property qualification or tax is imposed. Until the present century suffrage was greatly restricted in America. Massachusetts and the New Haven Colonies for a long time allowed none but church members to vote. There have been periods in the history of nearly all the Colonies when only freeholders were allowed to vote. When the States in the Federal Union first framed their constitutions some of them retained the church-membership qualification, while others permitted suffrage to freeholders only. In 1798 Georgia abolished the property qualification, and was followed by Maryland in 1801, Massachusetts and New York in 1821, Delaware in 1831, New Jersey in 1844, Connecticut in 1845, Virginia in 1850, North Carolina in 1854, South Carolina in 1865, and Rhode Island, except in municipal elections, in 1888,

The new States have mostly provided for manhood suffrage from the first. (See also Woman Suffrage.)

Suffren, The, French seamen on, accidentally killed by salute from the *United States*, III, 54.

Sugar:

Manufacture of—

Encouragement of, recommended, VII, 626.

From sorghum and sugar cane discussed, VIII, 798.

Manufacture of milk, in Switzerland referred to, VIII, 394.

Placed on free list discussed, IX, 191.

Probable retaliatory action of foreign governments for proposed imposition of duty on, IX, 478.

Protest of Germany to discriminating duty on, recommendations regarding, IX, 525.

Supervision provided by tariff law for domestic production of, transfer of, to Agricultural Department recommended, IX, 119.

Sugar-Beet Culture, VII, 582; IX, 119; X, 200.

Sugar Bounty:

Discussed, IX, 443, 532.

Payment of appropriation for, contained in sundry civil bill, referred to, IX, 663.

Suits Against Government, act regarding bringing of, vetoed, IX, 247.

Sullivan, John T., director of Bank of United States, nomination of, and reasons therefor, III, 41.

Sullivan, Mary, act granting pension to, vetoed, VIII, 651.

Sumatra.—An island of the Malay archipelago. It is south and west of the Malay peninsula, and it is separated from Java by the Strait of Sunda. It contains some mineral wealth and produces coffee, sugar, rice, pepper, etc. The religion is Mahommedan. In 1873 Sumatra made war against Acheen, which ended in the subjugation and annexation of the latter. Area, about 170,744 sq. miles; population, about 3,000,000.

Sumatra, attack on American vessels by pirates on coast of, II, 551, 596.

Instructions to commander of the *Potomac* regarding, II, 575.

Sumner, Edwin V., treaty with Indians concluded by, V, 191.

Sumpter, The, arrest of part of crew of, at Morocco referred to, VI, 144.

Sunday Laws.—Early in the history of the New England Colonies laws were passed enjoining a strict observance of the Sabbath. As early as 1649 a law of Massachusetts provided for the prohibition of labor, play, or travel on the Lord's Day, beginning on Saturday evening. The "Duke's Laws" of New York also forbade the profanation of the day by travel or labor. The Pennsylvania laws of 1682 forbade labor. Those of South Carolina in 1684 forbade profanation of the Sabbath. Virginia in 1692 forbade travel or profanation. The Colonies generally had such laws, remnants of which still survive in State legislation.

Superintendent of Finances. (See Finances, Superintendent of.)

Superintendent of Immigration, report of, discussed, IX, 445.

Superior, Lake. (See Lake Superior.)

Suplee, Edwin M., report of, on Navajo Indians transmitted, IX, 347.

Supplies, Public:

Distribution of, referred to, I, 149.

Officer should be placed in charge of, I, 149.

Supreme Court. (See Court, Supreme.)

Supreme Court Justices.—Chief and associate justices of the Supreme Court are appointed by the President, by and with the advice and consent of the Senate, and hold office during good behavior. The Chief Justice receives a salary of $10,500 per year and the associate justices $10,000. Since the establishment of the court the following have served as Chief Justice: John Jay, New York; Oliver Ellsworth, Connecticut; John Marshall, Virginia; Roger B. Taney, Maryland; Salmon P. Chase, Ohio; Morrison R. Waite, Ohio; Melville W. Fuller, Illinois. The following have served as associate justices: John Rutledge, South Carolina; William Cushing, Massachusetts; Robert H. Harrison, Maryland; James Wilson, Pennsylvania; John Blair, Virginia; James Iredell, North Carolina; Thomas Johnson, Maryland; William Paterson, New Jersey; Samuel Chase, Maryland; Bushrod Washington, Virginia; Alfred Moore, North Carolina; William Johnson, South Carolina; Brockholst Livingston, New York; Thomas Todd, Kentucky; Joseph Story, Massachusetts; Gabriel Duval, Maryland; Smith Thompson, New York; Robert Trimble, Kentucky; John McLean, Ohio; Henry Baldwin, Pennsylvania; James M. Wayne, Georgia; Philip P. Barbour, Virginia; John Catron, Tennessee; John McKinley, Alabama; Peter V. Daniel, Virginia; Samuel Nelson, New York; Levi Woodbury, New Hampshire; Robert C. Grier, Pennsylvania; Benjamin R. Curtis, Massachusetts; John A. Campbell, Alabama; Nathan Clifford, Maine; Noah H. Swayne, Ohio; Samuel F. Miller, Iowa; David Davis, Illinois; Stephen J. Field, California; William Strong, Pennsylvania; Joseph P. Bradley, New Jersey; Ward Hunt, New York; John M. Harlan, Kentucky; William B. Woods, Georgia; Stanley Matthews, Ohio; Horace Gray, Massachusetts; Samuel Blatchford, New York; Lucius Q. C. Lamar, Mississippi; David J. Brewer, Kansas; Henry B. Brown, Michigan; George Shiras, jr., Pennsylvania; Howell E. Jackson, Tennessee; Edward D. White, Louisiana; Rufus W. Peckham, New York, and Joseph McKenna, California.

Supreme Court Justices:

Salaries of, increase in, recommended, VII, 42.

Should be exempted from other duties, II, 261.

Supreme Court Reports.—The opinions and decisions of the Supreme Court are recorded in more than 100 large volumes. They comprise its work from its first session in 1790, to the present time. They begin with the volume numbered 2 Dallas and include 3 volumes by Dallas, covering the period between 1790 and 1800; 9 volumes by Cranch, 1800 to 1815; Wheaton, 12 volumes, 1816 to 1827; Peters, 16 volumes, 1828 to 1842; Howard, 24 volumes, 1843 to 1860; Black, 2 volumes, 1861 to 1862; Wallace, 23 volumes, 1863 to 1875. Up to that date the reports had reached 89 volumes by the different compilers. Since 1876 the reports have been styled 90 U. S., 91 U. S., etc.

Surgeon-General of Army:

Building for library of, recommended, VIII, 70, 246.

Ordered to accompany ex-President Jackson home, III, 323.

Surplus Revenue, Distribution of.—In his annual message of Dec. 1, 1834 (III, 97), President Jackson announced the extinguishment of the public debt. The compromise tariff measure of 1832, while it made some reduction in the revenue derived from import duties, produced a surplus in the Treasury. Jackson advocated the distribution of this surplus among the States rather than the appropriation of it to other purposes. A bill providing for such disposition of the surplus was attached to the bill regulating public deposits and passed by Congress in 1836. Under this law all the money in excess of $5,000,000 in the Treasury Jan. 1, 1837, was to be deposited with the States in proportion to their representation in the electoral college, and in four installments. The States were required to give certificates of deposit payable to the Secretary of the Treasury on demand. None of the banks selected by the Government as the custodians of public funds was under any kind of official supervision by the States which chartered them or by the General Government. The sum to be divided was $37,468,859. Three installments of the money were paid to all the States except the few that had refused to accept it on the conditions imposed. The return of these loans to the States has never been demanded.

Surplus Revenue in Treasury. (See Treasury.)

Surratt, John H.:

Discovery and arrest of, referred to, VI, 459, 461.

Reward offered for arrest of, revoked, VI, 353. Trial of, referred to, VI, 601.

Surratt, Mary E., implicated in assassination of President Lincoln, proceedings of trial of, and verdict of military commission, VI, 334, 335, 336, 342, 347, 348.

Surveyor of Public Buildings, report of, transmitted, X, 27, 29, 31, 33, 34, 37, 39.

Surveyors, Public, punishment of persons interrupting, discussed, II, 479.

Surveys, control and supervision of geographical and geological, discussed, VII, 264. (See also the several surveys.)

Susan Loud, The, seizure of, by Spanish or Cuban authorities referred to, V, 143.

Claims arising out of, referred to, V, 185, 367.

Suspension Bridge, N. Y., proclamation granting privileges of other ports to, V, 326.

Susquehanna, The, repair of, referred to, V, 231.

Susquehanna Company.—An organization, composed mostly of Connecticut farmers, formed in 1754 for the purpose of colonizing the Wyoming country. This was the name given to a strip of land bought by Connecticut from the Plymouth Company in 1631. Under the charter granted by James I to the Plymouth Company in 1620 their territory extended from the Atlantic to the Pacific and from lat. 40° to 46° north. The grant of Charles II to William Penn extended to 42° north, thus overlapping the Plymouth grant to more than the extent of the territory sold to Connecticut, which extended to 41° south. In 1754 the Susquehanna Company made a treaty with the Six Nations of Indians, securing the right to settlement upon their purchase. Charles II confirmed the sale to Connecticut, and Pennsylvania, though disputing the sale, made no effort to prevent a settlement. The first settlers in the disputed territory were driven off by the Indians in 1763. In 1769 some 40 more settlers arrived in the Wyoming region and were arrested by Pennsylvania officials. For the next 6 years a sort of civil warfare was kept up between the settlers of the disputed tract, and only suspended during the Revolution, after which the dispute was arranged between the States and the titles to the land confirmed. (See also Wyoming Controversy.)

Susquehanna, or Conestoga, Indians.—A tribe of the Iroquoian stock of Indians, now extinct. They formerly lived in Pennsylvania and Maryland, along the Susquehanna River and at the head of Chesapeake Bay. They were close allies of the Dutch and Swedes, but treacherous in their dealings with the English. The Susquehannas were overthrown by the Iroquois in 1675 after a desperate struggle. A remnant of the tribe was massacred by whites at Lancaster, Pa., in 1763.

Sutro Tunnel referred to, VII, 194.

Swamp Lands. (See Lands, Swamp.)

Swann, Thomas, mentioned, VI, 613.

Swanton, Vt., proclamation granting privileges of other ports to, V, 326.

Swartwout, Samuel, crimes charged against I, 417.

Swartwout, Samuel, default of, referred to, III, 506. (See also III, 492.)

Swartwout, Samuel, thanks of Congress to, recommended, VI, 76.

Sweden.—A Kingdom in the eastern part of the Scandinavian peninsula, in Europe. It is bounded on the north and west by Norway, on the east by Finland, the Gulf of Bothnia, and the Baltic Sea, and on the south and southwest by the Baltic and the Cattegat and Skager Rack channels. It extends from lat. 55° 20' to 69° 3' north and from long. 11° 6' to 24° 8' east. The surface is generally hilly and contains many lakes and rivers. For the purpose of dealing with foreign countries it is united with Norway, but otherwise it is independent. Sweden was one of the prominent European powers in the seventeenth century. It took a leading part in the Thirty Years' War under Gustavus Adolphus and his successor. It has an area of 172,876 sq. miles and a population (1897) of 5,009,632.

T.

fort, by 1,000 hostile Indians. Nov. 8, 1813, Jackson set out with 1,200 infantry and 800 cavalry to raise the siege. By 4 o'clock the next morning he had surrounded the enemy, who, 1,080 strong, were concealed in the thickets. At daylight the battle began. It resulted in the complete rout of the savages. As many as 290 dead warriors were found and many others doubtless perished in the woods of the surrounding mountains. The number of the wounded could not be ascertained, but was large. The loss to the whites was 15 killed and 85 wounded.

Tallasahatchee (Ala.), Battle of.—The massacre at Fort Mims spread consternation throughout the region inhabited by the Creeks, and hardy volunteers came forward thirsting for vengeance. Gen. Jackson led the Tennessee militia across the line into Alabama. Upon his arrival at the Coosa he was informed that the Creeks were assembled at Tallasahatchee, a town in an open woodland, not far from the present village of Jacksonville, the county seat of Benton County, Ala., on the southeast side of the Tallasahatchee Creek. Jackson sent Gen. Coffee with 1,000 horsemen to destroy the town. Nov. 3, 1813, Coffee's men surrounded the place and the Indians came out to meet them. The battle was short, sharp, and desperate. The victory for the whites was complete. Every warrior was killed. None asked for quarter, and each fought to the death. At the close of the battle 186 bodies were counted on the plain. It is belived that 200 were killed. Eighty-four women and children were made prisoners. The loss to the whites was 5 men killed and 41 wounded.

Talleyrand, Charles M., letter of, to Citizen Pichon regarding United States ministers in France, I, 283.

Tamarois Indians, treaty with, II, 47.

Tammany.—In 1789 the Columbian Order was organized in New York City by William Mooney. In 1805 it was incorporated under the name of Tammany Society. This was in memory of Tammany, an aged, wise, and friendly chief of the Delaware Indians. At this time charitable societies were also organized in Philadelphia and other cities and named in his honor. The only one of the number that survives is that in New York. William Mooney was the first grand sachem of Tammany, and was assisted by 13 sachems, representing the governors of the thirteen States. The members wore Indian insignia. In 1811 the society built the original Tammany Hall, fronting on City Hall Park. Since then a local political party, favored by a majority of the members of the Tammany Society, has always had its headquarters in the house of the society, and has been popularly known as "Tammany Hall." In theory the Tammany Hall general committee has no relation to the Tammany Society save as tenant of the latter's edifice, yet in practice they are coordinate branches of one political system, the society being in effect the citadel of the con-

trolling spirits of the Tammany Hall party. Tammany Hall claims to be the regular Democratic organization of the city and county of New York, though that claim has often been contested. By means of a thoroughly organized system of Tammany clubs and assembly district associations it has usually held a paramount place in city politics.

Taos (N. Mex.), Battle of.—Feb. 3, 1847, Col. Price, with about 400 Americans, arrived at the town of Don Fernando de Taos, on the top of the Taos Mountain, which had been the scene of the murder of Governor Bent and his party. The Mexicans, numbering 600, had taken refuge in a stone church and two other large buildings. They resisted the American assaults during Feb. 4 and on the morning of the 5th surrendered. The American loss was 54 killed and wounded; that of the Mexicans, 152 killed and many wounded.

Tappan, Samuel F., treaty with Indians concluded by, VI, 636.

Tariff.—The word "tariff" is generally applied to the customs duties levied by Congress on merchandise imported. Tradition identifies the word with the town of Tarifa, Spain. Here, during the Moorish occupancy of the country about Gibraltar, all vessels passing through the strait were compelled to put in and pay such duties as were demanded by the chiefs in possession. Among the Greeks and Romans a duty similar to the tariff of the present day was known, and in England as early as 980, during the reign of Ethelred, duties on ships and goods were levied, to be paid at Billingsgate. Charles II established a regular schedule of rates in 1663. After 1846 England gradually abolished her tariff duties, beginning with the repeal of the corn laws and continuing until 1891-92, when revenue duties alone were collected, and those upon less than twenty articles. In the United States the First Congress passed a tariff law levying on an average less than 8 per cent *ad valorem* on imports. This was approved by Washington July 4, 1789. Madison opened the discussion of this measure in Congress. South Carolina and Georgia favored a rate of 5 per cent, Pennsylvania one of 12 or more, while New England and Virginia succeeded in getting the rate raised a little above what the far South asked for, but placed it lower than the chief manufacturing States desired. The tariff of 1816 imposed duties of about 25 per cent on certain leading manufactures, under protest from the agricultural States of the South. In 1824 a new tariff act was passed, increasing, among the changes made, duties on metals and agricultural products. Jan. 31, 1828, the "tariff of abominations," as it was named by its enemies, was introduced in the House, embodying the recommendations of a national convention of manufacturers held at Harrisburg, Pa. This bill proposed a 41 per cent rate and was favored by Daniel Webster, who reversed his position of 1824. South Carolina protested against the proposed measure as unconstitutional, unjust, and oppressive. North Carolina also protested, and Alabama and Georgia denied the power of Congress to lay duties for protection. July 14, 1832, President Jackson approved a bill reducing the tax on iron, increasing that on woolens, making some raw wools free, and leaving cotton unchanged. This bill retained the protective feature of the law of 1828, but reduced the taxes somewhat. South Carolina passed an ordinance nullifying this act, but her ordinance was rescinded after the approval of the compromise tariff of 1833. This measure, introduced by Clay and supported by Calhoun, provided for a gradual reduction of duties to a uniform rate, to be reached in 1842. It secured a revenue tariff by successive reductions. In 1842, the Whigs being in a majority, Congress enacted a protective tariff, which President Tyler vetoed (IV, 180). July 30, 1846, a tariff law was enacted which subordinated the principle of protection to that of revenue. It passed the House by a vote of 114 to 95 and the Senate by the casting vote of Vice-President Dallas. The average rate of duty was fixed at about 25 per cent. This was lowered to about 20 per cent by an act of 1857. In 1861 the principle of protection was reasserted in the Morrill Act, which increased the rates of 1857 about one-third. During the Civil War the tariff rates were repeatedly raised to meet the expenses of Government and stimulate manufacture. These rates were continued long after the cessation of hostilities. In 1882 a tariff commission was appointed to visit different sections of the country in the interest of tariff revision. The commission recommended a reduction of 20 per cent in rates. President Cleveland, in his message of Dec. 8, 1885 (VIII, 341), recommended a reduction of the tariff, and his message of Dec. 6, 1887 (VIII, 580), was devoted exclusively to this topic. The Mills bill, framed largely in accordance with the President's views, passed the House, but failed in the Senate. The Fifty-first Congress passed in 1890 an act raising the duties to an average of about 48 per cent on dutiable goods. The tariff act of 1894 became a law without the President's signature, with an income-tax provision, which was declared unconstitutional by the Supreme Court. In 1897 the Dingley law was passed, which imposes the highest rates of duty on many articles ever known in our history.

Tariff. (See Foreign Import Duties; Import Duties.)

Tariff Acts. (See Import Duties.)

Tariff Commission discussed, VIII, 49, 135, 244.

Tariff Laws. (See Import Duties.)

Tariff of—
1816 referred to, II, 191.
1842 discussed and referred to, IV, 404, 451, 499, 552, 647.
1846 discussed and referred to, IV, 552, 647; V, 520.

Tarrateen Indians. (See Abnaki Indians.)

Tate, James H., consul at Buenos Ayres, nomination of, and reasons therefor, IV, 421.

Tattnall, Josiah, mentioned, II, 475.

Taussig, Edward D., member of board of management of Government exhibit at World's Columbian Exposition, IX, 401.

Tawakaro Indians, treaty with, III, 395.

Tax, Income. (See Income Tax.)

Tax, Poll. (See Poll Tax.)

Taxation.—The exaction of money from the individual for the use of the state is a function of all forms of government. The generally accepted theory of taxation in America is that money to be used in the service of all the citizens of the state is justly raised by taxation; that a tax which does not bear equally upon all or which, bearing equally upon all, is used only for the benefit of a few is unjust. The direction taken by all efforts at tax reform is toward self-taxation—i. e., the community as a whole to decide what is required of each individual for the public expense. Out of this principle grew the doctrine that no tax can be levied save by the representatives of the people who must pay it. It was in defense of this principle that the American colonists objected to the stamp tax imposed by Parliament and raised the claim that "taxation without representation is tyranny." The tax levied by a conquering nation upon a vanquished foe is tribute. Direct taxation is authorized by the Constitution in proportion to the population. The first direct tax was for $2,000,000, and was levied *pro rata* upon the sixteen States existing in 1798. Others have since been levied, notably that of 1861, when $20,000,000 was levied in this manner for prosecuting the war. Three-fourths of this amount was by act of Mar. 2, 1891, refunded to the States. Congress is forbidden by the Constitution to lay any tax or duty on exports (I, 26). States are forbidden to lay duties on either exports or imports, but may resort to direct taxation. Until the Civil War the Federal Government relied chiefly upon duties upon imports for its revenue, but since that time an internal-revenue tax has been collected. State taxation is direct and is assessed upon real and personal property, upon privileges, and upon individuals or polls. Before 1800 most of the States passed laws to regulate taxation. All except Delaware levied a tax on land, and nine of the original thirteen States collected a poll tax. The systems of county, State, and municipal taxation are numerous and constantly changing. According to the contention of those who favor the single-tax theory, taxation should be solely upon land values, exclusive of improvements.

Taxation (see also Import Duties):
Balance due from collectors, II, 51.
Consular reports on, VIII, 616.
Direct, discussed, I, 275, 278.
Increase in, IX, 114.
Recommended, I, 142; VII, 293.
Internal-revenue stamps referred to, VI, 705.
Joint resolution to correct clerical errors in internal-revenue act vetoed, VI, 270.
On capital and deposits of banks, repeal of, recommended, VIII, 49.

State;" motto, "Agriculture; Commerce." It lies between lat. 35° and 36° 35' north and long. 81° 37' and 90° 15' west. Tennessee is bounded on the north by Kentucky and Virginia, on the east and southeast by North Carolina (separated by the Great Smoky and Bald ranges of the Alleghanies), on the south by Georgia, Alabama, and Mississippi, and on the west by Arkansas and Missouri (separated by the Mississippi River). The eastern portion of the State is mountainous, while the extreme western part, bordering on the Mississippi River, consists of a flat alluvial plain, where vegetation grows with almost tropical luxuriance. Between these two extremes are the valley of the Tennessee in its southern course, an important agricultural region, and the Cumberland Plateau, a table-land with an elevation of 2,000 feet. Extending from this plateau to the Tennessee River in its northern course through the State lies the great central basin, sometimes called the Garden of the State. West of the Tennessee Valley rises another fertile plateau before the descent to the lowlands of the Mississippi. The leading productions are indian corn, wheat, cotton and tobacco, and live stock. Manufactures of cotton goods and iron have grown up since the Civil War. The first permanent settlement was made in 1769 at Wautauga by immigrants from North Carolina. When North Carolina proposed to cede this territory to the General Government these settlers objected and organized a State under the name of Franklin (q.v.). This government was overthrown and a Territory was organized in 1790. The State was admitted to the Union June 1, 1796. In January, 1861, a proposal to secede from the Union was defeated by popular vote, but carried in the election of June 8 of the same year. The State was the scene of some of the fiercest battles of the Civil War, including those of Island No. 10, Nashville, Lookout Mountain, Murfreesboro, Fort Donelson, Shiloh, Missionary Ridge, etc. It was readmitted to the Union in 1866. Area, 42,050 sq. miles; population (1890), 1,767,518.

Tennessee (see also Confederate States; Memphis):

Colored troops to be recruited in, order regarding, X, 110.

Commanding officers in, instructions to, as to conduct of war, VI, 275.

Government for, order of President Lincoln to Governor Johnson regarding, X, 109.

Home of Andrew Jackson tendered Government by, V, 421.

Insurrection in, declared suppressed by proclamation, VI, 317.

Joint resolution restoring, to Union approved and discussed, VI, 395.

Letter to governor of, respecting militia for suppression of troubles on Mississippi River, X, 101.

Murders committed by Indians in, X, 44.

Ratification of amendment to Federal Constitution by, referred to, I, 259.

Tennessee—Continued.

Relief for people in eastern section of, and address of East Tennessee Relief Association regarding, discussed, VI, 204.

Volunteers of—

Communication of President Jackson respecting apportionment of, X, 105.

Number of, in Indian wars greater than her proportion in general apportionment, III, 234.

Operation of, under Maj. Gen. Jackson against Indian allies of Great Britain, I, 548.

Recommendation that Government pay expenses incurred by, III, 235, 255.

Tennessee Bond Cases.—A series of 17 cases decided by the United States Supreme Court in 1885. In 1852 the Tennessee legislature passed an act making certain railroad bonds a statutory lien upon the property on which they were issued. Holders of State bonds afterwards brought suit to establish their lien upon the property in question. The Supreme Court held that the lien was created for the benefit of the State and not of the holders of State bonds issued under that act.

Tennessee River:

Canal from the Altamaha to, referred to, II, 464.

Survey of, referred to, II, 565.

Tenure-of-Office Act.—Under the terms of the Constitution the power of making appointments is vested in the President, to be exercised with the advice and consent of the Senate. In the course of his disputes with Congress President Johnson was charged with a corrupt use of the power of appointment and removal, and on the first day of the second session of the Thirty-ninth Congress a bill was introduced "to regulate the tenure of certain civil offices." It was passed over the President's veto Mar. 2, 1867, and was repealed in 1887. This act provided that, with certain exceptions, every officer appointed with the concurrence of the Senate should retain his office until a successor should be in like manner appointed. Johnson was impeached for violating the act in 1868 with regard to Secretary of War Stanton.

Tenure-of-Office Act:

Discussed by President—
Cleveland, VIII, 380.
Johnson, VI, 569.

Interpretation of, referred to, VI, 523.

Repeal of, recommended, VI, 673; VII, 38, 605.

Vetoed, VI, 492.

Terceira, claims of United States against Portugal arising out of blockade of, II, 535, 550; III, 24.

Terrill, William R., brigadier-general in Army, nomination of, and reasons therefor, VI, 161.

Territorial Expansion:

Annexation discussed. (See Alaska; California; Cuba; Florida; Gadsden Purchase; Hawaiian Islands; Louisiana Purchase; New Mexico; Philippine Islands; Puerto Rico; St. John Island; St. Thomas Island; Santo Domingo; Texas; Yucatan.)

Texas vs. White et al.—A case before the Supreme Court of the United States in which the acts of secession of the Southern States were declared void and the rights of a State of the Union held to be unimpaired by the acts of a revolutionary government within the State. In 1851 the United States issued to the State of Texas 5,000 coupon bonds for $1,000 each, payable to the State of Texas or bearer, with interest at 5 per cent semiannually, in settlement of certain boundary claims. Some of these bonds were seized by the officers of the State government during the Civil War and sold to White & Chiles and others of New York. The bonds were payable only when indorsed by the governor. The State convention in 1866 passed an ordinance looking to the recovery of these bonds. An act passed in October of that year authorized the governor to proceed in his discretion to carry out this intention. The agent appointed by the executive procured the filing of a bill the same year asking for an injunction and the recovery of the bonds in question. The case came before the Supreme Court of the United States at the December term, 1868, on the original bill. The injunction was granted on the general ground that the action of a revolutionary State government did not affect the right of Texas as a State of the Union having a government acknowledging her obligations to the Federal Constitution. The court pronounced the act of secession void, Chief Justice Chase rendering the opinion. Justice Grier dissented on all the points raised and decided. Justices Swayne and Miller concurred in dissenting on the capacity of the State of Texas, "in her present condition," to waive on an original suit. On the merits of the case they united with the majority. Further hearing was accorded to certain parties, and both complainant and defendants were granted liberty in the decree to apply for further directions in its execution. In one place in the court's opinion the Chief Justice said it was a historical fact that in 1862 the government of Texas in control was its only actual government, its acts in almost all respects valid, though unlawful and revolutionary as to the United States. December, 1869, the additional part of this celebrated case, known in the reports as Texas *vs.* Hardenberg, arose, the Chief Justice deciding for the court that upon the whole case the decree must be for the complainant as to the bonds claimed by Hardenberg. Further decisions of the Supreme Court on additional portions of the case are as follows, briefly: December, 1870, *In re* Paschal, Justice Bradley delivering the court's judgment, it was ordered that the motion to compel George W. Paschal to pay to the clerk of the court the money received by him be denied. An order was granted to discharge him as solicitor and counsel for the complainant in the second case. October, 1874, *In re* Chiles, Justice Miller rendering the court's opinion, Justices Field and Hunt dissenting, it was ordered that Chiles pay a fine of $250 and the costs of the proceeding and stand committed to the marshal's custody until the same be paid. This was for contempt in disobeying the court's decree.

Textiles and Glass, report on cost of producing, in United States and Europe transmitted, IX, 239.

Thacher, John M., report of, on International Patent Congress referred to, VII, 261.

Thames (Canada), Battle of.—After Perry's victory over the British fleet on Lake Erie, Gen. Harrison completed his preparations for the invasion of Canada. Sept. 21, 1813, the embarkation of the army on Perry's transports began. On the afternoon of the 27th the Army of the Northwest, consisting of 5,000 men, under the immediate command of Gen. Harrison and Gen. Shelby, governor of Kentucky, landed at Amherstburg (Malden), but found that Proctor's army, about 800 regulars and 1,200 Indians, had fled inland. Harrison started in hot pursuit. In response to the repeated demands of Tecumseh the British made a stand about

8 miles north of the river Thames. Here they were attacked on Oct. 5 by about 3,000 Americans. A short but decisive battle took place, in which the British and Indians were completely routed and Chief Tecumseh was killed. The precise number of casualties in this battle is not known. The American loss was probably about 15 killed and twice that number wounded. The British lost about 18 killed, 26 wounded, and 600 taken prisoners, of whom 25 were officers. Proctor made his escape. Thirty-three dead Indians were found upon the field after the battle.

Thanks of Congress:
Tender of, recommended to—
Alden, James, VI, 76.
Bailey, Theodorus, VI, 76.
Baldwin, Charles H., VI, 76.
Bell, Henry H., VI, 76.
Boggs, Charles S., VI, 76.
Breese, K. Randolph, VI, 76.
Caldwell, Charles H. B., VI, 76.
Craven, Thomas T., VI, 76.
Crosby, Pierce, VI, 76.
Cushing, William B., VI, 256.
Dahlgren, John A., VI, 83.
Davis, Charles H., VI, 83.
De Camp, John, VI, 76.
Dewey, George, etc., X, 155.
Donaldson, Edward, VI, 76.
Du Pont, Samuel F., VI, 64, 70.
Farragut, David G., VI, 75.
Foote, Andrew H., VI, 82.
Goldsborough, Louis M., VI, 65.
Guest, John, VI, 76.
Harrell, Abram, VI, 76.
Harrison, Napoleon, VI, 76.
Hobson, Richmond P., X, 159.
Lardner, James L., VI, 83.
Lee, Samuel P., VI, 76.
Morris, George U., VI, 144.
Morris, Henry, VI, 76.
Newcomb, Frank H., etc., X, 157.
Nichols, Edward F., VI, 76.
Porter, David D., VI, 76, 83, 151.
Preble, George H., VI, 76.
Queen, Walter W., VI, 76.
Ransom, George M., VI, 76.
Renshaw, William B., VI, 76.
Rodgers, John, VI, 191.
Rowan, Stephen C., VI, 83.
Russell, John H., VI, 76.
Smith, Albert N., VI, 76.
Smith, Melancton, VI, 76.
Smith, Watson, VI, 76.
Stringham, Silas H., VI, 83.
Swartwout, Samuel, VI, 76.
Wainwright, Jonathan M., VI, 76.
Wainwright, Richard, VI, 76.
Winslow, John A., VI, 256.
Woodworth, Selim E., VI, 76.
Worden, John L., VI, 143.
Tendered to—
Dewey, George, etc., X, 156.
Reply of, X, 157.
Grant, Ulysses S., VI, 231.
Lyon, Nathaniel, etc., VI, 99.

Thanks of President:
Tendered to—
Burnside, Ambrose E., VI, 104.
Canby, Edward R. S., VI, 239.
Dewey, George, etc., X, 208, 218.
Referred to, X, 155.
Farragut, David G., VI, 239.
Foote, Andrew H., VI, 104.
Goldsborough, Louis M., VI, 104.
Granger, Gordon, VI, 239.
Grant, Ulysses S., VI, 104.
Merritt, Wesley, etc., X, 217.
Militia of—
Illinois, VI, 241.
Indiana, VI, 241.
Iowa, VI, 241.
Ohio, VI, 239.
Wisconsin, VI, 241.
Sampson, William T., etc., X, 213.
Shafter, William R., etc., X, 214, 216.
Sherman, William T., VI, 238.
Wool, John E., VI, 112.
Worden, John L., VI, 112.
Thanksgiving Proclamations of President—
Adams, John, I, 268, 284.
Arthur, VIII, 36, 123, 159, 225.
Cleveland, VIII, 310, 491, 571, 743; IX, 433, 511, 593, 695.
Grant, VII, 18, 92, 138, 178, 228, 277, 325, 392, 397.
Harrison, Benj., IX, 19, 101, 162, 301.
Hayes, VII, 457, 490, 548, 599.
Johnson, VI, 332, 438, 550, 660.
Lincoln, VI, 89, 170, 172, 228. (See also Fasting and Prayer.)
McKinley, X, 207. (See also X, 213.)
Madison, I, 513, 532, 558, 560.
Washington, I, 64, 179.
Thayer, Sylvanus, brevet colonel in Army, nomination of, and reasons therefor, III, 479.
Thetis, The. (See Schley, Winfield S.)
Thomas, Francis, agreement with Peru signed by, VII, 258.
Thomas, George H., statue of, to be unveiled, VII, 557.
Thomas, Lorenzo, Secretary of War *ad interim,* directed to act as, VI, 663. (See also VI, 621.)
Thompson, Clark W., treaty with Indians concluded by, VI, 210.
Thompson, Elizabeth, Carpenter's painting of Lincoln and Cabinet at reading of Emancipation Proclamation presented to Congress by, VII, 483.
Thompson, Jacob:
Order exempting, from arrest during journey to Washington, VI, 237.
Reward offered for arrest of, VI, 307.
Revoked, VI, 353.
Thompson, Richard W., claim of, for alleged services to Menominee Indians, V, 366.
Thompson, Waddy, mentioned, IV, 233.
Thompsons Island. (See Key West.)
Thomson, Charles, informs Washington of his election as President, I, 42.
Thorn, Owen, claim of, against Great Britain referred to, VII, 10.

The bill to admit Kansas into the Union under the provisions of the Topeka constitution was introduced in the House of Representatives by Daniel Mace, of Indiana, Apr. 7, 1856, and in the Senate by Lewis Cass, of Michigan, Mar. 24. The bill passed the House, but failed in the Senate. (See also Lecompton Constitution; Wyandotte Constitution.)

Topeka Constitution. (See Kansas, Government of.)

Topographical Corps:
Increase in, recommended, II, 307; III, 255, 390.
Internal improvements, operations of, intrusted to, III, 559.
Reorganization of, recommended, III, 169.

Tornado, The. (See *Virginius*, The.)

Torpedo Boats. (See Vessels, United States.)

Torpedoes:
Adoption and construction of, discussed, IX, 324.
Appropriation for trial with, recommended, VII, 350.

Tortugas. (See Dry Tortugas.)

Tory.—The terms "Whig" and "Tory" had been in use in English politics for a great many years anterior to the American Revolution. The term "Whig" designated the party opposing the royal prerogative and who were generally in favor of reforms; the term "Tory," the party upholding the prerogative and adhering to old institutions. In our colonial days the term "Tory" was applied to those who were adherents of the Crown, and the term "Whig" to the opponents thereof, and so the American sympathizers were known as Whigs, the supporters of England as Tories.

Totten, Joseph G., correspondence regarding water supply for Washington and Georgetown, V, 162.

Tousig, Simon, claim of, to protection of United States, V, 228.

Town.—A word derived from the Anglo-Saxon word "tun," meaning "a place inclosed." The suffix still clings to the names of many English towns. In the United States the word has a varying signification. In Pennsylvania it is applied to any municipal government. In New York, Wisconsin, and most of the Western States a town is a subdivision of a county, and is often called a township (q. v.), but the town is not necessarily always coextensive with the latter. In New England the town is the unit of civil organization, a county being simply an aggregation of towns.

Town Meeting.—A peculiarly democratic institution of New England and some of the newly formed Western States. It is a meeting of the citizens to legislate for the town, levy taxes, elect the officers, usually a town clerk, selectmen, a treasurer, assessors, constables, overseers of the poor, and school commissioners. In some of the towns the cities, by their aldermen, are authorized to transact the business formerly attended to by the town meeting. That it still has a legal existence was demonstrated as recently as 1881, when the Labor

Reform Society of Boston secured a writ of mandamus to compel the city authorities to call a town meeting on petition, as required by its charter.

Towns, Seaport, protection for. (See Defenses, Public, provision for.)

Townsend, E. D., order for release of Clement C. Clay, jr., X, 113.

Townshend Acts.—At the instance of Charles Townshend, chancellor of the exchequer, two acts were passed by the British Parliament providing for the appointment of commissioners to enforce more effectually the laws relating to taxes in the Colonies. They authorized writs of assistance and increased the duties on many articles already taxed, besides imposing others on glass, paper, colors, and tea. The object of these taxes was to support the civil government in the territories.

Township.—In the older United States counties are divided, without reference to their inhabitants, into townships varying in size from 5 to 10 miles square. When in 1802 Col. Mansfield surveyed the Northwest Territory he divided the entire public domain into land districts made up of a varying number of tracts each 6 miles square. These were called townships. These townships were again divided into 36 equal squares, called sections, of 1 sq. mile each and containing 640 acres. A civil township may include more or less than 1 township in area.

Towson, Nathan, appointment of, to artillery discussed, II, 112.
Rejection of, discussed, II, 126, 133.

Tracy, Benjamin F., Secretary of Navy, mentioned, IX, 324.

Trade Dollar.—A silver coin issued by the United States from 1874 to 1878. It was coined for use in trade with China in competition with the Spanish and Mexican dollars. It was not intended for general circulation in the United States, though it was made a legal tender to the amount of $5 at the time of issue. The legal-tender provision was repealed in 1876. The weight of the trade dollar was 420 grains, while the standard American silver dollar weighed 412½ grains. An act of Mar. 1, 1887, authorized the Treasurer to redeem in standard silver dollars all trade dollars presented during the following 6 months.

Trade Dollars discussed, III, 180, 244.

Trade-Marks:
International convention at Paris on subject of, VIII, 127.
Treaty regarding, with—
Austria-Hungary, VII, 160.
Belgium, VIII, 212, 235.
Brazil, VII, 508.
France, VII, 13.
Germany, VII, 160, 188.
Great Britain, VII, 456, 467.
Italy, VIII, 202.
Roumania, VIII, 89.
Russia, VI, 689; VII, 266, 293.
Spain, VIII, 109.
  Referred to, VIII, 170.

up by Alexander Hamilton with such precision and comprehensiveness that few radical changes have since been found necessary. The law forbids the Secretary of the Treasury to engage in trade or commerce. He superintends the collection of the revenue, grants all warrants for moneys paid out of the Treasury in pursuance of appropriations made by law, and performs all such duties connected with the finances of the United States as are required by law. His business embraces the management of the national debt, the national currency and coinage, supervision of the national banks, the internal-revenue system, the customs revenue, the merchant marine, the light-house system, Coast and Geodetic Survey, inspection of steam vessels, Life-Saving Service, and marine hospitals. There are 2 Assistant Secretaries, and the routine work of the Department is divided among 8 divisions. The accounts for all receipts and disbursements by the United States or any of its officers are, according to law, examined in the office of one of the 6 Auditors of the Treasury. The Auditor for the Treasury Department has charge of all accounts relating to the customs service, the public debt, internal revenue, Treasurer and assistant treasurers, mints and assay offices, Bureau of Engraving and Printing, Coast and Geodetic Survey, Revenue-Cutter Service, Life-Saving Service, Light-House Board, Marine-Hospital Service, public buildings, Steamboat-Inspection Service, Immigration Service, Bureau of Navigation, Secret Service, and Alaskan fur-seal fisheries. The Auditor for the War Department receives and examines all accounts of salaries and incidental expenses of the Office of the Secretary of War and all bureaus and offices under his direction; all accounts relating to the military establishment, armories, and arsenals, national cemeteries, fortifications, public buildings and grounds under the Chief of Engineers, rivers and harbors, the Military Academy, and all other business within the jurisdiction of the Department of War. The Auditor for the Interior Department examines all accounts relating to salaries and incidental expenses of the Office of the Secretary of the Interior and all offices and bureaus under his direction, and all accounts relating to army and navy pensions, Geological Survey, public lands, Indians, Architect of the Capitol, patents, census, and all other business within the jurisdiction of the Department of the Interior. The Auditor for the Navy Department examines and settles all accounts of the Navy Department, including the Office of the Secretary of the Navy and all offices and bureaus under his direction. The Auditor for the State and Other Departments examines and certifies all accounts of salaries and incidental expenses of the offices of the Secretary of State, the Attorney-General, and the Secretary of Agriculture, and of all bureaus under their direction, the diplomatic and consular service, the judiciary, United States courts, judgments of United States courts, Executive Office, Civil Service Commission, Interstate Commerce Commission, Department of Labor, District of Columbia, Fish Commission, Court of Claims and its judgments, Smithsonian Institution, Territorial governments, Senate, House of Representatives, Library of Congress, Public Printing, Botanic Garden, and all boards, commissions, and establishments of the Government not included in any of the Executive Departments. The Auditor for the Post-Office Department examines and adjusts all accounts relating to the postal service. He superintends and when necessary takes legal measures to enforce the collection of all debts due the United States for the service of the Post-Office Department and all penalties imposed. All these accounts, after examination by an auditor, are referred to the Comptroller of the Treasury for his examination and approval. His decisions are final and conclusive upon the executive branch of the Government. The Register of the Treasury signs and issues all bonds, United States notes, and other securities, and receipts for their redemption, etc. The work of his office is performed in two divisions—first, the division of loans, and, second, the division of notes, coupons, and currency. The Comptroller of the Currency supervises the national-bank system. The Director of the Mint has charge of the coinage and kindred subjects. The Commissioner of Internal Revenue superintends the collection of internal taxes. The Solicitor of the Treasury has charge of the detection and punishment of frauds upon the customs revenue and counterfeiting. He is the law officer of the Treasury Department. The Chief of the Bureau of Statistics makes annual reports on immigration, shipping, commerce, etc. The Superintendent of the Coast and Geodetic Survey has charge of the survey of the coast and inland rivers and publishes sailing maps and charts. The Marine-Hospital Service is in charge of a Surgeon-General. The Supervising Architect draws designs and looks after the erection of all public buildings. The Life-Saving Service and the inspection of steam vessels are each in charge of a special superintendent. The Bureau of Engraving and Printing is under a chief and occupies a separate building. The Commissioner of Navigation is charged with superintendence of the merchant marine, the issuing of registers and enrollments, licenses of vessels, and the collection of tonnage taxes. The Treasurer of the United States is charged with the custody of all public moneys in the vaults at Washington and in the several subtreasuries in New York, Philadelphia, and other cities. The Department occupies a large freestone and granite structure in the Ionian style of architecture, just east of the Executive Mansion, at Washington. It employs some 16,000 persons, about 3,500 of whom are at the capital. Following is a list of the Secretaries of the Treasury from the establishment of the Department: Alexander Hamilton, New York; Oliver Wolcott, jr., Connecticut; Samuel Dexter, Massachusetts; Albert Gallatin, Pennsylvania; George W. Campbell, Tennessee; Alexander J. Dallas, Pennsylvania; William H. Crawford, Georgia; Richard Rush, Pennsylvania; Samuel D. Ingham, Pennsylvania; Louis McLane, Delaware; William J. Duane, Pennsylvania; Roger B. Taney, Maryland; Levi Woodbury, New Hampshire; Thomas Ewing, Ohio; Walter Forward, Pennsylvania; John C. Spencer, New York; George M. Bibb, Kentucky; Robert J. Walker, Mississippi; William M. Meredith, Pennsylvania, Thomas Corwin, Ohio; James Guthrie, Kentucky; Howell Cobb, Georgia; Philip F. Thomas, Maryland; John A. Dix, New York; Salmon P. Chase, Ohio; William P. Fessenden, Maine; Hugh McCulloch, Indiana; George S. Boutwell, Massachusetts; William A. Richardson, Massachusetts; Benjamin H. Bristow, Kentucky; Lot M. Morrill, Maine; John Sherman, Ohio; William Windom, Minnesota; Charles J. Folger, New York; Walter Q. Gresham, Indiana; Daniel Manning, New York; Charles S. Fairchild, New York; Charles Foster, Ohio; John G. Carlisle, Kentucky, and Lyman J. Gage, Illinois.

Treasury Department:

Appropriations for, transferred, III, 35, 185, 395, 555; IV, 51, 90, 272.

Vacancy occasioned by death of head of, recommendation regarding filling of, IX, 133.

Treasury Notes.—To meet the expenses of the War of 1812, $36,000,000 in Treasury notes bearing 5⅖ per cent interest were issued. They were receivable for all dues to the Government, but were not legal tender. Beginning with the panic of 1837 and extending through the Mexican War, $73,000,000 were issued, and following the panic of 1857 there was an issue of $53,000,000. The exigencies of the Civil War required the issue of Treasury notes in large amounts. An act of Feb. 25, 1862, authorized the issue of $150,000,000 of such notes with a legal-tender character and not bearing interest. These were called greenbacks (q. v.). The United States seven-thirties, of which $830,000,000 were issued, were a variety of Treasury note. Treasury notes were issued to pay for the monthly purchases of bullion authorized by the Sherman Act of 1890.

Treasury Notes:

Appropriation to meet outstanding, recommended, V, 542.

Issuance of, I, 564; IV, 266.

Additional, discussed, VI, 149.

Recommended, V, 458.

Purchase of, by banks referred to, X, 45.

Redemption of, referred to, III, 534.

Reissuance of, prohibition on, should be removed, III, 469.

Retirement of, issued in payment of silver purchased under act of 1890 recommended, IX, 646, 744.

Treasury Office of Accounts.—An important bureau under the Treasury Board as established by the Continental Congress. It was presided over by an auditor-general.

Treasury, Secretary of:

Duties of, discharged by Secretary of Navy, X, 47.

Power of, over deposits unqualified, III, 8.

Report of, I, 347, 479; II, 69, 83, and X, 121; II, 203, 231, 341, 343, 346, 535.

Vacancy occasioned by death of, recommendations regarding filling of, IX, 133.

Treasury, Solicitor of, office of, established, II, 527.

Operations of, referred to, IV, 689.

Treaties.—The modern definition of a treaty is an agreement or covenant between two or more nations or sovereignties formally signed by duly authorized commissioners and solemnly ratified by each. In ancient times terms of treaties were dictated rather than contracted. A conqueror with an army at the gates of a capital stated his terms and declared his intention of remaining and inflicting such punishment as he saw fit until he received satisfactory assurances that his wishes would be carried out. In the fifteenth century a jurisprudence of political treaties began to grow and was closely connected with the development of European statecraft. The treaty of Westphalia, which ended the Thirty Years' War, marked the turning point between ancient and modern diplomacy. Up to this time treaty negotiations had been based upon rights which had once existed and were recognized before rupture. After the treaties of Münster and Osnabrück the object of diplomacy was to establish a political equilibrium at the expense of preexistent rights and to maintain the *status quo*. The efforts of European diplomats during the early part of the nineteenth century were directed toward the suppression of the revolutionary spirit and the curbing of monarchical ambitions. Later the maritime rights of neutrals, suppression of slave trade, and the international emancipation of trade, navigation, arts, and labor became leading subjects for diplomatic consideration. The popularity of the principle of arbitration marks the latest step in diplomatic progress. The proposition made by the Czar of Russia in 1898 for the general disarmament of the world and the settlement of international disputes by a court of arbitration points to a culmination of the science of diplomacy. The first treaties of the United States were conceived before the Declaration of Independence was signed. Nov. 29, 1775, the Continental Congress appointed a committee on secret correspondence, charged with ascertaining whether, if the Colonies should be forced to form themselves into an independent State, France would enter into any treaty or alliance with them. Feb. 6, 1778, two treaties were concluded in Paris with France—a treaty of alliance and a treaty of amity and commerce. Oct. 8, 1782, a treaty of amity and commerce was concluded with the Netherlands, and Apr. 3, 1783, a similar treaty with Sweden. Jan. 20, 1783, an armistice with Great Britain was arranged, followed Sept. 3 by a definitive treaty of peace. Other treaties concluded before the adoption of the Constitution were a treaty of amity and commerce with Prussia, Dec. 10, 1785; a treaty of peace and friendship with Morocco in January, 1787, and a consular convention with France, Nov. 14, 1788. When Washington was called to the Presidency he found the northern frontier of the United States occupied by British military posts and Spain making encroachments on the south. With the outbreak of the French Revolution Spain joined England, and French sympathizers in America were attempting to fit out privateers to prey upon Spanish and English commerce. Washington was urged to cast the fortunes of the United States into one side of the struggle. To avoid any entangling alliances he sent John Jay, Chief Justice of the United States, as a special envoy to London (I, 154). Nov. 19, 1794, Jay concluded the treaty which has since borne his name. In consequence of the irritating conduct of Genêt, the French minister at Washington, Congress in 1798 abrogated the treaties and consular conventions with France. Another treaty was made in 1800, and in 1803 three conventions were signed, including the one ceding Louisiana. One of the most enduring treaties made by the United States was that of Oct. 27, 1795, with Spain, which stood for more than 100 years. This was the only treaty not swept away by the Napoleonic wars. The treaty of Ghent, signed in 1814, was important as settling some disputed boundary questions, as well as concluding peace between the United States and England. No mention was made of the right of search and the impressment of American seamen, though these were the especial causes of the war. Other notable treaties made by the United States were the Webster-Ashburton treaty, signed at Washington in 1842, defining the northeastern boundary between Canada and the United States, and the treaty of Guadalupe Hidalgo, in 1848, concluding the Mexican War, by which Mexico ceded territory now comprising Nevada, Utah, most of Arizona, a large part of New Mexico, parts of Colorado and Wyoming, and all of California. The treaty with Japan in 1854 secured humane treatment for American sailors shipwrecked on the coast of Japan and the right to appoint a consular agent; it also led to the establishment of important trading privileges with the United States and Great Britain in 1858. The treaties of Tientsin, concluded in 1858, and the Burlingame treaty of 1868 opened China to foreign travel and gave protection to Christians within her borders. The treaty of Washington was signed in 1871, and settled questions pending between the United States and Great Britain. It submitted the Alabama claims to a commission of arbitration and adjusted the fisheries question on a reciprocity basis. There was also a concession of important privileges by each to subjects of the other in America, and the question of the northwestern boundary of the United States was submitted to the arbitration of the German Emperor. At the close of the Spanish-American War, in 1898, Spain was forced to relinquish her sovereignty in Cuba and cede to the United States the island of Puerto Rico, together with the Philippine Islands and the island of Guam in the Ladrones, the United States paying to Spain $20,000,000. Under the Constitution treaties are made a part of the supreme law of the land and they have a legal status similar to that of contracts. Numerous treaties have been made with the Indians.

Treaties of United States (see also Indians; III, several powers):

Alleged violation of, memorial regarding, referred to, IV, 150.

Assent of House to, not required, I, 196.

Boundary survey made under treaty of Washington, VI, 390.

Contract for proposed edition of, referred to, IV, 423.

Power to make, vested in President with consent of Senate, I, 195.

Priority of one over another, law in regard to, I, 314.

Referred to, IV, 688, 690; VIII, 264.

Request of House for correspondence regarding, declined, I, 194.

Return of, requested, VIII, 303.

Withdrawn, VIII, 303, 337.

Trenholm, George A., pardon applied for by order regarding, VI, 352.

Trent Affair.—In the autumn of 1861 the government of the Confederate States sent J. M. Mason and John Slidell as commissioners to Great Britain and France, respectively. They went first to Havana, where they took passage on the British merchant ship *Trent* for St. Thomas, on their way to England. Nov. 8 the vessel was stopped in the Old Bahama Channel by the U. S. S. *San Jacinto*, Capt. Wilkes. The Confederate commissioners were seized and taken to Boston as prisoners. Wilkes's act was in violation of the rights of neutral nations, for which the United States had always contended. The British Government promptly instructed its minister at Washington to withdraw from the United States unless the prisoners were set at liberty and an apology tendered within 7 days. The United States disavowed the act of Capt. Wilkes and set the prisoners free.

Trent, The, removal of Confederate envoys from. (See Mason and Slidell.)

Trenton (N. J.), loss of, at Samoan Islands, IX, 44.

Trenton (N. J.), Battle of.—Washington's retreat through New Jersey left him with scarcely 3,000 men on the west bank of the Delaware River on Dec. 8, 1776. On the night of Dec. 13 Gen. Charles Lee was taken prisoner at Baskingridge by the British, and his army added to that of Washington gave the latter some 6,000 able-bodied soldiers. On the night of Dec. 25, 1776, Washington, with about 2,500 men, crossed the Delaware River and on the morning of the 26th attacked an outpost of 1,500 Hessians at Trenton under Col. Rahl and captured about

1,000 of them and killed 40. The American casualties were 2 killed, 2 frozen to death, and 3 wounded. The effect of this victory and that of Princeton following it was electrical. The Americans were uplifted and the British discouraged.

Trescot, William H. :
Mentioned, VII, 609.
Special envoy extraordinary to Peru, Chile, and Bolivia, referred to, VIII, 107.

Tresevant, L., mentioned, I, 281.

Trianon Decree.—A secret edict issued by Napoleon at the Grand Trianon Palace, at Versailles, Aug. 5, 1810. It placed a duty of 50 per cent on colonial products and ordered the immediate confiscation of all American vessels and merchandise brought into French ports prior to May 1, 1810, the date of the approval of the act excluding French vessels from American waters. It also ordered that until Nov. 1 American vessels were to be allowed to enter French ports, but not to unload without his permission, offering at the same time to revoke the Milan and Berlin decrees Nov. 1. The revocation was not carried into effect, and American ships and cargoes availing themselves of the promised protection were confiscated. (See also Berlin Decree; Embargo; Milan Decree; Orders in Council.)

Tribunal of Arbitration at Paris :
Acts to give effect to award of, proclaimed, IX, 494, 691.
Award of, discussed and recommendations regarding, IX, 526, 630.
Case of United States at, prepared by John W. Foster, IX, 313.
Convention for settlement of claims under, IX, 665.
Discussed, IX, 437.
Enforcement of regulations in accordance with decision of, referred to, IX, 568.
Failure of negotiations of, to protect fur seals of Alaska, IX, 750.
Reports of agent of United States to, transmitted, IX, 477.

Tribute paid Algeria by United States referred to, I, 123, 182, 337.

Triggs, Julia, act for relief of, vetoed, VIII, 824.

Trimble, Alexandria, demand of Mexico for extradition of, VIII, 204.

Trinidad, vessels from ports of, duties on, suspended by proclamation, VIII, 304.

Tripoli.—A province of the Turkish Empire in northern Africa. It is bounded on the north by the Mediterranean Sea, on the east by Egypt, on the west by Tunis, and on the south by the Desert of Sahara. The Oasis of Fezzan and some smaller oases are within its borders. It anciently belonged to Carthage and at a later date to Rome. It was overrun and conquered by the Arabs in the seventh century and by the Turks in the sixteenth century. It became an independent State in 1714, but was reconquered by the Turks about 1835. A war occurred between Tripoli and the United States 1801-1805 (q.v.). Population, about 800,000.

Tripoli :
Blockade of, by United States squadron referred to, I, 400, 401.
Citizens of United States imprisoned in, liberated, I, 385.
Claims of United States against, II, 462.
Corvette on coast of, destroyed by United States vessels, I, 365.
Ex-Bashaw of, treaty with United States relative to restoring family of, to, I, 430.
Hamet Caramalli, appeals of, to United States to place, on throne of, I, 392. (See also X, 29, 30.)
Philadelphia, wreck of the, on coast of, I, 368, 374.
Officers and crew of, fall into hands of citizens of, I, 368.
Treaty with, I, 245, 390.
War with. (See Tripolitan War.)

Tripolitan War.—A war between the United States and Tripoli, 1801-1805. During the latter part of the eighteenth century the United States, following the custom of the leading European nations, paid an annual tribute to the rulers of the various Barbary States as the price of immunity from their piratical depredations. In consequence of a refusal on the part of the United States to increase the tribute the Bashaw of Tripoli, June 10, 1801, declared war (I, 326). In anticipation of this event the United States had already sent a squadron to the Mediterranean. In October, 1803, the frigate *Philadelphia,* Capt. Bainbridge, while chasing a corsair into the harbor of Tripoli, struck a sunken rock and was captured with all on board. Commodore Decatur, of the *Intrepid,* ran his vessel into the harbor of Tripoli on the night of Feb. 16, 1804, and under the fire of the shore batteries burned the *Philadelphia.* Between July and September, 1804, Commodore Edward Preble made a series of attacks on the fortifications of Tripoli. Meantime Gen. William Eaton, United States consul at Tunis, joined Hamet, the rightful Bashaw of Tripoli, in an expedition against his usurping brother. Marching from Egypt across the desert, they took Derne Apr. 27, 1805. The success of this expedition made it possible to extort a highly favorable treaty from the Bashaw June 4, 1805, the United States agreeing to pay $60,000 ransom for the officers and crew of the *Philadelphia* and Hamet being induced to retire.

Tripolitan War :
Blockade established by United States referred to, I, 400, 401.
Discussed, I, 326, 343, 370, 391, 392.
Expenses in relation to, referred to, X, 50.
Letter of American consul regarding, transmitted, I, 375, and X, 120.
Treaty of peace transmitted, I, 390.

Trisarre, Mr., mentioned, V, 577.

Trist, N. P. :
Commissioner to Mexico—
Conduct of, discussed, IV, 573, 574.
Dispatches from, referred to, IV, 576, 577.
Recall of, discussed, IV, 573, 574.

Turkey—Continued.

American college at Scutari exempted from taxation, IX, 638.

American missionaries in, protection for and treatment of, discussed, VIII, 40, 505; IX, 440, 530, 637, 715.

Anatolia College partially destroyed by mobs in, and indemnity paid for discussed, IX, 440.

Arabian horses brought by Charles Rhind from, referred to, II, 536.

Armenian subjects of—

Cruelties and atrocities committed upon, by, IX, 557, 637, 715.

Investigation of, by American consul discussed, IX, 557, 637.

Referred to, IX, 658.

Obtaining citizenship in United States and returning to, expelled discussed, IX, 440, 530.

Treatment by, of naturalized citizens of United States of Armenian origin, IX, 663.

Capitulations of, referred to, VIII, 12, 77.

Claims of United States against, discussed, IX, 716; X, 190.

Commercial relations with, III, 515. (See also Black Sea.)

Consular courts of United States in, discussed, VI, 151.

Consuls of United States in, exequatur to, refused, IX, 638, 660, 716.

Investigation of atrocities committed on Armenians by, discussed, IX, 557, 637.

Referred to, IX, 658.

Relieved of judicial powers discussed, VII, 238.

Expulsion of Greeks from Constantinople referred to, V, 241.

Fugitive criminals, convention with, for surrender of, VII, 304, 342.

Immigration of citizens of United States into. (See Immigration.)

Invasion of, by Russia. (See Wars, Foreign.)

Jurisdictional rights of United States in, discussed, VIII, 128; IX, 37; X, 190.

Massacre by Turks in Bulgaria referred to, VII, 422.

Naturalization treaty with, referred to, VII, 304; VIII, 813.

Questions regarding, discussed, VIII, 335, 504; IX, 440, 530; X, 190.

Treatment by, of naturalized citizens of United States of Armenian origin referred to, IX, 663.

Relations with, VIII, 239.

Sultan of—

Death of, referred to, III, 533.

Visit of agent of, to United States referred to, V, 119.

Tariffs of, revision of, participated in by United States, VIII, 172.

Treaty with, transmitted and discussed by President—

Grant, VII, 304, 342.

Jackson, II, 504, 530, 551, 564, 574, 575, 594.

Lincoln, VI, 71, 128.

Construction of, referred to, VII, 43.

Turkey—Continued.

Treaty with—Continued.

Referred to, II, 530.

Termination of, VII, 403.

Sought by, VIII, 335.

War with—

Greece, hope for independence of latter entertained by United States, II, 193, 217, 259, 309, 384.

Russia—

Discussed by President—

Adams, J. Q., II, 407.

Hayes, VII, 466.

Neutrality preserved by United States in, VII, 466.

Threatening aspect of, discussed, II, 193.

Treaty of peace referred to, II, 445.

Turley, John A., act granting pension to widow of, vetoed, VIII, 681.

Turner, Junius T., act for relief of, vetoed, VII, 389.

Objections to bill withdrawn, VII, 389.

Turner, L. C., mentioned, VI, 121.

Turreau, Gen., letter of, concerning arrival of Cuban exiles in United States referred to, I, 471.

Turtle, Thomas, member of Board on Geographic Names, IX, 212.

Turtle Mountain Indians:

Agreement with, for cession of lands, IX, 346.

Referred to, VIII, 797.

Tuscaloosa, Ala., bill to provide for purchase of site and erection of public building at, vetoed, IX, 86.

Tuscany.—A compartimento of the Kingdom of Italy. Tuscany corresponds nearly to the ancient Etruria. It was ruled by the Romans, Goths, Byzantine Greeks, Lombards, and Franks. It became completely disintegrated about the eleventh century, but was afterward erected into the Grand Duchy of Tuscany. After several changes in its government it was taken by France and became a part of that country about 1808, and was restored to the Hapsburg-Lorraine line in 1814. Tuscany was annexed by Italy in 1860. Area, 9,304 sq. miles; population (1892), about 2,332,000.

Tuscany:

Treaty with France, I, 193.

Vessels of, discriminating duties on, suspended by proclamation, III, 233.

Tuscarora Indians.—A tribe of the Iroquois stock of Indians. Their name means "Unwilling to be with others." They early separated from the parent stock and emigrated to the South. They were first known to Europeans on the Neuse River, in North Carolina. In 1711 they attacked the whites and were almost annihilated. The survivors returned to the Iroquois in New York and became one of the Six Nations (q. v.). They number now about 700, about equally divided between New York and Canada.

Tuscarora Indians, treaty with, I, 356.

Tuttle, Joseph, act granting pension to, vetoed, VIII, 454.

U.

workman was asked the meaning of the initials "U. S.," which at that time were rarely used as an abbreviation for the United States. The prompt reply was "Elbert Anderson and Uncle Sam," referring to Sam Wilson. This interpretation became current among the workmen, many of whom afterwards enlisted and communicated the explanation to their comrades from all parts of the country as the mystic cipher elicited inquiry. The story went the rounds of the press and "Uncle Sam" became the popular appellation of the Government.

Uncompahgre Reservation, bill to change boundaries of, vetoed, IX, 87.

Underground Railroad.—A name commonly applied before the Civil War to an arrangement whereby fugitive slaves were assisted to escape to Canada. The idea originated in some one of the Northern States, and the plan consisted in harboring fugitives during the day and at night conducting them to the next "station" till they finally reached the border line. This "railroad" had many branches and the stations were a night's journey apart. The principal routes were from Kentucky, across Virginia and Ohio, and from Maryland through Pennsylvania and New York. This system of aiding escaping slaves was partially organized in 1838, but did not attain its highest activity until the passage of the fugitive-slave law, about 1850. A Quaker, Levi Coffin, the reputed president of the organization, is said to have aided in the escape of a large number of slaves annually for many years. A colored woman named Harriet Tubman is said to have made many journeys North, conducting bands of fugitives.

Union Flags, return of Confederate and, to respective States recommended, VIII, 578.

Proposition withdrawn, VIII, 579.

Union Labor Party.—A successor of the Greenback party. It was organized at Cincinnati Feb. 23, 1887, and promulgated a platform embodying the principles of the Knights of Labor. In 1891 it united with the Farmers' Alliance and other elements to form the Populist party.

United Confederate Veterans.—An association the objects and purposes of which are set forth in the constitution as finally adopted at the Houston reunion, May 23, 1895. It is a federation of all associations of Confederate veterans, soldiers and sailors. The purposes are the cultivation of ties of friendship between those who have shared common dangers, sufferings, and privations; the encouragement of the writing, by participators therein, of narratives, episodes, occurrences, etc., of the Civil War; the collection of authentic data for an impartial history, and the preservation of war relics and mementos, and the record, as far as possible, of every Confederate soldier who is dead; caring for the needy survivors and assisting and protecting Confederate widows and orphans; the erection of enduring monuments and marking with headstones the graves of Confederate dead, and instilling into descendants proper veneration for their fathers. Membership is by camps, and the latter are organized into departments, divisions, and brigades. There are 3 departments—Army of Northern Virginia, Army of the Tennessee, and Army of the Trans-Mississippi.

United Labor Party.—A local political party organized in New York City in 1886. It nominated Henry George for mayor on a platform based upon his theory that values arising from the growth of society belong to the community as a whole, and that therefore land values should bear the burden of taxation.

United States.—A Federal Republic composed of 45 States, 4 Territories, and 1 Federal District, together with the outlying territory of Alaska, the island of Puerto Rico, the Hawaiian group, the Philippines, and several small islands. The extreme limits of the continental possessions, excluding Alaska, are included between the parallels of 24° $20'$ and 49° north latitude and 66° $48'$ and 124° $32'$ west longitude. The United States proper is bounded on the north by the British American possessions (separated in part by the St. Lawrence River and the chain of lakes—Ontario, Erie, St. Clair, Huron, and Superior—with their connecting streams); on the east by the Atlantic Ocean; on the south by the Strait of Florida, Gulf of Mexico, and the Republic of Mexico, and on the west by the Pacific Ocean. Alaska, situated in the extreme northwest of the American continent, as well as the insular possessions, is treated of in separate articles (q. v.). The physical characteristics may be said briefly to consist of the Appalachian Mountain system in the eastern part, the Gulf slope on the south, the basin of the Great Lakes on the north, and between them the valleys of the Mississippi, Ohio, and Missouri rivers. West of this great central system of valleys and watersheds is the Rocky Mountain system, approached on the east by extensive treeless plains or prairies. West of the Rockies many fertile valleys diversify the slope to the Pacific. The leading agricultural products are grain, cotton, tobacco, and sugar. The mineral productions include iron, silver, copper, lead, gold, zinc, quicksilver, nickel, aluminum, platinum, antimony, coal, petroleum, natural gas, and mineral waters. It is the first country in the world in the production of steel, pig iron, cotton, wheat, and indian corn, and among the first in tobacco and sugar. A description and an epitome of the history of the Government are given in the present work. From 1774 to the Declaration of Independence, the title of the country was the "United Colonies." Sept. 9, 1776, the Continental Congress resolved that in all Continental commissions where theretofore the words "United Colonies" had been used the style should thereafterwards be "United States." The name United States, commonly supposed to have been first used in history in 1776, had been in fact sometimes applied to the European Dutch Republic, composed of what had been during the war for independence in the sixteenth century the United Provinces. The independence of the Government of the United States of America was first recognized by France in 1778. The area of the continental portion of the Republic is 3,025,600 sq. miles; including Alaska, 3,557,000 sq. miles. The population, exclusive of Indians and Alaskans, was, in 1890, 62,622,250; in 1899 (estimated), 70,000,000.

Pennsylvania, backed by the militia. In the case of Olmstead *et al. vs.* Rittenhouse's Executrixes (q.v.) Judge Peters, of the United States district court for Pennsylvania, decided in favor of the plaintiffs, but refrained, he stated, for prudential reasons, from carrying his judgment into execution. Apr. 2, 1803, a Pennsylvania statute was enacted forbidding the execution of the decree of the Federal court. A mandamus was then asked for against Peters. The Supreme Court granted it, Chief Justice Marshall declaring that the legislature of a State can not annul the judgment or determine the jurisdiction of a United States court. The execution of the original judgment required the payment of £11,496 9s. 9d., Pennsylvania currency, which had been placed in the custody of the State court. The Pennsylvania officials, with the militia, resisted payment for 26 days, when the marshal assembled a *posse comitatus* of 2,000 men, and the money was paid over without actual collision.

United States vs. Todd.—A case not printed, there having been no reporter at the time. It was possibly the first case in which the United States Supreme Court declared a Federal statute unconstitutional. Under an act of Congress passed in 1792 the name of Yale Todd was by the circuit court of Connecticut ordered to be placed upon the pension list. It was afterwards (Feb. 17, 1794) decided by the Supreme Court of the United States that the circuit court could not constitutionally make such a decree, nor could it act in the capacity of a commission not of judicial function.

Universal Expositions. (See Exhibitions.)

Universal Postal Union discussed, VII, 622; VIII, 53; IX, 539, 732.

Universities. (See National University; Seminaries of Learning.)

Unlawful Expeditions. (See Illegal Combinations.)

Upper Pend d'Oreille Indians:
Agreement with, for sale of lands, VIII, 153, 192.
Treaty with, V, 380.

Upshur, Abel P., death of, announced and honors to be paid memory of, IV, 279, 333.

Uruguay.—A Republic of South America. It lies between lat. 30° and 35° south and long. 53° and 58° west. It is bounded on the north by Brazil, on the east by Brazil and the Atlantic Ocean, on the south by the estuary of the Rio de la Plata, and on the west by Argentina (separated by the Uruguay River). Uruguay is also known as the Banda Oriental. The surface consists of extensive grassy plains, over which roam vast herds of cattle, horses, and sheep that constitute the wealth of the inhabitants. The chief exports are live stock, wool, beef, hides, tallow, etc. The government is vested in a President and a parliament consisting of a Senate and a Chamber of Representatives. The country was first settled by Spanish Jesuits in the seventeenth century. It became an independent State in 1828. Area, 72,172 sq. miles; population (1897), 827,485.

Uruguay:
American citizens aggrieved by acts of, referred to, IV, 161.
Treaty with, V, 167, 182, 280; VII, 118.
Delay in exchange of ratifications of, referred to, V, 382.

Usher, John P., treaty with Indians concluded by, VI, 193.

Utah.—One of the United States, often called Deseret, "The land of the honeybee;" motto, "Industry, 1847." It extends from lat. 37° to 42° north and from long. 109° to 114° west. It is bounded on the north by Idaho and Wyoming, on the east by Colorado and Wyoming, on the south by Arizona, and on the west by Nevada. The surface is mountainous and includes part of the Great Basin and the Great Salt Lake. The region formed a part of the territory ceded by Mexico in 1848. Lead and silver mining and agriculture are the principal industries. The first white settlements were made by Mormons in 1847. A Territorial government was organized in 1850. The polygamous practices of the Mormons kept the State out of the Union until Jan. 4, 1896. A large Gentile population has lately gone into the State. Area, 84,970 sq. miles; population (1890), 207,905.

Utah:
Admission of, into Union proclaimed, IX, 688.
Affairs in, correspondence regarding, referred to, V, 584, 592.
Appropriation bill passed by legislature of, and vetoed, discussed and recommendations regarding, VIII, 399.
Brigham Young, first governor of, V, 454.
Rebellion under leadership of. (See Rebellion in, *post.*)
Removal of, and successor appointed, V, 455, 503.
Difficulties with, terminated, V, 487, 503, 648.
Extraordinary session of legislature of, act authorizing, recommended, VIII, 399.
Gilsonite or asphaltum in, disposition of lands containing, discussed, IX, 736.
Government of, discussed by President—
Arthur, VIII, 250.
Buchanan, V, 454, 483, 493, 503.
Fillmore, V, 127.
Hayes, VII, 606.
Increase in numbers and influence of non-Mormon population in, discussed, IX, 118.
Industrial home in, report of board on, referred to, VIII, 601.
Information regarding, transmitted, V, 142.
Judiciary of, and administration of laws in, discussed, VII, 208, 250.
Land laws, extension of, over, recommended, V, 87, 506.
Land office in, recommended, V, 506.
Lands in, set apart as public reservation by proclamation, IX, 773.
Legal proceedings and condition of affairs in, referred to, V, 584.
Mormon Church in—
Commissioners appointed under "act in reference to bigamy," etc., referred to, VIII, 91, 144, 184, 214, 250, 361.

territory parceled out and confirmed by these treaties has been retained by the respective States to the present day. The clauses of particular interest to Americans were those by which France ceded to Great Britain Hudsons Bay and Straits, St. Kitts, Nova Scotia, Newfoundland, and the adjacent islands. Other important provisions of these treaties were: Philip V (of Bourbon) was confirmed King of Spain; the Kingdoms of France and Spain were to remain forever separate; France recognized the Protestant succession in England, and Prussia was recognized as a Kingdom. In addition to the possessions before mentioned, Great Britain received Gibraltar and Minorca. The Spanish Netherlands, Sardinia, the Milanese, and Naples were ceded to Austria. Spain ceded Sicily to Savoy. Prussia received Neuchâtel and part of Gelderland and renounced its claims to Orange, and Portugal was confirmed in certain South American possessions. A notable clause of the treaty between Great Britain and Spain was the granting to a company of British merchants the exclusive right to send negro slaves to Spanish America.

V.

Veto.—The act by which the executive refuses his approval of a measure of the legislative body with which he is associated. The Constitution gives the President of the United States power to veto any act of Congress by refusing to sign the bill after its passage. In the Colonies (except Rhode Island and Connecticut) the governors had power to veto acts of the colonial legislatures. Massachusetts was the first of the original States to grant the veto power to its governor. This was in 1780. In the Convention of 1787 several veto plans were discussed, one of which proposed to associate the Supreme Court with the President in the exercise of the power. The plan finally adopted resembled that in use in Massachusetts. If the President refuses to sign an act, it is returned to the House in which it originated with his reasons for refusing his signature. That House may then proceed to reconsider the act, and if it again passes both Houses with a majority of two-thirds it becomes a law. The Constitution also provides that "if any bill shall not be returned by the President within ten days (Sundays excepted) after it shall have been presented to him, the same shall be a law in like manner as if he had signed it, unless the Congress by their adjournment prevent its return, in which case it shall not be a law" (I, 24). The veto power was used quite sparingly by the early Presidents. Following is the number of veto messages sent to Congress by the several Presidents. Those whose names are not mentioned sent no veto: Washington, 2;

Madison, 6; Monroe, 1; Jackson, 9; Tyler, 8; Polk, 3; Pierce, 9; Buchanan, 7; Lincoln, 3; Johnson, 22; Grant, 46; Hayes, 8; Arthur, 4; Cleveland, first term, 301; Harrison, Benj., 19; Cleveland, second term, 42.

Veto Messages. (See the several Presidents; the several subjects.)

Veto, Pocket.—The power of the President to prevent the enactment into law of a bill presented to him within 10 days before the adjournment of Congress, without sending in a refusal to sign or his objections in writing, is known as a pocket veto.

Veto Power discussed by President—

Polk, IV, 662.

Taylor, V, 23.

Vetoes, Pension. (See Cleveland, Grover; Grant, Ulysses S.)

Vetoes, Pocket. (See the several Presidents; the several subjects.)

Vice-Admiral.—An honorary rank in the United States Navy created by Congress Dec. 21, 1864, and conferred upon David G. Farragut. At the time of its creation it was the highest grade in the Navy. Two years later (July 25, 1866) Congress created the rank of admiral and bestowed it upon Farragut, making David D. Porter vice-admiral. Oct. 17, 1870, after the death of Admiral Farragut, Porter was promoted to the vacancy and Rear-Admiral Stephen C. Rowan was made vice-admiral. On his death in 1890 the grade became extinct. During the colonial period it was customary for the royal governor to be appointed vice-admiral, which made him head of the colonial admiralty courts. (See also Admiral.)

Vice-Admiral, creation of grade of, recommended, VI, 249; X, 198.

Vice-President of United States.—The Constitution provides for the office of Vice-President. His duty is to preside over the Senate, and in case of the removal, death, resignation, or disability of the President succeed him. Until the adoption of the twelfth amendment, in 1804, the candidate for President receiving next to the highest number of votes was declared Vice-President. Four Vice-Presidents have succeeded to the Presidency by reason of the death of the President, viz: John Tyler, who succeeded William Henry Harrison in 1841; Millard Fillmore, who succeeded Zachary Taylor in 1850; Andrew Johnson, who succeeded Abraham Lincoln in 1865, and Chester A. Arthur, who succeeded James A. Garfield in 1881. The attempt was made in 1841 to give Tyler only the title and rights of "Acting President," but he claimed the full office of President. Five Vice-Presidents have died in office, namely: George Clinton, Elbridge Gerry, William R. King, Henry Wilson, and Thomas A. Hendricks. Only one resigned, John C. Calhoun. A list of Vice-Presidents follows: John Adams, Massachusetts; Thomas Jefferson, Virginia; Aaron Burr, New York; George Clinton, New York; Elbridge Gerry, Massachusetts; Daniel D. Tompkins, New York; John C. Calhoun, South Carolina; Martin Van Buren, New York; Richard M. Johnson, Kentucky; John Tyler, Virginia; George M. Dallas, Pennsylvania; Millard Fillmore, New York; William R. King, Alabama; John C. Breckenridge, Kentucky; Hannibal Hamlin, Maine; Andrew Johnson, Tennessee; Schuyler Colfax, Indiana; Henry Wilson, Massachusetts; William A. Wheeler, New York; Chester A. Arthur, New York; Thomas A. Hendricks, Indiana; Levi P. Morton, New York; Adlai E. Stevenson, Illinois; Garret A. Hobart, New Jersey.

Vice-President of United States:

Death of. (See Hendricks, Thomas A.; King, William R.; Wilson, Henry.)

Election of. (See President of United States.)

Vicksburg (Miss.), Siege and Capture of.—The night after the battle of the Big Black, May 17, 1863, McPherson's and McClernand's corps crossed the river on floating bridges made of bales of cotton covered with plank. Sherman, who carried the only pontoon train in the army, passed over at Bridgeport, a few miles above. The whole army then moved upon Vicksburg. Sherman, still holding the right, marched toward the Yazoo River, and on the 19th rested his right on the Mississippi, within plain view of Porter's gunboats. McPherson followed Sherman with the Seventeenth Army Corps, halting where the latter had turned off. McClernand came up by the Jackson road and deployed to the left. The investment of Vicksburg was thus completed by May 19, 1863. At this time Grant's army was over 30,000 strong. The Federal force was increased to nearly 70,000 during the siege. The Confederate garrison, commanded by Gen. Pemberton, consisted of about 25,000 or 30,000 men and 102 guns. Vicksburg's fortifications were bastioned earthworks. The place was provisioned for about two months. On the afternoon of the 19th Grant ordered a general assault, which was repulsed with a loss to the Federals of 942. Three days later he made another attack, but the assailants succeeded merely in planting their flags on the outer slopes of the bastions. The city was found to be too strong to be taken by assault. The Federal loss on the 22d was 3,199. During the skirmishing on the 18th, 20th, and 21st of May the Union army lost 241 men. Porter assisted materially in these attacks by a constant fire from his gunboats and mortar boats. Pemberton soon began to feel the effects of the siege. By the end of May his meat ration was reduced one-half, and not long thereafter the bacon supply was entirely exhausted. There were no signs of the arrival of reenforcements and 6,000 men lay sick and wounded in the hospitals and private houses. Some of his men had been in the trenches 47 days and nights. Besides, they were now constantly exposed to bursting shells and the fire of sharpshooters. Thus despairing of aid, his resources about exhausted, the Confederate commander resolved to capitulate. July 4, 1863, Vicksburg was surrendered to Grant. Gen. Grant accorded magnanimous terms. The entire garrison was paroled and was allowed to depart with rations to last them beyond the Union lines. The results of the campaign were the defeat of the Confederates in several engagements, the occupation of the capital of Mississippi, and the capture of the important post of Vicksburg with its garrison and munitions of war, a loss to the Confederates of over 30,000 prisoners and several thousand killed and wounded. Among the dead were Generals Tracy, Tilghman, and Green. Grant's losses in the campaign, from the first skirmish at Port Gibson, May 1, to the surrender of Vicksburg, were 1,511 killed, 7,396 wounded, and 453 missing—a total of 9,360.

Viel, Mary A., act granting pension to, vetoed, IX, 755.

Vienna, Austria:
International Exposition in, discussed, VII, 188, 236.
International Patent Congress in, VII, 261.

Villeré's Plantation (La.), Battle of.—After the battle of Lake Borgne, La. (q. v.), the British expedition pushed on toward New Orleans by way of the Bayou Bienvenu and Villerés Canal. Dec. 23, 1814, within an hour after hearing that the British were approaching, Jackson had 1,800 of his troops on the march to meet them. Half of the invading army, some 2,500 men, had approached to within 9 miles of New Orleans without serious check. The schooner *Carolina* dropped down the river to a point opposite Villeré's and opened a terrible fire upon the invading army, killing or maiming 100 men in 10 minutes. The general engagement lasted about 2 hours. Both combatants retired from the field in the darkness. The loss of the Americans was 213, while that of the British was about 400 men.

Vinton, David H., mentioned, II, 375.

Viollier, Lewis W., consular clerk, removal of, from office and reasons therefor, VII, 113.

Virginia.—One of the thirteen original States; nicknames, "Old Dominion," "Mother of States," "Mother of Presidents;" motto, "Sic semper tyrannis" ("Be it ever thus to tyrants"). It extends from lat. 36° 31' to 39° 27' north and from long. 75° 13' to 83° 37' west. Virginia is bounded on the northwest and north by West Virginia (separated by the Alleghany Mountains), on the north and northeast by Maryland and the District of Columbia (separated by the Potomac River), on the east by the Chesapeake Bay and the Atlantic Ocean, on the south by North Carolina and Tennessee, and on the southwest by Kentucky. The county of Accomac lies east of the Chesapeake. Virginia is traversed by the Blue Ridge Mountains from northeast to southwest. It is level toward the southeast. It is the second State in the Union in the production of tobacco. The State also produces largely wheat, corn, vegetables, fruit, timber, coal, iron, salt, and building stone, and manufactures flour, leather, iron, and tobacco. It was the first settled of the British American Colonies, the settlement having been made by the English at Jamestown in 1607. Virginia be-

came a royal colony in 1624. It was the largest and most influential of the Colonies. It took a conspicuous part in the events leading up to the Revolution. Virginia ceded to the United States all its territory beyond the Ohio River in 1784. It ratified the Constitution in 1788. This great State furnished 4 of the first 5 Presidents, and altogether 5 of the Presidents of the United States. It seceded from the Union Apr. 17, 1861, and became one of the principal battle grounds of the Civil War. The State was readmitted to the Union in 1870. Area, 42,450 sq. miles; population (1890), 1,655,980.

Virginia (see also Confederate States; Richmond):
Alexandria County retroceded to, by proclamation, IV, 470.
Application of loyal persons in, to remove within Union lines, VI, 159.
Authority of United States reestablished in, VI, 337.
Boundary line of, referred to, I, 133, 150.
Bounty lands of, referred to, I, 88.
Census of, incomplete, II, 85.
Claims of, for militia services in War of 1812, II, 237; X, 55.
Elections in, troops stationed at polling places referred to, VII, 413, 418.
Lands ceded to Indians by, I, 116.
Lands granted soldiers of, in Revolutionary War referred to, X, 63.
Mediation of, for settlement of questions threatening Union discussed, V, 661.
Negroes coming into Washington from, arrested as fugitives, order regarding, X, 108.
Persons in, attempting to exercise official powers of civil nature, order regarding, VI, 44.
Ratification of amendment to Federal Constitution by, referred to, I, 113, 114, 259.
Reconstruction of, recommendations regarding, VII, 11.
Referred to, VII, 46.
Time for submitting constitution to voters proclaimed, VII, 13.
Referred to, VII, 29.
War between the States, course regarding, pursued by, VI, 23.
Withdrawal of, from Union discussed, VI, 23.

Virginia Coupon Cases.—A series of eight cases in which the United States Supreme Court in 1884 denied the right of a State to pass laws impairing the obligation of contracts. An act of the Virginia legislature in 1871 authorized the receipt of coupons of the State's funded debt in payment of taxes and debts due the State. An act of 1882 required payment of tax dues in "gold, silver, United States Treasury notes, national-bank currency, and nothing else." The tax collectors thereupon refused to accept the coupons in payment of taxes, as authorized by the law of 1871. The court decided the law of 1882 void, and judgment was found for the plaintiff taxpayers.

Virginia Plan.—At the opening of the Convention of 1787 to amend the Articles of Confederation, Edmund Randolph, of Virginia, on behalf of his delegation, set forth the defects in the old articles and submitted a series of 15 resolutions drawn up by Madison. This was the first plan of revision presented to the convention and is sometimes called the "Randolph Plan" or the "National Plan." It provided for representation according to population in two branches of Congress—the first chosen by the people, the second by the State legislatures; Congressional control of taxation and commerce; Congressional veto of State enactments; an Executive chosen by Congress; a limited veto by the Executive and part of the judiciary upon acts of Congress. There were other and less important provisions. The Constitution as framed and ratified was based on the Virginia plan, but quite a number of its leading features were either rejected altogether or greatly modified.

Virginia Resolutions.—A set of nine resolutions drawn up by James Madison, then a member of the Virginia legislature, passed by that body, and signed by the governor Dec. 24, 1798. The reason for the passage of these resolutions and similar ones by Kentucky about the same time was to give expression to the feeling that had been growing since 1791 that the Federal party was endeavoring to obtain greater power than that conferred upon the Government by the Constitution. The direct cause of their adoption was the passage of the alien and sedition laws (q. v.) by Congress. The resolutions deplored the broad construction given to the Constitution, as tending toward monarchical government. They declared the Union to be a compact between the States composing it, and that when this compact was infringed each State might interpose to protect itself. The alien and sedition laws were denounced as "palpable and alarming infractions of the Constitution." (See also Alien and Sedition Laws; Kentucky Resolutions.)

Virginius, The.—Oct. 31, 1873, the *Virginius*, an American schooner suspected of carrying men and arms from New York to the Cuban insurgents, was captured by the Spanish gunboat *Tornado* on the high seas near Jamaica. Capt. Fry and 35 of the crew and 4 Cuban passengers were executed. The affair created much ill feeling between the United States and Spain. The latter country made such reparation as lay within her power by disclaiming any intention to insult the United States, by paying an indemnity, and by surrendering 102 remaining prisoners. It was proved that the *Virginius* was not entitled to sail under our flag. She foundered at sea off Cape Fear Dec. 19, 1873, while on her way to New York.

Virginius, The, seized by Spanish vessel and citizens of United States on, put to death discussed, VII, 235, 241, 256.

Claims regarding, settled, VII, 322.

Condition of indemnity fund referred to, VIII, 602; IX, 476.

Correspondence regarding, transmitted, VII, 484.

Virginius, The—Continued.
Distribution of indemnity to claimants discussed, VII, 336; VIII, 537.
Orders regarding, VIII, 492; X, 114.

Vizcaya, The, mentioned, X, 170.

Vogelsang, Sophia, act granting pension to, vetoed, VIII, 733.

Volunteers.—Persons who enter the military service of their own free will for temporary duty, as distinguished from regulars of a permanent military establishment. By an act passed in 1792 the American Congress recognized the existence in a number of States of volunteer organizations not included in the militia of those States. The Government has since from time to time raised volunteers for temporary purposes. Such troops are United States rather than State forces, and their officers are to be appointed by the President. A provisional force of 25,000 volunteers was authorized by Congress for the war with England in 1812. During the Mexican War 73,500 volunteers were enlisted. During the Civil War a number of calls were made for volunteers, aggregating nearly 2,800,000 enlistments. In the war with Spain over 200,000 volunteers were enlisted. (See also Militia.)

Von Scholten, Maj. Gen., Danish minister to United States, correspondence with Secretary of State referred to, II, 531.

Vote of Thanks. (See Thanks of Congress.)

W.

Wabash and Erie Canal, grant of land in aid of, to Indiana, III, 508.

Wabash Indians:
Expeditions against, I, 112, 115, 126, 134, 167.
Treaty with, I, 135.
Letter of Secretary of War regarding, transmitted, X, 15.
Troops must be called for to suppress, I, 61, 82.

Wabash River, act for improvement of navigation on, reasons for applying pocket veto to, III, 118.

Wade, James F., member of military commission to Cuba, X, 175.

Wadsworth, James S., military governor of District of Columbia, VI, 110.
Executive clerks to be organized under direction of, VI, 122.

Wadsworth, Jeremiah, commissioner to treat with Indians, I, 198, 259.

Wager, Peter, director of Bank of United States, nomination of, and reasons therefor, III, 41.

Wagner, Reinhardt, arrest of, at Lodz, Russia, VIII, 202, 206.

Wahpeton Indians, treaty with, VI, 470.

Wainwright, Jonathan M., thanks of Congress to, recommended, VI, 76.

Wainwright, Richard, thanks of Congress to, recommended, VI, 76.

Waishkey, John, jr., mentioned, VIII, 78.

Waite, Morrison R., Chief Justice, death of, announced and honors to be paid memory of, VIII, 764.

War between the States.—A four years' military conflict between the United States Government and the States adhering to it, on the one side, and the Confederate States Government (composed of the States of South Carolina, Mississippi, Florida, Alabama, Georgia, Louisiana, Texas, Virginia, Arkansas, North Carolina, and Tennessee) on the other. There was behind the war a constitutional struggle between the North and South, beginning nearly at the time of the formation of the Union and involving principles of politics, differences of origin and climate, of soil and social conditions, and the general circumstances of peoples who had been steadily drawing apart from the period when by the sword and self-sacrifice they had achieved a common liberty. The contest was unique among modern civil wars, and no ancient conflict between the members of a confederacy of republics was comparable with it, either in the magnitude of the questions involved or in the extent of the operations in the field and the results finally attained. While slavery was the apparent cause, or rather, it should be stated, the occasion, of the War between the States, the real causes were a combination of things inherent in the population, the nature of their surroundings, the structure of their Government, as well as the conditions of life and the objects and aims of a society not homogeneous but variant in many important respects. From the beginning of colonization in British America these differences appeared. The bond, slender in the colonial wars, was scarcely strengthened at the outset of the Revolution, and had distinctly lessened, except among the more cultivated classes, in the years immediately succeeding the peace of 1783. Jealousies between the New England and some of the Southern States well-nigh prevented a permanent union. In the Federal Convention of 1787 it required much mutual concession to avoid a dissolution of the feeble bonds of union. The Constitution as adopted lacked guaranties of perpetual peace and amity between the sections, but the amendments soon afterwards ratified reasonably satisfied the discontent. Discussions in all the early Congresses after the adoption of the Constitution are full of expressions of doubt as to the perpetuity of the federation, uttered by eminent men from New England as well as from other sections, many of whom had been prominent in the work of establishing the new frame of government. The assertion of the State-sovereignty doctrine was not confined to any one section or party, though it has been the custom to assign to the old Republican (now the Democratic) party the origination of this doctrine. The two sets of resolutions of Kentucky and Virginia, adopted in the years 1798 and 1799, which were attributed on good evidence to Jefferson and Madison, respectively, declared the fundamental principles of States rights as clearly and as boldly as they were ever proclaimed at any subsequent period. The report written

by Madison and presented to the Virginia legislature has often been referred to as the ablest official exposition of the doctrine that the State is the creator and sovereign component of the Union, and that it may on sufficient grounds withdraw from the compact, the latter having already been infracted and made of no binding effect. It is true that Mr. Madison subsequently denied that this construction could be placed upon the argument in the report. From 1803, the date of the acquisition of the Louisiana territory, to 1811, when the State of Louisiana was admitted into the Union, many New England public men and writers opposed to the extension of the Union, especially on the ground that it seemed to involve the extension of slavery, sometimes avowed secession sentiments. Josiah Quincy, in a speech in Congress in 1811, used the threat that the New England States would withdraw in a certain contingency, "peaceably if they can, forcibly if they must." Again, this doctrine of a separable union was advanced by the Hartford Convention (q. v.) in 1814, called by some of the New England States to protest against the continuance of the War of 1812 with Great Britain. When the question of admitting Missouri into the Union as a slave State (1817–1821) was being discussed, threats of disunion if she were refused admission were heard, this time proceeding from the South. In 1828 Congress passed a stringent tariff measure following the protective act of 1824. This was deemed by South Carolina inimical to her business interests. The State legislature called a convention and passed an ordinance of nullification (q. v.), which, however, she subsequently rescinded. As the question of slavery began to overshadow that of the tariff, Northern extremists, called by some "Abolitionists," contended for the overthrow of human bondage, although the Constitution conferred on Congress no power over the domestic institutions of the States. The first struggle occurred on the right of petition. Applications for the admission of new States organized from the public domain added fuel to the fire on both sides of the controversy. The occupation of the Territories by slavery and antislavery partisans kept the people there in a constant state of turmoil bordering on civil war. In the midst of this the John Brown raid (q. v.) occurred. In 1860 Abraham Lincoln was elected President on a platform of resistance to the extension of slavery. South Carolina, through her legislature, called a State convention which, on Dec. 20, 1860, declared that the State was no longer in the Union. Similar action was taken during that winter and the following months by Mississippi, Florida, Alabama, Georgia, Louisiana, Texas, Virginia, Arkansas, North Carolina, and Tennessee. Feb. 4, 1861, delegates from the States that had by that date seceded met at Montgomery, Ala., and organized the government of the Confederate States of America. The forts, military supplies, and provisions within the seceded States were seized, generally with little opposition until the attack on Fort Sumter, in Charleston Harbor, S. C. The war began, so far as military operations were concerned, with the effort of the Government at Washington to relieve the garrison at Fort Sumter and the firing upon that fort by order of the Confederate government. This event occurred Apr. 12-13, 1861. The war practically ended with the surrender of Gen. Robert E. Lee, commander of the Confederate forces, at Appomattox, Va., Apr. 9, 1865, and the subsequent surrender of the armies of Gen. Joseph E. Johnston in North Carolina and of Gen. E. Kirby Smith beyond the Mississippi River. Perhaps as clear a view of the position and attitude of the United States in the war as could be obtained in a few words from an official document is to be derived from the "memorandum" of Secretary of State William H. Seward in regard to the letter addressed to him by the Confederate Commissioners Forsyth and Crawford. Although filed earlier, it was delivered Apr. 8, 1861. In it the fact was stated that President Lincoln coincided generally with the views expressed by the Secretary of State. Frankly confessing, he said, that his understanding of recent events (meaning the attempted secession of the Southern States) was very different from the aspect in which they were presented to Messrs. Forsyth and Crawford, he proceeded, in the third person, to say that "he saw in them not a rightful and accomplished revolution, and an independent nation, with an established government, but rather a perversion of a temporary and partisan excitement to the inconsiderate purposes of an unjustifiable and unconstitutional aggression upon the rights and the authority vested in the Federal Government, and hitherto benignly exercised, as from their very nature they always must so be exercised, for the maintenance of the Union, the preservation of liberty, and the security, peace, welfare, happiness, and aggrandizement of the American people." Disavowing any authority to recognize the commissioners as diplomatic agents, or hold correspondence or other communication with them, Mr. Seward brought the memorandum to a close. President Lincoln in his first inaugural address combated the ideas of the Confederates and held that the States in the Union were in an analogous case with the counties in the States. He believed in the right of coercion, and as to slavery he is quoted as saying that he would save the Union "with or without slavery." The best official exposition of the views of the Confederate people is perhaps to be collected from the constitution of the Confederate States and from the inaugural address and messages of their President. Their constitution was professedly based on the principles of the Federal Constitution of 1787, with the amendments to the same. Its preamble, however, in order to put at rest all argument or dispute,

contained the pregnant words, "each State acting in its sovereign and independent character." It was expressly declared that no duties or taxes on importations from foreign nations should be laid to promote or foster any branch of industry. Export duties were allowed to be levied with the concurrence of two-thirds of both houses of congress. Any judicial or other federal officer resident and acting solely within the limits of a particular State was impeachable by two-thirds of both branches of the legislature thereof, as well as by two-thirds of the house of representatives in congress. Internal improvements by the general government were prohibited, except the improvement of harbors and local duties for lights, beacons, and buoys, the expenses to be borne by the navigation facilitated. Citizens of the several States were not permitted to sue each other in the federal courts. It required a two-thirds vote of each house of congress, the senate voting by States, to admit new States. A constitutional convention could meet to consider proposed amendments on the call of any 3 States legally assembled in their several conventions. The vote in convention was to be taken by States and afterwards ratified by the legislatures of two-thirds of the States or by conventions in them. The power of congress over Territories was settled explicitly, and it was provided that "in all such territory the institution of negro slavery * * * shall be recognized and protected by congress and by the Territorial government," etc. The constitution was adopted Mar. 11, 1861. In his inaugural address as provisional president, Feb. 18, 1861, Mr. Davis said in part: "Sustained by the consciousness that the transition from the former Union to the present Confederacy has not proceeded from a disregard on our part of just obligations or any failure to perform any constitutional duty; moved by no interest or passion to invade the rights of others; anxious to cultivate peace and commerce with all nations, if we may not hope to avoid war we may at least expect that posterity will acquit us of having needlessly engaged in it. We have changed the constituent parts but not the system of our Government. The Constitution formed by our fathers is that of these Confederate States in their exposition of it, and in the judicial construction it has received we have a light which reveals its true meaning." Some of the principal battles of the war were those of Bull Run, or first Manassas, July 21, 1861; Shiloh, Apr. 6-7, 1862; Antietam, or Sharpsburg, Sept. 17, 1862; Fredericksburg, Dec. 13, 1862; Stone River, or Murfreesboro, Dec. 31, 1862, to Jan. 2, 1863; the Seven Days' Battles around Richmond, June 25 to July 1, 1862; Chancellorsville, May 1-4, 1863; Gettysburg, July 1-3, 1863; Chickamauga, Sept. 19-20, 1863; Wilderness, May 5-7, 1864; Spottsylvania, May 8-18, 1864; Cold Harbor, June 1-12, 1864; Petersburg, June 15-19, 1864, and Five Forks, Apr. 1, 1865. The total number of enlistments in the Union armies was 2,688,523 (VII, 202). The number of enlistments in the Confederate army was between 650,000 and 700,000. The total number of deaths on the Federal side, including those killed in action, those who died of wounds received in action, and from disease and other causes, 9,584 officers and 349,944 men. The cost of the struggle to the United States during the four years was $6,500,000,000. It is interesting to note in this connection that the cost of the Revolutionary War was $135,193,703; of the War of 1812, $107,159,003, and of the Mexican War, $66,000,000. The public debt of the United States rose from $90,867,828.68 in July, 1861, to $2,682,593,026.53 in July, 1865, an increase in 4 years of $2,591,725,197.85. The results of the war were the restoration of the Union, the emancipation of the slaves, and the several amendments to the Constitution regarding the rights of the new citizens under the new conditions established. For a more detailed account of the causes and history of the war, see the messages of Presidents Buchanan and Lincoln. (See also Abolitionists; Confederate States; Missouri Compromise; Slavery; War between the States; the several battles.)

Congressional Library, the Smithsonian Institution, National Museum, Naval Observatory, Corcoran Art Gallery, National Soldiers' Home, Washington Monument, and many other objects of national interest. The White House, or Presidential residence, was first occupied by John Adams in 1800. The public buildings were burned by the British in 1814, and more imposing ones erected subsequently. (See also District of Columbia.)

Washington City (see also District of Columbia):

Act transferring duties of trustees of colored schools in Georgetown and, vetoed, VI, 705.

Bridge across Potomac River at. (See District of Columbia.)

Buildings in—

Commission of inquiry relative to, referred to, IV, 159.

Erection of, proclamation regarding, I, 324.

On three sides of Lafayette square recommended, VII, 626.

Referred to, I, 368; IV, 58, 104.

British invasion of, referred to in proclamation, I, 545.

Centennial anniversary of founding of, for capital to be held in 1900 discussed, X, 200.

Conference in, of representatives of Canada and United States regarding commercial exchanges, IX, 240, 243, 313.

Conspiracy to prevent inauguration of President-elect in, referred to, V, 669.

Defense of, clerks in Departments in, to be organized into companies for, VI, 122. (See also VI, 444.)

Expenditures, public, in, referred to, X, 31, 54.

Grand Army of Republic—

Appropriation for reception and entertainment of, in, recommended, IX, 237.

Order permitting members of, employed in public service to participate in parade of, IX, 305.

Parade of, discussed, IX, 328.

Improvement of Potomac flats and river front of, recommended, VII, 506, 580, 627; VIII, 64.

Bill for, submitted, VII, 581.

Improvements in, recommended, II, 262, 343; V, 174, 304.

Insane asylum in. (See Government Hospital for Insane.)

International American Conference at, VIII, 784; IX, 32.

Centennial celebration of discovery of America, resolution regarding, IX, 77.

Discussed, IX, 107.

Extradition, reports on subject of, adopted by, IX, 79.

Importations and exportations, recommendations of, regarding, IX, 71.

Intercontinental railroad, survey of route for, recommended by, IX, 69.

International American bank, establishment of, recommended by, IX, 70.

Discussed, IX, 125.

International American monetary union, establishment of, recommended by, IX, 78.

Washington City—Continued.

International American Conference at—Continued.

International arbitration, reports on, adopted by, IX, 83.

Referred to, IX, 188, 442.

International bureau of information, establishment of, at, recommended by, IX, 71.

International law, adoption of uniform code of, recommended by, IX, 78.

Latin-American library, establishment of, recommended by, IX, 71.

Memorial tablet in State Department to commemorate meeting of, erection of, recommended by, IX, 79.

Patents, trade-marks, and copyrights, report of, concerning protection of, IX, 77.

Port dues and consular fees, recommendations of, regarding uniform system of, IX, 79.

Postal and cable communication, establishment of improved facilities for, recommended by, IX, 76.

Public health, recommendations of, for protection of, IX, 78.

Reciprocal commercial treaties recommended by, IX, 74.

Steamship service, establishment of rapid, recommended by, IX, 76. (See also IX, 56.)

Weights and measures, report of, on, IX, 78.

International Marine Conference at, discussed, VIII, 595, 785; IX, 33, 58, 63, 108.

International Peace Congress at, discussed, VIII, 97, 130.

Invitation to countries of North and South America to attend, VIII, 98.

Postponement of, referred to, VIII, 130.

International Sanitary Conference at, discussed, VII, 612; VIII, 35, 44.

Jail erected in, I, 355.

Necessity for new one, III, 404.

Justices of the peace in, referred to, VI, 602.

Loan from Maryland, payment of, guaranteed by United States, I, 333.

Lots in, chargeable with, I, 333.

Referred to, II, 264.

Resales of lots for, deficiency in, I, 355.

Lots in, sale of, referred to, II, 264; III, 621.

Order regarding, X, 86.

Negroes coming into, from Virginia arrested as fugitives, order regarding, X, 108.

Officers of, salary of, I, 355.

Pennsylvania avenue in—

Bill for paving, vetoed, VII, 387.

Improvement of, referred to, III, 627.

Macadamizing of, referred to, IV, 162.

Repavement of, referred to, VII, 414, 480, 635.

Police system for, recommended. (See District of Columbia.)

Post-office building in, erection of, recommended, VIII, 778.

Postal congress to be held in, discussed, recommendation regarding, IX, 732.

Protection for, recommendations regarding, VI, 444. (See also VI, 122.)

Public schools in. (See District of Columbia.)

were opened to the people of both nations. It was also agreed to submit the disputed boundary line between the British possessions and the State of Washington to the arbitration of the German Emperor, who on Oct. 21, 1872, rendered a decision awarding the island of San Juan and the group of which it forms a part to the United States. (See also Alabama Claims; Geneva Tribunal.)

Washington Turnpike Road Co., act authorizing subscription of stock in, vetoed, II, 493.

Washington's Farewell Address to be read to Army, orders regarding, VI, 105.

Washita River, exploration of, I, 399.

Wasp, The.—An American war ship of 18 guns, built at Washington in 1806. Oct. 13, 1812, the *Wasp* left the Delaware for the West Indies, under Capt. Jacob Jones, with 137 men. Five days later she fell in with 6 merchantmen under convoy of the British brig *Frolic*, 18 guns and 110 men. The *Wasp* attacked, and in less than an hour the *Frolic* struck her colors, after a loss of 90 men. The fight was in a heavy sea. Within 2 hours the *Wasp* and its prize were captured by the British frigate *Poictiers*, 74 guns, and the Americans were sent to Bermuda as prisoners. In 1814 the United States built a naval vessel at Newburyport and christened it the *Wasp*. It was a ship-rigged sloop of war and carried 22 guns and 160 men. Leaving Portsmouth May 1, 1814, under Capt. Johnston Blakely, she ran into the English Channel to look for British merchantmen. June 28 she encountered the British sloop *Reindeer*, 18 guns and 118 men. In less than half an hour of fierce fighting the *Reindeer* struck her colors, having sustained a loss of 25 killed and 42 wounded. The American loss was 27 in all. Sept. 1, after a fight of about 2 hours, the *Wasp* captured the British brig *Avon*, 18 guns. Oct. 9, in lat. 18° 35′ north, long. 30° 10′ west, she spoke and boarded the Swedish brig *Adams* and took off Lieut. McKnight and a master's mate of the United States ship *Essex*, on their way from Brazil to England. The *Wasp* was never heard from again.

Wasp, The, engagement of, with the *Frolic*, I, 521.

Wasp, The, mentioned, X, 171.

Wasp, The, refused permission to enter ports of Paraguay by Brazilian blockade commander, VI, 685.

Water Supply. (See Irrigation.)

Water Witch, The, fired upon by Paraguayan fort, V, 449.

Commissioner sent to demand compensation, V, 519.

Demands of, acceded to, V, 560.

Discussed, V, 664.

Naval force sent to Paraguay, V, 519.

Watervliet Arsenal, N. Y., gun factory to be established at, VIII, 789.

Wautauga Association.—June 2, 1769, a company of North Carolina hunters formed an organization to settle the territory to the west of the Cumberland Mountains, which had been opened by the treaty of Fort Stanwix in the previous year. Their settlements were on the Wautauga, one of the tributaries of the Tennessee River, within the limits of what is now the State of Tennessee. The settlers framed a code of laws, which was signed by each of them, and the body politic thus formed was called the Wautauga Association. The tyranny of Governor Tryon, of North Carolina, caused many of the independent-spirited settlers of that Colony to cast their lot with the Wautauga Association. In 1784, at a convention held in Jonesboro, a separate State government was organized under the name of Franklin. (See also Franklin.)

Wayne, Anthony, treaty with Indians concluded by, I, 189.

Waxhaw (S. C.) Massacre.—After the capture of Charleston Sir Henry Clinton sent a detachment of 300 men under Col. Tarleton to disperse Col. Buford's command of 380 men, who, hearing of the fall of Charleston, had retired to a point near the North Carolina line. May 29, 1780, Tarleton, having overtaken Buford at the Waxhaw River, made a furious charge, while the Americans were awaiting flags of conference, believing hostilities suspended. Many of the Americans threw down their arms and begged for quarter; 113 were killed on the spot, 150 so badly wounded that it was impossible to move them, and only 53 were taken prisoners. Col. Buford and about 100 infantry and a few horse escaped. The British lost but 5 killed and 15 wounded.

Wea Indians:

Convention with, I, 478, 479.

Treaty with, I, 581, 582; II, 47, 81; V, 242; VI, 69, 518.

Trust lands of, referred to, VI, 199.

Weakley, Robert, commissioner to treat with Indians, nomination of, II, 51.

Weather Bureau.—A bureau of the Department of Agriculture. It was first suggested in 1817. In 1819 a cooperative movement was begun and the officers at the various military posts were required to make monthly reports of the weather. In 1870 Congress made an appropriation to establish a weather bureau at Washington and pay for telegraphic communication between posts of observation in different parts of the country. Until 1891 the Bureau remained under the War Department. In July of that year it was transferred to the newly created Department of Agriculture. This Bureau forecasts storms, floods, and all changes in the weather conditions, and publishes such climatic and meteorological data as the public interest seems to demand. It has about 1,000 paid employees, most of whom devote their entire time to its service. Its annual cost is more than $800,000. The annual saving to the agricultural and shipping interests of the country due to the forecasts of the Bureau is believed to be incalculable. The percentage of correct forecasts is about 4 out of 5. In hurricanes from the West Indies it reaches 5 out of 5, or 100 per cent.

party, but they preserved their power for another term by nominating a military candidate in the person of Zachary Taylor. He was elected, but the disintegration of the Whig party had begun. Many of the Northern Whigs became Free Soilers, and by 1856 Republicans, while many temporarily joined the American or Know-Nothing party. Large numbers of the Southern Whigs became Democrats. The factions of the old party united and nominated Winfield Scott for President in 1852, but he was defeated by Franklin Pierce. A small number of Whigs formed the Constitutional Union party and nominated Bell and Everett in 1860. Besides those already mentioned, the chief leaders of the party in the North were Webster, Winthrop, Choate, Seward, Greeley, and Weed; in the South, Mangum, Badger, Bell, Berrien, Forsyth, Stephens, Toombs, Prentiss, and Crittenden, and in the West, Giddings, Ewing, and Corwin.

Whipple, John, correspondence regarding Dorr's Rebellion, IV, 287, 288.

Whisky Insurrection.—A revolt against the enforcement of a Federal excise law by the people of 4 counties of western Pennsylvania. The Constitution gives Congress power to lay and collect excise taxes. The first bill for an excise law was defeated in Congress June 21, 1790. The project was revived the following year, and the first excise law was passed Mar. 3, 1791. The Senators from Pennsylvania were instructed by their legislature to oppose the law, "established on principles subversive of peace, liberty, and the rights of citizens." In Pennsylvania the law was violently opposed by one Bradford and his followers and condemned by more peaceable and reflecting citizens, following the lead of Albert Gallatin, afterwards Secretary of the Treasury, minister to France, envoy extraordinary to England, etc., and William Findley and John Smiley, members of Congress. Numerous meetings were held to protest against this law, which bore with particular force upon the settlers of western Pennsylvania because of their isolated position, distance from the seaboard, and the scarcity of money in that region. In response to repeated protests Congress on May 8, 1792, passed an act reducing the duties on whisky, but, on account of the threatening attitude of some of the settlers, empowering the President to use militia in suppressing disturbances within a State. The agents of the Government sent to collect the excise having been maltreated and driven from the country and the marshals refused office room and assistance in serving writs, President Washington, by a proclamation of Sept. 15, 1792 (I, 124), called upon the citizens to abandon their unlawful proceedings. Instead of complying, resistance to the service of writs continued and the officers were tarred and feathered. Aug. 1, 1794, a mass meeting of 7,000 armed insurgents was held on Braddock's Field, a county judge presiding, with Albert Gallatin as secretary and Bradford as the leading spirit. An emergency had now

arisen. Governor Mifflin, of Pennsylvania, having declined to take the initiative, a certificate of the existence of an insurrection was obtained from a Federal judge, and on Aug. 7, 1794, President Washington again called upon the insurgents to disperse and retire peaceably to their homes on or before Sept. 1, 1794 (I, 158). This warning was unheeded and was followed by a third proclamation on Sept. 25, 1794 (I, 161). A requisition for 15,000 militia was issued to the governors of Pennsylvania, Virginia, Maryland, and New Jersey. A Federal commission of 3 and a State commission of 2 preceded the troops with offers of amnesty on full submission. Bradford urged armed resistance, Gallatin counseled submission. Washington accompanied the troops, which were in command of Governor Lee, of Virginia, as far as Carlisle. Alexander Hamilton, then Secretary of the Treasury, accompanied the expedition to the scene of disorder. The troops arrived in the rebellious district early in November. After giving the people time to obey the President's proclamation, Lee's forces arrested many of those who failed to accept the proffered amnesty. Bradford and the more violent leaders escaped. Those captured were tried, convicted, and later pardoned by the President. The first show of Federal force had suppressed the insurrection.

Whisky Insurrection (see also Pennsylvania, insurrections in):

Discussed, I, 162, 168, 170.

Pardon granted insurgents, I, 181.

Referred to, I, 184.

Proclamations against, I, 124, 158, 161.

Whisky Ring.—A conspiracy of distillers and United States officials formed in St. Louis, Mo., in 1872 to defraud the Government of internal-revenue taxes. By 1874 the ring had attained national proportions, with branches in Milwaukee, Chicago, Peoria, St. Louis, Cincinnati, New Orleans, San Francisco, and Washington. Distillers who refused to enter the combination were trapped into technical violations of the revenue laws, and when made liable to seizure they were given their choice between ruin and surrender to the ring. The combination became so powerful that when Secretary Bristow ordered a transfer of supervisors, which would have thrown the ring into confusion, their agents at Washington procured a countermand of the order from President Grant. After diligent effort evidence was obtained against the distillers and revenue agents. Upon this evidence the Government seized $3,500,000 worth of property and procured indictments against 238 persons. It was shown that the Treasury had been defrauded of $1,650,000 between July 1, 1874, and May 1, 1875. When the papers were laid before President Grant he indorsed them with orders to "let no guilty man escape." The most important convictions were those of John A. Joyce, special revenue agent; John McDonald, supervisor, and William O. Avery, chief clerk in the Treasury Department.

and about 400 men. Early then marched on Chambersburg, Pa. In August, 1864, Sheridan took command of the Federal army in the valley, known as the Army of the Shenandoah. The Confederates under Early were encamped on the west bank of Opequan Creek, covering Winchester. They were attacked on Sept. 19 by Sheridan. The battle began about 10 a. m. and was maintained till nearly 3 p. m., when the Confederates retreated to and beyond Winchester. Sheridan took 2,500 prisoners and found 2,000 wounded in the hospitals at Winchester. The Confederate loss in all reached 5,500, while the Federal loss was 653 killed, 3,719 wounded, and 618 missing—a total of 4,990. This is also called the battle of Opequan.

Wind River Reservation. (See Shoshone Reservation.)

Windom, William, Secretary of Treasury, death of, announced and honors to be paid memory of, IX, 164.

Referred to, IX, 133.

Wines, E. C., commissioner to International Congress on Prevention of Crimes, report of, referred to, VII, 161.

Wines, duty on, discussed, II, 568; III, 102; IV, 274, 400.

Winnebago Indians.—A tribe of the Siouan stock of Indians. The name is a corruption of a word meaning "dirty water." They called themselves Hotcangara, meaning "parent speech." Early in the history of the Northwest Territory the Winnebagoes migrated eastward, but were forced back to the vicinity of Green Bay, Wis. They were nearly exterminated through wars with neighboring tribes in the seventeenth century. They aided the French in the wars between France and England and were allies of the British during both the Revolution and the War of 1812. The Winnebagoes were active in the Indian war of 1793-94 and were subdued by Gen. Wayne. A treaty of peace was made with them in 1816. In 1826 and 1827 treaties were made fixing the boundaries of their hunting grounds. In 1829 they ceded large tracts of land to the General Government, and after several removals they were in 1866 settled upon reservations in Nebraska and Wisconsin. Their number in 1893 was 2,184.

Winnebago Indians:

Agent for, recommended, VIII, 374.

Claim of Omahas against, VIII, 264.

Treaty with, II, 347, 395, 397, 423, 425, 430, 464, 466, 607; III, 395; V, 238, 242, 306, 578; VI, 376.

Winslow, Ezra D., refusal of Great Britain to surrender other fugitives and, VII, 371, 415.

Winslow, John A., thanks of Congress to, recommended, VI, 256.

Winslow, The, disabled in conflict in Cardenas Bay, Cuba, X, 157, 169.

Rescued by the *Hudson*, X, 157.

Thanks of Congress to officers and men of, recommended, X, 157.

Winthrop, Robert C., correspondence respecting presentation to United States of desk upon which Declaration of Independence was written, VII, 588.

Wisconsin.—One of the United States; nickname, "The Badger State;" motto, "Forward." It lies in the northern part of the country, between lat. 42° 27' and 47° north and long. 86° 53' and 92° 54' west, not including islands in Lakes Superior and Michigan. It is bounded on the north by Lake Superior and the upper peninsula of Michigan, on the northeast and east by the upper peninsula of Michigan and Lake Michigan, on the south by Illinois, and on the west by Iowa and Minnesota (separated mostly by the Mississippi and St. Croix rivers). Wisconsin is hilly in the north and southwest, but elsewhere is generally level. It has important agricultural, mining, and lumbering interests and extensive manufactures of flour and beer. It was visited as early as 1634 by Nicollet, La Salle, and French fur traders, who established a settlement at Green Bay in 1639. It was included in the Northwest Territory till 1800, when it became a part of Indiana Territory. In 1809 it was included in Illinois Territory, in 1818 in Michigan Territory, and in 1836 it was organized as Wisconsin Territory, and included, besides its present area, the territory now embraced in the States of Iowa and Minnesota and part of the Dakotas. It was admitted to the Union May 29, 1848. Area, 56,040 sq. miles; population (1890), 1,686,880.

Wisconsin:

Act for continuing certain works in, reasons for applying pocket veto to, IV, 610.

Boundary line with Michigan referred to, III, 629.

Constitution adopted by, transmitted, IV, 509, 577.

Volunteers from, thanks of President tendered, VI, 241.

Wisconsin River, act regarding improvement of, vetoed, VII, 282.

Wise, Henry A., minister to—

Brazil—

Correspondence of, referred to, IV, 576, 578, 688.

Dispatches from, regarding slave trade, IV, 362.

France, nomination of, and reasons therefor, IV, 233.

Witnesses:

Fees of, referred to, VIII, 143, 183, 249.

Protection of, from injury recommended, IX, 42.

Witt, William P., act granting pension to, vetoed, VIII, 648.

Wolcott, Oliver, commissioner of United States, nomination of, I, 300.

Wolford, Frank, Presidential elector of Kentucky, arrest and imprisonment of, VI, 259.

Woman Suffrage.—The claims for woman suffrage rest largely upon a dogma that suffrage is a natural right. The constitution of New Jersey, framed in 1776, and a statute passed in 1793 to regulate elections, permitted all inhabitants with certain qualifications to vote and stipulated how each should deposit "his or her ballot." This act was repealed in 1807. Advocates of woman suffrage argue that it is a natural right and that "the consent of the governed" is not the governed property holders, nor the governed voting men, but all the governed, men and women; that the voting of males is no longer conditioned upon military service, and that woman needs a vote to adequately protect and advance her interests. In reply to these claims it is held that "suffrage is not a natural right; that in all ages and countries it has been conditioned upon qualifications of expediency; that representation of taxpaying women practically exists; that the interests of the family and of the State will be best preserved by continuing the division of labor which hitherto has exempted women from military and political duty; that the interests of women are not so distinct from those of men as to make their representation as a class necessary, and that their interests can be adequately protected without their voting." The agitation has resulted in a partial enfranchisement of women, in elections involving property taxes and schools, in about half of the States and Territories. In Arizona, Delaware, Idaho, Illinois, Indiana, Kansas, Kentucky, Massachusetts, Michigan, Minnesota, Montana, Nebraska, New Hampshire, New Jersey, North Dakota, Oklahoma, Oregon, South Dakota, Texas, Vermont, Washington, and Wisconsin women have a modified and restricted form of suffrage. In Wyoming, Utah, and Colorado women have equal suffrage with men.

Woman's Rights.—The first woman's rights convention was held at Seneca Falls, N. Y., July 19, 1848. It demanded for women equal rights with men. The women based their claims on the Declaration of Independence. The first national woman's rights convention was held at Worcester, Mass., Oct. 23, 1850. In 1866 the American Equal Rights Association presented the first petition ever laid before Congress for woman suffrage. The New England Woman's Suffrage Association was formed in 1868, and the first systematic effort was then begun for memorializing legislatures and Congress. The Massachusetts Republican convention of 1868 admitted Lucy Stone and Mary A. Livermore as delegates. The following year the convention of the party in that State indorsed woman suffrage. In 1872 and again in 1876 the Republican National Convention resolved "that the matter of woman's rights should have respectful consideration." Besides the women mentioned above some of the more prominent leaders in the woman's rights movement have been Susan B. Anthony, Elizabeth Cady Stanton, Virginia L. Minor, Matilda Jocelyn Gage, and Julia Ward Howe. (See also Woman Suffrage.)

Wood, John E., correspondence of, referred to, V, 483.

Wood, Lafayette B., brevet second lieutenant, promotion of, to second lieutenant recommended, IV, 446.

Woodbridge, Sarah A., act granting restoration of pension to, vetoed, VIII, 727.

Woodbury, Harriet, act to pension, vetoed, IX, 756.

Woodbury, Levi, Secretary of Treasury:
Correspondence respecting interference in elections and pay of soldiers, III, 96.
Order of, regarding—
Circulation of small bank notes, X, 102.
Frauds in purchase of public lands, X, 104.

Woodcock, Amanda, act granting pension to, vetoed, IX, 681.

Woodford, Stewart L., minister to Spain, mentioned, X, 130, 142, 144.
Withdrawal of, X, 165.

Woodruff, Wilford, letter of, advising Mormons to refrain from contracting marriages forbidden by law referred to, IX, 118.

Woodson, Mary S., act granting pension to, vetoed, VIII, 449.

Woodworth, Mary, act granting pension to, vetoed, VIII, 732.

Woodworth, Selim E., thanks of Congress to, recommended, VI, 76.

Wool, John E.:
Communication of President Jackson to, respecting apportionment of militia and treaty with Cherokees, X, 105.
Correspondence regarding Department of Pacific, V, 296, 298, 483.
Inquiry in case of, III, 372.
Thanks of President tendered, VI, 112.

Wool and Woolens, import duty on, discussed, III, 28; VII, 293.

Woolley, Abram R., mentioned, II, 112.

Wooster, David, monument to memory of, information regarding, II, 232.

Worcester, Dean C., member of commission to Philippine Islands, X, 222.

Worcester, Frank D., act granting pension to, vetoed, VIII, 826.

Worcester vs. Georgia.—An important Supreme Court case involving the right of individual States to make laws at variance with treaties made by the Government of the United States. Samuel A. Worcester was a missionary among the Cherokees. In 1831 he was arrested by officers of the State of Georgia, tried, and sentenced to 4 years' imprisonment for living among the Indians in violation of an act of the State legislature which forbade any white person to reside among the Indians without a license from the governor of the State or some one else authorized to issue it. Worcester pleaded authorization by the President and by the Cherokees, also the unconstitutionality of the act itself. By a writ of error the case was brought before the United States Supreme Court. That tribunal reversed the decision of the State court and rendered judgment in favor of Worcester on the ground that the Georgia act, being repugnant to the Constitution, to the treaties made by the United States with the Cherokees, and to the laws of Congress in execution thereof, was unconstitutional and void. It was held that the treaties and laws of the United States contemplate the Indian

Wyandotte, now a part of Kansas City, Kans. (See also Lecompton Constitution; Topeka Constitution.)

Wyandotte Indians.—A tribe of the Iroquoian family of Indians. When first known to the whites they occupied a narrow strip of land in Ontario, but between 1615 and 1650 they were almost exterminated in war with neighboring tribes. They joined with another tribe and soon spread along the south and west shores of Lake Erie and acquired considerable influence. The Wyandottes sided with the French till the close of Pontiac's War and aided the British in the War of 1812. The word "Wyandotte" means "calf of the leg," and refers to the manner in which they cut their meat. They were called "Hurons" by the French on account of the arrangement of their hair, which resembled the bristles of a wild boar. They now number about 700, mostly at Quapaw Agency, Ind. T.

Wyandotte Indians:

Lands to be conveyed to, by Delawares, IV, 276.

Treaty with, I, 363, 390, 397, 434, 439, 460, 554, 569; II, 21, 47, 569; III, 226; IV, 157; V, 66, 301; X, 51.

Opinion of Senate concerning, requested, I, 62.

Referred to, V, 304.

Transmitted for exercise of powers for fulfilling, X, 32.

Wyld, Robert S., act for relief of, approved and reasons therefor, VIII, 152.

Wyoming.—One of the United States; motto, "Equal rights". It lies between lat. 41° and 45° north and long. 104° and 111° west. It is bounded on the north by Montana, on the east by South Dakota and Nebraska, on the south by Colorado and Utah, and on the west by Utah and Idaho. The surface being mountainous, the leading industries are stock raising and mining. Most of the present State was included in the Louisiana Purchase. It was organized as a Territory in 1868 from areas previously in Dakota, Idaho, and Utah, but derived more remotely from the original Territories of Nebraska, Utah, and Oregon, a portion having at one time also belonged to Washington. Wyoming was admitted to the Union in 1890. Area, 97,890 sq. miles; population (1890), 60,705.

Wyoming:

Admission of, into Union discussed, IX, 118.

Chinamen injured by lawless men in, VIII, 329, 383, 498.

Indemnity to, recommended, VIII, 634.

Appropriation for, VIII, 782.

Troops sent to protect, VIII, 348.

Lands in, set apart for public reservation by proclamation, IX, 142, 155, 789, 793.

Organized band of persons in, referred to, VII, 60.

Unlawful combinations in, proclamations against, IX, 290, 500.

Wyoming Controversy.—In the original charter granted by Charles I to William Penn the northern boundary of Pennsylvania was fixed at lat. 43° north. However, the proprietors of the colony accepted 42° as the northern boundary and extended the southern boundary to include the Chesapeake and Delaware bays. Connecticut claimed all the territory north of 41° in Pennsylvania, and asserted her rights by chartering the Susquehanna Company, organized in 1753, to form settlements in the disputed territory. In 1762 the company sent its first party of settlers, 200 in number, into the region, but they were driven out by the Indians, who repudiated a previous sale of their rights to Connecticut and made a sale to Pennsylvania. In 1769 the Susquehanna Company sent more colonists into the disputed country, and a desultory warfare began between them and the Pennsylvania settlers, to whom the territory had been leased. The former were several times driven out of the disputed district by the Pennsylvanians, but they finally obtained a permanent lodgment, as the Pennsylvania contestants were only lessees, while their opponents fought for their property rights. Hostilities with the mother country caused a suspension of civil strife for a time. In 1779 an act of the Pennsylvania legislature transferred all the proprietary lands to the State. Pennsylvania brought suit against Connecticut to decide the jurisdiction over Wyoming. The case was heard by 5 judges at Trenton. In November, 1782, their unanimous decision, afterwards confirmed by Congress, was in favor of Pennsylvania.

Wyoming Massacre.—July 3, 1778, Col. Zebulon Butler, of the Continental Army, with a force of about 300 militiamen, mostly old men and boys, marched out of Forty Fort, in the Wyoming Valley, about 3 miles above Wilkesbarre, Pa., to drive off an invading party of some 800 Indians and Tories under Chief Joseph Brant and the British Colonel Walter Butler. The Indians burned the forts in the upper part of the valley and forced the American militiamen to retreat in disorder. Of the 300 who left the fort in the morning the names of 162 officers and men are recorded as killed in action and the massacre which followed. Butler, the British officer in command, reported the taking of 227 scalps and only 5 prisoners. Col. Zebulon Butler with 14 men escaped from the valley.

X.

X. Y. Z. Mission.—An American embassy to France in 1797, consisting of Charles C. Pinckney, John Marshall, and Elbridge Gerry. Francis Dana declined appointment to this mission because of ill health. During the strained relations between the United States and the French Republic it became necessary to ask for the recall of Genêt, the French minister. In return France asked that Gouverneur Morris be recalled. Wishing to avoid rupture between the two Republics, President John Adams called a special session of Congress and announced his intention of sending a special mission to France to conciliate that country if possible (I, 245). In October the commission met at Paris and endeavored to open negotiations with Talleyrand, the minister of foreign affairs. Talleyrand deputed 3 special agents to treat with the Americans, and these were designated in dispatches to the United States Government as X., Y., and Z., respectively. They suggested that the American commissioners submit to Talleyrand a proposal from the United States to lend to France a large sum of money, or that the United States accept from France the assignment of a loan extorted from the Dutch, and that one of the envoys return to America to arrange the details of the business. The commissioners flatly refused the proposals, and their mission, which was fruitless, terminated. The correspondence was disclosed upon their return and aroused much indignation against France. While on this mission Charles Cotesworth Pinckney made the famous reply to an intimation that peace might be assured by a payment of money, "Millions for defense, but not a cent for tribute."

Y.

Yakama Indians, treaty with, V, 381.

Yakima Reservation, Wash., lands on, to be used by Northern Pacific Railway, VIII, 277, 369, 593.

Yale, The, mentioned, X, 171.

Yamgheim, Eli. J., act granting pension to, vetoed, VIII, 817.

Yancton Indians, treaty with, II, 346.

Yanctoni Indians, treaty with, II, 346.

Yangtse River, steamers sailing under American flag prohibited from passing through Straw Shoe Channel on, VI, 698, 704.

Yankee, The, mentioned, X, 170.

Yankee Doodle.—A popular national air of the United States. The words are said to have been written in derision of the ill-assorted Continental troops, about 1755, by Dr. Schuckburgh, a surgeon under Gen. Amherst in the French and Indian War. The original title was "The Yankee's Return from Camp," and there are several versions. The tune has undergone various changes.

Yankees.—A word of uncertain origin, first applied to the early English colonists, later by the English to Americans, and still later to Northerners by people of the South. According to common legend, Yankees is a corruption of Yengees, Yaunghees, or Yanghies, a name said to have been given by the Massachuset Indians to the English colonists in their efforts to pronounce the word "English" or the French word "Anglais." It was first applied to the New Englanders as a term of reproach by British soldiers.

Yard, James, consul to Santa Cruz, nomination of, I, 98.

Yazoo Frauds.—A term applied to the sale by the State of Georgia in 1795 of her western territory, now included in Alabama and Mississippi, to 4 land companies, known generally as the Yazoo companies, from the district in which they operated. The land extended from the Alabama and Coosa rivers to the Mississippi, and from the thirty-first to the thirty-fifth parallel, and the price paid to the State was $500,000, or about 1⅔ cents per acre. It was charged that many members of the legislature who voted for the sale had been bribed. President Washington made the alleged frauds the subject of a special message (I, 175). The people of the State were indignant and a party was formed to repeal the sale. In 1796 the records of the transaction were burned in the presence of the governor and legislature. Immediately numerous claims sprang up, which had to be decided by Congress. The territory was ceded to the United States in 1802. The next year President Jefferson appointed a commission to investigate the claims, and James Madison, chairman of the commission, recommended a compromise, but Georgia refused to compensate the claimants. Their claim was sustained by the Supreme Court, however, Chief Justice Marshall holding that allegations of bribery of the legislature could not be entertained, and that purchasers from the land companies were innocent holders; that the act of the Georgia legislature in 1796 repealing the sale of 1795 was an abrogation of contract, and therefore void. Finally an act was passed in 1814 appropriating $8,000,000, payable out of the proceeds of the sale of Mississippi lands, to satisfy the Yazoo claimants.

Yellow Fever (see also Contagious Diseases; International Sanitary Conference; Quarantine Regulations):

Commission to investigate causes, etc., of, recommended, X, 194.

In Southern States discussed, VII, 492.

Act legalizing issue of provisions to sufferers recommended, VII, 500.

Yellowstone National Park. (See National Parks.)

Yellowstone National Park, compensation to superintendent of, referred to, VIII, 82.

Yokum, William, report in case of, transmitted, VI, 211.

York (Canada), Capture of.—The plans for the prosecution of the war with Great Britain in 1813 contemplated an invasion of Canada from both the east and the west. Gen. Harrison successfully carried out the programme in the west, routed Proctor's army, and was in possession of the territory. Apr. 27 Gen. Dearborn, with about 1,700 men under the immediate command of Gen. Zebulon Pike, crossed Lake Ontario on Commodore Chauncey's transports and marched upon the British garrison at York (now Toronto), where Maj. Gen. Sheaffe was in command of 800 regulars and a body of Indians. A sharp conflict ensued. The British and Indians were routed. By the explosion of a magazine Gen. Pike was killed, together with 51 other Americans and 40 British; 180 Americans were wounded by the explosion. The American loss in the battle was 269 on land and 17 on water. The British